SUNDAYS AND SEASONS

YEAR C 2016

Sundays and Seasons
2016, Year C
Guide to Worship Planning

The Sundays and Seasons family of resources

Sundays and Seasons: Preaching, 2016, Year C (978-1-4514-2583-3)

Worship Planning Calendar, 2016, Year C (978-1-4514-2578-9)

Words for Worship, 2016, Year C (978-1-4514-2582-6)

Calendar of Word and Season 2016 (978-1-4514-2584-0)

Church Year Calendar, 2016, Year C (978-1-4514-2579-6)

Church Year Calendar, 2016, Year C PDF (978-1-4514-2580-2)

Bread for the Day: Daily Bible Readings and Prayers 2016 (978-1-4514-2581-9)

www.sundaysandseasons.com

Acknowledgments

Copyright © 2015 Augsburg Fortress. All rights reserved. Except as noted herein and for brief quotations in critical articles or reviews, no part of this book may be reproduced in any manner without prior written permission from the publisher. Write to: Permissions, Augsburg Fortress, Box 1209, Minneapolis, MN 55440-1209.

Unless otherwise indicated, scripture quotations are from the New Revised Standard Version Bible © 1989 Division of Christian Education of the National Council of the Churches of Christ in the United States of America. Used by permission. All rights reserved.

Revised Common Lectionary © 1992 Consultation on Common Texts. Used by permission.

The prayers of intercession (printed in each Sunday/festival section) may be reproduced for onetime, non-sale use, provided copies are for local use only and the following copyright notice appears: From *Sundays and Seasons*, copyright © 2015 Augsburg Fortress.

Evangelical Lutheran Worship (Augsburg Fortress, 2006): various prayers.

Evangelical Lutheran Worship Occasional Services for the Assembly (Augsburg Fortress, 2009): Welcoming People to Communion; various prayers.

Evangelical Lutheran Worship Prayer Book for the Armed Services (Augsburg Fortress, 2013): various prayers.

Holden Prayer Around the Cross: Handbook to the Liturgy, third ed. (Augsburg Fortress, 2009): Beside Still Waters.

Music Sourcebook for All Saints through Transfiguration (Augsburg Fortress, 2013): Thanksgiving for Saints of the Congregation.

Susan R. Briehl, *Come, Lord Jesus: Devotions for Advent, Christmas, Epiphany* (Augsburg Fortress, 1996): Blessing for a Home at Epiphany, adapt.

Diann L. Neu, co-director of WATER, "A Hand Blessing." Used by permission. The Women's Alliance for Theology, Ethics and Ritual, 8121 Georgia Ave, Suite 130, Silver Spring, MD 20910. www.waterwomensalliance.org. dneu@hers.com.

Annual and seasonal materials

The Year of Luke: Ray Pickett

Advent in November?: Craig M. Mueller

Treasuring the Revised Common Lectionary: Gail Ramshaw

Preparing for the Season: Mark Mummert (Advent–Time after Epiphany), Jennifer Baker-Trinity (Lent–Easter), Erik Christensen (Time after Pentecost), Linda Witte Henke (visual environment)

Seasonal Worship Texts: Martin A. Seltz; incorporating selected prayers from *Evangelical Lutheran Worship*, *Evangelical Lutheran Worship Occasional Services for the Assembly*, and *This Far by Faith*

Seasonal Rites: Clint A. Schnekloth (evening prayer series for Advent; graduate blessing); Lynn Bulock (lighting the Christmas tree; blessing the nativity scene); Melissa Moll (service for the Day of Epiphany; midweek Lenten series: Open My Life, Lord); Dennis Bushkofsky (continuing in the covenant of baptism); John Roberts (scripts for Maundy Thursday and Testing of Abraham)

Weekly materials

Prayers of Intercession: Lynn Bulock, Lawrence Clark, Brett Davis, Julie Kanarr, Jennifer Manis, Rachel Manke, Gail Ramshaw, Kyle Schiefelbein, Clint A. Schnekloth, Kevin Shock

Images in the Readings and Connections with the Liturgy: Gail Ramshaw

Ideas for the Day: Karen Bates-Olson, Tim Brown, Michael Coffey, Yehiel Curry, Melody Eastman, Anne Edison-Albright, Bryon Hansen, Jim Honig, Liv Larson Andrews, Nathan LeRud, Rebecca Liberty, Bekki Lohrmann, Anastasia McAteer, Patrick Shebeck, Harvard Stephens, David Vásquez-Levy, Paul E. Walters

Let the Children Come: Sharolyn Browning, Suzanne Guinn, Ruth Hetland, staff

Music materials

Assembly Song: Lorraine S. Brugh (global), Cheryl Dieter (psalmody), Julie Grindle (hymns), Omaldo Perez (praise/contemporary—Time after Pentecost), Clint A. Schnekloth (praise/contemporary—Advent through Day of Pentecost)

Music for the Day: Arletta Anderson (keyboard/instrumental), Michael Glasgow (handbell), Gwen Gotsch (children's choir), Timothy Shaw (choral)

Art and design

Cover art: Nicholas Wilton

Interior art: Claudia McGehee, Tanja Butler

Book design: Laurie Ingram, Jessica Hillstrom

Development staff

Suzanne Burke, Martin A. Seltz

Manufactured in the U.S.A.

978-1-4514-2577-2

INTRODUCTION

Lectionary Conversion Chart 7

Lectionary Color Chart. 8

Welcome 9

The Year of Luke 12

Advent in November? 15

Treasuring the Revised Common Lectionary 18

ADVENT

Preparing for Advent 23

Worship Texts for Advent. 26

Seasonal Rites for Advent 28

First Sunday of Advent. . . . . Nov 29, 2015 32

Second Sunday of Advent . . . . Dec 6 35

Third Sunday of Advent . . . . Dec 13 39

Fourth Sunday of Advent . . . . Dec 20 42

CHRISTMAS

Preparing for Christmas 47

Worship Texts for Christmas. 50

Seasonal Rites for Christmas 52

Nativity of Our Lord / Christmas Eve . . . . Dec 24 56

Nativity of Our Lord / Christmas Day. . . . . Dec 25 59

First Sunday of Christmas. . . . . Dec 27 63

Second Sunday of Christmas . . . . Jan 3, 2016. 66

Epiphany of Our Lord . . . . Jan 6. 69

TIME AFTER EPIPHANY

Preparing for the Time after Epiphany. 75

Worship Texts for the Time after Epiphany 78

Seasonal Rites for the Time after Epiphany 80

Baptism of Our Lord / Lectionary 1 . . . . Jan 10. 82

Second Sunday after Epiphany / Lectionary 2 . . . . Jan 17. 85

Third Sunday after Epiphany / Lectionary 3 . . . . Jan 24. 89

Fourth Sunday after Epiphany / Lectionary 4 . . . . Jan 31 92
Transfiguration of Our Lord / Last Sunday after Epiphany . . . . Feb 7 95

Lent

Preparing for Lent 101
Worship Texts for Lent 104
Seasonal Rites for Lent 106
Ash Wednesday . . . . Feb 10 112
First Sunday in Lent . . . . Feb 14 115
Second Sunday in Lent . . . . Feb 21 118
Third Sunday in Lent . . . . Feb 28 122
Fourth Sunday in Lent . . . . Mar 6 125
Fifth Sunday in Lent . . . . Mar 13 129
Sunday of the Passion / Palm Sunday . . . . Mar 20 132
Monday in Holy Week . . . . Mar 21 135
Tuesday in Holy Week . . . . Mar 22 136
Wednesday in Holy Week . . . . Mar 23 137

The Three Days

Preparing for the Three Days 141
Worship Texts for the Three Days 144
Seasonal Rites for the Three Days 146
Maundy Thursday . . . . Mar 24 150
Good Friday . . . . Mar 25 153
Resurrection of Our Lord / Vigil of Easter . . . . Mar 26 156
Resurrection of Our Lord / Easter Day . . . . Mar 27 160
Resurrection of Our Lord / Easter Evening . . . . Mar 27 163

Easter

Preparing for Easter 167
Worship Texts for Easter 170
Seasonal Rites for Easter 172
Second Sunday of Easter . . . . Apr 3 174
Third Sunday of Easter . . . . Apr 10 177
Fourth Sunday of Easter . . . . Apr 17 180
Fifth Sunday of Easter . . . . Apr 24 184
Sixth Sunday of Easter . . . . May 1 187
Ascension of Our Lord . . . . May 5 190
Seventh Sunday of Easter . . . . May 8 193
Vigil of Pentecost . . . . May 14 196
Day of Pentecost . . . . May 15 197

Time after Pentecost — Summer

Preparing for Summer 203
Worship Texts for Summer 206
Seasonal Rites for Summer 208
The Holy Trinity / First Sunday after Pentecost . . . . May 22 213
Time after Pentecost / Lectionary 9 . . . . May 29 216
Time after Pentecost / Lectionary 10 . . . . June 5 220
Time after Pentecost / Lectionary 11 . . . . June 12 224
Time after Pentecost / Lectionary 12 . . . . June 19 227
Time after Pentecost / Lectionary 13 . . . . June 26 231
Time after Pentecost / Lectionary 14 . . . . July 3 234
Time after Pentecost / Lectionary 15 . . . . July 10 238
Time after Pentecost / Lectionary 16 . . . . July 17 241
Time after Pentecost / Lectionary 17 . . . . July 24 244
Time after Pentecost / Lectionary 18 . . . . July 31 248
Time after Pentecost / Lectionary 19 . . . . Aug 7 251
Time after Pentecost / Lectionary 20 . . . . Aug 14 254
Time after Pentecost / Lectionary 21 . . . . Aug 21 258
Time after Pentecost / Lectionary 22 . . . . Aug 28 261

Time after Pentecost — Autumn

Preparing for Autumn 267
Worship Texts for Autumn 270
Seasonal Rites for Autumn 272
Time after Pentecost / Lectionary 23 . . . . Sept 4 274
Time after Pentecost / Lectionary 24 . . . . Sept 11 . . . 277
Time after Pentecost / Lectionary 25 . . . . Sept 18 . . . 281
Time after Pentecost / Lectionary 26 . . . . Sept 25 . . . 284
Time after Pentecost / Lectionary 27 . . . . Oct 2 287
Time after Pentecost / Lectionary 28 . . . . Oct 9 291
Time after Pentecost / Lectionary 29 . . . . Oct 16 294
Time after Pentecost / Lectionary 30 . . . . Oct 23 297
Reformation Sunday . . . . Oct 30 301
Time after Pentecost / Lectionary 31 . . . . Oct 30 304

Time after Pentecost — November

Preparing for November 311
Worship Texts for November 314
Seasonal Rites for November 316
All Saints Sunday . . . . Nov 6 318
Time after Pentecost / Lectionary 32 . . . . Nov 6 321
Time after Pentecost / Lectionary 33 . . . . Nov 13 325
Christ the King / Last Sunday after Pentecost / Lectionary 34 . . . . Nov 20 328
Day of Thanksgiving (U.S.A.) . . . . Nov 24 331

Resources. 334
Key to Hymn and Song Collections. 341
Key to Psalm Collections 342
Key to Music for Worship. 343
Key to Music Publishers. 343

INDEX OF SEASONAL RITES

A Service for the Day of Epiphany. 54
Blessing for a Home at Epiphany. 53
Blessing of Animals 273
Blessing of Backpacks 272
Blessing of Graduates 172
Blessing of the Nativity Scene 52
Blessings for Teachers and Students 272
Christmas Proclamation 52
Continuing in the Covenant of Baptism: A Midweek Plan for Lent 106
Farewell to Alleluia 81
Godparenting Sunday 80
Lighting the Christmas Tree. 52
Maundy Thursday: John 13:1-17, 31b-35 146
Midweek Lenten Series: Open My Life, Lord 107
Names for Holy Communion and What They Mean. 172
Practicing Prayer: An Evening Prayer Service for Advent. 29
Prayer Around the Cross: Beside Still Waters. 208
Presentation of the Bible 272
Resources for Labor/Labour Day 211
Resources for Memorial Day 211
Resources for Veterans Day 317
Testing of Abraham: Vigil of Easter 148
Thanksgiving for Saints of the Congregation. 316
The Advent Wreath 28
Week of Prayer for Christian Unity 81
Welcoming People to Communion 173

Lectionary Conversion Chart
Time after Pentecost, Year C, 2016

If today is . . .	. . . it falls within this date range.	The "lectionary" number assigned to this date range in *Evangelical Lutheran Worship* is . . .	. . . which is equivalent to "proper ____" in other printed lectionaries.	In 2016, this Sunday is the "____ Sunday after Pentecost."
Sunday, May 29	Sunday between May 29 & June 4 (*if after Holy Trinity*)	Lectionary 9	4	2nd
Sunday, June 5	Sunday between June 5 & 11 (*if after Holy Trinity*)	Lectionary 10	5	3rd
Sunday, June 12	Sunday between June 12 & 18 (*if after Holy Trinity*)	Lectionary 11	6	4th
Sunday, June 19	Sunday between June 19 & 25	Lectionary 12	7	5th
Sunday, June 26	Sunday between June 26 & July 2	Lectionary 13	8	6th
Sunday, July 3	Sunday between July 3 & 9	Lectionary 14	9	7th
Sunday, July 10	Sunday between July 10 & 16	Lectionary 15	11	8th
Sunday, July 17	Sunday between July 17 & 23	Lectionary 16	11	9th
Sunday, July 24	Sunday between July 24 & 30	Lectionary 17	12	10th
Sunday, July 31	Sunday between July 31 & Aug 6	Lectionary 18	11	11th
Sunday, August 7	Sunday between Aug 7 & 13	Lectionary 19	14	12th
Sunday, August 14	Sunday between Aug 14 & 20	Lectionary 20	15	13th
Sunday, August 21	Sunday between Aug 21 & 27	Lectionary 21	16	14th
Sunday, August 28	Sunday between Aug 28 & Sept 3	Lectionary 22	17	15th
Sunday, September 4	Sunday between Sept 4 & 10	Lectionary 23	18	16th
Sunday, September 11	Sunday between Sept 11 & 17	Lectionary 24	19	17th
Sunday, September 18	Sunday between Sept 18 & 24	Lectionary 25	20	18th
Sunday, September 25	Sunday between Sept 25 & Oct 1	Lectionary 26	21	19th
Sunday, October 2	Sunday between Oct 2 & 8	Lectionary 27	22	20th
Sunday, October 9	Sunday between Oct 9 & 15	Lectionary 28	23	21st
Sunday, October 16	Sunday between Oct 16 & 22	Lectionary 29	24	22nd
Sunday, October 23	Sunday between Oct 23 & 29	Lectionary 30	25	23rd
Sunday, October 30	Sunday between Oct 30 Nov 5	Lectionary 31	26	24th
Sunday, November 6	Sunday between Nov 6 & 12	Lectionary 32	27	25th
Sunday, November 13	Sunday between Nov 13 & 19	Lectionary 33	28	26th
Christ the King, Nov 20	Sunday between Nov 20 & 26	Lectionary 34	29	Last

Lectionary Color Chart
Year C, 2016

Advent

Nov 29	First Sunday of Advent	Blue
Dec 6	Second Sunday of Advent	Blue
Dec 13	Third Sunday of Advent	Blue
Dec 20	Fourth Sunday of Advent	Blue

Christmas

Dec 24/25	Nativity of Our Lord	White
Dec 27	First Sunday of Christmas	White
Jan 3	Second Sunday of Christmas	White
Jan 6	Epiphany of Our Lord	White

Time after Epiphany

Jan 10	Baptism of Our Lord	White
Jan 17	Second Sunday after Epiphany	Green
Jan 24	Third Sunday after Epiphany	Green
Jan 31	Fourth Sunday after Epiphany	Green
Feb 7	Transfiguration of Our Lord	White

Lent

Feb 10	Ash Wednesday	Purple
Feb 14	First Sunday in Lent	Purple
Feb 21	Second Sunday in Lent	Purple
Feb 28	Third Sunday in Lent	Purple
Mar 6	Fourth Sunday in Lent	Purple
Mar 13	Fifth Sunday in Lent	Purple
Mar 20	Sunday of the Passion	Scarlet/Purple
Mar 21	Monday in Holy Week	Scarlet/Purple
Mar 22	Tuesday in Holy Week	Scarlet/Purple
Mar 23	Wednesday in Holy Week	Scarlet/Purple

Three Days

Mar 24	Maundy Thursday	Scarlet/White
Mar 25	Good Friday	None
Mar 26/27	Resurrection of Our Lord	White/Gold

Easter

Apr 3	Second Sunday of Easter	White
Apr 10	Third Sunday of Easter	White
Apr 17	Fourth Sunday of Easter	White
Apr 24	Fifth Sunday of Easter	White
May 1	Sixth Sunday of Easter	White
May 5	Ascension of Our Lord	White
May 8	Seventh Sunday of Easter	White
May 15	Day of Pentecost	Red

Time after Pentecost

May 22	The Holy Trinity	White
May 29	Lectionary 9	Green
June 5	Lectionary 10	Green
June 12	Lectionary 11	Green
June 19	Lectionary 12	Green
June 26	Lectionary 13	Green
July 3	Lectionary 14	Green
July 10	Lectionary 15	Green
July 17	Lectionary 16	Green
July 24	Lectionary 17	Green
July 31	Lectionary 18	Green
Aug 7	Lectionary 19	Green
Aug 14	Lectionary 20	Green
Aug 21	Lectionary 21	Green
Aug 28	Lectionary 22	Green
Sept 4	Lectionary 23	Green
Sept 11	Lectionary 24	Green
Sept 18	Lectionary 25	Green
Sept 25	Lectionary 26	Green
Oct 2	Lectionary 27	Green
Oct 9	Lectionary 28	Green
Oct 10	Day of Thanksgiving (Canada)	Green
Oct 16	Lectionary 29	Green
Oct 23	Lectionary 30	Green
Oct 30	Reformation Sunday	Red
Oct 30	Lectionary 31	Green
Nov 6	All Saints Sunday	White
Nov 6	Lectionary 32	Green
Nov 13	Lectionary 33	Green
Nov 20	Christ the King (Lect. 34)	White/Green
Nov 24	Day of Thanksgiving (USA)	Green

WELCOME

Two decades and counting

This edition of *Sundays and Seasons* marks its twenty-first year of publication. Over those twenty-plus years, the mission of *Sundays and Seasons* has remained constant, even as its form and content have adapted to meet the changing needs of worship planners. *Sundays and Seasons* was introduced at a time when the ecumenical Revised Common Lectionary (1992) was being newly adopted by congregations and denominations and *Lutheran Book of Worship* (1978) was nearing its twentieth anniversary. More than twenty years later the church's worship continues to be enriched by this lectionary, and North American Lutherans have a new principal worship resource, *Evangelical Lutheran Worship* (2006).

Sundays and Seasons has expanded beyond a single print volume into a family of resources that includes a robust online planning tool, sundaysandseasons.com (see a list of the whole family on page 2 of this volume). In 2014, we introduced *Sundays and Seasons: Preaching*, an annual print resource that encourages and provides help for lectionary preaching, taking into account all the readings for the day, in addition to the rest of the service and the day itself in the church year.

As it has from the beginning, the Sundays and Seasons family of resources continues to support week-by-week planning for Lutherans with content and ideas shaped by the Revised Common Lectionary, the church year, and the assembly gathered around word and sacrament. Or, to say it the way its first editor, Samuel Torvend, said it, "*Sundays and Seasons* points us to that merciful place of encounter where God comes to abide among us in the holy gospel and the sacraments of grace: the worshiping assembly."

Welcome to the 2016 edition

Maybe you have been relying on *Sundays and Seasons* since its inception. Perhaps you are encountering it for the first time. While the basic form and content of *Sundays and Seasons* continues from previous years, this year's edition includes some things worth pointing out to both newcomers and longtime users.

This year, we are trying something new within the **seasonal introductions**. While *Sundays and Seasons* has always provided suggestions around **preparing the visual environment** for each season, this year the suggestions are accompanied by actual visuals (photographs, patterns, step-by-step instructions, and more) presented in PDF files that can be accessed online. You can access and download these files for free through the Augsburg Fortress web store: http://store.augsburgfortress.org/media/temp/Sundays Seasons/PDFs.zip. If you are a sundaysandseasons.com subscriber, these same files will be accessible through the seasonal rites section of the Library. These visual suggestions and ideas were created and curated by Linda Witte Henke. Linda is an award-winning mixed-media artist who creates commissioned liturgical art and exhibits her work within and beyond the United States (www.lindahenke.com). She lives in Indianapolis, where she also chairs the worship committee of the Indiana-Kentucky Synod.

The decision to omit a **seasonal greeting** beginning in 2014 came from widespread observation that many presiding ministers are so tied to the words on the page when speaking the words of an unfamiliar, regularly changing greeting that they do not actually look at the assembly when speaking these words. The intention here is to encourage presiders to use a greeting known by heart so they can be freed from the page and truly greet the assembly. The standard "The grace of our Lord Jesus Christ, the love of God, and the communion of the Holy Spirit be with you all" serves beautifully any Sunday of the year. And, there is great power in hearing the same words again and again, something especially the children in our assemblies remind us when we change the words to worship texts they know by heart.

With the whole church

This resource would not exist without the creative talents of many people across the church. Those who create content for *Sundays and Seasons* are people just like you. They are pastors, musicians, associates in ministry, members of worship committees and altar guilds, seminary professors, visual artists, diaconal ministers, and deaconesses. They work full time, part time, or are volunteers in their churches. They serve large and small congregations and campus ministries in rural areas, small towns, cities, and suburbs in the United States, Canada, and abroad. They come from various cultural contexts, and with different approaches to worship in word and sacrament. Over the past two decades literally hundreds of people have contributed to *Sundays and Seasons*. Here's this year's group.

Visual images

You may recognize **Tanja Butler**'s (weekly images) black and white icons from sundaysandseasons.com. We have already colorized Tanja's icons for years A and B; year C will be added in time for Advent 2015. **Claudia McGehee** (annual and seasonal images) contemplates and illustrates from her home studio in Iowa City, Iowa. Learn about her and see more of her work at claudiaillustration.blogspot.com. In creating the cover art for *Sundays and Seasons*, **Nicholas Wilton** believed that symbols of things were needed as, like poetry, we are trying to express something about the spiritual.

Annual and seasonal materials

Jennifer Baker-Trinity (Lent, Three Days, and Easter lectionary and music introductions) is a church musician who leads the people's song at Beaver Lutheran in Beaver Springs, Pennsylvania. **Lynn Bulock** (lighting the Christmas tree; blessing the nativity scene) is a diaconal minister in southern California. She is a member of New Hope Lutheran, a Stephen Leader, wife, mother, and grandmother. **Dennis Bushkofsky** (midweek Lenten plan: Continuing in the Covenant of Baptism) likes having a church office and home within one Wi-Fi signal where he also produces AF's annual *Bread for the Day*. **Erik Christensen** (Summer, Autumn, and November lectionary and music introductions) is the pastor of St. Luke's Lutheran of Logan Square in Chicago. He is learning to play guitar and waiting for the next season of Downton Abbey. Award-winning mixed-media artist, published author, and former parish pastor **Linda Witte Henke** (seasonal visual environment suggestions) creates commissioned liturgical art and exhibits her work within and beyond the U.S. **Melissa Moll** (Epiphany Day service; midweek Lenten series: Open My Life, Lord) is an organist, a librarian, and a member of First Lutheran in Lincoln, Nebraska. **Craig M. Mueller** (Advent in November?) is pastor of Holy Trinity Lutheran in Chicago and is interested in the intersection of liturgy, preaching, virtuality, and outreach to the millennial generation. **Mark Mummert** (Advent, Christmas, and Time after Epiphany lectionary and music introductions) is director of worship at Christ the King Lutheran in Houston. He served as seminary musician at Lutheran Theological Seminary at Philadelphia, 1990–2008. **Ray Pickett** (introduction to Luke) is professor of New Testament at Lutheran School of Theology at Chicago. **Gail Ramshaw** (Treasuring the Revised Common Lectionary) studies and crafts liturgical

language from her home in Washington, D.C. **John Roberts** (Maundy Thursday and Testing of Abraham scripts) is associate pastor of Unity Evangelical Lutheran in Chicago. **Clint A. Schnekloth** (evening prayer Advent series; graduate blessing) is lead pastor at Good Shepherd Lutheran, Fayetteville, Arkansas. He is the author of *Mediating Faith: Faith Formation in a Trans-media Era*.

Prayers of intercession

Rev. Dr. **Lawrence James Clark II** is senior pastor of St. Mark Lutheran in Chicago. **Brett Davis** is associate pastor of Muhlenberg Lutheran in Harrisonburg, Virginia. Pastor **Julie A. Kanarr** serves Christ Lutheran in Belfair, Washington. In addition to writing, she enjoys bicycling, camping, and sea kayaking. Diaconal minister **Jennifer Manis** serves at Lutheran Campus Ministry in Raleigh, North Carolina. She encounters God's grace daily through laughter, coffee, and walks in the wood. **Rachel Manke** is a parish pastor in the Boston area. In her free time she enjoys writing limericks and playing her ukuleles. **Kyle Schiefelbein** earned his PhD in liturgical studies from Graduate Theological Union and is a member of St. Mark's Lutheran in San Francisco. **Kevin Shock** enjoys many ministry opportunities with seniors, Penn State students, and others, but especially feels blessed as pastor for the people at St. Mark Lutheran in Pleasant Gap, Pennsylvania. **Lynn Bulock**, **Gail Ramshaw**, and **Clint A. Schnekloth** also contributed prayers of intercession to this volume.

Images in the readings, connections with the liturgy

Gail Ramshaw studies and crafts liturgical language from her home in Washington, D.C. She is the author of *Treasures Old and New*, *Christian Worship*, and *What Is Christianity?*

Ideas for the day

Pastor **Karen Bates-Olson** serves Lutheran Church of the Master in Pasco, Washington. She and her husband, Kevin, have two beautiful daughters, Amy and Katie. Pastor **Tim Brown** serves Luther Memorial Church in Chicago, and is a writer, dreamer, and occasional beer brewer. **Michael Coffey** serves as pastor of First English Lutheran in Austin, Texas. He enjoys writing, blogging, cooking, liturgical and ritual experimentation, Old Testament studies, and exploring spiritual formation. **Yehiel Curry** was ordained through the Theological Education for Emerging Ministries (TEEM) program after serving two years as mission developer of Shekinah Chapel in Riverdale, Illinois. He later earned his MDiv from the Lutheran School of Theology at Chicago. **Melody Eastman** is senior pastor of St. Paul Lutheran in Wheaton, Illinois. She and her husband Marty crave live music and camping. **Anne Edison-Albright** is wife to Sean, mom to Walter and Sally, friend to Hank the dog, and pastor to Redeemer Lutheran in Stevens Point, Wisconsin. **Bryon Hansen** is pastor of Phinney Ridge Lutheran in Seattle, a parish passionate about formation in and around the gift of baptism. His greatest delight is to preside, preach, and assist the catechumenate process. **James Honig** is pastor of Faith Evangelical Lutheran in Glen Ellyn, Illinois. He is a writer, blogger, and avid enjoyer of God's good creation. **Liv Larson Andrews** is an ELCA pastor serving in the West Central neighborhood of Spokane, Washington. Sunday worship is enlivened for her by her young son, Arlo, and spouse, Casey. **Nathan LeRud** is an Episcopal priest serving as canon for spiritual formation at Trinity Episcopal Cathedral in Portland, Oregon. **Rebecca Liberty** has served in congregations and campus ministries in the western United States and now lives in Bangor, Maine. **Bekki Lohrmann**, a 2014 LSTC graduate, is awaiting first call. She has served as interim pastor at Holden Village in Chelan, Washington, and Faith Lutheran in Joliet, Illinois. **Anastasia McAteer** is a liturgist, preacher, teacher, community organizer, and mommy. **Patrick Shebeck** is pastor of St. Paul–Reformation Lutheran in St. Paul. He has been a church musician in Roman Catholic, Episcopal, and Lutheran parishes in the Twin Cities. **Harvard Stephens**, an ELCA pastor, finds renewal through many forms of contemplative spirituality, including tai chi. He also enjoys playing the soprano saxophone. **David Vásquez-Levy** is president of Pacific School of Religion. A committed pastor, nationally recognized immigration leader, and sought after speaker, David loves intersections: church, academy, and world. **Paul E. Walters** is pastor of Lutheran Church of the Master in Troy, Michigan. He is a husband, father to three boys, and a knight of Sufferlandria.

Let the children come

Sharolyn Browning is a Godly Play storyteller and trainer. She holds a certificate in the spiritual guidance of children and a Master of Divinity degree. **Suzanne Guinn** is a pastor and chaplain in Fort Worth, Texas, and has two cats. She enjoys playing the keyboard, singing, and writing poetry. **Ruth E. Hetland** is a pastor, writer, wife, mom, skeptic, taphophile, and a Norwegian reality show participant (*Alt for Norge*, season 5).

Music suggestions

Arletta Anderson (keyboard/instrumental) is an associate in ministry in the ELCA and cantor at Queen Anne Lutheran in Seattle. **Lorraine S. Brugh** (global) is professor of music and director of chapel music at Valparaiso University. She serves as executive director of the University's Institute of Liturgical Studies, which annually brings church leaders across the country together to study and reflect upon worship practices. **Cheryl Dieter** (psalmody) is minister of worship and music at Trinity Lutheran in Valparaiso, Indiana, and business manager for the Association of Lutheran Church Musicians. **Michael J. Glasgow** (handbell) is an award-winning composer and internationally recognized conductor working in handbell, organ, orchestral, and choral settings (www.michaeljglasgow.com). **Gwen Gotsch** (children's choir) directs the youth choir and coordinates communications at Grace Lutheran in River Forest, Illinois. She has written devotions for *Christ in Our Home* and articles for *Gather*. **Julie Grindle** (hymns) is a lifelong church musician and serves as director of music ministries at St. Mark's Lutheran in Baldwinsville, New York. She is president-elect of the Association of Lutheran Church Musicians. **Omaldo Perez** (praise/contemporary songs, Holy Trinity through Christ the King) has served four Lutheran congregations in the last fifteen years in New Jersey, Arizona, Washington, and now Ohio, where he happily serves as the music director and organist at Zoar Lutheran in Perrysburg. The task of suggesting songs in the praise/contemporary category (Advent through Day of Pentecost) was shared by **Clint A. Schnekloth**. New Hampshire native **Timothy Shaw** (choral) is a composer, conductor, pianist, organist, and music educator (www.shawmusic.org).

You make it happen

Sundays and Seasons continues to be a collaborative endeavor each year. In our editorial conversations here at Augsburg Fortress we regularly evaluate the scope, format, and quality of the content provided in these pages. Your feedback, collected from you firsthand at events around this church, from postings in various forms of social media, from phone calls and emails to our sales and service representatives, and from surveys, helps us make decisions about how to adjust content so it is even more helpful. You, dear partners in ministry, make this resource happen. I welcome your ideas for future content, your suggestions for potential contributors (maybe you!), and your constructive feedback. Thank you for the trust you place in the changing roster of contributors who offer their time and talent to the whole church through *Sundays and Seasons*. Even more, thank you for the many and various ways in which you care for the Sunday assembly and its worship of the triune God.

Suzanne K. Burke, general editor

THE YEAR OF LUKE

The narrative arc of Luke's story of Jesus has much in common with the Gospel of Mark, one of its primary sources, and also with the Gospel of Matthew. However, Luke also has some distinctive traditions, themes, and perspectives that tell us something about how this gospel was designed to shape the communal life and practices of those for whom it was written. Although it is impossible to know precisely where and when the gospel was written, *how* the narrator has woven the disparate traditions about Jesus available to him into a coherent narrative that is interpreted in the light of Israel's scriptures and conceived of as a continuation of the ongoing story of God's people provides important clues as to *why* it was written, that is, its intended impact. All ancient texts, including scripture, were rhetorical in the sense that they were written and performed with a view to changing the way people think and act; their purpose was transformation. Paying attention to how Luke was constructed, its rhetorical strategy, and asking questions about what this narrative of Jesus is doing and the vision of reality it impels his followers to embrace and embody leads to a way of reading that involves the audience and engenders agency through the life-giving power of the Spirit—a prominent theme throughout Luke and Acts.

The first two chapters of Luke provide an introduction to the entire gospel as a story of the fulfillment of God's promises. They are saturated in the language of scripture with more than 90 percent of the vocabulary coming from the Septuagint, the Greek translation of Israel's scriptures. Three canticles set up many of the main themes that will be developed throughout the narrative. Mary's Song (Luke 1:46-55) voices confidence in the God of mercy and power who is cognizant of the humiliation and misery of God's people and will deliver on the promise to save them. The Magnificat indicates at the very outset that this story of Jesus' proclamation and enactment of God's kin(g)dom entails a new sociality that restores human dignity and a relational Spirit-power that breaks the bonds of subjugation. The second canticle comes in the form of Zechariah's prophecy, which, like Mary's Song, invokes the covenant with Abraham and also includes the Davidic covenant signaling continuity with and renewal of God's historic relationship with the people of God. Indeed, Simeon, in the third canticle, acclaims that ultimately this story of Jesus is about the restoration of Israel (2:25), and, echoing words from the prophet Isaiah, announces that this "salvation" to which Simeon is the first to bear witness will be "a light for revelation to the Gentiles and for glory to your people Israel" (2:32). Luke draws on Israel's scriptures to frame this gospel as a narrative of Jesus embodying God's purpose of bringing salvation to Israel and the nations and thereby fulfilling the covenant with Abraham. Hence the universal horizon of Luke's story of Jesus.

The term *salvation* and its cognates are used more in this gospel than any of the other gospels, and it is defined by the narrative itself, not only through the actions and teachings of Jesus but also by characters who respond faithfully to his message. So, for example, Jesus tells Zacchaeus, who gives half his possessions to the poor, "Today salvation has come to this house" (19:9). In the Gospel of Luke, as in the Bible generally, salvation is *communal*, *concrete*, and *cosmic*, encompassing all creation (3:6). Luke's vision of salvation is communal in that the aim is "to make ready a people prepared for the Lord" (1:17), that is, communities of disciples through which God accomplishes God's purposes because Jesus' followers hear his words and act on them (6:46-49). It is concrete because it involves tangible acts of physical healing, feedings, radical inclusivity, restoration, liberation, and prophetic action, and a pattern of communal life.

The Gospel of Luke develops the central theme of the restoration of Israel and the nations in a manner that raises questions for audiences about how this salvation will come about, what it will look like, and the role of Jesus' followers in making it a reality. That salvation has a political dimension in this gospel is evidenced in the fact that only Luke sets the stage by naming Augustus as emperor and other significant power brokers who preside over a draconian tax system connoted by the census (2:1-7). However, since the story of Jesus' ministry and its continuation by his followers in Acts occurs under Roman rule, salvation will not entail the hoped-for defeat of imperial power. On the road to Emmaus, Cleopas and the other disciple express their disappointment to the risen Jesus, whom they have yet to recognize: "We had hoped that he was the one to redeem

Israel" (24:21). Their response betrays the expectation that as Messiah, Jesus would be the one anointed to deliver God's people "from the hands of our enemies" (1:71, 74). The response of the risen Jesus to a final query, "Lord, is this is the time when you will restore the kingdom to Israel" (Acts 1:6) indicates that the hope and expectation of salvation must be recalibrated to focus on the empowerment of faithful followers to participate in God's reign in their own real-life contexts:

> "It is not for you to know the times or periods that the Father has set by his own authority. But you will receive power when the Holy Spirit has come upon you; and you will be my witnesses in Jerusalem, in all Judea and Samaria, and to the ends of the earth." (Acts 1:7-8)

So Luke's story of Jesus is a response to questions raised in Luke-Acts itself about the time and character of salvation by showing that the ministry, death, and resurrection of Jesus mark the dawning of a new age and a new chapter in the story of God's people that is continuous with Israel's story and is indeed a fulfillment of God's promises to restore not only Israel but all the nations of the earth.

The key themes of Jesus' teaching and enactment of the kingdom of God in Luke then serve the purpose of forming disciples who belong to the community of the new age, a community empowered by the Spirit to bear witness to God's ongoing work of redemption and restoration in the world. The clearest articulation of this vision is in the most programmatic passage in the gospel, where Jesus, having been baptized in the Spirit and tested by the devil who claims dominion over "all the kingdoms of the world" (4:5), returns to his hometown synagogue and identifies himself as the prophet called to fulfill Isaiah 61:

> "The Spirit of the Lord is upon me,
> because he has anointed me
>   to bring good news to the poor.
> He has sent me to proclaim *release to the captives*
>   and recovery of sight to the blind,
>   *to let the oppressed go free*,
> to proclaim the year of the Lord's favor."
> (Luke 4:18-19, emphasis added)

The whole of Jesus' ministry can be described as a ministry of "release" or liberation from the economic distress and social marginalization experienced by the populace of imperial society. As a prophet leading a community renewal movement in Galilee, Jesus proclaims an alternative future where interpersonal and communal relationships are reformed through new patterns and practices predicated on Jesus' exemplification of God's power, beneficence, mercy, and radical hospitality—some of the main themes in Luke's gospel.

Luke's account of Jesus' ministry begins with John's call for repentance, by which he means comprehensive social change (3:4-6). Only in Luke do those who are baptized ask, "What then should we do?" John replies with specific examples of how those with surplus goods, such as tax collectors and soldiers, must align their behavior with the new society God is forming (3:10-14). Repentance is a key theme throughout Luke-Acts, and it is frequently linked with forgiveness. Jesus' Sermon on the Plain in Luke 6 lays the foundation for this new sociality by challenging the Greco-Roman patronage system that kept people indebted and beholden by fostering a sense of loyalty to the patron that undermined cooperation and community. Jesus subverted the very foundation of Greco-Roman society, in which giving always obligated the recipient, when he exhorted followers to "love your enemies, do good, and lend, *expecting nothing in return*" (6:35, emphasis added). He advocated an alternative pattern of relating to those who were alienated or in need that promoted mutuality, solidarity, and interdependence predicated on God's boundless mercy and generosity: "Be merciful, just as your Father is merciful" (6:36).

Two other important features of God's new society Jesus is forming in Luke are hospitality and reformed economic relations. In Luke, Jesus is often seen going to a meal, leaving a meal, or sitting down at a meal, and meals are the occasion for demonstrating a radical inclusivity and the social reversal anticipated in Mary's Song (1:51-55). Jesus welcomes those who were otherwise *persona non grata* and also undermines Greco-Roman conventions of honor and status that were most evident at Greco-Roman meals (see 5:27-32; 7:36-50; 10:38-42; 11:37-44; 14:1-24; 22:14-27; 24:28-43). In Luke 14, Jesus' exhortation to eschew the quest for honor in favor of humility is followed by the parable of the great banquet, where those who refuse the invitation because they are too preoccupied with their possessions are replaced by "the poor, the crippled, the blind, and the lame." This is one of many passages signifying that the divine hospitality exhibited by Jesus reaches to the outermost socioeconomic margins of society.

Closely related to Jesus' emphasis on hospitality as a preeminent mark of God's new society are a number of passages dealing with economic relations that are unique to Luke (see 12:13-34; 14:25-33; 16:1-31; 18:18-30; 19:1-10, 11-27). In his inaugural sermon (4:18-19) and in the first beatitudes (6:20-21), Jesus made it clear that the poor and hungry were a priority in his ministry. However, what he has to say about the use of material possessions in Luke serves to inspire faithful practices of sharing and almsgiving that reveal divine compassion and magnanimity as intimations of the presence of God's future (11:1-4). All of these themes coalesce in Jesus' teaching on the centrality of the double command "Love the Lord your God with all your heart, and with all your soul, and with all your strength, and with all your mind; and your neighbor as yourself," which he elucidates with the parable of the good Samaritan (10:25-37). Followers of Jesus in every generation experience for themselves the power of the Spirit as they venture out of their comfort zones to show hospitality to strangers and discover the deep solidarity that binds us together as "children of the Most High" (6:35) as they learn what it means to love God by loving our neighbors.

The Gospel of Luke features the prophetic ministry of Jesus from his inaugural sermon in Nazareth (4:16-30) and the renewal movement he was leading in Galilee through his journey to Jerusalem, where he challenges the status quo of the capital city and is executed as an enemy of the Roman order, despite being declared innocent of the charges against him (23:4, 13-15, 47). However, from the outset Luke's portrait of Jesus' prophetic ministry simultaneously reflects a postresurrection perspective that this Galilean Jew is also "Lord." The story of the Crucified One whom God raised from the dead continues in Acts as he continues to "turn the world upside down" through followers who are baptized into his name and empowered by the Spirit.

Raymond Pickett
Lutheran School of Theology at Chicago

ADVENT IN NOVEMBER?
AN ECUMENICAL PROPOSAL, A HYBRID RESPONSE

Is it possible to meaningfully observe Advent in our culture when Christmas decorations begin appearing in stores in late August and then take center stage once Halloween décor is removed on November 1? The months of November and December have become an extended period of holiday advertisements, parties, shopping, and concerts. With an accelerated and extended Christmas season, many churches succumb by putting up trees and decorations, and begin singing carols at the beginning of Advent. Though Advent is recognized as preparation for the celebration of the nativity, within our cultural context the two seasons often fuse into in a four-week focus on the babe in the manger, angels, shepherds, and, since they make appearances in crèches and carols, the magi.

The only problem with the above scenario is that the essence of Advent is eschatological. Advent invites us to prepare for the coming of Christ at the end of time even as we welcome his appearance in our weekly assembly and in the world to which we are sent. Not until the fourth Sunday of Advent do the readings turn to texts we associate with the nativity. The spiritually rich themes of Advent are difficult to accentuate when our culture is fixated on merriment, not to mention crazed schedules and demands.

In response to the above challenges, the Advent Project proposes a seven-week Advent to afford an earlier and longer opportunity to glean the riches of the season's themes of waiting, expectation, preparation, and hope. Arguing that most churches are already on the way to Bethlehem at the beginning of December, the proposal argues that the primary focus of Advent is the full manifestation of the reign of God. If the culture of Christmas is in full swing by early December, perhaps we can begin to catch the attention of folks with some early weeks of eschatological (i.e., Advent) themes in November. The proposal does not suggest that December become a month to celebrate Christmas; rather, it provides an extended period to mine the riches of the Advent season.

The Advent Project began in 2006 as a continuing seminar of the North American Academy of Liturgy. Since then a number of congregations—mostly Episcopal and Methodist—have experimented with a seven-week Advent.

A website (theadventproject.org) provides background and resources. In 2013 the Reformed journal Call to Worship devoted an issue to the seven-week Advent proposal and related themes.

The ecumenical question

The Advent Project notes that the season of Advent has not always been four weeks and that Orthodox Christians still observe a longer Advent. Though the Advent Project is an ecumenical proposal, it appears there has not been a lot of traction so far. Whether a congregation experiments with the proposal or a denomination authorizes a seven-week Advent, either entity would be out of sync with the common Western liturgical calendar. To many, it would seem quite strange to announce that the first week of Advent begins on November 8, when most churches would be waiting three weeks to begin the season.

However, there is one essential and intriguing element to the proposal: it retains the current cycle of readings in the Revised Common Lectionary. Since the majority of the readings in November already have an eschatological focus, the final three Sundays of the church year are simply given an Advent overlay. In an expanded Advent, the first Sunday of the season would occur between November 5 and 12. Occasionally, this would overlap with All Saints Sunday and create either a difficult juxtaposition or one with creative possibilities, depending on the way you look at it.

On one hand, the question of catholicity seems integral to this proposal. When are we free to veer away from what we hold in common with others in our denomination or in the Western church? The same could be asked of those choosing to use the Narrative Lectionary. On the other hand, students of liturgical history note that in the early church there was much diversity in regard to rites and calendars, and local churches were not always in sync with one another. Is the Advent Project an example of local experimentation that could later lead to ecumenical discernment and an eventual calendar revision, or are local congregations simply going off on their own in the spirit of freedom and individualism that defines our culture?

November in *Sundays and Seasons*

In a somewhat unique move, since the mid-1990s some ELCA worship materials have set November apart as a quasi-liturgical season. In *Sundays and Seasons*, for example, the month of November is given its own chapter with suggested seasonal texts and worship planning ideas. Appropriately, the Sundays of November are seen as a unity with their emphasis on the communion of saints, death, judgment, and eschatology. Often these seasonal texts take images or scriptural references from All Saints and/or Christ the King and extend them throughout the month.

Since ELCA worship resources already highlight the uniqueness of the final Sundays of the church year, it is not a huge leap to see them within the scope of Advent and its eschatological themes. Furthermore, one of the assembly song sections in *Evangelical Lutheran Worship* is named End Time and includes a number of hymns that many would consider appropriate for Advent, such as "Lo! He comes with clouds descending," "My Lord, what a morning," "Soon and very soon," and "Wake, awake, for night is flying." The point: a number of hymns are appropriate both in November and during Advent. Perhaps the best example of the fluidity between November and Advent is Lectionary 32 in year A, with its gospel parable of the wise and foolish bridesmaids. Two of the most appropriate hymns for that day are "Rejoice, rejoice, believers" and "Wake, awake, for night is flying," no doubt Advent choices as well.

For those old enough to remember the one-year lectionary, in use for centuries until the three-year lectionary was introduced in 1973, the gospel on the last Sunday of the church year was the parable of the ten bridesmaids mentioned above. That explains why Bach's famous cantata, *Wachet auf, ruft uns die Stimme* (Wake, awake, for night is flying), was composed not for Advent but for the last Sunday of the church year. There is more permeability between the ending of one church year and the beginning of the next than we often acknowledge.

Hybrid option

An alternative to a full-blown, extended Advent is to link the seven Sundays together yet still retain the season of Advent in common with the Western catholic church. Here are a number of practical suggestions:

1. In the same way that some communities mark liturgical seasons with a change in musical settings and seasonal texts, link the seven weeks together. One musical option is Richard Proulx's *Missa Emmanuel*, which uses the chant melody from "O come, O come, Emmanuel" (available to those with a subscription to OneLicense.net). Throughout the seven weeks, the assembly response to the intercessions could be "Come, Lord Jesus," and this well-known table prayer could serve as an offering prayer or an invitation to communion:

> Come, Lord Jesus, be our guest.
> Let these gifts to us be blessed.
> Blessed be God who is our bread.
> May all the world be clothed and fed.

2. The Advent project suggests linking each of the seven Sundays with one of the O Antiphons. One of the antiphons—or the appropriate stanza of "O come, O come, Emmanuel"—could be sung at the beginning of the liturgy, perhaps connected to confession and forgiveness. *Music Sourcebook for All Saints through Transfiguration* (Augsburg Fortress, 2013) notes this option of tying the seven weeks together this way and provides several settings of the O Antiphons (see the notes, pp. 67–68). In order to connect the O Antiphon related to "king" to what is commonly called Christ the King Sunday, the Advent Project slightly rearranges the traditional order:

> Advent 1 (or third last Sunday): *O Sapientia* (Wisdom)
> Advent 2 (or second last Sunday): *O Adonai* (Lord)
> Advent 3 (or Christ the King): *O Rex Gentium* (King/ Ruler of nations)
> Advent 4 (or Advent 1): *O Radix Jesse* (Root/Branch of Jesse)
> Advent 5 (or Advent 2): *O Clavis David* (Key of David)
> Advent 6 (or Advent 3): *O Oriens* (Morning Star/ Dayspring)
> Advent 7 (or Advent 4): *O Emmanuel*

3. With so many fine Advent hymns, it is difficult to get them all scheduled during Advent. Be creative and think outside the box. Consider "The King shall come" and "Prepare the royal highway" on Christ the King Sunday. Hymns such as "Wait for the Lord," "Hark, the glad sound!" and "O Lord, how shall I meet you" work equally well in November. There are many others, considered appropriate for Advent but not in the Advent section in *Evangelical Lutheran Worship*, that work well in November. Take a look at the Topical Index of Hymns (pp. 1178ff.) under the categories of Advent, End Time, and Judgment.

4. Two practical concerns arise: color and wreath. If a full seven-week Advent is observed, it would be natural to use the color blue for the entire season, and to consider using a wreath with seven candles. The Advent Project website contains resources for the wreath lighting, but you would need to devise your own way to display seven candles. If a hybrid approach is employed, it would seem logical to use green for

the first three weeks and blue during Advent, and to retain the traditional wreath with four candles.

What about Christ the King?

What shall we do with Christ the King Sunday? Often preachers and hymn selectors fixate on the word "king"—either positively or negatively—and miss the many other themes related to eschatology or consummation on this day. The festival of Christ the King is a very late addition to the calendar, and various denominations have taken different approaches to the naming of the last Sunday of the church year. Examples include "The Reign of Christ" or "The Last Sunday after Pentecost." The Renewing Worship task force that prepared provisional church year resources prior to the publication of *Evangelical Lutheran Worship* proposed the term "Last Sunday of the Year," with the color green, but ultimately "Christ the King" was retained. This is all to say that in an extended seven-week November/Advent, one option is to not make the last Sunday after Pentecost a festival, to retain green as the liturgical color, and to use Last Sunday of the Year or something similar to name the day.

November in 2015 and 2016

Depending on when you read this, you may be considering ways to integrate some of these ideas either in November/Advent 2015 or 2016. In 2015, the final Sundays of year B include an assortment of eschatological texts that resonate with Advent themes. In particular, the gospels include:

November 8: Mark 12:38-44 *Judgment on hypocrisy and the rich (the poor widow)*
November 15: Mark 13:1-8 *Birth pangs, signs of consummation*
November 22: John 18:33-37 *Pilate and the kingship of Jesus*

The gospel on November 22 may seem most difficult to connect, particularly for those who have relied on images of kingship on this day. However, the first two readings include explicit references to the one coming with the clouds of heaven. Rather than dwelling solely on the image of Christ as king, consider themes of consummation and the kingdom that is not of this world.

The year 2016 is one of the interesting years when All Saints Sunday is November 6 and is also one of the final three Sundays before Advent. Instead of using the texts for All Saints, you may want to consider using the texts for Lectionary 32 (year C). The Job reading includes the well-known verse: "I know that my Redeemer lives, and that at the last he will stand upon the earth; and after my skin has been thus destroyed, then in my flesh I shall see God" (19:25-26). The second reading is eschatological, and in the gospel from Luke 20, Jesus speaks of the resurrection and the God of the living. Thus, it would be possible to observe All Saints Sunday with the readings from Lectionary 32C while also using seven-week seasonal texts. This juxtaposition would give the preacher an opportunity to address All Saints from a different perspective than may be customary. The readings for Lectionary 33C also work very well with the proposed trajectory. The assigned texts for the Last Sunday after Pentecost include Jeremiah 23:1-6 with its promise of coming days when the Lord will raise up a righteous Branch, reign as king, and execute justice and righteousness in the land.

If your congregation experiments with a seven-week Advent, a hybrid approach as suggested above, or something similar, consider sending feedback to the Advent Project via their website. May the observance of Advent lead not simply to a meaningful celebration of Christmas, but to a deeper reflection on the coming of Christ to our world both today and at the end of time.

Craig M. Mueller
Holy Trinity Lutheran Church, Chicago

TREASURING THE REVISED COMMON LECTIONARY

Why churches have lectionaries

What use has the Bible in our time? When a lector proclaims the story of the Israelites crossing the sea, and then on public television worshipers hear that a biblically described exodus never occurred, we might inquire about the contemporary use of the Bible. What parts of the Bible ought Christians know? Why? If believers are taught the story in Genesis 3 of the woman, the man, and the serpent in the garden, what about Genesis 6, in which angels mate with humans and produce giants? If believers hear in Genesis 22 that God saved Abraham's son from child sacrifice, should they know that in Judges 11 God did not save Jephthah's daughter from sacrifice? Ought Lutherans study Deuteronomic theology, in which God blesses the good guys and punishes the bad guys? Ought we admit that the infancy narratives in Matthew and in Luke do not cohere? How should we deal with the household codes in Ephesians and Colossians?

Throughout Christian history, the inquiry "Which parts of the Bible ought the faithful know?" has been asked this way: "Which Scriptures should be proclaimed at Sunday worship?" The practice has usually been to proclaim on Sunday, not those parts of the Bible that are interesting to scholars or that either confirm or shock people's sensibilities, but those passages judged necessary for the faith. Lectionaries are constructed with a specified use of the Bible in mind.

Yet scholars have unearthed little about the historical development of Christian lectionaries. Luke 4:17 says that in the synagogue Jesus was handed the scroll of Isaiah, perhaps indicating that in the 80s Luke's Christian assembly read preferred sections of the Hebrew Scriptures. In about 383, Egeria wrote that the readings proclaimed in Jerusalem during Holy Week were the same as those appointed in western France—without, alas, listing what those readings were. By medieval times, the churches in the West and the East had developed different systems of *lectio selecta*.

Martin Luther judged that the lectionary of his time should be retained, but that the salvation through Christ hidden in the texts be more clearly proclaimed. Ulrich Zwingli advocated instead *lectio continua*, urging preachers to proceed through the entire Bible one chapter at a time.

This not surprisingly quickly devolved into what one might call *lectio individua*, a practice common in the United States in which personal preference has high value. Preachers can choose their texts free from theological tradition, outside authority, or ecumenical collaboration, relying instead on their own autobiography. The intensification in the late nineteenth century of biblical literalism led to what one might call *lectio historica*, which uses the Bible as a history textbook: if by faith you accept this narrative as factually accurate, you will be saved.

A growing number of denominations are advocating use of a lectionary in hopes that wisely chosen biblical selections and trustworthy interpretation will unite the community in faith in the triune God. To develop, approve, promote, and teach a lectionary requires a massive amount of work. Granting with Augustine that the Bible is "of mountainous difficulty and enveloped in mysteries" (*Confessions* III.9), any attempt to assign to certain occasions of worship passages essential to the faith cannot be ideal. You wish to add an omitted passage? One other selection must go. However, the Bible always bursts out of the box we pack it into, and in many denominations believers of all ages undertake regular Bible study to support the little that Sunday morning allows.

Four characteristics of the Revised Common Lectionary

The Revised Common Lectionary is a revision of the Roman Catholic lectionary that was developed in the 1960s in response to a mandate of the Second Vatican Council for an enriched lectionary, with the intention that "the riches of the Bible are to be opened up more lavishly, so that richer fare may be provided for the faithful at the table of God's word" (*Constitution on the Sacred Liturgy*, II.51). According to the Roman and Revised Common lectionaries, the primary use of Scripture at worship is to call the baptized to renewed faith in Christ and to strengthen the community in the Spirit for its life of mission, and readings are chosen to support this goal.

The Revised Common Lectionary is the suggested lectionary for, among many others, the following church bodies: the Uniting Church of Australia, the Anglican Church of Australia, the Anglican Church of Canada, the Evangelical Lutheran Church in Canada, the Presbyterian Church in Canada, the United Church of Canada, the Church of England, the United Reformed Church of Great Britain, the Presbyterian Church in Korea, the Anglican Church of Melanesia; the Presbyterian Church of Venezuela; in New Zealand the Anglican, Methodist, and Presbyterian Churches; and in the United States, the Episcopal Church, the Disciples of Christ, the Christian Fellowship of the Unitarian Universalist Association, the Christian Reformed Church, the Evangelical Lutheran Church in America, the Presbyterian Church U.S.A., the Reformed Church in America, the United Church of Christ, and the United Methodist Church. Some church bodies, including the Lutheran Church–Missouri Synod, the Lutheran Church in Japan, and the Lutheran Church in Singapore, use the RCL with minor emendations, and several other churches are studying the RCL for possible adoption.

This list leads to the first characteristic of this lectionary: ecumenicity. The Revised Common Lectionary has been judged the profoundest and farthest-reaching ecumenical development of the twentieth century. We all repeatedly pray that the church may be one, and here, thanks to the astonishing acceptance by so many church bodies of one lectionary, we are granted this sign of the unity of Christ's church. The RCL, which appoints more of scripture than any previous lectionary except Zwingli's, which didn't work, supplants what had been in many places a denominationally narrow approach to the Bible, a rogue pattern for preaching, or individualist favorites.

An ecumenical lectionary engages us with other churches, connecting us with Christians across town and around the globe. In the interplay between ecumenical commonality and denominational distinctiveness, when, for example, Lutherans proclaim this common lectionary, they will interpret it according to the Lutheran template of law and gospel. Within those churches that advocate the RCL, any proposal to substitute a different method of Sunday proclamation must prayerfully consider whether what is gained by the innovation is more than what is lost by the rejection of ecumenical collaboration and the disregard of ecclesial decisions.

The second characteristic of the Revised Common Lectionary is its maintenance of the historic hermeneutic that scripture interprets scripture. This means that when probing a biblical passage, the first resource is always other uses in scripture of its vocabulary, imagery, and theology. The creeds are not acrylic blankets but patchwork quilts, one piece from the ancient scriptures, another from Paul, another from John. Thus, to ensure that Christians know the meaning of their creeds, certain parts of the Bible are enlisted to illumine other parts.

The principle that scripture interprets scripture derives from scripture itself. The New Testament continuously cites and interprets the Old. When Christians say, "Jesus Christ is Lord," the name "Jesus" recalls Joshua of Israelite history, the title "Christ" the ancient promise of an anointed king, and the honorific "Lord" the double use of the word *Kyrios*. "The rock was Christ," writes Paul (1 Cor. 10:4). What rock? So the lectionary ought to include the story of the water from the rock. "Look, here is the Lamb of God!" calls out John the Baptist (John 1:36), a meaningless metaphor unless we know about biblical animal sacrifices: yet even Raymond Brown requires pages of small print to probe which lamb the fourth evangelist meant (*The Gospel according to John*, I, 58–63).

The necessity of interweaving biblical texts leads logically to a lectionary that appoints not one but several biblical selections each Sunday. A single biblical passage can be chosen to prove almost any point one wishes to make. However, three readings demand careful comparison, deepening interpretation and correcting first reactions. Lutherans can be heartened that in year A there are thirteen Sundays on which the reading from Romans precedes the gospel from Matthew, as over these weeks the Bible debates with itself about the law. Three readings are not a burden but a gift, an interpretative aid in addressing the gospel reading. One reading is a swimming pool: three readings are the Pacific Ocean, filled with life great and small.

One way that scripture interprets scripture is that each gospel interprets the others. Rather than imagining the four gospels as somehow identical, poured into the preacher's blender so all the lumps get flattened into mush, the RCL receives from each canonical gospel its distinctive voice. As befits the church's theological development, the Christology of John's gospel is the central voice every year. John is joined by Matthew, Mark, and Luke, each adding its own testimony to Christ. For those church bodies that require of pastoral candidates critical study of the Bible, a lectionary of integrity must reflect, rather than ignore, such results. Through the RCL, the churches experience what Irenaeus taught in the second century: we need all four voices, each one proclaiming its theology to the others.

The third characteristic of the Revised Common Lectionary is its focus on the risen Christ. The world's sacred scriptures do not have some single meaning. Each religious community perceives its texts according to its own wisdom and for its own purposes. Thus it is, because of Mark 16:18 and Luke 10:19, that snake handling can become the primary sacrament of some Christian groups.

A study of women in the Bible encounters what men in the seventh century before Christ wrote about what God thought about women six hundred years prior. One cannot assume that studying such material will lead to Christ.

Indeed, the Revised Common Lectionary does not intend to be Bible study, with the purpose of educating students about the Bible's version of the ancient Near East. Rather, the RCL is selections chosen from scriptural memories, legends, poems, and theological proposals for the purpose of calling the baptized into more enduring faith in Christ and of leading them to the triune table of mercy. Inside the clothing of the Bible we find Christ. It is Christ, not the clothing, that saves.

The fourth characteristic of the Revised Common Lectionary is its proclamation of God as triune. We believe in a triune God. God is the creator of the universe, of plants and animals, of Israel, of the church, of life each day. God is the savior— in the biblical story, throughout church history, within the assembled community this Sunday, in our lives, and beyond our deaths. God is the animator, the loving Spirit who challenges the human desire for self-protection, a deity who goes out to the other to share divine life.

That the Revised Common Lectionary appoints three readings assists the church's proclamation of the Trinity. On some Sundays, the first person of the Trinity is especially evident in the first reading, the third person in the epistle, and the second person in the gospel, but often one hears a triune song through all three readings. Christians believe that God is creator of life, word of salvation, and power of mercy from before time, in Jesus Christ, and within the gathered assembly. As Ephrem the Syrian wrote in the fourth century (*Hymns on Faith*, LXVII.8–9):

> The scriptures are set up like a mirror;
> one whose eye is clear sees there the image of the truth.
> Set up there is the image of the Father;
> depicted there is the image of the Son, and of the Holy
>   Spirit.

It is easier to attend to only one single person of the Trinity. But even a devout focus on Christ—a favorite for Lutherans—is inadequate to the mystery of God, a shrinking of the divine, a god in an easier image.

To summarize: the Revised Common Lectionary is a stunning vehicle for proclaiming the gospel. The longer one lives in it, the more one finds, in texts widely ecumenical, hermeneutically biblical, centered in Christ, and revealing the Trinity. The three readings are holding hands, circling around us each week, and together we receive their images of salvation and their words of challenge. It may well be that in the future the churches will emend this lectionary. Yet now for us the RCL is already a treasure chest; we open the lid and discover gems shining with the triune mystery of God. I encourage you to use the Bible in this way, to read, mark, learn, and inwardly digest the Revised Common Lectionary, Sunday by Sunday, festival by festival, for some years to come.

Gail Ramshaw
Liturgical scholar

ADVENT

ADVENT

CHRISTMAS

TIME AFTER EPIPHANY

Preparing for Advent

Lectionary

Advent begins this year on November 29. The lectionary readings of Advent all point us to signs of God coming—whether we are ready or not—of days and times advancing toward us, of hopes and expectations for a future held in the promises of God. It may seem by November 29 that Advent will have already begun somehow, considering that at the end of the previous church year we have already been considering our lives in God's future. In early November we celebrate the saints who have died before us, awakening in us questions of what our own death and life in Christ might mean. And November's Sundays turn our eyes to final things, when God will bring to completion all that has begun. Even the festival of Christ the King at the end of the year can seem less like a culmination, given that Christ's reign is an "already but not yet" reality. Perhaps we need a longer Advent, a full six or seven Sundays, without altering the calendar of readings, beginning in early November, acknowledging our need to imagine a future, living and dying while awaiting the fulfillment of promises, and wondering if the diminishing sunlight will ever fully return.

During the season of Advent in this year of the gospels of Luke and John we have a feast of rich readings. On the first Sunday of Advent, Luke's Jesus points to the fig tree to see the signs (Luke 21), and on the second and third Sundays we proclaim the sequential narratives of John the Baptizer preparing the way with words of planetary reshaping—valleys filled, mountains lowered, trees felled, and wheat harvested (Luke 3). Only on the fourth Sunday of Advent do we begin the birth narratives from Luke (can we wait until then to mention a pregnancy?) with Mary's visit to Elizabeth, leading to the canticle filled with the promises of God's impending justice—Mary's Magnificat (Luke 1). The first and second readings on each Sunday complement the gospel readings, with prophecy from Jeremiah, Malachi, Zephaniah, and Micah, and pastoral counsel and consolation from the epistles to Thessalonica, Philippi, and the Hebrews. Advent is not a four-week exploration of waiting only for a baby. Advent is rather an annual time to consider God's coming in every way and time possible: in a meal, by a word, as a light, in the assembly gathered, as a complete surprise, following a long wait, suddenly, or as a child.

The pressures on worship planners to abandon Advent and orient worship in December to the cultural Christmas of consumer excess and exaggerated happiness devoid of any true joy or honest lament seem to increase each year. Some may argue that the church becomes more irrelevant when we do not orient worship to such cultural trends. Others feel that the church is responsible only when it offers a countercultural critique of the crass commercialism pervasive during December and the absence of either Christ or the meaning of the mass in Christmas. The rush to celebrate Christmas before Christmas corresponds to our penchant to have things our way, nearly immediately, without the need for waiting, prayer, patience, or longing. Keeping Advent in at least the weekly Sunday assembly (if not each day of the season) forms us to live in a world where patient waiting, intense prayer, and hopeful trust are Christian practices we are invited to hone.

Music

Music in the liturgies of Advent is filled with hope, expectation, longing, rejoicing (see especially the third Sunday of Advent), and honest lament. In Advent this year, the lectionary invites songs rooted in beloved psalms and biblical canticles. This year the gospels of Luke and John invite us to learn by heart the canticles from the infancy narrative in Luke—Zechariah's song, Benedictus (appointed as psalmody on the second Sunday of Advent), Mary's song, Magnificat (appointed as psalmody on the fourth Sunday of Advent), Simeon's song, Nunc dimittis (a possible canticle at the conclusion of the distribution of communion, highly recommended during the Advent and Christmas cycle), and the creedal hymn based on Luke's song of the angels, Gloria in excelsis Deo (which is best reserved for the twelve days of Christmas). The first song of Isaiah (Isa. 12:2-6) is the appointed psalmody for the third Sunday of Advent.

There are too many reports of congregations omitting the appointed psalmody in the Sunday liturgy. Sung psalmody is foundational to our congregational musical repertoire. If worship planning necessitates that the rite be edited for any reason, there are many musical and ritual options that are more disposable than psalms or the canticles that serve as response to the first appointed Bible reading. For instance, consider the length of the gathering rite, which can be quite lean if necessary, or consider how many spoken announcements or instructions need to be repeated or voiced at all.

A dietitian once advised a particularly grumpy client: "Do not continue to say, 'On this diet I can't eat cake.' Rather, say, 'On this diet, I get to eat turkey!'" Keeping Advent is not about limiting your singing of Christmas carols. Keeping Advent is about having the opportunity to sing amazing Advent hymns and songs. The repertoire of delightful, provocative, and meaningful Advent music for the assembly is growing, and with patient teaching, wise leadership, and creative thought, musicians can entice entire assemblies to the pleasures of Advent hymns easily. Savor the delicious turkey; you won't miss the cake.

Musical considerations for the time of Advent invite us to consider that there will also be time for silence. The danger set before most worship planners is that the rhythm established in most liturgies sets up an expectation that every moment will be filled up with sound. Trying to meet such an expectation, particularly in Advent, is ill-advised. It could be asserted that we need the practice of silence year-round. If a congregation needs help to be still and silent for a time of reflection and meditation, Advent is the perfect season to begin to learn. Some congregations will be helped to keep silence if there is a way to mark the period of silence with a sound, such as a bell, so that the assembly begins to trust that the space for silence is being monitored or honored. The holy communion rite in *Evangelical Lutheran Worship* appoints that silence be maintained before the corporate confession of sins, between the words "Let us pray" and the prayer of the day, and following the sermon. Since the hymn of the day commonly follows the sermon in the rite, worship planners will want to determine which ministers or musicians will hold the space for this most important silence of the liturgy.

Environment

Those who have experienced many Advent seasons may have diminished appreciation for the mystery of this season. Consider how the arts might be employed to connect worshipers with the wonder of the Word becoming flesh to dwell within and among us.

Sponsor an Advent Night in your parish that includes a simple meal, workshops for making child-friendly Advent wreaths (see 01_Advent.Wreath.pdf)* and/or Advent calendars (see 01_Advent.Calendar.pdf)*, and brief Evening Prayer worship. Encourage in-home use of the wreaths and calendars by making available a variety of Advent devotional resources, including some especially appropriate for families with young children.

If your space can accommodate banners, create one that employs images of light and darkness to depict subtle changes over the course of the season. 01_Advent.Banner.pdf* provides one possibility to prompt your imagination. Or invite a team of volunteers to create an Advent floor cloth or carpet runner that extends the full length of the center aisle and has the appearance of an ancient pathway. Consider leading the gathering from incremental positions (back to front) along the path as the congregation is urged to "prepare the way" for Christ's coming.

Make the Advent themes of anticipation and preparation more palpable by engaging parishioners of all ages in creating large numbers of simple paper stars (see 01_Advent.Stars.pdf)*. Assemble the stars into garlands and suspend them over or around the nave, putting worshipers in touch with the far-reaching significance of what is unfolding during this season. Perhaps start out with the stars sparsely spaced, adding more over the course of the season. And, because stars are an appropriate visual for Advent, Christmas, and Epiphany, don't be in a rush to pack them away.

The Great O Antiphons are a collection of ancient prayers, each one employing an Old Testament title for God and expressing a sense of longing for the coming of the Messiah. Although the precise origin of the prayers is unknown, they have been found in manuscripts dating back to the early church. In use, the O Antiphons became associated with Vespers (Evening Prayer) during the Advent season, when they were chanted, one each day from December 17 to 23. They have also become familiar in the form of the beloved Advent hymn "O come, O come, Emmanuel" (ELW 257). An online search will identify art, music, and inspiration for visual resources to enhance the sense of longing for the Messiah during this season.

If secular culture's seasonal fixation on vivid red has eclipsed your congregation's use of Advent blue, consider replacing those reds with elements of gold and white that will be compatible with Advent blue and anticipate the whites of Christmas and the Epiphany of Our Lord.

Look for ways to breathe new life into long-held traditions:
* Freshen use of the Advent wreath by adapting some of Herb Brokering's brief but captivating dialogues between Mary and the heard-but-not-seen Angel Messenger (*Unto Us Is Born: Christmas Conversations with the Mother of Jesus* [Augsburg Fortress, 1999]; available as an ebook) into brief, dramatic introductions to lighting the candles, just prior to the first reading.
* Position four torches around the nave, shaping the assembly into a living, breathing Advent wreath that anticipates the Messiah's coming. Incorporate a

lighting of the torches into the congregation's gathering rite or the singing of a special Advent hymn, such as "O come, O come, Emmanuel" (ELW 257), "Light one candle to watch for Messiah" (ELW 240), or "Come now, O Prince of peace" (ELW 247).

- Replace the Advent wreath with a Jesse tree. Here's one source to inspire your creativity: http://tiredneedsleep.blogspot.com/2012/11/advent-2012-jesse-tree.html.

Seasonal Checklist

- Plan special Advent and Christmas observances: caroling, midweek worship, children's pageant, service of lessons and carols.
- Order candles and greens for the Advent wreath.
- Arrange a day and time before the first Sunday of Advent (November 29) to prepare the seasonal environment in the worship space. Solicit volunteer help. Plan a subsequent day and time to prepare the environment for Christmas.
- Try a new setting of the liturgy, especially if you have used the same one for some time. Return to a familiar setting if you have been experimenting.
- Use the Kyrie. Omit the canticle of praise. Instead, sing an appropriate Advent hymn or refrain prior to the readings.
- Use the Nicene Creed.
- Consider especially Thanksgiving at the Table III in *Evangelical Lutheran Worship*.

WORSHIP TEXTS FOR ADVENT

Confession and Forgiveness

All may make the sign of the cross, the sign marked at baptism,
as the presiding minister begins.
Blessed be the holy Trinity, ✝ one God,
the Lord of Israel who comes to set us free,
the mighty Savior who comes to show mercy,
the Dawn from on high who guides us into peace.
Amen.

Let us come before God in confession.

Silence is kept for reflection.

To you, O God,
we lift up our souls.
You know us through and through;
we confess our sins to you.
Remember not our sins;
remember us with your steadfast love.
Show us your ways;
teach us your paths;
and lead us in justice and truth,
for the sake of your goodness
in Jesus Christ our Savior. Amen.

Sisters and brothers, come with joy
and draw water from the well of salvation.
Remember the gift of baptism:
your sin is washed away in the name of ✝ Jesus;
you belong to Christ;
you are anointed to serve.
Stand up and raise your heads!
The reign of God is near.
Amen.

Offering Prayer

God of abundance,
we bring before you the precious fruits of your creation,
and with them our very lives.
Teach us patience and hope as we care for all those in need
until the coming of your Son, our Savior and Lord.
Amen.

Invitation to Communion

God fills the hungry with good things.
Taste and see that the Lord is good.

Prayer after Communion

Holy One, we give you thanks
that in this bread and cup
we have feasted again on your endless love.
Let that love overflow more and more in our lives,
that we may be messengers to prepare your way,
harvesters of justice and righteousness,
and bearers of your eternal Word,
our Savior Jesus Christ.
Amen.

Sending of Communion

Gracious God,
whose mercy endures from generation to generation:
As Mary set out to visit Elizabeth
before she gave birth to her son,
bless those who go forth to share your word and sacrament
with our sisters and brothers who are
sick/homebound/imprisoned.
In your love and care, nourish and strengthen
those to whom we bring this communion,
that through the body and blood of your Son
we may all know the hope of your promised coming
in Jesus Christ our Lord.
Amen.

Blessing

May God direct your ways in peace,
make you abound in love for one another and for all,
and strengthen your hearts
until the coming of our Lord Jesus.
Almighty God, Father, ✝ Son, and Holy Spirit,
bless you now and forever.
Amen.

Dismissal

Go in peace. Christ is with you.
Thanks be to God.

SEASONAL RITES FOR ADVENT

The Advent Wreath

One of the best-known customs for the season is the Advent wreath. The wreath and winter candle-lighting in the midst of growing darkness strengthen some of the Advent images found in the Bible. The unbroken circle of greens is clearly an image of everlasting life, a victory wreath, the crown of Christ, or the wheel of time itself. Christians use the wreath as a sign that Christ reaches into our time to lead us to the light of everlasting life. The four candles mark the progress of the four weeks of Advent and the growth of light. Sometimes the wreath is embellished with natural dried flowers or fruit. Its evergreen branches lead the household and the congregation to the evergreen Christmas tree. In many homes, the family gathers for prayer around the wreath.

First Sunday of Advent

We praise you, O God, for this evergreen crown
that marks our days of preparation for Christ's advent.
As we light the first candle on this wreath,
rouse us from sleep, that we may be ready to greet our Lord
when he comes with all the saints and angels.
Enlighten us with your grace,
and prepare our hearts to welcome him with joy.
Grant this through Christ our Lord,
whose coming is certain and whose day draws near.
Amen.

Light the first candle.

Second Sunday of Advent

We praise you, O God, for this circle of light
that marks our days of preparation for Christ's advent.
As we light the candles on this wreath,
kindle within us the fire of your Spirit,
that we may be light shining in the darkness.
Enlighten us with your grace,
that we may welcome others as you have welcomed us.
Grant this through Christ our Lord,
whose coming is certain and whose day draws near.
Amen.

Light two candles.

Third Sunday of Advent

We praise you, O God, for this victory wreath
that marks our days of preparation for Christ's advent.
As we light the candles on this wreath,
strengthen our hearts
as we await the Lord's coming in glory.
Enlighten us with your grace,
that we may serve our neighbors in need.
Grant this through Christ our Lord,
whose coming is certain and whose day draws near.
Amen.

Light three candles.

Fourth Sunday of Advent

We praise you, O God, for this wheel of time
that marks our days of preparation for Christ's advent.
As we light the candles on this wreath,
open our eyes to see your presence
in the lowly ones of this earth.
Enlighten us with your grace,
that we may sing of your advent among us
in the Word made flesh.
Grant this through Christ our Lord,
whose coming is certain and whose day draws near.
Amen.

Light all four candles.

Practicing Prayer
An Evening Prayer Series for Advent

Overview

This Advent, consider a focus on prayer. If the congregation has a preferred musical setting for evening prayer, it can easily be woven into the service structure outlined here. Excellent musical settings for evening prayer include Marty Haugen's *Holden Evening Prayer*, Kent Gustavson's *Mountain Vespers*, Aaron David Miller's *Behold Our Light*, and the setting in *Evangelical Lutheran Worship*.

Week 1: Contemplative Prayer

Consider contemplation or meditation in some form this week. Invite all into a pattern of silence, repetitive prayer, or some other practice grounded in the spirituality of contemplation. Mary contemplated all things in her heart. We conform ourselves to her way of prayer.

Week 2: Embodied Prayer

Prayer is more than just a practice of the mind and spirit. It includes the body. Invite all into physical postures that pray with the whole body. Solomon prayed before the altar of the Lord with his whole body, and so we do likewise.

Week 3: Neighborhood Prayer

Prayer takes place in a specific place, among specific people. Pray for the needs of the congregation and neighborhood, and name specific places in the neighborhood in need of healing. James encouraged his community to trust that their prayers were effective and brought healing within the community and extending out from it.

Week 4: Praying the Hours

One of the most ancient patterns for prayer is the daily prayer cycle. Review the hours for prayer, and rehearse one or more patterns for the daily prayer offices. Paul encouraged his communities to pray in the Spirit at all times. Praying the daily hours is patterned after this encouragement.

Opening

Week 1

You speak to us in silence.
Open our hearts to your still, small voice.
Your word is inscribed on our hearts.
Remind us of the prayers we have learned by heart.
You are the Lord of time and space.
Give us patience to listen on your time, not ours.

Week 2

We stand to honor you. (*Stand*)
We kneel to adore you. (*Kneel*)
We raise our hands to worship you. (*Raise hands*)
We close our eyes to see you. (*Close eyes*)
We sit to hear you. (*Sit*)

Week 3

O God, you have called us to love our neighbors as ourselves.
Help us to see you in our neighbors.
Some of our neighbors' needs are unknown to us.
Forgive us our failure to inquire.
We have done more for our neighbors than we realize.
Help us to see your goodness and mercy shining through our actions.
We desire to pray for the good of our neighborhood.
Lord, bless and keep all who live and move around this church.

Week 4

Lord, you are with us in the morning.
Let our first thoughts and words be a prayer to you.
Lord, you are with us in the midday.
Keep us mindful of you as we work and play.
Lord, you are with us in the evening.
Prepare us for the night watches.
Lord, you are with us in the nighttime.
We commend our bodies and souls into your care.

Hymn of Light

Joyous light of glory   ELW 229, 230
O gracious Light   ELW 231
Light one candle to watch for Messiah   ELW 240

Prayer

Use the prayer of the day from the preceding Sunday.

Song

Wait for the Lord ELW 262

Reading

Week 1: Luke 2:19
Week 2: 1 Kings 8:54
Week 3: James 5:16
Week 4: Ephesians 6:18

Silence for reflection may be kept.

Reflection

Invite a guest speaker on each topic.

Week 1: A practitioner of meditation, a monk, or a contemplative prayer leader
Week 2: A yoga instructor, designer of labyrinths, imam, or rabbi
Week 3: A neighboring pastor, prayer room facilitator, or leader of a local prayer group
Week 4: A monk or other regular practitioner of the daily prayer cycle

Practicing Prayer

Ask the speaker to lead the community in the prayer practice they have spoken about.

Hymn

Week 1
Creator of the stars of night ELW 245
Unexpected and mysterious ELW 258

Week 2
Each winter as the year grows older ELW 252
He came down ELW 253

Week 3
Fling wide the door ELW 259
As the dark awaits the dawn ELW 261

Week 4
Hark, the glad sound! ELW 239
Awake! Awake, and greet the new morn ELW 242

Lord's Prayer

Blessing

The God to whom we pray enfold you in love.
The Christ through whom we pray lift you up.
The Spirit in whom we pray wing your prayers to God.
Amen.

Go in peace. Christ is coming soon.
Thanks be to God.

Suggested Resources

On contemplative prayer: Joann Nesser. *Contemplative Prayer: Praying When the Well Runs Dry*. Minneapolis: Augsburg Fortress, 2007.

On embodied prayer: Doug Pagitt and Kathryn Prill. *BodyPrayer: The Posture of Intimacy with God*. Colorado Springs, CO: WaterBrook Press, 2005.

On neighborhood prayer: Paul Sparks, Tim Soerens, and Dwight J. Friesen. *The New Parish: How Neighborhood Churches Are Transforming Mission, Discipleship, and Community*. Downers Grove, IL: InterVarsity Press, 2014.

On praying the hours: Robert Benson. *In Constant Prayer*. Nashville: Thomas Nelson, 2008.

Additional resources

Bread for the Day: Daily Bible Readings and Prayers. Minneapolis: Augsburg Fortress, annual publication.

Samuel Wells and Abigail Kocher. *Shaping the Prayers of the People: The Art of Intercession*. Grand Rapids, MI: Eerdmans, 2014.

Rowan Williams. *Being Christian: Baptism, Bible, Eucharist, Prayer*. Grand Rapids, MI: Eerdmans, 2014.

November 29, 2015
First Sunday of Advent

Advent is about the "coming days." God's people have always lived in great expectation, but that expectation finds specific, repeated enunciation in the texts appointed for these four weeks. The ancients anticipated a "righteous Branch to spring up for David." The Thessalonians awaited "the coming of our Lord Jesus with all the saints." Our Lord's contemporaries hoped for the time "to stand before the Son of Man." With them we eagerly await the coming days: another Christmas celebration, a second coming, and the advent of our Lord in word and supper.

Prayer of the Day

Stir up your power, Lord Christ, and come. By your merciful protection alert us to the threatening dangers of our sins, and redeem us for your life of justice, for you live and reign with the Father and the Holy Spirit, one God, now and forever.

Gospel Acclamation

Alleluia. Stand up and | raise your heads—* your redemption is | drawing near. *Alleluia.* (Luke 21:28)

Readings and Psalm
Jeremiah 33:14-16

In the Old Testament, "righteousness" often has to do with being faithful in relationship. God acts righteously both in punishing Israel for its sin and in having mercy. In today's reading, Jerusalem's future name—"The Lord is our righteousness"—proclaims that the Lord is even now working salvation for Israel.

Psalm 25:1-10

To you, O Lord, I lift up my soul. (Ps. 25:1)

1 Thessalonians 3:9-13

Upon Timothy's report from the congregation at Thessalonica, Paul is exuberant with gratitude for them. In this passage from his letter, Paul voices overflowing thanks, joy, and blessings for the people of this growing church.

Luke 21:25-36

God will fulfill God's purposes and, already, hidden signs of that fulfillment abound. On that great day there will be dismay, perplexity, confusion, and terror, but God's people shall be given strength to stand boldly and receive God's promised redemption.

Preface   Advent

Color   Blue

Prayers of Intercession

The prayers are prepared locally for each occasion. The following examples may be adapted or used as appropriate.

Emmanuel has come, is here, and is coming soon. Let us join in prayer for the church, the earth, and those who are in need, that all receive what God promises to give.

A brief silence.

Come to the church, saving God. Grant to your people your redemption. Stand with all Christians who are persecuted for the faith. Hear us, O God.

Your mercy is great.

Come to the earth, creating God. Protect the lands from environmental disasters. Nurture the animals and plants that you have made. Hear us, O God.

Your mercy is great.

Come to the nations of the world, sovereign God. Inspire all leaders to work for justice. Bring peace to Jerusalem. We pray for peace in (*here places or situations in need of peace may be named*). Hear us, O God.

Your mercy is great.

Come to all in need, mighty God. Protect those who suffer injustice. Comfort those who live in fear. Heal the sick. Accompany the dying. We pray especially for . . . . Hear us, O God.

Your mercy is great.

Reveal yourself to this congregation and to our community, gracious God. Deepen our love for one another. In this season, give us compassion for all who suffer, and keep us from selfish excess. Hear us, O God.

Your mercy is great.

Here other intercessions may be offered.

Loving God, you bring to yourself all the faithful who have died (*especially*). Strengthen us in holiness until with all the saints we come to see you face to face. Hear us, O God.

Your mercy is great.
Receive our prayers, merciful God, and make us ready to receive you when you come through Jesus Christ, our Savior and Lord.
Amen.

Images in the Readings

The four gospels repeatedly refer to the Jewish apocalyptic figure called the **Son of Man**, a mysterious humanlike judge who, as part of the cosmic upheaval at the end of time, will appear in the sky to represent God to the people and the people to God. The figure probably developed from speculation about the vision in Daniel 7. Despite popular misunderstanding that contrasts Son of God with Son of Man, "Son of Man" does not mean that Jesus was the human son of Mary. Today's readings describe the end of the world with the arrival of the Son of Man in both frightening and comforting language. Luke's description of the apocalypse emphasizes people's terror: the day will be like a trap. Yet the summer promises new life.

There are many biblical references to the **fig tree**. An image in ancient myth and literature for male fertility, the fig tree provided both food and shade for Israelites, and even clothing in the story of the fall. In Luke 21 the fig tree is a positive image for the arrival of God. What is now in bud will see its fruition.

It was common in the ancient Near East to depict a monarchy as a tree of life. The idea was that the virility of the king ensured the health and wealth of the nation. Also the Old Testament includes descriptions of David as the tree, and the future messiah as a **branch**. For Christians, Christ is that branch, and through him we all share the life of God's true tree.

Ideas for the Day

◆ As the people of God prepare for the coming of Jesus during Advent, many will focus on reclaiming the traditions of Christmases past. As families grow, tradition can pile upon tradition, ultimately creating expectations that become burdensome and wearying, making a call to lift one's head and be on guard even more difficult. A prayer of confession could be used to invite individuals to consider how they might prepare for Christ rather than preparing for Christmas.

◆ For congregations with the technical resources, consider setting up a live Twitter stream to project tweets from members about things they might give up to make more space for prayerful preparation. Alternately, invite members to post on a congregational Facebook page throughout the coming week, giving one another encouragement to make choices about activities during Advent.

◆ Jesus' words that "the powers of the heavens will be shaken" may evoke feelings of confusion or skepticism in an age when the study of the heavens reveals myriad wonders of quasars and black holes—and not so much of spiritual warfare. Biblical language about powers becomes less comprehensible in a scientific age, which leads to the danger of dismissing these words. Biblical scholar Walter Wink addresses the difficulty, and importance, of understanding "the powers" in biblical references and in our world in his book *The Powers That Be* (New York: Doubleday, 1998). He offers helpful insight into the "power struggle" that marks Christ's coming, today and every day.

◆ One has only to search the phrase "apocalyptic movies" online to see the impact the idea of the last days has on our collective consciousness. End-of-the-world movies range from the ridiculous (for example, *Night of the Comet*, 1984; *The World's End* and *This Is the End*, both released in 2013) to the poignant and/or disturbing (*The Road*, 2009, and *Melancholia*, 2011). Many of these movies contain profanity, violence, and sexual content—and as such certainly aren't marketed to a Christian audience. But their prevalence raises interesting questions about whether we dread "the end," think that it's inevitable, hope for it, or consider it merely a matter of fantasy.

Connections with the Liturgy

In the Lord's Prayer we ask God to "save us from the time of trial." It is precisely the dangers and terrors of the eschatological end to which this petition refers. If your assembly is still praying the historic translation of the prayer about "temptation," this Sunday is a good time to begin use of the 1975 translation, which more accurately conveys the meaning of the prayer ascribed to Jesus. Most Christians will indeed experience "a time of trial."

Let the Children Come

The church tells time with colors as well as with calendars. Colors mark the progression of days and seasons, an immediate signal that something different is happening. Like people of any age, children respond to color with interesting interpretations. And one color may contain many meanings. Invite children and their parents to meet the presiding minister after worship for a brief chat about the color for Advent. What does or could this deep blue signify? How does the color make you feel? Where do you see it in the worship space? Could we "wear the season" too?

Assembly Song
Gathering

Fling wide the door   ELW 259, LBW 32
Blessed be the God of Israel   ELW 552
O come, O come, Emmanuel   ELW 257, LBW 34, LS 10, LLC 281

Psalmody and Acclamations

Jennings, Carolyn. "Psalm 25:1-10" from PWC.

Parker, Val. "Psalm 25: To You, O Lord, I Lift My Soul." SATB, assembly, kybd, gtr. OCP 21060.

Shute, Linda Cable. "Psalm 25:1-10," Refrain 1, from PSCY.

(GA) Pishner, Stephen. "Advent Gospel Acclamation" from *Psalm and Gospel Acclamation for Advent*. SATB, cant, assembly, kybd. GIA G-5259.

Hymn of the Day

Lo! He comes with clouds descending ELW 435, LBW 27 *HELMSLEY*
Wake, awake, for night is flying ELW 436, LBW 31 *WACHET AUF*
He came down ELW 253 *HE CAME DOWN*

Offering

Light one candle to watch for Messiah ELW 240, st. 1, WOV 630, st. 1
Blessed be the God of Israel ELW 250, sts. 1-2, WOV 725, sts. 1-2

Communion

My Lord, what a morning ELW 438, TFF 40, WOV 627
Wait for the Lord ELW 262
Bread of life, our host and meal ELW 464

Sending

Rejoice, rejoice, believers ELW 244, LBW 25
Hark! A thrilling voice is sounding! ELW 246, LBW 37

Additional Assembly Songs

Blessed be the Lord God of Israel W&P 20

Caminamos hacia el sol LLC 275

¡Despertad! Que a todos llama LLC 276

Cuban tune. "El es nuestra paz" from *Laudate Omnes Gentes/Praying Together*. U. Gütersloher Verlagshaus. Out of print; available on Amazon.com.

Shaha, Bart. "Come, Lord Jesus Christ" from *Sound the Bamboo*. U. GIA G-6830.

Bruxvoort Colligan, Richard. "To You (Psalm 25)" from *Shout for Joy*. AFP 9780806698632. psalmimmersion.bandcamp.com.

Grundy, Christopher. "Stepping In" from *Stepping In*. christopher grundy.com.

Hansen, Holly. "Song of Praise" from *Resonance Mass*. nemercy .org/resonance.

Kurtz, Rachel. "Save Us All" from *For Crying Out Loud*. rachel kurtz.org.

Rundman, Jonathan. "Texas Kyrie" from *A Heartland Liturgy*. jonathanrundman.bandcamp.com.

Wilson, Tay. "All Things New" from *Stay the Course*. Available on Amazon.com.

Music for the Day
Choral

p ● Bach, Johann Sebastian. "Zion Hears the Watchmen Singing" from *Bach for All Seasons*. U, kybd. AFP 9780800658540.

p Benson, Robert. "My Lord, What a Morning." SATB, pno. AFP 9780800623876.

p Ferguson, John. "Rejoice, Rejoice, Believers." SAB, org. AFP 9781451401684.

p Haugen, Kyle. "Lost in the Night." SAB, pno, opt solo. AFP 9781451483215.

Children's Choir

Handel, G. F./arr. Michael Burkhardt. "Daughter of Zion." U/SSA, org, opt 2 C inst/2 B-flat inst/2 hrn. MSM 50-8875.

p ● Kadidlo, Phil. "He Came Down" from *ChildrenSing Around the World*. 2 pt, pno, perc. AFP 9781451491951.

Lowenberg, Kenneth. "Creator of the Stars of Night." 2 pt, opt C inst, kybd. GIA G-6873.

Keyboard / Instrumental

p ● Organ, Anne Krentz. "Helmsley" from *Piano Reflections on Advent Tunes*. Pno. AFP 9781451462647.

p ● Osterland, Karl. "Helmsley" from *Augsburg Organ Library: Advent*. Org. AFP 9780800658953.

● Sowash, Bradley. "He Came Down" from *Piano Plus: Hymns for Piano and Treble Instrument, Advent/Christmas*. Pno, inst. AFP 9780800638542.

● Walther, Johann. "Wachet auf." Org. Various editions.

Handbell

p Hopson, Hal H. "Advent Carol." 3 or 5 oct, L2. CG CGB154.

● Mallory, Ron. "Wake, Awake, for Night Is Flying." 3-5 oct hb, opt 3 oct hc, L2+. LOR 20/1661L.

● Nelson, Susan T. "Lo, He Comes with Clouds Descending." 3-6 oct hb, opt 3-4 oct hc, L3+. HOP 2253.

Monday, November 30
Andrew, Apostle

Andrew was the first of the Twelve. He is known as a fisherman who left his net to follow Jesus. As a part of his calling, he brought other people, including Simon Peter, to meet Jesus. The Byzantine church honors Andrew as its patron and points out that because he was the first of Jesus' followers, he was, in the words of John Chrysostom, "the Peter before Peter." Together with Philip, Andrew leads a number of Greeks to speak with Jesus, and it is Andrew who shows Jesus a boy with five barley loaves and two fish. Andrew is said to have died on a cross saltire, an X-shaped cross.

⊕ = global song   ☼ = praise song
● = relates to hymn of the day   p = available in Prelude Music Planner

Thursday, December 3

Francis Xavier, missionary to Asia, died 1552

Francis Xavier (SAYV-yehr) was born in the Basque region of northern Spain. Francis's native Basque language is unrelated to any other, and Francis admitted that learning languages was difficult for him. Despite this obstacle he became a missionary to India, Southeast Asia, Japan, and the Philippines. At each point he learned the local language and, like Martin Luther, wrote catechisms for the instruction of new converts. Another obstacle Francis overcame to accomplish his mission work was a propensity to seasickness. All his travels to the Far East were by boat. Together with Ignatius Loyola and five others, Francis formed the Society of Jesus (Jesuits). Francis spoke out against the Spanish and Portuguese colonists when he discovered their oppression of the indigenous people to whom he was sent as a missionary.

Friday, December 4

John of Damascus, theologian and hymnwriter, died around 749

Born to a wealthy family in Damascus and well educated, John left a career in finance and government to become a monk in an abbey near Jerusalem. He wrote many hymns as well as theological works. Foremost among the latter is a work called *The Fount of Wisdom*, which touches on philosophy, heresy, and the orthodox faith. This summary of patristic theology remained influential for centuries.

December 6, 2015
Second Sunday of Advent

Forerunners and messengers advance the advent of our God. While John the Baptizer's voice in the wilderness may be the principal focus of the day, Malachi's prophecy could as easily herald the coming Lord Jesus as forerunner of the Lord of hosts. Finally all the baptized are called to participate in the sharing of the gospel. In so doing we prepare the way for the coming of the Lord and assist all flesh in capturing a vision of the "salvation of God."

Prayer of the Day

Stir up our hearts, Lord God, to prepare the way of your only Son. By his coming give to all the people of the world knowledge of your salvation; through Jesus Christ, our Savior and Lord, who lives and reigns with you and the Holy Spirit, one God, now and forever.

Gospel Acclamation

Alleluia. Prepare the way ¦ of the Lord.* All flesh shall see the salva- ¦ tion of God. *Alleluia.* (Luke 3:4, 6)

Readings and Psalm
Malachi 3:1-4

The Lord announces a covenant with Israel. A messenger like Malachi (his name means "my messenger") shall prepare the way for the coming of the Lord by purifying and refining God's people, as silver and gold are refined.

or Baruch 5:1-9

A poem of hope from the school of the prophet Jeremiah speaks of the return of scattered Israel from Babylon, but also looks beyond that to the end times when God's kingdom will be established.

Luke 1:68-79

In the tender compassion of our God the dawn from on high shall break upon us. (Luke 1:78)

Philippians 1:3-11

The apostle Paul was the pastor of many new churches. He writes in this letter about his joy to be in partnership with the Christians of Philippi. Listen to how tender-hearted Paul, sometimes a stern preacher, is with his friends as he encourages them to grow in love and knowledge.

Luke 3:1-6

John the Baptist is a herald of the saving Lord, whose way is prepared by "repentance for the forgiveness of sins." As we hear the careful record of human leaders, we sense the spectrum of political and religious authority that will be challenged by this coming Lord.

Preface Advent

Color Blue

Prayers of Intercession

The prayers are prepared locally for each occasion. The following examples may be adapted or used as appropriate.

Emmanuel has come, is here, and is coming soon. Let us join in prayer for the church, the earth, and those who are in need, that all receive what God promises to give.

A brief silence.

O God, our hope of unity, come to your church around the world. Purify your people and give to all the wisdom and courage to proclaim your word of forgiveness and renewal. Lord, in your mercy,

hear our prayer.

O God our Savior, come to the earth that you made. Nurture the health of lands and seas. Give to plants and animals favorable weather. Lord, in your mercy,

hear our prayer.

O God of peace, come to all the nations. Inspire heads of state and regional leaders with a passion for justice. Bring peace throughout the world. We pray especially for (*here places or situations in need of peace may be named*). Lord, in your mercy,

hear our prayer.

O God of love, come to everyone in need. Heal the sick. Answer the cries of those who are poor, those without housing, and those who have fled from violence or famine. We pray especially for . . . . Lord, in your mercy,

hear our prayer.

O God of compassion, come to our congregation and our community. This Advent, help us to prepare for your coming. Make us gifts to one another, that no one remains destitute or despairing. Lord, in your mercy,

hear our prayer.

Here other intercessions may be offered.

O Lord of hosts, we praise you for the lives of all the faithful (*especially Nicholas, Bishop of Myra, and . . .*). Bring us with them to your feast of eternal compassion. Lord, in your mercy,

hear our prayer.

Receive our prayers, merciful God, and make us ready to receive you when you come through Jesus Christ, our Savior and Lord.

Amen.

Images in the Readings

The citation from Isaiah sets God's prophet in the **wilderness**, an inhospitable terrain symbolic of much human life. Yet in such a barren place we hear God's promise. It is best if your worship space is not yet decorated for Christmas: we are still in the desert. The wilderness is an honest image, and it is good to let it speak.

Yet, paradoxically, Luke situates John the Baptist by the **Jordan** River. Thus also the years of nomadic wanderings were coming to an end as the Israelites crossed the Jordan into the promised land. Led by Jesus (who bears the same name as Joshua) who entered the wilderness of our lives, Christians, too, cross a river in baptism, and so enter into the kingdom of God. Law, gospel: wilderness, river.

In the ancient Near East and the Roman Empire, **highways** were constructed by conquering monarchs to facilitate the movement of troops and celebratory parades. Similarly, paths in the wilderness must be marked out by those who have gone before us. But on this highway, Jesus walks toward the cross, and on this pathway walked the fascinating crew of saints we commemorate in December: Francis Xavier, John of Damascus (ELW 361), Nicholas ("Santa Claus"), Ambrose (ELW 263, 559, 571), Lucy (think of candles in a young girl's hair), John of the Cross, and Katherine von Bora Luther, to name a few. We join them, walking to God, and meeting Christ on the way.

Ideas for the Day

◆ The book *Crazy Talk: A Not-So-Stuffy Dictionary of Theological Terms* defines repentance: "The change in a person's behavior that follows recognition of having sinned and immediately precedes further sinning" (Rolf Jacobson, ed. [Minneapolis: Augsburg, 2008], 144). Luther says that the entire life of the believer should be one of repentance. While the liturgical color of Advent has shifted from purple (symbolizing repentance) to blue (symbolizing hope), this theme of repentance *alongside* hope helps us reinforce the distinction between merely preparing for Christmas and preparing for God.

◆ *Fight Club* (Fox, 1999) is a movie many people avoided because of its violence, profanity, and sexual content. Yet it was immensely popular with young adults, in part because of its deep (and largely unacknowledged) spiritual themes. Near the movie's end, the headquarters of several credit card companies are demolished, erasing the debt of millions of people. This "great leveling" brings to mind the jubilee year of the Old Testament and reminds us that the promise that "every valley shall be filled, and every mountain and hill shall be made low" could well represent a massive upheaval in current accepted social structures. How might we resist preparing the way of the Lord at the same time that we cry out for it?

◆ Along with individual repentance, corporate/communal repentance is desperately needed in our world—but we struggle to understand how to engage in and act on it. Yet the prophets make clear that God's promise of renewal is not just for us as individuals, but for us as community. The

ELCA social statement, *The Church in Society: A Lutheran Perspective*, states, "This church must . . . discern when to support and when to confront society's cultural patterns, values, and powers" (p. 3). The full text of the social statement is available on the ELCA's website (www.elca.org). A congregation may choose to read this statement and/or other social statements and identify a point of communal confession and repentance to act on during Advent, such as environmental stewardship, antiracism workshops, or a study of how to transform charity into justice.

Connections with the Liturgy

Paul wrote that he constantly thanked God for the Philippi community and prayed for their continued faithfulness. Each Sunday in the intercessions we join with Paul by including a petition for the church universal, its ministry, and the mission of the gospel. This week we can also pray for everyone who is rightly or wrongly imprisoned.

Let the Children Come

Plant small bulbs—paper whites or narcissus—in a clay pot filled with rich soil. Set it near a sunny window. During Advent, watch the shoots emerge. During the twelve days of Christmas, delicate white flowers will bloom and fill the room with sweet fragrance, a reminder of God's promise to make all things new in Christ Jesus. Send children home with this Advent prayer: "Here I wait in quiet hope that you will come, water the field of my heart, and make your love blossom. Amen."

Assembly Song
Gathering

Come, thou long-expected Jesus   ELW 254, LBW 30
Prepare the royal highway   ELW 264, LBW 26
Hark, the glad sound!   ELW 239, LBW 35

Psalmody and Acclamations

Byzantine chant/arr. John A. Melloh, s.m. "You Have Come to Your People" from PAS.
Gospel canticle from Morning Prayer, *ELW*, p. 303.
Joncas, Michael, and James Quinn. "Canticle of Zechariah." SATB, assembly, hrn, br qrt, timp. GIA G-7138.
(GA) Pishner, Stephen. "Advent Gospel Acclamation" from *Psalm and Gospel Acclamation for Advent*. SATB, cant, assembly, kybd. GIA G-5259.
Wentzel, Brian. "Blessed Are You, Lord." MSB2 S525

Hymn of the Day

On Jordan's bank the Baptist's cry   ELW 249, LBW 36   *PUER NOBIS*
There's a voice in the wilderness   ELW 255   *ASCENSION*
Prepare the royal highway   ELW 264, LBW 26   *BEREDEN VÄG FÖR HERRAN*

Offering

Light one candle to watch for Messiah   ELW 240, sts. 1-2, WOV 630, sts. 1-2
Come now, O Prince of peace   ELW 247, LS 13

Communion

Comfort, comfort now my people   ELW 256, LBW 29
All earth is hopeful   ELW 266, TFF 47, WOV 629
Drawn to the light   ELW 593

Sending

People, look east   ELW 248, LS 11, WOV 626
Lost in the night   ELW 243, LBW 394

Additional Assembly Songs

Somebody's knockin' at your door   TFF 44
Vendrá una nueva luz   LLC 278
A story for all people   W&P 2
⊕ Feliciano, Francisco. "Who Will Set Us Free?" from *Sound the Bamboo*. U. GIA G-6830.
⊕ Lee, Geonyong. "Come Now, O Prince of Peace." ELW 247.
✧ Dakota Road. "Prepare the Way" from *Dakota Road Music Anthology*. dakotaroadmusic.com.
✧ Grundy, Christopher. "Every Step of the Way" from *Stepping In*. christophergrundy.com.
✧ Gustavson, Kent. "Prayer of Good Courage" from *Mountain Vespers*. kentgustavson.com.
✧ Koza, Chris. "Every Little Blade of Grass" from *Song of the Earth Mass*. nemercy.org.
✧ Munson, Scott. "Sanctus" from *The Middle America Mass*. nemercy.org.
✧ Tangled Blue. "Behold, the Lamb" from *Storm Home: A Collection of Music from Humble Walk Artists-in-Residence*. humble walk.bandcamp.com.

Music for the Day
Choral

p ● Bell, John. "A Voice Proclaims." SATB, kybd, cl, opt assembly. GIA G-5499.
p   Erickson, Richard. "Light One Candle to Watch for Messiah." SATB, org. AFP 9780800657512.
p ● Organ, Anne Krentz. "There's a Voice in the Wilderness." 2 pt mxd, pno, ob. AFP 9780800676537.
   Proulx, Richard. "Comfort, Comfort Now My People." SAB, fc, tamb. MSM AE-110.

Children's Choir

How, Martin. "It Is My Prayer." 2 pt/3 pt, org. GIA G-4313.
Music, David W. "Make Straight in the Desert a Highway." 2 pt trbl, 2 opt inst, kybd. CPH 983499WEB.

⊕ = global song   ✧ = praise song
● = relates to hymn of the day   p = available in Prelude Music Planner

p   Page, Anna Laura. "The World's True Light: Dona nobis pacem" from *ChildrenSing in Worship*, vol. 3. U/2 pt, kybd, opt fl. AFP 9781451462548.

Keyboard / Instrumental

● Cool, Jayne Southwick. "Bereden väg för Herran" from *Piano Plus: Hymns for Piano and Treble Instrument, Advent/Christmas*. Pno, inst. AFP 9780800638542.

p ● Dahl, David P. "Ascension" from *The Organ Sings*. Org. AFP 9781451462609.

● Miller, Aaron David. "Puer nobis" from *Augsburg Organ Library: Advent*. Org. AFP 9780800658953.

p ● Shields, Valerie, and Lynette Maynard. "Puer nobis" from *Introductions and Alternate Accompaniments for Piano*, vol. 3. Pno. AFP 9780800623616.

Handbell

p ● Afdahl, Lee J. "Ascension (There's a Voice in the Wilderness)" from *Hymn Accompaniments for Handbells: Advent and Christmas*. 3-5 oct, L3+. AFP 9780806698076.

p ● Page, Anna Laura. "Prepare the Royal Highway" from *I Heard the Bells*. 2-3 oct hb, opt hc, L2+. CG CGB860. 3-5 oct hb, opt hc, L2+. CG CGB861.

p ● Phillips, Judy. "Advent Fantasy." 3-6 oct hb, opt 2 oct hc, opt tamb, opt tri, L3. CG CGB751.

Sunday, December 6

Nicholas, Bishop of Myra, died around 342

Though Nicholas is one of the church's most beloved saints, little is known about his life. In the fourth century he was a bishop in what is now Turkey. Legends that surround Nicholas tell of his love for God and neighbor, especially the poor. One famous story tells of Nicholas secretly giving bags of gold to the three daughters of a father who was going to sell them into prostitution because he could not provide dowries for them. Nicholas has become a symbol of anonymous gift giving.

Monday, December 7

Ambrose, Bishop of Milan, died 397

Ambrose was a governor of northern Italy and a catechumen when he was elected bishop of Milan. He was baptized, ordained, and consecrated a bishop all on the same day. While bishop, he gave away his wealth and lived in simplicity. He was a famous preacher and is largely responsible for the conversion of Augustine. He is also well known for writing hymns. On one occasion, Ambrose led people in a hymn he wrote while the church in which they were secluded was threatened by attack from Gothic soldiers. The soldiers turned away, unwilling to attack a congregation that was singing a hymn. Ambrose is credited with authorship of three hymns in *Evangelical Lutheran Worship*, including "Savior of the Nations, Come" (ELW 263).

December 13, 2015
Third Sunday of Advent

The presence of the Lord "in your midst" in the wonder of the holy supper is cause for singing. The nearness of the Lord in prayer, in every circumstance, is cause for rejoicing. The coming of one "more powerful" than John, even with his winnowing fork in his hand, is good news—and cause for exultation—for us who are being saved. Great joy is the tone for the third Sunday of Advent.

Prayer of the Day

Stir up the wills of your faithful people, Lord God, and open our ears to the preaching of John, that, rejoicing in your salvation, we may bring forth the fruits of repentance; through Jesus Christ, our Savior and Lord, who lives and reigns with you and the Holy Spirit, one God, now and forever.

Gospel Acclamation

Alleluia. I am sending my messen- | ger before you,* who will prepare your | way before you. *Alleluia.* (Matt. 11:10)

Readings and Psalm

Zephaniah 3:14-20

The prophet Zephaniah's message is mostly one of judgment for sin. This reading, however, which comes from the conclusion of the book, prophesies joy for Judah and Jerusalem. Judgment has led to repentance, and God's salvation is at hand.

Isaiah 12:2-6

In your midst is the Holy One of Israel. (Isa. 12:6)

Philippians 4:4-7

Despite being in prison, Paul is remarkably upbeat as he writes this letter. Here, he urges his friends in Philippi to trust God with all their worries and concerns, with the hope they will experience God's joy and peace.

Luke 3:7-18

John the Baptist heralds the mighty one "who is coming." John teaches that preparation for God's reign is not a matter of identity but of bearing fruits of merciful justice, radical generosity, and vocational integrity.

Preface   Advent

Color   Blue

Prayers of Intercession

The prayers are prepared locally for each occasion. The following examples may be adapted or used as appropriate.

Emmanuel has come, is here, and is coming soon. Let us join in prayer for the church, the earth, and those who are in need, that all receive what God promises to give.

A brief silence.

For the church throughout the world, for bishops, pastors, and seminaries, for the courage to live out the challenges of our baptism, and for the inspiration of the Holy Spirit, let us pray.

Have mercy, O God.

For the earth, for glaciers, for the protection of dormant vegetation and hibernating animals, and for wisdom in the use and care of the creatures and landscapes we live among, let us pray.

Have mercy, O God.

For the nations of the world, for soldiers and police, for all who suffer political oppression, for our enemies, and especially for (*here places or situations in need of peace may be named*), let us pray.

Have mercy, O God.

For all those in need, for those who are sick or cold, injured or outcast, for victims of fraud or extortion, for all who will die today, and especially for . . . , let us pray.

Have mercy, O God.

For this congregation, for joy in Christ, and for our community, for an increase in practices that truly enact justice and compassion, let us pray.

Have mercy, O God.

Here other intercessions may be offered.

We praise you, O God, for the lives of all the faithful departed (*especially the martyr Lucy and . . .*). That we complete our baptismal journey in you, let us pray.

Have mercy, O God.

Receive our prayers, merciful God, and make us ready to receive you when you come through Jesus Christ, our Savior and Lord.

Amen.

Images in the Readings

When watered by baptism, we can be trees that bear good **fruit**. At holy communion, we take into ourselves the fruit of the vine to strengthen our resolve to be productive trees.

Since many Christians connect baptism with helpless infants, John the Baptist's talk of **fire** is unsettling. What burns away is our inherent selfishness, for we humans instinctively choose our own desires over the concerns of others. Augustine wrote that even in the infant crying for milk, we can see a human caring only for the self. The good news is that the Lord is near.

The Bible's **sexual imagery**, such as in Zephaniah, was cherished especially by the celibate clergy, monks, and nuns in medieval Europe. These believers gave up the marital covenant and wrote extensively of either themselves as individuals or of the feminized church as having married Christ. Some contemporary Christians find the sexual imagery beautiful as religious imagery and helpful in its surprising earthiness. Other Christians hesitate to use it, either out of an embarrassed restraint (given contemporary cultural media?) or because traditionally the image always construes the male as the dominant partner. Yet the couple becomes one: and so perhaps we can revive use of this imagery with careful gusto.

Ideas for the Day

◆   For a very long time, the church celebrated the third Sunday of Advent as *Gaudete* Sunday (taken from the Philippians reading: Rejoice, which in Latin is *gaudete*). The color was changed from either purple or blue to pink, and the general seriousness of the season was lessened. In this same vein, what are some glimpses of rejoicing that are trying to break through? Indeed, there is a rush to Christmas that ignores the integrity of Advent, and this is generally to be avoided. However, might one be able to preach or do some thinking with our assemblies about how incarnation (*gaudate!*) is trying to break through into all things, even when we do our best to restrain it?

◆   The *gaudete* of Philippians is a far cry from John's fire and brimstone in today's gospel from Luke. Among all his talk of wrath, unquenchable fire, and winnowing forks, might there be promise in the burning of chaff? In short, might the gospel that is coming (the Word made flesh) be right on course to remove from us the things (chaff) that are killing us? Often read as terrifying, how might we reimagine this notion to be freeing? After all, the gospel reading ends by telling us that John "proclaimed the good news to the people" (Luke 3:18). Can the burning of what is unnecessary or harmful be good news?

◆   One part of Luke's gospel that is overlooked (because we are terrified of all the wrath?) is the issue of *sharing*, which John the Baptist mentions twice: once regarding clothing and once regarding food. This is an interesting parallel considering that John is specifically identified with his clothing (camel's hair) and the food he eats (locusts and wild honey). Perhaps the lesson here is that not only others who lived in poverty needed these things, but so did John. Might this be an admonition to listen to those in need about what they need, rather than declaring from a place of privilege what it is we *think* they need? Might holiday toy drives be less innocuous than they seem?

Connections with the Liturgy

Each Sunday, in both the passing of the peace and the closing blessing and dismissal, we repeat Paul's prayer for the indwelling of God's peace. The peace we envision is the peace of Christ, the peace experienced in Christ, beyond understanding, thus a peace that is far more than a morning hello or good-bye.

Let the Children Come

By third grade, many children are able to read a Bible passage clearly and meaningfully. When possible, schedule children to serve as readers on Sundays when the readings will easily make sense to them. The second reading for this Sunday is such a passage. Children need the same instruction and practice adults need. In addition, they might need a stool to stand on at the ambo and a good microphone. Teach them how to introduce the reading and to allow silence for reflection following the reading. Instruct them to close with the phrase "The word of the Lord" so the assembly, including the children, can respond, "Thanks be to God."

Assembly Song
Gathering

Rejoice, for Christ is king!   ELW 430, LBW 171

People, look east   ELW 248, LS 11, WOV 626

Come, we that love the Lord   ELW 625, LS 164, TFF 135, WOV 742

Psalmody and Acclamations

Haugen, Marty. "You Will Draw Water Joyfully" from LP:S.

p   Highben, Zebulon M. "With Joy You Will Draw Water (Isaiah 12:2-6)." MSB1 S483.

Rusbridge, Barbara. "Sing a Song to the Lord" from PS1.

(GA) Pishner, Stephen. "Advent Gospel Acclamation" from *Psalm and Gospel Acclamation for Advent*. SATB, cant, assembly, kybd. GIA G-5259.

Hymn of the Day

Hark, the glad sound!   ELW 239, LBW 35   CHESTERFIELD

Joy to the world   ELW 267, LBW 39   ANTIOCH

Rejoice, rejoice, believers   ELW 244, LBW 25   HAF TRONES LAMPA FÄRDIG

Offering

Light one candle to watch for Messiah   ELW 240, sts. 1-3, WOV 630, sts. 1-3

O day of peace   ELW 711, WOV 762

Communion

O Lord, how shall I meet you   ELW 241, LBW 23

As the dark awaits the dawn   ELW 261, OBS 46

My Lord, what a morning   ELW 438, TFF 40, WOV 627

Sending

The King shall come   ELW 260, LBW 33, LS 5

Soon and very soon   ELW 439, LS 2, TFF 38, W&P 128, WOV 744

Additional Assembly Songs

Come by here   TFF 42, 43

Tiempo de esperanza   LLC 279

Arriba los corazones   LLC 396

⊕ Feliciano, Francisco. "Maranatha" from *Sent by the Lord: Songs of the World Church*, vol. 2. U. GIA G-3740.

⊕ Maraschin, Jaci. "Come to Be Our Hope, O Jesus" from *Global Songs 2*. U. AFP 9780800656744.

✿ Bruxvoort Colligan, Richard. "Prepare the Way for Love (The Baptizer's Rant)" from *Seeds of Faith*. worldmaking.net.

✿ Dakota Road. "Stir Us, Lord" from *All Are Welcome, Disc 2*. dakotaroadmusic.com.

✿ Gungor, Michael. "Beautiful Things" from *Beautiful Things*. gungormusic.com.

✿ Hansen, Holly. "Under the Son" from *Storm Home: A Collection of Music from Humble Walk Artists-in-Residence*. humblewalk .bandcamp.com.

✿ Haugen, Marty. "As the Grains of Wheat." ELW 465.

✿ Kurtz, Rachel. "Make a Difference" from *Broken & Lowdown*. rachelkurtz.org.

Music for the Day

Choral

p   Haugen, Kyle. "Lost in the Night." SAB, pno, opt solo. AFP 9780800659240.

p   Keesecker, Thomas. "Hail to the Lord's Anointed" from *The New Gloria Deo*, vol. 2. 2 pt mxd, pno, opt second kybd, gtr. AFP 9781451424133.

p ● Shaw, Timothy. "Hark, the Glad Sound!" SATB. AFP 9781451485837.

p   Smith, Alan. "Come, Jesus, Come." SATB, org. AFP 9781451423952.

Children's Choir

p   Handel, G. F. "Good News Is in the Air." U, kybd. AFP 9780800664077.

●   Kohrs, Jonathan. "Hark the Glad Sound!" U/2 pt, org/pno. CPH 984187POD.

Kosche, Kenneth. "Rejoice in the Lord Always." 2 pt trbl, kybd. CPH 983091PODWEB.

Keyboard / Instrumental

p ● Carlson, J. Bert. "Chesterfield" from *Introductions and Alternate Accompaniments for Piano*, vol. 1. Pno. AFP 9780800623593.

●   Cherwien, David M. "Chesterfield" from *Organ Plus One*. Org, inst. AFP 9780800656188.

●   Diemer, Emma Lou. "Antioch" from *Augsburg Organ Library: Advent*. Org. AFP 9780800658953.

●   Organ, Anne Krentz. "Haf trones lampa färdig" from *Piano Plus: Hymns for Piano and Treble Instrument, Advent/Christmas*. Pno, inst. AFP 9780800638542.

Handbell

p ● Afdahl, Lee J. "Antioch (Joy to the World)" from *Hymn Accompaniments for Handbells: Advent and Christmas*. 3-5 oct, L3+. AFP 9780806698076.

p ● Geschke, Susan E. "Hark, the Glad Sound!" 2-3 oct, L1+. CG CGB346.

●   Page, Anna Laura. "Rejoice, Rejoice, Believers." 3-5 oct hb, opt 3 oct hc, L2. CG CGB642.

Sunday, December 13

Lucy, martyr, died 304

Lucy was a young Christian of Sicily who was martyred during the persecutions under Emperor Diocletian. Apparently she had decided to devote her life to God and her possessions to the poor. Beyond that, however, little is known for certain about Lucy. However, her celebration became particularly important in Sweden and Norway, perhaps because the feast of Lucia (the name means "light") originally fell on the shortest day of the year. A tradition arose of a girl in the household, wearing a crown of candles, bringing saffron rolls to her family early in the morning on the day of Lucia.

Monday, December 14

John of the Cross, renewer of the church, died 1591

John was a monk of the Carmelite religious order who met Teresa of Ávila when she was working to reform the Carmelite Order and return it to a stricter observance of its rules. He followed Teresa's lead and encouraged others to follow her reform. He was imprisoned when he encountered opposition to the reform. His writings, like Teresa's, reflect a deep interest in mystical thought and meditation. In one of John's poems, "The Spiritual Canticle," he cried, "Oh, that my griefs would end! Come, grant me thy fruition full and free!"

⊕ = global song   ✿ = praise song
● = relates to hymn of the day   p = available in Prelude Music Planner

December 20, 2015
Fourth Sunday of Advent

Cradle and cross are inextricably connected on the fourth Sunday of Advent. Between a lovely tribute to the little town of Bethlehem and the blessed virgin Mary's magnificent song of praise, the letter to the Hebrews reminds us in no uncertain terms that Christ's advent is for "the offering of the body of Jesus Christ once for all." It is the kind of tension in which the church always lives as when in the holy communion—with high delight—"we proclaim the Lord's death."

Prayer of the Day

Stir up your power, Lord Christ, and come. With your abundant grace and might, free us from the sin that binds us, that we may receive you in joy and serve you always, for you live and reign with the Father and the Holy Spirit, one God, now and forever.

Gospel Acclamation

Alleluia. Here I am, the servant ¹ of the Lord;* let it be with me according ¹ to your word. *Alleluia.* (Luke 1:38)

Readings and Psalm

Micah 5:2-5a

The prophet Micah, having pronounced judgment upon Judah, speaks of a future shepherd-king who, like David, will come from the small town of Bethlehem. (Ephrathah refers to the area around Bethlehem.) This king will restore Israel and bring peace. New Testament writers understood this passage to be referring to Jesus.

Luke 1:46b-55

You, Lord, have lifted up the lowly. (Luke 1:52)

or Psalm 80:1-7

Let your face shine upon us, and we shall be saved. (Ps. 80:7)

Hebrews 10:5-10

The author of Hebrews uses the image of religious sacrifice to convey the significance of Christ's coming. Through obedient acceptance of God's will, Christ allows his own body to become the greatest sacrifice of all, one through which we are made a holy people.

Luke 1:39-45 [46-55]

We are presented with Elizabeth, John's mother, and Mary, the mother of Jesus, two women filled with the Holy Spirit and with faith. In Elizabeth's inspired greeting and Mary's song of praise we hear of a saving God who remembers, scatters, lifts up, and fulfills all things.

Preface   Advent

Color   Blue

Prayers of Intercession

The prayers are prepared locally for each occasion. The following examples may be adapted or used as appropriate.

Emmanuel has come, is here, and is coming soon. Let us join in prayer for the church, the earth, and those who are in need, that all receive what God promises to give.

A brief silence.

O God our Wisdom, give to all the baptized knowledge of your truth and the power of your presence. Inspire worship leaders and church musicians toward ever-deepening praise. Hear us, O God.

Your mercy is great.

O God, Lord of might, hold the cosmos in your care. Give the earth both darkness and light, cold and warmth. Protect the mountains from exploitation. Hear us, O God.

Your mercy is great.

O God, King of nations, bring peace and justice to all the countries of the world. Guide all leaders toward honest and merciful rule. Raise up those who are poor. We pray especially for . . . . Hear us, O God.

Your mercy is great.

O God, Key of David, look from your throne upon all in need. Mend the broken and the brokenhearted. Free those imprisoned by anxiety or illness. We pray especially for . . . . Hear us, O God.

Your mercy is great.

O God, Tree of Jesse, nurture our community. Give us joy in one another, and make us servants of all in need. Bless our holy day celebrations with your Spirit. Hear us, O God.

Your mercy is great.

Here other intercessions may be offered.

O God, Dayspring, we remember all who have died and now live in your light (*especially Katharina von Bora Luther and . . .*). Gather us to yourself and teach us to sing together Mary's song of praise. Hear us, O God.

Your mercy is great.
Receive our prayers, merciful God, and make us ready to receive you when you come through Jesus Christ, our Savior and Lord.
Amen.

Images in the Readings

The **pregnant woman** can be a symbol of the life that comes from God. In the Bible, many women, from Eve in Genesis 4:1 on, conceive and bear children with the help of God. Here both the virgin Mary and the postmenopausal Elizabeth are pregnant. When we acclaim God as creator, we attest that God is continually creating life on this earth.

What has been termed "the visitation" is observed also on May 31. Recently many women have found inspiration in this story of **two women**, each in some way outside the mainstream, supporting one another.

The **arm of the Lord** is a repeated image in the Old Testament. Biblical imagery describes God's activities as if God has a humanlike body, although with scarce reference to male or female generative organs. By the fifth century, theologians, quite aware of polytheisms in which the deities have bodies, opposed any literal belief in God as a superhuman. Singing Mary's Magnificat in Advent, we think of the infant's arms as the almighty power of God.

Bethlehem means "house of bread." We come each week to the table, welcomed to Christ's house of bread.

Ideas for the Day

◆   Today's readings are rich, and while preachers and musicians could reasonably focus on Mary (a recovery of Marian theology in the Lutheran tradition is important), some time could also be spent specifically on the second reading and the issue of supersessionism (Heb. 10:9b); that is, the notion that the second covenant replaces the first. This is not only bad theology but can give rise to a host of evils. The number of people who believe this in our assemblies (whether they can name it or not) may be higher than one might think. Preaching on the continuation of the covenanting God might be one way to go today.

◆   The Marian theology cherished by Martin Luther himself (for example, in his *Commentary on the Magnificat*) has largely been lost to Lutherans as a reaction to Roman Catholicism. Nonetheless, the story of the visitation that is heard today is primarily centered around *blessing*; blessed is Mary and blessed is the child she will bear. In reaction to the overreaction of Lutherans regarding Mary, how might she—whom the text calls "blessed"—be recovered as a "blessing" to us? Her blessing fits hand-in-glove with Lutheran theology, specifically due to her belief (Luke 1:45). Far from being the poster child for another tradition, Mary

is recovered and held in high esteem by churches of the Reformation.

◆   Mary's Magnificat is appointed to be sung every day at evening prayer, the time when one day is ending and a new liturgical day (beginning at sunset) is about to be born in time. This is not lost within the incarnation itself, as one day passes (dominated by empires, inequality, and vengeance) and a new day comes into being in time (the birth of Jesus and the reign of God). Might your community consider celebrating evening prayer during Advent, and if so, might Mary's song be lifted up as particularly appropriate for the incarnational day that is quickly coming?

Connections with the Liturgy

In the Nicene Creed we acclaim Jesus Christ "the only Son of God . . . incarnate of the Holy Spirit and the virgin Mary."

In evening prayer for centuries, Christians have sung Mary's Song, as if no matter what happened during the day, we conclude by praising God for the gift of mercy.

Let the Children Come

Children have many ways to literally leap for joy on happy occasions, depending on their abilities—skipping, jumping, clapping, hugging, waving their arms. This is a good day for children to express joy actively in church. Imagine with children what worship would be like if people jumped with joy at the reading of the gospel, for example, or skipped on their way to communion, or hugged one another happily following a baptism. God loves bodies so much that God became flesh; the gospel text reminds us to use our bodies in service to the gospel. In this, children can be excellent guides for adults.

Assembly Song
Gathering

Awake! Awake, and greet the new morn   ELW 242, WOV 633
Creator of the stars of night   ELW 245, LBW 323
O come, O come, Emmanuel   ELW 257, LBW 34, LS 10, LLC 281

Psalmody and Acclamations

Burkhardt, Michael. "Psalm 146" from *Psalms for the Church Year.* U or 3 pt canon a cap. MSM 80-708.
Cooney, Rory. "Praise the Lord, My Soul (Psalm 146)" from PCY, vol. 4.
Wold, Wayne. "Psalm 80:1-7," Refrain 1, from PSCY.
(GA) Pishner, Stephen. "Advent Gospel Acclamation" from *Psalm and Gospel Acclamation for Advent.* SATB, cant, assembly, kybd. GIA G-5259.

Hymn of the Day

Unexpected and mysterious   ELW 258   *ST. HELENA*

My soul proclaims your greatness   ELW 251, WOV 730   *KINGSFOLD*

My soul does magnify the Lord   ELW 882, TFF 168   *GOSPEL MAGNIFICAT*

Offering

Light one candle to watch for Messiah   ELW 240, WOV 630

My soul proclaims the greatness of the Lord / Magnificat   ELW 234–236, LBW 6

Communion

Each winter as the year grows older   ELW 252, WOV 628

Praise to the Lord, all of you   ELW 844

My soul now magnifies the Lord   ELW 573, LBW 180

Sending

Canticle of the Turning   ELW 723, GS2 46, W&P 26

Savior of the nations, come   ELW 263, LBW 28

Additional Assembly Songs

Emmanuel   TFF 45, W&P 36

Ya viene la Navidad   LLC 282

El Dios de paz, Verbo divino   LLC 277

⊕ Bell, John. "No Wind at the Window" from *Glory to God*. U. WJK 9780664238971.

⊕ Kiley, Henry W. "Mary's Salidummay" from *Sound the Bamboo*. U. GIA G-6830.

⊕✿ Bell, John. "Magnificat" from *We Walk His Way: Shorter Songs for Worship*. GIA G-7403.

✿ Bruxvoort Colligan, Richard. "Turn and Restore Us (Psalm 80)" from *Shout for Joy*. AFP 9780806698632. psalmimmersion .bandcamp.com.

✿ Grundy, Christopher. "Jesus Is There" from *Stepping In*. christo phergrundy.com.

✿ Hansen, Tim. "Trust in You" from *Is Anybody Listening?* timhan senproject.com.

✿ Rundman, Jonathan. "Four Candles" from *Sound Theology*, vol. 1. jonathanrundman.com.

✿ Stevens, Sufjan. "We're Goin' to the Country" from *Songs for Christmas*. sufjan.com.

Music for the Day
Choral

p Busarow, Donald. "Let All Mortal Flesh Keep Silence" from *Augsburg Choirbook for Advent, Christmas, and Epiphany*. 2 pt mxd, org, opt assembly. AFP 9780800678586.

Helvey, Howard. "O Come, Divine Messiah!" SATB, org. OXF X-521.

p Raabe, Nancy. "Come, Thou Long-Expected Jesus." S(A)B, kybd, opt fc. AFP 9781451462319.

p Raney, Joel. "Come, Come, Emmanuel." SATB, pno, opt inst. HOP C-5841.

Children's Choir

Handel, G. F./arr. Michael Burkhardt. "He Shall Feed His Flock." U trbl, kybd, opt 2 C inst, opt vc/bass inst. MSM 50-9404.

p Kemp, Helen. "Magnificat." U, pno, C inst, hc, hb. CG CGA954.

Schulz-Widmar, Russell. "Visitation Carol." 2 pt, tri. GIA G-4740.

Keyboard / Instrumental

● Keesecker, Thomas. "Kingsfold" from *Sing It Simply*. Pno, gtr, hb, opt C inst. MSM 80-790.

p Kerr, J. Wayne. "Aria" from *Organ Celebrations*. Org. AFP 9781451451740.

p ● Lasky, David. "St. Helena" from *The King of Glory*. Org. AFP 9781451462579.

● Organ, Anne Krentz. "Kingsfold" from *Woven Together*, vol. 2. Pno, inst. AFP 9780800677664.

Handbell

Larson, Lloyd. "Come, O Come, Emmanuel" from *Ringing the Church Year*. 3-5 oct, L2+. LOR 20/1671L.

p Moklebust, Cathy. "Lo, How a Rose." 3-5 oct hb, L2+, CG CGB844. Opt kybd, opt org or synth, opt str, CG CGRP30. Opt full score, CG CGB843.

● Wagner, H. Dean. "Fantasy on 'Kingsfold'." 3-6 oct hb, opt 3 oct hc, L2+, HOP 2134. Opt full score with fl, ob, hrn, tpt, perc, hp, str, HOP 2134O.

Sunday, December 20

Katharina von Bora Luther, renewer of the church, died 1552

Born to an impoverished nobleman, when Katharina (Katie) was five her mother died and she was sent to live in a convent. She later took vows as a nun, but around age twenty-four she and several other nuns who were influenced by the writings of Martin Luther left the convent. Six children were born to Katie and Martin. Though initially Luther felt little affection for Katie, she proved herself a gifted household manager and became a trusted partner. She was so influential that Luther took to calling her "my lord Katie."

CHRISTMAS

ADVENT

CHRISTMAS

TIME AFTER EPIPHANY

PREPARING FOR CHRISTMAS

Lectionary

When one speaks the word *Christmas*, most people inevitably imagine a single day of robust celebration. When one speaks the word *Epiphany*, at least in circles of people connected with the church, many people imagine a season stretching from Christmas until Lent begins. Interestingly, by *Evangelical Lutheran Worship* and by the calendars of most Western Christians, Christmas is a season and Epiphany a day, and not the other way around. Christmas is twelve full days, if you will, a day for each month of the year, and the feast of Epiphany brings the Christmas season to a festal close. Certainly, in the Time after Epiphany we are experiencing *epiphanies*; that is, God in Christ is revealed to us in the flesh and personhood of Jesus. And, it must be said, observing the Epiphany of Our Lord as a major day does help bridge the church in the West with the church in the East. Understanding the calendar in this way will help make sense of our current lectionary and its wisdom.

At the primary festivals of the year, we retell the primary biblical stories. Christians tell the central stories of Christ, as told in one of the four gospel books, on each Sunday and festival. The stories in those gospels are similar but also interestingly different. In Holy Week each year, the lectionary appoints that we tell the story of Jesus' betrayal, suffering, death, and burial in two ways: on the Sunday of the Passion/Palm Sunday, the story is read from either Matthew, Mark, or Luke, depending on the year. On Good Friday in the same week, the story is told from John's gospel. The stories are marvelously different, the scripts and characters changed, and each gospel writer tells the story through a particular lens or viewpoint. Also, at the celebration of the Resurrection of Our Lord (Easter Vigil and Easter Day), the lectionary appoints that we read John's gospel at the Vigil and the story of the empty tomb from either Matthew, Mark, or Luke on Easter Day in the morning. The point of telling these stories in at least two ways, from the pens of at least two different writers, is to make note that the Bible is made up of diverse narratives. These diverse narratives invite us to consider that the Bible is not a report of the way things actually happened, but stories to invite us

into the ways of God, through the lens of a storyteller, that we might come to believe.

During the season of Christmas, we tell the stories of Christ's birth among us in particularly diverse ways. Each year on Christmas Eve, the lectionary appoints that we read the birth narrative from Luke 2. Two options are given in *Evangelical Lutheran Worship* on Christmas Day in the morning: either more of Luke 2 or the prologue from John's gospel (John 1:1-14). The classic choice would have been to read Luke in the evening and John in the morning. The two ways of proclaiming the incarnation could not be more different. In Luke's gospel, we have the vivid characters of shepherds and angels, of Mary and Joseph, of fields and inns, of both "Glory to God" and "Do not be afraid." In John's gospel, the Word becomes flesh and life, full of light, grace, truth, and glory; John testifies to this light, and the world does not recognize the light. And—now here is a most wondrous thing—on the Epiphany of Our Lord, the day set apart that brings our Christmas season to a close, we tell the story through the eyes of Matthew: magi from the east, gifts of gold, a conniving King Herod, and a marvelous star. (Note: there is no star in Luke's gospel narrative of the birth of Jesus.) Each year, at Christmas and Epiphany, we tell the story of Jesus' birth in at least three ways. Why? Because each way invites us to see Jesus a bit differently, to encounter Christ present to us as a child, in the flesh, as a gravitational center strong enough even to pull stars to his presence. And because we tell these stories in assemblies made up of diverse people, the stories will resonate more with some than with others. Or, at the very least, hearing the diverse stories will invite us into the diversity of a unified triune God, whose complexity is rivaled only by remarkable simplicity. Such is the mystery of the lectionary and the appointed gospel readings at Christmas and Epiphany, but also all through the year.

It may be that scheduling and enacting the liturgies of the Christmas season have become a burden in some places. With all of the excesses of the commercial season and the pressures that mount on us individually and collectively, just getting to Christmas Eve might seem a major victory. Planning a full and robust Christmas season with holiday travel, family plans, or even the postholiday doldrums can seem impossible. Some congregations have given up. In some places, worship is full and rich only on Christmas Eve, but a liturgy on Christmas Day in the morning is not observed, the Sundays of Christmas are indeed "low Sundays," and when Epiphany falls midweek, as it does this year on Wednesday, the major festival is bypassed altogether. When this happens, we have fallen into the trap set for us by the culture that began "Christmas" in late October or early November, such that we are exasperated by December 25. Or, for worship planners and professional staff in congregations, the demands of December are so great that anything but a nap (hibernation?) after December 26 seems unlikely. Maybe the weather has been particularly harsh, or the nostalgia that infects our expectations of Christmas has only made us more jaded. As worship planners, we can resist these traps and temptations. Planning and enacting robust liturgies throughout the twelve days of Christmas can reinvigorate congregational life and feed a spiritual hunger among the people in our assemblies who have only been beaten up or abused this season. Keep the days of Christmas, all of them, with the wondrous and diverse biblical stories, and in them encounter Christ: alive, human, wondrous, and for you (or, as in Texas, for y'all).

Evangelical Lutheran Worship does allow for the transference of Epiphany of Our Lord to Sunday, January 3, if it seems impossible for congregational worship to be scheduled midweek on Wednesday, January 6. (See page 10 in the notes on the church year in *Evangelical Lutheran Worship*, Leaders Desk Edition.) When a congregation makes this transference, the appointed Sunday readings are displaced, which means the gospel reading, John 1:[1-9]10-18 would not be proclaimed. It is wise to consider, then, if the prologue from John's gospel will be read on Christmas Day if the Epiphany festival is transferred, retaining the principle that we hear the diverse gospel readings each year.

Music

The music of Christmas worship may seem to many planners as predetermined. There are so many expectations of the requisite carols sung at the requisite moments, it could seem as though there are no real choices to be made, or no moments for creativity or something new (or at least newer). Do not be afraid. Make room for the expectations, but take every opportunity in Christmas days to plan music that will be new. The psalms appointed for the Nativity of Our Lord each year are Psalms 96, 97, and 98, two of which begin with the words, "Sing a *new* song to the LORD." It is too easy to repeat only the music that worked well last year. More than that, it can get terribly boring. Reinvigorate your plans this year and make it a point to plan new things, so that everyone who worships in your assemblies will hear the

good news anew. And when you must repeat certain carols at certain moments in worship each year, musicians could work to make them sound fresh, with varied introductions or harmonizations that will shake things up a bit.

If you have reveled in the Advent hymns during Advent, then make every effort to schedule and plan the beloved Christmas carols throughout the twelve days. Some congregations plan an additional carol sing on the Sundays in the season, either before or after worship, to augment the Christmas hymns sung in the liturgies. If it seems impossible to gather choirs, bands, or other musicians for worship during the twelve days, make provision for an intergenerational Christmas choir or ensemble that rehearses only before worship. In this way, singers or instrumentalists who may be traveling to visit family in other cities or in other congregations can participate in an ensemble during the festival season.

Music during Christmas does not always need to be joyous and celebratory. Leave some room in Christmas music to express the not yet realized hopes and dreams that remain for most people. Let Christmas music bring to expression the wonder and mystery of the incarnation, the diversity of song present among the diverse people of the world, the disappointment of expectations not met or prayers not yet answered. At Christmastime, people are still sick, dying, wounded, abused, depressed, addicted, tormented, oppressed, and at war. The Christmas song sings hope and promise to such situations, but it does not deny that such realities continue to plague our lives and communities.

Environment

If your congregation's celebration includes poinsettias, consider transitioning from red to ivory blooms and requesting gold sleeves for the plants. This subtler coloration complements the beauty of many worship settings, as well as the white paraments and vestments of the season.

Be intentional about crafting worship on the Nativity of Our Lord as distinctive from Christmas Eve. Whereas Christmas Eve worship typically focuses on the nativity characters, the birth of the Christ child, and "light in the darkness," Christmas Day worship might focus more intentionally on the incarnation, the Word made flesh, and the far-reaching impact of this child's coming. Encourage reflection on the eucharist as one concrete means by which Christ takes up residence within and among us.

Use a variety of ribbons and bells to create a tintinnabularium. See 02_Christmas.Tintinnabularium.pdf* for ideas on how to proceed in fashioning this visual and melodic focal point for worship. If you opt to create a mobile tintinnabularium, incorporate it into processions, right behind the cross. If your tintinnabularium is stationary, explore how you might position it over the font as a kinetic reminder of the Spirit's movement within and among God's people.

If your congregation's celebration of the Sundays of Christmas has drifted into a pattern of predictable sameness, introduce a gathering rite informed by *Las Posadas*, a reenactment of Mary and Joseph's journey from place to place in search of lodging (see 02_Christmas.Preparation.pdf*). Explore linking its use with initiatives to provide assistance to persons who are homeless and/or to facilitate reflection on our own experiences of displacement, alienation, and hunger.

Amid the joyful celebrations of Christ's birth, be mindful that Christmas is not a happy time for everyone. On the weekdays immediately following Christmas, assemble a few carolers to visit homebound members, members who have lost loved ones during the past year, and/or residents in the neighborhoods near your church.

Throughout the twelve days of Christmas, cultivate deeper awareness of God-with-us by encouraging increased attention to God's presence and activity within and beyond the faith community. Anchor that awareness in an invitation for worshipers to record their observations throughout the coming year, either on slips of paper to be collected in an identified spot or in a common "God Sightings" notebook located in or near the worship space. Make occasional, ongoing references to the entries, celebrating how these sightings give shape to the gospel according to your congregation.

Encourage households to make use of the twelve days of Christmas to delve more deeply into the significance of Emmanuel's coming. Parents of young children will find a variety of printable resources and craft ideas on Pinterest.

In some contexts, the Epiphany of Our Lord is a time for conferring a house blessing that includes making an inscription in chalk over the lintel of the main entrance (an order for such a blessing is provided on page 53). Invite parishioners to gather in groups of three to five households to experience together a progressive house blessing. The groups move from house to house, asking God to bless each home and those who dwell there.

Seasonal Checklist

- Publicize Christmas services in outdoor signage, local newspapers, and online listings, on your church website and Facebook page, and perhaps in a special mailing to area residents.
- As many communities enter flu season, consider making antibacterial wipes or gel available to worshipers.
- Prepare materials for Christmas flower sponsorship.
- Repair or replace seasonal environment materials and decorations as needed.
- If handheld candles are used by worshipers on Christmas Eve, ensure that you have an adequate supply of candles on hand, and that fire extinguishers and detectors are up-to-date.
- Order service folder covers if needed for services on Christmas Eve, Christmas Day, and Epiphany.
- Design service folders that guests will be able to follow easily, including specific instructions for communion distribution. For tips on preparing excellent worship folders, consult *Leading Worship Matters: A Sourcebook for Preparing Worship Leaders* (Augsburg Fortress, 2013, pp. 268–72).
- Make arrangements for adequate seating, along with additional worship books and service folders for larger assemblies on Christmas Eve.
- Determine the communion distribution procedure for services with large numbers of communicants. Rehearse communion assistants if necessary.
- Use the canticle of praise ("Glory to God"). In addition to the form in the communion setting, see options in the service music section of *Evangelical Lutheran Worship* (162–164).
- Use the Nicene Creed.
- Consider especially Thanksgiving at the Table III in *Evangelical Lutheran Worship*.

Worship Texts for Christmas

Confession and Forgiveness

All may make the sign of the cross, the sign marked at baptism, as the presiding minister begins.

Blessed be the holy Trinity, ☩ one God,
the Maker of heaven and earth,
the Word made flesh,
the Lord and giver of life.
Amen.

Let us come into the light of Christ,
confessing our need for God's mercy.

Silence is kept for reflection.

God of peace,
we confess that we are not at peace—
with others or with ourselves.
We bring to you all that tears us apart:
discord in our families,
violence in our world,
our own conflicted hearts.
In your mercy, mend us.
Reconnect us to one another and to you.
Let peace reign over all the earth,
through the Prince of peace,
our Savior Jesus Christ. Amen.

In the Word who has come to dwell with us,
God has given us grace upon grace:
forgiveness that is stronger than our sins,
love that can heal every broken heart.
Hear this word of God's pardon and peace:
in the name of ☩ Jesus our Savior,
you are free from all your sins.
Rise, shine, for your light has come.
Amen.

Offering Prayer

Good and loving God,
we rejoice in the birth of Jesus,
who came among the poor to bring the riches of your grace.
As you have blessed us with your gifts,
let them be blessing for others.
With the trees of the field, with all earth and heaven,
we shout for joy at the coming of your Son,
Jesus Christ our Lord.
Amen.

Invitation to Communion

The mystery hidden for the ages
is revealed for us in this meal.
Come, behold and receive your God.

Prayer after Communion

We give you thanks, O God,
that in this bread and cup of Christ's very life,
you give us food for our journey.
As you led the magi by a star,
as you brought the holy family home again,
guide us on the way unfolding before us.
Wherever we go, may our lives proclaim
good news of great joy in Jesus Christ our Lord.
Amen.

Sending of Communion

O God,
whose grace and truth are revealed
in the Word-made-flesh,
bless those who go forth to share your word and sacrament
with those who are *sick/homebound/imprisoned*.
Nourish and strengthen
those who receive this holy communion,
that through the body and blood of your Son
all may rejoice at his birth
and in his presence among us now and forever.
Amen.

Blessing

May the Word that Mary brought to birth
carry you into new and abundant life.
Amen.
May the Word that Joseph cradled in his arms
enfold you with love and strength.
Amen.
May the Word that angels proclaimed in song
bring harmony to our world.
Amen.
And the blessing of almighty God,
the Father, the + Son, and the Holy Spirit,
be upon you and remain with you always.
Amen.

Dismissal

Go in peace. Christ is with you.
Thanks be to God.

SEASONAL RITES FOR CHRISTMAS

Lighting the Christmas Tree

Use this prayer when you first illumine the tree or when you gather at the tree.

Holy God,
we praise you as we light this tree.
It gives light to this place
as you shine light into darkness through Jesus,
the light of the world.

God of all,
we thank you for your love,
the love that has come to us in Jesus.
Be with us now as we remember that gift of love
and help us to share that love with a yearning world.

Creator God,
you made the stars in the heavens.
Thank you for the light that shines on us in Jesus,
the bright morning star.
Amen.

Blessing of the Nativity Scene

This blessing may be used when figures are added to the nativity scene and throughout the days of Christmas.

Bless us, O God, as we remember a humble birth. With each angel and shepherd we place here before you, show us the wonder found in a stable. In song and prayer, silence and awe, we adore your gift of love, Christ Jesus our Savior.
Amen.

Christmas Proclamation

This contemporary version of an ancient proclamation places the birth of Christ into human history yet avoids a literalistic accounting of time. The last phrase makes it clear that the nativity of Jesus is not only then but now, today, in our own time. The proclamation may be chanted by a presiding or assisting minister, cantor(s), or choir at the beginning of the Christmas Eve or Christmas Day liturgy, perhaps before the gathering hymn. Music Sourcebook for All Saints through Transfiguration (Augsburg Fortress, 2013) includes two musical settings for the Christmas proclamation.

Many ages from the time when God created
the heavens and the earth
and then formed man and woman in his own image;
long after the great flood,
when God made the rainbow shine forth
as a sign of the covenant;
twenty-one centuries from the time the promise was given
to Abraham and Sarah;
thirteen centuries after Moses led the people of Israel
out of Egypt and Miriam danced in freedom;
eleven hundred years from the time of Ruth and the judges;
one thousand years from the anointing of David as king,
in fulfillment of the times and years and months and days
discerned by the prophets;
in the one hundred and ninety-fourth Olympiad;
the seven hundred and fifty-second year from the
foundation of the city of Rome;
the forty-second year of the reign of Octavian Augustus;
while the whole world enjoyed a span of peace,
Jesus Christ, eternal God and Son of the eternal Father,
desiring to sanctify the world by his most merciful coming,
being conceived by the Holy Spirit
and nine months of growth in the womb of his mother—
now in our own times is the nativity of our Lord Jesus
Christ, God made flesh.

Text: Traditional, adapt. Brian T. Johnson

Blessing for a Home at Epiphany

Matthew writes that when the magi saw the shining star stop overhead, they were filled with joy. "On entering the house, they saw the child with Mary his mother" (Matt. 2:10-11). In the home, Christ is met in family and friends, in visitors and strangers. In the home, faith is shared, nurtured, and put into action. In the home, Christ is welcome.

Twelfth Night (January 5), Epiphany of Our Lord (January 6), or another day during the time after Epiphany offers an occasion for gathering with friends and family members for a blessing for the home. Someone may lead the greeting and blessing, while another person may read the scripture passage. Following an eastern European tradition, a visual blessing may be inscribed with white chalk above the main door; for example, 20 + CMB + 16. The numbers change with each new year. The three letters stand for either the ancient Latin blessing Christe mansionem benedicat, *which means "Christ, bless this house," or the legendary names of the magi (Caspar, Melchior, and Balthasar).*

Greeting

May peace be to this house and to all who enter here.
By wisdom a house is built
and through understanding it is established;
through knowledge its rooms are filled
with rare and beautiful treasures. (*Proverbs 24:3-4*)

Reading

As we prepare to ask God's blessing on this household,
let us listen to the words of scripture.

In the beginning was the Word,
and the Word was with God, and the Word was God.
He was in the beginning with God.
All things came into being through him,
and without him not one thing came into being.
What has come into being in him was life,
and the life was the light of all people.

The Word became flesh and lived among us,
and we have seen his glory,
the glory as of a father's only son, full of grace and truth.
From his fullness we have all received,
grace upon grace. (*John 1:1-4, 14, 16*)

Inscription

This inscription may be made with chalk above the entrance:
20 + C M B + 16
Write the appropriate character (left) while speaking the text (right).
The magi of old, known as
C   Caspar,
M   Melchior, and
B   Balthasar,
followed the star of God's Son who came to dwell among us
20   two thousand
16   and sixteen years ago.
✝   Christ, bless this house,
✝   and remain with us throughout the new year.

Prayer of Blessing

O God, you revealed your Son to all people
by the shining light of a star.
We pray that you bless this home and all who live here
with your gracious presence.
May your love be our inspiration,
your wisdom our guide,
your truth our light,
and your peace our benediction;
through Christ our Lord.
Amen.

Then everyone may walk from room to room, blessing the house with incense or by sprinkling with water, perhaps using a branch from the Christmas tree.

An acclamation may be sung during the procession, such as Music Sourcebook for All Saints through Transfiguration #S560.

Adapted from Come, Lord Jesus: Devotions for the Home *(Augsburg Fortress, 1996). See also "Blessing for a Home" in* Evangelical Lutheran Worship Pastoral Care, *pp. 337–353.*

A Service for the Day of Epiphany

The opening dialogue is based on the Tribus miraculis orna-tum, an ancient Latin text remembering the three traditional revelations of Epiphany. Christopher Wordsworth's hymn text, "Songs of thankfulness and praise" (ELW 310) and the proper preface for Epiphany within the great thanksgiving in Evangeli-cal Lutheran Worship also reference these three epiphanies: the magi following a star to Jesus, the baptism of Jesus, and the miracle of water turned to wine. A musical setting of the dialogue is available in Music Sourcebook for All Saints through Transfiguration #S556 (Augsburg Fortress, 2013).

Epiphany Dialogue

The dialogue may be spoken or sung, and led by a presiding or assisting minister, cantor, or choir.

We give thanks on this holy day, adorned with epiphanies:
for the star that led the magi to the manger,
that the nations may see the light of Christ;
for the water turned to wine at Cana's wedding,
that the people taste the goodness of the Lord;
for the baptism of our Lord Jesus Christ in the Jordan,
that the Christ would save us all.
This is the day that the Lord has made,
we will rejoice and be glad in it. Alleluia.

Gathering Song

O Morning Star, how fair and bright!   ELW 308, LBW 76

Greeting

God who sent the Light into our world,
God who shone in the Bethlehem manger,
God who spreads the Spirit's rays,
be with you all.
And also with you.

Prayer of the Day

Everlasting God, the radiance of all faithful people, you brought the nations to the brightness of your rising. Fill the world with your glory, and show yourself to all the world through him who is the true light and the bright morning star, your Son, Jesus Christ, our Savior and Lord, who lives and reigns with you and the Holy Spirit, one God, now and forever. **Amen.**

First Reading   Isaiah 60:1-6

Psalmody   Psalm 72:1-7, 10-14

Second Reading   Ephesians 3:1-12

Gospel Acclamation

**As a star, God's holy word
leads us to our King and Lord;
brightly from its sacred pages
shall this light throughout the ages
shine upon our path of life,
shine upon our path of life.**
Tune: *DEJLIG ER DEN HIMMEL BLÅ* (LBW 75, st. 6)

Gospel   Matthew 2:1-12

Sermon

Hymn of the Day

Songs of thankfulness and praise   ELW 310
Christ, Be Our Light   ELW 715

Creed

Prayers of Intercession

Guided by the star, together with the whole people of God in Christ Jesus, let us pray for the church, those in need, and all of creation.
A brief silence.
O Splendor of God's glory, shine your radiance within our world. Remove the barriers that divide us, and teach us to love with all our might. Lead us, O God:
lead us by your light.
True Dawn from on high, set us free from the power of guilt and grave. Shine your light in our lives and grant us your grace. Lead us, O God:
lead us by your light.
O living Spring of light from light, renew the strength of all who suffer: the poor, the sick, and those who mourn (*especially*). Lead us, O God:
lead us by your light.
Here other intercessions may be offered.

God of light, into your hands we place all for whom we pray, trusting in your radiant mercy; through Jesus Christ our Savior and Lord.
Amen.

Peace

Offering Song

**As they offered gifts most rare
at thy cradle, rude and bare,
so may we with holy joy,
pure and free from sin's alloy,
all our costliest treasures bring,
Christ, to thee, our heav'nly king.**
(ELW 302, LBW 82, st. 3)

Communion

The presiding minister may address the assembly in these or similar words.
The light of Christ came into our world
and shines in the darkness.
Come now to feast at Christ's table.

Communion Song

Brightest and best of the stars   ELW 303, LBW 84
I want to walk as a child of the light   ELW 815, WOV 649
Now the silence   ELW 460, LBW 205

Prayer after Communion

O Lord, you look upon us in love and refresh our souls through the gifts of bread and wine. Send us out, reflecting the light of your grace, to tell the story of Jesus Christ, our bright morning star.
Amen.

Blessing

Beloved children of God, what came into being in Christ was life, and the life was the light of all people. The light shines in the darkness, and the darkness did not overcome it. The light of Christ shine on you with grace and mercy and fill you with joy and peace. (*John 1:1, 3-5*)
Amen.

Sending Song

Bright and glorious is the sky   ELW 301, LBW 75, sts. 1-5

Dismissal

Go in peace, guided by the light of Christ.
Thanks be to God.

"Epiphany Dialogue" text: traditional, adapt. Zebulon M. Highben.

Bright and glorious is the sky" (LBW 75). Text © 1958 Service Book and Hymnal, admin. Augsburg Fortress.

Some of the prayers of intercession are based on the text of "O Splendor of God's glory bright" (ELW 559). Text © 2000 Augsburg Fortress.

December 24, 2015

Nativity of Our Lord
Christmas Eve

On a long winter evening we gather to proclaim the coming of the light. Isaiah announces that the people who walked in darkness have seen a great light. Paul reminds us that the grace of God has appeared, bringing salvation to all. In the familiar account of Christ's birth, the evening sky is bright with the heavenly host singing, "Glory to God in the highest." Amid our broken world we proclaim that the Prince of peace is born among us. God comes to us in human flesh—in Christ's body and blood—so that we may be bearers of divine light to all the world.

I
Particularly appropriate for Christmas Eve

Prayer of the Day

Almighty God, you made this holy night shine with the brightness of the true Light. Grant that here on earth we may walk in the light of Jesus' presence and in the last day wake to the brightness of his glory; through your Son, Jesus Christ our Lord, who lives and reigns with you and the Holy Spirit, one God, now and forever.

Gospel Acclamation

Alleluia. I am bringing you good news of great joy for ¹ all the people:* to you is born this day in the city of David a Savior, who is the Messi- ¹ ah, the Lord. *Alleluia.* (Luke 2:10-11)

Readings and Psalm

Isaiah 9:2-7

This poem promises deliverance from Assyrian oppression, a hope based on the birth of a royal child with a name full of promise. While Judah's king will practice justice and righteousness, the real basis for faith lies in God's passion for the people: The zeal of the Lord of hosts will do this!

Psalm 96

Let the heavens rejoice and the earth be glad. (Ps. 96:11)

Titus 2:11-14

The appearance of God's grace in Jesus Christ brings salvation for all humanity. Consequently, in the present we live wisely and justly while also anticipating the hope of our Savior's final appearance.

Luke 2:1-14 [15-20]

God's greatest gift comes as a baby in a manger. Angels announce the "good news of great joy" and proclaim God's blessing of peace.

Preface   Christmas

Color   White

Prayers of Intercession

The prayers are prepared locally for each occasion. The following examples may be adapted or used as appropriate.

Rejoicing with all the faithful, let us pray for the church, the world, and all who are in need.

A brief silence.

Let us pray for the church throughout the world; for those who proclaim the gospel; for teachers of the faith; for poets, artists, and musicians; and for all the baptized. Lord, in your mercy,

hear our prayer.

For the earth, your beloved creation and our fragile home; for rivers and woods, mountains and valleys; for marshes and oceans, towns and cities; for shepherds, ranchers, and all who care for animals. Lord, in your mercy,

hear our prayer.

For those who govern and for all in authority; for those who work to bring lasting peace to the land of Jesus' birth; and for all who protect the lives of children. Lord, in your mercy,

hear our prayer.

For innkeepers and travelers; for those whose needs for food or shelter depend upon the generosity of others; for those struggling with addiction; for those who suffer neglect, and for all who are sick (*especially*). Lord, in your mercy,

hear our prayer.

For this assembly; for those celebrating their first Christmas; for those whose joy is diminished by loneliness or loss; for those absent from us; and for those who are far from home. Lord, in your mercy,

hear our prayer.

Here other intercessions may be offered.

With thanksgiving, we remember all who have died (*especially*) and those whose lives have inspired us to deeper faith, more passionate service, and stronger love. Lord, in your mercy,
hear our prayer.
Pondering the mystery of your love, we offer our prayers in the name of Christ, the Word made flesh.
Amen.

Images in the Readings

Luke's gospel presents images of **the poor**: those oppressed by Roman government, women giving birth in a place that houses both people and barn animals, newborns wrapped only in strips of cloth, the socially despised and religiously unclean shepherds. In our society where Christmas suggests unrestricted spending and continual feasting, Luke's image of the poor is striking.

Both the gospel and the first reading suggest the image of the **mother** bearing new life. Often in the Bible, childbirth is credited to God's power. All Christians are now Mary, bearing Christ for the world.

The Hebrew word ***Bethlehem*** means "house of bread." From this historic city famous for its connection to King David comes the one who will feed the people forever. In the liturgy, we enter that house of bread and eat.

Ideas for the Day

◆ Christians sometimes hear that shepherds were outcasts in first-century society. But Jewish tradition presents a very different image of the shepherd, who is a figure of honor associated with many of the great heroes of the Torah: Abraham, Isaac, Jacob, Rachel, Joseph and his brothers, Moses, and King David were all responsible for the well-being of sheep and goats. In the article "Shepherd Consciousness," Jewish educator Fivel Yedidya Glasser highlights the shepherd's opportunity for *hitbodedut*, self-reflective prayer: "The silence of the shepherd is not just the absence of speech. It is a sublime language of silence, flowing from an outpouring of the soul" (www.canfeinesharim.org, January 29, 2014). Perhaps this kind of contemplative prayer is what the Bethlehem shepherds were practicing before the angels appeared on their hillside long ago.

◆ Welsh poet and clergyman R. S. Thomas (1913–2000) is noted for his unsentimental, often fierce theological imagery. His Christmas poems present a stark winter landscape and reflect the longings and doubts of many contemporary churchgoers. In a culture besotted with candy canes and gingerbread, Thomas offers a different vision of the incarnation. "Blind Noel" begins: "Christmas; the themes are exhausted. Yet there is always room on the heart for another snowflake to reveal a pattern" (*No Truce with the Furies* [London: Bloodaxe Books, 1996]). The preacher might hear in this poem a meditation on the difficulty of preaching such familiar texts year after year. Is there still room in her heart—in the hearts of her congregation—for another snowflake to reveal its pattern?

◆ On Christmas Eve, faced with a packed worship space and many visitors, the preacher is not likely to focus on the Letter to Titus, one of the shorter and less familiar epistles. Nevertheless, the writer asks a question that resonates with regular and occasional churchgoers alike: Beyond the familiar stories and candlelit scenes of Christmas, what does the miracle of incarnation say about how we should live today? The writer of the letter seems influenced by Stoic philosophers who were concerned with self-control and the renunciation of worldly passions. For some, Christianity has been reduced to a set of behavioral guidelines, and Titus may seem to reinforce this belief. But the letter imagines God's grace "training us" in a way of life that has less to do with moralism and more to do with maintaining focus while waiting for the fulfilment of a promise. Might Titus present an invitation to a kind of spiritual gymnasium whereby we learn the exercises and tools we need to maintain our focus while we wait for the fulfillment of God's promises? What if our new year's resolution was to begin a membership in the kind of training program that Titus outlines?

Connections with the Liturgy

The standard canticle of praise quotes today's gospel: "Glory to God in the highest, and peace to God's people on earth." Every Sunday that we sing this canticle, we join with the angels at the birth of Jesus.

Let the Children Come

If your church displays a nativity scene or crèche in the worship space, it would be appropriate to offer a prayer of blessing after the sermon or after communion. Children may be invited to gather at the manger as the community sings. Consider one of these hymns: "Infant holy, infant lowly" (ELW 276), "Your little ones, dear Lord" (ELW 286), "Once in royal David's city" (ELW 269), or "Away in a manger" (ELW 277/278). A blessing of the nativity scene is provided in the seasonal rites section for Christmas (p. 52).

Assembly Song
Gathering

Hark! The herald angels sing ELW 270, LBW 60, LS 25
Let all together praise our God ELW 287, LBW 47
It came upon a midnight clear ELW 282, LBW 54

Psalmody and Acclamations

Alonso, Tony. "Today Is Born Our Savior" from TLP:S.
Cable Shute, Linda. "Psalm 96," Refrain 4, from PSCY.

Hobby, Robert A. "Psalm 96" from PWC.

(GA) Chepponis, James J. "Christmastime Alleluia." Cant, assembly, kybd, opt SATB, gtr, B flat or C inst, hb. GIA G-4453.

Hymn of the Day

Peace came to earth   ELW 285, WOV 641   *SCHNEIDER*

On Christmas night   ELW 274   *SUSSEX CAROL*

Love has come   ELW 292   *UN FLAMBEAU*

Offering

Infant holy, infant lowly   ELW 276, LBW 44

Away in a manger   ELW 277/278, LBW 67, WOV 644, LS 17/18

Communion

I am so glad each Christmas Eve   ELW 271, LBW 69, LS 22

Midnight stars make bright the skies   ELW 280

O little town of Bethlehem   ELW 279, LBW 41

Sending

Angels, from the realms of glory   ELW 275, LBW 50

Silent night, holy night!   ELW 281, LBW 65, LS 26, LLC 301

Additional Assembly Songs

Jesus, the light of the world, TFF 59

The virgin Mary had a baby boy   TFF 53, LS 29

Pastores: a Belén   LLC 305

⊕ Puerto Rican traditional. "Glory in the Highest/Gloria en las alturas" from *Worship and Song*. SAB. Abingdon Press 9781426709951.

⊕ Venezuelan traditional. "Child So Lovely/Niño lindo" from *My Heart Sings Out*. SA. Church Publishing 9780898694741.

✧ Bruxvoort Colligan, Richard. "Sing a New Song for God (Psalm 96)" from *Shout for Joy*. AFP 9780806698632. psalmimmersion .bandcamp.com.

✧ Mohr, Joseph/Matt Maher. "Silent Night (Emmanuel)" from WT.

✧ Stevens, Sufjan. "Put the Lights on the Tree" from *Songs for Christmas*. music.sufjan.com.

✧ The Welcome Wagon. "Nature's Goodnight" from *Precious Remedies Against Satan's Devices*. asthmatickitty.com.

✧ Ylvisaker, John. "A Child This Day Is Born" from *Borning Cry Second Edition*. Available on Amazon.com.

Music for the Day
Choral

Head, Michael. "The Little Road to Bethlehem." SATB, div. B&H (HAL) M-060032448.

● Hopson, Hal. "On Christmas Night." 2 pt mxd, kybd, opt hb. MSM 50-1204.

Martin, Gilbert. "Dost Thou in a Manger Lie?" SATB, opt trbl solo. SMP AM-118.

p Wentzel, Brian. "Silken Sounds." SAB, kybd. AFP 9781451462470.

Children's Choir

Bock, Almon. "Angels' Advent Carol." U, pno. GIA G-4899.

p Herman, David. "Maria Walks amid the Thorn" from *Augsburg Choirbook for Advent, Christmas, and Epiphany*. SA, org, fl, glock. AFP 9780800678586.

Holman, Derek. "Carol of the Shepherds." U/2 pt/3 pt, pno/org. HIN HMC1902.

p Hopson, Hal H. "O Come, Little Children." U/2 pt, pno, opt hb. CG CGA1366.

Keyboard / Instrumental

● Milford, Robin. "Sussex Carol" from *Augsburg Organ Library: Christmas*. Org. AFP 9780800659356.

p ● Miller, Aaron David. "Un flambeau" from *Eight Chorale Preludes for Manuals Only*, vol. 2. Org. AFP 9780800678470.

● Raabe, Nancy M. "Sussex Carol" from *Grace and Peace*, vol. 1. Pno. AFP 9780800677602.

● Roberts, Al. "Un flambeau" from *Piano Plus: Hymns for Piano and Treble Instrument, Advent/Christmas*. Pno, 2 inst. AFP 9780800638542.

Handbell

Honoré, Jeffrey. "Canon of Peace." 3-5 oct hb, opt C inst, L3. CPH 97-6657.

● Osman, Terry. "Sussex Carol." 2-3 oct, L1+. LOR 20/1719L.

● Smith, James C. "Bring a Torch, Jeanette, Isabella." 3-5 oct, L3. RR BL5020.

December 25, 2015
Nativity of Our Lord
Christmas Day

On this Christmas morning the people of God gather to celebrate the birth of the Word made flesh, Christ our Lord. Luke recounts the familiar story of shepherds and angels; John's gospel tells of the Word that dwells among us, full of grace and truth. The meaning of Christmas is made clear: the light shines in the darkness. It is in the liturgy that we encounter the Word made flesh—in the people of God gathered together as the body of Christ, and in the meal around the holy table. We go forth to be bearers of light as we proclaim this good news to all the ends of the earth.

II
Particularly appropriate for Christmas Day

Prayer of the Day

All-powerful and unseen God, the coming of your light into our world has brightened weary hearts with peace. Call us out of darkness, and empower us to proclaim the birth of your Son, Jesus Christ, our Savior and Lord, who lives and reigns with you and the Holy Spirit, one God, now and forever.

Gospel Acclamation

Alleluia. A holy day has dawned upon us. Come, you nations, and a- | dore the Lord.* For today a great light has come up- | on the earth. *Alleluia.*

Readings and Psalm

Isaiah 62:6-12

The prophet invites the people to give God no rest until God reestablishes Jerusalem. In turn, they will receive names full of promise: Holy People, the Redeemed of the Lord, a City Not Forsaken.

Psalm 97

Light dawns for the righteous, and joy for the honest of heart. (Ps. 97:11)

Titus 3:4-7

God saves us not because of what we do. Rather, God is a God of mercy and salvation who graciously cleanses us in baptism and renews our lives through the Holy Spirit.

Luke 2:[1-7] 8-20

The world's deep night is shattered by the light of God's new day. The glory of God is revealed to poor shepherds, who share the good news with others.

III
Particularly appropriate for Christmas Day

Prayer of the Day

Almighty God, you gave us your only Son to take on our human nature and to illumine the world with your light. By your grace adopt us as your children and enlighten us with your Spirit, through Jesus Christ, our Redeemer and Lord, who lives and reigns with you and the Holy Spirit, one God, now and forever.

Gospel Acclamation

Alleluia. I am bringing you good news of great joy for | all the people:* to you is born this day in the city of David a Savior, who is the Messi- | ah, the Lord. *Alleluia.*
(Luke 2:10-11)
or
Alleluia. A holy day has dawned upon us. Come, you nations, and a- | dore the Lord.* For today a great light has come up- | on the earth. *Alleluia.*

Readings and Psalm
Isaiah 52:7-10

A messenger races home to Jerusalem with the marvelous words: "Your God reigns!" In comforting the people, God proves to be the best brother or sister (redeemer) they have ever known. Everyone will witness the victory (salvation) of God.

Psalm 98

All the ends of the earth have seen the victory of our God. (Ps. 98:3)

Hebrews 1:1-4 [5-12]

This letter opens with a lofty declaration of Jesus' preeminent status as the Son through whom God created the world and through whom our sins are cleansed. God speaks to us now through the Son, who is exalted even above the angels.

John 1:1-14

The prologue to the Gospel of John describes Jesus as the Word of God made flesh, the one who reveals God to be "full of grace and truth."

Preface Christmas

Color White

Prayers of Intercession

The prayers are prepared locally for each occasion. The following examples may be adapted or used as appropriate.
Rejoicing with all the faithful, let us pray for the church, the world, and all who are in need.
A brief silence.
Let us pray for new communities of faith and for long-established congregations; for pastors and mission developers, missionaries and teachers, bishops and associates in ministry, those in diaconal ministry; and for all the baptized. Lord, in your mercy,
hear our prayer.
For plants, animals, and people adapting to changing environments; for those affected by storms or droughts; for farmers, ranchers, seafood harvesters, and all whose labor brings food to our tables. Lord, in your mercy,
hear our prayer.
For the people of every nation; for leaders and decision makers; for those who protect the dignity and safety of others; and for peacemakers, especially those whose efforts are met with resistance and fear. Lord, in your mercy,
hear our prayer.
For those who face prejudice, abuse, or neglect; for those who experience depression; for those yearning for light within dark spaces in their lives; for those who grieve; and for all who are sick (*especially*). Lord, in your mercy,
hear our prayer.
For this assembly; for those who help us to recognize and respond to the needs of our community; for those who lead us in reaching out in love and service to our neighbors. Lord, in your mercy,
hear our prayer.
Here other intercessions may be offered.
With thanksgiving, we remember all who have died (*especially*) and those whose lives have borne witness to your love revealed to us in Christ. Lord, in your mercy,
hear our prayer.
Pondering the mystery of your love, we offer our prayers in the name of Christ, the Word made flesh.
Amen.

Images in the Readings
II

Luke writes that **angels**, messengers from heaven, a link between God and humankind, announce Christ and sing praise to God. It is a challenge to describe and, especially, to depict angels in a worthy manner. Contrary to popular notions, Christian doctrine does not teach that dead Christians become angels, but rather that angels are supernatural beings that signify and convey the power of God. In Luke, the angels proclaim the meaning of the incarnation.

Although in some places in the Bible cities are described as evil and filled with temptations, in Isaiah 62 the city **Jerusalem** symbolizes God's protection, God's very presence on earth. Throughout history, the church has used the image of Jerusalem as a picture of itself: we are like Jerusalem, a magnificent city, protected by the arms of God, thriving on word and sacrament. This imagery might not be clear to all worshipers, who might think that we are referring to the actual city of the twenty-first century. Sometimes in our worship "Jerusalem" is a metaphor for the church, and sometimes it is the name of a current city filled with international religious conflict.

On a day that we think about the **birth** of Jesus, we recall also the water of our rebirth in baptism.

III

During the fourth century, Christians chose the festival at the winter solstice as an appropriate time to celebrate the birth of Jesus. The prologue of John praises the Word of God as this **light** come to illumine the world. What has been born into the darkness on the earth is its light—an image especially appropriate for Christians in the northern hemisphere. The light of Christmas awaits the light of the resurrection.

Too often the church speaks about **creation** as if it were the task of only God the Father. However, the prologue of John and the introduction to Hebrews see the fullness of God as having created the world. Jesus Christ, the Son of God, "the exact imprint of God's very being," is lauded as creator of all things. For Christians, God is triune.

The gospel of John demonstrates its Greek context in its reliance on the imagery of Jesus as the **Son of God**. Christian theologians stressed that calling Jesus the Son of God does not mean what it commonly signified in Greco-Roman polytheism, where superhumans were born from a human mother who had been impregnated by a god like Jupiter. Rather, the image is supreme metaphor. John claims that Jesus, as the Father's only Son, makes all believers into children of God.

For John, Christ is the **Word**, and when he speaks, we hear God. When God speaks, we encounter Jesus. Worshipers receive this word at Sunday worship.

Ideas for the Day

◆ The Saint John's Bible is the first handwritten and illuminated Bible produced in the modern world. Over a period of thirteen years, master calligrapher Donald Jackson worked with teams of scholars, theologians, graphic artists, illustrators, calligraphers, and naturalists to create one of the most dramatic pieces of religious art in the twenty-first century. The illumination accompanying John 1 is particularly evocative, and Susan Sink's guide to the Saint John's Bible provides helpful commentary that may illuminate the text for congregations (*The Art of the Saint John's Bible* [Collegeville, MN: Liturgical Press, 2013], 260). In the illumination for John 1, titled "The Word Made Flesh," a golden Christ seems to step forth from the chaos of darkness as pure light: the texture behind Christ's head is inspired by images taken from the Hubble space telescope. The Saint John's Bible is itself an attempt to illuminate the word in language reflected in John's prologue, and may provide inspiration to preacher and assembly alike.

◆ One of the most striking musical illustrations of John's prologue can be found in the opening passages of Haydn's oratorio *The Creation*. Pizzicato strings create shimmering tension before a sudden C major chord bombs forth as the chorus intones the word *Licht*: "light." This moment in the oratorio was staged—and received—with great dramatic effect at the Vienna premiere in 1798: "No one, not even Baron van Swieten, had seen the page of the score wherein the birth of light is described," Haydn's friend Fredrick Silverstolpe reported. "And in that moment when light broke out for the first time, one would have said that rays darted from the composer's burning eyes. The enchantment of the electrified Viennese was so general that the orchestra could not proceed for some minutes" (Mary Hunter and Richard Wayne Will, eds., *Engaging Haydn: Culture, Context and Criticism* [Cambridge: Cambridge University Press, 2012], 170).

◆ If at this point in the Christmas season the preacher is faced with the daunting task of coming up with fresh things to say about the incarnation, one recourse may be to mine the tradition for classic sermons that can fall fresh on modern ears. One could do worse than the famous Christmas morning homily of St. John Chrysostom, the "golden-mouthed" preacher of the fourth century. "For this God assumed my body, that I may become capable of God's Word; taking my flesh, God gives me God's spirit; and so God bestowing and I receiving, I am prepared for the treasure of Life," Chrysostom preached in 386, when the liturgical commemoration of the incarnation was still a new idea. Hundreds of years later, his words resonate. The homily is readily available on the internet; www.patheos.com reprints it regularly around the Christmas season.

Connections with the Liturgy

II

For the dismissal today, we call out, "Go in peace. Share the good news. Thanks be to God." We are the shepherds.

III

In the Nicene Creed we confess that our one Lord, Jesus Christ, is "the only Son of God, eternally begotten of the Father, God from God, Light from Light, true God from true God."

Let the Children Come

"O Lord, how shall I receive you?" the old Christmas hymn asks. Today and throughout this season, offer gentle table instructions to children and other communicants. Show them how to make a manger with their open hands so as to receive the gift of Christ.

Assembly Song
Gathering

Once in royal David's city   ELW 269, WOV 643
O come, all ye faithful   ELW 283, LBW 45, LS 27, LLC 309
Angels we have heard on high   ELW 289, LBW 71, LS 16

Psalmody and Acclamations

Alonso, Tony. "A Light Will Shine on Us This Day" from TLP:S.
Beckett, Debbie. "This Day New Light Will Shine" from PS1.
Pavlechko, Thomas. "Psalm 97" from SMP.
(GA) Chepponis, James J. "Christmastime Alleluia." Cant, assembly, kybd, opt SATB, gtr, B flat or C inst, hb. GIA G-4453.

Hymn of the Day

O come, all ye faithful   ELW 283, LBW 45, LLC 309   *ADESTE FIDELES*
Good Christian friends, rejoice   ELW 288, LBW 55   *IN DULCI JUBILO*
From heaven above   ELW 268, LBW 51   *VOM HIMMEL HOCH*

Offering

Jesus, what a wonderful child   ELW 297, TFF 51
Your little ones, dear Lord   ELW 286, LBW 52

Communion

Lo, how a rose e'er blooming   ELW 272, LBW 58
In the bleak midwinter   ELW 294
The bells of Christmas   ELW 298, LBW 62

Sending

Go tell it on the mountain   ELW 290, LBW 70, TFF 52, LS 23
Of the Father's love begotten   ELW 295, LBW 42

Additional Assembly Songs

Mary had a baby   TFF 55

There's a star in the east   TFF 58, WOV 645

Cristianos: alegrémonos   LLC 289

Kalinga melody. "In the Heavens Shone a Star" from *Glory to God*. U. WJK 9780664238971.

Loh, I-to. "Child of Christmas Story" from *Sound the Bamboo*. U. GIA G-6830.

Bell, John. "He Came Down." ELW 253.

Badham, Raymond. "Emmanuel" from CCLI.

Bruxvoort Colligan, Richard. "Shout for Joy (Psalm 98)" from *Shout for Joy*. AFP 9780806698632. psalmimmersion.bandcamp.com.

Glover, Ben/Reuben Morgan. "We Have a Saviour" from CCLI.

Malicsi, Jonathan/Ellsworth Chandlee. "In the Heavens Shone a Star" from *Sound the Bamboo*. GIA G-6830.

Stevens, Sufjan. "I Saw Three Ships" from *Songs for Christmas*. music.sufjan.com.

Music for the Day
Choral

Forrest, Dan. "There Is Faint Music." SATB, pno. HAL 08749800.

p   Larson, Lloyd. "Christmastime." 2 pt, pno, opt U vcs, hb. HOP C-5828.

p   Miller, Aaron David. "The Hills Are Bare at Bethlehem" from *The New Gloria Deo: Music for Small Choirs*. 2 pt mxd, pno. AFP 9780806698403.

Shaw, Timothy. "We Praise You, Jesus, at Your Birth." SAB, pno. CPH 98-4170.

Children's Choir

Burkhardt, Michael. "Awake! Arise!" 2 pt, kybd/Orff, opt hb. MSM 50-1425A.

Florindez, Lorraine. "Sweetest Song of This Bright Season." SA, kybd. CPH 983504PODWEB.

Larson, Lloyd. "Angels Are Singing." 2 pt, kybd. FB BG2314.

Tucker, Sondra. "Gentle Mary Laid Her Child." U, fl/C inst, kybd. GIA G-6515.

Keyboard / Instrumental

Dupré, Marcel. "In dulci jubilo" from *Augsburg Organ Library: Christmas*. Org. AFP 9780800659356.

p   Raabe, Nancy M. "Vom Himmel hoch" from *Day of Arising*. Pno. AFP 9780800637460.

Walther, Johann. "Vom Himmel hoch." Org. Various editions.

Wasson, Laura. "Adeste fideles" from *A Christmas Season Tapestry*. Pno. AFP 9780800657253.

Handbell

p   Afdahl, Lee J. "Vom Himmel hoch (From Heaven Above)" from *Hymn Accompaniments for Handbells: Advent and Christmas*. 3-5 oct, L3+. AFP 9780806698076.

p   Keller, Michael R. "O Come, All Ye Faithful." 3-5 oct, L3. HOP 2645.

Turner, Julie. "Variations on 'In dulci jubilo.'" 3-6 oct hb, opt 3-5 oct hc, L3. RW 8234.

Saturday, December 26

Stephen, Deacon and Martyr

Stephen was a deacon and the first martyr of the church. He was one of those seven upon whom the apostles laid hands after they had been chosen to serve widows and others in need. Later, Stephen's preaching angered the temple authorities, and they ordered him to be put to death by stoning, with Saul (later Paul) as one of the observers. As he died, he witnessed to his faith and spoke of a vision of heaven.

December 27, 2015
First Sunday of Christmas

On the first Sunday of Christmas we find the boy Samuel and the boy Jesus, both in the temple, both growing in wisdom and stature and in favor with God and humankind. We too have returned to the house of God "to sing psalms, hymns, and spiritual songs to God," who has gifted us with a savior. As the festival continues, "let the peace of Christ rule in your hearts." It is Christmas, still.

Prayer of the Day

Shine into our hearts the light of your wisdom, O God, and open our minds to the knowledge of your word, that in all things we may think and act according to your good will and may live continually in the light of your Son, Jesus Christ, who lives and reigns with you and the Holy Spirit, one God, now and forever.

Gospel Acclamation

Alleluia. Let the peace of Christ rule ¹in your hearts,* and let the word of Christ dwell ¹in you richly. *Alleluia.* (Col. 3:15, 16)

Readings and Psalm

I Samuel 2:18-20, 26

Having dedicated her son Samuel to God's service, Hannah visits him every year when she and her husband, Elkanah, come to the Lord's house to offer sacrifices. God grants Hannah more children, and Samuel himself gains favor in the sight of all.

Psalm 148

The splendor of the Lord is over earth and heaven. (Ps. 148:13)

Colossians 3:12-17

Just as newly baptized Christians in the early church were clothed with white robes upon arising from the baptismal waters, so all who have received God's gift of life in Jesus Christ are covered with the character of Christ.

Luke 2:41-52

Jesus grew up in a family that went to the Passover festival each year. It was in this environment of faithful adherence to the law that Jesus grew into spiritual maturity and an understanding of his identity and mission.

Preface   Christmas

Color   White

Prayers of Intercession

The prayers are prepared locally for each occasion. The following examples may be adapted or used as appropriate.

Rejoicing with all the faithful, let us pray for the church, the world, and all who are in need.

A brief silence.

Let us pray for evangelists and pastors; for teachers and story-tellers; for seminarians and those discerning their call to ministry; and for all who proclaim the gospel in word and deed. Lord, in your mercy,

hear our prayer.

For the earth and all its creatures; for those seeking refuge from damaging storms; for those who work outdoors in weather that is hard to bear, in winter cold or summer heat; and for all whose labor provides us with food, clothing, shelter, and transportation. Lord, in your mercy,

hear our prayer.

For all nations and their leaders; for those who bring harmony within division; for those who challenge injustice and prejudice; and for those who are sent far from home to serve and protect others. Lord, in your mercy,

hear our prayer.

For parents of missing children; for youth who have no safe place to call home; for travelers; for those who are anxious; for those who grieve and all who are sick *(especially)*. Lord, in your mercy,

hear our prayer.

For this assembly; for musicians and poets; for elders and youth; for those who ask questions and those who mentor others to deeper faith and compassionate service. Lord, in your mercy,

hear our prayer.

Here other intercessions may be offered.

With thanksgiving, we remember all who have died, especially *(the apostle and evangelist John and)* those whose lives have helped us to see your love and compassion. Lord, in your mercy,

hear our prayer.

Pondering the mystery of your love, we offer our prayers in the name of Christ, the Word made flesh.

Amen.

Images in the Readings

In place of the shrine at Shiloh and the **temple** in Jerusalem, Christians meet to worship in any structure or in the open air. Christ is our temple, and we need only to gather around him to be in God's house.

For **three days** we search for Jesus, and we find him alive, asking and answering questions. Each Sunday is the third day, Easter.

After several centuries with many clergy wearing a black academic robe to signify their learning, many churches have returned to **clothing** their ministers, assistants, choir, confirmands, and new members in the white robe of baptism. White ponchos, with or without a cross, and donned after plenteous water has been poured, work well if the candidates—whether infants, youth, or adults—are baptized already clothed.

Ideas for the Day

◆ Hannah made a new robe every year for her longed-for son to wear as he worked in the temple. A granddaughter wore the last pajamas her grandmother made for her until they couldn't be stretched out any further. A woman got news of a friend's miscarriage and knitted a baptismal blanket, hoping and praying that there would be another baby. Men and women, old and young are making things. People have always made things, but there has been a resurgence of interest around a new Maker Movement. What are the stories in your congregation about the love and prayers that go along with making something for someone?

◆ Can you imagine the anxiety Jesus' parents felt when they realized their son wasn't with them? Parental anxiety is in the news a great deal, with some experts arguing that children are being overprotected—not developing enough grit and resilience to deal with life's problems—and others arguing that children, and childhood itself, isn't being protected enough, as children are forced to grow up too fast. Search for the National Public Radio story from March 20, 2014, "Kids These Days: Growing Up Too Fast or Never at All?" (www.npr.org). Parenting has changed in many ways since Jesus' time, but the emotions and anxieties are universal.

◆ Samuel and Jesus grew in stature, favor, wisdom, and years actively participating and being mentored in their faith. How are children mentored in your congregation? How are they active participants and leaders in worship and in congregational life?

Connections with the Liturgy

Recalling the passage from Colossians, *Evangelical Lutheran Worship*'s rite of baptism (p. 231) suggests that the newly baptized receive a white robe, which among the wealthy evolved into the elaborate baptismal gown. Although baptizing naked adults would not sit well in our culture, infants can be baptized naked or wearing only a diaper. The white robe of baptism is the alb that ministers regularly wear. The robe of our baptisms covers the one body of the faithful.

Let the Children Come

Hannah made Samuel a robe "each year" and took it to him when she and her husband made the yearly sacrifice. "Every year" Jesus' parents went to Jerusalem for the festival of the Passover. Children are formed spiritually through repeated ritual even before they have words to put to the experience. At baptism, parents promise to live with their children among God's faithful people, to bring them to the word of God and the holy supper, to nurture them in faith and prayer so that their children may learn to trust God (*ELW*, p. 228). The body of Christ helps them in this important work.

Assembly Song
Gathering

Savior of the nations, come   ELW 263, LBW 28
Let our gladness have no end   ELW 291, LBW 57
From heaven above   ELW 268, LBW 51

Psalmody and Acclamations

Arnatt, Ronald. "Psalm 148." SATB, assembly, org. ECS 5674.
Gelineau, Joseph. "Psalm 148" from ACYG.
Makeever, Ray. "Praise and Exalt God (Psalm 148)" from DH.
(GA) Chepponis, James J. "Christmastime Alleluia." Cant, assembly, kybd, opt SATB, gtr, B flat or C inst, hb. GIA G-4453.

Hymn of the Day

Let all together praise our God   ELW 287, LBW 47   *LOBT GOTT, IHR CHRISTEN*
In a lowly manger born   ELW 718, LBW 417   *MABUNE*
That boy-child of Mary   ELW 293, TFF 54   *BLANTYRE*

Offering

Beloved, God's chosen   ELW 648, OBS 48
The bells of Christmas   ELW 298, sts. 1, 4; LBW 62, sts. 1, 4

Communion

When long before time   ELW 861, WOV 799
All my heart again rejoices   ELW 273
Our Father, by whose name   ELW 640, LBW 357

Sending

Cold December flies away   ELW 299, LBW 53, LLC 292
Joy to the world   ELW 267, LBW 39

Additional Assembly Songs

Sing of Mary, pure and lowly WOV 634

Hush, little Jesus boy TFF 56

Yo conozco un pueblito chiquito LLC 296

◉ Caribbean folk melody. "Now Go in Joy" from *Glory to God*. U. WJK 9780664238971.

◉ Tibimenya, Leonidas. Rwanda. "Munezero/Sing Out Gladly" from *Love and Anger: Songs of Lively Faith and Social Justice*. SATB, cant. GIA G-4947.

✧ Bruxvoort Colligan, Richard. "Creation's Hallelujah (Psalm 148)" from *Shout for Joy*. AFP 9780806698632. psalmimmersion .bandcamp.com.

✧ Card, Michael. "Now That I've Held Him in My Arms" from CCLI.

✧ Dakota Road. "Glory to the Love" from *Dakota Road Music Anthology*. dakotaroadmusic.com.

✧ Hansen, Holly. "Song of Praise" from *Resonance Mass*. nemercy .org/resonance.

✧ Stevens, Sufjan. "Only at Christmas Time" from *Songs for Christmas*. music.sufjan.com.

✧ Stevens, Sufjan. "Jupiter Winter" from *Songs for Christmas*. music .sufjan.com.

Music for the Day

Choral

p ● Denis, Kimberley. "That Boy-Child of Mary." SATB, pno, opt assembly. AFP 9781451485981.

Hyslop, Scott. "Hallelujah! Praise God with Singing." U, opt hb, perc, assembly. MSM 50-7401.

p Kadidlo, Phil. "Jesus, What a Wonderful Child/Go Tell It on the Mountain" from *Wade in the Water: Easy Choral Music for All Ages*. SAB, kybd, opt gtr. AFP 9780800678616.

Lovelace, Austin. "A Christmas Roundelay." 2 pt mxd, kybd. ECS 7316.

Children's Choir

Burkhardt, Michael. "A Prayer to Jesus." U, org/pno. MSM 50-1985.

Cherwien, David. "Your Little Ones, Dear Lord." SA, org, fl. CPH 983356WEB.

● Highben, Zebulon M. "In a Lowly Manger Born." 2 pt trbl, 2 inst/ org. MSM 50-1915.

p Patterson, Mark. "Living God's Love." U/2 pt, pno, opt hb. CG CGA1367.

Keyboard / Instrumental

● Buxtehude, Dietrich. "Lobt Gott, ihr Christen." Org. Various editions.

p ● Nelson, Ronald A. "Blantyre" from *Easy Hymn Settings for Organ*, vol. 3. Org. AFP 9781451462562.

● Rowland-Raybold, Roberta. "Lobt Gott, ihr Christen" from *Introductions and Alternate Accompaniments for Piano*, vol. 1. Pno. AFP 9780800623593.

p ● Shaw, Timothy. "Blantyre" from *All Praise for Music*. Org. AFP 9781451401127.

Handbell

Morris, Hart. "West Indies Carol." 4-5 oct hb, L4, Ring Out! Press RO0116. Opt perc, Ring Out! Press RO1010.

Page, Anna Laura. "Christ Is Born!" from *Ringing the Church Year*. 3-5 oct hb, opt 2-3 oct hc, L2+. LOR 20/1671L.

Tucker, Sondra. "O Morning Star, How Fair and Bright" from *Ringing the Church Year*. 3-5 oct, L2+. LOR 20/1671L.

Monday, December 28

The Holy Innocents, Martyrs

The infant martyrs commemorated on this day were the children of Bethlehem, two years old and younger, who were killed by Herod, who worried that his reign was threatened by the birth of a new king. Augustine called these innocents "buds, killed by the frost of persecution the moment they showed themselves." Those linked to Jesus through their youth and innocence encounter the same hostility Jesus encounters later in his ministry.

Tuesday, December 29

John, Apostle and Evangelist (transferred)

John, the son of Zebedee, was a fisherman and one of the Twelve. John, his brother James, and Peter were the three who witnessed the light of the transfiguration. John and James once made known their desire to hold positions of power in the kingdom of God. Jesus' response showed them that service to others was the sign of God's reign in the world. Tradition has attributed authorship of the gospel and the three epistles bearing his name to the apostle John. John is a saint for Christmas through his proclamation that the Word became flesh and lived among us, that the light of God shines in the darkness, and that we are called to love one another as Christ has loved us.

Friday, January 1, 2016

Name of Jesus

The observance of the octave (eighth day) of Christmas has roots in the sixth century. Until the recent past, Lutheran calendars called this day "The Circumcision and Name of Jesus." The emphasis on circumcision is the older emphasis.

Every Jewish boy was circumcised and formally named on the eighth day of his life. Already in his youth, Jesus bears the mark of a covenant that he makes new through the shedding of his blood on the cross. That covenant, like Jesus' name, is a gift that marks the children of God. Baptized into Christ, the church begins a new year in Jesus' name.

Saturday, January 2

Johann Konrad Wilhelm Loehe, renewer of the church, died 1872

Loehe (approximate pronunciation: LAY-uh) was a pastor in nineteenth-century Germany. From the small town of Neuendettelsau, he sent pastors to North America, Australia, New Guinea, Brazil, and the Ukraine. His work for a clear confessional basis within the Bavarian church sometimes led to conflict with the ecclesiastical bureaucracy. Loehe's chief concern was that a congregation find its life in the holy communion, and from that source evangelism and social ministries would flow. Many Lutheran congregations in Michigan, Ohio, and Iowa were either founded or influenced by missionaries sent by Loehe.

January 3, 2016
Second Sunday of Christmas

Within the gospel reading's profound words lies the simple message that God is revealed in a human person. Though we may try to understand how the Word existed with God from the beginning of time, the wonder we celebrate at Christmas is that the Word continues to dwell among us. Christ comes among us in the gathered assembly, the scriptures, the waters of new birth, and the bread and the wine. Through these ordinary gifts we receive the fullness of God's grace and truth.

Prayer of the Day

Almighty God, you have filled all the earth with the light of your incarnate Word. By your grace empower us to reflect your light in all that we do, through Jesus Christ, our Savior and Lord, who lives and reigns with you and the Holy Spirit, one God, now and forever.
or
O God our redeemer, you created light that we might live, and you illumine our world with your beloved Son. By your Spirit comfort us in all darkness, and turn us toward the light of Jesus Christ our Savior, who lives and reigns with you and the Holy Spirit, one God, now and forever.

Gospel Acclamation

Alleluia. All the ends | of the earth* have seen the victory | of our God. *Alleluia.* (Ps. 98:3)

Readings and Psalm
Jeremiah 31:7-14

God promises to bring Israel back to its land from the most remote parts of exile. In Zion Israel will rejoice over God's

gift of food and livestock. Young women will express their joy in dancing; God will give gladness instead of sorrow.

or Sirach 24:1-12

The figure of Wisdom played a major role in early discussions of Christology. Wisdom is the divine word, coming from the mouth of God, and ruling over all of creation. Wisdom, created at the beginning of time, made her dwelling place in Jerusalem among God's people.

Psalm 147:12-20

Worship the LORD, O Jerusalem; praise your God, O Zion. (Ps. 147:12)

or Wisdom 10:15-21

We sing, O Lord, to your holy name. (Wis. 10:20)

Ephesians 1:3-14

In Jesus, all of God's plans and purposes have been made known as heaven and earth are united in Christ. Through Jesus, we have been chosen as God's children and have been promised eternal salvation.

John 1:[1-9] 10-18

John begins his gospel with this prologue: a hymn to the Word through whom all things were created. This Word became flesh and brought grace and truth to the world.

Preface   Christmas

Color   White

Prayers of Intercession

The prayers are prepared locally for each occasion. The following examples may be adapted or used as appropriate.

Rejoicing with all the faithful, let us pray for the church, the world, and all who are in need.

A brief silence.

Let us pray for the church throughout the world; for bishops, pastors, ministers of word and service, and all other leaders; for teachers and missionaries; for the newly baptized and those preparing for baptism. Lord, in your mercy,
hear our prayer.

For coastlands and mountains, rivers and deserts, prairies and valleys; for wilderness and cities, lakes and oceans; for farmlands and pastures, forests and rangelands; and for orchards, vineyards, and gardens. Lord, in your mercy,
hear our prayer.

For those who live in the north and the south, the east and the west; for all who work for peace; for those whose safety is threatened by warfare; and for immigrants and refugees. Lord, in your mercy,
hear our prayer.

For those who are hungry; for those who live with disabilities; for those who fear what the future holds for them; for those who grieve; and for all who are sick (*especially*). Lord, in your mercy,
hear our prayer.

For this assembly; for council members and all other leaders; for those who help us learn from our past and plan for the future; and for all whose faithful stewardship sustains this congregation's ministry. Lord, in your mercy,
hear our prayer.

Here other intercessions may be offered.

With thanksgiving, we remember all who have died (*especially*) and those who have pointed us toward the light of Christ and the truth of your love. Lord, in your mercy,
hear our prayer.

Pondering the mystery of your love, we offer our prayers in the name of Christ, the Word made flesh.
Amen.

Images in the Readings

Once again this Sunday, **light** is a primary image for the power of God to transform the earth and us in it. Even the smallest light shines through a field of darkness.

Again, becoming **children of God** recurs in the readings. Although many contemporary people think of God as being naturally father of humankind, this was not a cultural idea in the first century, and the Bible understands this extraordinary claim only as a consequence of the incarnation. God is not, as many people imagine, the alien and uncaring other. Rather, thanks to Christ, God loves us as children.

The church is a **watered garden**. A garden is more personal, more beautiful, than a field of crops. We think ahead to Good Friday and the Easter Vigil, when according to John's gospel Jesus is buried and raised to life in a garden.

Ideas for the Day

◆   Jeremiah imagines life after exile as "a watered garden"—an experience of being planted, rooted, tended, nourished, and cared for. With pictures or plants, create a garden in your sanctuary. Be sure to water it well! What else, or who else, in your congregation needs watering, tending, and caring for?

◆   Today's readings from Ephesians and John both speak of adoption. Invite a Lutheran Social Services representative, an adoptive parent, or an adopted child to talk about the experience of adoption and how they relate to the themes of and references to adoption throughout the New Testament.

◆   The song "Take Up Your Spade" by Sara Watkins (*Sun Midnight Sun* [Nonesuch, 2012]) connects the image of the watered garden from Jeremiah with the exhortation to be thankful from Ephesians: "Give thanks, for all that you've been given. / Give thanks, for who you can become. / Give thanks, for each moment and every crumb. / Take up your spade and break ground."

Connections with the Liturgy

Christians are watered at baptism. In the words of the presentation of candidates for baptism, "By water and the Holy Spirit we are reborn children of God."

Christians are enlightened at baptism. In the words of the baptismal welcome, "Whoever follows me will have the light of life."

Let the Children Come

Much of North American culture has finished its midwinter festival of consumerism and consumption, while the church is in the midst of its celebration of the incarnation. Encourage the people of your parish to keep their homes awash with the light of their Christmas trees, their walkways or doorways illumined, and their tables brightened with candles until Epiphany. This helps children see that they are keeping the same feast at home and at church.

Assembly Song
Gathering

O Word of God incarnate   ELW 514, LBW 231

O Splendor of God's glory bright   ELW 559, LBW 271

Once in royal David's city   ELW 269, WOV 643

Psalmody and Acclamations

Pavlechko, Thomas. "Psalm 147:12-20" from SMP.

Polyblank, Christopher. "Praise the Lord" from PS3.

Sedio, Mark. "Wisdom 10:15-21" from PWA.

(GA) Chepponis, James J. "Christmastime Alleluia." Cant, assembly, kybd, opt SATB, gtr, B flat or C inst, hb. GIA G-4453.

Hymn of the Day

Of the Father's love begotten   ELW 295, LBW 42 *DIVINUM MYSTERIUM*

Word of God, come down on earth   ELW 510, WOV 716 *LIEBSTER JESU, WIR SIND HIER*

Let our gladness have no end   ELW 291, LBW 57 *NARODIL SE KRISTUS PÁN*

Offering

What feast of love   ELW 487, WOV 701

Let the whole creation cry   ELW 876, LBW 242

Communion

Peace came to earth   ELW 285, WOV 641

Let all mortal flesh keep silence   ELW 490, LBW 198

We eat the bread of teaching   ELW 518

Sending

Love divine, all loves excelling   ELW 631, LBW 315

Thy strong word   ELW 511, LBW 233

Additional Assembly Songs

I wonder as I wander   TFF 50, WOV 642

Fruto del amor divino   LLC 318

Christ, burning wisdom   OBS 51

⊕ Iona Community. "Word of the Father" from *Come, All You People: Shorter Songs for Worship*. SATB. GIA G-4391.

⊕ Loh, I-to. "Hunger Carol" from *Sound the Bamboo*. U. GIA G-6830.

✧ Bruxvoort Colligan, Richard. "Praise and Thanks to You (Psalm 147)" from *Shout for Joy*. AFP 9780806698632. psalmimmersion.bandcamp.com.

✧ Dakota Road. "Light Shines in the Darkness" from *Dakota Road Music Anthology*. dakotaroadmusic.com.

✧ Sampson, Marty/Matt Crocker. "Light Will Shine" from CCLI.

✧ Sotto, Angel/arr. Elena G Maquiso. "Let Us Even Now Go" from *Sound the Bamboo*. GIA G-6830.

✧ Stevens, Sufjan. "Bring a Torch, Jeanette, Isabella" from *Songs for Christmas*. music.sufjan.com.

✧ Stevens, Sufjan. "All the Kings' Horns" from *Songs for Christmas*. music.sufjan.com.

Music for the Day
Choral

● Mann, Brian. "Of the Father's Love Begotten." SATB, org. FB BG-2590.

p Mozart, Wolfgang Amadeus/arr. Patrick Liebergen. "Cantate Domino." SATB, pno. CG 1290.

p Scott, K. Lee. "In the Bleak Midwinter" from *Sing Forth God's Praise*. U (vocal solo), kybd. AFP 9780800675387.

p Spurlock, William. "Christ Was Born on Christmas Day." SATB, pno. AFP 9781451423945.

Children's Choir

Coleman, Gerald Patrick. "Light of the World." U/2 pt, pno, fl, opt hb. CPH 983887WEB.

Hildebrand, Kevin. "Where Shepherds Lately Knelt." 2 pt/3 pt, org/pno, opt hb. CPH 984188PODWEB.

Hurlbutt, Patricia. "Let Every Heart Awake and Sing." 2 pt, kybd, opt hb. BP BP1112.

Keyboard / Instrumental

● Held, Wilbur. "Divinum mysterium" from *Augsburg Organ Library: Christmas*. Org. AFP 9780800659356.

● Hyslop, Scott M. "Divinum mysterium" from *Piano Plus: Hymns for Piano and Treble Instrument, Advent/Christmas*. Pno, inst. AFP 9780800638542.

p ● Powell, Robert J. "Liebster Jesu, wir sind hier" from *Our Cheerful Songs*. Org. AFP 9781451486070.

p ● Rowland-Raybold, Roberta. "Divinum mysterium" from *All Praise for Music*. Pno. AFP 9781451486087.

Handbell

p ● Geschke, Susan E. "O Come, O Come, Emmanuel" with "Of the Father's Love Begotten." 2-3 oct, L2. CG CGB857.

Glasgow, Michael J. "Gaudete!" 3-7 oct hb, opt 3 oct hc, opt tamb, opt tri. Level TBD. CG CGBTBD.

Waugh, Timothy. "Past Three O'Clock." 3-5 oct, L2. JEF JHS9109.

January 6, 2016
Epiphany of Our Lord

Epiphany means "manifestation." On this day we celebrate the revelation of Christ to the Gentiles—that is, to all nations. Some Christian traditions celebrate three great epiphanies on this day: the magi's adoration of the Christ child, Jesus' baptism in the Jordan River, and his first miracle, in which he changes water into wine. The word and sacraments are for us the great epiphany of God's grace and mercy. We go forth to witness to the light that shines brightly in our midst.

Prayer of the Day

O God, on this day you revealed your Son to the nations by the leading of a star. Lead us now by faith to know your presence in our lives, and bring us at last to the full vision of your glory, through your Son, Jesus Christ our Lord, who lives and reigns with you and the Holy Spirit, one God, now and forever.

or

Almighty and ever-living God, you revealed the incarnation of your Son by the brilliant shining of a star. Shine the light of your justice always in our hearts and over all lands, and accept our lives as the treasure we offer in your praise and for your service, through Jesus Christ, our Savior and Lord, who lives and reigns with you and the Holy Spirit, one God, now and forever.

or

Everlasting God, the radiance of all faithful people, you brought the nations to the brightness of your rising. Fill the world with your glory, and show yourself to all the world through him who is the true light and the bright morning star, your Son, Jesus Christ, our Savior and Lord, who lives and reigns with you and the Holy Spirit, one God, now and forever.

Gospel Acclamation

Alleluia. We have observed his star [|] at its rising,* and have come to [|] worship him. *Alleluia.* (Matt. 2:2)

Readings and Psalm
Isaiah 60:1-6

Jerusalem is assured that nations will make a pilgrimage to her, because the light of God's presence is in her midst. The bountiful food of the sea and the profits of international trade will come streaming to Jerusalem and thereby declare God's praise.

Psalm 72:1-7, 10-14

All kings shall bow down before him. (Ps. 72:11)

Ephesians 3:1-12

What had been hidden from previous generations is now made known through the gospel ministry of Paul and others. In Christ both Jews and Gentiles participate in the richness of God's promised salvation.

Matthew 2:1-12

God's promise shines bright in the night as magi follow a star to honor a new king. Strangers from a faraway land, they welcome the long-awaited messiah of Israel.

Preface   Epiphany of Our Lord

Color   White

Prayers of Intercession

The prayers are prepared locally for each occasion. The following examples may be adapted or used as appropriate.

Rejoicing with all the faithful, let us pray for the church, the world, and all who are in need.

A brief silence.

Let us pray for the church throughout the world; for those who proclaim the gospel; for those seeking faith and those looking for hope; for congregations in communities large and small, near and far. Lord, in your mercy,

hear our prayer.

For the land and the seas; for all plants and animals; for astronomers and other scientists; for explorers and map makers; for librarians and all who seek to increase and preserve knowledge. Lord, in your mercy,

hear our prayer.

For wise leaders and tireless peacemakers; for those whose lives are threatened by violence; and for those who leave their homelands in search of safety or to provide for their families. Lord, in your mercy,

hear our prayer.

For those who face prejudice, abuse, or neglect; for those who experience depression; for those yearning for light

within dark spaces in their lives; for those who grieve; and for all who are sick (*especially*). Lord, in your mercy,
hear our prayer.

For this assembly; for those who offer their gifts to your service; for those who lead us in worship; for all who reach out to welcome those who are seeking; and for those who guide us in faith. Lord, in your mercy,
hear our prayer.

Here other intercessions may be offered.

With thanksgiving, we remember all who have died (*especially*) and those whose lives have inspired us to follow you with joy and hope. Lord, in your mercy,
hear our prayer.

Pondering the mystery of your love, we offer our prayers in the name of Christ, the Word made flesh.
Amen.

Images in the Readings

The main image is **light**. The star symbolizes a new light in the cosmos. The dawn pierces the thick darkness that has obscured our vision. During January, the northern hemisphere is experiencing a gradual lightening of the darkest time of the year, an appropriate time for the church to praise Christ as the light. This light shines again in the night of the Easter Vigil.

Made popular in hymns, pageants, and crèche sets are the gifts of the magi: **gold**, **frankincense**, and **myrrh**. Gold denotes Jesus as a king. Frankincense and myrrh are sweet-smelling resins that were used in offerings to gods and at status burials. These are symbolic gifts for the divine king who had come to die. The birth narratives contain in them the death of Christ.

The ancient political idea was that monarchs were supposed to ensure safety for their subjects. Christ, not Herod, is the true **king** who gives life, rather than death, to the people.

Ideas for the Day

◆   Have a star processional, involving all the children and anyone else who wants to participate. Simple wooden dowels or even straws with a decorated star can be carried in procession following the cross during the gathering song or paraded around during the hymn of the day. These real-time journeyers following the star to Bethlehem could then end their procession at the crèche.

◆   Consider reading poetry as part of a gathering rite, during the offering, or before the final blessing, as a way to highlight the unusual visit of these travelers and their prophetic gifts. Walter Brueggemann's "Epiphany" in *Prayers for a Privileged People* ([Nashville: Abingdon, 2008], 163) would be a wonderful option.

◆   The Epiphany story may be full of nostalgia for many. So consider the day from the magi's point of view: as strangers in a strange land. Reflecting from this angle, Mark Searle writes, "In this strange land, amid these unfamiliar faces, there is a way to see the Epiphany: the way of the magi, of these strangers who came in from the night. It is to see ourselves and to recognize our condition in these otherwise alien people. It is to know ourselves compacted with them in a common destiny . . . heirs of the promise through the Child marked for death" ("A Sermon for Epiphany," *A Christmas Sourcebook* [Chicago: Liturgy Training Publications, 1984], 126).

◆   Incense is used in some churches for festive occasions, and while you should take health concerns seriously, today would be a great day to burn some frankincense and invite the assembly to smell the perfume that the magi carried. Have a magi processional (combined with a star processional?) as the gifts are brought forward, accompanied by the singing of "Bright and glorious is the sky" (ELW 301, sts. 3, 5-6), "As with gladness men of old" (ELW 302), or "Brightest and best of the stars" (ELW 303, sts. 3-5). One of the magi could cense the congregation with incense in a thurible or set it in a bowl full of sand.

Connections with the Liturgy

Even when today's churches encourage parish contributions via automatic withdrawals from individuals' bank accounts, the liturgy hopes to make clear that at every service, whenever believers celebrate God's gift of grace, they make donations for those in need. Our offerings to help those in need and to pay for the ministries of the church are like the magi's gold, frankincense, and myrrh: they are gifts of financial value that come in symbolic praise to God and in recollection of the death of Christ.

Let the Children Come

Epiphany is a traditional time for the family ritual of "chalking the door." This is a short service of prayer to ask God's blessing on the home and all who dwell there. It includes writing in chalk above the doorway. To encourage worshipers to do this ritual in their homes, give out bags with a copy of the service (see p. 53 in the seasonal rites section) and a piece of chalk. Consider using a ritual of blessing for your own church building too. Carry symbols of the faith as you go—a cross, a light, and water for sprinkling. Invite children into holy play as they sprinkle people and spaces with remembrances of baptismal living.

Assembly Song
Gathering

Bright and glorious is the sky   ELW 301, LBW 75

The only Son from heaven   ELW 309, LBW 86

O Morning Star, how fair and bright!   ELW 308, LBW 76

Psalmody and Acclamations

Haugen, Marty. "Every Nation on Earth." Cant, assembly, opt SAB, kybd, gtr, perc. GIA G-5241.

Hobby, Robert A. "Psalm 72:1-7, 10-14" from PWC.

Mummert, Mark. "Psalm 72:1-7, 10-14," Refrain 1, from PSCY.

(GA) Chepponis, James J. "Christmastime Alleluia." Cant, assembly, kybd, opt SATB, gtr, B flat or C inst, hb. GIA G-4453.

Hymn of the Day

The first Noel   ELW 300, LBW 56   *THE FIRST NOWELL*

Come, beloved of the Maker   ELW 306   *JILL*

Brightest and best of the stars   ELW 303, LBW 84   *MORNING STAR*

Offering

What child is this   ELW 296, LBW 40

Hail to the Lord's anointed   ELW 311, sts. 1, 4; LBW 87, sts. 1, 4

Communion

Light shone in darkness   ELW 307

'Twas in the moon of wintertime   ELW 284, LBW 72, LS 15

In Christ there is no east or west   ELW 650, LBW 359, TFF 214

Sending

As with gladness men of old   ELW 302, LBW 82

We are marching in the light of God   ELW 866, TFF 63, W&P 148, WOV 650

Additional Assembly Songs

We three kings of Orient are   WOV 646, LS 30, LLC 321

Sister Mary had-a but one child   TFF 60

Van hacia el pesebre   LLC 314

⊕ Aguiar, Ernani. "Acalanto para o Menino Jesus/Carol for the Baby Jesus" from *World Carols for Choirs*. SATB. OXF 019353231X.

⊕ Puerto Rican traditional. "Los magos que llegaron a Belén/The Magi Who to Bethlehem Did Go" from *My Heart Sings Out*. SA. Church Publishing 9780898694741.

✪ Bruxvoort Colligan, Richard. "How Great Is Your Name (Psalm 8)" from *Shout for Joy*. AFP 9780806698632. psalmimmersion.bandcamp.com.

✪ Dakota Road. "Made for Love" from *Dakota Road Music Anthology*. dakotaroadmusic.com.

✪ Deconto, Jesse James. "A Beautiful World" from *A Beautiful World*. pinkertonraid.bandcamp.com.

✪ Kurtz, Rachel. "Save Us All" from *For Crying Out Loud*. rachelkurtz.org.

✪ Morris, Michael. "We Need Jesus' Light Every Day" from *Storm Home: A Collection of Music from Humble Walk Artists-in-Residence*. humblewalk.bandcamp.com.

✪ Stevens, Sufjan. "The Friendly Beasts" from *Songs for Christmas*. music.sufjan.com.

Music for the Day
Choral

● Forrest, Dan. "The First Noel." SATB, pno. BP 1857.

p Larter, Evelyn. "A Babe Is Born." SATB, pno, fl. AFP 9781451462296.

p Pooler, Marie. "O How Beautiful the Sky" from *Unison and Two-Part Anthems*. U or 2 pt, kybd. AFP 9780800648916.

● Schwandt, Daniel. "O Lord of Light, Who Made the Stars." 2 pt mxd, org. MSM 50-9932.

Children's Choir

Blersch, Jeffrey. "Bright and Glorious Is the Sky" from *Children Rejoice and Sing*. U/2 pt, kybd, hc. CPH 977074WEB.

James, Donald. "The Three Kings" from *Three Carols for Children*. U/2 pt, pno. PAR PPMO9717.

Music, David. "Follow the Star to Bethlehem." U/2 pt, pno. GIA G-8176.

Oliver, Curt. "Sun Had No More Light to Offer." U, kybd. SEL 405-364.

Keyboard / Instrumental

p ● Ashdown, Franklin. "Jill" from *Bright and Guiding Star*. Org. AFP 9781451462593.

● Nelhybel, Vaclav. "The First Nowell" from *Festival Hymns and Processionals*. Org, br qnt, timp. Conductor Score. HOP 750.

● Wasson, Laura E. "The First Nowell" from *A Christmas Season Tapestry*. Pno. AFP 9780800657253.

● Wold, Wayne L. "Morning Star" from *Augsburg Organ Library: Epiphany*. Org. AFP 9780800659349.

Handbell

● McFadden, Jane. "Brightest and Best of the Stars of the Morning." 3-5 oct hb, opt 3 oct hc, L3. BP HB322.

Prins, Matthew. "Adoration of the Wise Men." 3-5 oct, L2. GIA G-7624.

p ● Sherman, Arnold. "The First Noel." 3-6 oct, L2+. HOP 2644.

TIME AFTER EPIPHANY

ADVENT

CHRISTMAS

TIME AFTER EPIPHANY

PREPARING FOR THE TIME AFTER EPIPHANY

Lectionary

The title of this collection of worship materials is exactly right: *Sundays and Seasons*. The ordering of those words is precisely right: the primary Christian observance is the Sunday assembly. Every eight days, Christians gather to proclaim that the God who created the world also raised Jesus from the dead and pours out the Spirit on all peoples. On this eighth day, the triune God is celebrated, made present, heard, and tasted. Seasons throughout the year sometimes group Sundays in an order or toward a common purpose. But there are other times throughout the year, such as this Time after Epiphany, which are not seasons at all, but successions of Sundays. Some speak of this time as *ordinary*, but no Sunday is really ordinary at all.

The Time after Epiphany this year is a succession of five Sundays, shortened by the early Lent determined by the timing of Passover. Each year, this grouping of Sundays is surrounded by two festivals: Baptism of Our Lord and Transfiguration of Our Lord. The same sort of pattern is repeated in the Time after Pentecost later in the year, where that succession of Sundays is also surrounded by two festivals: Holy Trinity and Christ the King. It is perhaps notable that the festivals surrounding the Time after Epiphany are centered around events in the life of Jesus, while the festivals surrounding the Time after Pentecost reflect theological convictions about the nature and reign of God as triune.

Because we are in the year of Luke (and John), the gospel readings appointed for the Time after Epiphany this year are all from Luke, except on the second Sunday after Epiphany. On this Sunday, the classic narrative of the wedding at Cana is appointed. This sweep of assigned gospel readings from Epiphany of Our Lord through the second Sunday after Epiphany (Matt. 2:1-12; Luke 3:15-17, 21-22; and John 2:1-11) shows how Christopher Wordsworth (1807–1885) understood the sweep of the lectionary in his day, exhibited in his hymn "Song of thankfulness and praise" (ELW 310). These are the classic stories of God in flesh made manifest: by a star, in Jordan's stream, at Cana's feast.

It is customary in the Time after Epiphany and the Time after Pentecost for the lectionary to appoint a semicontinuous reading through one of the New Testament letters as the second reading. Such is the case on the non-festival Sundays of this time, where continuous portions of 1 Corinthians are read. (We would read more of 1 Corinthians this year had Lent not begun so early.) Unlike the seasonal times of the year, when the appointed second reading is chosen to harmonize with the other readings, this time after Epiphany applies a different principle. Such a discovery might help preachers and other worship planners make sense of the appointed readings, and not force an expectation that the readings are complementary every week. In the case of the first readings appointed on these Sundays, however, complementary resonance with the appointed gospel reading is intended. See, for instance, the resonances between the first readings and the gospel readings in this time:

Baptism of Our Lord
Isaiah 43:1-7 *Passing through the waters*
Luke 3:15-17, 21-22 *The baptism of Jesus*

Second Sunday after Epiphany
Isaiah 62:1-5 *God like a bridegroom and the bride*
John 2:1-11 *The wedding at Cana*

Third Sunday after Epiphany
Nehemiah 8:1-3, 5-6, 8-10 *Ezra reads the law*
Luke 4:14-21 *Jesus reads the prophet Isaiah*

Fourth Sunday after Epiphany
Jeremiah 1:4-10 *A prophet to the nations*
Luke 4:21-30 *The prophet Jesus not accepted*

Transfiguration of Our Lord
Exodus 34:29-35 *Moses' face shines*
Luke 9:28-36 [37-43a] *Jesus transfigured on the mountain*

Some worship planners expect that the preachers will be the ones to make these resonances plain. There has been an increase in encouragement that preaching in the Sunday liturgy consider all of the appointed readings and not just one reading, perhaps only the assigned gospel reading. Sometimes it is unwieldy for a preacher to accept the full responsibility for showing forth these harmonizations, so it then falls to all other worship leaders and planners to be persistent in proclaiming as much of the scriptures as possible each week. The language of prayers of intercession, hymns and other music, other ritual texts, art and image—all of these can contribute to the full proclamation of the lectionary's readings.

During this time each year occurs the Week of Prayer for Christian Unity, set off by the festivals of the Confession of Peter (January 18) and the Conversion of Paul (January 25). Prayer for Christian unity is appropriate weekly, if not daily, but the annual observance is a particularly fine time to enlarge our prayers for unity. Perhaps it is possible for diverse congregations of Christians to come together during this time for a joint prayer service (see "Environment," below, and page 81 for suggestions). In such an ecumenical service, prayers could also be made that the whole human family throughout the world find a common unity, even beyond the unity of Christians.

Music

Choosing assembly song for the Sundays of the year is of immense importance. The songs and hymns we sing, because of the wedding of text and tune, get into our bodies and remain with us for a long time, perhaps forever. We cannot overestimate how important assembly song is to Christian formation, faith, and life. In the Time after Epiphany, it may be well to take stock of those hymns that each assembly knows well, which songs ought to be learned over the coming year, and which hymns may have served their purpose and could be retired from the repertoire.

The particularly Lutheran inheritance of the placement and purpose of the hymn of the day ought to be treasured among us. That the rite for our Sunday worship calls for the assembly to take up the task of proclaiming the gospel in song, placed as an especially important event paired with the preached sermon, is a true gift. Too often we let this opportunity pass by without careful thought and planning. Such thought should involve not only the selection of the hymn of the day, but also how it will be sung and supported. Not only should the hymn have resonance with the themes in the appointed readings and the sermon based on those readings, but the hymn should involve the fullest possible musical resources of the assembly. Stanzas of the song or hymn can be sung by alternating voices to allow singers to both sing and listen to the words. Instrumental accompaniment, when carefully planned, can draw attention to the text of the hymn. Other music for the liturgy can be based on the tune of the hymn of the day so as to draw the ears of the assembly to this primary tune. Every Sunday, the hymn of the day is the primary musical expression of the assembly, so the text should be able to bear the weight of that proclamation, the tune should be durable enough to linger in the ears and imagination, and the singing of the hymn should be planned, robust, and thoughtful, such that the hymn anchors the liturgy musically to the gospel we proclaim.

Evangelical Lutheran Worship includes ten musical settings that are possible ways to musically make our way through Sunday worship. These ten settings are not an exhaustive canon but invite us to see that there *at least* ten different ways and styles of singing the liturgy. A scan of the service music section of the hymnal allows worship planners to dream up even more such settings. However, in the Time after Epiphany, especially on the Sundays for which the appointed color is green, it may be wisest to plan a leaner rite with less music. In too many places, week after week (for example), a full gathering rite is offered, complete with a gathering song, Kyrie, and canticle of praise. On these green Sundays, one musical element may suffice. It would certainly be preferable to simplify the gathering rite rather than to eliminate a biblical reading or sung psalmody. The Time after Epiphany is a most appropriate time to set priorities and attend to only the central things. Then, when worshipers come to seasons and festivals, they will sense the fullness and find meaning in the more robust character of the day or time when all of the musical and ritual elements return.

Environment

Beginning with the Baptism of Our Lord, the readings for the Time after Epiphany prompt heightened awareness of *journey* as a metaphor for the life of faith. If your worship space accommodates flexible seating arrangements, consider creating a winding aisle that will invite mindfulness of the journey undertaken by the holy family, as well as the journey of the magi who followed the star in search of the Christ child and then received divine guidance to return home by another route. Other journey-related ideas:

- Use the Isaiah 43 text as inspiration for a gathering rite that could be used on all of the Sundays after Epiphany.
- Sing "Bless now, O God, the journey" (ELW 326).
- Incorporate a prayer from the service of Evening Prayer ("O God, you have called your servants to ventures of which we cannot see the ending . . . ," *ELW*, p. 317) into the Sending on the Sundays after Epiphany.
- Construct a simple walking labyrinth (search "walking labyrinth design" online). Encourage parishioners to use the labyrinth to reflect on experiences that have been important to their journeys of faith and life.

The *baptismal journey* could also be a source of inspiration for these Sundays after Epiphany:

- Does your congregation maintain a list of members' baptismal anniversaries? If not, the Sundays after Epiphany might be a good time to gather that information. Make a plan and initiate a process for sending out baptismal anniversary cards to arrive on or near the date of each person's baptismal anniversary (see 03_AfterEpiphany.BaptismCard.pdf* for a print-ready example).
- Plan an affirmation of baptism by the assembly (*ELW*, p. 237) for the Baptism of Our Lord.
- Bring the stone water jars referenced in the story of the wedding at Cana (Epiphany 2) to visual prominence through an arrangement of large pottery vessels in the worship space. If pottery vessels aren't feasible, consider creating smaller paper vessels using the technique showcased in 03_AfterEpiphany.Pots.pdf*.

To observe the Week of Prayer for Christian Unity (January 18–25), consider these ideas:

- Schedule evening prayer worship in a space where seating can be arranged in a circle. On the floor inside the circle, spread out a large map of the world. Place lighted candles throughout the space. As worship begins, invite the assembly to identify some of the nations, places, and peoples in need of healing, hope, and peace, perhaps by placing a lighted tea candle on the map. Then encourage mindfulness of those concerns during the prayers.
- Sponsor an ecumenical hymn festival for churches in your area. Sing hymns commonly known across Christian denominations. Invite each church's choir to provide one musical offering, or to prepare something together as a combined choir. Recognize each church and its pastoral leader(s). Invite contributions toward refreshments for a time of shared fellowship following the festival.

If you made a mobile tintinnabularium for Christmas (see p. 48), bring it back on Transfiguration of Our Lord, once again incorporating it in the procession, right behind the cross. Gather the children to explain that this visual celebration of Christ's birth will disappear, along with the alleluias, during Lent. You might even consider engaging the children's help in "burying" the alleluias in two large pots of soil, along with some amaryllis bulbs. Why two pots? See the Environment suggestions for Lent on pages 102–103.

Seasonal Checklist

- If the Baptism of Our Lord (January 10) will be observed as a baptismal festival, publicize the festival for the congregation and arrange for baptismal preparation with parents, sponsors, and candidates. See *Washed and Welcome: A Baptism Sourcebook* (Augsburg Fortress, 2010) for suggestions on ways to organize and structure baptismal preparation sessions.
- Order a sufficient annual quantity of *Welcome, Child of God* (a board book for infants and toddlers) and *Living the Promises of Baptism: 101 Ideas for Parents* (both Augsburg Fortress), and present them as baptismal gifts from the congregation to children and parents. A gift subscription to *The Little Lutheran* could also be given (thelittlelutheran.org).
- If a form of baptismal remembrance is used, evergreen branches for sprinkling may be desired.
- On the festivals of the Baptism of Our Lord and Transfiguration, consider using thanksgiving for baptism instead of confession and forgiveness during the gathering rite.
- Use the Kyrie on the festivals of the Baptism of Our Lord and Transfiguration; omit it on the green Sundays after Epiphany.
- Use the canticle of praise ("Glory to God").
- Use the Nicene Creed for festivals; use the Apostles' Creed for the green Sundays.
- Increasingly, Martin Luther King Jr. Day (observed January 18) is observed as a day of service in many locales. Plan to participate as a church in local observances or organize your own.
- If you are hosting a catechumenal process and have a group of inquirers, use Welcome to Baptism (*ELW*, pp. 232–233) prior to the beginning of Lent.
- If the alleluia will be symbolically buried or bid farewell on the festival of the Transfiguration, make appropriate arrangements (for example, prepare for the burial of an alleluia banner).

WORSHIP TEXTS FOR THE TIME AFTER EPIPHANY

Confession and Forgiveness

All may make the sign of the cross, the sign marked at baptism,
as the presiding minister begins.
Blessed be the holy Trinity, ✝ one God,
who creates us and forms us,
who redeems us and calls us,
who unites us and sends us.
Amen.

Gathered in God's presence, let us confess our sin.

Silence is kept for reflection.

Mighty and loving God,
we confess that we are captive to sin
and cannot free ourselves.
We seek our own way.
We divide the body of Christ.
In your mercy, cleanse us and heal us.
Let the words of our mouths,
the thoughts of our hearts,
and everything that we do
be filled with faith, hope, and love. Amen.

Hear the voice of Jesus:
"The Spirit of the Lord is upon me
to proclaim release to the captives."
In the name of ✝ Jesus Christ,
I proclaim to you
that your sins are forgiven and you are released.
The joy of the Lord is your strength,
and the gifts of the Holy Spirit are yours forever.
Amen.

Offering Prayer

Merciful God, as grains of wheat scattered upon the hills
were gathered together to become one bread,
so let your church be gathered together
from the ends of the earth into your kingdom,
for yours is the glory through Jesus Christ, now and forever.
Amen.

Invitation to Communion

Come to the table.
Feast on God's abundant life for you.

Prayer after Communion

We thank you, O God,
that you have fed us at your banqueting table
with bread and wine beyond compare,
the very life of Christ for us.
Send your Spirit with us now,
that we may set the captive free,
use your gifts to build one another up,
and in everything reflect your glory
revealed in Jesus Christ, our Savior and Lord.
Amen.

Sending of Communion

Compassionate God, as Jesus called disciples to follow him,
bless those who go forth to share your word and sacrament
with those who are *sick/homebound/imprisoned*.
May these gifts be signs of our love and prayers,
that through the sharing of the body and blood of Christ,
all may know your grace and healing
revealed in Jesus Christ our Lord.
Amen.

Blessing

God Almighty send you light and truth
to keep you all the days of your life.
The hand of God protect you;
the holy angels accompany you;
and the blessing of almighty God,
the Father, the ✝ Son, and the Holy Spirit,
be with you now and forever.
Amen.

Dismissal

Go in peace. Remember the poor.
Thanks be to God.

SEASONAL RITES FOR THE TIME AFTER EPIPHANY

Godparenting Sunday

One of the ways to recognize and support the lifelong relationship between godparent and godchild is to celebrate a "Godparenting Sunday" regularly, where the godparent-godchild relationship can be lifted up in various ways. When this was done for the first time at one Lutheran church, an older man told the pastor afterward that he had taken his responsibilities as a godparent very seriously in all the decades since his godchild had been baptized, but that no one in church had ever once spoken to him about his being a godparent since the baptism! That's a strong argument for having such Sunday celebrations.

Ideas

- Schedule your Godparenting Sunday once a year, or once every three years (picking one Sunday in the three-year lectionary). Choose a day with baptismal readings. The Sunday of the Baptism of Our Lord (first after Epiphany) is one possibility, though it may be too soon after the Christmas holidays to gather people and energy. Lent's baptismal focus makes that a natural time. In year C, Lent 3 is one possibility: Isaiah 55, "come to the waters," and Paul connecting baptism with the Red Sea and the water-giving rock.
- Announce the celebration in advance, giving people time to invite godparents and godchildren who might be able to visit.
- Have sticky name tags with "I am the godparent of . . ." for godparents to wear, on which they can write their godchildren's names.
- In the prayers of intercession, include a petition for godparents and one for "our godchildren." Pause so that godparents may name their godchildren aloud. Or when they fill out their name tags before the service, have them also write their godchildren's names on slips of paper that will be put in a beautiful bowl, and have the prayer leader hold up that bowl during the petition for the godchildren.

- Have godchild-godparent pairs (or threesomes) perform roles in worship together: splitting up a single scripture reading between the two of them, or bringing up the gifts, distributing communion, ushering, or performing musically together.
- Identify everyone named in the worship folder as "*Name*, godchild of *name/s*, and (if applicable) godparent of *name/s*."
- Make available the handouts "10 Ways to Godparent an Adult Godchild" and "Ways to Celebrate Your Godchild's Baptismal Anniversary" from *Washed and Welcome: A Baptism Sourcebook* (Augsburg Fortress, 2010).
- "Remember and rejoice" (ELW 454) and "O blessed spring" (ELW 447) are especially appropriate hymns for a day celebrating the lifelong nature of the baptismal promise.
- You don't need to make godparenting the main focus of the sermon, but you might include an anecdote about a godchild-godparent relationship. (This will get you asking your members if they have such stories, which is itself a good thing!)
- Gather photos of members' godchildren, or of members with their godchildren or godparents. Make color photocopies of them and create a collage to display near the font (if they are digital photos, the collage can be created on the computer). The collage could be saved and added to each year.
- Have postcards (almost any watery scene will do) that people can take to mail to godparents or godchildren who are not present, and suggest they can just write, "Today was Godparenting Sunday at our church, so I thought of you!"
- If it is Lent, provide or have people make Easter cards to send to godchildren, perhaps with a water, dove, or candle design. Add Romans 6:4 for adult godchildren, or simpler words linking Easter's new life with baptism for young godchildren.
- Get your worship-planning committee or education folks to brainstorm variations on these ideas or other things to do each year.

Week of Prayer for Christian Unity

The Week of Prayer for Christian Unity is January 18–25. Liturgical resources and materials for use in congregations are available from the Pontifical Council for Promoting Christian Unity and the Commission on Faith and Order of the World Council of Churches. Worship resources, biblical reflections, and prayers for each day of the week are available at www.oikoumene.org/en/resources/week-of-prayer/week-of-prayer.

Resources for observing this week of prayer may also be obtained from the Graymoor Ecumenical and Interreligious Institute, 475 Riverside Dr., Room 1960, New York, NY 10115; email: lmnygeii.org@aol.com; phone: 212/870-2330; or at www.geii.org. Resources on the website include a brief history of the Week of Prayer for Christian Unity, an ecumenical celebration of the word of God, music suggestions, bulletin announcements, and more.

Farewell to Alleluia

Congregations that keep the ancient practice of fasting from singing or speaking "alleluia" through the forty days of Lent may consider the practice of "burying" the alleluia at the end of the liturgy on the last Sunday before Ash Wednesday. This might mean simply singing an appropriate song at the end of the service. Or it might include the actual lowering of a visual alleluia (a banner created by children, perhaps) while singing. The alleluia may literally be buried in a box in the church yard or hidden away somewhere in the church (where only the children know where it is!). The alleluia should return with great joy at the first alleluias of the Easter season, perhaps at the Vigil of Easter liturgy.

Hymns and songs

Alleluia, song of gladness   ELW 318, WOV 654

Halle, halle, hallelujah   ELW 172

Gospel Acclamation / Celtic Alleluia   ELW 174

Schwandt, Daniel. "Farewell to Alleluia." *Music Sourcebook for All Saints through Transfiguration* S571.

January 10, 2016
Baptism of Our Lord
Lectionary 1

The Baptism of Our Lord cannot help but recall our own and all baptismal blessings. We recall and celebrate our adoption as daughters and sons, the gift of the Holy Spirit, and the promised company of almighty God when we "pass through the waters . . . the rivers . . . fire." On this day the heavens open again, for this assembly, and we receive the gift of the beloved Son of God in bread and wine.

Prayer of the Day

Almighty God, you anointed Jesus at his baptism with the Holy Spirit and revealed him as your beloved Son. Keep all who are born of water and the Spirit faithful in your service, that we may rejoice to be called children of God, through Jesus Christ, our Savior and Lord, who lives and reigns with you and the Holy Spirit, one God, now and forever.

Gospel Acclamation

Alleluia. A voice from heaven said, "This is my Son, ˡ the Beloved,* with whom I ˡ am well pleased." *Alleluia.* (Matt. 3:17)

Readings and Psalm

Isaiah 43:1-7

Near the end of Israel's exile in Babylon, God promises to bring them home. They need no longer be afraid, because the one who formed, created, and called them by name now redeems them from all their enemies. God declares them precious and honored, and God loves them.

Psalm 29

The voice of the LORD is upon the waters. (Ps. 29:3)

Acts 8:14-17

Peter and John are sent to support the new Christians in Samaria, a group that was recently baptized after hearing the good news of Christ through the preaching of Philip. Here the Samaritans receive the gift of the Holy Spirit in the laying on of hands.

Luke 3:15-17, 21-22

The reading opens with questions about the identity of the Messiah. John the Baptist insists that he is not the Messiah; instead he points ahead to one who is coming. And whether the voice of God was heard by all or only by Jesus, God settles the matter: Jesus is God's beloved Son.

Preface   Baptism of Our Lord

Color   White

Prayers of Intercession

The prayers are prepared locally for each occasion. The following examples may be adapted or used as appropriate.

Giving thanks for the gift of baptism and the gifts of grace in the world, we pray for the church, the world, and all those in need.

A brief silence.

For your church on earth, that your Spirit guides your children. Unite us in our common call to live out your justice and stand with our siblings of every faith community. Lord, in your mercy,

hear our prayer.

For this world, which you redeemed, that the powerful in all nations foster its health and care for all its creatures. Lord, in your mercy,

hear our prayer.

Give your people of every land the tools and strength to care for one another. Give passion to strive for justice to your people. Bless all countries with the courage to follow what is wise and good. Lord, in your mercy,

hear our prayer.

Lift up the poor and oppressed, ease the troubled minds and hearts of those in turmoil, and surround those who are ill with the comforts of good medicine and good friends, signs of your healing. We pray especially for . . . . Lord, in your mercy,

hear our prayer.

Guide those preparing for baptism, their sponsors, and this assembly so that we all live into the promises made in baptism. Lead us all to scripture, the holy supper, and toward justice and peace. Lord, in your mercy,

hear our prayer.

Here other intercessions may be offered.

We give you thanks for the lives of the faithful departed and for the assurance of the same resurrection by our baptism into Christ's death. Lord, in your mercy,

hear our prayer.

Into your hands, gracious God, we commend all of your beloved for whom we pray, trusting in your mercy; through Christ our Lord.

Amen.

Images in the Readings

Life on planet Earth must have **water**. Christians see in the waters of baptism the matrix of our new life in Christ. The font is like the Jordan River that leads us to the new land of promise, like the primeval waters over which the Spirit of God hovered in creation. We stand in the river, but we are also with the baptizer in the wilderness.

In several Bible stories, the **dove** symbolizes the presence of God's Holy Spirit. The white color matches the baptismal garment. Secular culture associates the dove especially with peace, which is the word from God that concludes the tumultuous Psalm 29.

Yet we do not forget the message of John the Baptist that God comes with **fire**, which both destroys and purifies. A forest must periodically burn so that dormant seeds can be released to sprout and grow. So what in us must be burned?

Once again **light** is an image for the power of God. God's voice brings light into the earth's darkness. Early Christians referred to baptism by water as enlightenment.

Ideas for the Day

◆ In the movie *Shawshank Redemption* (Warner Bros., 1994), Tim Robbins's character Andy Dufresne crawls through a sewer line to escape prison. When he makes it past the gates, he stands in the pouring rain, the stench of the sewer washing off him, with his hands outstretched to the sky as he gives thanks for his new freedom. This is a striking image for baptism, especially for adult baptism. How might we see baptism as a freeing act of God's grace through such an image?

◆ Baptism connects the church, not just with Jesus' baptism, but also with all the ancient water stories of scripture: the Spirit brooding over the waters at creation, the flood and salvation, water from the rock flowing to the Israelites in Exodus, the streams of the Psalms, and many more. In the prayers of intercession today, give thanks for any local water sources near your congregation, connecting the day to your geographic location. You may even be able to bring water from one or more of those sources into worship to use as an illustration of how baptism connects us with this primal source of life and the God who gives true life.

◆ Have you ever celebrated a "Godparenting Sunday"? Today is a natural day to do so. Invite everyone to extend an invitation to their godparents and godchildren to join them at church as you celebrate the gift of baptism. You could provide postcards with a water image on one side and "Thinking of you, godchild!" on the other that worshipers could send to godchildren who can't be present. You can find more ideas for Godparenting Sunday and for supporting godparents in their roles in the seasonal rites section

(p. 80) and in *Washed and Welcome: A Baptism Sourcebook* (Minneapolis: Augsburg Fortress, 2010).

◆ Gregory of Nazianzus wrote about Jesus' baptism, "Jesus comes out of the water, drawing the world with him, as it were, and raising it up when it had hitherto been sunk in the abyss" (*A Christmas Sourcebook* [Chicago: Liturgy Training Publications, 1984], 146). This idea of Jesus' baptism drowning the whole world in God's love is a beautiful illustration that may help people wrestle with why Jesus, who was without sin, would be baptized. Maybe it was not for him, but for us.

Connections with the Liturgy

The Thanksgiving at the Font at baptism (*ELW*, p. 230) describes the baptism of Jesus in the Jordan as one of the precursors of our own baptisms. "Pour out your Holy Spirit," we pray, just as God did at Jesus' baptism.

Let the Children Come

Baptisms are always special. Some churches with aging populations do not get to experience them often, and so it can be both wonderful and educational for young and old alike to spend some time during worship learning about the various parts of the baptismal service and the meaning behind the symbols and ritual. Even if you don't have a baptism scheduled today, you could invite children up to the font so they can get a close-up view of this liturgical space. Share the significance of the water, the candles, the anointing oil, the white garment, and any other objects your congregation uses at a baptism.

Assembly Song
Gathering

We know that Christ is raised   ELW 449, LBW 189

Crashing waters at creation   ELW 455

This is the Spirit's entry now   ELW 448, LBW 195

Psalmody and Acclamations

Gelineau, Joseph, or Michel Guimont. "Baptism of the Lord / ABC" from PS:W4.

Hopson, Hal H. "Psalm 29" from TP.

Smith, Geoffrey Boulton. "Give Strength to Your People, Lord" from PS1.

p   (GA) Friesen-Carper, Paul. "A Voice from Heaven Said." MSB2 S557.

Hymn of the Day

When Jesus came to Jordan   ELW 305, WOV 647   *KING'S LYNN*

I bind unto myself today   ELW 450, LBW 188   *ST. PATRICK'S BREASTPLATE*

You Are Mine   ELW 581, W&P 158   *YOU ARE MINE*

Offering

Remember and rejoice   ELW 454, sts. 1, 4
Baptized in water   ELW 456, WOV 693, LS 87

Communion

Waterlife   ELW 457, W&P 145
O blessed spring   ELW 447, WOV 695, OBS 71
Wade in the water   ELW 459, TFF 114

Sending

Christ, when for us you were baptized   ELW 304
Baptized and Set Free   ELW 453, W&P 14

Additional Assembly Songs

I've just come from the fountain   TFF 111, LS 89, WOV 696
Free at last   TFF 116
Manantial de vida nueva   LLC 379

⊕ Florián, Lorenzo. "Hijos de Dios/Angels on High" from *Psalms for All Seasons: A Compete Psalter for Worship*. SATB. Brazos Press 9781592554447.

⊕ Tanzanian traditional/arr. Mark Sedio. "Nimemwona Bwana/We Have Seen the Lord" from *Global Choral Sounds*. SATB. CPH 98-3610. Also ELW 869.

✿ Bruxvoort Colligan, Richard. "In My Heart Is the Road (Psalm 84)" from *Our Roots Are in You*. worldmaking.net.

✿ Dakota Road. "Child of the Water" from *Dakota Road Music Anthology*. dakotaroadmusic.com.

✿ DeConto, Jesse James. "Voice of Silver" from *A Beautiful World*. pinkertonraid.bandcamp.com.

✿ Hansen, Holly. "River of Fervor" from *Storm Home: A Collection of Music from Humble Walk Artists-in-Residence*. humblewalk .bandcamp.com.

✿ Kurtz, Rachel. "Healing River" from *For Crying Out Loud*. rachelkurtz.org.

✿ Rimbo, Justin. "Born, Reborn" from *Storm Home: A Collection of Music from Humble Walk Artists-in-Residence*. humblewalk .bandcamp.com.

Music for the Day
Choral

• Borwick, Susan. "As Jesus Walked into the Stream." 2 pt, kybd, opt trbl inst, vc. MSM 50-9201.

• Herman, David. "When Jesus Went to Jordan's Stream." SAB, kybd, ob. GIA G-3421.

p Keesecker, Thomas. "Oh, Love, How Deep." SATB, org. AFP 9781451420760.

p • Pasch, William Allen. "Baptized in Jordan." SATB. AFP 9780800664169.

Children's Choir

Coleman, Gerald Patrick. "You Are My Own." U, C inst, pno. CPH 982881PODWEB.

p Highben, Zebulon M. "I'm Going on a Journey." U, pno, bass gtr, sax, opt assembly. AFP 9781451435993.

Weber, Paul D. "When You Pass through the Waters." U/2 pt trbl/2 pt mxd, pno. MSM 50-0501.

Keyboard / Instrumental

• Cherwien, David M. "King's Lynn" from *Augsburg Organ Library: Baptism and Communion*. Org. AFP 9780800623555.

p Dahl, David P. "Nordic Aria" from *A Scandinavian Suite*. Org, inst. AFP 9780800678435.

• Peek, Richard. "Prelude on St. Patrick's Breastplate." Org. MSM 10-845.

• Schaffner, John Hebden. "St. Patrick's Breastplate" from *Augsburg Organ Library: Epiphany*. Org. AFP 9780800659349.

Handbell

Delancy, Lauran. "God's Own Child." 3-5 oct, L2. CPH 97-7271.

Glasgow, Michael J. "Quietude (Solemn Stillness)." 3-7 oct hb, opt 3-6 oct hc, L3-. GIA G-8494.

• Larson, Lloyd. "You Are Mine." 3-5 oct, L2+. HOP 2696.

Friday, January 15

Martin Luther King Jr., renewer of society, martyr, died 1968

Martin Luther King Jr. is remembered as an American prophet of justice among races and nations, a Christian whose faith undergirded his advocacy of vigorous yet nonviolent action for racial equality. A pastor of churches in Montgomery, Alabama, and Atlanta, Georgia, his witness was taken to the streets in such other places as Birmingham, Alabama, where he was arrested and jailed while protesting against segregation. He preached nonviolence and demanded that love be returned for hate. Awarded the Nobel Peace Prize in 1964, he was killed by an assassin on April 4, 1968. Though most commemorations are held on the date of the person's death, many churches hold commemorations near Dr. King's birth date of January 15, in conjunction with the American civil holiday honoring him. An alternate date for the commemoration would be his death date, April 4.

January 17, 2016
Second Sunday after Epiphany
Lectionary 2

The Sundays after Epiphany continue to celebrate the revelation of the glory of God to us as it was made known to the magi and to those on Jordan's banks at the baptism of Jesus—today using wedding imagery. Our God rejoices over God's people "as the bridegroom rejoices over the bride." By the power of the Spirit there are gifts galore for everyone. In Christ Jesus the best wine is saved for last. Taste and see.

Prayer of the Day

Lord God, source of every blessing, you showed forth your glory and led many to faith by the works of your Son, who brought gladness and salvation to his people. Transform us by the Spirit of his love, that we may find our life together in him, Jesus Christ, our Savior and Lord.

Gospel Acclamation

Alleluia. Jesus re- ¹ vealed his glory,* and his disciples be- ¹ lieved in him. *Alleluia.* (John 2:11)

Readings and Psalm

Isaiah 62:1-5

The people's return to Judah after the exile was marred by economic and political troubles. Nevertheless, the prophet declares, Jerusalem and Judah will be restored. God will rejoice over Jerusalem as a bridegroom rejoices over his bride; and the people are called to the celebration.

Psalm 36:5-10

We feast upon the abundance of your house, O Lᴏʀᴅ. (Ps. 36:8)

1 Corinthians 12:1-11

The congregation at Corinth experienced division as people were comparing one another's spiritual gifts, thinking some to be superior to others. Paul invites this fractured community to trust that God's Holy Spirit has gifted them all perfectly for their mission together.

John 2:1-11

Turning water to wine at the wedding at Cana is described as the first of Jesus' signs. Through many such epiphanies, Jesus reveals that he bears God's creative power and joyful presence into the world.

Preface   Sundays

Color   Green

Prayers of Intercession

The prayers are prepared locally for each occasion. The following examples may be adapted or used as appropriate.

Giving thanks for God's great gifts, we pray for the church, the world, and all those in need.

A brief silence.

You enliven your church. Inspire the body of Christ to rejoice in and make good use of the various gifts and vocations with which you have entrusted it. Lord, in your mercy,

hear our prayer.

You are the fountain that brings forth life. Guide us to be good stewards of all plant and animal life entrusted to our care. Lord, in your mercy,

hear our prayer.

In your light we see light. Shine on the path for all nations to seek peace, justice, and the well-being of all your children. Lord, in your mercy,

hear our prayer.

You are a refuge to those in peril. Grant help, healing, and wholeness to all who are in need of your care. We pray especially for . . . . Lord, in your mercy,

hear our prayer.

Bless the leaders of this assembly. Help them to use their gifts in this community to the glory of your holy name. Lord, in your mercy,

hear our prayer.

Here other intercessions may be offered.

We give thanks for the faithful departed who have gone to join the marriage feast that has no end (*especially Antony of Egypt and Pachomius, renewers of the church*). May their lives inspire us to trust always in your promise of eternal life. Lord, in your mercy,

hear our prayer.

Into your hands, gracious God, we commend all of your beloved for whom we pray, trusting in your mercy; through Christ our Lord.

Amen.

Images in the Readings

About the **175 gallons of wine**: Christian use of the Cana story usually has avoided any symbolic references to Dionysus or much honesty about the immense volume of wine created. Instead, the detail that this miracle occurs at a wedding has been interpreted as God's blessing of marriage as an example of the joy of those who live in Christ. Medieval celibate Christians welcomed any biblical passages that could serve the imagery of Christ's marriage to the church. Christians can use this delightful story as standing behind the weekly communion of the millions of believers who together drink the good wine of Jesus Christ. Would it be a good idea on this Sunday to encourage communicants to drink two full swallows of wine, rather than the usual meager sip? In antiquity, and still today in some places of the world, wine is safer to drink than water and is thus the standard drink at table. Churches that make grape juice an option at communion can still use the symbol of wine—its effect on the body of the person and on the body of the community—to suggest divine power and joy.

We are **married** to God: that is, we are chosen in love and bonded until death in mutual service and joy. For Christians, human marriage becomes a welcome metaphor for our relationship with God, and, conversely, the ideal relationship with God informs what we hope Christian marriage to be.

Ideas for the Day

◆   When the best wine is saved for last, it isn't the married couple alone who is touched. All the guests are made glad and changed. When have you witnessed Cana moments in weddings where new beginnings took place for the guests as well as the couple? A pastor tells of the reconciliation of two wedding guests separated by months of cold silence. Other Cana moments have occurred when families or friends were reunited or when guests, unfamiliar with the Christian tradition, were struck by the words, gestures, and symbols of the wedding liturgy. Can you remember such a Cana moment? New beginnings at weddings are some of the new beginnings Jesus provides in all of life's journeys.

◆   Jesus changes water into wine. What changes when we gather for holy communion? Is it the bread and wine or substantially more? As Jesus gladdened the wedding at Cana and the guests were transformed, so the guests who gather around Jesus' table are touched in mysterious ways. We are changed. Read the various thanksgivings at the table in *Evangelical Lutheran Worship*. Note how the prayer of invocation for the Holy Spirit petitions God to bless not just bread and wine, but the community sharing bread and wine. An example: "Holy God, we long for your Spirit. Come among us. Bless this meal. May your Word take flesh in us. Awaken your people. Fill us with your light. Bring the gift of peace on earth" (Thanksgiving at the Table III, p. 110).

◆   The wedding at Cana reveals who God is and what God gives in great abundance when we gather around word and table: healing, forgiveness, compassion, joy, newness, community, and energy for mission. The gifts of God overflow from the wine that only Jesus can provide. We are blessed to be a blessing.

◆   "When we leave church, or rise from prayer, would people mistake us for wedding guests? For party-goers? Why not? Did we 'do whatever he tells' us? Did we see his glory and believe?" (N. T. Wright, *Twelve Months of Sundays* [Harrisburg, PA: Morehouse, 2012]).

Connections with the Liturgy

In *Evangelical Lutheran Worship*'s Thanksgiving at Table X (p. 69), we pray, "O God, you are Wine: warm our hearts and make us one." In the various services that celebrate baptism, we invoke the Spirit of God to enter one another with gifts that serve the community.

The rite of Christian marriage is the occasion when the Christian community asks God to bless the couple. John 2 is a suggested gospel reading (*Occasional Services for the Assembly*, p. 370), as if we have invited Christ to be a guest at also this wedding banquet.

Let the Children Come

Jesus calls out to all the hungry, "Come and dine." Who is welcome at your communion table and why? If you have a certain age stipulation, how long has that been in place? Could it be time to revisit that conversation and think together about how your congregation's communion policies do or do not reflect Jesus' radical hospitality?

Assembly Song
Gathering

Hail to the Lord's anointed   ELW 311, LBW 87

Now the feast and celebration   ELW 167, WOV 789

Praise ye the Lord   ELW 872

Psalmody and Acclamations

Hopson, Hal. "Psalm 36" from TPP.

Refrain from PAS 36A with ELW tone 2 in G.

Watts, Isaac. "High in the Heavens, Eternal God" (*TRURO*) from PAS 36B.

p   (GA) Friesen-Carper, Paul. "A Voice from Heaven Said." MSB2 S557.

Hymn of the Day

Jesus, come! For we invite you   ELW 312, WOV 648   *UNION SEMINARY*

Songs of thankfulness and praise   ELW 310, LBW 90   *SALZBURG*

Soul, adorn yourself with gladness   ELW 488, LBW 224   *SCHMÜCKE DICH*

Offering

Now the silence   ELW 460, LBW 205

God extends an invitation   ELW 486, LLC 397

Communion

In the singing   ELW 466

What feast of love   ELW 487, WOV 701

Around you, O Lord Jesus   ELW 468, LBW 496

Sending

Oh, sing to the Lord   ELW 822, LLC 598, TFF 274, LS 178, WOV 795

Arise, my soul, arise!   ELW 827, LBW 516

Additional Assembly Songs

Living thanksgiving   DH 99

Now we offer you, our Father   TFF 129, WOV 761

Agua, Dios nuestra   LLC 380

⊕ Ascencio, Rodolfo. "Yo soy la luz del mondo/I Am the World's True Light" from *My Heart Sings Out*. U. Church Publishing 9780898694741.

⊕ Vas, Charles. "Give Us Light/Jyothi dho" from *Sound the Bamboo*. U. GIA G-6830.

✿ Beech, Jay. "Alleluia We Are Listening." store.baytonemusic.com.

✿ Bell, John. "Will You Come and Follow Me." ELW 798.

✿ Hansen, Holly. "Song of Praise" from *Resonance Mass*. nemercy.org.

✿ Gungor, Lisa/Michael Gungor. "In Every Breath" from WT.

✿ Noel, Dexter. "Lord, Make Us One" from *Let the People Sing*, vol. 1. AFP 9780800675394.

✿ Tangled Blue. "Kyrie" from *Storm Home: A Collection of Music from Humble Walk Artists-in-Residence*. humblewalk.bandcamp.com.

Music for the Day
Choral

Morris, Sally Ann. "Come, Join in Cana's Feast." SATB, kybd. GIA G-4608.

Patterson, Joy. "Each One Has a Gift." U, kybd, fl, opt assembly. MSM 80-844.

p ● Perkins, Scott. "Soul, Adorn Yourself with Gladness." SATB, org. AFP 9781451424041.

p Schalk, Carl. "Thine the Amen, Thine the Praise." SATB, pno, opt assembly. AFP 9780800646127.

Children's Choir

● Bach, J. S./arr. Michael Burkhardt. "Soul, Adorn Yourself with Gladness." U/2 pt, two trbl inst, kybd, opt brass inst. MSM 50-8370.

p Holland, Kevin B. "Uyai Mose, Come All You People." U/SATB, perc. CG CGA1373.

Kirkland, Terry. "The Fruits of the Spirit." U/2 pt, kybd. LOR 10/2700K.

Wagner, Douglas E. "God Is So Good." U/2 pt, kybd, opt hb/hc. LOR 10/3988L.

Keyboard / Instrumental

● Biery, James. "Union Seminary" from *Augsburg Organ Library: Autumn*. Org. AFP 9780800675790.

● Manz, Paul. "Union Seminary" from *Three Hymn Settings for Organ*, vol. 2. Org. MSM 10-525.

● Organ, Anne Krentz. "Salzburg" from *Come to Us, Creative Spirit*. Pno. AFP 9780800659042.

p ● Wonacott, Glen. "Schmücke dich" from *Introductions and Alternate Accompaniments for Piano*, vol. 4. Pno. AFP 9780800623623.

Handbell

p ● Afdahl, Lee J. "Salzburg (Songs of Thankfulness and Praise)" from *Hymn Accompaniments for Handbells: Advent and Christmas*. 3-5 oct, L3+. AFP 9780806698076.

Behnke, John. "Jesus Has Come." 3-5 oct hb, opt drm, L2+. CPH 97-7423.

● Buckwalter, Karen. "Songs for the Feast." 4-5 oct, L4-. BP HB192.

Sunday, January 17
Antony of Egypt, renewer of the church, died around 356

Antony was born in Qemen-al-Arous, Upper Egypt, and was one of the earliest Egyptian desert fathers. Born to Christian parents from whom he inherited a large estate, he took personally Jesus' message to sell all that you have, give to the poor, and follow Christ. After making arrangements to provide for the care of his sister, he gave away his inheritance and became a hermit. Later, he became the head of a group of monks who lived in a cluster of huts and devoted themselves to communal prayer, worship, and manual labor under Antony's direction. The money they earned from their work was distributed as alms. Antony and his monks also preached and counseled those who sought them out. Antony and the desert fathers serve as a reminder that certain times and circumstances call Christians to stand apart from the surrounding culture and renounce the world in service to Christ.

Sunday, January 17

Pachomius, renewer of the church, died 346

Another of the desert fathers, Pachomius (puh-KOME-ee-us) was born in Egypt about 290. He became a Christian during his service as a soldier. In 320 he went to live as a hermit in Upper Egypt, where other hermits lived nearby. Pachomius organized them into a religious community in which the members prayed together and held their goods in common. His rule for monasteries influenced both Eastern and Western monasticism through the Rule of Basil and the Rule of Benedict, respectively.

Monday, January 18

Confession of Peter
Week of Prayer for Christian Unity begins

The Week of Prayer for Christian Unity is framed by two commemorations, the Confession of Peter (a relatively recent addition to the calendar) and the older Conversion of Paul. Both apostles are remembered together on June 29, but these two days give us an opportunity to focus on key events in each of their lives. Today we remember that Peter was led by God's grace to acknowledge Jesus as "the Christ, the Son of the living God" (Matt. 16:16). This confession is the common confession that unites us with Peter and with all Christians of every time and place.

Tuesday, January 19

Henry, Bishop of Uppsala, martyr, died 1156

Henry, an Englishman, became bishop of Uppsala, Sweden, in 1152 and is regarded as the patron of Finland. He traveled to Finland with the king of Sweden on a mission trip and remained there to organize the church. He was murdered in Finland by a man he had rebuked and who was disciplined by the church. Henry's burial place became a center of pilgrimage. His popularity as a saint is strong in both Sweden and Finland.

Thursday, January 21

Agnes, martyr, died around 304

Agnes was a girl of about thirteen living in Rome, who had chosen a life of service to Christ as a virgin, despite the Roman emperor Diocletian's ruling that had outlawed all Christian activity. The details of her martyrdom are not clear, but she gave witness to her faith and was put to death as a result, most likely by the sword. Since her death, the church has honored her as one of the chief martyrs of her time.

January 24, 2016
Third Sunday after Epiphany
Lectionary 3

The glory of the Lord is revealed in the reading of scripture. People stand at attention. People weep. People prostrate themselves in prayer. The unity of the church is another reflection of the glory of God. Most gloriously, the promises of God are fulfilled in the person of Jesus Christ. Gather round. Listen up. Glimpse the glory of God.

Prayer of the Day

Blessed Lord God, you have caused the holy scriptures to be written for the nourishment of your people. Grant that we may hear them, read, mark, learn, and inwardly digest them, that, comforted by your promises, we may embrace and forever hold fast to the hope of eternal life, through your Son, Jesus Christ our Lord.

Gospel Acclamation

Alleluia. The Spirit of the Lord has anointed me to bring good news ⌐ to the poor,* and to proclaim release ⌐ to the captives. *Alleluia.* (Luke 4:18)

Readings and Psalm

Nehemiah 8:1-3, 5-6, 8-10

The exiles have returned and rebuilt Jerusalem. Now Ezra, the priest, reads the law of Moses to them in the public square. When they hear it, they weep for their sins and for the long years in exile, but Ezra reminds them that the joy of the Lord is their strength.

Psalm 19

The teaching of the LORD revives the soul. (Ps. 19:7)

1 Corinthians 12:12-31a

The apostle and pastor Paul uses the metaphor of the human body to describe how intimately connected we are in the church. For this struggling congregation in Corinth, Paul delivers a vital message of unity that is a mark of the church today.

Luke 4:14-21

Near the beginning of Jesus' public ministry, he visits his hometown of Nazareth. In the words of Isaiah, he states and claims his identity, purpose, and mission.

Preface   Sundays

Color   Green

Prayers of Intercession

The prayers are prepared locally for each occasion. The following examples may be adapted or used as appropriate.

Gathered together by God's Spirit, we pray for the church, the world, and all those in need.

A brief silence.

Grant unity in the body of Christ, your church. Replace dissension with reconciliation, and strengthen its witness to the world. Lord, in your mercy,

hear our prayer.

When your creation is harmed, all suffer together. Guide your people to make wise choices that protect the land, sea, and all life. Lord, in your mercy,

hear our prayer.

Put an end to strife, violence, and hate in nations where there is turmoil (*especially*). Guide leaders and movements for change to seek peace above all else. Lord, in your mercy,

hear our prayer.

Be present where there is loneliness. Be comfort where there is pain. Be healing where there is brokenness. We pray especially for . . . . Lord, in your mercy,

hear our prayer.

Grant health and new life in this assembly. Send us to share the good news of your abundant love in Christ. Lord, in your mercy,

hear our prayer.

Here other intercessions may be offered.

We give thanks for the faithful departed who have come to know the fulfillment of your promises. Assure us of your hope until we join the saints in light. Lord, in your mercy,

hear our prayer.

Into your hands, gracious God, we commend all of your beloved for whom we pray, trusting in your mercy; through Christ our Lord.

Amen.

Images in the Readings

Scholars suggest that perhaps the **synagogue** developed especially in the diaspora as a substitute for the temple, which was too distant to attend. At the synagogue the community gathered for word and prayer, and a Christian church building echoes much of what the synagogue intended.

In antiquity, most books were inscribed on **scrolls** of parchment or leather. It was largely Christians at worship who popularized the codex, that is, what we call a book, since finding the appropriate reading at public worship was easier when the text was on pages.

Ezra dismissed the crowd in Jerusalem so they could **eat and drink**. We Christians remain, one body of Christ, eating and drinking the body of Christ.

At the weekly handshake of peace and the annual footwashing, Christians at worship honor each other's **body** as if it is one's own.

Ideas for the Day

◆ Jesus' sermon in the synagogue is met not merely with resistance, but with rejection. When we hear the gospel, we take the risk of hearing a word that may give us offense. The prophetic word of the Bible is often at odds with conventional notions of reality. Perhaps the Bible or lectionary book is lifted high at the reading of the gospel. In unpacking such a gesture, we may point to a word that is unlike any other. God invites us to be so shaped by the Bible that we dwell first in God's kingdom instead of the kingdom of empire. Can we take the risk of lifting up this word above all others, not so much to understand it, but to stand under it?

◆ The words of the prophet echo in Jesus' proclamation about himself: "The Spirit of the Lord is upon me." Proclaiming Jesus is Spirit-led and Spirit-shaped. Just as we pray an invocation for the Spirit in the thanksgiving at the table, what might it be like to pray for the outpouring of God's Spirit around the proclamation of God's word? Some traditions call this the "prayer for illumination." Examples may be found in the Presbyterian *Book of Common Worship* ([Louisville: Westminster John Knox, 1994], 60, 90–91). Placed prior to the first reading, the prayer calls on the Spirit to open us that we may receive God's word. In his *Deutsche Messe*, Luther suggested a hymn be sung to the Holy Spirit between the readings. How might you create a sense of wonder or a sense of expectation around preaching and receiving the word of God?

◆ Daniel Erlander provides both an artistic and a theological picture of Jesus' sermon in the synagogue. You can download his image "The Year of Jubilee" at http://daniel erlander.com to project on a screen or print in a worship folder (see the usage terms on the site).

Connections with the Liturgy

Every Sunday is modeled after the Nehemiah reading: the entire community gathers on the holy day, the scriptures are read, God is praised, and the people call out "Amen" and later give food to those in need. Although in Nehemiah the assembly goes home for a meal, Christians remain in the body that Paul describes, sharing in the joy of the wine of salvation.

Let the Children Come

The gospel could be effectively read in parts today with a narrator, an attendant handing the scroll to Jesus, and someone reading Jesus' part from the scroll. Older children who are confident readers could be invited to do this and rehearse ahead of time. Or maybe a family could do this together with each member reading a part. The reading could be proclaimed from its usual place in your worship space, or, if your worship space is small, readers might stand and read from their place in the assembly.

Assembly Song
Gathering

Listen, God is calling   ELW 513, LS 79, TFF 130, WOV 712

Open your ears, O faithful people   ELW 519, LS 84, WOV 715

Word of God, come down on earth   ELW 510, WOV 716

Psalmody and Acclamations

Furlong, Sue. "God of Hosts, Bring Us Back" from PS1.

Horman, John D. "Psalm 80" from *ChildrenSing Psalms*. U, kybd, opt tamb.

Makeever, Ray. "Behold and Tend This Vine (Psalm 80)" from DH.

p   (GA) Friesen-Carper, Paul. "A Voice from Heaven Said." MSB2 S557.

Hymn of the Day

Hail to the Lord's anointed   ELW 311, LBW 87   *FREUT EUCH, IHR LIEBEN*

Christ, Be Our Light   ELW 715   *CHRIST, BE OUR LIGHT*

When our song says peace   ELW 709   *JENKINS*

Offering

The Word of God is source and seed   ELW 506, WOV 658

Break now the bread of life   ELW 515, LBW 235

Communion

Come, beloved of the Maker   ELW 306

One bread, one body   ELW 496, TFF 122, W&P 111, WOV 710

The only Son from heaven   ELW 309, LBW 86

Sending

Arise, your light has come!   ELW 314, WOV 652

The Spirit sends us forth to serve   ELW 551, WOV 723

Additional Assembly Songs

Thy word is a lamp unto my feet   TFF 132, W&P 144

Palabra que fue luz   LLC 398

Praise to you, O Christ, our Savior   W&P 118, WOV 614

⊕ Bouknight, Lillian. "The Lord Is My Light." SATB. TFF 61.

⊕ Cortez, Jaime. "Somos el cuerpo de Cristo/We Are the Body of Christ" from *Glory to God*. U. WJK 9780664238971.

✿ Beech, Jay. "Alleluia We Are Listening." store.baytonemusic.com.

✿ Dakota Road. "Build Up" from *Dakota Road Music Anthology*. dakotaroadmusic.com.

✿ Hansen, Tim. "Enter In" from *Bring On the Light*. thetimhansenproject.com.

✿ Tangled Blue. "Kyrie" from *Storm Home: A Collection of Music from Humble Walk Artists-in-Residence*. humblewalk.bandcamp.com.

✿ Webb, Derek. "She Must and Shall Go Free" from *She Must and Shall Go Free*. derekwebb.com.

Music for the Day
Choral

p deSilva, Chris. "The Greater Glory of God." SAB, assembly, kybd, gtr, opt inst. GIA G-8280.

p Hirten, John Karl. "For Glory Dawns upon You" from *The Augsburg Choirbook: Sacred Choral Music of the Twentieth Century*. SATB, kybd. AFP 9780800656782.

p Martinson, Joel. "By All Your Saints" from *Augsburg Easy Choirbook*, vol. 2. 2 pt mxd, org. AFP 9780800677510.

p ● Raney, Joel. "Christ, Be Our Light!" SATB, readers, pno, opt hb, assembly. HOP C-5851.

Children's Choir

Lindner, Jane. "O Love, How Deep." U, fl, kybd. GIA G-6253.

p Miller, Aaron David. "Many Are the Lightbeams." U, pno. AFP 9781451459883.

Wienhorst, Richard. "The Spirit of the Lord Is on Me" from *Two Pieces for Children's Choir*. U, hb, kybd. GIA G-3364.

Keyboard / Instrumental

● Burkhardt, Michael. "Freut euch, ihr lieben" from *Five Christmas Hymn Improvisations*, set 1. Org. MSM 10-111.

p ● Cherwien, David M. "Jenkins" from *We Sing of God*. Org. AFP 9780806698052.

● Organ, Anne Krentz. "Jenkins" from *Eight for Eighty-Eight*, vol. 3. Pno, inst. AFP 9780800623495.

p ● Raabe, Nancy M. "Christ, Be Our Light" from *Foot-Friendly Preludes*. Org. AFP 9781451479539.

Handbell

Edwards, Dan. "Praise and Exaltation." 2-3 oct, L3. CG CGB384.

p Moklebust, Cathy. "Peace in Our Time." 3-6 oct hb, opt 3-6 oct hc, L3, CG CGB801. Opt vln, CG CGB801V.

Roberts, Philip. "Inward Light." 3-5 oct, L2. GIA G-7583.

⊕ = global song   ✿ = praise song
● = relates to hymn of the day   p = available in Prelude Music Planner

Monday, January 25
Conversion of Paul
Week of Prayer for Christian Unity ends

Today the Week of Prayer for Christian Unity comes to an end. The church remembers how a man of Tarsus named Saul, a former persecutor of the early Christian church, was turned around by God's grace to become one of its chief preachers. The risen Christ appeared to Paul on the road to Damascus and called him to proclaim the gospel. The narratives describing Paul's conversion in the Acts of the Apostles, Galatians, and 1 Corinthians inspire this commemoration, which was first celebrated among the Christians of Gaul.

Tuesday, January 26
Timothy, Titus, and Silas, missionaries

On the two days following the celebration of the Conversion of Paul, his companions are remembered. Timothy, Titus, and Silas were missionary coworkers with Paul. Timothy accompanied Paul on his second missionary journey and was commissioned by Paul to go to Ephesus, where he served as bishop and overseer of the church. Titus was a traveling companion of Paul, accompanied him on the trip to the council of Jerusalem, and became the first bishop of Crete. Silas traveled with Paul through Asia Minor and Greece and was imprisoned with him at Philippi, where they were delivered by an earthquake.

Wednesday, January 27
Lydia, Dorcas, and Phoebe, witnesses to the faith

On this day the church remembers three women who were companions in Paul's ministry. Lydia was Paul's first convert at Philippi in Macedonia. She was a merchant of purple-dyed goods, and because purple dye was extremely expensive, it is likely that Lydia was a woman of some wealth. Lydia and her household were baptized by Paul, and for a time her home was a base for Paul's missionary work. Dorcas is remembered for her charitable works, particularly making clothing for needy widows. Phoebe was a *diakonos*, a deaconess in the church at Cenchreae, near Corinth. Paul praises her as one who, through her service, looked after many people.

Thursday, January 28

Thomas Aquinas, teacher, died 1274

Thomas Aquinas (uh-ᴋᴡʏ-nus) was a brilliant and creative theologian of the thirteenth century. He was first and foremost a student of the Bible and profoundly concerned with the theological formation of the church's ordained ministers. As a member of the Order of Preachers (Dominicans), he worked to correlate scripture with the philosophy of Aristotle, which was having a renaissance in Aquinas's day. Some students of Aristotle's philosophy found in it an alternative to Christianity. But Aquinas immersed himself in the thought of Aristotle and worked to explain Christian beliefs in the philosophical culture of the day.

January 31, 2016

Fourth Sunday after Epiphany
Lectionary 4

The glory of God is often revealed when and where it is least expected. God uses our lips to declare that glory, inexperienced and hesitant though they may be. God uses our love to demonstrate that glory and so urges us to exercise it. God uses Jesus of Nazareth, water and the word, bread and wine, to reveal God's glory where and when God chooses. Take heed, lest the glory of God slip through our midst unnoticed.

Prayer of the Day

Almighty and ever-living God, increase in us the gifts of faith, hope, and love; and that we may obtain what you promise, make us love what you command, through your Son, Jesus Christ, our Savior and Lord.

Gospel Acclamation

Alleluia. You shall go to all to ˈ whom I send you.* Do not be afraid, for ˈ I am with you. *Alleluia.* (Jer. 1:7, 8)

Readings and Psalm

Jeremiah 1:4-10

God calls Jeremiah to be a prophet and consecrates him in the womb. Jeremiah's task is to preach God's word in the midst of the difficult political realities of his time, before the Babylonian exile. He is to make God known not only to Judah, but also to the nations.

Psalm 71:1-6

From my mother's womb you have been my strength. (Ps. 71:6)

1 Corinthians 13:1-13

Christians in Corinth prided themselves on their spiritual gifts. Paul reminds them that God gives us many gifts through the Holy Spirit, but the purpose behind all of them is love, the kind of love that God showed us in Jesus Christ.

Luke 4:21-30

People in Jesus' hometown are initially pleased when he says that God will free the oppressed. Their pleasure turns to rage when he reminds them that God's prophetic mission typically pushes beyond human boundaries so that mercy and healing are extended to those regarded as outsiders.

Preface   Sundays

Color   Green

Prayers of Intercession

The prayers are prepared locally for each occasion. The following examples may be adapted or used as appropriate.

Gathered as children of the same Lord, we pray for the church, the world, and all those in need.

A brief silence.

Make your church a prophetic voice for the voiceless, a bold witness of love to the neighbor, and a force for hope in all the world. Lord, in your mercy,

hear our prayer.

Guard all creatures that fly, swim, creep, and walk upon the earth. Defend and preserve threatened lands and waters (*especially*). Lord, in your mercy,

hear our prayer.

Stir leaders of all nations to compassion and righteous anger in the face of injustice and lead them to rejoice in the truth that all people are beloved children of the Most High. Lord, in your mercy,

hear our prayer.

Grant patience, endurance, healing, and hope to all those in any need. Give strength to those living with addictions and comfort to those who have lost jobs, homes, health, and hope. We pray especially for . . . . Lord, in your mercy,
hear our prayer.
Guide the ministries of this congregation (*especially*). Curb our impatience, our envy, and our insistence on our own way, and give us patience, kindness, and love in service to others. Lord, in your mercy,
hear our prayer.
Here other intercessions may be offered.
We give thanks for the faithful departed who have come to know the fulfillment of your promises. Strengthen us in faith, hope, and love until we join the saints in light. Lord, in your mercy,
hear our prayer.
Into your hands, gracious God, we commend all of your beloved for whom we pray, trusting in your mercy; through Christ our Lord.
Amen.

Images in the Readings

Not only in the seventh century BCE but still today people hope for a **prophet**, someone who will speak truth, whose words can conquer evil by the very power of divine authority. We see this archetypal hope, for example, in films when magical words spoken by the good guys are able to obliterate what is wicked and hateful. In the Bible, a prophet is not primarily a seer who foretells the future, but someone who is inspired to distinguish truth from falsehood and who speaks honestly about the outcomes of ignoring such a word of God. Over the centuries, it remains true that most prophets are ignored by most people.

The first-century **mirrors** that Paul mentions did not reflect as precisely as do ours. Yet whether visually clear or not, a mirror reflects only ourselves back to us. So it is that even our beloved images for God reflect our own minds, languages, denominations, traditions, and cultures. We pray, however, that even these mirrors will bring something to us of the very face of God. ("Face" of God is, of course, another metaphor that mirrors our humanity.)

The gospel includes two common biblical images of human need: the **widow** and the **leper**. Both were persons in some ways excluded from the wider society. Paul urged that the Christian community be known for an inclusive love.

Ideas for the Day

◆ The people of Nazareth hope that Jesus, "one of their own," will share his powerful gifts with them, as he has done elsewhere. Perhaps they think he owes that to his own people. In response, Jesus tells stories that show God's powerful gifts to outsiders instead. To help hearers imagine the rage this provoked, use a current event. One can almost always find a news story about a group keeping good gifts for "their own" and away from "outsiders," however that is defined—by immigration status, sexual orientation, class, education or work history, or political party, for example.

◆ Jesus' return to Nazareth is in some ways a "local boy makes good" story. However, people also question, "Is not this Joseph's son?" It's easy for a community to overlook the talents and prophetic gifts of young people they have watched grow up. Even as Epiphany calls us to see the manifestation of God in Jesus, how might we also be called to see the Holy Spirit manifested in our own "local" boys and girls? With Jeremiah's story also in mind, this Sunday would be a good opportunity for youth to share their gifts, passions, and convictions in worship.

◆ In today's gospel, people move from speaking well of Jesus to feeling rage strong enough to kill. What makes people speak well of your congregation, and what could trigger rage? Ask a few people in your wider community for their impressions of your congregation. Reflect on the ways "public relations" do or do not shape the choices you make in ministry.

◆ Injustice calls us to practice "faith, hope, and love" by speaking truth as a prophet does. "Whistleblowers" who reveal unjust corporate practices may be compared to prophets like Jeremiah—often reluctant, threatened, and persistent—and even to Jesus who risks the rage of his own people in order to speak the truth of God's loving and expansive reign. The film *The Insider* (Touchstone, 1999) tells the story of a whistleblower in the tobacco industry; read a review at www.spiritualityandpractice.com.

Connections with the Liturgy

At baptism, the parents and sponsors are enjoined to bring the children to the word of God and the holy supper, to place in their hands the holy scriptures, and to nurture them in faith and prayer so they grow in the Christian faith and life. These words of commission recall both the child Jeremiah and the maturation of which Paul speaks in 1 Corinthians.

Let the Children Come

God calls us regardless of age. Imagine a child reading Jeremiah today ("I am only a boy"), or even a visibly pregnant woman ("Before I formed you in the womb I knew you"). To engage with the 1 Corinthians text, children could make paper hearts with "love" on one side and the various descriptors on the back: "is patient," "is kind," "is not rude." Ask the children to join in greeting people on the way out of worship and hand out the hearts.

Assembly Song

Gathering

I love to tell the story   ELW 661, LBW 390, LS 154, TFF 228

Rise, shine, you people!   ELW 665, LBW 393

O God of light   ELW 507, LBW 237

Psalmody and Acclamations

"My Lips Will Tell of Your Justice" from *Psallite* C-105.

Duck, Ruth C. "God, My Help and Hiding Place" (*TOKYO*) from PAS 71B.

Hopson, Hal. "Psalm 71" (verses 1-2) from TPP.

p   (GA) Friesen-Carper, Paul. "A Voice from Heaven Said." MSB2 S557.

Hymn of the Day

O Word of God incarnate   ELW 514, LBW 231   *MUNICH*

Son of God, eternal Savior   ELW 655, LBW 364   *IN BABILONE*

Although I speak with angel's tongue   ELW 644   *O WALY WALY*

Offering

Heaven is singing for joy   ELW 664, LLC 575

As the grains of wheat   ELW 465, WOV 705

Communion

By gracious powers   ELW 626, WOV 736

He comes to us as one unknown   ELW 737, WOV 768

Where charity and love prevail   ELW 359, LBW 126, TFF 84

Sending

Hallelujah! We sing your praises   ELW 535, LLC 420, TFF 158, WOV 722

Lord, speak to us, that we may speak   ELW 676, LBW 403

Additional Assembly Songs

Lord, this day we've come to worship   TFF 137

Come and see   W&P 29

Now in this banquet   W&P 104

⊕   Ghanian melody. "Praise God, All You Nations/Da n'ase" from *Glory to God*. U. WJK 9780664238971.

⊕   Shona Traditional. "There's No One in This World Like Jesus/ Hakuna Wakaita sa Jesu" from *Worship and Song*. SATB. Abingdon Press 9781426709951.

✧   Beech, Jay. "Alleluia We Are Listening." baytonemusic.com.

✧   Dakota Road. "Savior's Song" from *Dakota Road Music Anthology*. dakotaroadmusic.com.

✧   Hansen, Tim. "Open Your Eyes" from *Bring On the Light*. thetim hansenproject.com.

✧   Tangled Blue. "Kyrie" from *Storm Home: A Collection of Music from Humble Walk Artists-in-Residence*. humblewalk.band camp.com.

✧   Tenth Avenue North. "Healing Begins" from *The Light Meets the Dark*. Available on Amazon.com.

Music for the Day

Choral

•   Hopson, Hal. "The Gift of Love." U or 2 pt mxd, kybd. HOP CF-148.

p   Mendelssohn, Felix/arr. Sue Ellen Page. "For the Mountains Shall Depart." 2 pt mxd, org, ob, opt str qrt. GIA G-8004.

p   Scroggins, Debra. "An Instrument of Thy Peace." SATB, pno. CG 1331.

p   Wood, Dale. "Rise, Shine!" from *The Augsburg Choirbook: Sacred Choral Music of the Twentieth Century*. SATB, org. AFP 9780800656782.

Children's Choir

Archer, Malcolm. "Faith, Hope, and Love Remain." SA, pno. OXF 9780193401655.

Gieseke, Richard W. "May the Peoples Praise You, O God." 2 pt, kybd. CPH 982929PODWEB.

p   Horman, John D. "Jeremiah's Lament" from *Sing the Stories of God's People*. U, kybd. AFP 9781451460469.

Keyboard / Instrumental

p •   Harbach, Barbara. "O Waly Waly" from *Augsburg Organ Library: Marriage*. Org. AFP 9781451486025.

•   Miller, Aaron David. "Munich" from *Augsburg Organ Library: Autumn*. Org. AFP 9780800675790.

•   Roberts, Al. "O Waly Waly" from *Organ Plus Anthology*, vol. 1. Org, inst. AFP 9781451424256.

p •   Shaw, Timothy. "In Babilone" from *My Redeemer Lives*. Pno. AFP 9781451451795.

Handbell

p   Dobrinski, Cynthia. "Glorious Celebration." 3-6 oct, L2+. HOP 2678.

•   Eithun, Sandra. "Reflection on 'O Waly Waly.'" 3-6 oct hb, opt 3 or 5 oct hc, L2+. CPH 97-7489.

•   Griffin, Jackie. "Festive Celebration." 5 oct hb, L3, FTT 201885HB. Br qnt, FTT 201885B. Org, FTT 201885O. Timp, FTT 201885P. Full score, FTT 201885M. Complete set (8 hb pt, 1 of each other pt), FTT 201885.

Tuesday, February 2

Presentation of Our Lord

Forty days after the birth of Christ we mark the day Mary and Joseph presented him in the temple in accordance with Jewish law. There a prophetess named Anna began to speak of the redemption of Israel when she saw the young child. Simeon also greeted Mary and Joseph. He responded to the presence of the consolation of Israel in this child with the words of the Nunc dimittis. His song described Jesus as a "light for the nations."

Because of the link between Jesus as the light for the nations, and because an old reading for this festival contains a line from the prophet Zephaniah, "I will search Jerusalem with candles," the day is also known as Candlemas, a day when candles are blessed for the coming year.

Wednesday, February 3

Ansgar, Bishop of Hamburg, missionary to Denmark and Sweden, died 865

Ansgar was a monk who led a mission to Denmark and later to Sweden, where he built the first church. His work ran into difficulties with the rulers of the day, and he was forced to withdraw into Germany, where he served as a bishop in Hamburg. Despite his difficulties in Sweden, he persisted in his mission work and later helped consecrate Gothbert as the first bishop of Sweden. Ansgar had a deep love for the poor. He would wash their feet and serve them food provided by the parish.

Friday, February 5

The Martyrs of Japan, died 1597

In the sixteenth century, Jesuit missionaries, followed by Franciscans, introduced the Christian faith in Japan. But a promising beginning to those missions—perhaps as many as 300,000 Christians by the end of the sixteenth century—met complications from competition between the missionary groups, political difficulty between Spain and Portugal, and factions within the government of Japan. Christianity was suppressed. By 1630, Christianity was driven underground.

Today we commemorate the first martyrs of Japan, twenty-six missionaries and converts who were killed by crucifixion. Two hundred and fifty years later, when Christian missionaries returned to Japan, they found a community of Japanese Christians that had survived underground.

February 7, 2016
Transfiguration of Our Lord
Last Sunday after Epiphany

Witnesses to the glory of God in the face of Jesus will be unable to avoid reflecting that glory in the world. It was true for Moses. It was doubtless true for Peter, James, and John. We pray that it will be true of all of us who see the glory of the Lord in the word and in the supper and who are being "transformed into the same image" by the Spirit of God.

Prayer of the Day

Holy God, mighty and immortal, you are beyond our knowing, yet we see your glory in the face of Jesus Christ. Transform us into the likeness of your Son, who renewed our humanity so that we may share in his divinity, Jesus Christ our Lord, who lives and reigns with you and the Holy Spirit, one God, now and forever.

Gospel Acclamation

Alleluia. This is my ¹ Son, my Chosen,* lis- ¹ ten to him! *Alleluia.* (Luke 9:35)

Readings and Psalm
Exodus 34:29-35

Moses' face shone with the reflected glory of God after he received the ten commandments on Mount Sinai. The sight caused the Israelites to be afraid, so Moses wore a veil to mask the radiance of God's glory, taking it off when he spoke directly with God.

Psalm 99

Proclaim the greatness of the LORD; worship upon God's holy hill. (Ps. 99:9)

2 Corinthians 3:12—4:2

In his debates with the Corinthians, Paul contrasts the glory of Moses with the glory of Christ. The Israelites could not see Moses' face because of the veil. But in Christ we see the unveiled glory of God and are transformed into Christ's likeness.

Luke 9:28-36 [37-43a]

The conversation about Jesus' suffering and death is enclosed in a dazzling foreshadowing of the resurrection. God affirms Jesus' identity, the disciples are stunned speechless, and Jesus resumes his mission with a demonstration of his power over evil.

Preface Transfiguration

Color White

Prayers of Intercession

The prayers are prepared locally for each occasion. The following examples may be adapted or used as appropriate.

Rejoicing with all the faithful, we pray for the church, the world, and all those in need.

A brief silence.

God of glory, guide and empower your church's leaders to trust your promises as Moses and Elijah did. Shine the light of Christ through your church to the world. Lord, in your mercy,

hear our prayer.

God of majesty, from the highest mountain to the lowest valley, your power is seen in your creation. Help us to protect and care for soil, air, water, and all the creatures you have made. Lord, in your mercy,

hear our prayer.

God of hope and freedom, give just laws; fair leaders; sufficient food, water, and shelter; and abundant peace to all nations in poverty, strife, or at war (*especially*). Lord, in your mercy,

hear our prayer.

God of wholeness, bring clarity to those in confusing times, healing to those in painful times, and peace to those in trying times. We pray especially for . . . . Lord, in your mercy,

hear our prayer.

God of new life, show us your will for the ministries in this place (*especially*), and transform us for mission and witness. Lord, in your mercy,

hear our prayer.

Here other intercessions may be offered.

God of glory, we give thanks for all the beloved who rest in your loving arms. Keep us from losing heart and strengthen our faith in your promise of everlasting life. Lord, in your mercy,

hear our prayer.

Into your hands, gracious God, we commend all of your beloved for whom we pray, trusting in your mercy; through Christ our Lord.

Amen.

Images in the Readings

The readings include the central biblical images of light and **mountain**. In the Bible, significant religious events occur on a mountain because, according to the ancient cosmology, God was described as dwelling above the earth and, when appearing on earth, coming as far down as the top of the mountain. Still today people speak of "mountaintop experiences."

God is not only brilliant light, but also **cloud**. Although contemporary people tend to think of clouds as relating to weather conditions, in the Bible the cloud is a mysterious sign of the presence of God. It is as if God covers the earth, brings life, yet suddenly vanishes. Christians can add that, from God as cloud, the waters of baptism rain down.

The first and second readings refer to a face **veil** that humans needed to don if they were to be in God's presence. A recurring claim in biblical Judaism is that one cannot look at God and live—although in one story (Exod. 24:11) the elders not only survive their experience of seeing God, but also eat with God. Religion itself can be thought about as the veil that people don so that with safety they can approach the utterly inexplicable presence of spiritual reality. For Luther, convinced of the absolute distance between God and humanity, a veil was indeed necessary, and that veil is Christ. As the confession and forgiveness says it, if we have turned ourselves away from God's view, we need to be turned again through Christ toward God. Many contemporary people who view God as a benign uncle see no need for any veil of any kind.

Ideas for the Day

◆ The story of the transfiguration can seem quite foreign to our experience when we struggle to imagine details like Jesus' appearance, the dwellings, and a mysterious cloud. Yet there are also elements common to Christian witnesses through the centuries: the "mountaintop experience" of God's presence, the challenge of staying awake, and a sense of being enveloped or surrounded by mystery. Invite testimony from someone with such an experience, or share your own. Starting with our liturgy's proclamation, "Heaven and earth are full of your glory," share how you see God's glory on earth.

◆ Paul declares to the Corinthians that "all of us . . . are being transformed into the same image from one degree of glory to another." Acknowledge how difficult that can be for us to hear, with the help of Thomas Merton's revelation: "I have the immense joy of being man, a member of a race in which God Himself became incarnate. . . . And if only everybody could realize this! But it cannot be explained. There is no way of telling people that they are all walking around shining like the sun" (*Conjectures of a Guilty Bystander* [New York: Doubleday Religion, 1965], 155).

◆ Baptismal living presents countless opportunities to be transformed. Lenten discipline, soon to begin, invites spiritual growth in heart, mind, and action. With both those themes in mind, this would be an appropriate day for a communal affirmation of baptism. People could mark each other with the sign of the cross, reminding one another that in baptism they are chosen and beloved by God.

◆   When we begin the more somber and reflective season of Lent, we bring with us the brightness of transfiguration. It can light our way in the dark, helping us see what we need to see—the reality of sin and brokenness and our need for Christ's redemption—and keeping alive our hope of resurrection dawn. On this day when some communities bury the "alleluia" until Easter, consider "burying" the word within or around a flashlight that can silently light the way through Lent.

Connections with the Liturgy

At baptism, the minister calls each of the baptized a "child of God," and the welcome may be worded, "Jesus said, I am the light of the world." So each baptism contains an echo of the transfiguration.

Let the Children Come

Invite children to go with you on a tour of hidden treasures. A good place to begin or end is the communion table (or the place where the bread and wine are kept before the table is set for communion). Why does cloth cover the communion elements? Where are the bread and wine kept during the week? Point out any meaningful iconography "hidden" in glass, wood, marble, or cloth, especially images and symbols that most people might not notice. How do these hidden treasures reveal God in surprising ways?

Assembly Song
Gathering

Oh, sing to God above   ELW 555, LLC 600, WOV 726
Christ, whose glory fills the skies   ELW 553, LBW 265
Give to our God immortal praise   ELW 848, LBW 520

Psalmody and Acclamations

Hopson, Hal. "Psalm 99" from TPP.
Mathis, William H. Refrain for "Psalm 99" from *After the Prelude: Year A*. U/cant, hb. CG CGB659 (digital version), CGB658 (printed version). Use with ELW psalm tone 6 or 10 (in C).
Seltz, Martin A. "Psalm 99" from PWC.
p   (GA) Friesen-Carper, Paul. "A Voice from Heaven Said." MSB2 S557.

Hymn of the Day

Jesus on the mountain peak   ELW 317   *BETHOLD*   WOV 653
   ST. ALBINUS
Shine, Jesus, shine   ELW 671, TFF 64, W&P 123, WOV 651   *SHINE, JESUS, SHINE*
How good, Lord, to be here!   ELW 315, LBW 89   *POTSDAM*

Offering

Lord of light   ELW 688, sts. 1, 3; LBW 405, sts. 1, 3
Love divine, all loves excelling   ELW 631, sts. 1, 4; LBW 315, sts. 1, 4

Communion

I want to walk as a child of the light   ELW 815, LS 36, WOV 649
Beautiful Savior   ELW 838, LBW 518, LS 174
Oh wondrous image, vision fair   ELW 316, LBW 80

Sending

Alleluia, song of gladness   ELW 318, WOV 654
This little light of mine   ELW 677, LS 33, TFF 65

Additional Assembly Songs

Yo soy la luz del mundo   LLC 319
To God be the glory   TFF 264/272
⊕   Syrian traditional. "Halle, Hallelujah." from *Pave the Way: Global Songs 3*. U. AFP 9780800676896.
⊕   Zulu traditional. "Walking in the Light of God" from *Worship and Song*. SATB. Abingdon Press 9781426709951.
✧   Bruxvoort Colligan, Richard. "O Tender God, Have Mercy" from *Worldmaking*. worldmaking.net.
✧   Dakota Road. "Messiah" from *Dakota Road Music Anthology*. dakotaroadmusic.com.
✧   Haugen, Marty. "Gather Us In." ELW 532.
✧   Houge, Nate. "Be with Us Now" from *Storm Home: A Collection of Music from Humble Walk Artists-in-Residence*. humblewalk .bandcamp.com.
✧   Hughes, Tim. "God of Justice" from CCLI.
✧   Morris, Michael. "We Need Jesus' Light Every Day" from *Storm Home: A Collection of Music from Humble Walk Artists-in-Residence*. humblewalk.bandcamp.com.

Music for the Day
Choral

p   Bouman, Paul. "God Is Light." SATB, org. AFP 9780800653255.
p ●   Forsberg, Charles. "Fairest Lord Jesus." SATB div, pno. AFP 9780800656966.
p   Miller, Aaron David. "Eternal Light" from *The New Gloria Deo: Music for Small Choirs*. SAB, pno. AFP 9780806698403.
p ●   Sedio, Mark. "Jesus on the Mountain Peak" from *Augsburg Choirbook for Advent, Christmas, and Epiphany*. SATB, org, assembly. AFP 9780800678586.

Children's Choir

Anderson, Shari. "I Want to Walk as a Child of the Light" from *ChildrenSing in Worship*, vol. 2. 2 pt, pno, fl, AFP 9781451461213.
Mauersberger, Erhard. "We Saw His Glory" from *A Second Morning Star Choir Book*. 2 pt, kybd. CPH 974702WEB.
Walker, Christopher. "Cry Out with Joy." U, pno/org. OXF 9780193853799.

⊕ = global song   ✧ = praise song
● = relates to hymn of the day   p = available in Prelude Music Planner

Keyboard / Instrumental

p • Dahl, David P. "Bethold" from *The Organ Sings*. Org. AFP
    9781451462609.

p • Greene, J. William. "Potsdam" from *New Year Joy*. Org, tpt. AFP
    9781451462555.

•   Rotermund, Donald. "Potsdam" from *Introductions, Interludes,
    and Codas*, set 4. Org. MSM 10-544.

p • Sedio, Mark. "Bethold" from *Come and Praise*, vol. 2. Org. AFP
    9780806696928.

Handbell

p   Geschke, Susan E. "This Glorious Day." 2-3 oct, L2-. HOP 2623.

p   Lamb, Linda. "Glorify Thy Name." 3-5 oct hb, opt 3 oct hc, L3-.
    HOP 2661.

•   McChesney, Kevin. "Shine, Jesus, Shine." 3-5 oct hb, opt 1 or 2 bell
    trees, opt pno, opt bass, L3. CG CGB778.

LENT

PREPARING FOR LENT

Treasuring Lent

Close the door to your room and pray in secret. Blow a trumpet and invite all, even the aged and nursing children, to an assembly. Right away in Lent, hearing scripture from the prophet Joel and Matthew's gospel, it seems as though signals have gotten crossed, the messages mixed up. Do we line up in a sanctuary or at a subway station to receive an ashen cross on our forehead, a very public sign of our mortality and our faith? Or do we purchase a new Lenten devotional booklet and carve out times for solitude, prayer, and meditation?

Yes and yes. In the book *Worship Matters: An Introduction to Worship*, an exploration of Lutheran worship begins with the premise that we are both/and people. "Lutherans live in the beautiful tension of *and*. We are simultaneously sinner *and* saint. We need the law that tells us the truth about our sinfulness *and* the gospel that tells us we are a new creation in Christ, freed and forgiven by God's grace" (Augsburg Fortress, 2012, pp. 16–17). As you contemplate Lenten worship in your assembly, consider this both/and: What does it mean to connect with God in private? What does it mean to be church, Christ's body, in public? How do we treasure both faithfully?

Lent, liturgy, and private devotion

"For where your treasure is, there your heart will be also." (Matt. 6:21)

"Anything on which your heart relies and depends, I say, that is really your God." (Martin Luther, commentary on the first commandment)

"Jesus, priceless treasure, source of purest pleasure, truest friend to me." (ELW 775)

Where is your treasure? This is one of those questions requiring self-examination, a searching of the heart. We encounter this straightforward theme on Ash Wednesday, but as we move through Lent, the gospel readings offer us variations on the theme. We encounter revealing stories of Jesus as God's treasured one and the world, especially the sinner, as loved beyond measure.

The devil tempts Jesus to treasure his divinity by exploiting it: If you are the Son of God, unleash your grand power (Lent 1). Unique to Luke's gospel, Jesus is the mother hen looking out for the wayward ones, attempting to gather those who are not willing (Lent 2). A lackluster fig tree is left alone, given one more year to bear fruit; it is too precious to be cut down (Lent 3). The father treasures his prodigal son (Lent 4), and Mary adores Jesus in a manner that appears wasteful (Gospel of John, Lent 5).

Where are we in these stories? Are we willing to be gathered under Jesus' wings this Lent? Like the fig tree given that extra time and like the wayward son welcomed home, we are given Lent to discover to whom and what we cling.

While worship certainly includes self-examination, much of our devotion happens privately. Notice the pocket-sized devotionals published for Lent, not Easter. Lent can indeed be a time to nurture prayer life and contemplation with greater intentionality. How can we connect with the God we treasure and who treasures us? How does this devotion happen in worship and beyond it? As you plan and lead worship in Lent, consider:

- How can silence and reflection be nurtured in worship? During confession and forgiveness? At other times?
- Can a smaller, midweek Lenten service have a different character that values self-reflection and examination? *Holden Prayer Around the Cross* could be one possibility (Augsburg Fortress, 2009).
- Does your congregation open its doors at specific times during the week for private prayer?
- Could members of your congregation contribute to a written Lenten devotional in print or online format?
- Is your congregation familiar with the daily lectionary readings (*ELW*, pp. 1121–1153)?

Lent, liturgy, and public witness

On the fifth Sunday in Lent, we move from the Gospel of Luke to John's gospel, encountering a story of great devotion: Mary's generous anointing of Jesus. Less than two weeks later, we hear of an act of devotion by Jesus, the washing of his disciples' feet. This second act is intimate yet shared: "So if I, your Lord and Teacher, have washed your feet, you also ought to wash one another's feet" (John

13:14). We are warned about public piety on Ash Wednesday. The warning, however, is not a complete dismissal of public acts of piety. The danger lies in the temptation to lord such piety over another, much in the way Jesus was tempted in the wilderness.

The readings for the Sundays in Lent and the passages from Luke in particular call us to an outward piety: welcoming sinners and eating with them. The church is the treasured gathering given away as bread in the wilderness. This giving away as told in the story of the waiting father and his sons is unique to Luke. Biblical scholar Luke Timothy Johnson says of this story, "It is the father whose mercy and openness to both children stands as the emblem for Jesus' prophetic mission from God to restore the people with an open invitation to all" (*Sacra Pagina: The Gospel of Luke* [Collegeville, MN: Liturgical Press, 1991], p. 241). Our private devotion to God flows forth in public love to one another.

This public piety, this turning toward others, finds its origins in our baptism. When baptism is affirmed publicly in an assembly, those making affirmation are asked if they intend

to live among God's faithful people,
to hear the word of God and share in the Lord's supper,
to proclaim the good news of God in Christ through
    word and deed,
to serve all people, following the example of Jesus,
and to strive for justice and peace in all the earth.
    (*ELW*, p. 236)

Lent, a season of baptismal preparation and renewal, calls us to ask what we treasure, yet this treasuring has a public dimension. It is not that we do not need the private devotion; we do. Yet honoring this relationship leads to public witness, both in the liturgy (the public work of the people) and beyond. As you plan worship for the season of Lent, how can these weeks form us as the body that welcomes sinners and eats with them? Consider:

- Use the midweek worship plan presented on page 106 of this volume, which is based on the questions asked at baptism and affirmation of baptism.
- "Go in peace. Remember the poor," is one of the options for the dismissal. How is this remembering rooted in the baptismal promises?
- "Lord, have mercy." How do we regard this as a communal plea for God's continual help?
- How does your congregation publicly support those who are preparing for baptism? (See Welcome to Baptism, *ELW*, p. 232).
- If you hold Lenten midweek meals, are they open to the public?

- How can worship-related ministries—art, music, and hospitality—find a place in the wider community at other times and places?

Music

Those who make musical decisions in Lent and at all times must bear in mind music's intensely personal dimension and its powerfully public potential. For example, a hymn might be chosen because it is a favorite of individuals or congregations; it resonates with them deeply because of its connection to human experience. At the same time, the words we sing shape our Christian identity. Song selection is not unlike a diet in this way; how we are fed contributes to our overall health. Hymns and songs of different styles nourish us in different ways; a Taizé refrain differs from a robust, German chorale, which differs from an American gospel song. Singing from the wide treasury of songs available to us can be a gift to us individually and as the church.

Sharing the story behind a hymn or song, whether familiar or new, can broaden and deepen our connection to music and the community of saints past and present. Consider purchasing the *Hymnal Companion to Evangelical Lutheran Worship* (Augsburg Fortress, 2010) for a church library and publishing notes about a hymn in a worship folder, online newsletter, or via other media. If your assembly creates its own Lenten devotional, include a hymn as well as a prayer for each day in Lent.

Could a sung communal response during the prayers of intercession be introduced in Lent? See ELW #178–180, 751–752. Other resources include *Singing Our Prayer* (Augsburg Fortress, 2010) and *Hear Our Prayer* (Augsburg Fortress, 2007). As you look ahead to the Three Days, what music specific to those days could be introduced in the Sundays in Lent? See *Music Sourcebook for Lent and the Three Days* (Augsburg Fortress, 2009).

Environment

Lent is a season when we are challenged to examine our loyalties and allegiances. Most of us are challenged from the outset, quickly realizing that we must say no to something just in order to say yes to self-examination. Because such self-examination nudges us toward uncomfortable realignments, Lent has earned a reputation as a somber season. The good news is that we anchor our struggles in readings that assure us of the profound joy that accompanies our "fasting from" the world's empty promises in order to "feast on" the trustworthy promises of our faithful, loving, and merciful God.

Search "Lent: Fast and Feast" online to discover various lists of practices and behaviors worshipers might be invited to "fast from" and "feast on" during Lent. Provide opportunities for worshipers to record their experiences of fast and feast throughout the season on strips of paper or fabric that may be woven into a simple Lenten prayer loom (see 04_Lent.PrayerLoom.pdf)*. Encourage reflection on how fasting and feasting shape both private devotion and public witness.

If meals preceding midweek Lenten worship have lost their original simplicity, consider paring back, perhaps limiting offerings to soups and bread. Encourage participants to use the change as an opportunity to talk about fasting and feasting and to consider how less can be more.

Visually signal the conversion ("turning around") to which we are called during Lent by altering the seating arrangement in the worship space if you can. Congregations with flexible seating options might reconfigure seating toward the font, or change the location of the font and then turn in this new direction for confession and forgiveness. Congregations without flexible seating might turn to face one another during the confession, an uncomfortable but effective reminder of the impact our sinfulness has on others.

Stories that unfold in the Sunday gospels present powerful and compelling images. Consider how the story of the prodigal son or Mary's extravagant love in anointing Jesus' feet might be dramatized in a silent tableau that serves as a visual companion to a sermon. Such visuals may invite further reflection on how the father's welcome anticipates God's welcoming embrace of all who return and how Mary's action anticipates the ultimate extravagance of Jesus' love for us poured out on the cross.

In lieu of floral arrangements during Lent, create arrangements of thorns or bare branches; arrange pussy willow branches in water so that worshipers may watch them for signs of new life; or display potted Crown of Thorns cacti. On Passion Sunday, consider using large potted palms or arrangements of greenery in which palms are prominently featured.

If you buried the alleluias with some amaryllis bulbs on the Transfiguration of Our Lord, place one pot in the sunlight and water it throughout Lent. Place the other pot in a darker spot, and don't water the bulbs. Throughout Lent, invite the children to help with the watering and ask them to report on any changes they observe in either pot. Anchor the significance of this exercise by learning the song by Natalie Sleeth, "In the bulb there is a flower" (*LifeSongs*, #56).

Seasonal Checklist

- Review the liturgies for Ash Wednesday and the Sunday of the Passion in *Evangelical Lutheran Worship* (Assembly Edition, pp. 247–257; Leaders Edition, pp. 611–627).
- Purchase resources for Lent and the Three Days that contain insights, images, ideas, commentary, practical tips, songs, and responses to help your congregation deepen its worship life during the days from Ash Wednesday to Easter. Consider *Worship Guidebook for Lent and the Three Days* and *Music Sourcebook for Lent and the Three Days*, both from Augsburg Fortress.
- Arrange to simplify the worship environment during Lent. Center attention on the font and table.
- Consider a Lenten fast from extra committee meetings or other events that could be postponed to give greater time for prayer and worship.
- Use the Apostles' Creed.
- Consider especially Thanksgiving at the Table IV in *Evangelical Lutheran Worship*.
- Order worship participation leaflets if used for the Ash Wednesday and/or Passion Sunday liturgies.
- Burn palms from the previous Passion Sunday or obtain ashes from a church supplier for use on Ash Wednesday (February 10).
- If midweek services will be held during Lent, determine style, content, and leadership. See the seasonal rites section for possibilities (pp. 106–111).
- If corporate or individual confession and forgiveness will be offered during Lent, consider using the orders provided in *Evangelical Lutheran Worship*, pages 238–244. Publicize times for individual confession and forgiveness, or information on how to schedule a time.
- Consider ordering eco-palms for Passion Sunday (www.lwr.org/palms/). If long, individual palm fronds are used, they will need to be separated ahead of time. Reserve leftover palm branches to be burned for ashes next year.
- Determine how and where the procession with palms will take place on Passion Sunday. Prepare signs or recruit volunteers to help direct people. Determine how those with physical disabilities will participate in the procession or be seated ahead of time.
- Schedule a rehearsal of readers in preparation for the passion reading on Passion Sunday.

---

* Download at http://store.augsburgfortress.org/media/temp/SundaysSeasons/PDFs.zip

WORSHIP TEXTS FOR LENT

Confession and Forgiveness

All may make the sign of the cross, the sign marked at baptism,
as the presiding minister begins.
Blessed be the holy Trinity, + one God,
who brings us safely through the sea,
who gives us water from the rock,
who leads us into the land of milk and honey.
Amen.

Let us come home to God, confessing our sin.

Silence is kept for reflection.

Merciful Father,
we have sinned against heaven and before you.
We do not fully live as your sons and daughters.
We use your gifts to our own ends.
Forgive us and restore us,
that we may resist all that draws us away from you,
and be at peace with one another. Amen.

We are reconciled to God through Christ;
for his sake, God does not count our trespasses against us.
Once dead in sin, we are now alive to God.
Once lost, we now are found.
God clothes you in the finest robe of all,
the righteousness of + Jesus Christ,
forgiving you all your sins
and making of you a new creation.
Amen.

or, especially on Ash Wednesday

All may make the sign of the cross, the sign marked at baptism,
as the presiding minister begins.
Blessed be the holy Trinity, + one God,
who brings us safely through the sea,
who gives us water from the rock,
who leads us into the land of milk and honey.
Amen.

Let us confess our sin
in the presence of God and of one another.

Silence is kept for reflection.

Holy God, holy and mighty, holy and immortal,
have mercy on us.

For self-centered living,
and for failing to walk with humility and gentleness:
Holy God, holy and mighty, holy and immortal,
have mercy on us.

For longing to have what is not ours,
and for hearts that are not at rest with ourselves:
Holy God, holy and mighty, holy and immortal,
have mercy on us.

For misuse of human relationships,
and for unwillingness to see the image of God in others:
Holy God, holy and mighty, holy and immortal,
have mercy on us.

For jealousies that divide families and nations,
and for rivalries that create strife and warfare:
Holy God, holy and mighty, holy and immortal,
have mercy on us.

For reluctance in sharing the gifts of God,
and for carelessness with the fruits of creation:
Holy God, holy and mighty, holy and immortal,
have mercy on us.

For hurtful words that condemn,
and for angry deeds that harm:
**Holy God, holy and mighty, holy and immortal,
have mercy on us.**

For idleness in witnessing to Jesus Christ,
and for squandering the gifts of love and grace:
**Holy God, holy and mighty, holy and immortal,
have mercy on us.**

In the mercy of almighty God,
Jesus Christ was given to die for us,
and for his sake God forgives us all our sins.
Through the Holy Spirit God cleanses us
and gives us the power to proclaim
the mighty acts of the one who called us
out of darkness into his marvelous light.
As a called and ordained minister of the church of Christ,
and by his authority,
I therefore declare to you
the entire forgiveness of all your sins,
in the name of the Father, and of the + Son,
and of the Holy Spirit.
Amen.

Offering Prayer

God our provider,
you have not fed us with bread alone,
but with words of grace and life.
Bless us and these your gifts,
which we receive from your bounty,
through Jesus Christ our Lord.
Amen.

Invitation to Communion

All who thirst, all who hunger,
come and be filled with the goodness of God.

Prayer after Communion

O God, we thank you for gathering and feeding us
as a mother hen embraces her young.
Release us now to go on our way in these forty days,
ready to see our work as prayer,
ready to fast from complacency,
and ready to share with those in need;
through Jesus Christ, our Savior and Lord.
Amen.

Sending of Communion

Eternal God,
whose glory is revealed in the crucified and risen Lord,
bless those who go forth to share your word and sacrament
with our sisters and brothers
who are *sick/homebound/imprisoned.*
In your love and care, nourish and strengthen
those to whom we bring this communion
in the body and blood of your Son,
that we may all feast upon your abundant love
made known in Jesus Christ our Lord.
Amen.

Blessing

The blessing of God Almighty,
the wisdom and power of + Christ Jesus,
and the light of the Holy Spirit
be among you and remain with you always.
Amen.

Dismissal

Go in peace. Remember the poor.
Thanks be to God.

Seasonal Rites for Lent

Continuing in the Covenant of Baptism
A Midweek Plan for Lent

The focus for each week is a portion of the baptismal covenant from the order for Affirmation of Baptism (Evangelical Lutheran Worship, p. 236). Purchase enough pads of sticky notes so that each worshiper has several to write or draw on for each of the five weeks. Pens or pencils will need to be available for each worshiper as well.

The following weekly suggestions may be used within the service of Evening Prayer (ELW, pp. 309–319).

Opening (p. 310)

Behold, now is the accept- ˡ able time;
now is the day ˡ of salvation.
Turn us again, O God of ˡ our salvation,
that the light of your face may ˡ shine on us.
May your justice shine ˡ like the sun;
and may the poor be ˡ lifted up.

Hymn of Light (p. 310)

Thanksgiving for Light (pp. 310–311)

Midweek after the first Sunday in Lent

Focus: To live among God's faithful people
Psalmody: Psalm 133
Song: God is here! ELW 526
     or All Are Welcome ELW 641
Reading: Acts 2:37-47

Midweek after the second Sunday in Lent

Focus: To hear the word of God and share in the Lord's
     supper
Psalmody: Psalm 119:97-104
Song: Word of God, come down on earth ELW 510
     or What is this place ELW 524
Reading: Luke 24:28-32

Midweek after the third Sunday in Lent

Focus: To proclaim the good news of God in Christ
     through word and deed
Psalmody: Psalm 71:15-24

Song: Abide, O dearest Jesus ELW 539
     or O Zion, haste ELW 668
Reading: Luke 24:44-49

Midweek after the fourth Sunday in Lent

Focus: To serve all people, following the example of Jesus
Psalmody: Psalm 25:1-10
Song: The Son of God, our Christ ELW 584
     or Lord, whose love in humble service ELW 712
Reading: John 13:31-35

Midweek after the fifth Sunday in Lent

Focus: To strive for justice and peace in all the earth
Psalmody: Psalm 85
Song: Christ, Be Our Light ELW 715
     or Where cross the crowded ways of life ELW 719
Reading: Micah 6:6-8

Reflection: Guided Conversation

The leader may offer a few brief comments or homily related to the week's focus. Conclude the comments by asking worshipers what the week's focus looks like in each of their lives. Ask worshipers to reflect on this question silently for a period of time, then to write or draw short responses on sticky notes (and optionally to talk about their responses in groups of two or three people). Place the sticky notes on a large sheet of newsprint or poster board each week. If it is possible to leave the notes in place from one week to the next, then worshipers will have a broader sense of what it means to live in the covenant of baptism.

Scriptural Dialogue (p. 314)

Gospel Canticle (pp. 314–315)

Prayers (pp. 316–318)

A petition related to the earlier time of reflection may be added each week.

Lord's Prayer (p. 318)

Blessing (p. 319)

Midweek Lenten Series:
Open My Life, Lord
Planning Note

As the season of Lent begins, teach the youngest members of the congregation the action prayer used in Week 5. Encourage the children and their parents and caregivers to use the action prayer at home as part of their Lenten devotions.

Overview

Week of Lent 1: Open My Eyes, Lord
Paul saw the light of Christ shining around him on the road to Damascus. As individuals and communities, what do we have difficulty seeing? How does our perspective change when we view the world through the eyes of Christ?

Consider placing artwork or projecting images in the worship space that speak of transformation and new vision. Allow for an extended time during worship to view the artwork and reflect with opened eyes.

Week of Lent 2: Open My Hands, Lord
We use our hands to pick up a child, to serve a meal, to play an instrument, to wipe away a tear. Jesus used his hands for healing and for deeds of great power, and the psalmist reminds us that we are always held fast in God's hands. In Deuteronomy, Moses encourages us to open our hands in service to others.

Consider anointing the hands of the gathered community during worship.

Week of Lent 3: Open My Ears, Lord
Ancient Greek philosophy notes that we have two ears and one mouth so that we can listen twice as much as we speak. Jesus reminds us that we sometimes hear but don't listen, listen but don't understand. Opening our ears isn't as easy as it sounds.

Consider including an extended time of silence, listening, prayer, and meditation.

Week of Lent 4: Open My Heart, Lord
Listening to Paul's teaching, Lydia opened her heart to God and was baptized. Her willing, trusting faith echoes down through the centuries as we witness her "open heart procedure."

Responding with open eyes, hands, ears, and hearts, consider including an ingathering of items for those in need locally, regionally, nationally, or globally.

Week of Lent 5: Open My Life, Lord
Moses presents us with a choice: death and adversity, or a life cracked open to the love of God. Writing to the Galatians, Paul tells us that we have died to the law so that we might live to God. It is no longer we who live, but Christ who lives in us.

Consider inviting a member of the congregation to share one way in which God has opened his or her life. Conclude by bringing the children forward to lead the congregation in an action prayer:
Open my eyes, Lord. (*Point toward your eyes*)
Open my hands, Lord. (*Stretch out your hands*)
Open my ears, Lord. (*Point toward your ears*)
Open my heart, Lord. (*Place your hands over your heart*)
Open my life, Lord. (*Raise your arms up to God*)
Amen.

Opening Dialogue
Week 1
We look but do not see.
Lord, open our eyes.
We stumble at noon as in the twilight.
Lord, open our eyes.
God turns our darkness into light.
Lord, open our eyes.
We are not forsaken: look up and see!
Lord, open our eyes.
(Based on Isaiah 59:10; 42:16-18)

Week 2

Into your hands, almighty God, we place ourselves:
our minds to know you, our hearts to love you,
our wills to serve you, for we are yours.
Into your hands, incarnate Savior, we place ourselves:
receive us and draw us after you,
that we may follow your steps.
Into your hands, O hovering Spirit, we place ourselves:
take us and fashion us after your image;
let your comfort strengthen us and your fire cleanse us.
Into your hands, almighty God, we place ourselves:
gather us in your light eternal.
(Based on the commitment prayer, ELW, p. 86)

Week 3

As children, we hear:
Don't touch! Slow down!
As teenagers, we hear:
Your curfew begins in an hour.
As adults, we hear:
Cash or credit?
In the water and the word, we hear:
You are loved, my precious child.

Week 4

Open our hearts, Lord, to behold your laws.
Teach us to walk in your commandments.
Grant us grace to know and understand your will,
for all that we are in body and soul is a gift from you.
Lord, you are the everlasting Truth,
the one who speaks the words of eternal life.
Open our hearts, Lord, to behold your laws.
Teach us to walk in your commandments.
(Based on Thomas à Kempis, 1380–1471, The Imitation of Christ, trans. Richard Whitford, ca. 1530)

Week 5

When our lives are joyous and laughter abounds,
Christ is dwelling there.
When the news is grim and we have nowhere to turn,
Christ is dwelling there.
In the water and word, the bread and wine,
Christ is dwelling there.
In our life and our death, in the new life to come,
Christ is dwelling there.

Gathering Song

Week 1: Be thou my vision   ELW 793, WOV 776
Week 2: God, whose giving knows no ending   ELW 678
Week 3: Open now thy gates of beauty   ELW 533, LBW 250
Week 4: Lord, let my heart be good soil   ELW 512, LS 83,
   TFF 131, W&P 52, WOV 713
Week 5: Lord, Be Glorified   ELW 744, TFF 248, W&P 89

Greeting

The grace of our Lord Jesus Christ, the love of God,
and the communion of the Holy Spirit be with you all.
And also with you.

Prayer

Week 1

Open our eyes, Lord, to perceive your desire for the world. Remove those things that block our vision and widen our gaze to encompass all you would have us see. In Jesus' name we pray. **Amen.**

Week 2

Open our hands, Lord, to reach out to a world in need. May our arms enfold those who sorrow, our palms bear mercy and grace, and our fingers point to your love. In Jesus' name we pray. **Amen.**

Week 3

Open our ears, Lord, to heed your will for our lives. Help us not only to hear, but to listen and understand with our hearts. In Jesus' name we pray. **Amen.**

Week 4

Open our hearts, Lord, and fill us with your love. Grant us strength and courage, remove our hard-heartedness, and turn us always to you. In Jesus' name we pray. **Amen.**

Week 5

Open our lives, Lord, to reflect your glory. Lead us to the cross, to the grave, to the empty tomb, and into the world as imitators of Christ. In Jesus' name we pray. **Amen.**

Reading

Week 1: Isaiah 42:5-9
Week 2: Deuteronomy 15:7-11
Week 3: Isaiah 50:4-5
Week 4: 2 Corinthians 6:1-13
Week 5: Deuteronomy 30:15-20

Psalmody

Week 1: Psalm 119:17-24
Week 2: Psalm 139:1-10
Week 3: Psalm 40:1-8
Week 4: Psalm 28
Week 5: Psalm 16

Reading

Week 1: Acts 26:4-18
Week 2: Mark 6:1-5
Week 3: Matthew 13:10-17
Week 4: Acts 16:11-15
Week 5: Galatians 2:15-21

Reflection

Hymn of the Day

Week 1: Stay with us   WOV 743
Week 2: We raise our hands to you, O Lord   ELW 690
Week 3: Dearest Jesus, at your word   ELW 520, LBW 248
Week 4: Lift up your heads, ye mighty gates   HFW 717
Week 5: Take my life, that I may be   ELW 583/685,
    LBW 406

Optional

Week 1: Extended time to view and reflect on artwork
    placed or projected in the worship space
Week 2: Anointing of hands
Week 3: Extended time of silence, listening, prayer, and
    meditation
Week 4: Ingathering for those in need
Week 5: Brief testimonial from a congregational member
    and action prayer led by the children

Prayers

Lord of all life,
when we cannot see the beauty of your creation,
open our eyes, that all living things thrive and grow.
When we neglect the poor, the sick, and the grieving,
open our hands to do your work in the world.
When we ignore the cries of injustice in our midst,
open our ears, that all will know your love.
When we are hardened against our neighbor,
open our hearts and heal our resentment.
When we are closed to the grace you long to give us,
**open our lives and turn us to follow in the way of the
cross.**
Here other prayers may be offered.
Into your hands, gracious God, we commend all for whom
we pray, trusting in your mercy; through Jesus Christ, our
Savior.
Amen.

Lord's Prayer

Peace

Offering

Offering Prayer (*ELW*, p. 64, adapt.)
God of mercy and grace, the eyes of all wait upon you, and
you open your hand in blessing. Fill us with good things
that we may come to the help of all in need, through Jesus
Christ, our redeemer and Lord. **Amen.**

Blessing

Go into the world with eyes open to the transforming light
of Christ, hands open to serve those you meet, ears open to
the call of the Spirit, hearts open to the bountiful love of
God, and lives open to follow Christ to the cross.
The God who opened for us the way of everlasting life
✛ bless you now and forever.
Amen.

Sending Song

Week 1: Eternal Spirit of the living Christ   ELW 402,
    LBW 441
Week 2: The Lord now sends us forth   ELW 538, LLC 415

Week 3: Listen, God is calling   ELW 513, LS 79, TFF 130, WOV 712

Week 4: On my heart imprint your image   ELW 811, LBW 102

Week 5: That priceless grace   ELW 591, TFF 68

Dismissal

Go in peace. Christ is with you.
Thanks be to God.

Additional Assembly Songs

Week 1

God, whose almighty word   ELW 673, LBW 400
Amazing grace, how sweet the sound   ELW 779, LBW 448
O Lord, open my eyes   TFF 134
Open our eyes, Lord   LS 31, TFF 98, W&P 113

Week 2

In the singing   ELW 466
Here, O Lord, your servants gather   ELW 530
We Are an Offering   ELW 692, W&P 146
The people walk   ELW 706, LLC 520
Come to me, all pilgrims thirsty   ELW 777
Wide open are your hands   LBW 489

Week 3

God of our life, all-glorious Lord   LBW 270
May you look beyond seeing   ASG 22
You made every part of me   LS 115
Lord, my strength   W&P 93

Week 4

Fling wide the door   ELW 259, LBW 32
Great God, your love has called us   ELW 358, WOV 666
Joyous light of heavenly glory   ELW 561
O Christ, your heart, compassionate   ELW 722
Beloved, God's chosen   ELW 648, OBS 48
Change my heart, O God   ELW 801, W&P 28
We Are Called   ELW 720, LS 37, W&P 147
Song Over the Waters   W&P 127
O God beyond all praising   ELW 880, WOV 797

Week 5

When we are living   ELW 639, LLC 462
Yours, Lord, is the glory (sts. 1-3)   ELW 849, LLC 605
Come, my way, my truth, my life   ELW 816, LBW 513
God, here is my life and my will   BOL 6
Father, I adore you   W&P 37
Christ is the life   OBS 52
King of my life   TFF 86

Music for the Series

Choral

Althouse, Jay L. "Lord, I Stretch My Hands to You." SATB, pno, opt 3-5 oct hb acc, HOP PP131. SAB, HOP PP140. 2 pt trbl/mxd, HOP C5277. TTBB, HOP C5704.

p Garber, Aaron. "On My Heart Imprint Your Image." SATB, pno, vln. AFP 9780800621513.

Hayes, Mark. "Open the Eyes of My Heart with Be Thou My Vision." SATB, pno, opt perc. Monarch Music LO.10-3449M.

p Hobby, Robert. "Lord, Let Us Listen." U, kybd. AFP 9780800659233.

Miller, Aaron David. "A Heart of Grace." SATB, pno. MSM 50-8545.

Moore, Bob. "Christ, the Way of Life." SATB. GIA G-4942.

Scott, K. Lee. "Open My Eyes." SATB, kybd. CPH 982904PODWEB.

p Sedio, Mark. "Take My Life, That I May Be: Toma, oh Dios, mi voluntad." SATB, pno, fl. AFP 9780800658298.

Young, Philip M. "Open Our Hearts, Lord." SATB, org. MSM 50-6022.

Children's Choir

Landis, Priscilla Lamparter. "Loving Hands of Jesus" from ChildrenSing in Worship, vol. 1. U, kybd. AFP 9781451401806.

Page, Sue Ellen. "Jesus' Hands Were Kind Hands." U, fl, kybd. CG CGA485.

p Patterson, Mark. "I Will Give My Heart to the Lord" from Young ChildrenSing. U, kybd, opt orff, opt ch. AFP 9780800676803.

Keyboard / Instrumental

Ashdown, Franklin D. "Slane" from Augsburg Organ Library: Lent. Org. AFP 9780800658977.

p Lasky, David. "That Priceless Grace" from That Priceless Grace: Lenten Hymn Settings. Org. AFP 9781451479577.

Organ, Anne Krentz. "Give Thanks/Lord, Be Glorified" from Come to Us, Creative Spirit: Piano Reflections. Pno. AFP 9780800659042.

Smith, Douglas. "Jesus' Hands Were Kind Hands." 2 fl, 2 cl. David E. Smith Publications 130412.

Handbell

Cota, Patricia. "Purify My Heart." 3-5 oct hb, L2. Ring Praise Publications MRP7507.

Eithun, Sandra. "Open My Eyes That I May See." 3-5 oct hb, L3. SF 279083.

McChesney, Kevin. "Come, My Way, My Truth, My Life." 2-3 oct hb, L2. LOR MLC201554L.

Rogers, Sharon Elery. "Bind Us Together/Open Our Eyes, Lord." 2-3 oct hb, L2. HOP 2254.

p = available in Prelude Music Planner

February 10, 2016
Ash Wednesday

Lent begins with a solemn call to fasting and repentance as we begin our journey to the baptismal waters of Easter. As we hear in today's readings, now is the acceptable time to return to the Lord. During Lent the people of God will reflect on the meaning of their baptism into Christ's death and resurrection. The sign of ashes suggests our human mortality and frailty. What seems like an ending is really an invitation to make each day a new beginning, in which we are washed in God's mercy and forgiveness. With the cross on our brow, we long for the spiritual renewal that flows from the springtime Easter feast to come.

Prayer of the Day

Almighty and ever-living God, you hate nothing you have made, and you forgive the sins of all who are penitent. Create in us new and honest hearts, so that, truly repenting of our sins, we may receive from you, the God of all mercy, full pardon and forgiveness through your Son, Jesus Christ, our Savior and Lord, who lives and reigns with you and the Holy Spirit, one God, now and forever.

or

Gracious God, out of your love and mercy you breathed into dust the breath of life, creating us to serve you and our neighbors. Call forth our prayers and acts of kindness, and strengthen us to face our mortality with confidence in the mercy of your Son, Jesus Christ, our Savior and Lord, who lives and reigns with you and the Holy Spirit, one God, now and forever.

Gospel Acclamation

Return to the ¹ Lord, your God,* who is gracious and merciful, slow to anger, and abounding in ¹ steadfast love. (Joel 2:13)

Readings and Psalm
Joel 2:1-2, 12-17

Because of the coming Day of the Lord, the prophet Joel calls the people to a community lament. The repentant community reminds God of his gracious character and asks God to spare the people, lest the nations doubt God's power to save.

or Isaiah 58:1-12

Shortly after the return of Israel from exile in Babylon, the people were troubled by the ineffectiveness of their fasts. God reminds them that outward observance is no substitute for genuine fasting that results in acts of justice, such as feeding the hungry, sheltering the homeless, and clothing the naked. Sincere repentance will lead to a dramatic improvement of their condition.

Psalm 51:1-17

Have mercy on me, O God, according to your steadfast love. (Ps. 51:1)

2 Corinthians 5:20b—6:10

The ministry of the gospel endures many challenges and hardships. Through this ministry, God's reconciling activity in the death of Christ reaches into the depths of our lives to bring us into a right relationship with God. In this way, God accepts us into the reality of divine salvation.

Matthew 6:1-6, 16-21

In the Sermon on the Mount, Jesus commends almsgiving, prayer, and fasting, but emphasizes that spiritual devotion must not be done for show.

Preface Lent

Color Purple

Prayers of Intercession

The prayers are prepared locally for each occasion. The following examples may be adapted or used as appropriate.

Hearing the call to return to the Lord, let us join the whole people of God in prayer for all who cry out in pain and in hope.

A brief silence.

Merciful Lord, where people ask, "Where is their God?" send your church. Equip us with compassion and boldness to listen to our neighbors. Make our speech and actions witness to your eternal presence. Hear us, O God.

Your mercy is great.

Merciful Lord, where the soil cries for rain, send relief. Restore depleted water tables and cleanse waterways around the world. Teach us to treasure all creation as you do. Hear us, O God.

Your mercy is great.

Merciful Lord, where terror shouts, send peace. Deliver all from the threat of bloodshed and the trauma of violence. Reconcile nation with nation and neighbor with neighbor. Wash us in your peace. Hear us, O God.
Your mercy is great.
Merciful Lord, where bellies rumble, send food. Bless Lutheran World Relief and all who work to ensure no one goes to bed hungry. Provide for all who suffer in body, mind, or spirit (*especially*). Hear us, O God.
Your mercy is great.
Merciful Lord, when hearts and minds call for you, send faithful disciples. Walk with all who prepare for baptism. Uphold them with a community rooted in your word and nourished by bread and wine. Hear us, O God.
Your mercy is great.
Here other intercessions may be offered.
Merciful Lord, where death stings, send comfort. Be with all who mourn. In the midst of their sorrow and pain, sustain their trust in the eternal life you give. Hear us, O God.
Your mercy is great.
To you, gracious God, we commend all for whom we pray, trusting in your boundless mercy; through Jesus Christ, our Savior.
Amen.

Images in the Readings

Although cited only in the reading from Isaiah 58, **ashes** are the primary image for the day. Since the eleventh century, the ashes, made by burning last year's palms, cycle around from the triumphant celebration of Jesus' entry into Jerusalem to the humiliation of sinners covering their heads with the burnt greens. Ashes also bring to mind the fire of the Easter Vigil. Honesty is always good, if sometimes painful: this day we are honest about sin and death. The ash cross marks one's forehead as if it is the brand of one's owner. We journey forward wearing the sign of the cross.

The gospel reading is the source for the three **disciplines of Lent** that have proved useful for many of Christ's disciples. To increase one's giving to the poor, to increase one's attention to prayer, and to decrease one's focus on the self: the idea is that such disciplines open up the self to God and to the neighbor.

The **acceptable time**, the day of salvation, are ways Paul describes the here and now of the life of the baptized. Ash Wednesday calls us each day into life in Christ.

Several beloved hymns call Christ our **treasure**. The treasure described by both Matthew and Paul—"poor, yet making many rich"—is the countercultural value of the baptized life.

Ideas for the Day

◆   Even as requirements to turn off electronic devices during takeoff and landing are eased, "airplane mode" is still a powerful symbol about the value of focusing during moments of transition. Lent is the ancient version of airplane mode. In today's gospel, Jesus invites us into conversation with God through prayer and scripture, that we may pay attention to well-worn advice about breathing and staying afloat even in an emergency. He calls us to fasting, that we may stow away any extra baggage we are carrying around. He challenges us to give alms, that we may provide for those in need and, in gratitude, become aware of the gifts right out our window.

◆   "This is the only place I can breathe," said Isabel, who migrated to the United States more than twenty years ago. "Church is the one place where I am defined as a child of God, and not by the fact that I crossed a border without papers." Capturing our Lenten longing to be cleansed from sin, rid of its stain, freed from its power over us, the psalmist pleads: "blot out . . . wash . . . cleanse . . . purge me" (Ps. 51:1, 2, 7). He asks to be forgiven so that he might be able to rejoice once more and be freed to "do good to Zion." That's what Isabel longs for—the opportunity to be freed from the defining guilt of a difficult decision to migrate illegally made more than twenty years ago. How might Ash Wednesday's proclamation shape our engagement with the way we deal with those who have transgressed?

◆   In *Toy Story 2* (Pixar, 1999), Woody is stolen by a toy collector who plans to sell him to a museum in Japan. Disheartened that his owner, Andy, is growing up and will soon forget about him, Woody refuses to go with his friends when they attempt to rescue him. In a scene that captures the power of music, ritual, and naming, Woody recovers his courage when he sees the indelible mark Andy made on his boot years earlier (www.youtube.com/watch?v=uiPNEL9ealA). How will our Lenten journey be shaped by the retracing with ashes of God's mark and the claim on us at baptism?

Connections with the Liturgy

Ash Wednesday is an intensification of our regular rite of confession and forgiveness, a rare time in our culture during which we acknowledge our sin and beg for renewal. The Kyrie also recalls Ash Wednesday: "Lord, have mercy, Lord, have mercy," over and over. At communion we sing, "Lamb of God, you take away the sin of the world. Have mercy on us." There is always more and more need for mercy.

Let the Children Come

Prayer is one of the three traditional Lenten disciplines (the others are fasting and works of love). Lead children (and adult children of God) in experiencing two traditional prayer postures: kneeling and *orans* (Latin for "prayer"). The latter posture is done standing up with arms outstretched, hands open and cupped, and is viewed as openness to God and the gathering of the assembly into prayer. Ask children to describe the differences they experience between the two postures. How could either posture be used to "show off"? How could either be used genuinely in prayer?

Assembly Song and Music for the Day

Because of the nature of this day, music suggestions are listed by place in the service and categorized by type of leadership (in brackets): Ch=Choral; CC=Children's Choir; KI=Keyboard/Instrumental; HB=Handbell. Many suggestions require assembly participation.

Gathering

Psalm 51 (see Psalmody and Acclamations)
Kyrie   ELW 151–158 or from communion settings
Our Father, we have wandered   ELW 606, WOV 733
✧ Rundman, Jonathan. "Texas Kyrie" from *A Heartland Liturgy*. jonathanrundman.bandcamp.com.

Psalmody and Acclamations

Cherwien, David. "Psalm 51:1-17," Refrain 2, from PSCY.
p Raabe, Nancy. "Have Mercy on Me, O God (Psalm 51:1-17)." MSB1 S402.
Schalk, Carl, or May Schwarz. "Psalm 51:1-17" from PWC.
⊕ Grullón, Rafael. "Ten piedad de mí/Lord, Have Mercy on Me" from *Psalms for All Seasons: A Compete Psalter for Worship*. SATB. Brazos Press 9781592554447.
✧ Bruxvoort Colligan, Richard. "Wash Me Clean (Psalm 51)" from *Sharing the Road*. AFP 9780800678630. psalmimmersion.bandcamp.com.
✧ Bruxvoort Colligan, Richard. "O Tender God, Have Mercy (Psalm 51)" from *Worldmaking*. worldmaking.net.
p Schram, Ruth Elaine. "Psalm 51: Brighter Than Snow." U/2 pt, pno. AFP 9781451484069. [Ch]
p (GA) Organ, Anne Krentz. "Return to the Lord." MSB1 S419.

Hymn of the Day

Savior, when in dust to you   ELW 601, LBW 91   ABERYSTWYTH
Eternal Lord of love, behold your church   ELW 321   OLD 124TH
Restore in us, O God   ELW 328   BAYLOR   WOV 662   CATECHUMEN
p ● Shaw, Timothy. "Old 124th" from *Introductions and Alternate Accompaniments for Piano*, vol. 2. Org. AFP 9780800623606. [KI]

Confession of Sin

Music Sourcebook for Lent and the Three Days (MSB1) includes four musical settings of texts for corporate confession of sin, one using the text in the Ash Wednesday service (S408) and others using the text from Corporate Confession and Forgiveness, Evangelical Lutheran Worship Leaders Edition, p. 603 (S409–S411).

Imposition of Ashes

Lord Jesus, think on me   ELW 599, LBW 309
Out of the depths I cry to you   ELW 600, LBW 295
✧ DeConto, Jesse James. "Sins of the Fathers" from *A Beautiful World*. pinkertonraid.bandcamp.com.
Byrd, William. "Ne irascaris Domine" (Do not be angry beyond measure, O Lord). SATTB. CPDL. [Ch]
Messick, Pat. "Treasures in Heaven." U/2 pt, pno. CG CGA1252. [CC]
● Bliem, William. "Aberystwyth" from *Piano Plus Through the Year*, vol. 2. Pno, inst. AFP 9780800663728. [KI]
p Bettcher, Peggy. "The Power of the Cross." 2-3 oct, L3-, HOP 2629. 3-5 oct, L3-, HOP 2513. [HB]

Setting the Table

Music Sourcebook for Lent and the Three Days (MSB1) includes an appendix with hymn stanzas appropriate for use during the setting of the table on this and other days. These stanzas are also included on the CD-ROM that accompanies the volume.

✧ Tangled Blue. "Thankful and Broken" from *Storm Home: A Collection of Music from Humble Walk Artists-in-Residence*. humblewalk.bandcamp.com.
p Cool, Jane Southwick. "O Lord, I Call to You." SAB, pno, opt assembly. AFP 9781451479423. [Ch]
p Hurlbutt, Patricia. "At the Cross." 2 pt mxd, solo. AFP 9781451479317. [CC]
● Near, Gerald. "Aberystwyth" from *Augsburg Organ Library: Lent*. Org. AFP 9780800658977. [KI]
p ● Ingram, Bill. "Draw Near and Take the Body of the Lord (Old 124th)" from *Communion Hymns for Handbells*. 2-3 oct, L1+. CPH 97-7136. [HB]

Communion

Once we sang and danced   ELW 701
You, dear Lord   ELW 702, LLC 429
Softly and tenderly Jesus is calling   ELW 608, TFF 155, WOV 734
⊕ Jortack, Victor. "Cordero de Dios/Lamb of God" U. *ELW*, p. 182.
✧ Rimbo, Justin. "When It Seems the Day Will End" from *Storm Home: A Collection of Music from Humble Walk Artists-in-Residence*. humblewalk.bandcamp.com.

- Schultz, Ralph. "Create in Me." SATB, org. MSM 50-30340. [Ch]
  Reeves, Jeff. "Create in Me a Clean Heart." U/2 pt, pno. CG CGA879.
  [CC]
- Organ, Anne Krentz. "Aberystwyth" from *Christ, Mighty Savior.*
  Pno. AFP 9780800656805. [KI]
- Morris, Hart. "Jesus, Lover of My Soul." 5 oct, fl or ob, L3+. BP
  HB90. [HB]

Sending

Bless now, O God, the journey ELW 326
Through the night of doubt and sorrow ELW 327, LBW 355

February 14, 2016
First Sunday in Lent

These forty days called Lent are like no other. It is our opportune time to return to the God who rescues; to receive the gifts of God's grace; to believe with the heart and confess with the mouth the wonder of God's love in Jesus; and to resist temptation at every turn. This is no small pilgrimage on which we have just embarked. It is a struggle Jesus knew. It is a struggle Jesus shares. The nearness of the Lord, in bread and wine, water and word, will uphold and sustain us.

Prayer of the Day

O Lord God, you led your people through the wilderness and brought them to the promised land. Guide us now, so that, following your Son, we may walk safely through the wilderness of this world toward the life you alone can give, through Jesus Christ, our Savior and Lord, who lives and reigns with you and the Holy Spirit, one God, now and forever.

Gospel Acclamation

One does not live by ' bread alone,* but by every word that comes from the ' mouth of God. (Matt. 4:4)

Readings and Psalm
Deuteronomy 26:1-11

The annual harvest festival, called the Feast of Weeks, provides the setting for this reading. This festival celebrates the first fruits of the produce of the land offered back to God in thanks. In this text, worshipers announce God's gracious acts on behalf of Israel.

Psalm 91:1-2, 9-16

God will give the angels charge over you, to guard you in all your ways. (Ps. 91:11)

Romans 10:8b-13

Paul reminds the Christians at Rome of the foundation of their creed, the confession of faith in the risen Christ as Lord.

Luke 4:1-13

After being filled with the Holy Spirit at his baptism, Jesus is led in the wilderness. Through his responses to the temptations of the devil he defines what it means to be called "the Son of God."

Preface Lent

Color Purple

Prayers of Intercession

The prayers are prepared locally for each occasion. The following examples may be adapted or used as appropriate.

Hearing the call to return to the Lord, let us join the whole people of God in prayer for all who cry out in pain and in hope.

A brief silence.

Break down and mend divisions within your church, Holy One. Bring together rich and poor, homeless and housed, and those who hold differing political views as the one body of Christ. Unite us in worship of you. Lord, in your mercy,
hear our prayer.

Sustain citrus groves and orchards, divine Gardener. Provide rich soil and water in due season for an abundant harvest. Help us share the fruit of your harvest with all people. Lord, in your mercy,
hear our prayer.

Raise up peacemakers, almighty God. In nations ravaged by war, pour out your Spirit of wisdom on their leaders. Equip

them to respond with your mercy and justice. Make peace flourish in all the world (*especially*). Lord, in your mercy,
hear our prayer.

Protect all who flee oppression, eternal Father. Grant refuge on their journey. Provide shelter as there is need. Turn the hearts of those who oppress. Lord, in your mercy,
hear our prayer.

Teach us to love as you love, gracious Lord. Open us to encounter our enemies as our neighbors. Give us courage to trust in your redeeming love and proclaim your gospel to all people. Lord, in your mercy,
hear our prayer.

Here other intercessions may be offered.

Show all people your salvation, Alpha and Omega. Bring us to eternal joy with all the saints who have gone before us (*especially the missionaries Cyril and Methodius*). Lord, in your mercy,
hear our prayer.

To you, gracious God, we commend all for whom we pray, trusting in your boundless mercy; through Jesus Christ, our Savior.
Amen.

Images in the Readings

Luke writes that Jesus was tested for **forty days and forty nights**. In the Bible, forty is always the time between, the necessary span before the gracious conclusion. It is forty, days or years, that numbers the rain of Noah's flood; Moses on Mount Sinai; Israel in the wilderness; the spies scouting out Canaan; Israel in the hands of the Philistines; Goliath's taunting; the reigns of Saul, David, and Solomon; Elijah going to Mount Horeb; Ezekiel lying on his right side; Nineveh's repentance; and Jesus' appearance after Easter. For us, it is forty days until the resurrection—since the church does not count Sundays as time in the wilderness.

The gospel reading describes the **devil** as the tempter, the power that seeks to lure us away from God by throwing obstacles in our paths. The tradition of art has not given us profound enough depictions of this primordial evil, but the devil is the opposite reality of the angels, who protect the faithful. Jews developed a belief in the devil as the source of evil from their contact with especially the Zoroastrians, for whom the powers of good and of evil were in perpetual conflict. For Jews and Christians, evil is never an equal power to God.

The idea of presenting **first fruits** in gratitude to God develops over Israelite history into an obligation that supports the temple priests. A parallel in Canaanite practice was to offer one's firstborn child to the deities. Many Christians continue to speak of their monetary offerings as first fruits, for some the first 10 percent of one's earnings. Lent has traditionally been a time to encourage almsgiving, since

Christians recognize that giving to the needy is how the faithful give to God.

Ideas for the Day

◆ The account of Jesus' temptation is familiar, yet it can seem quite distant. Few of us identify with a nagging desire to turn stones into bread. The words of scripture roll so easily off Jesus' tongue that we feel he is more able than we are to just say no. What might be some ways to help listeners feel the tension and excitement in this story? Staying a bit longer with each temptation, as if we don't know how Jesus might respond, can help avoid the sense that Jesus is simply making clear choices between good and evil.

◆ In the prologue to his controversial novel, *The Last Temptation of Christ*, author Nikos Kazantzakis says, "This book was written because I wanted to offer a supreme model to the [one] who struggles" ([New York: Touchstone, 1998], 4). Many reacted negatively to Kazantzakis's novel, and decades later to the film adaptation by Martin Scorsese. Yet the last verse in our gospel reading leaves the door open for Kazantzakis's approach to this story: "When the devil had finished every test, he departed from him until an opportune time" (Luke 4:13). The temptations out in the desert were just the beginning. Jesus wasn't done, any more than a smoker is done with cigarettes after he or she has managed to go one day without lighting up. His temptations, like ours, were not so clear-cut.

◆ Jesus was famished when the devil proposed he turn stones into bread (Luke 4:2). To eat when hungry is hardly a clear choice between good and evil. Real temptation is to eat when hungry, to drink when thirsty, to desire power over others, to go out on a limb and hope God will protect us. These are not easy choices between good and evil, rather between doing what comes naturally and what we really ought to do. Temptation is the desire to do the kind of stuff nobody could blame you for doing: exercise power when we are in authority over others, pride when we have accomplished something great, rudeness to the poor, impatience with the elderly, reluctance in giving. Our temptation is to give in to being less than we are called to be, less bold, less gracious, less passionate and compassionate, less than children of God.

Connections with the Liturgy

In the Lord's Prayer, we recall the testing of Jesus when we pray that God "save us from the time of trial." We pray to be saved from tests that we will fail.

Let the Children Come

What is different in worship today? What tells us "It's Lent"? The color, pared down liturgy, no alleluias, a simplified worship space? Prepare children for these changes and then ask them what they notice today. Purple is the color of royalty. Jesus is a king who reigns from the cross. Ask the children how the color makes them feel. Where do the colors go when they are not in the worship space? Plan a time during Lent for the children to visit the sacristy with members of the altar guild so they can see where the things we use in worship are cared for.

Assembly Song
Gathering

Bless now, O God, the journey ELW 326
The glory of these forty days ELW 320, WOV 657
Lord of our life ELW 766, LBW 366

Psalmody and Acclamations

Gelineau, Joseph. "Psalm 91" from ACYG.
Haugen, Marty. "Two Simple Songs of Hope." Choir or 2 cant, assembly, kybd, gtr. GIA G-6935.
Shute, Linda Cable. "Psalm 91," Refrain 2, from PSCY.
p (GA) Organ, Anne Krentz. "Return to the Lord." MSB1 S419.

Hymn of the Day

O Lord, throughout these forty days ELW 319 *CONSOLATION*
    LBW 99 *CAITHNESS*
I want Jesus to walk with me ELW 325, TFF 66, WOV 660
    SOJOURNER
Abide with me ELW 629, LBW 272 *EVENTIDE*

Offering

God, whose giving knows no ending ELW 678, LBW 408
We give thee but thine own ELW 686, LBW 140

Communion

As the sun with longer journey ELW 329, WOV 655
Lord Jesus, you shall be my song ELW 808
How sweet the name of Jesus sounds ELW 620, LBW 345

Sending

Guide me ever, great Redeemer ELW 618, LBW 343
Lord, dismiss us with your blessing ELW 545, LBW 259

Additional Assembly Songs

Satan, we're going to tear your kingdom down TFF 207
Yield not to temptation TFF 195
Estos cuarenta días hoy LLC 323
☻ Cassina, Miguel. "I Depend upon Your Faithfulness/Tu fidelidad" from *Glory to God*. U. WJK 9780664238971.
☻ Shona traditional. "Rakanaka Vhangeri/Come and Hear Now the Gospel" from *Agape: Songs of Hope and Reconciliation*. SATB. Lutheran World Federation. Out of print. Available on Amazon.com.

☼ Dakota Road. "Take Up Your Cross" from *Dakota Road Music Anthology*. dakotaroadmusic.com.
☼ Hansen, Holly. "Song of Praise" from *Resonance Mass*. nemercy.org/resonance.
☼ Houge, Nate. "Be with Us Now" from *Storm Home: A Collection of Music from Humble Walk Artists-in-Residence*. humblewalk.bandcamp.com.
☼ Kurtz, Rachel. "Come Ye Sinners" from *Come All Ye Sinners*. rachelkurtz.org.
☼ Larkin, Kenneth. "I'm Going on a Journey." ELW 446
☼ Rundman, Jonathan. "Texas Kyrie" from A *Heartland Liturgy*. jonathanrundman.bandcamp.com.

Music for the Day
Choral

p ● Cornish, John. "Abide with Me." SATB, pno. AFP 9781451451528.
p Hanson, Brian. "The Very Thought of Thee." SATB, pno. CG 1375.
● Scott, K. Lee. "Who at My Door Is Standing?" 2 pt mxd, kybd. HIN HMC-728.
p ● Trinkley, Bruce. "I Want Jesus to Walk with Me" from *Augsburg Choirbook for Men*. TB, pno. AFP 9780800676834.

Children's Choir

p ● Miller, Aaron David. "I Want Jesus to Walk with Me" from *ChildrenSing in Worship*, vol. 3. U/opt desc, pno. AFP 9781451476552.
Nagy, Russell. "'Someone' Song." U, opt desc, kybd, opt hb/C inst. BP JH505.
p Patterson, Mark. "Guide Us, Lord." U/2 pt, pno, opt vla. CG CGA1357.

Keyboard / Instrumental

● Frahm, Frederick. "Consolation" from *Faith Alive*, vol. 2. Org. AFP 9780800678788.
● Glick, Sara. "Sojourner" from *Piano Arrangements for Worship: Lent/Easter*. Pno. AFP 9780800658809.
● Peterson, Lynn. "Eventide" from *Augsburg Organ Library: Healing and Funeral*. Org. AFP 9781451462616.
● Shehi, Christina. "Eventide" from *Piano Plus Through the Year*, vol. 2. Pno, inst. AFP 9780800663728.

Handbell

p ● Moklebust, Cathy. "Abide with Me." 3-5 oct hb, opt 3-6 oct hc, opt fl, L2+. CG CGB777.
p ● Waldrop, Tammy. "I Want Jesus to Walk with Me." 3-6 oct hb, opt 2 oct hc, L2+. HOP 2635.
Whitehill, Erik. "There Is a Balm in Gilead." 3-5 oct, L2. AGEHR AG35324.

☻ = global song   ☼ = praise song
● = relates to hymn of the day   p = available in Prelude Music Planner

Sunday, February 14

Cyril, monk, died 869; Methodius, bishop, died 885; missionaries to the Slavs

These two brothers from a noble family in Thessalonika in northeastern Greece were priests and missionaries. After some early initial missionary work by Cyril among the Arabs, the brothers retired to a monastery. They were later sent to work among the Slavs, the missionary work for which they are most known. Since Slavonic had no written form at the time, the brothers established a written language with the Greek alphabet as its basis. They translated the scriptures and the liturgy using this Cyrillic alphabet. The Czechs, Serbs, Croats, Slovaks, and Bulgars regard the brothers as the founders of Slavic literature. The brothers' work in preaching and worshiping in the language of the people are honored by Christians in both East and West.

Thursday, February 18

Martin Luther, renewer of the church, died 1546

On this day in 1546, Martin Luther died at the age of sixty-two. For a time, he was an Augustinian monk, but it is his work as a biblical scholar, translator of the Bible, public confessor of the faith, reformer of the liturgy, theologian, educator, and father of German vernacular literature that holds him in our remembrance. In Luther's own judgment, the greatest of all of his works was his catechism, written to instruct people in the basics of faith. And it was his baptism that sustained him in his trials as a reformer.

February 21, 2016
Second Sunday in Lent

Though we sometimes doubt and often resist God's desire to protect and save us, our God persists. In holy baptism, God's people have been called and gathered into a God-initiated relationship that will endure. Lent provides the church with a time and a tradition in which to seek the face of the Lord again. Lent provides another occasion to behold the God of our salvation in the face of the Blessed One who "comes in the name of the Lord."

Prayer of the Day

God of the covenant, in the mystery of the cross you promise everlasting life to the world. Gather all peoples into your arms, and shelter us with your mercy, that we may rejoice in the life we share in your Son, Jesus Christ, our Savior and Lord, who lives and reigns with you and the Holy Spirit, one God, now and forever.

Gospel Acclamation

The Son of Man must be ¹ lifted up,* that whoever believes in him may have e- ¹ ternal life. (John 3:14-15)

Readings and Psalm
Genesis 15:1-12, 17-18

God promises a childless and doubting Abram that he will have a son, that his descendants will be as numerous as the stars, and that the land of Canaan will be their inheritance. Abram's trust in God is sealed with a covenant-making ceremony, a sign of God's promise.

Psalm 27

In the day of trouble, God will give me shelter. (Ps. 27:5)

Philippians 3:17—4:1

Although Paul's devotion to Christ has caused him to be persecuted, he does not regret the course he has taken. Writing from prison, he expresses confidence in a glorious future and encourages other Christians to follow in his footsteps.

Luke 13:31-35

Neither Herod's plotting nor Jerusalem's resistance to maternal love will deter Jesus from his sacrificial mission.

Preface   Lent

Color   Purple

Prayers of Intercession

The prayers are prepared locally for each occasion. The following examples may be adapted or used as appropriate.

Hearing the call to return to the Lord, let us join the whole people of God in prayer for all who cry out in pain and in hope.

A brief silence.

For an end to killings because of faith, we turn to you, O Lord. Protect all those who risk their lives each time they worship you. Give new vision to the intolerant. Hear us, O God.

Your mercy is great.

For the beauty of the stars, we turn to you in thanksgiving, O Lord. By their vast number and light, remind us of your covenant with Abram and deep love for all creation. Hear us, O God.

Your mercy is great.

For peace and justice in our neighborhoods, we turn to you, O Lord. Where gangs, domestic violence, or kidnappings cause your children to live in fear, give courage and wisdom to those in authority. Hear us, O God.

Your mercy is great.

For older adults with no family to care for them, we turn to you, O Lord. Surround them with social workers, medical professionals, and neighbors to support them. Embrace them with compassion and quell any fear. Hear us, O God.

Your mercy is great.

For the sick in our congregation and our community, we turn to you, O Lord. Gather all who live with illness under your wings (*especially*). Make us instruments of your healing. Hear us, O God.

Your mercy is great.

Here other intercessions may be offered.

For the prophets and all the faithful departed, we turn to you in thanks, O Lord. Empowered by their witness, may we stand firm in you until the day we see you face-to-face. Hear us, O God.

Your mercy is great.

To you, gracious God, we commend all for whom we pray, trusting in your boundless mercy; through Jesus Christ, our Savior.

Amen.

Images in the Readings

There are lots of animals in this Sunday's readings. Like other evils that lurk around, a **fox** is a clever predator that lives off the death of the unsuspecting meek. The young of **chickens** are notoriously weak, and the mother **hen** protects them under her wings. Many Old Testament poetic passages speak of God as having outstretched wings. Now in the Louvre in Paris is the 1562 painting by Frans Floris, *Allegory of the Trinity,* in which God the Father and

the dove of the Spirit attend Christ, whose arms extended on the cross are superimposed on immense wings, under which all the faithful are gathered. You can find a photo of this most interesting painting on the internet. Israel, like its pagan neighbors, conducted **animal sacrifices** in which the life of the valuable animal symbolized the devotion of the worshiper. This practice of animal sacrifice is recalled when Christians compare Christ to a lamb.

God is present to Abram as a flaming torch. From the burning bush of Moses to the tongues "as of fire" on the forehead of each believer, **fire** functions in the Bible as a symbol of the power of God. Fire not only burns refuse away but also occasions human community: gathering around the fire, we share heat and light, and we cook food to eat together.

A Roman **citizen** was a freeborn male who enjoyed numerous legal rights: the right to vote, to sue, to appeal a trial verdict, to function as paterfamilias. A Roman citizen could not be tortured or whipped, nor executed by crucifixion. These and many other rights meant that Roman citizenship was a coveted privilege. Paul uses the imagery of citizenship when describing the benefits of faith.

Ideas for the Day

◆ Jesus' desire to gather God's people together in safety, love, and protection is reflected in the feminine image of a hen gathering her chicks under her wing. This motherly, passionate desire—rather than the resistance we or others may show toward it—lies at the heart of the gospel message in this text. Even today, feminine images for God are not common in Christian worship. Consider ways to use this expression of divine, motherly care in liturgy, prayers, and preaching, and how it might expand or heal some individuals' understanding of God's love.

◆ Thanksgiving at the Table V from *Evangelical Lutheran Worship* includes these lines: "In great love you sent to us Jesus, your Son, who reached out to heal the sick and suffering, who preached good news to the poor, and who, on the cross, opened his arms to all" (p. 65). The image of Jesus opening his arms on the cross as a welcome to all expresses beautifully the image of the hen gathering her flock under her wings. Simply using this prayer could help the assembly make connections from the gospel reading to the cross to the eucharist.

◆ Abram questions God when the promise of an heir is not fulfilled according to Abram's time frame. God shows Abram the stars of the night sky to help him see and trust the promise will come true. At times, the Milky Way and a night full of stars can feel like the arms of God wrapping around us and holding us in love. Reminding the assembly to look at the stars tonight and remember they are held and loved could give a meaningful Sunday evening ritual to do at home.

◆   In many communities, light pollution prevents people from seeing stars at night. Some cities are changing laws to minimize lights that ruin the night sky. What might be "light pollution" for our lives of faith that keeps us from seeing and trusting God's love and care for us? Invite the assembly to think of what blocks out their ability to trust God's promises in faith, and explore how to "turn off" whatever spoils our trust in God.

Connections with the Liturgy

Luke cites Psalm 118:26 in his hidden reference to the passion of Christ. Each Sunday when we sing the "Holy, holy, holy," we sing these words as we attend the bread and wine. Here on the altar, in our hands and mouths, is the body of the one who bears the divine name of God.

Let the Children Come

Jesus' comparing himself to a mother hen is a beautiful image. Have the children ever seen a mother hen with her chicks? How does she protect them? Invite a farmer in the congregation to tell the children about how mother hens protect their chicks, or invite some parents to talk about what it means to them to protect their own children. Then ask, "How does God shelter us from harm?" Send home this bedtime prayer: "Dear Jesus, as a hen covers her chicks with her wings to keep them safe, protect us this night under your golden wings; for your mercy's sake. Amen" (*ELW*, p. 86).

Assembly Song
Gathering

Lord Christ, when first you came to earth   ELW 727, LBW 421
The God of Abraham praise   ELW 831, LBW 544
Shout to the Lord   ELW 821, W&P 124

Psalmody and Acclamations

Behnke, John A. "The Lord Is My Light and My Salvation." SAB, assembly, kybd, opt 2-3 oct hb. CG CGA981.
Burkhardt, Michael. "Psalm 27" from *Psalms for the Church Year*. U, org. MSM 80-708.
Forman, Bruce. "Hear Me, O Lord." SATB, cant, assembly, kybd, opt gtr. CG CGA578.
p   (GA) Organ, Anne Krentz. "Return to the Lord." MSB1 S419.

Hymn of the Day

Lord, thee I love with all my heart   ELW 750, LBW 325   *HERZLICH LIEB*
The numberless gifts of God's mercies   ELW 683   *JAG KAN ICKE RÄNKA DEM ALLA*
Mothering God, you gave me birth   ELW 735, WOV 769   *NORWICH*

Offering

Be thou my vision   ELW 793, sts. 1, 3; WOV 776, sts. 1, 3
Day by day   ELW 790, WOV 746

Communion

Thy holy wings   ELW 613, WOV 741
How small our span of life   ELW 636
Jesus, still lead on   ELW 624, LBW 341

Sending

Blessed assurance   ELW 638, TFF 188, WOV 699
My God, how wonderful thou art   ELW 863, LBW 524

Additional Assembly Songs

Oh, how he loves you and me   TFF 82
Junto a los rios de Babilonia   LLC 328
Why should I feel discouraged   TFF 252
⊕ Kenyan melody. "Here on Jesus Christ I Will Stand/Dwake Yesu nasimama" from *Glory to God*. U. WJK 9780664238971.
⊕ South African traditional. "Woza nomthwalo wakho/Come, Bring Your Burdens to God" from *We Walk His Way*. SATB. GIA G-7403.
✿ Bruxvoort Colligan, Richard. "All of My Life (Psalm 27)" from *Sharing the Road*. AFP 9780800678630. psalmimmersion.band camp.com.
✿ Bruxvoort Colligan, Richard. "My Heart Will Not Fear (Psalm 27)" from *Our Roots Are in You*. worldmaking.net.
✿ Bruxvoort Colligan, Richard. "Wait for God (Psalm 27)" from *Shout for Joy*. AFP 9780806698632. psalmimmersion.bandcamp.com.
✿ Dakota Road. "Lord of Light" from *Dakota Road Music Anthology*. dakotaroadmusic.com.
✿ Hansen, Holly. "Under the Son" from *Storm Home: A Collection of Music from Humble Walk Artists-in-Residence*. humblewalk .bandcamp.com.
✿ Westendorf, Omer. "We Eat the Bread of Teaching." ELW 518.

Music for the Day
Choral

Larter, Evelyn. "O Jesus, I Have Promised." SATB, pno, vln. ABP 9780687648801.
p ● Miller, Aaron David. "Bow Down Your Ear." U, pno. AFP 9780800677954.
p   Simmons, David. "Jesus, Lover of My Soul." 2 pt mxd, kybd. AFP 9781451451627.
p   Weber, Paul. "It Is the Lord." SATB, org, fl. AFP 9781451479379.

Children's Choir

Leavitt, John. "In the Shadow of Your Wings." 2 pt, pno, opt ob/C inst. GIA G-4302.
Lowenberg, Kenneth. "Can You Count the Stars?" U/2 pt/SATB, kybd. LOR AM814.

⊕ = global song   ✿ = praise song
● = relates to hymn of the day   p = available in Prelude Music Planner

Wetzler, Robert. "As the Hart." U/2 pt, kybd, opt fl, opt assembly. LOR AM762.

Keyboard / Instrumental

- Cherwien, David M. "Norwich" from *Organ Plus One*. Org, inst. AFP 9780800656188.
- p • Kolander, Keith. "Norwich" from *Introductions and Alternate Accompaniments for Piano*, vol. 8. Pno. AFP 9780800623661.
- Manz, Paul. "Herzlich lieb" from *Augsburg Organ Library: Healing and Funeral*. Org. AFP 9781451462616.
- Scott, Mark. "Lord, Let Your Angels Shelter Me" (Herzlich lieb). Org, br qrt. MSM 20-841.

Handbell

Moklebust, Cathy. "Thee We Adore, O Hidden Savior." 2-3 oct, L1+, CG CGB372. 3-5 oct, L1+, CG CGB714.

Tucker, Margaret. "Comfort Ye." 4-5 oct hb, opt 2 oct hc, opt vc, L2+. CG CGB788.

Tucker, Sondra. "God Himself Is with Us (God Is Present with Us)." 3-5 oct, L1. CG CGB784.

Tuesday, February 23

Polycarp, Bishop of Smyrna, martyr, died 156

Polycarp was bishop of Smyrna (in present-day western Turkey) and a link between the apostolic age and the church at the end of the second century. He is said to have been known by John, the author of Revelation. In turn he was known by Iranaeus, bishop of Lyon in France, and Ignatius of Antioch. At the age of eighty-six he was martyred for his faith. When urged to save his life and renounce his faith, Polycarp replied, "Eighty-six years I have served him, and he never did me any wrong. How can I blaspheme my king who saved me?" The magistrate who made the offer was reluctant to kill a gentle old man, but he had no choice. Polycarp was burned at the stake, his death a testimony to the cost of renouncing temptation.

Thursday, February 25

Elizabeth Fedde, deaconess, died 1921

Fedde was born in Norway and trained as a deaconess. In 1882, at the age of thirty-two, she was asked to come to New York to minister to the poor and to Norwegian seafarers. Her influence was wide-ranging, and she established the Deaconess House in Brooklyn and the Deaconess House and Hospital of the Lutheran Free Church in Minneapolis. She returned home to Norway in 1895 and died there.

February 28, 2016
Third Sunday in Lent

The warnings are plentiful and blunt on the third Sunday in Lent. Lent is a season of repentance. Cut it out or get cut down! The warnings are accompanied by God's invitation to attentiveness: "Incline your ear, and come to me; listen, so that you may live." The landowner's ultimatum is forestalled by the gardener's readiness to till the ground one more year. That is good news for all of us. Thanks be to God!

Prayer of the Day

Eternal God, your kingdom has broken into our troubled world through the life, death, and resurrection of your Son. Help us to hear your word and obey it, and bring your saving love to fruition in our lives, through Jesus Christ, our Savior and Lord, who lives and reigns with you and the Holy Spirit, one God, now and forever.

Gospel Acclamation

Jesus began | to proclaim,* Repent, for the kingdom of heaven | has come near. (Matt. 4:17)

Readings and Psalm

Isaiah 55:1-9

To those who have experienced long years in exile, the return to their homeland is a celebration of abundant life. God calls them into an everlasting covenant of love. Those who return to the Lord will enjoy new life and forgiveness, because God's ways are not our ways.

Psalm 63:1-8

O God, eagerly I seek you; my soul thirsts for you. (Ps. 63:1)

1 Corinthians 10:1-13

Paul uses images from Hebrew story and prophecy to speak the truth of Jesus Christ: He is our rock, our water, our food, and our drink. Christ is the living sign of God's faithfulness.

Luke 13:1-9

Asked about current tragic events, Jesus turns a lesson about whether suffering is deserved into a hard call to obedience. He then tells a parable that holds out hope that the timeline for ultimate judgment will be tempered by patience.

Preface   Lent

Color   Purple

Prayers of Intercession

The prayers are prepared locally for each occasion. The following examples may be adapted or used as appropriate.

Hearing the call to return to the Lord, let us join the whole people of God in prayer for all who cry out in pain and in hope.

A brief silence.

Incline our ears to you, faithful God. Open us to receive your word. Transform our thoughts into your thoughts and our ways into your ways for the glory of your kingdom. Lord, in your mercy,

hear our prayer.

Send rain to dry and weary lands, faithful God. Quench the thirst of the earth and every living creature. Lord, in your mercy,

hear our prayer.

Make all governments thirst for your justice, faithful God. Bring citizens and elected officials together to create communities where all people may live in peace. Sustain us by your grace in this work. Lord, in your mercy,

hear our prayer.

Fill the cups of the thirsty, faithful God. Fill the plates of the hungry. Give peace to all who mourn and healing to all who live with mental illness. Be with all who suffer (*especially*). Lord, in your mercy,

hear our prayer.

Gather the hungry around your table, faithful God. Satisfy and unite us with the body and blood of your Son. Send us out to share the bountiful feast you give to us. Lord, in your mercy,

hear our prayer.

Here other intercessions may be offered.

Keep us in your steadfast love, faithful God. We give thanks for all who mentored each of us in the faith and now celebrate life eternal with you (*especially*). By their witness we know you more fully. Lord, in your mercy,

hear our prayer.

To you, gracious God, we commend all for whom we pray, trusting in your boundless mercy; through Jesus Christ, our Savior.

Amen.

Images in the Readings

Throughout the Bible, the **fig tree** is cited both for its fruit and for its broadleaf shade. Other historic literature also uses the fig tree as especially significant: for example, both Augustine and the Buddha were sitting under fig trees when they came to their enlightenment. In Luke's parable, the gardener is surprisingly merciful to the unproductive fig tree. That the fig tree is in a vineyard would suggest to first-century Jews the tradition of describing Israel as God's vineyard.

Although much in Christian history has used the Bible to condemn Judaism, Paul's hermeneutic exemplifies one original Christian use of the Hebrew Scriptures: the first Testament is interpreted as proclaiming the same divine mercy as was embodied in Christ. So the church fathers wrote of Isaiah's reference to **water**, **wine**, and **bread** as helping Christians reflect on baptism and eucharist, and Paul describes the history of Israel using Christian vocabulary of **baptism** and **spiritual food** and **drink**. Paul believed that Christians have been incorporated into God's pattern of mercy, thus allowing Christians to use Jewish history, legend, and poetry to illumine the life, death, and resurrection of Christ. For this reason, the lectionary illumines the gospel readings with selections from the Old Testament.

Especially since 9/11, the sentence in Luke about the **tower of Siloam** calls us to refrain from blaming the victims of tragedy. God's ways are not our ways. The human desire to find a reason for suffering often leads to conclusions that Christianity cannot support theologically.

Ideas for the Day

◆   In this harsh-sounding gospel reading, grace is expressed as the gift of time. Jesus preaches the hard call to repentance and obedience. Then he tells a parable that says it is not too late. It is both gracious and urgent. Because this is the middle of Lent, the assembly can be reminded that "one more year" is this year. Now is the time for returning to the Lord. At the same time, every Lent is "one more year" when we live under the gracious rule of God in Christ. Time is grace.

◆   Jesus mentioned tragic events that seemed to be the reason for wrongly blaming others—as if those who suffered were at fault for their suffering. In the movie *Good Will Hunting* (Miramax, 1997), Will sees a therapist to deal with his difficult past, which included physical abuse. In one key scene, the therapist tells Will over and over, "It's not your fault. It's not your fault." How liberating a message it is to hear when one lives with guilt and blame for their own suffering to hear it is not their fault.

◆   Where and when are we not reflecting God's love and giving life and hope to others? A large barren branch could be placed in a planter in the nave. For confession, the assembly may be invited to hang strips of paper that name parts of their lives that feel barren and fruitless. This could then be cut down and removed in silence followed by an absolution.

◆   Like the gospel text, Isaiah says now is the time to seek the Lord and let go of foolish ways. Isaiah uses the curious image of wine and milk without price, and bread that satisfies offered freely. During the sermon or during the presentation of the gifts, bread and wine could be brought forward with large price tags on them. The price tags can then be removed to emphasize the free grace of God in Christ. There is no price for what is priceless. The invitation to communion could be "Come, receive wine and bread without price."

Connections with the Liturgy

In the upcoming Easter Vigil, the reading from Isaiah 55 is one of the preferred Old Testament passages appointed to proclaim, in the words of Paul, that "Christ was raised in accordance with the scriptures."

In the daily morning psalm (*ELW*, p. 300), we praise God as the rock of our salvation, an image found repeatedly in the Psalms. For Christians, that rock is Christ. We can stand on this Rock before God.

Let the Children Come

Invite the children to join in a procession that "sets the stage" for today's gospel. Several children carry in vases containing bare branches. Others carry in bowls of ripe fruit. Have them place both in front of the altar. At the end of the service, enlist the children's help in handing out fruit to worshipers as they leave as a reminder to bear fruit that lasts. If your baptismal font is near the entrance to the worship space, you could stand there to make the connection to baptismal living more prominent.

Assembly Song
Gathering

Eternal Lord of love, behold your church   ELW 321

Jesus, keep me near the cross   ELW 335, TFF 73

In the cross of Christ I glory   ELW 324, LBW 104

Psalmody and Acclamations

Cooney, Rory. "My Soul Is Longing" from PCY, vol. 4.

Iona Community. "O God, You Are My God Alone" (Gratus) from LUYH.

Krisman, Ronald. "My Soul Is Thirsting" with refrains in Spanish and English. Cant, assembly, org, opt SATB, eng hrn. GIA G-5425.

p   (GA) Organ, Anne Krentz. "Return to the Lord." MSB1 S419.

Hymn of the Day

We raise our hands to you, O Lord ELW 690 *VI REKKER VÅRE HENDER FREM*

As the deer runs to the river ELW 331 *JULION*

As the sun with longer journey ELW 329, WOV 655 *NAGEL*

Offering

Tree of Life and awesome mystery ELW 334, sts. 1 and Lent 3

For the fruit of all creation ELW 679, WOV 760, LBW 563

Communion

Give me Jesus ELW 770, TFF 165, WOV 777

There's a wideness in God's mercy ELW 587/588, LBW 290

Let us break bread together ELW 471, LBW 212, TFF 123

Sending

Restore in us, O God ELW 328

On my heart imprint your image ELW 811, LBW 102

Additional Assembly Songs

Por los caminos sedientos de luz LLC 531

Down at the cross TFF 72

How can I be free from sin W&P 65

⊕ Kim, Seung Nam. "Soft Rains of Spring Flow" from *Glory to God*. U. WJK 9780664238971.

⊕ Koizumi, Isao. Japanese Gagaku mode. "Here, O Lord, Your Servants Gather/Sekai no tomo to te o tsunagi" U. ELW 530.

✿ Bruxvoort Colligan, Richard. "You Are My God (Psalm 63)" from *Sharing the Road*. AFP 9780800678630. psalmimmersion .bandcamp.com.

✿ Cuéllar, Guillermo. "Let Us Go Now to the Banquet." ELW 523.

✿ Dakota Road. "Right by the Water" from *Dakota Road Music Anthology*. dakotaroadmusic.com.

✿ Hansen, Tim. "It's Time" from *Bring On the Light*. thetimhansen project.com.

✿ Houge, Nate. "Metanoia" from *Reform Follows Function*. natehouge.com.

✿ Kernsey. "Paradox" from *Storm Home: A Collection of Music from Humble Walk Artists-in-Residence*. humblewalk.bandcamp .com.

Music for the Day
Choral

Hoffman, Stanley. "In the Shadow of Your Wings." SATB. ECS 7394.

p Pooler, Marie. "Wondrous Love" from *Unison and Two-Part Anthems*. U, kybd. AFP 9780800648916.

p ● Schalk, Carl. "As the Sun with Longer Journey." SATB, kybd, fl. AFP 9780800621384.

p Schrader, Jack. "Remember, Remember Me." SATB, pno. HOP C-5809.

Children's Choir

Handel, G. F./arr. Walter Ehret. "All Who Are Thirsty, Come to the Spring." 2 pt, kybd. GIA G-5838.

p Keesecker, Thomas. "Make Me a Vessel" from *ChildrenSing in Worship*, vol. 2. 2 pt, pno. AFP 9781451461244.

Summers, Roger. "Take My Heart." U/2 pt, kybd. LOR 10/2771K.

Keyboard / Instrumental

● Cherwien, David M. "Nagel" from *Organ Plus One*. Org, inst. AFP 9780800656188.

p ● Langlois, Kristina. "Julion" from *Ride On in Majesty*. Org. AFP 9781451451771.

● Raabe, Nancy M. "Julion" from *Grace and Peace*, vol. 1. Pno. AFP 9780800677602.

Schumann, Clara. "Prelude in G Minor" from *Women Composers' Album*. Org. MSM 10-774.

Handbell

p Bettcher, Peggy. "How Deep the Father's Love for Us." 2-3 oct, L3+, HOP 2630. 3-5 oct, L3+, HOP 2588.

Phillips, Judy. "Arioso (In the Shadow of Thy Wings)." 3-6 oct, L2. AGEHR AG36038.

Wissinger, Kathleen. "Love's Reflection." 3-6 oct hb, opt 1-6 oct hc, L3+. HOP 2342.

Tuesday, March 1

George Herbert, hymnwriter, died 1633

As a student at Trinity College, Cambridge, England, George Herbert excelled in languages and music. He went to college with the intention of becoming a priest, but his scholarship attracted the attention of King James I. Herbert served in parliament for two years. After the death of King James and at the urging of a friend, Herbert's interest in ordained ministry was renewed. He was ordained a priest in 1630 and served the little parish of St. Andrew Bremerton until his death. He was noted for unfailing care for his parishioners, bringing the sacraments to them when they were ill, and providing food and clothing for those in need. Herbert is best remembered, however, as a writer of poems and hymns such as "Come, My Way, My Truth, My Life" (ELW 816).

Wednesday, March 2

John Wesley, died 1791; Charles Wesley, died 1788; renewers of the church

The Wesleys were leaders of a revival in the Church of England. Their spiritual discipline (or method) of frequent communion, fasting, and advocacy for the poor earned them the name "Methodists." The Wesleys were missionaries in the American colony of Georgia for a time, but returned to England discouraged. Following a conversion experience while reading Luther's *Preface to the Epistle to the Romans*, John was perhaps the greatest force in eighteenth-century revival. The brothers' desire was that the Methodist Societies would be a movement for renewal in the Church of England, but after their deaths the societies developed a separate status.

Charles wrote more than six hundred hymns, including "Hark! The Herald Angels Sing" (ELW 270), "Christ, Whose Glory Fills the Skies" (ELW 553), and "Love Divine, All Loves Excelling" (ELW 631).

March 6, 2016
Fourth Sunday in Lent

The psalm sets the tone this day: "Happy are they whose transgressions are forgiven, and whose sin is put away!" Happy are those who have "become the righteousness of God" in the merits of Christ Jesus. Happy are those for whom the forgiveness of God has "rolled away . . . the disgrace" of former times. Happy is the father at the return of his prodigal son. Happy are we that our sins are forgiven for Jesus' sake. Rejoice!

Prayer of the Day

God of compassion, you welcome the wayward, and you embrace us all with your mercy. By our baptism clothe us with garments of your grace, and feed us at the table of your love, through Jesus Christ, our Savior and Lord, who lives and reigns with you and the Holy Spirit, one God, now and forever.

Gospel Acclamation

I will arise and go to my fa- | ther and say,* I have sinned against heaven | and before you. (Luke 15:18)

Readings and Psalm

Joshua 5:9-12

By celebrating the Passover and eating the produce of the promised land instead of the miraculous manna that had sustained them in the desert, the Israelites symbolically bring their forty years of wilderness wandering to an end at Gilgal.

Psalm 32

Be glad, you righteous, and rejoice in the Lord. (Ps. 32:11)

2 Corinthians 5:16-21

One way to describe the gospel is the promise that in Christ everything is transformed into newness. All mistakes, all deliberate sins, all old history is reconciled with Christ's resurrection. This is Paul's strong message to the congregation in the city of Corinth.

Luke 15:1-3, 11b-32

Jesus tells a parable about a son who ponders his father's love only after he has spurned it. The grace he receives is beyond his hopes. That same grace is a crisis for an older brother who believed it was his obedience that earned his place in the father's home.

Preface   Lent

Color   Purple

Prayers of Intercession

The prayers are prepared locally for each occasion. The following examples may be adapted or used as appropriate.

Hearing the call to return to the Lord, let us join the whole people of God in prayer for all who cry out in pain and in hope.

A brief silence.

For campus ministries, we give you thanks, eternal Lord. Equip the students, staff, and ministers to share your steadfast love with their university community and all whom they meet. Hear us, O God.

Your mercy is great.

For polluted oceans and rivers, we seek your healing, creative Lord. Restore the homes of manatees and sea turtles. Teach us to love the earth as you do. Hear us, O God.
Your mercy is great.

For conflicts between political parties, we ask for your discernment and wisdom, merciful Lord. Enable citizens and elected officials to listen to one another and to work together for your justice. Hear us, O God.
Your mercy is great.

For the unemployed, the working poor, and all who struggle to make ends meet, we pray for your provision, gracious Lord. Break down systems that shame, and hold all in the truth that they are your children. Hear us, O God.
Your mercy is great.

For all who engage in the disciplines of Lent, we seek your strength and grace, loving Lord. Even as we rest in your mercy, create a new heart within us. Hear us, O God.
Your mercy is great.

Here other intercessions may be offered.

For all the saints, sinners of your own redeeming, we praise your name, faithful Lord. Grant that we continue to grow as your people by their teaching and example. Hear us, O God.
Your mercy is great.

To you, gracious God, we commend all for whom we pray, trusting in your boundless mercy; through Jesus Christ, our Savior.
Amen.

Images in the Readings

Repeatedly in the Bible a **feast** is the image for our communal joy in sharing the life of God. Today a sign of this feast is offered us in holy communion. The details of the allegory can be mined: the distant country, the pigs, the robe, the ring, the sandals, the fatted calf, the working slaves, the righteous indignation of the obedient son. Thinking of the son wearing a festive robe, some Christians dress each week in their "Sunday best," in a celebrative mood because they are joining others to feast with God.

The **Passover** is the annual Jewish commemoration of God's saving their ancestors from the angel of death, from capture by the Egyptian army, and from death by drowning. Early Christians always called the celebration of Christ's resurrection *pascha*, Passover. Our designation "Easter" derives from the name of a pagan goddess of springtime. Each Sunday we keep the feast of the resurrection: for us, each Sunday is Passover.

Paul calls us **ambassadors** for Christ. An ambassador is empowered to be the presence of the one in authority. Just as Christ brought about reconciliation with God, as Christ's ambassadors we are now to effect reconciliation in the new world that Christ has inaugurated.

Do contemporary people seek **reconciliation** with God? How do you know?

Ideas for the Day

◆ The absence of women in today's gospel text is probably a reflection of the social landscape in Jesus' day. Theologian Walter Brueggemann empowers us to revise the text for an alternative community in his book *The Prophetic Imagination* (Minneapolis: Fortress, 2001). Let's give voice to those silent women by reimagining the prodigal son in today's society. How would the mother or a sister respond to the request of the younger son or the financial decision of the father?

◆ The younger son decided to return home and ask his father for forgiveness. What led to this kairos moment? Was it a moment of isolation that led him to reflect on his current situation? In *Caring for God's People*, Philip Culbertson states, "Only as we know ourselves can we recognize God and find our centeredness there" ([Minneapolis: Augsburg Fortress, 2000], 3). It is not until the son is standing in the mud that he takes the time to reflect and take self-inventory. How many of us have experienced a kairos moment in the midst of "muddy" circumstances? A circumstance in which we found it was difficult to maneuver, and yet where that stillness allowed for reflection and as a result made it easier to take steps toward beginning anew? Imagine the process of receiving a mud facial, in which one lies still with eyes closed, taking the opportunity to reflect as mud saturates the skin, transforming the rough surface to a smoother one. The feeling of restriction is most likely the process of transformation.

◆ The younger son accepted a job that he would have previously passed on upon coming to a new community. The sluggish economy put the young man in a desperate position because he had squandered his assets. The labor-intensive, low-paying job could not adequately provide for his needs; however, he found value in his debased situation. God's grace spoke above the situation and prepared the unworthy son who was wasteful and reckless to receive his father's love, which had never wavered. Is it possible that the hope one finds in moments of despair is the same hope that has always been?

Connections with the Liturgy

The rite of Welcome to Baptism (*ELW*, pp. 232–233) provides a way for the full assembly to celebrate a baptism that is scheduled for the future. As with a pregnant mother, as with the watchful father in the parable, we wait expectantly for each one's arrival. In the name of Christ, we welcome those who are preparing for baptism. We give them, not a literal robe, ring, and sandals, but the sign of the cross and our communal support, for we are ambassadors of Christ's reconciliation to the whole world.

Let the Children Come

Running in church is recommended this Sunday. A vivid telling of this story could enlist a narrator, two sons, and the father running to meet the lost son. Encourage children and adults to wear running shoes to church this Sunday because we remember that God runs to us to forgive us in the same way the father ran to meet his lost-and-found son. The word *prodigal* means "recklessly extravagant." The lost son is prodigal in his spending; the waiting father is prodigal too—extravagant and lavish in his love for his son, just as God loves us. Is your congregation being prodigal in love and service?

Assembly Song
Gathering

God loved the world   ELW 323, LBW 292

Come, thou fount of every blessing   ELW 807, LBW 499, TFF 108

What wondrous love is this   ELW 666, LBW 385

Psalmody and Acclamations

Anderson, Mark. "Psalm 32," Refrain 3, from PSCY.

Helgen, John. "Psalm 32" from *ChildrenSing Psalms*. U, assembly, kybd.

Keesecker, Thomas. "Psalm 32" from PWC.

p   (GA) Organ, Anne Krentz. "Return to the Lord." MSB1 S419.

Hymn of the Day

Our Father, we have wandered   ELW 606, WOV 733   *HERZLICH TUT MICH VERLANGEN*

Softly and tenderly Jesus is calling   ELW 608, TFF 155, WOV 734   *THOMPSON*

I heard the voice of Jesus say   ELW 332, LBW 497   *THIRD MODE MELODY*   ELW 611   *KINGSFOLD*   TFF 62   *SHINE ON ME*

Offering

Just as I am   ELW 592, LBW 296

God of the sparrow   ELW 740, sts. 1, 4, 7

Communion

We sing to you, O God   ELW 791

I want Jesus to walk with me   ELW 325, TFF 66, WOV 660

We who once were dead   ELW 495, LBW 207

Sending

God, when human bonds are broken   ELW 603, WOV 735

Amazing grace, how sweet the sound   ELW 779, LBW 448, LLC 437

Additional Assembly Songs

For God so loved   W&P 39

Days are filled with sorrow and care   TFF 74

Heme aquí, Jesús bendito   LLC 444

⊕ Lee, Geonyong. "Come Now, O Prince of Peace." SATB. ELW 247.

⊕ Puerto Rican folk hymn. "Oh, How Good Is Christ the Lord/Oh, qué bueno es Jesús" from *My Heart Sings Out*. U. Church Publishing 9780898694741.

✿ Bruxvoort Colligan, Richard. "Unfailing Love (Psalm 32)" from *Sharing the Road*. AFP 9780800678630. psalmimmersion .bandcamp.com.

✿ Dakota Road. "All Are Welcome" from *Dakota Road Music Anthology*. dakotaroadmusic.com.

✿ Houge, Nate. "Redemption" from *Reform Follows Function*. natehouge.com.

✿ MacIntosh, Jonathan/Sarah MacIntosh/Vicky Beeching. "Salvation Day" from CCLI.

✿ Olivar, José Antonio. "When the Poor Ones." ELW 725.

✿ Webb, Derek. "Saint and Sinner" from *She Must and Shall Go Free*. derekwebb.com.

Music for the Day
Choral

● Cherwien, David. "Softly and Tenderly Jesus Is Calling." SATB, solo. MSM 50-6304.

p Johnson, David. "O Dearest Lord, Thy Sacred Head." SATB, org, opt fl. AFP 9780800645793.

p Organ, Anne Krentz. "How Can I Keep from Singing" from *Augsburg Choirbook for Women*. SSA, pno. AFP 9780800620370.

Schalk, Carl. "Out of the Depths." SAB, org. MSM 50-3410.

Children's Choir

p Edwards, Rusty/arr. Wayne L. Wold. "Rejoice! I Found the Lost." U/2 pt, kybd. AFP 9780800653545.

Marcello, Benedetto. "Oh, Hold Thou Me Up" from *The Morningstar Choir Book*. 2 pt, kybd. CPH 976287WEB.

p Paris, Twila/arr. Lloyd Larson. "Lamb of God." SSA, pno. HOP C5865.

Keyboard / Instrumental

● Ferguson, John. "Thompson" from *Augsburg Organ Library: Healing and Funeral*. Org. AFP 9781451462616.

p ● Hobby, Robert A. "Thompson" from *For All the Saints*, vol. 2. Org, opt 1 hb. AFP 9780800679101.

● Pachelbel, Johann. "Herzlich tut mich verlangen." Org. Various editions.

p ● Raabe, Nancy M. "Thompson" from *Day of Arising*. Pno. AFP 9780800637460.

⊕ = global song   ✿ = praise song
● = relates to hymn of the day   p = available in Prelude Music Planner

Handbell

- Lamb, Linda. "Softly and Tenderly." 3-5 oct hb, opt 3 oct hc, L2. SF 279059.
- McChesney, Kevin. "Kingsfold." 3-5 oct, L2+. RW 8212.
  Stewart, Kevin, and Tammy Waldrop. "You Are My Hiding Place." 3 or 5 oct hb, opt 3 oct hc, L2. ALF 33938.

Monday, March 7

Perpetua and Felicity and companions, martyrs at Carthage, died 202

In the year 202 the emperor Septimius Severus forbade conversions to Christianity. Perpetua, a noblewoman, Felicity, a slave, and other companions were all catechumens at Carthage in North Africa. They were imprisoned and sentenced to death. Perpetua's father, who was not a Christian, visited her in prison and begged her to lay aside her Christian convictions in order to spare her life and spare the family from scorn. Perpetua responded by telling her father, "We know that we are not placed in our own power but in that of God."

Thursday, March 10

Harriet Tubman, died 1913; Sojourner Truth, died 1883; renewers of society

Harriet Tubman was born into slavery in Maryland and remained a slave until about age thirty when, fearing she would be sold and moved farther south, she escaped with the help of the Underground Railroad. After that, she helped about three hundred others to escape until slavery was abolished. After the Civil War, her home in Auburn, New York, became a center for women's rights and served the aged and poor.

Sojourner Truth, too, was born a slave, in New York state. Her birth name was Isabella. After slavery was abolished in New York in 1827, she was freed and, while working as a housekeeper, became deeply involved in Christianity. A number of years later, she discerned a call to become a preacher. Taking the name Sojourner Truth, she set out on an evangelistic journey, where people found her testimony to be deeply moving. In later life, she also became a popular speaker against slavery and for women's rights.

Saturday, March 12

Gregory the Great, Bishop of Rome, died 604

Gregory was born into a politically influential family. At one time he held political office and at another time he lived as a monk, all before he was elected to the papacy. Gregory's work was extensive. He influenced public worship through the establishment of a lectionary and prayers to correlate with the readings. He established a school to train church musicians. Gregorian chant is named in his honor. He wrote a treatise underscoring what is required of a pastor serving a congregation. He sent missionaries to preach to the Anglo-Saxons who had invaded England. And at one time he organized distribution of grain during a shortage of food in Rome.

March 13, 2016
Fifth Sunday in Lent

The Lord our God makes all things new. In the first reading God promises it. In the gospel Mary anticipates it, anointing Jesus' feet with costly perfume in preparation for the day of his burial. In the second reading we recall the transformation of Saul, the persecutor, into Paul, the apostle. In baptism, God's new person (you!) rises daily from the deadly mire of trespasses and sins.

Prayer of the Day

Creator God, you prepare a new way in the wilderness, and your grace waters our desert. Open our hearts to be transformed by the new thing you are doing, that our lives may proclaim the extravagance of your love given to all through your Son, Jesus Christ, our Savior and Lord, who lives and reigns with you and the Holy Spirit, one God, now and forever.

Gospel Acclamation

Forgetting what lies behind and straining forward to what
¹ lies ahead,* I press on toward the goal for the prize of the heavenly call of God ¹ in Christ Jesus. (Phil. 3:13-14)

Readings and Psalm
Isaiah 43:16-21

The prophet declares that long ago the Lord performed mighty deeds and delivered Israel from Egyptian bondage through the waters of the sea. Now, the Lord is about to do a new thing, bringing the exiles out of Babylon and through the wilderness in a new exodus.

Psalm 126

Those who sowed with tears will reap with songs of joy. (Ps. 126:5)

Philippians 3:4b-14

Writing to Christians in Philippi, Paul admits that his heritage and reputation could give him more reason than most people to place confidence in his spiritual pedigree. But the overwhelming grace of God in Jesus calls Paul to a new set of values.

John 12:1-8

Judas willfully misinterprets as waste Mary's extravagant act of anointing Jesus' feet with costly perfume. Jesus recognizes that her lavish gift is both an expression of love and an anticipation of his burial.

Preface   Lent

Color   Purple

Prayers of Intercession

The prayers are prepared locally for each occasion. The following examples may be adapted or used as appropriate.

Hearing the call to return to the Lord, let us join the whole people of God in prayer for all who cry out in pain and in hope.

A brief silence.

Holy God, in times of both joy and sorrow you call us to worship you. Bless the work of musicians, altar guilds, readers, presiding and assisting ministers, and all who serve in worship. Sustain them with your Spirit as we journey toward Holy Week. Lord, in your mercy,
hear our prayer.

Creative God, you made every living creature and saw that it was good. Teach us to care for the homelands of animals in the wild. Lord, in your mercy,
hear our prayer.

Living God, you require mercy and justice. Bless the work of all organizations that work to restore cities and countries, especially Lutheran Volunteer Corps and Lutheran Disaster Response. Lord, in your mercy,
hear our prayer.

Compassionate God, you make a way out of no way. Give your peace and vision to all who struggle with addiction, depression, grief, or illness (*especially*). Make plain that in the midst of suffering, you are suffering, and that your desire is wholeness and life. Lord, in your mercy,
hear our prayer.

Shepherding God, you tend your flock with mercy and love. Guide the outreach ministries of this congregation (*especially*). Strengthen our relationships in this community as we serve our neighbors in love. Lord, in your mercy,
hear our prayer.

Here other intercessions may be offered.

Triune God, in you there is abundant life. Deepen our union with you, that in living we may die and in dying we may live with all your saints. Lord, in your mercy,
hear our prayer.
To you, gracious God, we commend all for whom we pray, trusting in your boundless mercy; through Jesus Christ, our Savior.
Amen.

Images in the Readings

The **anointing woman** has been an extremely popular image in Christian art and imagination, especially since Pope Gregory in the sixth century tied together several New Testament stories of women as all referring to Mary of Magdala, whom he identified as a reformed prostitute. Thus in the history of art, the anointing woman is usually named Mary Magdalene and is often shown with wild red hair, an off-the-shoulder dress, and her jar of ointment. Recent scholarship has demonstrated that this conflation of stories has defamed Mary of Magdala, whom the New Testament identifies as one of the witnesses to the resurrection, and has intensified a stereotypical depiction of women as being either sinless, like Mary of Nazareth, or sexually sinful, like a prostitute. In John's account, Jesus is being honored in the home of close friends and supporters of his movement. This year's proclamation of John's account of the anointing woman ought not muddy Lent's baptismal waters by identifying this faithful woman as a prostitute.

Isaiah's poem is filled with images: the Red **Sea** opened; the Egyptian **army** drowned; a **candle** extinguished; a new **plant** springing up; a **path** in the **wilderness**; a **river** in the **desert**; the **wild animals**, jackals, and ostriches that honor their creator; the **water** from the rock, nourishing the nomads. Perhaps the most astonishing image is the idea of newness: God continually creates new things. We Christians see all these images as reflecting the new reality released into the world in the resurrection of Jesus Christ.

Perhaps some of you cannot bluntly indicate what Paul really wrote for our word *rubbish*. We are more comfortable with less disruptive language. Yet Paul's image proclaims the countercultural Christian conviction that what comes from us is more like excrement than like something that could grant us the prize of God's call.

Ideas for the Day

◆ The Gospel of John makes reference to the Passover and the raising of Lazarus prior to focusing attention on Jesus' anointing by Mary of Bethany. It is as if the writer of John is providing context clues to remind us that he already knows how the story ends with the death and resurrection of Jesus Christ after the Passover. John 12:1 prepares the reader for the verses that follow, which unveil the certainty and reality of Jesus' impending death. The writer carefully inserts resurrection hope as a prelude to the notion of death as Mary lavishly prepares her Lord. How do Christians today take the biblical story and/or a contemporary context to help unveil the resurrection promise and the promise of Christ's return? How do we draw others into the gospel story and gospel promise?

◆ In her earnest worship, Mary performed a rite of preparation for Jesus' death. Jesus used this outpouring of love to foretell his death. Do we worship sparingly so that we do not appear foolish to those around us? Mary does not explain her action but is defended by Jesus for the sake of God's plan. Perhaps we should worship without fear and see how God uses it to unveil the mystery of faith. In what ways do we honor the living God so that our actions, thoughts, and words are in remembrance of him?

◆ If our actions are directed toward worrying about our tribulations or impressing others, then who or what have we professed as Lord? Mary surely had things in her life that needed attention. Perhaps there were major and minor needs that she could have been addressing. Or there may have been something pleasurable that could have consumed her time. Instead, she focused on her Lord. Kneeling to anoint Jesus' feet, she placed herself in a vulnerable position—a position of humility. She was acknowledging Jesus is Lord. Jesus is Lord—not our buildings, the pastor, our gender, our hymnal, or our tribulations. Do we give God our undivided attention?

Connections with the Liturgy

To be Christian is to be named by Christ, the Anointed One. So the rite of baptism suggests that oil be used in marking the newly baptized with a cross. We are now anointed, chosen by God—as was Jesus Christ—to serve in the kingdom. The cross is the sign of our baptism. Jesus is the Anointed One whose death on the cross and "the power of his resurrection" transfer that status of authority to believers.

Let the Children Come

Mary of Bethany is extravagant, over the top in showing love for Jesus with this expensive oil. Are we showing abundance or stinginess in our love toward God and neighbor? What do our congregations' actions and priorities say? Remind the children that they received the sign of the cross at their baptism, a sign that God's love is stronger than death and that they belong to God no matter what. Anoint each child's hand with an oily cross. Each can carry the scent with them through the day as a reminder of their baptism and the story of Mary of Bethany.

Assembly Song
Gathering
Christ, the life of all the living   ELW 339, LBW 97

When I survey the wondrous cross   ELW 803, TFF 79, LBW 482

A lamb goes uncomplaining forth   ELW 340, LBW 105

Psalmody and Acclamations
Daw, Carl P., Jr. "When God First Brought Us Back" (tune: *WAYFARING STRANGER*) from PAS 126A.

Pavlechko, Thomas. "Psalm 126" from SMP.

Smith, Alan. "The Lord Has Done Great Things" from PS1.

p   (GA) Organ, Anne Krentz. "Return to the Lord." MSB1 S419.

Hymn of the Day
Holy God, holy and glorious   ELW 637 *NELSON*

Seed that in earth is dying   ELW 330 *SÅKORN SOM DØR I JORDEN*

Now behold the Lamb   ELW 341, TFF 128 *NOW BEHOLD THE LAMB*

Offering
Come to the table   ELW 481, W&P 33

Eat this bread   ELW 472, TFF 125, WOV 709

Communion
Eat this bread, drink this cup   ELW 492, WOV 706

For by grace you have been saved   ELW 598

My song is love unknown   ELW 343, LBW 94, WOV 661

Sending
Lord, thee I love with all my heart   ELW 750, LBW 325

O Christ, your heart, compassionate   ELW 722

Additional Assembly Songs
What can wash away my sin?   TFF 69

Amazing love   W&P 8

Rich in promise   OBS 75

⊕ Lim, Swee Hong. "Lord, Have Mercy" from *Sound the Bamboo*. U. GIA G-6830. ELW 158.

⊕ Park, Chung Kwan. "To My Precious Lord" from *Glory to God*. U. WJK 9780664238971.

✿ Bruxvoort Colligan, Richard. "When We Share God's Dream (Psalm 126)" from *Shout for Joy*. AFP 9780806698632. psalmimmersion.bandcamp.com.

✿ Bruxvoort Colligan, Richard. "Rivers in the Desert (Psalm 126)" from *Shout for Joy*. AFP 9780806698632. psalmimmersion.bandcamp.com.

✿ Dakota Road. "Praise to You" from *Dakota Road Music Anthology*. dakotaroadmusic.com.

✿ Gungor, Michael. "Beautiful Things" from *Beautiful Things*. gungormusic.com.

✿ Houge, Nate. "Your Work in Me" from *Reform Follows Function*. natehouge.com.

✿ Kurtz, Rachel. "Save Us All" from *For Crying Out Loud*. rachelkurtz.org.

Music for the Day
Choral
p ● Ellingboe, Bradley. "Seed That in Earth Is Dying." SAB, pno. AFP 9780800638849.

p   Harlan, Benjamin. "Beneath the Cross of Jesus." SATB, org, vl. AFP 9780800678005.

p   Highben, Zebulon. "My Hope Is Built." SATB, perc. AFP 9781451462395.

p   Larson, Lloyd. "Lamb of God" from *Women in Song*, IV. SSA, pno. HOP 8581.

Children's Choir
Carter, Sydney/arr. Hal Hopson. "One More Step Along the World I Go." U/2 pt, C inst, pno. GIA G-8198.

p   Gilpin, Greg. "Little Innocent Lamb." U/2 pt, pno. CG CGA1359.

p   Patterson, Mark. "I Will Give My Heart to the Lord" from *Young ChildrenSing*. U, kybd, opt Orff/hc. AFP 9781451460247.

Keyboard / Instrumental
●   Childs, Edwin T. "Now Behold the Lamb" from *For Manuals Only: Lent and Easter*. Org. AFP 9780800621629.

●   Gehring, Philip. "Såkorn som dør i jorden" from *Five Hymn Preludes for Organ*. Org. AFP 9780800678777.

p ● Organ, Anne Krentz. "Nelson" from *Reflections on Hymn Tunes for Holy Communion*, vol. 2. Pno. AFP 9780800679095.

●   Raabe, Nancy M. "Nelson" from *Piano Plus Through the Year*, vol. 2. Pno, inst. AFP 9780800663728.

Handbell
p   Moats, William. "In the Shadow of the Cross." 3-5 oct hb, opt 3 or 5 oct hc, L2+. CG CGB821.

p   Olstad, Brent. "How Great Thou Art." 3 oct, L3. HOP 2672.

p   Page, Anna Laura. "Joys Are Flowing Like a River (Blessed Quietness)." 3-5 oct hb, opt 3-5 oct hc, L2+. CG CGB822.

Thursday, March 17

Patrick, bishop, missionary to Ireland, died 461
At sixteen, Patrick was kidnapped by Irish pirates and sold into slavery in Ireland. He himself admitted that up to this point he cared little for God. He escaped after six years, returned to his family in southwest Britain, and began to prepare for ordained ministry. He later returned to Ireland,

this time to serve as a bishop and missionary. He made his base in the north of Ireland and from there made many missionary journeys, with much success. In his autobiography he denounced the slave trade, perhaps from his own experience as a slave. Patrick's famous baptismal hymn to the Trinity, "I Bind unto Myself Today" (ELW 450), can be used as a meditation on Lent's call to return to our baptism.

Saturday, March 19

Joseph, Guardian of Jesus

The gospels are silent about much of Joseph's life. We know that he was a carpenter or builder by trade. The Gospel of Luke shows him acting in accordance with both civil and religious law by returning to Bethlehem for the census and by presenting the child Jesus in the temple on the fortieth day after his birth. The Gospel of Matthew tells of Joseph's trust in God, who led him through visionary dreams. Because Joseph is not mentioned after the story of a young Jesus teaching in the temple, it is assumed that he died before Jesus reached adulthood.

March 20, 2016
Sunday of the Passion
Palm Sunday

The voice of the suffering savior, Jesus, can be heard in the prophet Isaiah's words and the pleading of the psalm. We are invited into the agony of our Lord in the extended reading of the story of Jesus' passion. In the second reading, we who have put on Christ in holy baptism are urged to let the mind of Christ be our own. Lent leads us to this holy moment. Embrace it.

Prayer of the Day

Everlasting God, in your endless love for the human race you sent our Lord Jesus Christ to take on our nature and to suffer death on the cross. In your mercy enable us to share in his obedience to your will and in the glorious victory of his resurrection, who lives and reigns with you and the Holy Spirit, one God, now and forever.

or

Sovereign God, you have established your rule in the human heart through the servanthood of Jesus Christ. By your Spirit, keep us in the joyful procession of those who with their tongues confess Jesus as Lord and with their lives praise him as Savior, who lives and reigns with you and the Holy Spirit, one God, now and forever.

or

O God of mercy and might, in the mystery of the passion of your Son you offer your infinite life to the world. Gather us around the cross of Christ, and preserve us until the resurrection, through Jesus Christ, our Savior and Lord, who lives and reigns with you and the Holy Spirit, one God, now and forever.

Gospel Acclamation

Christ humbled himself and became obedient to the point of death—even death | on a cross.* Therefore God also

highly exalted him and gave him the name that is above | every name. (Phil. 2:8-9)

Readings and Psalm

Procession with Palms: Luke 19:28-40

Isaiah 50:4-9a

This text, the third of the four Servant Songs in Isaiah, speaks of the servant's obedience in the midst of persecution. Though the servant has been variously understood as the prophet himself or a remnant of faithful Israel, Christians have often recognized the figure of Christ in these poems.

Psalm 31:9-16

Into your hands, O LORD, I commend my spirit. (Ps. 31:5)

Philippians 2:5-11

Paul quotes from an early Christian hymn that describes Jesus' humble obedience in his incarnation as a human being, even to death, and his exaltation and glory as Lord of all.

Luke 22:14—23:56 or Luke 23:1-49

Through the teachings and events of the passion story we see and hear the great contradictions that characterize the coming of God's reign. The leader serves, the empty disciples are able to fill others, proud Peter is revealed in his cowardice, and Jesus—the innocent bringer of life—is arrested, beaten, executed, and buried.

Preface   Sunday of the Passion

Color   Scarlet *or* Purple

Prayers of Intercession

The prayers are prepared locally for each occasion. The following examples may be adapted or used as appropriate.

Hearing the call to return to the Lord, let us join the whole people of God in prayer for all who cry out in pain and in hope.

A brief silence.

Be with all who wave palm branches and walk the road to the cross. For the mission of the gospel where your church is forgotten, for disciples wrestling with betrayal, for all who seek the Lord, let us pray.

Have mercy, O God.

Renew the waters of the earth and restore us to right relationship with all creation. For villages without access to clean water, for cities with an abundance, for flood lands and drought lands, let us pray.

Have mercy, O God.

End human trafficking in every nation. For children taken from their families, for men and women without hope, for governments and nonprofits seeking resolutions, let us pray.

Have mercy, O God.

Comfort the afflicted. For those imprisoned, for those waiting on death row, for all overwhelmed by sorrow, and for all who live with disease, chronic pain, and anxiety in this world (*especially*), let us pray.

Have mercy, O God.

Enrich the children and youth of our congregation with an abundance of your Spirit. For each child in our community, for parents and guardians, for confirmation mentors and faith formation leaders, let us pray.

Have mercy, O God.

Here other intercessions may be offered.

Sustain the weary. For all who mourn, for all who yearn to be with you in paradise, for funeral home staff, for hospital chaplains and grief counselors, let us pray.

Have mercy, O God.

To you, gracious God, we commend all for whom we pray, trusting in your boundless mercy; through Jesus Christ, our Savior.

Amen.

Images in the Readings

Two opposite images of Christ come in the readings. First, Christ is **king**. In Luke's passion narrative, he is acclaimed as king; he is the apocalyptic Son of Man, who will judge the world at the end of time; he is accused of being the Son of God (in the religious worldview of the ancient Near Eastern world, the king was a son of the deity), the "king of the Jews," and the Messiah. He is prominent enough to interact with King Herod. He is served by Simon of Cyrene. Much in North American culture resists seeing "king" as a positive image. Yet the hope that someone has ultimate power, absolute justice, and endless mercy persists in human imagination.

In an image that derives from the first and second readings, Christ is **servant**. God will vindicate the servant, even though he is now suffering. We are to adopt the mind of Christ Jesus, who became a servant, indeed a slave, for us. Once again, much in North American culture resists "servant" as a positive image. Martin Luther's essay "The Freedom of the Christian" can help us here: through our baptism, we are free, slaves to none, and yet simultaneously servants to all.

In Luke's passion account, Jesus forgives, now and in **paradise**. There is considerable exegetical and theological discussion of what Luke meant by the term *paradise*, a word that occurs only three times in the New Testament, both other times in the context of visions. That Jesus promises to see the forgiven criminal in paradise probably referred to God's forgiveness in the coming parousia, albeit that it has come to signify the Christian hope that life with God in heaven occurs immediately after death.

Ideas for the Day

◆   The Gathering on this Sunday heightens the significance of this part of every Sunday's worship pattern. We gather, perhaps outside the church building or in a space other than the nave, to symbolize that we come from the world to enter the church. When we read one of the biblical accounts of Jesus' entry into Jerusalem, it is not that we are propelled back in time, but rather that today Jesus enters our city, our assembly, our lives, and we laud him as king (*Worship Guidebook for Lent and the Three Days* [Minneapolis: Augsburg Fortress, 2009], 79).

◆   Jesus' final table consists of those followers who would betray him, deny knowing him, and abandon him. What about the tables we prepare? How should our communion tables resemble Jesus' final table? Who do we need to reinvite to the table?

◆   There are big moments in our lives that are defined by ordinary things like a rooster crowing. Jesus told Peter that he would deny him three times before the cock crowed. It was true. The crowing of a rooster, a reminder of his sin, could have held Peter hostage to a mistake for the rest of his life. What are some negative triggers in our lives that remind us of past pain, a particular sinful act or inaction, a date someone died, the termination or resignation of a job, or a bad relationship? Peter did not let this reality impede him from serving God. As children of God, we need to take notice of when these reminders impede our actions and rejoice in God's forgiveness as we move forward in mission like Peter, who went on to serve God faithfully.

◆ Both Matthew 27:45-46 and Mark 15:33-34 suggest that Jesus' cry from the cross was the first line of Psalm 22, "My God, my God, why have you forsaken me?" Was Jesus singing, in the midst of darkness, to God? Consider the words of the gospel song "His eye is on the sparrow." The song begins with a series of questions and ends with the conviction that God watches over the singer. Can you sing to God during your darkest hours?

Connections with the Liturgy

Each Sunday's thanksgiving at the eucharistic table, like the song in Philippians, retells the Christian gospel. Jesus Christ is God for us, his death a living reality that gives us salvation. "This is my body," we speak each week over the bread, broken for us, as was the body of Jesus on the cross. A faithful Christian assembly worshiping on Sunday remembers and honors the passion and death of Christ. Our life comes from and through his death.

Let the Children Come

This day is full of movement, objects, and ritual action that helps everyone, not just children, enter into the worship of these coming days. There are palm branches to wave, there is perhaps a walk around the church outside, there is a long reading to hear, perhaps proclaimed by many different voices. If your assembly sings "All glory, laud, and honor" (ELW 344) as its processional hymn, be sure the children learn the refrain by heart ahead of time; they will love the line "to whom the lips of children made sweet hosannas ring."

Assembly Song
Gathering

Bless now, O God, the journey   ELW 326
All glory, laud, and honor   ELW 344, LBW 108, LS 48
Prepare the royal highway   ELW 264, LBW 26

Psalmody and Acclamations

Gelineau, Joseph. "Psalm 31" from ACYG.
Haugen, Marty. "Father, into Your Hands" from LP:S.
Rossi, Richard Robert. "Father, I Put My Life in Your Hands." SATB, assembly. GIA G-5716.
p   (GA) "Christ Humbled Himself." ELW, tone 12. MSB1 S431.

Hymn of the Day

My song is love unknown   ELW 343, WOV 661   *LOVE UNKNOWN* LBW 94   *RHOSYMEDRE*
A lamb goes uncomplaining forth   ELW 340, LBW 105   *AN WASSERFLÜSSEN BABYLON*
Lamb of God   ELW 336   *YOUR ONLY SON*

Offering

O sacred head, now wounded   ELW 351/352, sts. 1, 3; LBW 116/117, sts. 1, 3
Lord of glory, you have bought us   ELW 707, sts. 1-2; LBW 424, sts. 1-2

Communion

Jesus, I will ponder now   ELW 345, LBW 115
They crucified my Lord   ELW 350, TFF 80
Beneath the cross of Jesus   ELW 338, LBW 107

Sending

Ride on, ride on in majesty   ELW 346, LBW 121
Through the night of doubt and sorrow   ELW 327, LBW 355

Additional Assembly Songs

Alas! And did my Savior bleed   TFF 71
On a hill far away   TFF 77
Gloria sea a Cristo   LLC 327
⊕ Traditional. "'Sanna" from *My Heart Sings Out*. SATB. Church Publishing 9780898694741.
⊕ Wu, Mabel. "O Lamb of God." ELW 198.
✿ Bruxvoort Colligan, Richard. "Into Your Hands (Psalm 31)" from *Sharing the Road*. AFP 9780800678630. psalmimmersion .bandcamp.com.
✿ Dakota Road. "Messiah" from *Dakota Road Music Anthology*. dakotaroadmusic.com.
✿ Harling, Per. "You Are Holy." ELW 525. (Gathering)
✿ Tangled Blue. "Behold, the Lamb" from *Storm Home: A Collection of Music from Humble Walk Artists-in-Residence*. humblewalk.bandcamp.com.
✿ Tomlin, Chris/Daniel Carson/Jason Ingram. "Jesus My Redeemer" from CCLI.
✿ The Welcome Wagon. "I'm Not Fine" from *Precious Remedies Against Satan's Devices*. asthmatickitty.com.

Music for the Day
Choral

● Childs, Edwin. "My Song Is Love Unknown." SATB, kybd. MSM 50-3044.
p Jennings, Carolyn. "Ah, Holy Jesus" from *Augsburg Choirbook for Women*. SA, vc. AFP 9780800620370.
p Roesch, Robert. "Alas! And Did My Savior Bleed." SAB, org. AFP 9780800675400.

p   Willan, Healey. "Behold the Lamb of God." SATB, org. CPH
        98-1509.

Children's Choir

•   Archer, Malcolm. "My Song Is Love Unknown." 2 pt. GIA G-4646.
        Avila, Rubén Ruiz/arr. Aaron David Miller. "Filled with
        Excitement" from *ChildrenSing Around the World*. U, pno,
        opt gtr, opt perc. AFP 9781451491944.
        Campbell, Jonathan Strommen. "Fair and Eloquent Flowers." 2 pt,
        pno. GIA G-8615.

Keyboard / Instrumental

•   Leavitt, John. "Love Unknown" from *Organ Plus Anthology*, vol. 1.
        Org, inst. AFP 9781451424256.

•   Osterland, Karl. "Love Unknown" from *Augsburg Organ Library:
        Lent*. Org. AFP 9780800658977.

•   Porter, Rachel Trelstad. "Love Unknown" from *Introductions
        and Alternate Accompaniments for Piano*, vol. 2. Pno. AFP
        9780800623609.

•   Sedio, Mark. "An Wasserflüssen Babylon" from *Music for the
        Paschal Season*. Org. AFP 9780800656232.

Handbell

p   Hanson, Nicholas A. "Triumphant Spirit." 2-3 oct, L3, CG CGB841.
        3-6 oct, L3, CG CGB842.

•   Moklebust, Cathy. "My Song Is Love Unknown." 3-5 oct, L3. CG
        CGB203.

•   Ryan, Michael. "Lamb of God." 2-3 oct, L2. LOR 20/1457L.

March 21, 2016
Monday in Holy Week

*During Holy Week some communities gather each day to meditate
on Jesus' final days before his death on the cross. Today's gospel
commemorates the anointing of Jesus by Mary, a foreshadowing
of his death and burial. Isaiah speaks of the suffering servant who
is a light for the nations and who faithfully brings forth justice.
For Christians, Jesus' suffering is the path to resurrection and
new life. We eagerly await the celebration of the great Three Days
later this week.*

Prayer of the Day

O God, your Son chose the path that led to pain before joy
and to the cross before glory. Plant his cross in our hearts,
so that in its power and love we may come at last to joy and
glory, through Jesus Christ, our Savior and Lord, who lives
and reigns with you and the Holy Spirit, one God, now and
forever.

Gospel Acclamation

May I never boast of ¹anything* except the cross of our
Lord ¹ Jesus Christ. (Gal. 6:14)

Readings and Psalm
Isaiah 42:1-9

God's servant Israel is endowed with the Spirit in order to
bring justice to the nations. The servant will not exercise
authority boisterously or with violence, nor will weariness
ever keep it from fulfilling its task. God's old promises have
been fulfilled; the new assignment of the servant is to bring
light to the nations.

Psalm 36:5-11

All people take refuge under the shadow of your wings.
(Ps. 36:7)

Hebrews 9:11-15

Prior to Christ, forgiveness was mediated through animal
sacrifice. Christ came as the great high priest to establish a
new covenant. Through his blood we are liberated from our
sins and promised eternal life.

John 12:1-11

A few days after raising Lazarus from the dead, Jesus visits
the man's home. Lazarus's sister Mary is criticized when she
anoints the feet of Jesus with costly perfume.

Preface   Sunday of the Passion

Color   Scarlet *or* Purple

Monday, March 21

Thomas Cranmer, Bishop of Canterbury, martyr, died 1556

Cranmer was serving as bishop of Taunton in England when he was chosen by King Henry VIII to become archbishop of Canterbury, largely because Cranmer would agree to the king's divorce from Catherine of Aragon. Cranmer's lasting achievement is contributing to and overseeing the creation of the Book of Common Prayer, which in revised form remains the worship book of the Anglican Communion. He was burned at the stake under Queen Mary for his support of the Protestant Reformation.

March 22, 2016
Tuesday in Holy Week

As the great Three Days draw near, some communities gather each day of Holy Week for worship. Paul proclaims Christ crucified as the wisdom and power of God. Jesus speaks of the grain of wheat that falls into the earth and dies in order that it may bear fruit. We die with Christ in baptism that we may be raised with him to new life. We will celebrate this great mystery of death and resurrection at the Easter Vigil later this week.

Prayer of the Day

Lord Jesus, you have called us to follow you. Grant that our love may not grow cold in your service, and that we may not fail or deny you in the time of trial, for you live and reign with the Father and the Holy Spirit, one God, now and forever.

Gospel Acclamation

May I never boast of ¹ anything* except the cross of our Lord ¹ Jesus Christ. (Gal. 6:14)

Readings and Psalm

Isaiah 49:1-7

Here the servant Israel speaks for herself and acknowledges herself as God's secret weapon. Called like Jeremiah and John the Baptist before her birth, the servant is not only to restore Israel itself, but the servant's ultimate assignment is to bring news of God's victory to the ends of the earth. God in faithfulness has chosen Israel for this task.

Psalm 71:1-14

From my mother's womb you have been my strength. (Ps. 71:6)

1 Corinthians 1:18-31

To the world, the word of the cross is silly, because it claims God's power is most fully revealed in complete, utter weakness. For those who are being saved, however, the word of the cross unveils God's true wisdom, power, and source of true life.

John 12:20-36

Knowing that his hour has come, Jesus announces that his death will be an exaltation. God's name will be glorified when his death draws people to new life.

Preface   Sunday of the Passion

Color   Scarlet *or* Purple

Tuesday, March 22

Jonathan Edwards, teacher, missionary to American Indians, died 1758

Edwards was a minister in Connecticut and is described as the greatest of the New England Puritan preachers. One of Edwards's most notable sermons found its way into contemporary anthologies of literature. In this sermon, "Sinners in the Hands of an Angry God," he spoke at length about hell. However, throughout the rest of his works and his preaching he had more to say about God's love than God's wrath. His personal experience of conversion came when he felt overwhelmed with a sense of God's majesty and grandeur, rather than a fear of hell. Edwards served a Puritan congregation, where he believed that only those who had been fully converted ought to receive communion; his congregation thought otherwise. Edwards left that congregation and carried out mission work among the Housatonic Indians of Massachusetts. He became president of the College of New Jersey, later to be known as Princeton University.

March 23, 2016
Wednesday in Holy Week

This day was formerly called "Spy Wednesday," an allusion to the gospel accounts in which Judas is identified as the betrayer of Jesus. As Jesus endured the suffering of the cross, we are called to run the race of life with perseverance, confident of the joy to come. In the Three Days, which begin tomorrow evening, we will journey with Christ from darkness to light, from captivity to freedom, from death to life.

Prayer of the Day

Almighty God, your Son our Savior suffered at human hands and endured the shame of the cross. Grant that we may walk in the way of his cross and find it the way of life and peace, through Jesus Christ, our Savior and Lord, who lives and reigns with you and the Holy Spirit, one God, now and forever.

Gospel Acclamation

May I never boast of | anything* except the cross of our Lord | Jesus Christ. (Gal. 6:14)

Readings and Psalm
Isaiah 50:4-9a

The servant of the Lord expresses absolute confidence in his final vindication, despite the fact that he has been struck and spit upon. This characteristic of the servant played an important role in the early church for understanding the suffering, death, and resurrection of Jesus.

Psalm 70

Be pleased, O God, to deliver me. (Ps. 70:1)

Hebrews 12:1-3

In the way of the cross, Jesus has blazed the trail for our salvation. With faithful perseverance, we follow in his footsteps.

John 13:21-32

At the last supper, Jesus identifies Judas Iscariot as the one who will betray him, and sends him on his way.

Preface   Sunday of the Passion

Color   Scarlet *or* Purple

THE THREE DAYS

PREPARING FOR THE THREE DAYS

In academic settings, students often need to fit in more coursework than a semester's schedule allows. One solution is to take an intensive course, which is, as the name implies, intense. The student will be tired at the end but also richer for the focused learning. Every liturgical year, the church gathers for an *intensive* in Christian identity. The liturgies of Maundy Thursday, Good Friday, and the Vigil of Easter with their intense hearing, singing, washing, eating, and praying school us as cross and resurrection people. The days' readings and rituals may not change from year to year, but *we* have changed in the past year. This worship meets our changed identities, re-forming us into Christ's body for the sake of the world.

Maundy Thursday: mandate and grace

"Great God, your love has called us here, as we, by love, for love were made" (ELW 358). Loving as we have been loved. This is Jesus' command, the mandate (Lat., *mandatum*) for which Maundy Thursday is named. Living into our Christian identity is both mandate and grace. The words and rituals of this night make demands of us. We begin in confession. We hear the command to the Israelites to sacrifice a lamb and mark their doorposts. We hear our Lord's command to "do this in remembrance of me." We are commanded to love one another, a command enacted in the washing of another's feet.

With Peter, we go on the defense: "You will not wash my feet." Some congregations observe Maundy Thursday without footwashing or include only a symbolic footwashing of the worship leaders. Lutherans claim law and gospel; therefore, with the mandate of Maundy Thursday comes great love. God loves us in spite of our defensiveness. A footwashing can be a life-changing ritual action, but notice that the command is not to observe the washing itself but to love one another as Christ has loved us. Whether beginning this rite or continuing in a well-established footwashing tradition, be aware of the intense intimacy of this act, an intensity that can elicit fear in some. Take care that the teaching and ritual of footwashing invite rather than compel.

Practicing footwashing beforehand could help your congregation embrace this ritual more fully. Consider washing feet during an education time. If your congregation celebrates first communion on Maundy Thursday, have the children assist with the footwashing. If coming "up front" is too intense for some, provide multiple footwashing stations, including a station or two at the rear or sides of your worship space.

If footwashing is not a part of your congregation's Maundy Thursday practice, consider enlisting a small circle of diverse participants to carefully prepare and prayerfully enact this rite. Either "Great God, your love has called us" (ELW 358) or "Where charity and love prevail" (ELW 359) would provide effective auditory reinforcement of this rite's significance and power.

God's great love is poured out for us as forgiveness, as water over our feet and as the wine of suffering and gladness. In the words of Brian Wren's hymn, this love comes "not through some merit, right, or claim, but by [God's] gracious love alone" (ELW 358).

Good Friday: suffering and healing

Children are often the first to notice the paradox of Good Friday. "Mom, why is this day called good if Jesus died?" How do we live into this paradox as grown children of God? Can we claim that the cross is simultaneously an instrument of suffering and a tree of life offering healing?

Which passion?

One way to live into the paradox is by taking a closer look at the passion narrative, a key element of this liturgy. Here is a practical matter that deserves attention. Both Good Friday and the Sunday of the Passion/Palm Sunday include the passion narrative. What is your response to someone in your congregation who asks, "Why should I come to church on Good Friday when I've already heard the passion story on Sunday?"

A biblical professor once called the Bible an authorized argument; it is not one voice, but a chorus of many voices, voices that clash at times. We have not one passion narrative but four, each one telling a slightly different story. When we worship on Passion/Palm Sunday this year, we hear the passion according to Luke. Yet on Good Friday, we hear the passion according to John. These gospel accounts share the basic plotlines but have distinct moods and emphases.

We are richer for being drawn into both stories, the more chaotic, human drama in Luke and what Jonathan Linman calls the "serene confidence" of John (*New Proclamation, Year C 2013: Advent through Holy Week* [Augsburg Fortress, 2012], 217).

Enrich this day's reading of John's passion narrative by presenting it in a manner distinct from Passion Sunday's reading from Luke. One possibility would be to recruit a team to present the text as a subdued but dramatic readers' theater. Recruit the team well in advance and schedule a rehearsal in the worship space at the same time of day as the Good Friday service, if possible. Encourage team members to read at a steady pace and to integrate timely pauses at appropriate points in the reading.

The need for two songs

We benefit not only from hearing contrasting passion narratives days apart, but also from responding in song. So much of the piety of Good Friday (and Passion Sunday) is contained in what we sing. Spend some time with "O sacred head, now wounded" (ELW 351/352) and "There in God's garden" (ELW 342). The first is often suggested as part of Passion Sunday, the second as the sending hymn on Good Friday. Notice the very personal human suffering of Gerhardt's hymn and the triumph and healing of the cross in "There in God's garden." How can both open up the paradox of suffering and healing in Holy Week?

Easter Vigil: death and life

This is *the* night, the night to be immersed in who we are as God's people. This night overflows with biblical images of a world redeemed in Jesus Christ. We come not to get all the answers, but to be filled to the brim with stories that both refresh and perplex us. At first it could appear that the Vigil is a simple movement from dark to light, from death to life. We await the magic moment when the lights come on and, yes, it is Easter. Yet it remains dark outside when we leave worship. Just as Good Friday contains elements of both suffering and triumph, so does the Vigil. The stories central to this night are not without suffering; what about those who miss the ark? Those on the other side of the sea? The unfortunate ones who lift Shadrach, Meshach, and Abednego into the flames? We identify with suffering; we know it in our bones. Yet we are given a new heart and a new spirit; light shines in the darkness.

The Vigil in time and space

Practical matters guide our thinking and planning about this service. Context will vary, but especially with this service, planning well in advance and involving people of all ages in leadership roles will make for more enriching worship.

- When will the service be held? An earlier time allows for greater participation for families with young children and the elderly. A later time allows for gathering in darkness, a service similar in character to a midnight Christmas Eve liturgy. Know your context and choose a time that will work best.
- How long will it be? Will your service have numerous baptisms? This might influence the number of readings you choose. If this is the first time your congregation has held a Vigil, will you build gradually, perhaps beginning with a service of light and readings only? Or will you hold the Vigil in its fullness, spending time in advance teaching and planning?
- Where will the service be held? Much can be gained from a Vigil that begins in one place and ends in another. The fire might begin outside, the readings in a fellowship hall, and baptism and communion in the main worship space. If you are able to experience the Easter Vigil readings somewhere other than in the main worship space, you could arrange the seating so that it encircles the reader. Children can relax with cushions on the floor, and subdued lighting can be augmented by candlelight. Again, these questions are especially contextual. Your space and people will determine what will work best.

Music

Worship over the Three Days includes a great deal of movement, such as processions, footwashing, and communion. Because of this complexity in action, music for these liturgies can be simpler; less may be more. The sheer amount of music that enriches the Three Days will be complex enough. At all times, but especially in these days, music serves the word and actions of worship. Questions of fittingness come to the forefront: Why will this song work here and not there?

Context is especially important in services that involve changes in space or lighting. As you make plans for what the assembly will sing, ask the following:

- Where will this be sung?
- What instruments will lead the singing? From where?
- What is the lighting in the room?
- Will the people be holding candles? Will they need books or a worship folder?

Paperless music—music sung without the aid of printed materials—would be fitting for these liturgies when well prepared and skillfully led. Such music is often less complex but intense in its own way. For more on how such practices enrich assembly worship, look into Music that Makes Community (musicthatmakescommunity.org).

Without rests, music makes no sense. Likewise, silence has a role to play in worship. How can the worship leaders in your place invite gracious silence? How can silence be welcomed so that it is "not a terrible void, but full of glorious, cruciform, divine presence" (Linman, *New Proclamation, Year C 2013*, 220)?

Environment

If your building infrastructure allows you to adjust the relative intensity and brightness of lighting in your worship space, explore how you can make choices that will have a dramatic and meaningful impact on worship. Experiment with using inexpensive spotlights placed on the floor.

If you made a mobile tintinnabularium for Christmas, bring it back for the Easter Vigil to amplify the return of the alleluias. If there is a procession associated with alleluia's return, include the tintinnabularium in the procession. Encourage worshipers to bring bells to the Vigil and ring them whenever an alleluia is spoken or sung.

If you planted amaryllis bulbs at the beginning of Lent, gather the children on Easter Day and reflect with them about the changes that have taken place in the flowerpots in recent weeks. Sing "In the bulb there is a flower" (*LifeSongs*, #56) one more time.

Here are three ideas for visual art in the worship space that could be unveiled or used for the first time at the Easter Vigil and then left in place throughout the Easter season:

- If your parish includes people with gifts for crafting and sewing, consider engaging them to weave together a variety of white and gold ribbons to create fabric from which to construct paraments and vestments (05_Easter.Textiles.pdf)*. The ribbons, which intersect to form many crosses, will remind worshipers of our calling to become signs of the risen Christ in the world.
- Consider engaging broad participation in creating a volume of paper butterflies (see 05_Easter.Butterfly.pdf)* and using them to construct a cascading mobile. If possible, position the mobile over the font as a reminder of baptism as our participation in Christ's dying and rising.
- The readings for the Easter season include numerous references to the creative power of God in fashioning newness within and among God's people. If your liturgical arts team is ready to take on a project, invite them to consider fashioning a three-dimensional, cruciform sculpture to capture the energy of the new creation that Christ ushers into our world (see 05_Easter.Sculpture.pdf* for examples to spark your creativity). Install the sculpture over the font or table for a season-long reminder of the newness that Christ secures for us at Easter.

Seasonal Checklist

- Review the liturgies for Maundy Thursday, Good Friday, and the Vigil of Easter in *Evangelical Lutheran Worship* (Assembly Edition, pp. 258–270; Leaders Edition, pp. 628–653).
- See extensive backgrounds and practical helps for these days in *Worship Guidebook for Lent and the Three Days*, as well as additional music for the services in the companion *Music Sourcebook for Lent and the Three Days* (both Augsburg Fortress, 2009).
- Arrange rehearsals for all the liturgies of the Three Days. These services are unique and happen only once each year, so all worship leaders, even those who have been involved in previous years, need to prepare for their roles.
- Be sure that altar guild members are well equipped and informed about their tasks for these busy days.
- Order worship participation leaflets if used for the Good Friday service.
- Order worship folder covers for Holy Week services.
- It is helpful to prepare printed materials for worship leaders for the Three Days. Consider placing all the texts and musical resources needed into three-ring binders (ceremonial binders in liturgical colors are available from Augsburg Fortress). Highlight speaking parts and instructions for each worship leader in individual copies.
- Publicize Holy Week and Easter services in local newspapers, online (church website, Facebook, Twitter), and through other media.
- Determine whether additional handheld candles are needed for the Easter Vigil.
- Purchase a new paschal candle.
- Prepare extra communion elements and communionware needed for large numbers of communicants during Holy Week and Easter.
- If the Easter Vigil (or Easter Sunday) is to be observed as a baptismal festival or the culmination of a catechumenal process, see the suggestions in the Time after Epiphany seasonal checklist, p. 77, as well as the Easter Vigil planning resources in *Go Make Disciples: An Invitation to Baptismal Living* ([Augsburg Fortress, 2012], pp. 108–123).

---

* Download at http://store.augsburgfortress.org/media/temp/SundaysSeasons/PDFs.zip

WORSHIP TEXTS FOR THE THREE DAYS

MAUNDY THURSDAY

Confession and Forgiveness

Friends in Christ,
in this Lenten season we have heard our Lord's call
to struggle against sin, death, and the devil—
all that keeps us from loving God and each other.
This is the struggle to which we were called at baptism.
[We have shared this discipline of Lent with new brothers
and sisters in Christ who will be baptized at the Easter Vigil.]

Within the community of the church,
God never wearies of forgiving sin
and giving the peace of reconciliation.
On this night
let us confess our sin against God and our neighbor,
and enter the celebration of the great Three Days
reconciled with God and with one another.

Silence is kept for reflection.

Most merciful God,
**we confess that we are captive to sin
and cannot free ourselves.
We have sinned against you in thought, word, and deed,
by what we have done and by what we have left undone.
We have not loved you with our whole heart;
we have not loved our neighbors as ourselves.
For the sake of your Son, Jesus Christ,
have mercy on us.
Forgive us, renew us, and lead us,
so that we may delight in your will
and walk in your ways,
to the glory of your holy name. Amen.**

In the mercy of almighty God,
Jesus Christ was given to die for us,
and for his sake God forgives us all our sins.
As a called and ordained minister of the church of Christ
and by his authority, I therefore declare to you
the entire forgiveness of all your sins,
in the name of the Father, and of the ☩ Son,
and of the Holy Spirit.
Amen.

Greeting

The grace of our Lord Jesus Christ, the love of God,
and the communion of the Holy Spirit be with you all.
And also with you.

Offering Prayer

God of glory,
receive these gifts and the offering of our lives.
As Jesus was lifted up from the earth,
draw us to your heart in the midst of this world,
that all creation may be brought from bondage to freedom,
from darkness to light, and from death to life;
through Jesus Christ, our Savior and Lord.
Amen.

Invitation to Communion

Where charity and love abide, there is God.
Rejoice in this holy communion.

Prayer after Communion

Lord Jesus, in a wonderful sacrament
you strengthen us with the saving power
of your suffering, death, and resurrection.
May this sacrament of your body and blood
so work in us that the fruits of your redemption
will show forth in the way we live,
for you live and reign with the Father and the Holy Spirit,
one God, now and forever.
Amen.

VIGIL OF EASTER

Greeting

The grace of our Lord Jesus Christ, the love of God,
and the communion of the Holy Spirit be with you all.
And also with you.

Sisters and brothers in Christ, on this most holy night
when our Savior Jesus Christ passed from death to life,
we gather with the church throughout the world
in vigil and prayer. This is the passover of Jesus Christ.
Through light and the word,
through water and oil, bread and wine,
we proclaim Christ's death and resurrection,
share Christ's triumph over sin and death,
and await Christ's coming again in glory.

Offering Prayer

Blessed are you, O God, ruler of heaven and earth.
Day by day you shower us with blessings.
As you have raised us to new life in Christ,
give us glad and generous hearts,
ready to praise you and to respond to those in need,
through Jesus Christ, our Savior and Lord.
Amen.

Invitation to Communion

This is the feast of victory for our God. Alleluia.

Prayer after Communion

Mighty and compassionate God,
you have brought us over from death to life
through your Son, our risen Savior,
and you have fed us with the food of life
in the sacrament of his body and blood.
Send us now into the world in peace,
and grant us strength and courage
to love and serve you
with gladness and singleness of heart;
through Jesus Christ our Lord.
Amen.

Blessing

The blessing of the Lord God Almighty,
the blessing of + Christ, the Lamb who was slain,
and the blessing of the Spirit of truth
be among you and remain with you always.
Amen.

Dismissal

Alleluia. Go in peace. Share the good news.
Thanks be to God. Alleluia.

Worship texts for Easter Day and Easter Evening begin on page 170.

SEASONAL RITES FOR THE THREE DAYS

Maundy Thursday

John 13:1-17, 31b-35

Preparation

You will need six readers. If presented simply by a chorus of six, one rehearsal should suffice. If mimes or dancers are added, more rehearsal time will be needed.

This reading is proposed as a chorus. All six readers stand together. It is also possible to have another group mime the actions of the characters or to accompany the reading with liturgical dance.

Script

All Readers: The holy gospel according to John.

1: Now before the festival of the Passover, Jesus knew that his hour had come to depart from this world and go to the Father.

2: Having loved his own who were in the world, he loved them to the end.

3: The devil had already put it into the heart of Judas son of Simon Iscariot to betray him.

4: And during supper, Jesus, knowing that the Father had given all things into his hands, and that he had come from God and was going to God, got up from the table,

5: took off his outer robe,

6: and tied a towel around himself.

1: Then he poured water into a basin and began to wash the disciples' feet and to wipe them with the towel that was tied around him.

2: He came to Simon Peter, who said to him, "Lord, are you going to wash my feet?"

3: Jesus answered, "You do not know now what I am doing, but later you will understand."

4: Peter said to him, "You will never wash my feet."

5: Jesus answered, "Unless I wash you, you have no share with me."

6: Simon Peter said to him, "Lord, not my feet only but also my hands and my head!"

1: Jesus said to him, "One who has bathed does not need to wash, except for the feet, but is entirely clean. And you are clean, though not all of you."

2: For he knew who was to betray him; for this reason he said, "Not all of you are clean."

3: After he had washed their feet, had put on his robe, and had returned to the table, he said to them, "Do you know what I have done to you?

4: You call me Teacher and Lord—and you are right, for that is what I am.

5: So if I, your Lord and Teacher, have washed your feet, you also ought to wash one another's feet.

6: For I have set you an example, that you also should do as I have done to you.

1: Very truly, I tell you, servants are not greater than their master, nor are messengers greater than the one who sent them.

2: If you know these things, you are blessed if you do them.

3: Now the Son of Man has been glorified, and God has been glorified in him.

4: If God has been glorified in him, God will also glorify him in himself and will glorify him at once.

5: Little children, I am with you only a little longer. You will look for me; and as I said to the Jews so now I say to you, 'Where I am going, you cannot come.'

6: I give you a new commandment,

6, 1: that you love one another.

6, 1, 2: Just as I have loved you,

6, 1, 2, 3: you also should love one another.

6, 1, 2, 3, 4: By this everyone will know that you are my disciples,

All readers: if you have love for one another."
A brief pause.
The gospel of the Lord.

Testing of Abraham
Vigil of Easter

Genesis 22:1-18

Preparation

You will need five readers. If presented without movement, one rehearsal should suffice. If presented with movement, possibly a second rehearsal is needed.

If presented without movement, the Narrator, Abraham, and Isaac (a young person if possible) could stand together. Or the Narrator may stand at the lectern, pulpit, or ambo. God and the Angel are unseen (placed in a balcony, outside the worship space, or otherwise hidden), but heard over a sound system. Directions for movement by Abraham and Isaac are indicated within the script.

Script

Narrator: A reading from Genesis.

God tested Abraham.

God: Abraham!

Abraham and Isaac are seated in the assembly; Abraham stands.
Abraham: Here I am.

God: Take your son, your only son Isaac, whom you love, and go to the land of Moriah, and offer him there as a burnt offering on one of the mountains that I shall show you.

Abraham and Isaac leave their places and walk through the assembly to a place in front of it.
Narrator: So Abraham rose early in the morning, saddled his donkey, and took two of his young men with him, and his son Isaac; he cut the wood for the burnt offering, and set out and went to the place in the distance that God had shown him. On the third day Abraham looked up and saw the place far away. Then Abraham said to his young men,

Abraham speaks to the assembly.
Abraham: Stay here with the donkey; the boy and I will go over there; we will worship, and then we will come back to you.

Abraham and Isaac walk to a different place in front of the assembly.
Narrator: Abraham took the wood of the burnt offering and laid it on his son Isaac, and he himself carried the fire and the knife. So the two of them walked on together. Isaac said to his father Abraham,

Isaac: Father!

Abraham: Here I am, my son.

Isaac: The fire and the wood are here, but where is the lamb for a burnt offering?

Abraham: God himself will provide the lamb for a burnt offering, my son.

Narrator: So the two of them walked on together.

When they came to the place that God had shown him, Abraham built an altar there and laid the wood in order. He bound his son Isaac, and laid him on the altar, on top of the wood. Then Abraham reached out his hand and took the knife to kill his son. But the angel of the Lord called to him from heaven and said,

Angel: Abraham, Abraham!

Abraham: Here I am.

Angel: Do not lay your hand on the boy or do anything to him;

Angel and God: for now I know that you fear God, since you have not withheld your son, your only son, from me.

Narrator: Abraham looked up and saw a ram, caught in a thicket by its horns. Abraham went and took the ram and offered it up as a burnt offering instead of his son. So Abraham called that place

Narrator, Abraham, and Isaac: "The Lord will provide";

Narrator: as it is said to this day, "On the mount of the Lord it shall be provided."
A brief pause.

The angel of the Lord called to Abraham a second time from heaven, and said,

Angel: By myself I have sworn, says the Lord:

Angel and God: Because you have done this, and have not withheld your son, your only son,

God: I will indeed bless you, and I will make your offspring as numerous as the stars of heaven and as the sand that is on the seashore. And your offspring shall possess the gate of their enemies, and by your offspring shall all the nations of the earth gain blessing for themselves, because you have obeyed my voice.

Narrator: The word of the Lord.

March 24, 2016
Maundy Thursday

With nightfall our Lenten observance comes to an end, and we gather with Christians around the world to celebrate the Three Days of Jesus' death and resurrection. At the heart of the Maundy Thursday liturgy is Jesus' commandment to love one another. As Jesus washed the feet of his disciples, we are called to follow his example as we humbly care for one another, especially the poor and the unloved. At the Lord's table we remember Jesus' sacrifice of his life, even as we are called to offer ourselves in love for the life of the world.

Prayer of the Day

Holy God, source of all love, on the night of his betrayal, Jesus gave us a new commandment, to love one another as he loves us. Write this commandment in our hearts, and give us the will to serve others as he was the servant of all, your Son, Jesus Christ, our Savior and Lord, who lives and reigns with you and the Holy Spirit, one God, now and forever.

or

Eternal God, in the sharing of a meal your Son established a new covenant for all people, and in the washing of feet he showed us the dignity of service. Grant that by the power of your Holy Spirit these signs of our life in faith may speak again to our hearts, feed our spirits, and refresh our bodies, through Jesus Christ, our Savior and Lord, who lives and reigns with you and the Holy Spirit, one God, now and forever.

Gospel Acclamation

I give you a ¹ new commandment,* that you love one another just as I ¹ have loved you. (John 13:34)

Readings and Psalm
Exodus 12:1-4 [5-10] 11-14

Israel remembered its deliverance from slavery in Egypt by celebrating the festival of Passover. This festival featured the Passover lamb, whose blood was used as a sign to protect God's people from the threat of death. The early church described the Lord's supper using imagery from the Passover, especially in portraying Jesus as the lamb who delivers God's people from sin and death.

Psalm 116:1-2, 12-19

I will lift the cup of salvation and call on the name of the Lord. (Ps. 116:13)

1 Corinthians 11:23-26

In the bread and cup of the Lord's supper, we experience intimate fellowship with Christ and with one another, because it involves his body given for us and the new covenant in his blood. Faithful participation in this meal is a living proclamation of Christ's death until he comes in the future.

John 13:1-17, 31b-35

The story of the last supper in John's gospel recalls a remarkable event not mentioned elsewhere: Jesus performs the duty of a slave, washing the feet of his disciples and urging them to do the same for one another.

Preface   Maundy Thursday

Color   Scarlet *or* White

Prayers of Intercession

The prayers are prepared locally for each occasion. The following examples may be adapted or used as appropriate.

At this service of communion at Christ's table, let us join together in prayer for the church, the world, and all in need. *A brief silence.*

Blessed are you, O God, for the church. Bring all people into your fellowship of love. Make us worthy to share your food. Pass us over from death into life. Hear us, O God.
Your mercy is great.

Blessed are you for this good earth. Protect the waters from pollution. Bless the growing crops with your rain and sun. Hear us, O God.
Your mercy is great.

Blessed are you for our nation. Inspire us and all nations to live in peace and concord. Free those who are enslaved by injustice. We pray especially for . . . . Hear us, O God.
Your mercy is great.

Blessed are you for this table. We pray for the hungry, those in need, the sick (*especially*), and for those alienated from you. Answer their cries. Hear us, O God.
Your mercy is great.

Blessed are you for this community of faith. Form us into servants for this neighborhood. Give us your spirit of service. Hear us, O God.
Your mercy is great.
Here other intercessions may be offered.
Blessed are you for all believers who have gone before us (*especially Archbishop Oscar Romero and . . .*). Bring us all at the end into your everlasting glory. Hear us, O God.
Your mercy is great.
Receive, O loving God, our prayers, and grant that we and all people may know the mercy of your Son, Jesus Christ, our Savior and Lord.
Amen.

Images in the Readings

A primary image for Maundy Thursday is the **servant**. We recall from Passion Sunday's Servant Song that the image of servant is not a readily accessible symbol in today's society. Even the waitstaff in many restaurants now present themselves not as servants but as personal friends. John's gospel offers us a lowly, even dirty, task as appropriate for a true servant.

The readings are filled with **body**: the body of the dead lamb, cooked and eaten; the body of Christ, shared in the bread; the body of the neighbor's actual feet. For people who like to keep their individual space, it is countercultural to share in one another's body in this public way.

The first reading says that it is the lamb's **blood** that reminds God not to punish the Israelites, and Paul says that the wine is a new covenant in Jesus' blood. In the ancient world, life was seen as residing in the blood. Thus pouring out of blood is giving up of life. Isn't it interesting that small children lick a bleeding wound in hopes of keeping their blood inside their body?

In all three readings, the people of God experience themselves as a **meal** community. Humans must eat to live, and humans eat together to become and maintain community. The Israelites are to keep the Passover meal "as a perpetual ordinance"; Paul assumes and corrects the meal practice of the Corinthians; John describes the last loving meal Jesus had with his disciples before his arrest. So it is over the centuries most Christian assemblies have shared a meal at their weekly meeting. The liturgy of the Three Days begins with this meal.

Ideas for the Day

◆ Perhaps you have heard the old joke about the Easter ham, how the ends must be cut off just so. Why? No one knows. (Three generations ago, the pan was too small. Ha-ha.) Tonight, an elaborate recipe for lamb is included in our holy book for a deeper purpose: to remember the journey of freedom. Our ancestors ate it with haste, sandals on their feet, ready to go, for Pharaoh's tyranny over them was beginning to fail. From this feast, the band of slaves walked through parted Red Sea waters and into freedom. Do our meals still tell stories?

◆ The story that takes us from death to life begins on Maundy Thursday, and our whole bodies are involved in the telling. Our heads will be touched when the pastor pronounces absolution. Our feet will be bathed by a neighbor during footwashing. Our mouths and bellies will receive the bread and wine. Blessing, washing, eating, and then darkness. Our whole selves will be disoriented for a time as the lights darken while the space is stripped. We speak of muscle memory, and it's true. Our bodies retain knowledge that our minds often neglect. Walk through this liturgy with your leaders, and with those preparing for baptism. Help the bodies of those who are gathered find their way through the occasional—or brand-new—actions of each ritual.

◆ Susan Briehl describes tonight this way: "Setting aside our shoes, our reluctance to serve, and our objections to being served, we take up the towel and fill the basin. Washing and being washed, we enact the love we pray to embody every day" (*Worship Guidebook for Lent and the Three Days* [Minneapolis: Augsburg Fortress, 2009], 93).

Connections with the Liturgy

In *Evangelical Lutheran Worship*'s Thanksgiving at the Table I, adapted from the 1958 *Service Book and Hymnal*'s compilation from ancient Christian sources, we cite this day's words of Paul: "For as often as we eat of this bread and drink from this cup, we proclaim the Lord's death until he comes."

Let the Children Come

You hardly need to welcome children into this liturgy. The readings, the music, the footwashing, the meal, and the stripping of the altar engage every sense. The meaning of servanthood is not lost on the young when another bends to wash their feet in warm water. Let children carry the gifts of bread and wine to the table. Eight- to eleven-year-olds often are drawn to the solemnity of this night. With adequate rehearsal, they and older children could help with the stripping of the table (and the dressing of the table at the Vigil).

Assembly Song and Music for the Day

Because of the nature of this day, music suggestions are listed by place in the service and categorized by type of leadership (in brackets): Ch=Choral; CC=Children's Choir; KI=Keyboard/Instrumental; HB=Handbell. Many suggestions require assembly participation.

Laying On of Hands

Come, ye disconsolate ELW 607, TFF 186
Eternal Spirit of the living Christ ELW 402, LBW 441

p Anonymous. "Forgive Your People/Perdona a tu pueblo." MSB1
      S437.

✧ Tangled Blue. "Thankful and Broken" from *Storm Home: A
      Collection of Music from Humble Walk Artists-in-Residence.*
      humblewalk.bandcamp.com.

p ● Busarow, Donald. "Great God, Your Love Has Called Us." SATB,
      org, 2 trbl inst. AFP 9781451479355. [Ch]

● Cherwien, David M. "Song 1" from *Augsburg Organ Library:
      Baptism and Communion.* Org. AFP 9780800623555. [KI]

p Bettcher, Peggy. "Alas! and Did My Savior Bleed." 3-5 oct, opt 2 oct
      hc, L2+. HOP 2677. [HB]

Psalmody and Acclamations

Bell, John L. "I Love the Lord." SATB, assembly, kybd, vc. GIA
      G-8013.

Farlee, Robert Buckley. "Psalm 116:1-2, 12-19" from PWC.

Mummert, Mark. "Psalm 116:1-2, 12-19," Refrain 1, from PSCY.

✧ Bruxvoort Colligan, Richard. "Now to God I Make My Vows
      (Psalm 116)" from *Sharing the Road.* AFP 9780800678630.
      psalmimmersion.bandcamp.com.

p (GA) "I Give You a New Commandment." ELW, tone 11. MSB1 S438.

Hymn of the Day

Great God, your love has called us   ELW 358, WOV 666   RYBURN
Lord, who the night you were betrayed   ELW 463, LBW 206   SONG 1
When twilight comes   ELW 566, WOV 663   DAPIT HAPON

Footwashing

Where charity and love prevail   ELW 359, LBW 126, TFF 84
Love consecrates the humblest act   ELW 360, LBW 122

✧ Jobe, Kari/Mia Fieldes/Paul Baloche. "Beautiful" from CCLI.

p Nelson, Ronald. "Whoever Would Be Great among You." SAB, gtr or
      kybd. AFP 9780800645809. [Ch]

Schalk, Carl. "Where Charity and Love Prevail." 2 pt trbl, org, ob.
      CPH 982701PODWEB. [CC]

Setting the Table

*Music Sourcebook for Lent and the Three Days (MSB1) includes
an appendix with hymn stanzas appropriate for use during the
setting of the table on this and other days. These stanzas are
also included on the CD-ROM that accompanies the volume.*

◉ Lee, Hyun Chul. "Come to the Table" from *Glory to God.* U. WJK
      9780664238971.

✧ Kurtz, Rachel. "Make a Difference" from *Broken & Lowdown.*
      rachelkurtz.org.

✧ The Welcome Wagon. "Up on a Mountain" from *Welcome to the
      Welcome Wagon.* asthmatickitty.com.

p Scott, K. Lee. "As We Gather at Your Table." SAB, org. AFP
      9780800678081. [Ch]

Adams, Aaron. "Remember Me." U/2 pt, kybd, opt fl. LOR
      10/2459K. [CC]

● Farlee, Robert Buckley. "Song 1" from *Augsburg Organ Library:
      Lent.* Org. AFP 9780800658977. [KI]

● Organ, Anne Krentz. "Dapit hapon" from *Global Piano Reflections.*
      Pno, wch, fc. AFP 9780800658014. [KI]

p Glasgow, Michael J. "Reminiscence." 3-7 oct hb, opt 3, 6 or 7 oct hc,
      L3+. CG CGB814. [HB]

Communion

Lord, who the night you were betrayed   ELW 463, LBW 206
Jesu, Jesu, fill us with your love   ELW 708, LS 146, TFF 83, WOV 765
Thee we adore, O Savior   ELW 476, LBW 199

◉ Hurd, Bob, and Pia Moriarty. "Pan de Vida" from *My Heart Sings
      Out.* U. Church Publishing 9780898694741.

✧ Houge, Nate. "Out on the Plains" from *Reform Follows Function.*
      natehouge.com.

Lovelace, Austin. "An Upper Room." SATB, kybd. GIA G-5885. [Ch]

p Pooler, Marie. "Lamb of God" from *Unison and Two-Part Anthems.*
      U/2 pt, kybd. AFP 9781451421149. [CC]

p ● Shields, Valerie. "Dapit hapon" from *Introductions and Alternate
      Accompaniments for Piano,* vol. 5. Pno. AFP 9780800623630.
      [KI]

p Moklebust, Cathy. "When You Do This, Remember Me." 3-5 oct
      hb, opt 3 oct hc, L2, CG CGB866. Opt full score with org, CG
      CGB865. [HB]

Stripping of the Altar

Miller, Aaron David. "Psalm 22" from PWC.

Mummert, Mark. "Psalm 22," Refrain 1, from PSCY.

p Highben, Zebulon M. "Lord, I Cry to You (Psalm 88)." MSB1 S446.

Hopkins, Edward. "Psalm 22" from *Anglican Chant Psalter.* Church
      Publishing 9780898691351.

Sending

None

Thursday, March 24

Oscar Arnulfo Romero, Bishop of El Salvador, martyr, died 1980

Romero is remembered for his advocacy on behalf of the
poor in El Salvador, though it was not a characteristic of his
early priesthood. After being appointed as archbishop of
San Salvador, he preached against the political repression in
his country. He and other priests and church workers were
considered traitors for their bold stand for justice, especially defending the rights of the poor. After several years of
threats to his life, Romero was assassinated while presiding
at the eucharist. During the 1980s thousands died in El Salvador during political unrest.

March 25, 2016
Good Friday

At the heart of the Good Friday liturgy is the passion according to John, which proclaims Jesus as a triumphant king who reigns from the cross. The ancient title for this day—the triumph of the cross—reminds us that the church gathers not to mourn this day but to celebrate Christ's life-giving passion and to find strength and hope in the tree of life. In the ancient bidding prayer we offer petitions for all the world for whom Christ died. Today's liturgy culminates in the Easter Vigil tomorrow evening.

Prayer of the Day

Almighty God, look with loving mercy on your family, for whom our Lord Jesus Christ was willing to be betrayed, to be given over to the hands of sinners, and to suffer death on the cross; who now lives and reigns with you and the Holy Spirit, one God, forever and ever.

or

Merciful God, your Son was lifted up on the cross to draw all people to himself. Grant that we who have been born out of his wounded side may at all times find mercy in him, Jesus Christ, our Savior and Lord, who lives and reigns with you and the Holy Spirit, one God, now and forever.

Gospel Acclamation

Look to Jesus, who for the sake of the joy that was set before him endured the cross, disregard- | ing its shame,* and has taken his seat at the right hand of the | throne of God. (Heb. 12:2)

Readings and Psalm

Isaiah 52:13—53:12

The fourth servant poem promises ultimate vindication for the servant, who made his life an offering for sin. The early church saw in the servant's pouring himself out to death and being numbered with the transgressors important keys for understanding the death of Jesus.

Psalm 22

My God, my God, why have you forsaken me? (Ps. 22:1)

Hebrews 10:16-25

In the death of Jesus, forgiveness of sins is worked and access to God is established. Hence, when we gather together for worship and when we love others we experience anew the benefits of Jesus' death.

or Hebrews 4:14-16; 5:7-9

In his death Jesus functions as great high priest who experiences temptation and suffering in order that we would receive mercy and find grace, because he is the source of true salvation.

John 18:1—19:42

On Good Friday, the story of Jesus' passion—from his arrest to his burial—is read in its entirety from the Gospel of John.

Holy communion is normally not celebrated on Good Friday; accordingly, no preface is provided. The worship space having been stripped on the preceding evening, no paraments are used today.

Prayers of Intercession

On Good Friday, the church's ancient Bidding Prayer is said or sung. See Evangelical Lutheran Worship Leaders Edition, pp. 636–638.

Images in the Readings

The **cross** was the electric chair of the Roman Empire, the means of execution for low-class criminals. Other cultures have seen in the shape of the cross a sign of the four corners of the earth itself. Christians mark the newly baptized with this sign, God coming through suffering and death, aligned with all who are rejected, and surprisingly in this way bringing life to the whole earth. In the suggested sixth-century hymn "Sing, my tongue," the cross is paradoxically likened to the archetypal tree of life.

In John's passion narrative, Jesus of Nazareth is called King of the Jews, the Son of God, and most significantly, I Am, the very **name** of God. Christians see in the man dying on the cross the mystery of God's self-giving love. Along with the witnesses in John's passion, we can sing with the hymn writer Caroline Noel, "At the name of Jesus every knee shall bow, every tongue confess him king of glory now" (ELW 416).

In the Israelite sacrificial system, the **lamb** represented the life of the nomadic herders, and killing the lamb symbolized a plea that God would receive the animal's death as a gift to prompt divine mercy. The New Testament often uses the image of the lamb as one way to understand the meaning of Jesus' death. The book of Revelation recalls Good Friday and Easter in its paradoxical vision of a lamb seated on a throne and "standing as if it had been slaughtered."

But any single image—such as the lamb—is not sufficient. Thus we are given the opposite image, Christ as the **high priest** who does the slaughtering. According to Israelite religion, the people needed an intermediary to approach God. Christ then is the mediator who prays to God for us. Yet for John, Christ is the God whom our prayers address. Good Friday lays each image next to another one, for no single metaphor can fully explain the mystery of Christ.

Ideas for the Day

◆ Why have we come together on a Friday night when we could be out at the movies or home enjoying supper? And why have we gathered around such a disturbing story? Bloodshed, torture, death. And lest we have tuned out the most difficult image from the passion narrative, in a few moments we will bring it front and center—a large cross—into the room. What are we doing?

◆ In reverencing the cross, in bringing a rough-hewn instrument of death into the room, we are not giving praise to death and destruction. Quite the opposite. By drawing near this cross, we recall that much of the world is on a cross, also suffering and dying. When we show honor to this wood, we pray for all those who are in terrible pain. As leaders, model some of the ways your assembly can show reverence to the cross. Bow, kneel, offer votive candles or flowers for worshipers to bring forward.

◆ In bending our bodies toward this sign of bodily harm, we pray to be grafted into the nonviolent way of the one who hung on this tree, Christ, the Savior of the whole world. Amphilochius, a fourth-century bishop of Iconium, put it this way, "He is stretched out upon a cross who by his words stretched out the heavens. He is crowned with thorns who crowned the earth with flowers. They enclose him in a tomb whom creation cannot contain" (*The Sunday Sermons of the Great Fathers*, vol. 2, ed. and trans. M. F. Toal [Chicago: Henry Regnery, 1958], 92). Here, in our bodies, on this night, we anticipate the healing and redemption of the whole wide world.

Connections with the Liturgy

The Sunday liturgy opens "in the name" of the triune God; we are baptized into this triune name of God. Christians say that it is because of the exaltation of Christ on the cross that we can call upon and be sheltered within the power of God's saving name. Each time Christians assemble, it is the mystery of the life-giving cross around which we gather.

For Christians, no meeting can be so totally celebrative that it does not have at its core our faith in the salvific death of Christ.

For each day's morning and evening prayer, Martin Luther wrote, "You are to make the sign of the holy cross and say . . ." (*ELW*, pp. 1166, 1167). Many Christians choose, whenever they hear the name of God, the Father, the Son, and the Holy Spirit, to make the sign of the cross. With this hand gesture, we place the cross of Good Friday on our very bodies.

Let the Children Come

Good Friday's passion narrative is filled with violence and terror. Many parents will struggle to talk with their children about the event at the cross in ways that will build faith and foster hope. Help them by focusing children's attention on John 19:25-27. Jesus' mother and friends stick with him when everyone else has fled. This is an image of the church, which promises all its children that it will stand with them when the world is at its cruelest.

Assembly Song and Music for the Day

Because of the nature of the Good Friday liturgy, music suggestions are listed by place in the service. Many suggestions require assembly participation. For services other than the liturgy of Good Friday, see "Additional Music Suggestions" below.

Gathering

None

Psalmody and Acclamations

Hopkins, Edward. "Psalm 22" from *Anglican Chant Psalter*. Church Publishing 9780898691351.

Mummert, Mark. "Psalm 22" from PSCY.

p   Witte, Marilyn. "My God, My God (Psalm 22)." MSB1 S448.

☼   Bruxvoort Colligan, Richard. "My God, O My God (Psalm 22)" from *Sharing the Road*. AFP 9780800678630. psalmimmersion.bandcamp.com.

p   (GA) Weidler, Scott. "Look to Jesus." MSB1 S450.

Hymn of the Day

Sing, my tongue ELW 355 *PANGE LINGUA* ELW 356, LBW 118 *FORTUNATUS NEW*

Calvary ELW 354, TFF 85 *CALVARY*

Ah, holy Jesus ELW 349, LBW 123 *HERZLIEBSTER JESU*

Procession of the Cross: Dialogue

p   Organ, Anne Krentz. "Behold the Life-Giving Cross" and "We Adore You, O Christ." MSB1 S459.

p   Pavlechko, Thomas. "Behold the Life-Giving Cross" and "We Adore You, O Christ." MSB1 S458.

Procession of the Cross: Solemn Reproaches

Farlee, Robert Buckley. "Solemn Reproaches of the Cross." Solo, SATB, pno. AFP 9780800674724.

Sanders, John. "The Reproaches." SSAATTBB, org. RSCM RS362.

p Witte, Marilyn. "Solemn Reproaches." MSB1 S461.

Procession of the Cross: We Glory in Your Cross

p Haugen, Marty. "Adoramus te Christe." MSB1 S469.

Pearson, Donald. "We Glory in Your Cross, O Lord." SAB, a cap. OCP 4537.

p Weidler, Scott. "We Glory in Your Cross." MSB1 S465.

Procession of the Cross: Other Choral Music

Frahm, Frederick. "Crux Fidelis (Faithful Cross)." SAB a cap. CPH 98-3478.

McGoff, Kevin G. "This Is the Wood of the Cross." SATB, assembly. GIA G-7794.

Nicholson, Paul. "Velum Templi." SATB a cap. GIA G-7592.

Hymn of Triumph

There in God's garden   ELW 342, WOV 668

Goodness is stronger than evil   ELW 721

Jesus, keep me near the cross   ELW 335, TFF 73

Additional Music Suggestions

The suggestions listed below may also be appropriate, especially for services other than the liturgy of Good Friday.

Assembly Songs

⏚ Hontiveros, Eduardo P. "Behold the Man We Nailed on the Cross" from *Sound the Bamboo*. U. GIA G-6830.

⏚ Sato, Taihei. "Why Has God Forsaken Me?" from *Glory to God*. U. WJK 9780664238971.

✿ Bell, John L. "Lo, I Am with You" from *There Is One Among Us: Shorter Songs for Worship*. GIA G-5111.

✿ Hansen, Holly. "Under the Son" from *Storm Home: A Collection of Music from Humble Walk Artists-in-Residence*. humblewalk .bandcamp.com.

✿ Houge, Nate. "Your Work in Me" from *Reform Follows Function*. natehouge.com.

Choral

Govenor, Deborah. "Alas, and Did My Savior Bleed." SATB, fl. BP 1323.

Larsen, Libby. "God So Loved the World." SATB. OXF 9780193856646.

p Pasch, William Allen. "We Sing the Praise of Him Who Died." 2 pt mxd, opt SATB, kybd. AFP 9781451479492.

p ● Shaw, Timothy. "Ah, Holy Jesus." SATB. AFP 9781451451535.

Children's Choir

● Jennings, Carolyn. "Ah, Holy Jesus" from *Augsburg Choirbook for Women*. 2 pt trbl, vc. AFP 9781451461381.

Leo, Leonardo. "Christus factus est." SA, org. GIA G-1974.

McMillan, Alan. "O vos omnes." 2 pt trbl, org. PAR PPMO9805.

Pooler, Marie. "Wondrous Love" from *Unison and Two-Part Anthems*. U, kybd. AFP 9781451421477.

Keyboard / Instrumental

● Arnatt, Richard. "Pange lingua" from *Augsburg Organ Library: Lent*. Org. AFP 9780800658977.

p ● Lind, Richard. "Herzliebster Jesu" from *Piano Impressions for Worship*. Pno. AFP 9781451435054.

p ● Powell, Robert J. "Calvary" from *Mixtures: Hymn Preludes for Organ*. Org. AFP 9781451479553.

● Young, Jeremy. "Pange lingua" from *At the Foot of the Cross*. Pno. AFP 9780800655396.

Handbell

● Glasgow, Michael J. "Lenten Reflection" from *Ringing the Church Year*. 3-6 oct hb, opt 3 or 5 oct hc, L2+. LOR 20/1671L.

p ● Larson, Lloyd. "The Wonderful Cross with Near the Cross." 3-5 oct, L3-, HOP 2676. Opt SATB, HOP C5867.

● Nelson, Susan. "Psalm" from *A Plainchant Meditation: Morning Suite*. 3 oct, L3. AFP 9780800655464.

March 26, 2016

Resurrection of Our Lord
Vigil of Easter

This is the night! This is our Passover with Christ from darkness to light, from bondage to freedom, from death to life. Tonight is the heart of our celebration of the Three Days and the pinnacle of the church's year. The resurrection of Christ is proclaimed in word and sign, and we gather around a pillar of fire, hear ancient stories of our faith, welcome new sisters and brothers at the font, and share the food and drink of the promised land. Raised with Christ, we go forth into the world, aflame with the good news of the resurrection.

Prayer of the Day

Eternal giver of life and light, this holy night shines with the radiance of the risen Christ. Renew your church with the Spirit given us in baptism, that we may worship you in sincerity and truth and may shine as a light in the world, through your Son, Jesus Christ our Lord, who lives and reigns with you and the Holy Spirit, one God, now and forever.

or

O God, you are the creator of the world, the liberator of your people, and the wisdom of the earth. By the resurrection of your Son free us from our fears, restore us in your image, and ignite us with your light, through Jesus Christ, our Savior and Lord, who lives and reigns with you and the Holy Spirit, one God, now and forever.

Gospel Acclamation

Alleluia. Let us sing to the Lord, who has ┃ triumphed gloriously;* our strength and our might, who has become ┃ our salvation. *Alleluia.* (Exod. 15:1-2)

Vigil Readings and Responses

Readings marked with an asterisk are not omitted.

*1 Genesis 1:1—2:4a

Creation

Response: Psalm 136:1-9, 23-26

God's mercy endures forever. (Ps. 136:1)

2 Genesis 7:1-5, 11-18; 8:6-18; 9:8-13

Flood

Response: Psalm 46

The Lord of hosts is with us; the God of Jacob is our stronghold. (Ps. 46:7)

3 Genesis 22:1-18

Testing of Abraham

Response: Psalm 16

You will show me the path of life. (Ps. 16:11)

*4 Exodus 14:10-31; 15:20-21

Deliverance at the Red Sea

Response: Exodus 15:1b-13, 17-18

I will sing to the Lord, who has triumphed gloriously. (Exod. 15:1)

*5 Isaiah 55:1-11

Salvation freely offered to all

Response: Isaiah 12:2-6

With joy you will draw water from the wells of salvation. (Isa. 12:3)

6 Proverbs 8:1-8, 19-21; 9:4b-6
or Baruch 3:9-15, 32—4:4

The wisdom of God

Response: Psalm 19

The statutes of the Lord are just and rejoice the heart. (Ps. 19:8)

7 Ezekiel 36:24-28

A new heart and a new spirit

Response: Psalms 42 and 43

I thirst for God, for the living God. (Ps. 42:2)

8 Ezekiel 37:1-14

Valley of the dry bones

Response: Psalm 143

Revive me, O Lord, for your name's sake. (Ps. 143:11)

9 Zephaniah 3:14-20

The gathering of God's people

Response: Psalm 98

Lift up your voice, rejoice, and sing. (Ps. 98:4)

10 Jonah 1:1—2:1

The deliverance of Jonah

Response: Jonah 2:2-3 [4-6] 7-9

Deliverance belongs to the Lord. (Jonah 2:9)

11 Isaiah 61:1-4, 9-11

Clothed in the garments of salvation
Response: Deuteronomy 32:1-4, 7, 36a, 43a
Great is our God, the Rock, whose ways are just. (Deut. 32:3-4)

*12 Daniel 3:1-29

Deliverance from the fiery furnace
Response: Song of the Three 35–65
Praise and magnify the Lord forever. (Song of Thr. 35)

New Testament Reading and Gospel
Romans 6:3-11

We were incorporated into the death of Jesus Christ in baptism and so were liberated from the dominion of sin. We also anticipate that we will be incorporated into the resurrection of Christ and so will be liberated from the hold death has over our mortal bodies.

John 20:1-18

John's gospel describes the confusion and excitement of the first Easter: the stone is moved, disciples race back and forth, and angels speak to a weeping woman. Then, Jesus himself appears.

Preface Easter

Color White *or* Gold

Prayers of Intercession

The prayers are prepared locally for each occasion. The following examples may be adapted or used as appropriate.
On this most holy night, let us pray to God for the church, the earth, and all in need, that the whole world may know the resurrection that God promises to give.
Amen.
A brief silence.
We pray for the church throughout the world. *A brief silence.*
For the spirit of resurrection within all believers. *A brief silence.*
For the newly baptized. *A brief silence.*
For the health of plants and animals. *A brief silence.*
For all who care for the earth. *A brief silence.*
For peace throughout the world. *A brief silence.*
For an increase of justice in every land. *A brief silence.*
For those in need, those close to home, those far away. *A brief silence.*
For those who are hungry. *A brief silence.*
For the sick and the dying. *A brief silence.*
For our neighborhood. *A brief silence.*
For this assembly of worshipers. *A brief silence.*
For the desires of our hearts. *A brief silence.*
Here other intercessions may be offered.

We give thanks for the lives of all the faithful who have died and who now enjoy the full presence of God. We pray that at the end we may join them in the resurrection. *A brief silence.* On this most holy night, O God of resurrection, receive our prayers and praises, and give us your Spirit, that our lives may be signs of the new life you give through Jesus Christ, our Savior and Lord.
Amen.

Images in the Readings

At the beginning of the Vigil, Christ is symbolized by the candle, which gives **light** to our darkness and remains bright even when we all share in its flame. The early church called baptism enlightenment. Sharing this light outdoors in darkness makes the image emotionally effective.

Each reading offers an image with which to picture salvation: the earth is God's perfect creation; we are saved in the ark during the flood; we are granted a reprieve from sacrifice; we escape the enemy army; we are enlivened by spring rains; we are instructed by Woman Wisdom; we are given a new heart; our bones are brought back to life; we enjoy a homeland; swallowed by the fish, we do not drown but are coughed up on dry ground; we wear party clothes; thrown into a furnace, we emerge untouched by the fire; we are risen with Christ; and although we do mistake Christ for the gardener, he appears to us and enlivens our faith.

Ideas for the Day

◆ The Easter Vigil showers us with so many readings, so many stories. How does one choose a reading on which to concentrate for preaching? Maybe this is not a time to focus specifically on any one of the readings, but rather to focus on the liturgical experience of God overcoming darkness, evil, and death. As Christ is raised from the tomb, so are we raised from all that would bind us to the ways of death. Mystagogical preaching, a practice from the early church, calls attention to the images, words, and actions of the liturgy. In the process, it opens their significance for the Christian life. In his mystagogical preaching, Ambrose of Milan asked his hearers, "What did we do?" "What did you see?" "What did you say?" (Craig A. Satterlee, "Mystagogical Preaching," 2, craigasatterlee.com/mystagogy-complete.pdf).

◆ The text of the Easter proclamation is a rich resource for reflection on the joy of the Easter Vigil. In addition to its powerful proclamation of the resurrection, it calls on multiple nonhuman creatures and created things to join in praise of God who brings life from death. For instance, the bees are lauded for the gift of wax to make the candles used to chase away the darkness and begin the celebration of resurrection light. Have you considered using real beeswax candles for your Vigil? Read the full text of the Easter proclamation in *Evangelical Lutheran Worship* Leaders Edition ([Minneapolis: Augsburg Fortress, 2006], 646–47).

◆ Consider presenting the Vigil readings in the styles of various storytelling traditions. To highlight the intimacy of the storytelling experience, a separate room could be set up with a small platform or even just a simple rug and chair to designate the space for the storytelling. The purpose of the storytelling is to make familiar biblical stories come alive for the hearer in a new and fresh way; the biblical narratives may take on new meaning when heard differently.

Connections with the Liturgy

Since the first century, the primary day for Christians to assemble around word and sacrament has been Sunday, because every Sunday is understood as the day of resurrection. The preface to the eucharistic prayer for standard Sundays says that Jesus Christ "on this day overcame death and the grave, and by his glorious resurrection opened to us the way of everlasting life."

Let the Children Come

The Vigil is a perfect opportunity to teach children (and adults) about the paschal candle, its symbolic connection to the resurrection, and its use during the Great Fifty Days, baptisms, and funerals. If possible, allow the children to participate in the preparation of the new paschal candle prior to the Vigil service. Let them gather close to the presiding minister during the gathering rite to see the inscription traced on the candle.

Assembly Song and Music for the Day

Because of the nature of this day, music suggestions are listed by place in the service and categorized by type of leadership (in brackets): Ch=Choral; CC=Children's Choir; KI=Keyboard/Instrumental; HB=Handbell. Many suggestions require assembly participation.

Fire and Procession

p Abbey of Gethsemani. "Song for the Lighting of the Fire." MSB1 S470.

p Haugen, Marty. "Light of Christ, Rising in Glory." MSB1 S472.

Easter Proclamation

Alonso, Tony. "Procession of the Paschal Candle and Exsultet." SATB, cant, assembly, kybd, gtr, opt fl, ob, vc. WLP 005314.

Farrell, Bernadette. "Christ, Be Our Light (Easter Vigil Text)." Assembly, opt cant, kybd, gtr, fl, tpt. OCP 11502.

p Haugen, Marty. "Easter Proclamation." MSB1 S474.

Hillebrand, Paul. "Exsultet." Cant, SATB, assembly, kybd, gtr. OCP 30113062.

Trapp, Lynn. "The Easter Proclamation (Exsultet)." SATB, cant, org, opt tmp. MSM 80-320.

Vigil Readings and Responses

Responses to each reading are included in Music Sourcebook for Lent and the Three Days (MSB1). Related hymns are listed in Indexes to Evangelical Lutheran Worship. The responses listed below are from other resources.

1 Creation

Boyd, Glen T. "Psalm 136, Wimbo Wa Shukrani (Hymn of Thanks)" from *Four African Hymns*. SATB, drm, shaker. CG CGA686. [Ch]

Cooney, Rory. "Genesis Reading for the Great Vigil." SATB, cant, assembly, kybd, gtr, fl. GIA G-5018.

Haugen, Marty. "Your Love Endures." SATB, cant, assembly, kybd, gtr, 2 ww in C. GIA G-4842.

p Hopson, Hal H. "Many and Great" from *ChildrenSing Around the World*. 2 pt trbl, pno, drum, opt fl. AFP 9781451492040. [CC]

⊕ Amis tribe, Taiwan. "O Give Thanks to the Lord" from *My Heart Sings Out*. U. Church Publishing 9780898694741.

✿ Bruxvoort Colligan, Richard. "God Who Remembers (Psalm 136)" from *Our Roots Are in You*. worldmaking.net.

2 Flood

"A River Flows" from *Psallite* A-238. Cant or SATB, assembly, kybd.

Moore, James E., Jr. "Be Still." SATB, assembly, kybd, gtr. GIA G-5731.

Patterson, Mark. "Psalm 46" from *ChildrenSing Psalms*. U, kybd, assembly.

✿ Bruxvoort Colligan, Richard. "God Our Home and Help (Psalm 46)" from *Our Roots Are in You*. worldmaking.net.

✿ Bruxvoort Colligan, Richard. "God Is Our Shelter and Strength (Psalm 46)" from *Sharing the Road*. AFP 9780800678630. psalmimmersion.bandcamp.com.

✿ Bruxvoort Colligan, Richard. "There Is a River (Psalm 46)" from *Sharing the Road*. AFP 9780800678630. psalmimmersion.bandcamp.com.

Summers, Roger. "It Wasn't Even Raining!" U or 2 pt, pno. LOR 10/2664K. [CC]

3 Testing of Abraham

Alonso, Tony. "You Are My Inheritance" from LP:S.

Gelineau, Joseph. "Psalm 16" from ACYG.

"My Portion and My Cup" from *Psallite* A-54. Cant or SATB, assembly, kybd.

4 Deliverance at the Red Sea

Cooney, Rory. "Exodus Reading for the Great Vigil." SATB, cant, assembly, kybd, gtr, opt fl. GIA G-4117.

Gibbons, John. "Canticle of Moses" from PS2.

Haugen, Marty. "Let Us Sing to the Lord" from LP:S.

Pischner, Stephen. "The Easter Vigil in the Holy Night: After the Third Reading" from COJ:S.

Keesecker, Thomas. "Go Down, Moses." U/2 pt, pno. CG CGA1368. [CC]

5 Salvation freely offered to all

Cherwien, David. "Surely God Is My Salvation." SATB, opt assembly, org. MSM 80-710.

Haugen, Marty. "You Will Draw Water Joyfully" from LP:S.

"Joyfully You Will Draw Water" from *Psallite* A-57. Cant or SATB, assembly, kybd.

6 The wisdom of God

Haas, David. "Lord, You Have the Words" from PCY, vol. 1.

Birks, Thomas R. "The Heavens Declare Your Glory" (tune: FAITHFUL; alternate tunes: AURELIA, ELLACOMBE) from LUYH.

p de Lassus, Rudolf. "Stars in the Sky Proclaim" from *Augsburg Motet Book*. SAB. AFP 9781451423709. [Ch]

7 A new heart and a new spirit

Hurd, Bob. "As the Deer Longs" from PS2.

Joncas, Michael. "As the Deer." Cant, SATB, assembly, org, opt str, ww, hp. GIA G-4883.

Toolan, S. Suzanne. "Living Waters" from *Living Spirit*. SSAA or SATB, kybd, opt assembly. GIA G-1676 (SSA/A), G-1625 (SATB).

Salinas, Juan. "Como el ciervo/Like a Deer" from *Psalms for All Seasons: A Compete Psalter for Worship*. SATB. Brazos Press 9781592554447.

8 Valley of the dry bones

Gelineau, Joseph. "Psalm 143" from ACYG.

Hopson, Hal. "Psalm 143" from TPP.

Makeever, Ray. "Show Me the Way (Psalm 143)" from DH.

9 The gathering of God's people

Behnke, John. "Psalm 98: Sing to the Lord a New Song." SATB, cant, assembly, kybd, 2 tpt, hb. CPH 983666WEB.

Hesla, Bret. "Shout unto God (Psalm 98)" from *Justice, Like a Base of Stone*. AFP 9780800623562.

Trapp, Lynn. "All the Ends of the Earth." SATB, assembly, kybd, tr, 2 C inst. GIA G-5623.

☼ Bruxvoort Colligan, Richard. "Shout for Joy (Psalm 98)" from *Shout for Joy*. AFP 9780806698632. psalmimmersion.bandcamp.com.

10 The deliverance of Jonah

Guimont, Michel. "Easter Vigil X" from PRCL.

Horman, John D. "Jonah" from *Sing the Stories of God's People*. U, kybd. AFP 9780806698397. [CC]

Pavlechko, Thomas. "Jonah 2:2-3 [4-6] 7-9" from PSCY.

11 Clothed in the garments of salvation

Guimont, Michel. "Easter Vigil XI" from PRCL.

Mummert, Mark. "Deuteronomy 32:1-4, 7, 36a, 43a" from PSCY.

12 Deliverance from the fiery furnace

Consiglio, Cyprian. "Song of the Thee Young Men." Cant, assembly, perc. OCP 10199.

Joncas, Jan Michael. "Canticle of the Three Young Men." SATB, assembly, 2 cant, org. GIA G-8441.

Proulx, Richard. "Song of the Three Children." U, 2 pt, assembly, org, tamb, tri, fc, drm. GIA G-1863.

p Larter, Evelyn. "Didn't My Lord Deliver Daniel?" SATB, pno, fl, vc. AFP 9780806697307. [Ch]

MacKenzie, Valerie. "Cool Under Fire." U, pno. Canadian International Music, dist. LOR. CIM 1051. [CC]

Gospel Acclamation

Browning, Carol/arr. Tom Andino. "Deo Gloria Alleluia (Easter Gospel Acclamation)." SATB, cant, assembly, kybd, gtr, opt fl and 2 tr. GIA G-6402.

Procession to the Font

Springs of water, bless the Lord   ELW 214

Wade in the water   ELW 459, TFF 144

Handel, George Frederic/arr. Walter Ehret. "All Who Are Thirsty, Come to the Spring." 2 pt, kybd. GIA G-5838.

Hughes, Howard. "We Have Put on Christ." Cant, assembly, 2 C inst, opt 3 oct hb. GIA G-7745.

Setting the Table

Music Sourcebook for Lent and the Three Days *includes an appendix with hymn stanzas appropriate for use during the setting of the table on this and other days. These stanzas are also included on the CD-ROM that accompanies the volume.*

Now the feast and celebration   ELW 167, WOV 789

Now the green blade rises   ELW 379, LBW 149, LS 55

p Keesecker, Thomas. "Washed Anew" from *Augsburg Easy Choirbook*, vol. 2. SATB, pno, opt hb, assembly. AFP 9780800677510. [Ch]

Coleman, Gerald Patrick. "The Lamb." U/2 pt, kybd. MSM 50-4045. [CC]

Powell, Robert J. "The Strife Is O'er" from *Reflections throughout the Church Year: Nine Pieces for Solo Instrument and Organ or Piano*. Pno, inst. MSM 20-915. [KI]

Stults, Tyleen. "Haleluya." 3-5 oct, perc, L3-. RR SM7007. [HB]

Communion

Alleluia! Christ is arisen   ELW 375, LLC 361

At the Lamb's high feast we sing   ELW 362, LBW 210

Come, let us eat   ELW 491, LBW 214, LS 103, TFF 119

⊕ = global song   ☼ = praise song
p = available in Prelude Music Planner

p   Whitehill, Erik. "Now the Green Blade Rises" from *Wade in the Water: Easy Choral Music for All Ages*. SAB, kybd. AFP 9780800678616. [Ch]

James, Gary. "The Lamb's High Banquet." U, desc, kybd. MSM 50-4600. [Ch or CC]

Krebs, Johann Ludwig. "Christ lag in Todesbanden" from *Klavierübung*. Org. Various editions. [KI]

McChesney, Kevin. "The Strife Is O'er." 3-5 oct, L3. BP HB215. [HB]

Sending

Christ has arisen, alleluia   ELW 364, WOV 678, TFF 96

Be not afraid   ELW 388

Thine the amen   ELW 826, WOV 801

Hobby, Robert A. "Jesus Christ Is Risen Today." Org, br qnt, timp. MSM 20-402. [KI]

Vogt, Emanuel. "Mfurahini, Haleluya" from *Augsburg Organ Library: Easter*. Org. AFP 9780800659363. [KI]

Gramann, Fred. "Alleluia! The Strife Is O'er." 3-6 oct hb, org. L2+ LOR 201377L. [HB]

March 27, 2016
Resurrection of Our Lord
Easter Day

"This is the day that the Lord has made; let us rejoice and be glad in it." God has indeed raised from the dead the one who was put to death "by hanging him on a tree." Alleluia! God allows Jesus to appear "to us who were chosen by God as witnesses" in holy baptism and invites us to eat and drink at the table of the risen Christ. Alleluia!

Prayer of the Day

O God, you gave your only Son to suffer death on the cross for our redemption, and by his glorious resurrection you delivered us from the power of death. Make us die every day to sin, that we may live with him forever in the joy of the resurrection, through your Son, Jesus Christ our Lord, who lives and reigns with you and the Holy Spirit, one God, now and forever.

or

God of mercy, we no longer look for Jesus among the dead, for he is alive and has become the Lord of life. Increase in our minds and hearts the risen life we share with Christ, and help us to grow as your people toward the fullness of eternal life with you, through Jesus Christ, our Savior and Lord, who lives and reigns with you and the Holy Spirit, one God, now and forever.

Gospel Acclamation

Alleluia. Christ, our paschal lamb, | has been sacrificed.* Therefore, let us | keep the feast. *Alleluia*. (1 Cor. 5:7, 8)

Readings and Psalm
Acts 10:34-43

Peter's sermon, delivered at the home of Cornelius, a Roman army officer, sums up the essential message of Christianity. Everyone who believes in Jesus, whose life, death, and resurrection fulfilled the words of the prophets, receives forgiveness of sins through his name.

or Isaiah 65:17-25

Through the prophet, God promises a new heaven and a new earth. Weeping will pass away, life will be abundant for God's people, and the world—including the wild animals—will be at peace.

Psalm 118:1-2, 14-24

This is the day that the Lord has made; let us rejoice and be glad in it. (Ps. 118:24)

1 Corinthians 15:19-26

Paul describes the consequences of the resurrection, including the promise of new life in Christ to a world that has been in bondage to death. He celebrates the destruction of evil and the establishment of God's victorious rule over all.

or Acts 10:34-43

See above.

Luke 24:1-12

Evidently expecting to find Jesus' corpse, some of his women followers go to the tomb with embalming spices. After a perplexing encounter with the empty tomb and angelic visitors, the women become the first to proclaim the amazing news of resurrection.

or John 20:1-18

This morning began with confusion: the stone was moved and the tomb was empty. Disciples arrive, then angels, and finally Jesus himself. Out of the confusion, hope emerges, and a weeping woman becomes the first to confess her faith in the risen Lord.

Preface Easter

Color White *or* Gold

Prayers of Intercession

The prayers are prepared locally for each occasion. The following examples may be adapted or used as appropriate.

On this most holy day, let us pray to God for the church, the earth, and all in need, that the whole world may know the resurrection that God promises to give.

A brief silence.

O God of life, pour the life of your Son's resurrection into the churches. Make visible the unity we have in you. Show to each denomination the strengths of the others. Hear us, O God.

Your mercy is great.

Give to the lands and seas the life of your continuing creation. Water the flowers of springtime, and nurture the growing crops. Bless all who protect your plants and animals. Hear us, O God.

Your mercy is great.

Grant to all nations your life of peace. Keep us from war. Lead us into justice. Turn enemies into friends. We pray especially for . . . . Hear us, O God.

Your mercy is great.

Visit the needy with your compassionate life. Feed the hungry. Nurse the sick. Protect the weak. Comfort the sorrowful. Attend the dying. Especially we pray for . . . . Hear us, O God.

Your mercy is great.

Raise up this assembly with the life of your Spirit. Reveal in our community the signs of Christ's resurrection. Hear us, O God.

Your mercy is great.

Here other intercessions may be offered.

O God of life, we praise you for the faithful who have met you in death (*especially*). Bring us all through death into the life of your resurrection. Hear us, O God.

Your mercy is great.

O God, we praise your life. We bless your mercy. We honor your power. Transform all that is dying with the joy of the resurrection of Jesus Christ, our Savior and Lord.

Amen.

Images in the Readings

The language of being **raised** from death relies on the commonplace human idea, evident in speech and story, that up is good and down is bad. The ancient three-tier universe placed divine powers on the top level, humans in the middle—between life and death—and the dead below the earth. In today's readings (Luke, Paul, Acts), Jesus has been raised up from death. Current scientific understandings of the universe teach us that there is no "up." Yet many languages maintain this imagery: the brain is up, dirty feet are down. Thus this language must function for us symbolically: up is life, down is death.

Jews during intertestamental times developed the belief in a final **resurrection**. The situation under foreign powers was so intractable that there was no present hope. Rather, at the end of time, God would bring an end to this evil and in a general resurrection would raise to new life all the righteous dead. Influence from especially Zoroastrianism added the idea that those who were evil would be raised to eternal punishment. The New Testament speaks of Christ's resurrection as the beginning of this phenomenon.

The noun **Jerusalem** has many meanings. It was the site of the temple, where Israelites and later Jews connected with God. Isaiah used it as shorthand for the restored life in the promised land. It is the location of Jesus' crucifixion and the origin of the Christian mission. Especially in their use of the Psalms, Christians interpret it to mean the church. It is also a contemporary deeply troubled city that functions in different ways for competing religious pieties.

In 1 Corinthians 15 and Romans 5, Paul contrasts **Adam** with Christ. Adam is the sinful human, Christ the second Adam who reversed the effects of sin by divine grace. Paul is not interested in the narrative details of Genesis 3, but rather interprets the Genesis story in the light of Christ. For Paul, those who are baptized are now enlivened not by the natural Adam but by Christ, the Son of God.

Ideas for the Day

◆ Easter is not the time to engage in debates about what actually happened in the garden or to provide an apology for bodily resurrection. Resurrection is a matter of faith, neither proven nor arrived at through rational argument. At Easter, proclaim the flourishing life that God offers to all creation through Christ's death and resurrection. Easter provides the opportunity to flesh out, so to speak, the implications of resurrection for all the places of death that our hearers must live in. The events of Holy Week are concrete places: Gethsemane, Golgotha, the high priest's courtyard, Pilate's headquarters, the burial garden, and others. Name the Calvarys, the courtyards, and the judgment halls in the lives of the hearers. Even more importantly, name their specific places of resurrection. Even though the hard places have not disappeared, they look very different in the light of resurrection morning.

◆ "Remember how he told you . . ." (Luke 24:6). Dr. John Ratey suggests that stress tends to block from our memory anything but the most immediate crisis (*Spark: The Revolutionary New Science of Exercise and the Brain* [New York: Little, Brown and Company, 2013], 66–68). For example, in the middle of a fire alarm, people may not remember the location of the exits, even if they know well the locations. Perhaps it makes sense that the disciples couldn't remember Jesus' predictions of suffering and death. Now, in the joy of resurrection, they remember. We can never hear too much of the resurrection. It must be embedded deep within us so that we can remember when it is most important and hardest to remember.

◆ When confronted by the resurrection of Jesus, who rises to new life and who inaugurates a new age, we cannot be silent or sit on our hands in the face of the ways of death that permeate the world. When we see oppression, injustice, poverty, or the careless exploitation of the earth, the resurrection of Jesus challenges us to confront death. Julia Esquivel has written poignantly and evocatively of such confrontation in her poem "They Have Threatened Us with Resurrection" (*Spiritus: A Journal of Christian Spirituality* 3, no. 1 [Spring 2003]: 96–101).

Connections with the Liturgy

Every Sunday is a celebration of the resurrection. Thus each Sunday's worship includes references to today's readings. "On the third day he rose again," we affirm in the Nicene Creed. "He descended to the dead. On the third day he rose again," says the Apostles' Creed. "Christ has died. Christ is risen," we call out during the eucharistic prayer. When we receive the dismissal, it is as if we are the women witnessing to the others: "Go in peace. Share the good news."

Let the Children Come

This is the day that the Lord has made; let us rejoice and be glad in it! The Easter story is for all people at all times! Invite children to participate in many ways during today's worship. Older children could process in with the paschal candle or with festive banners or streamers. A younger child could lead the assembly in the Easter greeting. A middle schooler could proclaim the reading from 1 Corinthians. All children could ring bells or shake tambourines or claves at the gospel acclamation. The good news of Christ's resurrection is for all ages. Make sure all ages are represented among your worship leaders today.

Assembly Song
Gathering

Jesus Christ is risen today   ELW 365, LBW 151, LS 57

Christ the Lord is risen today; Alleluia!   ELW 369, LBW 128

Hail thee, festival day!   ELW 394, LBW 142

Psalmody and Acclamations

Barry, Martin. "This Is the Day." SATB, cant, assembly, kybd, gtr, opt ww qnt. GIA G-6395.

Proulx, Richard. "Psalm for Easter Day." SATB, cant, assembly, org, br qrt or sextet, opt hp. GIA G-5383.

Shields, Valerie. "Psalm for Easter." SATB, cant, assembly, org, opt tpt, hb, perc. MSM 80-405.

(GA) Browning, Carol/arr. Tom Andion. "Deo Gloria Alleluia (Easter Gospel Acclamation)." SATB, cant, assembly, kybd, gtr, opt fl and 2 tr. GIA G-6402.

Hymn of the Day

Christ is risen! Alleluia!   ELW 382, LBW 131   MORGENLIED

Christ has arisen, alleluia   ELW 364, TFF 96, WOV 678   MFURAHINI, HALELUYA

Hallelujah, Jesus lives!   ELW 380, LBW 147   FRED TIL BOD

Offering

Now all the vault of heaven resounds   ELW 367, LBW 143

Christ is arisen   ELW 372, LBW 136

Communion

Christ Jesus lay in death's strong bands   ELW 370, LBW 134

Awake, my heart, with gladness   ELW 378, LBW 129

I know that my Redeemer lives!   ELW 619, LBW 352

Sending

Good Christian friends, rejoice and sing   ELW 385, LBW 144

The strife is o'er, the battle done   ELW 366, LBW 135

Additional Assembly Songs

They crucified my Savior   TFF 90

Low in the grave he lay   TFF 94

A los tres días   LLC 349

⊕ Sosa, Pablo. "This Is the Day" from *Glory to God*. U. WJK 9780664238971.

⊕ South African/arr. Anders Nyberg. "We Walk His Way" from *Worship and Song*. SATB. Abingdon Press 9781426709951.

✿ Bruxvoort Colligan, Richard. "God's Love Endures Forever (Psalm 136)" from *Sharing the Road*. AFP 9780800678630. psalmimmersion.bandcamp.com.

✿ Kernsey. "You've Arrived" from *Storm Home: A Collection of Music from Humble Walk Artists-in-Residence*. humblewalk.bandcamp.com.

✿ Kurtz, Rachel. "Hallelujah" from *Broken and Low Down*. rachelkurtz.org.

✿ Morris, Michael. "Hallelujah! Praises to the Son!" from *Storm Home: A Collection of Music from Humble Walk Artists-in-Residence*. humblewalk.bandcamp.com.

⊕ = global song   ✿ = praise song
● = relates to hymn of the day   p = available in Prelude Music Planner

☼ The Welcome Wagon. "The Strife Is O'er" from *Precious Remedies Against Satan's Devices*. asthmatickitty.com.

☼ Wilson, Tay. "All Things New" from *Stay the Course*. Available on Amazon.com.

Music for the Day
Choral

- Arnatt, Ronald. "Christ Is Risen." SAB, org. ECS 7050.
- Ferguson, John. "Christ the Lord Is Risen Today." SATB, snare drm, picc. AFP 9780800646363.
- p ● Frahm, Frederick. "Now Is Christ Risen from the Dead." 2 pt mxd, kybd. AFP 9780800678920.
- p Grieg, Edvard/arr. Oscar Overby. "God's Son Has Made Me Free" from *The Augsburg Choirbook: Sacred Choral Music of the Twentieth Century*. SATB. AFP 9780800656782.

Children's Choir

Bach, J. S. "With Loudest Rejoicing." SA, org/kybd. CPH 981846WEB.

Breedlove, Jennifer Kerr. "Early Easter Morning." 2 pt, hb, kybd. GIA G-5894.

Hopson, Hal H. "Rejoice and Be Glad." U/2 pt, kybd, opt hb. LOR AM663.

Ziegenhals, Harriet. "Now Let the Heavens Be Joyful." U/3 pt, kybd, opt fl/vln. HOP JR220.

Keyboard / Instrumental

- p ● Frahm, Frederick. "Fred til bod" from *Faith Alive*, vol. 2. Org. AFP 9780800678788.
- ● Helgen, John. "Morgenlied" from *Introductions and Alternate Accompaniments*, vol. 3. Pno. AFP 9780800623616.
- p ● Lasky, David. "Morgenlied" from *All Glory, Laud, and Honor*. Org. AFP 9780800637484.
- p ● Raabe, Nancy M. "Mfurahini, haleluya" from *Grace and Peace*, vol. 2. Pno. AFP 9780800679019.

Handbell

- p Buckwalter, Karen. "Alleluia! Amen!" 3-5 oct, L1+. CG CGB817.

Morris, Hart. "Hymn of Victory" from *Ringing the Church Year*. 3-5 oct, L2+. LOR 20/1671L.

- ● Stults, Tyleen. "Haleluya." 3-5 oct, opt perc. L3-. RR SM7007.

March 27, 2016
Resurrection of Our Lord
Easter Evening

Isaiah proclaims the great feast to come, when God will swallow up death forever. Paul invites us to celebrate the paschal feast with the unleavened bread of sincerity and truth. The Easter evening gospel tells of the risen Christ being made known to the disciples in the breaking of the bread. Our hearts burn within us as the hope of the resurrection is proclaimed in our midst, and as Jesus appears to us at the holy table.

Prayer of the Day

O God, whose blessed Son made himself known to his disciples in the breaking of bread, open the eyes of our faith, that we may behold him in all his redeeming work, Jesus Christ, our Savior and Lord, who lives and reigns with you and the Holy Spirit, one God, now and forever.

Gospel Acclamation

Alleluia. Our hearts ¹ burn within us* while you open to ¹ us the scriptures. *Alleluia*. (Luke 24:32)

Readings and Psalm
Isaiah 25:6-9

The prophet portrays a wonderful victory banquet at which death, which in ancient Canaan was depicted as a monster

swallowing everyone up, will be swallowed up forever. The prophet urges celebration of this victory, which is salvation.

Psalm 114

Tremble, O earth, at the presence of the Lᴏʀᴅ. (Ps. 114:7)

I Corinthians 5:6b-8

In preparation to celebrate Passover, God's people cleaned out all the old leaven from their homes. Paul draws on this practice to portray Christ as our Passover lamb whose sacrifice means that we now clean out the old leaven of malice and wickedness from our lives and replace it with sincerity and truth.

Luke 24:13-49

> On the day of his resurrection, Jesus joins two disciples on the road to Emmaus and makes himself known to them in the breaking of bread.

Preface   Easter

Color   White *or* Gold

Monday, March 28

Annunciation of Our Lord (transferred)

> Nine months before Christmas the church celebrates the annunciation. In Luke the angel Gabriel announces to Mary that she will give birth to the Son of God, and she responds, "Here am I, the servant of the Lord." Ancient scholars believed that March 25 was also the day on which creation began and was the date of Jesus' death on the cross. Thus, from the sixth to eighth centuries, March 25 was observed as New Year's Day in much of Christian Europe.

Tuesday, March 29

Hans Nielsen Hauge, renewer of the church, died 1824

> Hans Nielsen Hauge was a layperson who began preaching about "the living faith" in Norway and Denmark after a mystical experience that he believed called him to share the assurance of salvation with others. At the time, itinerant preaching and religious gatherings held without the supervision of a pastor were illegal, and Hauge was arrested several times. He also faced great personal suffering: his first wife died, and three of his four children died in infancy.

Thursday, March 31

John Donne, poet, died 1631

> This priest of the Church of England is commemorated for his poetry and spiritual writing. Most of his poetry was written before his ordination and is sacred and secular, intellectual and sensuous. He saw in his wife, Anne, glimpses of the glory of God and a human revelation of divine love. In 1615 he was ordained and seven years later he was named dean of St. Paul's Cathedral in London. By that time his reputation as a preacher was firmly in place. In his poem "Good Friday, 1613. Riding westward," he speaks of Jesus' death on the cross: "Who sees God's face, that is self life, must die; What a death were it then to see God die?"

EASTER

PREPARING FOR EASTER

Fullness and hope

Are you full? Have you had enough? After the devotion of Lent and the intensity of the Three Days, it might seem like we've had enough on our plates. And yet there is more. There is Easter.

> City of God, Easter forever,
> golden Jerusalem, Jesus the Lamb,
> river of life, saints and archangels,
> sing with creation to God the I Am!
> Jesus is risen and we shall arise.
> Give God the glory! Alleluia! (ELW 377)

Herbert Brokering's hymn with its buffet of images invites us into the season of Easter, a season of abundance.

In year C of the Revised Common Lectionary, the church reads from Revelation. It is a perplexing book, yet one we need to sink our teeth into. As biblical scholar Barbara Rossing reminds us, "Revelation's gift to us is a story of a God who loves us and comes to live with us" (*The Rapture Exposed* [Boulder, CO: Westview, 2004], xi). Revelation, like Easter, is not ultimately about absence, about Jesus' or our going away, but about presence and fullness.

One might be struck by the fullness of images and descriptors in the Easter readings from Revelation: myriads, thousands, blessing, honor, glory, multitudes, nations, and more and more. The tree in the city that we hear about in Revelation 21 bears not one but twelve kinds of fruit for the healing of the nations.

Fullness abounds in Easter, but even then we feel emptiness. We sing with the psalmist on Easter 4, "The Lord is my shepherd; I shall not be in want," but we still want for many things. So did the disciples. They hunkered down in a locked room, in the dark, afraid. Yet Jesus comes to them. Throughout the season of Easter, we will hear of Jesus coming among the disciples and promising peace. How will your Easter worship convey the fullness of God? How will it take seriously the wants, known and unknown, of a people hungering for more?

Historically, the church prepares for baptism during Lent, welcoming seekers to baptism at the Easter Vigil. Coming to the waters leads to the table. The postresurrection stories with Jesus' followers often include a meal. It is in these meals that his followers recognize him. Easter would be an appropriate time for digging deeper into the rich meanings of holy communion (see "Names for Holy Communion and What They Mean" in the seasonal rites section, page 172). If your congregation does not practice weekly communion, consider communion every week during the season of Easter as a first taste.

Ascension: the fullness of all things

The image of Jesus ascending into heaven adorns many churches, but this Easter festival may get passed over in the congregation, especially if the focus becomes mired in scientific versus biblical debates. If the universe is more complicated than a heaven above, a hell beneath, and the earth in between, what do we make of Jesus' ascension? We read in Ephesians: "I pray that the God of our Lord Jesus Christ, the Father of glory, may give you a spirit of wisdom and revelation as you come to know him. . . . He has put all things under his feet and has made him the head over all things for the church, which is his body, the fullness of him who fills all in all" (Eph. 1:17, 22-23).

The ascension paradox claims that fullness in Christ comes through Christ's going away. We are now Christ's body, witnesses of God's abundance. Instead of avoiding this day or seeking to explain its mystery away, how might preaching shift from explanation to wonder and witness: wondering at the fullness of God and witnessing to God's presence even when we fear God's absence?

Take care with musical choices for this festival. Many hymns and songs, both ancient and of the praise-and-worship genre, enforce a three-tiered universe. Can we retain these images if they are embraced as metaphor? How might they be balanced with hymns that challenge prescientific understandings (see, for example, "Christ is alive," ELW 389)?

The gift of Easter spills over. In the words of Laurence Hull Stookey, "We divide this wonderful action of God into parts that we may better approach the fullness of a mystery we can never fathom" (*Calendar: Christ's Time for the Church* [Nashville: Abingdon, 1996], 66). Celebrating the ascension gives us another way to ponder what Christ's resurrection means for us.

Pentecost: filled with the Spirit

The finale of the Easter season echoes with the theme of abundance: "How manifold are your works. . . . The earth is full of your creatures. . . . All of them look to you to give them their food in due season" (Ps. 104:24, 27, *ELW*). Pentecost is indeed a culmination of Easter fullness. The myriad languages and nations described in Revelation return anew in this Sunday's readings from Acts or Genesis. It is the pouring out of the Spirit that leads to both perplexity and amazement. The signs of hope we see in Revelation infuse our Pentecost celebration; the Spirit is at work, renewing the face of the earth.

The gospel reading for Pentecost recalls Maundy Thursday: "If you love me, you will keep my commandments." Yet with this commandment comes the Advocate, the Holy Spirit who guides us. We celebrate baptisms and affirmation of baptism on this day, trusting in the Spirit who abides in us as the Three-in-One abides in unity.

Themes of unity and diversity mark the Day of Pentecost. How does our worship life on this day and at all times reflect both unity and diversity? The Nairobi Statement on Worship and Culture (Lutheran World Federation, 1996) suggests that worship is both contextual and transcultural. The Spirit is at work in your time and place with your particular people. How do your choices for worship reflect this diversity? Your church's Pentecost celebration will not look like one across town or across the globe. Yet at the same time, we are one in the Spirit of the Lord, joint heirs with Christ, as we hear in Romans. What elements of our worship connect us to Christians across time and space?

Music

Alleluia! This word cries out to be sung. If your assembly keeps the tradition of burying the alleluia in Lent, celebrate its return with lavish alleluias during the Easter season. The word rolls easily off the tongue, making it a perfect word to sing with young children. Engage the assembly in vocal expressions of resurrection joy by making unabashed use of the Easter call and response (Alleluia! Christ is risen. / Christ is risen indeed. Alleluia!) in the greeting, the peace, the invitation to communion, and the dismissal.

An assembly sings in full voice the songs they know deep in their bones. As you plan music for this season, think about the unity of the season and what musical elements hold up well to repetition for eight Sundays. How do you balance singing the familiar with the new? The fullness of Christ can be experienced as we sing a variety of hymns and songs, led by diverse instrumentation. Our knowledge and understanding of cultures different from us are limited.

As you teach and learn songs from other cultures, consult the *Hymnal Companion* (Augsburg Fortress, 2010) and *Musicians Guide* (Augsburg Fortress, 2007) to *Evangelical Lutheran Worship* for background information and leading tips.

Congregations might sing in different languages on Pentecost as a way to embody the fullness of the Spirit. If this is new for you, have a soloist or choir sing in the new language and the assembly in the more familiar language. You might teach a simple refrain to the assembly that they can learn by ear.

"This is the feast of victory for our God. Alleluia!" How does your assembly sing during communion? Robustly? A little? Not at all? The voices in Revelation call us to sing at the feast, but singing during communion has its challenges. Part of this is practical; people are moving and walking. For this reason, new hymns with many stanzas are not ideal. Instead, choose songs with refrains (such as "I am the Bread of life," ELW 485) or repeated ostinatos ("Be not afraid," ELW 388).

Another challenge of singing during communion is theological. If your congregation regards communion as solely introspective and penitential, singing seems out of place. Without dismissing the need for silence and reflection, communion during the season of Easter carries a different flavor than communing on Maundy Thursday. We are feasting with the risen Christ! Could your assembly learn a hymn for this season that celebrates the banquet of the Lord? Could you sing it at either the beginning or conclusion of distribution? Possibilities in *Evangelical Lutheran Worship* include:

375 Alleluia! Christ is arisen
491 Come, let us eat
498 United at the table
500 Now we remain
525 You are holy
531 The trumpets sound, the angels sing
869 We have seen the Lord

See also *The Sunday Assembly* (Augsburg Fortress, 2008, pp. 220–224) for a helpful list of communion hymns and songs.

Environment

See page 143 in this volume for visual art suggestions that can be introduced at the Easter Vigil and carried through the entire Easter season.

Let your worship environment appeal not just to the eyes and ears, but also to the nose. The lilies, tulips, and hyacinths that typically adorn worship spaces on Easter Day and perhaps a Sunday or two after may need to be replaced with fresh blooming plants. Plan and budget for this in advance so that the Easter garden does not completely disappear before the season is half over. And what about freshly baked bread? In the account of Christ's interaction with the two disciples on the road to Emmaus (Luke 24:13-49, Easter Evening), we find a powerful description of "how he had been made known to them in the breaking of the bread." Recruit a team to bake fresh, fully leavened bread for communion on all the Sundays of Easter, a reminder that "Jesus is risen and we shall arise" (ELW 377).

Pentecost

In Moses' encounter with God in the burning bush (Exod. 3), Moses asks God's name. Although God's reply has traditionally been translated as "I AM WHO I AM," it may also be translated "I will be present where I will be present." The latter option is clearly descriptive of God's presence at Pentecost. The rush of a violent wind, the appearance of dancing tongues of fire, the swirling sounds of multiple languages miraculously understood—each bears powerful testimony that God's Holy Spirit is unpredictable, uncontainable, and uncontrollable; each reminds us of the endless possibilities for the Holy Spirit's movement within and among God's people. How might worship on this day invite the assembly into fuller experience of and appreciation for "I will be present where I will be present" in our midst? Some ideas:

- If climate and circumstances permit, consider scheduling Pentecost worship outdoors.
- During the weeks leading up to Pentecost, engage broad congregational participation in creating folded paper doves (see www.origami-instructions.com/origami-dove.html). Construct a mobile of doves to be hung over or near the baptismal font as a reminder of the Spirit's gifts poured out in baptism (see www.pinterest.com/pin/271412315015138815 for an example).
- During the weeks leading up to Pentecost, collect old metal keys that worshipers are willing to discard, then use them to create a simple wind chime. Invite reflection on what forces, situations, or attitudes hold us captive and hinder the Spirit's movement within and among us.
- A month or so in advance, solicit donations to fund the purchase of potted red geraniums; use them to decorate the worship space on Pentecost, then plant them on the church grounds or give them away to homebound members and neighborhood residents.
- Before worship on Pentecost or on another Sunday before Pentecost, plan an intergenerational gathering where worshipers of all ages can create Pentecost windsocks, pinwheels, and streamers together

(see 06_Pentecost.WindToys.pdf)*. Incorporate these floating, blowing, dancing objects into processions today: at the gathering, the reading of the gospel, the offering, the sending.
- Create vividly colored, flame-shaped flags and display them outdoors and/or indoors on lightweight fiberglass fishing poles (see 06_Pentecost.Flags.pdf)*.
- Create a red paper banner with a fiery sun surrounding the cross (see 06_Pentecost.Banner.pdf)*.
- Use many yards of skinny, translucent ribbons in shades of vivid red and gold to create 30-foot-long streamers. Use a swivel hook to affix the streamers to lightweight (flexible) fiberglass fishing poles. Recruit and prepare worship leaders to move through the worship space with the streamers at the gathering, during the hymn of the day, and/or at the sending. Have them practice casting the ribbon streamers across the space to dance over the heads of the assembly.
- Conclude your Pentecost celebration with a community meal to which participants contribute foods whose aromas and flavors speak the languages of many cultures.

Seasonal Checklist

- It is particularly appropriate during the Easter season to use thanksgiving for baptism as an alternative to confession and forgiveness.
- Use the canticle of praise ("This is the feast"). Unify the season by singing one setting of the liturgy throughout.
- Use the Nicene Creed.
- Consider especially Thanksgiving at the Table IV in *Evangelical Lutheran Worship*.
- Publicize Ascension and Pentecost services, helping the congregation understand the importance of these festivals.
- If you will use a diversity of languages for the Day of Pentecost, make preparations in advance with musicians and readers.
- If your congregation celebrates affirmation of baptism (confirmation) during this season, review the rite in *Evangelical Lutheran Worship*.

* Download at http://store.augsburgfortress.org/media/temp/SundaysSeasons/PDFs.zip

Worship Texts for Easter

Confession and Forgiveness

Thanksgiving for baptism (ELW, pp. 97, 119) is especially appropriate for use during the Easter season instead of confession and forgiveness. The following is provided for occasions during the Easter season when an order for confession and forgiveness is desired.

All may make the sign of the cross, the sign marked at baptism, as the presiding minister begins.

Blessed be the holy Trinity, ✝ one God,
the fountain of living water,
the rock who gave us birth,
our light and our salvation.
Amen.

Let us come into the light,
the revealing and healing light of God.

Silence is kept for reflection.

God of grace and glory,
you have brought us through the night of sin
into the light of Jesus' resurrection.
Yet our lives are still shadowed by sin.
Make us alive in Christ, O God.
Make us new as you make all things new.
Rescue us from evil and the gloom of sin,
renew us in grace,
and restore us to living in your holiness,
through Jesus Christ, our risen Lord.
Amen.

Rejoice with all creation around God's throne!
The light of the risen Christ
puts to flight all evil deeds, washes away sin,
restores innocence to the fallen,
casts out hate, brings peace,
and humbles earthly pride.
Jesus Christ loves you
and ✝ frees you from your sins by his blood.
To him be glory and dominion forever and ever!
Amen.

Offering Prayer

Blessed are you, O God, ruler of heaven and earth.
Day by day you shower us with blessings.
As you have raised us to new life in Christ,
give us glad and generous hearts,
ready to praise you and to respond to those in need,
through Jesus Christ, our Savior and Lord.
Amen.

Invitation to Communion

The table of life is spread before you.
Feast on the goodness and mercy of God.

Prayer after Communion

We give you thanks, O God,
that you make your home with us,
bringing heaven to earth in this holy meal.
Fill us with your Spirit as we go from here,
that we may wipe away tears,
tend to those in mourning and pain,
seek the healing of the nations,
and bring to earth the presence of your Son,
Jesus Christ, our Savior and Lord.
Amen.

Sending of Communion

Eternal God,
whose glory is revealed in the crucified and risen Lord,
bless those who go forth to share your word and sacrament
with our sisters and brothers
who are *sick/homebound/imprisoned.*
In your love and care, nourish and strengthen
those to whom we bring this communion
in the body and blood of your Son,
that we may all feast upon your abundant love
made known in Jesus Christ our Lord.
Amen.

Blessing

The blessing of the Lord God Almighty,
the blessing of + Christ, the Lamb who was slain,
and the blessing of the Holy Spirit of truth
be among you and remain with you always.
Amen.

Dismissal

Alleluia. Go in peace. Share the good news.
Thanks be to God. Alleluia.

SEASONAL RITES FOR EASTER

Blessing of Graduates

All-wise and loving God, we give thanks for your gifts to us: for creating us, for saving us in Christ, for calling us in baptism as your people. Look with love on these graduates and bless them as they complete this season of their studies. By your Spirit, help them to use their gifts for your glory and for the good of all people. In your lovingkindness, guide them in their journey. We ask these blessings through Christ our Lord. **Amen.**

O God, you have called your servants to ventures of which we cannot see the ending, by paths as yet untrodden, through perils unknown. Give us faith to go out with good courage, not knowing where we go, but only that your hand is leading us and your love supporting us; through Jesus Christ our Lord. **Amen.**

"O God, you have called your servants" from Evangelical Lutheran Worship *(admin. Augsburg Fortress, 2006), pp. 304, 317.*

Names for Holy Communion and What They Mean

We use several names for the communion meal because one name alone can't capture the depth of meaning of this meal. Just as we appreciate the beauty of a diamond when we see all its facets together, we come to a deeper understanding of the communion meal when we understand its many different aspects. Every name for the communion meal recognizes that this meal is a means of grace in which we encounter and receive the love of God shown to us in the presence of our Lord Jesus Christ in the eating and drinking of bread and wine.

Holy Communion

This name emphasizes the relationship between the assembly and Christ and the relationship among those who eat the meal. When we eat and drink the bread and wine of the meal, we receive the body of Christ as the presence of Jesus and become the body of Christ as a community. We are bound together as one community by sharing this meal together, now and with those from every time and place.

Lord's Supper

This name emphasizes the one who hosts this meal: the crucified and risen Lord, Jesus Christ, who invites us into his presence and to share in the meal. "Lord's supper" recalls the story when Jesus instituted this meal with his disciples and also indicates a feast yet to come when Jesus comes again to share a great feast with all who believe in him. The Lord's supper in which we participate today connects past events, present reality, and the future hope. In all time, it is Jesus who gives us the gift of the feast.

Eucharist

"Eucharist" comes from the Greek word for thanksgiving, and it describes both the communion meal and the whole worship service. "Eucharist" emphasizes the assembly's celebration and thanksgiving in word and song for all of God's creation, for the gift of salvation in Jesus Christ, and for God's gift of the communion meal.

Mass

"Mass" comes from the Latin word "missa" which means "mission." In the communion meal, we are not only connected to the death and resurrection of Jesus Christ, but we are also connected to all the joys and needs of others who gather at the meal and throughout the world. "Mass" points toward the mission of Christ in service to the world. The meal strengthens us to serve those in need, including those who are hungry, hurting, lonely, and hopeless. After sharing the meal, the assembly is sent into the world to serve with the command, "Go in peace. Serve the Lord."

Sacrament of the Altar

The altar is representative of Christ's presence in the worship space. Altars are traditionally used as a place of sacrifice and offering, and using "Sacrament of the Altar" emphasizes the gift Jesus Christ gives by offering himself as a final sacrifice for the sake of the world. The gift of the body and blood of Christ in the meal then assures us of the forgiveness of sins, life, and salvation. The altar of sacrifice is transformed, once and for all, into a meal table where we gather at Christ's invitation.

From Fed and Forgiven: Communion Preparation and Formation Leader Guide *(Augsburg Fortress, 2009).*

Welcoming People to Communion

At a service in which individuals or a group of people who have been baptized on another occasion mark the beginning of their regular participation in holy communion, the presiding minister may acknowledge the event with an announcement (for example, before the service or before the readings) that is baptismal in orientation. The prayers of intercession may include a suitable petition for the occasion.

Example of a welcome

Today this community of faith rejoices with the following people who join in sharing the meal of holy communion: *names*. In the sacrament of holy baptism, we are welcomed into the body of Christ and sent to share in the mission of God. In the sacrament of holy communion, God unites us in Jesus Christ and nourishes us for that mission. Living among God's faithful people, we are strengthened by God's word and this holy supper to proclaim the good news of God in Christ through word and deed, to serve all people, following the example of Jesus, and to strive for justice and peace in all the earth.

Let us welcome *these sisters and brothers* in Christ to holy communion.
Welcome to the Lord's table. We thank God for you. We pray that you will find joy and strength in this meal, until we feast forever at God's heavenly banquet.

Examples of petitions for the prayers of intercession

For those who join in sharing the meal of holy communion this day [*names*], we thank you. As you made them your own in baptism, feed and nourish them always with your forgiveness, grace, and love.
or
For those who join in sharing the meal of holy communion this day [*names*], we thank you. May they know you are near. Make them one with all your people. Help them share with others the new life you give them in baptism, in your word, and at your table.

When coming to participate in communion on this day, it is most natural for those being welcomed to come to the table with those who are accompanying them on their journey of faith—such as parents, families, and sponsors.

Blessing at the Table

Some congregations have the practice of offering a blessing at the table to those who are not yet communing, whether children or adults. The sign of the cross may be traced on the person's forehead, with or without accompanying words. This sign is both a reminder of baptism for the baptized and a symbol of the love of Christ that extends to all people.

A baptismal reminder is also appropriate for words that may be spoken by a communion minister. If words are used, they may vary significantly depending on the age and circumstances of the one coming for a blessing. Suggestions for such a blessing—when the minister knows that the person is baptized—include the following or similar words.

Remember your baptism, and be joyful.
You belong to Christ, in whom you have been baptized.
Blessed be God, who chose you in Christ.
Remember your baptism. Jesus loves you.

Words that may be appropriate whether or not a person is baptized include the following.

(*from Welcome to Baptism:*)
Receive the sign of the cross, a sign of God's endless love and mercy for you.
(*from Luther's Small Catechism:*)
God the Father, Son, and Holy Spirit watch over you.
Jesus loves you and cares for you.
God be with you and bless you.

When speaking the words of a blessing, in the same way as when giving the elements of communion, it is not necessary to address the person by name. Not only is it burdensome for communion ministers to be expected to know the names even of those who come regularly, it is difficult to avoid making distinctions between those who come regularly and those who come occasionally or who are visiting the worshiping community for the first time.

April 3, 2016
Second Sunday of Easter

In spite of all we have heard and all that we have seen, it is often hard to believe. Because it is hard to believe, we will invest ourselves in the Easter mystery for fifty days (a week of weeks). Because it is hard to believe, John the evangelist will provide sign after sign celebrating Jesus' victory over death. Because it is hard to believe, the Lord Jesus will return to us again and again in the mystery of the holy communion, inviting us to touch and taste his presence, and offering us his peace.

Prayer of the Day

O God of life, you reach out to us amid our fears with the wounded hands of your risen Son. By your Spirit's breath revive our faith in your mercy, and strengthen us to be the body of your Son, Jesus Christ, our Savior and Lord, who lives and reigns with you and the Holy Spirit, one God, now and forever.

Gospel Acclamation

Alleluia. Blessed are those who ¹ have not seen* and yet have come ¹ to believe. *Alleluia.* (John 20:29)

Readings and Psalm

Acts 5:27-32

Peter has been arrested for proclaiming the good news of Jesus' death and resurrection. His response to the charges of the high priest summarizes the early church's proclamation of forgiveness of sin through repentance.

Psalm 118:14-29

You are my God, and I will exalt you. (Ps. 118:28)

or Psalm 150

Let everything that has breath praise the Lord. (Ps. 150:6)

Revelation 1:4-8

The book of Revelation recounts a mystical vision of the risen Christ, experienced by a Christian prophet named John. Here he describes Christ as a timeless redeemer, the beginning, present, and end of all time.

John 20:19-31

The unprecedented events of the day of resurrection continue as the risen Jesus appears to his fearful disciples. A week later, after Thomas worships Jesus, Jesus pronounces that the blessings of the resurrection are also for those who "have not seen and yet believe."

Preface   Easter

Color   White

Prayers of Intercession

The prayers are prepared locally for each occasion. The following examples may be adapted or used as appropriate.

Rooted in the abundant life and love of Christ Jesus, we pray for the life of the church, the lives of people in need, and the life of all creation.

A brief silence.

Holy God of resurrection, fill us with your Holy Spirit to announce the new life you give through Christ Jesus. Lead us to people who need to hear good news. Hear us, O God.
Your mercy is great.

Breathe new life into all of creation. Send sun to warm and water to saturate yards, fields, and mountains. Set all things in order, that abundance may come forth. Hear us, O God.
Your mercy is great.

Open paths for cooperation between nations to care for refugees, survivors of natural disaster, and people living through war. Bless the efforts of peacemaking troops, diplomats, and relief organizations to foster peace in the world. Hear us, O God.
Your mercy is great.

Pour out your enduring mercy to strengthen those who persevere in difficult times (*especially*). Guide them to places where they may find shelter in your presence. Hear us, O God.
Your mercy is great.

Gather together the various gifts of this community and unite us in praise. Harmonize the sound and movement of instruments, voices, hands, feet, and, bodies. Hear us, O God.
Your mercy is great.

Here other intercessions may be offered.

You have united yourself with the saints at rest through Jesus Christ, the firstborn of the dead. Join us all together in his resurrection on the last day. Hear us, O God.

Your mercy is great.
We deliver all this into your care, O God, trusting in the work of your Holy Spirit to bring all things into the risen life of Christ our Lord.
Amen.

Images in the Readings

Usually depictions of the crucified or risen Christ include the marks on his **hands and side**. Our archaeological knowledge of crucifixions tells us that nails were driven through the wrist, but this knowledge should not negate the symbolism of the palm, which is central to a person's hand. We also do not need to get fascinated by the accounts of the stigmata, for we all carry the mark of the crucified and risen Christ on our palm each time we receive the body of Christ at communion. Easy talk about healing from one's wounds can be replaced with the Johannine image of the wounds: like Christ, we may scar rather than heal. In John 19:34, blood and water flow from the wound on Jesus' side, and church tradition has seen in this detail not an erroneous description of human anatomy but rather the proclamation that baptism and eucharist flow from the death of Christ.

Each year on the second Sunday of Easter, we meet **doubting Thomas**. He is all of us, and we doubters are glad to share with all other doubters the peace of the risen Christ. It is not easy to believe that we, too, have felt the wounds of Christ. Faith is trust in what is unseen.

According to John, the believing community assembles each **first day** of the week, which was not until the mid-fourth century a holiday. Christians have continued this practice, thus to meet the risen Christ.

No single description of God is sufficient, and today two opposite depictions are superimposed: the **wounded Jesus** comforting his disciples after the resurrection, and the **triumphant Lord** who will judge the earth at the end of time and now rules the world with divine authority ("at God's right hand"). The doctrine of the two natures of Christ is an attempt to hold together these truths of faith.

Today's readings include a wealth of divine titles: Christ is Leader, Savior, God's right-hand man, faithful witness, firstborn of the dead, ruler of kings, Messiah, Son of God; God is Father, Lord, Alpha and Omega, the Almighty.

Ideas for the Day

◆   In a sense, Thomas and his doubts speak to all humanity and their doubts. Obtain a large framed mirror. Hold it with the glass facing away from the assembly and tell them you have discovered a picture of Thomas. Then turn it around so they can see their reflection in the mirror. Remind them that Jesus is the one who comes to all humanity, even in the midst of our questions and doubts, bringing his grace and peace.

◆   Yes this is often a low attendance Sunday, but that does not mean you have to give in or encourage it. For example, you could welcome a new group of children to regular participation in holy communion, plan a Godparenting Sunday (see Baptism of Our Lord, p. 83), or invite a guest musician or musical ensemble to assist in leading the assembly's song. Give people a special reason to be present so they will not miss out like Thomas did.

◆   Thomas thought he needed to reach out and touch Jesus' wounds before he could believe in the resurrection. Confronted with the risen Christ, Thomas realized that was enough. What do people in these days think they need in order to believe? How does Jesus enter the locked rooms of our hearts these days? Through song, through eucharist, through baptism, through scripture, through prayer. When has Jesus been most real to you? When have you seen lives touched by the risen Christ? Could it be the celebration of a newborn infant? Loving care of the dying? The gift of healing? Christ is risen and entering our lives daily. Show Jesus to your people.

Connections with the Liturgy

Each Sunday Christians exchange with one another the peace of the risen Christ. In some assemblies, the peace has become a kind of seventh-inning stretch during which everyone chats with everyone else about the week's news. It is important to remember the liturgical intention of this greeting: we are enacting John 20, receiving from one another the peace that Christ gave to the disciples. We fill the room with the life of the Holy Spirit, breathing to one another the meaning of Christ's death and resurrection.

Let the Children Come

Early Orthodox churches gathered on the Monday after Easter to tell stories, jokes, and anecdotes. They celebrated the "joke" that God pulled on Satan. It is known as Bright Monday, White Monday, Dyngus Day, and Emmaus Day in various countries. The Latins call it *risus paschalis*—God's joke, the Easter laugh. Make this second Sunday of Easter a time to laugh! Prepare plastic Easter eggs with simple jokes in them that children and adults can open and read during worship. Hang streamers from font, pulpit, balcony. Rejoice! Christ is risen indeed!

Assembly Song
Gathering

This joyful Eastertide   ELW 391, WOV 676, LBW 149

The day of resurrection   ELW 361, LBW 141

Come, you faithful, raise the strain   ELW 363, LBW 132

Psalmody and Acclamations

Farlee, Robert Buckley. "Psalm 118:14-29" from PWC.

Gelineau, Joseph. "Psalm 150" from ACYG.

Mummert, Mark. "Psalm 118:14-29," Refrain 2, from PSCY.

(GA) Browning, Carol/arr. Tom Andion. "Deo Gloria Alleluia (Easter Gospel Acclamation)." SATB, cant, assembly, kybd, gtr, opt fl and 2 tr. GIA G-6402.

Hymn of the Day

The risen Christ   ELW 390   *WOODLANDS*

O sons and daughters, let us sing   ELW 386/387, LBW 139   *O FILII ET FILIAE*

We walk by faith   ELW 635   *SHANTI*   WOV 675   *DUNLAP'S CREEK*

Offering

You are holy   ELW 525

The trumpets sound, the angels sing   ELW 531, W&P 139

Communion

O Savior, precious Savior   ELW 820, LBW 514

Bread of life from heaven   ELW 474

Now We Remain   ELW 500, W&P 106

Sending

That Easter day with joy was bright   ELW 384, LBW 154

Thine is the glory   ELW 376, LBW 145

Additional Assembly Songs

God sent his Son   TFF 93

We praise thee, O God   TFF 100

Aleluya, es la fiesta del Señor   LLC 364

⊕ Bruxvoort Colligan, Richard. "Peace of God Be with You/As-salaamu lakum" from *Glory to God*. U. WJK 9780664238971.

⊕ Puerto Rican folk hymn. "Oh, How Good Is Christ the Lord/Oh, qué bueno es Jesús" from *My Heart Sings Out*. U. Church Publishing 9780898694741.

✿ Bruxvoort Colligan, Richard. "God's Love Endures Forever (Psalm 136)" from *Sharing the Road*. AFP 9780800678630. psalmimmersion.bandcamp.com.

✿ Dakota Road. "Blessed Are Those Who Do Believe" from *Dakota Road Music Anthology*. dakotaroadmusic.com.

✿ Hansen, Holly. "Song of Praise" from *Resonance Mass*. nemercy .org/resonance.

✿ Kurtz, Rachel. "Hallelujah" from *Broken and Lowdown*. rachelkurtz.org.

✿ Morris, Michael. "Hallelujah! Praises to the Son!" from *Storm Home: A Collection of Music from Humble Walk Artists-in-Residence*. humblewalk.bandcamp.com.

Music for the Day
Choral

p ● Pasch, William Allen/Robert Weaver. "What Can It Mean That Jesus Is Arisen?" SATB, kybd, opt tpt, assembly. AFP 9781451451702.

Rutter, John. "Psalm 150." 2 pt, org. OXF E-135.

p ● Scott, K. Lee. "O Sons and Daughters of the King." SATB, br, org. AFP 9780800677053.

p Vaughan Williams, Ralph/arr. Erik Whitehill. "Come My Way" from *Wade in the Water: Easy Choral Music for All Ages*. SAB, kybd. AFP 9780800678616.

Children's Choir

p Ferguson, John. "Jesus, My Lord and God" from *ChildrenSing in Worship*, vol. 3. U/2 pt, kybd. AFP 9781451476569.

p Shepperd, Mark. "We Thank You, Dear God." U/2 pt, pno. AFP 9781451434279.

Vaughan Williams, Ralph. "Unto Him That Loved Us" from *The Morningstar Choir Book*. U, kybd. CPH 976287WEB.

Keyboard / Instrumental

● Biery, Marilyn. "O filii et filiae" from *The Lord Is Risen*. Pno or org. MSM 10-428.

● Cherwien, David M. "Shanti" from *Six Organ Preludes*. Org. GIA G-4291.

p ● Culli, Benjamin. "Woodlands" from *Praise the One*, vol. 3. Org. AFP 9781451424195.

● Held, Wilbur. "O filii et filiae" from *Augsburg Organ Library: Easter*. Org. AFP 9780800659363.

Handbell

Glasgow, Michael J. "Whimsical Praise." 3-7 oct hb, opt 2-3 oct hc, L3. CG CGB883.

● Gramann, Fred. "O Sons and Daughters, Let Us Sing." 4-5 oct, L5. AGEHR AG45038.

p Zabel, Albert. "The Strife Is O'er." 3-5 oct, L3. AFP 9781451432282.

Monday, April 4

Benedict the African, confessor, died 1589

Born a slave on the island of Sicily, Benedict first lived as a hermit and labored as a plowman after he was freed. When the bishop of Rome ordered all hermits to attach themselves to a religious community, Benedict joined the Franciscans, where he served as a cook. Although he was illiterate, his fame as a confessor brought many visitors to the humble and holy cook, and he was eventually named superior of the community. A patron saint of African Americans, Benedict is remembered for his patience and understanding when confronted with racial prejudice and taunts.

Wednesday, April 6

Albrecht Dürer, died 1528; Matthias Grünewald, died 1529; Lucas Cranach, died 1553; artists

These great German artists revealed through their work the mystery of salvation and the wonder of creation. Dürer's work reflected the apocalyptic spirit of his time. Though he remained a Roman Catholic, he was sympathetic to Martin Luther's reforming work. Grünewald's paintings are known for their dramatic forms, vivid colors, and depiction of light. Cranach's work includes many fine religious examples and several portraits of Martin Luther. Cranach was also widely known for his woodcuts.

Saturday, April 9

Dietrich Bonhoeffer, theologian, died 1945

Bonhoeffer (BON-heh-fer) was a German theologian who, at the age of twenty-five, became a lecturer in systematic theology at the University of Berlin. In 1933, and with Hitler's rise to power, Bonhoeffer became a leading spokesman for the Confessing Church, a resistance movement against the Nazis. He was arrested in 1943. He was linked to a failed attempt on Hitler's life and sent to Buchenwald, then to Schönberg prison. After leading a worship service on April 8, 1945, at Schönberg prison, he was taken away to be hanged the next day. His last words as he left were, "This is the end, but for me the beginning of life." *Evangelical Lutheran Worship* includes a hymn (626) by Bonhoeffer, "By Gracious Powers."

April 10, 2016
Third Sunday of Easter

The disciples make a big splash and breakfast with the risen Jesus in the gospel. Wading in the water (remembering our baptism) and eating with Jesus (celebrating the holy communion) is our weekly encounter with the risen Christ. Jesus asks us, with Peter, again and again: Do you love me? And Jesus invites us, again and again, to follow him bringing the Easter life to others.

Prayer of the Day

Eternal and all-merciful God, with all the angels and all the saints we laud your majesty and might. By the resurrection of your Son, show yourself to us and inspire us to follow Jesus Christ, our Savior and Lord, who lives and reigns with you and the Holy Spirit, one God, now and forever.

Gospel Acclamation

Alleluia. Our hearts ǀ burn within us* while you open to ǀ us the scriptures. *Alleluia.* (Luke 24:32)

Readings and Psalm
Acts 9:1-6 [7-20]

Each of us has a story of meeting God's grace. Saul (later called Paul) was an ardent persecutor of all who followed the Way of Christ. This reading recounts the story of his transformation, beginning with an encounter with Jesus Christ on the way to Damascus.

Psalm 30

You have turned my wailing into dancing. (Ps. 30:11)

Revelation 5:11-14

The vision of John recorded in Revelation offers a glimpse of cosmic worship on the Lord's Day. At its center is "the Lamb who was slain."

John 21:1-19

The risen Christ appears again to his disciples by the sea where they were first called. After echoes of the fishing and feeding miracles, he gives a final reminder of the cost of a disciple's love and obedience.

Preface Easter

Color White

Prayers of Intercession

The prayers are prepared locally for each occasion. The following examples may be adapted or used as appropriate.

Rooted in the abundant life and love of Christ Jesus, we pray for the life of the church, the lives of people in need, and the life of all creation.

A brief silence.

Holy God, you supply everything we need, and more. Equip us to do the work you intend with the confidence that you will multiply the outcome. Hear us, O God.

Your mercy is great.

Open our eyes to the promise of new life all around us. Make sprouting plants, awakening animals, and swimming fish all bear witness to your glorious abundance. Hear us, O God.

Your mercy is great.

Preserve the lives of those who are persecuted for their devotion to you. Use the faithfulness and insight you have given them to transform their persecutors. Hear us, O God.

Your mercy is great.

Restore the well-being of people who cry out to you in suffering and in want (*especially*). Pour out your mercy upon them, and turn their wailing into dancing. Hear us, O God.

Your mercy is great.

Inspire the work of translators, authors, and composers who bring your word to others (*as you inspired Mikael Agricola, whom we commemorate today*). Reveal your life through their work. Hear us, O God.

Your mercy is great.

Here other intercessions may be offered.

Remembering the saints who praised you in life and in death, bring us also to the day when you will gather all people to sing hymns of praise in your presence. Hear us, O God.

Your mercy is great.

We deliver all this into your care, O God, trusting in the work of your Holy Spirit to bring all things into the risen life of Christ our Lord.

Amen.

Images in the Readings

Fish became a significant symbol in Christianity's early centuries, perhaps in memory of disciples having been fishermen, but perhaps because of a Jewish metaphoric tradition that described fish as the main course served at the messianic banquet. Eating fish may have symbolized faith in the demise of the ancient evil sea monster. The acronym for "Jesus Christ, God's Son, Savior," spelled the Greek noun for fish, *ichthus*. Some early Christian art depicting the last supper shows a great fish on the plate in front of Jesus, as does the frontispiece for Holy Communion by He Qi in *Evangelical Lutheran Worship* (p. 89). Although we do not know where Jerome got this data, the great biblical interpreter wrote that God had created 153 varieties of fish; thus the reference in John 21:11 means that all of creation comes to serve God.

Later trinitarian doctrine made the language of Jesus as **Son** of God privileged divine speech. But earlier Christian writing (for example, Acts 9:20) understood that Jesus' sonship was his messianic status, which ensured salvation to all believers: using categories important in a patriarchal society, we all were to become sons of God who would inherit what the Father bestowed.

Even Luke's narrative details can function as symbols: Saul is **blind** for three days. There is considerable discussion now about the church's traditional use of blindness as a symbol for being spiritually unaware. Some Christians who are blind welcome the imagery; others criticize its use.

Ideas for the Day

◆ The name change from Saul to Paul is a reflection of the Jewish Saul, with a Hebrew name, understanding his call as a missionary to the Gentiles. So he takes on the Greek version of his name: Paul. What changes does the church need to make to speak the truth of Jesus to the culture of today? This is a question for the whole church, but also one answered differently in different settings.

◆ In the gospel, it is the resurrected Jesus coming to the disciples and bringing them to faith, again. In the reading from Acts, it is Ananias who is sent to care for Saul in his time of blindness. Everyone has someone who helped lead them to faith. Could this be an opportunity for folks to share a brief story about that person with their neighbor during the sermon? Or could this be an opportunity to interview a handful of members about a person who helped shape and ground their faith?

◆ It is only a short time after the crucifixion and resurrection, and already the disciples seem to have forgotten Jesus and returned to the lives they left when they first followed him. Sunday mornings may touch people, but how soon Monday comes and the rush of life takes over. Still Jesus continues to seek out the disciples, feeding them and sending them out. This is what happens as the Holy Spirit gathers God's people for worship. This happens as Jesus gives himself in the bread and wine. This happens as the hungry are fed, the homeless given shelter, and the sick healed. We may forget, we may try to return to ordinary life, but Jesus continues finding us, feeding us, and sending us out for service in his name.

Connections with the Liturgy

The Sunday Assembly ([Minneapolis: Augsburg Fortress, 2008], 124) suggests that especially during the weeks of Easter "This is the feast" be sung as the initial canticle of praise. The stanzas of this canticle (*ELW*, p. 101) are adapted from today's second reading. We join with every creature in heaven and on earth and under the earth and in the sea to praise God with these beloved words.

Let the Children Come

Jesus says, "Follow me." What are ways that we feed Jesus' lambs and tend Jesus' sheep as he asks Peter to do to show his love? Are we intentional about doing this and teaching our children and youth to develop lives of service? Talk about what it means to serve one another and follow Jesus—and that it is more than just raising funds or food for this cause or that charity, but it is finding ways to build connections with people. How does your congregation not only help others, but build Christ-centered relationships with others?

Assembly Song
Gathering

Blessing and honor   ELW 854, LBW 525
Blessing, honor, glory to the Lamb   ELW 433, W&P 21
With high delight   ELW 368, LBW 140

Psalmody and Acclamations

Haugen, Marty. "Psalm 30," Refrain 3, from PSCY.
Louis, Kenneth W. "Third Sunday of Easter / C" from LP:LG.
Schalk, Carl. "Psalm 30" from PWC.
(GA) Browning, Carol/arr. Tom Andion. "Deo Gloria Alleluia (Easter Gospel Acclamation)." SATB, cant, assembly, kybd, gtr, opt fl and 2 tr. GIA G-6402.

Hymn of the Day

Christ is alive! Let Christians sing   ELW 389, LBW 363   *TRURO*
That Easter day with joy was bright   ELW 384   *PUER NOBIS*
  LBW 154   *ERSCHIENEN IST*
Amen, we praise your name, O God   ELW 846, TFF 279, WOV 786
  AMEN SIAKUDUMISA

Offering

Signs and wonders   ELW 672, sts. 1, 3
Christ is risen! Shout hosanna!   ELW 383, WOV 672

Communion

Come, let us eat   ELW 491, LBW 214, LS 103, TFF 119
Praise the One who breaks the darkness   ELW 843, ASG 34
Soul, adorn yourself with gladness   ELW 489, LLC 388

Sending

Rise, O church, like Christ arisen   ELW 548, OBS 76
Let us talents and tongues employ   ELW 674, TFF 232, WOV 754

Additional Assembly Songs

Toma mi mano, hermano   LLC 390
The Lamb   TFF 89
Feed my lambs   ASG 8

⊕ Monteiro, Simei. "O choro pode durar/Though Weeping and Deepest Sorrow" from *Psalms for All Seasons: A Compete Psalter for Worship*. SATB. Brazos Press 9781592554447.

⊕ South African/arr. Anders Nyberg. "Hamba nathi" from *Global Songs 2*. SATB with cantor. AFP 9780800656744.

✿ Crowder, David/Mark Waldrop/Matt Maher. "Oh, Great Love of God" from CCLI.

✿ Dakota Road. "Communion Response" from *Dakota Road Music Anthology*. dakotaroadmusic.com.

✿ Dakota Road. "To Be Alive" from *Dakota Road Music Anthology*. dakotaroadmusic.com.

✿ Kendrick, Graham. "Here Is Bread." ELW 483.

✿ Kernsey. "Paradox" from *Storm Home: A Collection of Music from Humble Walk Artists-in-Residence*. humblewalk.bandcamp.com.

✿ Wilson, Tay. "All Things New" from *Stay the Course*. Available on Amazon.com.

Music for the Day
Choral

p   Haydn, Johann Michael/arr. Patrick Liebergen. "Come Follow Me Forever." 2 pt mxd, kybd. GIA G-5387.

p ● Highben, Zebulon. "Christ Is Alive! Let Christians Sing." SATB, org, br qrt, assembly. AFP 9781451451580.

p ● Pavlechko, Thomas. "That Easter Day with Joy Was Bright" from *Choral Stanzas for Hymns*, vol. 1. SATB. AFP 9780806698410.

p   Wentzel, Brian. "The Day of Resurrection!" SAB, kybd. AFP 9781451451665.

Children's Choir

Corp, Ronald. "Give to My Eyes, Lord." SA, pno. OXF 9780193359215.

Paterson, Suzanne Hunt. "Come, Feed My Lambs." U/2 pt, kybd. BP BP1248.

p   Simpson, F. Thomas. "Nets of Love." U/2 pt, pno. CG CGA1301.

Keyboard / Instrumental

● Hobby, Robert A. "Puer nobis" from *Twenty Hymn Introductions for Organ*. Org. MSM 10-613.

● Miller, Aaron David. "Truro" from *Eight Chorale Preludes for Manuals Only*, vol. 1. Org. AFP 9780800677560.

● Nelhybel, Vaclav. "Truro" from *Festival Hymns and Processionals*. Org, br qnt, timp. Conductor Score. HOP 750.

p ● Organ, Anne Krentz. "Puer nobis" from *Be Thou My Vision*. Pno. AFP 9780800678524.

Handbell

● Kinyon, Barbara B. "Christ Is Alive (Truro)." 3-5 oct hb, opt 3 oct hc, L3+. HOP 2070.

Laurence, Eileen. "Lament and Dance." 3-5 oct hb, opt fl, L3+. AGEHR AG35262.

● Moklebust, Cathy. "That Easter Day with Joy Was Bright." 2-3 oct, L1. CG CGB281.

⊕ = global song   ✿ = praise song
● = relates to hymn of the day   p = available in Prelude Music Planner

Sunday, April 10

Mikael Agricola, Bishop of Turku, died 1557

Agricola was consecrated as the bishop of Turku in 1554, without papal approval. As a result, he began a reform of the Finnish church along Lutheran lines. He translated the New Testament, the prayerbook, hymns, and the mass into Finnish, and through this work set the rules of orthography that are the basis of modern Finnish spelling. His thoroughgoing work is particularly remarkable in that he accomplished it in only three years. He died suddenly on a return trip from negotiating a peace treaty with the Russians.

April 17, 2016
Fourth Sunday of Easter

The gift of new life, of eternal life, is the gift of the risen Christ. It is the promise of Jesus. It was true for Dorcas in Joppa. It was true for those "who have come out of the great ordeal" in the Revelation vision. It is true for us and for all the baptized: Surely goodness and mercy shall follow me all the days of my life, and I will dwell in the house of the Lord forever.

Prayer of the Day

O God of peace, you brought again from the dead our Lord Jesus Christ, the great shepherd of the sheep. By the blood of your eternal covenant, make us complete in everything good that we may do your will, and work among us all that is well-pleasing in your sight, through Jesus Christ, our Savior and Lord, who lives and reigns with you and the Holy Spirit, one God, now and forever.

Gospel Acclamation

Alleluia. Jesus says, I am | the good shepherd.* I know my own and my | own know me. *Alleluia.* (John 10:14)

Readings and Psalm

Acts 9:36-43

Dorcas was a faithful and devoted woman of charity in the community of Joppa. Her kindness and her work with clothing was well-known, especially to the widows in town. When she fell ill and died, Peter raised her back to life through the power of prayer.

Psalm 23

The Lord is my shepherd; I shall not be in want. (Ps. 23:1)

Revelation 7:9-17

Christ is the shepherd who leads his faithful to springs of the water of life. Christ is also the lamb who vanquishes sin and suffering, in whose blood the saints have washed their robes and made them white.

John 10:22-30

Jesus responds to questions about his identity with the remarkable claim that he and the Father are one. Those who understand this are his sheep; they hear his voice, follow, and will never be snatched from his hand.

Preface   Easter

Color   White

Prayers of Intercession

The prayers are prepared locally for each occasion. The following examples may be adapted or used as appropriate.

Rooted in the abundant life and love of Christ Jesus, we pray for the life of the church, the lives of people in need, and the life of all creation.

A brief silence.

Holy and mighty God, fulfill your saving work on behalf of all who give thanks for your great love for this creation. Make our song strong enough to invite all hurting people into your family. Hear us, O God.

Your mercy is great.

Make us ever conscious of how we use and consume the gifts you have given us on the earth and in the oceans. Open our eyes to see creation as good, useful, and worthy of care. Hear us, O God.

Your mercy is great.

Give your wisdom to people who make decisions that affect others. Fill human institutions with your reconciling justice. When we oppress people, disrupt us and heal our hearts. Hear us, O God.

Your mercy is great.

Respond to the call of people who cry out in grief, in loneliness or despair, or in chronic pain or illness (*especially*). Embrace them with your compassion. Hear us, O God.
Your mercy is great.

With your very presence sustain communities that are formed out of common struggle: among those who are widowed, among children without parents, and among people who have no permanent shelter. Hear us, O God.
Your mercy is great.

Here other intercessions may be offered.

You give strength to the saints by fulfilling your promise of eternal life. Shepherd us in paths of righteousness, that we may know life now and in the age to come. Hear us, O God.
Your mercy is great.

We deliver all this into your care, O God, trusting in the work of your Holy Spirit to bring all things into the risen life of Christ our Lord.
Amen.

Images in the Readings

To deepen our contemplation of the metaphor of Christ as **shepherd**, it is good to review the positive use the Bible makes of the image of **sheep**. The Hebrew Scriptures remembered the past as a nomadic life of herders of sheep and goats. Sheep signified the communal life of the people, constituted a source of food and clothing, and functioned as the primary sacrificial gifts to God. The single wandering lamb from Luke's parable of the lost sheep is not the image in John 10; nor does the Bible describe sheep as being dirty; nor is a barefoot, white-robed man a realistic depiction of the shepherd, who by the first century was thought of as lower class and religiously unclean. Shepherds were both male and female: see Genesis 29. Christians adapted pagan religious sculpture to depict Jesus as the divine good shepherd. The early Christian movement was largely an urban phenomenon, and thus shepherding was a distant reality, readily available for the religious imagination.

Dorcas's contribution of **clothes** for the needy set the example for providing clothing for the needy as a primary Christian charity throughout history.

The **white robe** worn by the blessed dead is recalled in contemporary albs, which mean to signify not clerical status but baptismal identity. Many artists have depicted Jesus as wearing white, which is unlikely considering the difficulty of keeping white clean. This imagery is symbolic, as if Jesus shines with the light of God.

Around the throne the martyrs carry **palm branches**. We all carried palms a month ago, to join with the Jerusalem crowd on Passion Sunday. As is usual, the religious symbolism has double meaning: lauding Christ on his way to the cross and honoring the Lamb on the throne of heaven.

In the Bible, God is described as having human body parts, in John 10 a **hand**. In contrast to Greco-Roman paganism, although God is referred to as a "he," the biblical God does not have or use male sexual organs.

Ideas for the Day

♦   The promise that Jesus' sheep will hear his voice (John 10:27) can be difficult when God feels distant. Looking back to verse 25, Jesus explains that his "works" confirm his relationship to the Father. Likewise, our service to others places us in the hand of Christ, and the more we emulate his works the clearer his voice will become. On the Dear Working Preacher blog, David Lose suggests passing out a checklist of service opportunities that people can join this week, to help them begin hearing Christ's voice more clearly.

♦   Dorcas's ministry included making clothes for the needy (Acts 9:36, 39). She receives new life in today's story, and her charity work has taken on an eternal life of its own, continuing throughout history and leading to such places as the Salvation Army's thrift stores. Consider how you might create a Dorcas ministry in your context: you might do a clothing drive to send items on a mission trip, provide school uniforms and shoes for underprivileged children, or collect outerwear for the homeless. You might discover knitters in your congregation who could create prayer shawls for prisoners, or folks interested in starting a sewing club that would donate whatever they make to those in need. Name and celebrate the important work of this special disciple.

♦   Today's reading from Revelation easily lends itself to a reader's theater arrangement for multiple readers and/or assembly and leader(s). It is a marvelous call to worship or invitation to the meal: for when we gather around God's table, we are gathering around the glorified Christ present in the bread and wine, just as the worshipers surround the Lamb on the throne. The reading is dramatic and builds to a beautiful climax. It's especially nice to have the voices pull back in volume—perhaps to only one young voice—for the final phrase "and God will wipe away every tear from their eyes."

Connections with the Liturgy

The commendation spoken at the close of Christian burial (*ELW*, p. 283) asks the Savior to receive "a sheep of your own fold, a lamb of your own flock," and the final blessing (p. 285) refers to our Lord Jesus as "the great shepherd of the sheep."

Let the Children Come

It was once commonplace for children to memorize scripture both at Sunday school and at home. There are benefits for people of all ages to commit certain passages to memory.

Psalm 23 is one of the most beloved and well-known psalms. Invite Sunday school families to work together to commit it to memory. Whether families work on this at the dinner table, in the car, or at bedtime, ultimately children love knowing they memorized something, and they (and their parents) will remember the text the rest of their lives. Lay the groundwork for memorizing more passages in the future.

Assembly Song
Gathering

Christ the Lord is risen today; Alleluia! ELW 369, LBW 128

Thine is the glory ELW 376, LBW 145

Alleluia! Voices raise ELW 828

Psalmody and Acclamations

Comer, Marilyn. "Psalm 23" from *ChildrenSing Psalms*. U, assembly, kybd.

Ollis, Peter. "The Lord Is My Shepherd" from PS2.

Roberts, Leon C. "The Lord Is My Shepherd (Psalm 23)." TFF 3.

(GA) Browning, Carol/arr. Tom Andion. "Deo Gloria Alleluia (Easter Gospel Acclamation)." SATB, cant, assembly, kybd, gtr, opt fl and 2 tr. GIA G-6402.

Hymn of the Day

The King of love my shepherd is ELW 502, LBW 456 *ST. COLUMBA*

My Shepherd, you supply my need ELW 782 *RESIGNATION*

The Lord's my shepherd ELW 778, LBW 451 *BROTHER JAMES' AIR*

Offering

To God our thanks we give ELW 682

Praise the Lord, rise up rejoicing ELW 544, sts. 1-2; LBW 196, sts. 1-2

Communion

You satisfy the hungry heart ELW 484, WOV 711

Shepherd me, O God ELW 780

Savior, like a shepherd lead us ELW 789, TFF 254, LBW 481

Sending

Christ Jesus lay in death's strong bands ELW 370, LBW 134

Have no fear, little flock ELW 764, LBW 476, LS 171

Additional Assembly Songs

My good shepherd is the Lord ASG 23

How lovely on the mountains TFF 99

He leadeth me TFF 151, LBW 501

◉ African-Caribbean traditional. "You Hear the Lambs a-Cryin'" from *The Courage to Say No: 23 Songs for Lent and Easter*. U. GIA G-4244.

◉ Villarreal, Ricardo. "El Señor is mi pastor/My Shepherd Is the Lord" from *Psalms for All Seasons: A Compete Psalter for Worship*. SATB. Brazos Press 9781592554447.

✷ Bruxvoort Colligan, Richard. "My Love Is My Shepherd (Psalm 23)" from *Sharing the Road*. AFP 9780800678630. psalmimmersion.bandcamp.com.

✷ Bruxvoort Colligan, Richard. "Surely Goodness and Mercy (Psalm 23)" from *Our Roots Are in You*. worldmaking.net.

✷ Bruxvoort Colligan, Richard. "All of My Days" from *Psalm 23 Cycle*. worldmaking.net.

✷ Dakota Road. "Your Love Is Everlasting" from *Dakota Road Music Anthology*. dakotaroadmusic.com.

✷ Rimbo, Justin. "When It Seems the Day Will End" from *Storm Home: A Collection of Music from Humble Walk Artists-in-Residence*. humblewalk.bandcamp.com.

Music for the Day
Choral

p Evans, David/arr. C. J. Adams. "Be Still." SATB, pno. HOP C-5792.

● Shaw, Timothy. "The Twenty-Third Psalm." 2 pt mxd, kybd, opt trbl inst. CPH 98-4065.

● Thomson, Virgil. "My Shepherd Will Supply My Need." SATB. ALF GCMR-02046.

p Whitehill, Erik. "Wind of the Spirit" from *Wade in the Water: Easy Choral Music for All Ages*. SAB, assembly, kybd. AFP 9780800678616.

Children's Choir

p Bakken, Jeremy S. "Children of the Heavenly Father." U/2 pt, pno. CG CGA1380.

Schalk, Carl F./arr. Michael Burkhardt. "Someone Special." U/2 pt, org, hb. CPH 984135WEB.

Schram, Ruth Elaine. "You Renew My Soul." U/2 pt, pno. SHW 884088949396.

Keyboard / Instrumental

● Christiansen, David. "St. Columba" from *Organ Plus Anthology*, vol. 1. Org, fl. AFP 9781451424256.

p ● Hobby, Robert A. "Resignation" from *For All the Saints*, vol. 2. Org. AFP 9780800679101.

● Porter, Emily Maxson. "Resignation" from *Piano Plus Through the Year*, vol. 2. Pno, inst. AFP 9780800663728.

p ● Wright, M. Searle. "Brother James' Air" from *Augsburg Organ Library: Marriage*. Org. AFP 9781451486025.

Handbell

● Eithun, Sandra. "Shepherd's Peace" from *Ringing the Church Year*. 3-5 oct hb, opt 3-5 oct hc, L2+. LOR 20/1671L.

● Larson, Lloyd. "Meditation on 'Brother James' Air.'" 3-5 oct, L2+. BP HB459.

p ● Moklebust, Cathy. "The King of Love My Shepherd Is." 3-5 oct hb, opt 3-5 oct hc, L3+. CG CGB825.

◉ = global song   ✷ = praise song
● = relates to hymn of the day   p = available in Prelude Music Planner

Tuesday, April 19

Olavus Petri, priest, died 1552; Laurentius Petri, Bishop of Uppsala, died 1573; renewers of the church

These two brothers are commemorated for their introduction of the Lutheran movement to the Church of Sweden after studying at the University of Wittenberg. They returned home and, through the support of King Gustavus Vasa, began their work. Olavus published a catechism, hymnal, and a Swedish version of the mass. He resisted attempts by the king to gain royal control of the church. Laurentius was a professor at the university in Uppsala. When the king wanted to abolish the ministry of bishops, Laurentius persuaded him otherwise. The historic episcopate continues in Sweden to this day. Together the brothers published a complete Bible in Swedish and a revised liturgy in 1541.

Thursday, April 21

Anselm, Bishop of Canterbury, died 1109

This eleventh- and twelfth-century Benedictine monk stands out as one of the greatest theologians between Augustine and Thomas Aquinas. He is counted among the medieval mystics who emphasized the maternal aspects of God. Of Jesus Anselm says, "In sickness you nurse us and with pure milk you feed us." Anselm is perhaps best known for his "satisfaction" theory of atonement. He argued that human rebellion against God demands a payment, but because humanity is fallen it is incapable of making that satisfaction. But God takes on human nature in Jesus Christ, Anselm proposed, in order to make the perfect payment for sin.

Saturday, April 23

Toyohiko Kagawa, renewer of society, died 1960

Toyohiko Kagawa (toy-oh-hee-koh ka-ga-wah) was born in 1888 in Kobe, Japan. Orphaned early, he was disowned by his remaining extended family when he became a Christian. Kagawa wrote, spoke, and worked at length on ways to employ Christian principles in the ordering of society. His vocation to help the poor led him to live among them. He established schools, hospitals, and churches. He also worked for peace and established the Anti-War League. He was arrested for his efforts to reconcile Japan and China after the Japanese attack of 1940.

April 24, 2016
Fifth Sunday of Easter

Easter initiates a new day. It anticipates a new heaven and a new earth. The risen Lord is making all things new. In the mystery of holy baptism God has made new people of us. Today the Lord Jesus invites us to see everyone in a new light—through the lens of love.

Prayer of the Day

O Lord God, you teach us that without love, our actions gain nothing. Pour into our hearts your most excellent gift of love, that, made alive by your Spirit, we may know goodness and peace, through your Son, Jesus Christ, our Savior and Lord, who lives and reigns with you and the Holy Spirit, one God, now and forever.

Gospel Acclamation

Alleluia. Everyone will know that you are ¹ my disciples* if you have love for ¹ one another. *Alleluia.* (John 13:35)

Readings and Psalm

Acts 11:1-18

In defense of his earlier baptism of pagan believers, Peter demonstrates to the members of the Jerusalem church that God's intention to love Gentiles as well as Jews is revealed in Jesus' own testimony. In this way the mission to the Gentiles is officially authorized.

Psalm 148

The splendor of the LORD is over earth and heaven. (Ps. 148:13)

Revelation 21:1-6

John's vision shows us that in the resurrection the new age has dawned; God dwells with us already. Yet we wait for the time when the tears that cloud our vision will be wiped away. Then we will see the new heaven, new earth, and new Jerusalem.

John 13:31-35

After washing the disciples' feet, predicting his betrayal, and then revealing his betrayer, Jesus speaks of his glorification on the cross. This deep, complicated love of Jesus, even to death on the cross, will be the distinctive mark of Jesus' community.

Preface   Easter

Color   White

Prayers of Intercession

The prayers are prepared locally for each occasion. The following examples may be adapted or used as appropriate.

Rooted in the abundant life and love of Christ Jesus, we pray for the life of the church, the lives of people in need, and the life of all creation.

A brief silence.

Holy God, by your Holy Spirit reveal to us the saving work of Christ. Strengthen your church with the good news that leads to limitless life for all. Hear us, O God.

Your mercy is great.

Send us to places far and near, and join our voices in chorus with all creation. Use us to show others your abundant goodness in the created world. Hear us, O God.

Your mercy is great.

End war and the human desire to hold on to power. Free all people to love both neighbor and enemy, and make your church an example of such love. Hear us, O God.

Your mercy is great.

Surround people who are hurting with agents of your healing and messengers of your peace. Provide safe communities for all who are in any need (*especially*). Hear us, O God.

Your mercy is great.

Strengthen the bonds of shared service between congregations and social ministry organizations (*here specific social ministry organizations may be named*). Guide us in doing your work together. Hear us, O God.

Your mercy is great.

Here other intercessions may be offered.

In Christ's death and resurrection you have fulfilled your work for the sake of your saints. Come swiftly to dwell among us and to make all things new. Hear us, O God.

Your mercy is great.

We deliver all this into your care, O God, trusting in the work of your Holy Spirit to bring all things into the risen life of Christ our Lord.

Amen.

Images in the Readings

John's gospel teaches Christians to redefine the word **glory**. Often in typical religious speech, *glory* refers to the unutterable power of the divine, and it is contrasted with the human condition of weakness and death. Sometimes in the Old Testament, the phrase "the glory of the Lord" describes overwhelming natural phenomena that indicate God's powerful presence. However, in the fourth gospel, divine glory is seen not only in the signs Jesus performed but also in his passion, death, and resurrection. Fourth-century Christians saw in the Easter celebration of the Three Days one way to express the single meaning of this threefold event, the single glory through which Christ conquered evil. A stranger to Christianity may find a large crucifix morbid, but the New Testament teaches that in this paradoxical cross is the glory of God.

The book of Revelation includes the image of the **marriage** between God and humanity. "This is the night in which heaven and earth are joined, things human and things divine," is how the Easter proclamation says it (*Evangelical Lutheran Worship* Leaders Edition [Minneapolis: Augsburg Fortress, 2006], 647). Especially medieval monastics delighted in this image, since their celibacy allowed them to speak easily of marriage only with God. Several women mystics even spoke of their sense of wearing a wedding ring. But all imagery for God, because partial, is to some degree problematic, and some contemporary Christians see the marriage imagery as then suggesting that a human bride is to be subservient to her husband, just as the church is to Christ. In light of John 13, we can stress the love between spouses as a sign of God's bonds with humankind.

Ideas for the Day

◆ There is no Sermon on the Mount in John's gospel; instead, all of Jesus' teachings are encapsulated in one verse: "I give you a new commandment, that you love one another. Just as I have loved you, you also should love one another" (13:34). Explore the ramifications of living with love as the center of your faith community. Are you more concerned with saving money on the coffee you serve than on loving your global neighbors who need a fair price paid for their labor? Are the clergy expected to handle all pastoral care, leaving no space for laity to support their church family? How is your church council doing at loving one another? Intentionally putting love as your top priority will both challenge and reward your congregation.

◆ The glory of Christ—and of his followers—is rooted in sacrificial love. The 2013 blockbuster animated film *Frozen* features several examples of true love expressed through sacrifice. First, the snowman Olaf is willing to give his life to help Princess Anna, saying, "Some people are worth melting for." At the film's climax, Anna sacrifices herself to save her sister, Elsa's, life, which Olaf describes as "an act of true love." After this, Elsa realizes that her strongest power comes from showing love instead of living in fear, changing her life and her kingdom forever.

◆ The radical inclusivity of God's mission is illustrated by Peter's vision and accepted by the Jews hearing his report. Likewise, the hospitality of church life must extend beyond our imagined categories for who "fits" or our intended "audience." True hospitality looks to those on the margins and reaches out in healing love. Who is on the margins of ministry in your church? Perhaps women's voices are not fully included, or maybe children have no clear role in your worship. Does your congregation include a cross-section of socioeconomic statuses that reflects the neighborhood you serve? For an excellent theology on the topic of inclusive hospitality, see Letty M. Russell's *Just Hospitality: God's Welcome in a World of Difference*, ed. J. Shannon Clarkson and Kate M. Ott (Westminster John Knox, 2009).

Connections with the Liturgy

The final verse of today's gospel is the same as that of Maundy Thursday, when the community has enacted the love of Christ in the footwashing.

Although some Christians teach that a personal emotional experience of the indwelling of God is necessary for salvation, the rite of Holy Baptism repeats Luke's emphasis that baptism itself brings the gift of the Holy Spirit. Thus there is no requirement for a subsequent personal experience or any extraordinary manifestations of the Spirit.

Let the Children Come

Whoever proclaims the gospel reading today should be prepared to emphasize and perhaps pause after the words "Little children" (John 13:33). Watch to see if children's demeanors or facial expressions change or perk up when they hear these words. Place a note in the worship folder encouraging parents to prepare their children to hear these words. The reader might consider using a tone that is both instructive and saturated with love. Help the hearers sense these words are meant for them as well.

Assembly Song
Gathering

We Are Called   ELW 720, LS 37, W&P 147

All Are Welcome   ELW 641

Christ the Lord is risen today! ELW 373, LBW 130, LS 64

Psalmody and Acclamations

Arnatt, Ronald. "Psalm 148." SATB, assembly, org. ECS 5674.

Leckebusch, Martin. "Let All Creation's Wonders" (tune: *THAXTED*) from LUYH.

Makeever, Ray. "Praise and Exalt God (Psalm 148)" from DH.

(GA) Browning, Carol/arr. Tom Andion. "Deo Gloria Alleluia (Easter Gospel Acclamation)." SATB, cant, assembly, kybd, gtr, opt fl and 2 tr. GIA G-6402.

Hymn of the Day

Alleluia! Jesus is risen! ELW 377, TFF 91, WOV 674 *EARTH AND ALL STARS*

Now all the vault of heav'n resounds ELW 367, LBW 143 *LASST UNS ERFREUEN*

We know that Christ is raised ELW 449, LBW 189 *ENGELBERG*

Offering

Although I speak with angel's tongue ELW 644

We are all one in Christ ELW 643, LLC 470, LS 130, TFF 221

Communion

Come, my way, my truth, my life ELW 816, LBW 513

I received the living God ELW 477, LS 105, WOV 700

United at the table ELW 498, LLC 408

Sending

Awake, O sleeper ELW 452, WOV 745

Oh, praise the gracious power ELW 651, WOV 750

Additional Assembly Songs

Hoy celebramos con gozo LLC 353

There is a name I love to hear TFF 249

No longer strangers W&P 102

⊕ Batak melody. "Hallelujah! Sing Praise to Your Creator" from *Glory to God*. SATB. WJK 9780664238971.

⊕ Sosa, Pablo. "Cristo vive/Christ Is Risen" from *Éste es el Día*. U. GIA G-7021.

✧ Colvin, Tom. "Jesu, Jesu, Fill Us with Your Love." ELW 708.

✧ Bell, John L. "Love One Another" from *One Is the Body: Songs of Unity and Diversity*. GIA G-5790.

✧ Bruxvoort Colligan, Richard. "Creation's Hallelujah (Psalm 148)" from *Shout for Joy*. AFP 9780806698632.

✧ Dakota Road. "Come and See" from *Dakota Road Music Anthology*. dakotaroadmusic.com.

✧ Grundy, Christopher. "Garments of Love" from *Stepping In*. christophergrundy.com.

Music for the Day
Choral

p ● Behnke, John. "Now All the Vault of Heaven Resounds." SATB, assembly, br qnt, timp, hb, org. MSM 60-4020.

p Burrows, Mark. "Bwana Asifiwe." U or 2 pt, pno, perc. CG 1311.

p Erickson, Richard. "Come Away to the Skies" from *The Augsburg Choirbook*. SATB, fl, fc. AFP 9780800656782.

p Leaf, Robert. "Come with Rejoicing." U, kybd. AFP 9780800645755.

Children's Choir

Aston, Peter. "I Give You a New Commandment." SS/2 pt mxd, org/pno. GIA G-4331.

Savoy, Thomas. "Walk Softly in Springtime." 2 pt, org. GIA G-4785.

Saylor, Bruce. "In the Spirit." U, org, hp/pno. PAR PPMO 0223.

Keyboard / Instrumental

p ● Cherwien, David M. "Engelberg" from *Augsburg Organ Library: Easter*. Org. AFP 9780800659363.

p ● Hobby, Robert A. "Earth and All Stars" from *For All the Saints*, vol. 3. Org. AFP 9781451486056.

● Larkin, Michael. "Lasst uns erfreuen" from *All Creatures of Our God and King*. Pno. MSM 15-765.

● Organ, Anne Krentz. "Earth and All Stars" from *On Eagle's Wings*. Pno. AFP 9780800655525.

Handbell

p ● Moklebust, Cathy. "When in Our Music God Is Glorified." 3-7 oct hb, L2+, CG CGB712. Opt full score, CG CGB711.

p ● Organ, Anne K. "Earth and All Stars." 3 oct hb, opt 2 oct hc, L2. AFP 9781451431346.

p ● Ryan, Michael. "Easter Bells." 2-3 oct, L2+. HOP 2675.

Monday, April 25
Mark, Evangelist

Though Mark himself was not an apostle, it is likely that he was a member of one of the early Christian communities. It is possible that he is the John Mark of Acts 12 whose mother owned the house where the apostles gathered. The gospel attributed to him is brief and direct. It is considered by many to be the earliest gospel. Tradition has it that Mark went to preach in Alexandria, Egypt, became the first bishop there, and was martyred.

Friday, April 29
Catherine of Siena, theologian, died 1380

Catherine of Siena was a member of the Order of Preachers (Dominicans), and among Roman Catholics she was the first woman to receive the title Doctor of the Church. She was a contemplative and is known for her mystical visions of Jesus. This gift of mysticism apparently extended back into her childhood, much to the dismay of her parents, who wanted her to be like other children. Catherine was a humanitarian who worked to alleviate the suffering of the poor and imprisoned. She was also a renewer of church and society and advised both popes and any persons who told her their problems. Catherine's contemplative life was linked to her concern for the poor and suffering. She is a reminder that prayer and activism belong together.

May I, 2016
Sixth Sunday of Easter

Visions abound in the readings for the sixth Sunday of Easter. Paul has a vision about what to do. John has a vision of what will be. The risen Lord Jesus provides visions of peace that passes human understanding and power beyond human imagination.

Prayer of the Day

Bountiful God, you gather your people into your realm, and you promise us food from your tree of life. Nourish us with your word, that empowered by your Spirit we may love one another and the world you have made, through Jesus Christ, our Savior and Lord, who lives and reigns with you and the Holy Spirit, one God, now and forever.

Gospel Acclamation

Alleluia. Those who love me will keep my word, and my Fa-
I ther will love them,* and we will come to them and make our I home with them. *Alleluia.* (John 14:23)

Readings and Psalm

Acts 16:9-15

A vision compels Paul to move his ministry into Greece. There he meets Lydia, an important person in the business community, whose heart has been opened by God to receive the gospel. Her conversion and baptism provide the impetus for the founding of the church at Philippi.

Psalm 67

Let the nations be glad and sing for joy. (Ps. 67:4)

Revelation 21:10, 22—22:5

John's vision of a new Jerusalem coming out of heaven pro-vides continuity with God's past actions. Yet in this new city, God's presence replaces the temple, and the glory of God and the Lamb supplant sun and moon.

John 14:23-29

As Jesus talks of returning to the Father, he promises to send the Advocate, the Holy Spirit, who will teach Jesus' fol-lowers and remind them of all that Jesus taught. Even more, those in whom God makes a home will experience a peace that overcomes fear.

or John 5:1-9

Jesus performs a healing miracle on the sabbath. In doing so he both reveals divine creative power and teaches a richer,
deeper meaning for the sabbath as a healing and creative time.

Preface   Easter

Color   White

Prayers of Intercession

The prayers are prepared locally for each occasion. The following examples may be adapted or used as appropriate.

Rooted in the abundant life and love of Christ Jesus, we pray for the life of the church, the lives of people in need, and the life of all creation.

A brief silence.

Holy God, ruler of the nations, renew your call to all people. Raise up leaders who are eager to follow you into justice, love, and truth (*as the apostles Philip and James did*). Hear us, O God.

Your mercy is great.

Nourish all lands through springs, rivers, lakes, pools, and irrigation systems. Produce abundant food by the flowing of your Spirit throughout creation. Hear us, O God.

Your mercy is great.

Help us to extend your hospitality and inspire us to share the grace of Christ in places near and far. Use even small interactions to usher in peace for all people. Hear us, O God.

Your mercy is great.

Send compassionate servants to those who live with health concerns in body, mind, or spirit. Deliver your healing and peace to all in need (*especially*). Hear us, O God.

Your mercy is great.

Bear the burdens of people who long to work, yet remain unemployed or underemployed. Give them dignity when they seek help, and place them where their gifts may be used. Hear us, O God.

Your mercy is great.

Here other intercessions may be offered.

You have given blessed salvation to all your saints. Thank you for writing our names also in the book of life. Make us

Christ's presence for others while we await his coming. Hear us, O God.

Your mercy is great.

We deliver all this into your care, O God, trusting in the work of your Holy Spirit to bring all things into the risen life of Christ our Lord.

Amen.

Images in the Readings

Once again the risen Christ extends **peace** to the assembled believers.

Most of us at some time in our lives will be like the **invalid**, lying helplessly, hoping for healing. May we trust not in some hazy legend but in the power of Christ's resurrection.

Many religions include stories of the legendary **tree of life**. To see the universal interest across time and place in this image, spend some time on Google Images. In the Bible, the reason that God expels Adam and Eve from the garden is to prohibit their enjoying the fruit of the tree of life. Yet later Jewish scholars called the Torah itself the tree of life. That tree returns in the last chapter of the Bible, its fruits miraculously ripening all twelve months of the year, and its soothing leaves healing the nations. Christian tradition has superimposed the cross onto such a tree, and countless churches display art in which the crucifix is a flowering fruited tree.

Traditionally biblical scholars have described Luke as particularly positive about the ministry of **women**. More recently some scholars have noted that Luke praises especially women who are supportive of male leadership, either by their attitude (for example, the mother of Jesus) or by their considerable resources (for example, Lydia). In either case, Lydia offers us an image of a faithful believer and an independent woman who was not identified by any connection to a male. Historians have confirmed that from its origins the Christian movement attracted such women: among the biblical examples are Mary of Magdala, Mary and Martha of Bethany, Susanna, Dorcas, Phoebe, Mary (Rom. 16:6), Junia, Tryphaena, Tryphosa, Persis, and Julia. During early centuries, some Christian men were ridiculed for their faith, given a perception that Christianity was a women's religion.

Ideas for the Day

◆ Notice the transitional nature of these texts. In Acts, Paul travels between two places. When he gets to Macedonia, he meets some women outside the gate. In Revelation, a New Jerusalem is being ushered in. Again we are on the cusp of change between one reality and another. And in both of the gospel texts, the space is liminal. In John 5, Jesus meets the man by the Sheep Gate at the pool of Bethesda, not really inside but not entirely outside either. In John 14, Jesus himself seems to be a liminal space; his presence among us is in a state of transition as he is preparing to depart and the Advocate is about to arrive. What do you make of the transitional, liminal nature of these texts? What liminal space is your congregation straddling? What liminal spaces are occupying our national or international news?

◆ Put John 5 (the alternate gospel text) in conversation with the texts for Easter Sunday. In this text, what functions as the tomb and who is being crucified? Who is the resurrected character in this text? And what shape does the resurrected life take in this story? You may have to read on to answer these questions, and you may be surprised and a little discouraged by what you find. It turns out that this man's rising is not good news for everyone. Resurrection appears to be offensive.

◆ Sabbath observance set God's chosen people apart from the rest of society. In the alternate gospel text from John 5, Jesus defies the sabbath law and also commands the now-healed man to pick up his mat and walk, which means that now both men are guilty! Both Jesus and the healed man have committed the crime of working on the sabbath, putting them outside of Israel's covenant relationship. What does it mean and how is it good news that Jesus has placed both himself and the healed man outside of God's covenant people?

Connections with the Liturgy

In several places, *Evangelical Lutheran Worship* includes the image of the tree of life: the frontispiece to the calendar (p. 11); the frontispiece to the Easter Vigil (p. 266); the frontispiece to the Psalms (p. 333); Thanksgiving at the Table VII (p. 67); and Thanksgiving at the Table X (p. 69). Some hymns refer also to God's promised salvation as like the tree of life.

Let the Children Come

Today's second reading from Revelation includes a reference to "those who are written in the Lamb's book of life" (Rev. 21:27). If children were baptized in your congregation, their names are recorded in the parish register. If they transferred to the congregation from another, their names should also be in the records. Bring out the parish register and show children their names. Even those who were baptized elsewhere, or whose baptismal day is still in the future, can be assured that their names are written in the Lamb's book of life.

Assembly Song
Gathering

Alleluia! Jesus is risen!   ELW 377, TFF 91, WOV 674

Glorious things of you are spoken   ELW 647, LBW 358

Christ is alive! Let Christians sing   ELW 389, LBW 363

Psalmody and Acclamations

Chepponis, James. "Let Nations Sing Your Praise." Cant, assembly, opt SATB, kybd, gtr, 17 hb, B flat or C inst. GIA G-4226.

Harbor, Rawn. "Let the Peoples Praise You, O God (Psalm 67)." TFF 7.

Horman, John D. "Psalm 67." U and SATB, assembly, pno, opt fl, hb. CG CGA589.

(GA) Browning, Carol/arr. Tom Andion. "Deo Gloria Alleluia (Easter Gospel Acclamation)." SATB, cant, assembly, kybd, gtr, opt fl and 2 tr. GIA G-6402.

Hymn of the Day

I want to walk as a child of the light   ELW 815, WOV 649   *HOUSTON*

O blessed spring   ELW 447, WOV 695   *BERGLUND*

In Christ called to baptize   ELW 575   *ST. DENIO*

Offering

The peace of the Lord   ELW 646, LLC 471

Day of arising   ELW 374, sts. 1, 3, 4; OBS 54, sts. 1, 3, 4

Communion

There in God's garden   ELW 342, WOV 668

Tree of Life and awesome mystery   ELW 334

Wash, O God, our sons and daughters   ELW 445, TFF 112, WOV 697

Sending

We are marching in the light of God   ELW 866, TFF 63, W&P 148, WOV 650

Go, my children, with my blessing   ELW 543, TFF 161, WOV 721

Additional Assembly Songs

Alabaré   LLC 582, WOV 791

Cristo ha vencido a la muerte   LLC 360

I've got peace like a river   TFF 258, LS 159

Honduran melody. "Alleluia" from *Glory to God*. SATB. WJK 9780664238971.

Suderman, Bryan Moyer. "Our God Is a God Who Makes Friends" from *Sing with the World: Global Songs for Children*. U. GIA G-7339.

Bruxvoort Colligan, Richard. "Creation's Hallelujah (Psalm 148)" from *Shout for Joy*. AFP 9780806698632. psalmimmersion.bandcamp.com.

Cartford, Gerhard. "O Sing to the Lord." ELW 822

Dakota Road. "Your River, O God" from *Dakota Road Music Anthology*. dakotaroadmusic.com.

Dakota Road. "Hope of All Creation (Prayer Response)" from *Dakota Road Music Anthology*. dakotaroadmusic.com.

Rundman, Jonathan. "Forgiveness Waltz" from *Jonathan Rundman*. jonathanrundman.com.

Music for the Day
Choral

p ● Erickson, Richard. "I Want to Walk as a Child of the Light." SATB, org. AFP 9780800658397.

Hahn, Mark. "I Am Bound for the Kingdom." SATB div. LOR 104221-R.

Pinkham, Daniel. "God Be Merciful unto Us." U, org. ECS 5394.

p Proulx, Richard. "Christ Sends the Spirit" from *The Augsburg Choirbook: Sacred Choral Music of the Twentieth Century*. SAB, org, fl, opt assembly. AFP 9780800656782.

Children's Choir

Mozart, W. A./arr. Walter Ehret. "Lord, Grant Peace to All Your Servants." 3 pt canon, kybd. BP BP1545.

Powell, Robert J. "Peace between Neighbors." U, org. PAR PPMO 0209.

Proulx, Richard. "Happy Are Those." 2 pt, org, fl, ob. GIA G-5336.

Keyboard / Instrumental

● Carter, John. "St. Denio" from *From the British Isles: Nine Traditional Melodies for Solo Piano*. Pno. MSM 15-851.

● Cherwien, David M. "Berglund" from *Organ Plus One*. Org, inst. AFP 9780800656188.

● Organ, Anne Krentz. "Houston" from *Woven Together*, vol. 1. Pno, inst. AFP 9780800658168.

● Thomas, David Evan. "St. Denio" from *Augsburg Organ Library: Autumn*. Org. AFP 9780800675790.

Handbell

p Glasgow, Michael J. "Giusto con vivo." 3-7 oct hb, opt 3 oct hc, L3. CG CGB839.

p ● Moklebust, Cathy. "I Want to Walk as a Child of the Light." 2-3 oct, opt Bflat or C inst, L2, CG CGB831. 3-5 oct, opt Bflat or C inst, L2, CG CGB832.

● Smith, Douglas Floyd. "Fantasy on 'Immortal, Invisible' (St. Denio)." 3 or 5 oct, L2. HOP 2346.

Monday, May 2

Philip and James, Apostles (transferred)

Philip was one of the first disciples of Jesus, who after following Jesus invited Nathanael to "come and see." According to tradition, Philip preached in Asia Minor and died as a martyr in Phrygia. James, the son of Alphaeus, is called "the Less" (meaning "short" or "younger") to distinguish him from another apostle named James who is commemorated July 25. Philip and James are commemorated together because the remains of these two saints were placed in the Church of the Apostles in Rome on this day in 561.

Monday, May 2

Athanasius, Bishop of Alexandria, died 373

Athanasius (ath-an-AY-shus) attended the Council of Nicaea in 325 as a deacon and secretary to the bishop of Alexandria. At the council, and when he himself served as bishop of Alexandria, he defended the full divinity of Christ against the Arian position held by emperors, magistrates, and theologians. Because of his defense of the divinity of Christ, he was considered a troublemaker and was banished from Alexandria on five occasions. As bishop, one of his paschal letters to surrounding bishops gives a list for books that should be considered canonical scripture. He lists the twenty-seven New Testament books that are recognized today.

Wednesday, May 4

Monica, mother of Augustine, died 387

Monica was married to a pagan husband who was ill-tempered and unfaithful. She rejoiced greatly when both her husband and his mother became Christian. But it is because she is the mother of Augustine that she is best known. Monica had been a disciple of Ambrose, and eventually Augustine came under his influence. Almost everything we know about Monica comes from Augustine's *Confessions*, his autobiography. She died far from her home but said to her son, "Do not fret because I am buried far from our home in Africa. Nothing is far from God, and I have no fear that God will not know where to find me, when Christ comes to raise me to life at the end of the world." Her dying wish was that her son remember her at the altar of the Lord, wherever he was.

May 5, 2016
Ascension of Our Lord

In today's gospel the risen Christ ascends into heaven and his followers are assured that the Spirit will empower them to be witnesses throughout the earth. The disciples were told to not gaze up into heaven to look for Jesus; we find his presence among us as we proclaim the word and share the Easter feast. We too long for the Spirit to enliven our faith and invigorate our mission.

Prayer of the Day

Almighty God, your only Son was taken into the heavens and in your presence intercedes for us. Receive us and our prayers for all the world, and in the end bring everything into your glory, through Jesus Christ, our Sovereign and Lord, who lives and reigns with you and the Holy Spirit, one God, now and forever.

or

Almighty God, your blessed Son, our Savior Jesus Christ, ascended far above all heavens that he might fill all things. Mercifully give us faith to trust that, as he promised, he abides with us on earth to the end of time, who lives and reigns with you and the Holy Spirit, one God, now and forever.

Gospel Acclamation

Alleluia. Go and make disciples of all nations, ¹ says the Lord;* I am with you always, to the end ¹ of the age. *Alleluia.* (Matt. 28:19, 20)

Readings and Psalm

Acts 1:1-11

Before he is lifted into heaven, Jesus promises that the missionary work of the disciples will spread out from Jerusalem to all the world. His words provide an outline of the book of Acts.

Psalm 47

God has gone up with a shout. (Ps. 47:5)

or Psalm 93

Ever since the world began, your throne has been established. (Ps. 93:2)

Ephesians 1:15-23

The risen and exalted Christ reigns over the entire universe. The author of Ephesians prays that we would be given the wisdom to comprehend this and display it through love toward others.

Luke 24:44-53

On the day of his ascension, Jesus leaves his disciples with a commission, a blessing, and a promise of the Holy Spirit.

Preface   Ascension

Color   White

Prayers of Intercession

The prayers are prepared locally for each occasion. The following examples may be adapted or used as appropriate.

Rooted in the abundant life and love of Christ Jesus, we pray for the life of the church, the lives of people in need, and the life of all creation.

A brief silence.

Holy and ever-present God, your messengers promised the apostles that Jesus would come again. Reveal his presence to us each day while we await his coming in fullness. Hear us, O God.

Your mercy is great.

As you did for Noah and his family and for the Israelites crossing into freedom, make a way through raging waters for those in the path of floods or storms. Hear us, O God.

Your mercy is great.

Sustain the leaders of every nation with your righteousness and abundant mercy. Humble those who seek to use power for gain, and foster work among leaders for the well-being of all. Hear us, O God.

Your mercy is great.

Come swiftly with compassion and healing to all who suffer in any way (*especially*). Comfort those for whom death draws near, and bring peace to all who struggle. Hear us, O God.

Your mercy is great.

Breathe your Holy Spirit throughout all expressions of Christ's church, in order to move us toward greater visible unity. Teach us to welcome, pray for, and learn from one another. Hear us, O God.

Your mercy is great.

Here other intercessions may be offered.

Gather all the witnesses of your saving work from every time and every place. Join our voices in proclamation and praise of the good things you have done for all people. Hear us, O God.

Your mercy is great.

We deliver all this into your care, O God, trusting in the work of your Holy Spirit to bring all things into the risen life of Christ our Lord.

Amen.

Images in the Readings

Ascension Day plays with the ancient cosmological picture of the three-tier universe, the highest level of which is heaven, or "the heavens." Over the centuries, Christians have speculated in quite different ways about what this heaven is. By the nineteenth century, heaven came to be described as a kind of family summer camp, perfection in populist human terms. However, in the Bible, "heaven" is often a synonym for God, a way to speak about divine majesty and mercy. In Acts, the ascending Jesus is covered with a cloud, which in the Hebrew Scriptures usually refers to the elusive presence yet cosmic power of God. It is important that today's references to heaven not suggest that it is a place that is far away. The risen Christ is here in the assembly of believers.

Luke has two men in **white robes** speaking with the disciples. The Christian church has regularized the wearing of white robes as the sign of baptism. We all can speak of the power of the ascended Christ.

In Ephesians, the **body of Christ** is the church imagined like Atlas, a giant standing on earth holding up the skies, the head being Christ and the body being the church that fills the world. Today we blend this understanding of "body of Christ" with the bread we eat and the assembly gathered to worship.

Ideas for the Day

◆   The word *witnesses* appears in two of our three readings for today. This word functions in two ways. First, a witness is one who gives testimony, like a witness on the stand in court. Second, a witness is one who has seen something firsthand, as in "I witnessed a police chase on my way to work." There are two parts to witnessing: speaking and seeing. Today we hear a great deal about going out and sharing the good news (the speaking part). But we'll never be effective witnesses of the gospel if we haven't taken the time to see the risen Christ in our midst. In this text, Jesus is affirming the disciples as ones who are presently seeing the realities of the Messiah. What if discipleship emphasized what we have seen more than what we say? When have you seen the risen Christ at work forgiving sins, suffering, dying, and rising? When have you witnessed Christ in your midst?

◆   What's the deal with Jesus ascending up into the sky? We've been to outer space. Astronauts have not yet run into the ascended Christ. What if we understood this directional cue less in spatial terms and more in theological terms? It's possible that *up* is less about the direction that Christ ascends and more a statement that Christ is the highest, that he's above the whole cosmos. It's possible that it is more a theological statement about Christ's cosmic position than his postresurrection location.

◆   In community organizing, power is defined as the ability to act (Edward Chambers, *Roots for Radicals: Organizing for Power, Action, and Justice* [London: Bloomsbury, 2004], 27). Community organizers also distinguish "power-over" from "power-with" (*Roots*, 28). In Acts, the apostles ask Jesus if he is going to restore the kingdom to them. They are looking for power-over the Romans. Jesus responds by promising them the power of the Holy Spirit, which is power-with. In the ascension, Jesus ascends over all the earth, but he uses his position over us to give us power. Jesus' power is different from the power of empire.

Connections with the Liturgy

"He ascended into heaven and is seated at the right hand of the Father," says the Nicene Creed. "He ascended into heaven, he is seated at the right hand of the Father," says the Apostles' Creed.

Let the Children Come

The geography of Ascension Day is puzzling to adults and any children who understand that "up there" is not just heaven but planets, stars, and space stations. Jesus' ascension is not so much about Jesus "going up" as it is about his message "going out"—"to all nations, beginning from Jerusalem." Jesus is not just here; he is able to be with us *everywhere*. Whether or not your congregation worships today, invite children to send a message of love—or a gift of concrete assistance—to the "ends of the earth" as a reminder that the risen Jesus is present *anywhere* his love is proclaimed in word or deed.

Assembly Song
Gathering

Rejoice, for Christ is king! ELW 430
Crown him with many crowns ELW 855, LBW 170
Lord, I lift your name on high ELW 857, W&P 90

Psalmody and Acclamations

Gelineau, Joseph. "Psalm 47" from ACYG.
Haugen, Marty. "God Mounts His Throne" from LP:S.
Inwood, Paul. "A Blare of Trumpets" from PS2.
(GA) Browning, Carol/arr. Tom Andion. "Deo Gloria Alleluia (Easter Gospel Acclamation)." SATB, cant, assembly, kybd, gtr, opt fl and 2 tr. GIA G-6402.

Hymn of the Day

A hymn of glory let us sing! ELW 393, LBW 157 *LASST UNS ERFREUEN*
Lord, enthroned in heavenly splendor ELW 475, LBW 172 *BRYN CALFARIA*
Jesus shall reign ELW 434, LBW 530 *DUKE STREET*

Offering

Create in me a clean heart ELW 185
Let us talents and tongues employ ELW 674, TFF 232, WOV 754

Communion

Alleluia! Sing to Jesus ELW 392, LBW 158
Send me, Lord ELW 809, TFF 244, WOV 773
My Lord of light ELW 832, WOV 796

Sending

Lord, you gave the great commission ELW 579, WOV 756
Go, make disciples ELW 540, W&P 47

Additional Assembly Songs

Go ye therefore W&P 49
You are the seed TFF 226, LS 139, WOV 753
Lift up your heads W&P 88

🌐 Anon./arr. Howard S. Olson. "He's Ascended into Heaven" from *Set Free: A Collection of African Hymns*. SATB. AFP 9780806600451.

🌐 Yoruba folk melody. "Open Your Mouth and Praise the Lord!" from *Glory to God*. SATB. WJK 9780664238971.

✡ Dakota Road. "Go Now" from *Dakota Road Music Anthology*. dakotaroadmusic.com.

✡ Gungor, Michael. "Brighter Day" from *Beautiful Things*. gungormusic.com.

✡ Rimbo, Justin. "When It Seems the Day Will End" from *Storm Home: A Collection of Music from Humble Walk Artists-in-Residence*. humblewalk.bandcamp.com.

✡ Rundman, Jonathan. "The Serious Kind" from *Public Library*. jonathanrundman.com.

✡ The Welcome Wagon. "Lo He Comes with Clouds Descending" from *Precious Remedies Against Satan's Devices*. asthmatickitty.com.

Music for the Day
Choral

p ● Biery, James. "Lord, Enthroned in Heavenly Splendor" from *Choral Stanzas for Hymns*, vol. 1. SATB, org. AFP 9780806698410.
Helvey, Howard. "Jesus, My All, to Heaven Is Gone." 2 pt mxd, pno, ob. BP 1562.
p Riegel, Friedrich Samuel. "See God to Heaven Ascending" from *Chantry Choirbook*. SATB. AFP 9780800657772.
p Roberts, Leon. "He Has the Power!" SATB, pno, gtr, opt bass. GIA G-2476.

Children's Choir

p Kerrick, Mary Ellen. "We Hear Singing." U/2 pt, pno. CG CGA1351.
Stearns, Peter Pindar. "The Day Thou Gavest." 2 pt trbl, org. PAR PPMO 0313.
Todd, Will. "The Call of Wisdom." U, org. OXF 9780193389724.

Keyboard / Instrumental

● Cherwien, David M. "'Variations on 'Jesus Shall Reign.'" Org. MSM 10-570.

🌐 = global song   ✡ = praise song
● = relates to hymn of the day   p = available in Prelude Music Planner

- Cool, Jayne Southwick. "Bryn Calfaria" from *Piano Plus Through the Year*, vol. 2. Pno, inst. AFP 9780800663728.
- Ferguson, John. "Lasst uns erfreuen" from *Festival Hymns*, set III. Org, br qrt. GIA G-4124.
- p ● Raabe, Nancy M. "Lasst uns erfreuen" from *Foot-Friendly Preludes*. Org. AFP 9781451479539.

Handbell

- Krug, Jason W. "Christ the King" from *Ringing the Church Year*. 3-5 oct hb, opt 3-5 oct hc, L2+. LOR 20/1671L.
- Lamb, Linda. "Bell Peal on 'Lasst uns erfreuen.'" 3-5 oct, L1. SHW HP5453.
- Noller, Donald. "Variations on 'Bryn Calfaria.'" 3-5 oct, L2+. GIA G-8744.

May 8, 2016
Seventh Sunday of Easter

It is possible to hear in Jesus' high priestly prayer, a prayer he offered shortly before his death, the petitions of the ascended Lord for his own throughout history—to our day—and beyond. Jesus prays for us. In holy baptism we become believers in God, have our robes washed in the flood of Christ's forgiveness, and receive the gift of life forever with all the saints.

Prayer of the Day

O God, form the minds of your faithful people into your one will. Make us love what you command and desire what you promise, that, amid all the changes of this world, our hearts may be fixed where true joy is found, your Son, Jesus Christ our Lord, who lives and reigns with you and the Holy Spirit, one God, now and forever.

Gospel Acclamation

Alleluia. I will not leave you orphaned, [|] says the Lord.*
I am com- [|] ing to you. *Alleluia.* (John 14:18)

Readings and Psalm

Acts 16:16-34

The owners of a slave-girl who used her powers to tell fortunes threw Paul and Silas into jail for "healing" her and, consequently, ruining their business. In prison, Paul and Silas bring the good news of the gospel to the jailer and his family.

Psalm 97

Rejoice in the LORD, you righteous. (Ps. 97:12)

Revelation 22:12-14, 16-17, 20-21

The ascended Christ, hidden from our sight, promises to come again. We eagerly pray, "Come, Lord Jesus," with all who respond to this invitation.

John 17:20-26

Jesus prays that the life of his followers will be characterized by an intimate unity of identity with God. To be so identified with God means also to share in God's mission: to proclaim the word that will bring others into this same unity.

Preface   Ascension

Color   White

Prayers of Intercession

The prayers are prepared locally for each occasion. The following examples may be adapted or used as appropriate.

Rooted in the abundant life and love of Christ Jesus, we pray for the life of the church, the lives of people in need, and the life of all creation.

A brief silence.

God of renewal, fill us to overflowing with the grace we receive in word, in water, in the meal. Draw others to join the life we share in your church. Hear us, O God.

Your mercy is great.

Declare your righteousness through the blossoming of creation. By the wind's blowing and birds' singing, inspire us to join in the hymn of all creation. Hear us, O God.

Your mercy is great.

Be the source of all strength and peace for people who are imprisoned. Renew them with the overwhelming power of your salvation, and give them release for their spirits. Hear us, O God.

Your mercy is great.

Reveal yourself to those who feel isolated because of illness, grief, status, or the prejudice of others. (*Especially we pray* for . . .). Comfort and welcome them into your Spirit-filled community. Hear us, O God.

Your mercy is great.

Bless those who serve in a mothering role for others. Send your Spirit to those who mourn, who have not known their mothers, or who long to be a mother. Hear us, O God.

Your mercy is great.

Here other intercessions may be offered.

You draw (*Julian of Norwich, whom we commemorate today, and*) all the saints into your presence. Draw us into the mystery and wonder of your presence until Christ comes again. Hear us, O God.

Your mercy is great.

We deliver all this into your care, O God, trusting in the work of your Holy Spirit to bring all things into the risen life of Christ our Lord.

Amen.

Images in the Readings

In polytheism, even the divine is multiple. But in monotheism, God and divine truth are understood as one. Thus Christian theology develops the theme of **unity**: the Trinity is one, and believers are one in a unity created by and shared with the one God. Christians have struggled with this image, since even in the first century the church was not visibly a single unified organization. In spite of our words in the Nicene Creed, "We believe in one holy catholic and apostolic church," separate denominations flourish, and sociologists suggest that this very diversity has led to more active membership. We can at least pray that God, looking at the church, sees us as one in Christ, and we can look at one another across denominational lines with gratitude for the various ways the Spirit leads us to live within that oneness.

We join Paul and Silas, for we are all, at some time, in some way, in **prison**.

This is the last Sunday, until the next year C, to focus on the **Johannine images** of Alpha and Omega, washed robes, the tree of life, the city gates, the bright morning star, the Spirit and the bride.

"**Come, Lord Jesus**," we say this Sunday. "Come, Lord Jesus," says Thanksgiving at the Table III, VI, VII (*ELW*, pp. 110, 66, 67). "Come, Lord Jesus," pray many Christians when they sit down at home for dinner. We pray for more of what we already have, for the body of Christ is here with us.

Ideas for the Day

◆ Today's reading from Acts is about conversion. Father Richard Rohr, in his work *The Naked Now*, defines conversion as "*one who has moved from mere belief systems or belonging systems to actual inner experience*" (St. Louis: Crossroad, 2009, 29–30). Perhaps the jailer's conversion can

be thought of in this way, as one who saw the belief of Paul and Silas and, in their call for him to live and not die, experienced that belief within himself for the first time. How can we talk today about conversion as less a change of mind and more a life-giving experience we're invited to live into and live out every day? Could someone share their own conversion story today?

◆ In today's gospel, Jesus says that he gives humanity his glory so that we may be one as God is one. The "one" here, as the Greek indicates, is one of purpose or mission. Consider playing U2's song "One" (from the album *Achtung Baby*, 1991) during worship today. Use the lyrics as a launching point for wondering with the community in the sermon how our unity in Jesus mirrors the very intimate unity Jesus has in God. Specifically the words "We're one but we're not the same" and "We get to carry each other, carry each other / One" might provide for great communal reflection.

◆ Today would be a great day to do an extended thanksgiving at the table. The Revelation text provides some wonderful images the presiding minister might use to craft one for the day. For example, Alpha and Omega, tree of life, bright morning star, water of life. Several thanksgivings at the table in *Evangelical Lutheran Worship* already use "Come, Lord Jesus" (Rev. 22:20) as an assembly acclamation (form III, p. 110; form VI, p. 66; and form VII, p. 67).

◆ Henri Nouwen's short work *With Open Hands* (Notre Dame, IN: Ave Maria Press, 1972) is a great resource to encourage the understanding and practice of prayer in the congregation, and could help the preacher with sermon preparation, mirroring the prayer emphasis of the Acts and John readings. Perhaps the whole congregation could take it on as a reading discipline over the next month and hear it referenced in preaching.

Connections with the Liturgy

It is usual for thanksgivings at the table, in the petition for the coming of the Holy Spirit, to include a prayer for the unity of the church. For example, the historic prayer ascribed to Hippolytus in the third century includes the words "Gather into one all who share this bread and wine" (*ELW*, form XI, p. 70).

Let the Children Come

One of the oldest prayers in the Christian community is found in today's second reading from Revelation: "Come, Lord Jesus!" In Aramaic, the language that Jesus spoke, one word—*Maranatha*—said two things. It was a prayer for help in time of need: Come, Lord, save us. It was also used as a joyous and confident welcome to the risen Christ: Come, Lord Jesus, be our guest. Teach the children the word

Maranatha and its meanings, and ask them to listen for the words "Come, Lord Jesus" in today's worship.

Assembly Song
Gathering
Faith of our fathers   ELW 813
Evening and morning   ELW 761, LBW 465
Christ is risen! Shout hosanna!   ELW 383, WOV 672

Psalmody and Acclamations
Anderson, Mark. "Psalm 93" from PSCY.
Duncan, Norah IV. "Seventh Sunday of Easter / C" from LP:LG.
Roberts, William Bradley. "Psalm 97," Refrain 1, from PSCY.
(GA) Browning, Carol/arr. Tom Andion. "Deo Gloria Alleluia (Easter Gospel Acclamation)." SATB, cant, assembly, kybd, gtr, opt fl and 2 tr. GIA G-6402.

Hymn of the Day
Thine the amen   ELW 826, WOV 801   *THINE*
Alleluia! Sing to Jesus   ELW 392, LBW 158   *HYFRYDOL*
Come now, O Prince of peace   ELW 247   *OSOSŎ*

Offering
Now we join in celebration   ELW 462, LBW 203
Behold, how pleasant   ELW 649, LLC 468

Communion
One bread, one body   ELW 496, TFF 122, W&P 111, WOV 710
Father, we thank you   ELW 478, WOV 704
O Christ the same   ELW 760, WOV 778

Sending
I come with joy   ELW 482
Blest be the tie that binds   ELW 656, LBW 370

Additional Assembly Songs
Bind us together   LS 127, TFF 217, W&P 18, WOV 748
Unidos en tu nombre   LLC 480
I will sing, I will sing   W&P 73, LS 180
Moon, Sung Mo. "Praise to the Lord" from *Glory to God*. SATB. WJK 9780664238971.
Puerto Rican traditional. "Le lo le lo lay lo" from *Pave the Way: Global Songs 3*. U. AFP 9780800676896.
Bell, John L. "One Is the Body" from *One Is the Body: Songs of Unity and Diversity*. GIA G-5790.
Dakota Road. "Go Now" from *Dakota Road Music Anthology*. dakotaroadmusic.com.
Hansen, Handt. "Lord, Listen to Your Children Praying" from CCLI.
The Welcome Wagon. "Jesus" from *Welcome to the Welcome Wagon*. asthmatickitty.com.
Ylvisaker, John. "God's Community" from *Borning Cry Second Edition*. ylvisaker.com.
Ylvisaker, John. "Borning Cry." ELW 732.

Music for the Day
Choral
p   Cherwien, David. "O Blessed Spring." SATB or 2 pt mxd, org, opt C inst, assembly. AFP 9781451420753.
p   Larson, Lloyd. "Come, Share the Lord." SATB, pno. HOP C5842.
Manz, Paul. "E'en So, Lord Jesus, Quickly Come." SATB. MSM 50-0001.
p ● Schalk, Carl. "Thine the Amen, Thine the Praise." SATB, org, opt assembly. AFP 9780800646127.

Children's Choir
Beck, John Ness. "In Heavenly Love." U, kybd, opt gtr, opt C inst. BP BP1404.
p   Leaf, Robert. "Come with Rejoicing." U, org, pno. AFP 9781451484045.
p   Wold, Wayne. "Sisters and Brothers, Family of God" from *ChildrenSing in Worship*, vol. 1. U/2 pt, kybd. AFP 9781451461282.

Keyboard / Instrumental
p ● Dahl, David P. "Hyfrydol" from *The Organ Sings*. Org. AFP 9781451462609.
p ● Hamilton, Gregory. "Hyfrydol" from *Piano Stylings on Hymn Tunes*. Pno. AFP 9781451486094.
p ● Raabe, Nancy M. "Thine" from *How Good It Is*. Pno. AFP 9781451401165.
● Roberts, Al. "Thine" from *Organ Plus Anthology*, vol. 1. Org, inst. AFP 9781451424256.

Handbell
Compton, Matthew. "Lauda Spiritoso." 4-7 oct, L4+. BP HB410.
p   Eithun, Sandra. "When Morning Gilds the Skies." 2-3 oct (5-7 ringers), L2. CG CGB789.
● Tucker, Sondra. "Meditation on 'Hyfrydol.'" 3 oct, L2. CG CGB182.

Sunday, May 8

Julian of Norwich, renewer of the church, died around 1416

Julian (or Juliana) was most likely a Benedictine nun living in an isolated cell attached to the Carrow Priory in Norwich (NOR-rich), England. Definite facts about her life are sparse. However, when she was about thirty years old, she reported visions that she later compiled into a book, *Sixteen Revelations of Divine Love*, a classic of medieval mysticism. The visions declared that love was the meaning of religious

⦿ = global song   ✧ = praise song
● = relates to hymn of the day   p = available in Prelude Music Planner

experience, provided by Christ who is love, for the purpose of love. A prayer and a hymn attributed to Julian are included in *Evangelical Lutheran Worship* (p. 87, #735).

Monday, May 9

Nicolaus Ludwig von Zinzendorf, renewer of the church, hymnwriter, died 1760

Count Zinzendorf was born into an aristocratic family and after the death of his father was raised by his Pietistic grandmother. This influence was a lasting one, and he moved away from what he felt was an overly intellectual Lutheranism. When he was twenty-two, a group of Moravians asked permission to live on his lands. He agreed, and they established a settlement they called *Herrnhut*, or "the Lord's watch." Eventually worldwide Moravian missions emanated from this community. Zinzendorf participated in these missions and is also remembered for writing hymns characteristic of his Pietistic faith, including "Jesus, Still Lead On" (ELW 624).

May 14, 2016
Vigil of Pentecost

At this liturgy we gather in vigilant prayer as the disciples did in the days preceding Pentecost. Our world waits for an end to war and violence. The whole creation waits for an end to suffering. With undying hope we pray for the crowning gift of Easter—the Spirit of the risen Christ among us.

Prayer of the Day

Almighty and ever-living God, you fulfilled the promise of Easter by sending the gift of your Holy Spirit. Look upon your people gathered in prayer, open to receive the Spirit's flame. May it come to rest in our hearts and heal the divisions of word and tongue, that with one voice and one song we may praise your name in joy and thanksgiving; through Jesus Christ, our Savior and Lord, who lives and reigns with you and the Holy Spirit, one God, now and forever.

Gospel Acclamation

Alleluia. Come, Holy Spirit, fill the hearts | of your faithful,* and kindle in us the fire | of your love. *Alleluia.*

Readings and Psalm
Exodus 19:1-9

At Sinai God assured Israel that they were God's prized possession and commissioned them to serve as mediating priests for the nations. God's word spoken to Moses is the basis of the people's trust.

or Acts 2:1-11

Believers are filled with the Spirit to tell God's deeds.

Psalm 33:12-22

The LORD is our helper and our shield. (Ps. 33:20)

or Psalm 130

There is forgiveness with you. (Ps. 130:4)

Romans 8:14-17, 22-27

The Holy Spirit has made us God's children who eagerly await the glorious future God has prepared for all of creation. Although we cannot fully see what God has in store for us and creation, we eagerly anticipate it in hope. Even when we are unable to pray, the same Spirit prays for us.

John 7:37-39

Jesus describes the Holy Spirit as living water, quenching the thirst of all who come to him and filling the hearts of believers till they overflow.

Preface   Vigil and Day of Pentecost

Color   Red

Saturday, May 14

Matthias, Apostle

After Christ's ascension, the apostles met in Jerusalem to choose a replacement for Judas. Matthias was chosen over Joseph Justus by the casting of lots. Little is known about Matthias, and little is reported about him in the account of his election in Acts 1:15-26. Matthias traveled among the disciples from the beginning of Jesus' ministry until his ascension. His task, after he was enrolled among the eleven remaining disciples, was to bear witness to the resurrection.

May 15, 2016
Day of Pentecost

Pentecost is a day of promises fulfilled. The promised Spirit of God is poured out. The baptized have become "children of God" and "joint heirs with Christ." By the power of the Spirit we have seen the face of the Father in his only begotten Son and been saved by him. Bless the Lord, O my soul.

Prayer of the Day

God our creator, the resurrection of your Son offers life to all the peoples of earth. By your Holy Spirit, kindle in us the fire of your love, empowering our lives for service and our tongues for praise, through Jesus Christ, our Savior and Lord, who lives and reigns with you and the Holy Spirit, one God, now and forever.

Gospel Acclamation

Alleluia. Come, Holy Spirit, fill the hearts ¹ of your faithful,* and kindle in us the fire ¹ of your love. *Alleluia.*

Readings and Psalm

Acts 2:1-21

Before Jesus ascended into heaven, he told his disciples they would be filled with the Holy Spirit. Now, surrounded by signs of fire, wind, and a variety of languages in their midst, the people were amazed and astonished at Jesus' promise coming true.

or Genesis 11:1-9

The builders of the tower of Babel try to make a name for themselves by building their tower to the heavens. God scatters them, confusing their language so that they cannot understand one another. The miracle at Pentecost reverses this story, drawing many different peoples together into the new people of God.

Psalm 104:24-34, 35b

Send forth your Spirit and renew the face of the earth. (Ps. 104:30)

Romans 8:14-17

Here Paul speaks about the mystery of baptism: through the Holy Spirit we are claimed, gathered, and welcomed into Christ's body, the church. And we receive new names in our adoption: brother, sister, child of God.

or Acts 2:1-21

See above.

John 14:8-17 [25-27]

Though the disciples struggle with Jesus' nature and identity, they receive the promise that they too will be identified with God and God's mission. Though he must leave them now, Jesus promises the coming of the Advocate whom God will send to comfort and enlighten them.

Preface   Vigil and Day of Pentecost

Color   Red

Prayers of Intercession

The prayers are prepared locally for each occasion. The following examples may be adapted or used as appropriate.

Rooted in the abundant life and love of Christ Jesus, we pray for the life of the church, the lives of people in need, and the life of all creation.

A brief silence.

O God, move among your people and send forth your Spirit to make your church a holy place where people find welcome, Christ's compassion, and new life. Hear us, O God. **Your mercy is great.**

Send forth your Spirit to renew the earth in the wake of storms, earthquakes, or human misuse. Breathe life into every mountain and valley, stream and ocean (*especially*). Hear us, O God.

Your mercy is great.

Send forth your Spirit to unite all nations in caring for those who are vulnerable or in need. Help us to put aside our differences and to seek your will. Hear us, O God.

Your mercy is great.

Send forth your Spirit to aid people in distress (*especially*). Sweep them up in the movement of your Spirit, and fulfill your everlasting promises for all. Hear us, O God.

Your mercy is great.

Send forth your Spirit to knock down barriers that prevent people from receiving your good news. Guide interpreters and cultural ambassadors who open lines of communication. Hear us, O God.

Your mercy is great.

Here other intercessions may be offered.

Send forth your Spirit to unite us with the saints of every time and place. By the gifts of your Spirit, rouse us to deeds of mercy and words of kindness. Hear us, O God.

Your mercy is great.

We deliver all this into your care, O God, trusting in the work of your Holy Spirit to bring all things into the risen life of Christ our Lord.

Amen.

Images in the Readings

Anthropologists describe **fire** as one of the markers of the human species. For tens of thousands of years, humans gathered around fire for light, warmth, protection, community, and cooked food. Many passages in the Bible liken God to fire. The Holy Spirit of God appeared on Sinai in flames of fire, which on Pentecost appeared on the forehead of each believer. Moses experienced God in fire; through fire the Israelites presented offerings to God; God led the people through the wilderness with a pillar of fire. Seraphim are fire-spirits, extensions of the divine. Yet fire is also a sign of divine judgment: the angel in Eden hides the tree of life from humanity with a sword of fire, and John the Baptist predicts that fire will consume the chaff. Fire both occasions human life and has the power to destroy. Think fire, think God.

The Hebrew noun *ruach* can be translated into English as **spirit**, breath, or wind. Spirit is the most amorphous of these words. In Christian theology, the Spirit we experience is the Spirit of the risen Christ, a spirit of service, a spirit of love, a spirit of resurrection beyond death.

According to the New Testament, the resurrection of Christ has inaugurated the very end of this world. In Acts 2, Luke uses characteristic eschatological imagery to describe the **last days** and the Day of the Lord. Throughout much of Christian history, those believers who find the anticipation of the Day of the Lord most comforting are those suffering the most from their current situation and seeing no way out. The immensely popular *Left Behind* novels are based on a fundamentalist view of the rapture and the last days, but there is no way to know how fully this theology is accepted by the series' millions of readers.

Ideas for the Day

◆ The global dimension of today's worship can be highlighted in assembly song. *Evangelical Lutheran Worship* includes many songs from around the world, as do the resources *Global Songs, Global Songs 2,* and *Pave the Way* (all from Augsburg Fortress). Include notes about the sources of the texts and tunes in your worship folder, or make brief spoken introductions about their origins (*Hymnal Companion to Evangelical Lutheran Worship* can help here). If you have a song leader who can teach songs in languages other than English, give that a try too. Pentecost was surely uncomfortable for those first disciples. Perhaps we can stretch ourselves too.

◆ Worship's global dimension can be highlighted in the eucharist. Choose a bread from a different culture today, like a traditional breakfast bread from Mexico, a fry bread from Africa, or Indian naan. You could also choose a wine from somewhere else in the world, a Chilean red or a South African chenin blanc, for example.

◆ The Pentecost event is described as wind and fire. The two are often incompatible, but actually feed off of one another. Without air a fire dies. Without fire or heat, air turns cold and life becomes impossible. How can the relationship between the Holy Spirit and humanity be envisioned similarly? How is God's Spirit necessary for our work, and our work necessary for God's message? It seems paradoxical to think that the divine would work with the mortal, and yet this is God's way.

◆ Today is a day for streamers and processions, mimicking the movement of the Spirit over the disciples. Paper streamers in red, yellow, orange, and pink are inexpensive. Tear off a good length, and hand them to children and any adults who want them as they come into church. Then invite everyone with a streamer to process around the church during the gathering song, waving these streamers high as the Spirit falls on the congregation. If you have a balcony, you could even have some people tossing streamers onto the assembly.

Connections with the Liturgy

In *Evangelical Lutheran Worship*'s Thanksgiving at the Table X (p. 69), we praise God with these words: "O God, you are Breath: send your Spirit on this meal.... O God, you are Fire: transform us with hope." Each eucharistic prayer asks for the Spirit to come into the bread and wine, into the believing community, and into the wider world.

In the thanksgivings at the font (*ELW*, pp. 70–71), we ask God to send the Spirit into the water and into the candidates for baptism. Thanksgiving III includes the words "Breathe new life into those who are here baptized," as if the candidates now are only dry bones.

Let the Children Come

Along with Christmas and Easter, Pentecost is one of the three most important and celebratory days of the church year. Do not treat this Sunday as just another day! Pentecost demands we pull out all the stops and go crazy with red. There are many ideas for adding red to your celebrations in the "Preparing for Easter" essay on page 169. Do not underestimate the impact such preparations can make on children: this is a special—red letter—day!

Assembly Song
Gathering

Come, gracious Spirit, heavenly dove ELW 404, LBW 475
O Holy Spirit, enter in ELW 786, LBW 459
Come, Holy Ghost, God and Lord ELW 395, LBW 163

Psalmody and Acclamations

"Alleluia, Send Out Your Spirit" from *Psallite* A-93. Cant or SATB, assembly, kybd.
Haas, David. "Lord, Send Out Your Spirit" from PCY, vol. 1.
Joncas, Michael. "Lord, Send Out Your Spirit (Psalm 104)." SATB, cant, assembly, org or str qrt, hp. GIA G-7141.
(GA) Browning, Carol/arr. Tom Andion. "Deo Gloria Alleluia (Easter Gospel Acclamation)." SATB, cant, assembly, kybd, gtr, opt fl and 2 tr. GIA G-6402.

Hymn of the Day

O living Breath of God ELW 407, LLC 368 *VÅRVINDAR FRISKA*
Creator Spirit, heavenly dove ELW 577 *VENI CREATOR SPIRITUS*
ELW 578, LBW 284 *KOMM, GOTT SCHÖPFER*
O Holy Spirit, root of life ELW 399, WOV 688 *PUER NOBIS*

Offering

Like the murmur of the dove's song ELW 403, WOV 685
Come down, O Love divine ELW 804, LBW 508

Communion

Loving Spirit ELW 397, WOV 683
Spirit of gentleness ELW 396, LS 68, WOV 684
Draw us in the Spirit's tether ELW 470, WOV 703

Sending

God of tempest, God of whirlwind ELW 400
O day full of grace ELW 627, LBW 161, LS 71

Additional Assembly Songs

Enter, Holy Spirit! ASG 31
I'm goin'-a sing TFF 109
En un aposento alto LLC 369
Lim, Swee Hong. "As the Wind Song" from *Glory to God*. U. WJK 9780664238971.
Zimbabwe/arr. John L. Bell. "If You Believe and I Believe" from *Worship and Song*. SATB. Abingdon Press 9781426709951.
Dakota Road. "Your River, O God" from *Dakota Road Music Anthology*. dakotaroadmusic.com.
Grundy, Christopher. "Pour Out Your Spirit" from *Sing! Prayer and Praise*. ucc.org/music-arts.
Houge, Nate. "Be with Us Now" from *Storm Home: A Collection of Music from Humble Walk Artists-in-Residence*. humblewalk.bandcamp.com.
Kernsey. "You've Arrived" from *Storm Home: A Collection of Music from Humble Walk Artists-in-Residence*. humblewalk.bandcamp.com.
Rundman, Jonathan. "Narthex" from *Public Library*. jonathanrundman.com.
Ylvisaker, John. "Every Time I Feel the Spirit" from *Borning Cry*, 2nd ed. Available on Amazon.com.

Music for the Day
Choral

Farlee, Robert Buckley. "Spirit of God, Descend upon My Heart." 2 pt mxd, kybd. MSM 50-5555.
p ● Miller, Aaron David. "Creator Spirit, Who Gave Us Life." SATB, pno. AFP 9781451420678.
p ● Scott, K. Lee. "Gracious Spirit, Dwell with Me." 2 pt mxd, org. AFP 9780800646134.
p Vaughan Williams, Ralph/arr. Philip Dietterich. "Come Down, O Love Divine." SATB, org. HOP APM-241.

Children's Choir

Blersch, Jeffrey. "Holy Spirit, Light Divine" from *Children Rejoice and Sing*. U, desc, pno, C inst. CPH 977074WEB.
Staden, Johann. "Nun bitten wir den Heiligen Geist/To God the Holy Spirit." 2 pt/3 pt, opt vc/org. GIA G-6853.
p Taylor, Terry. "I'm Gonna Sing with Over My Head." 2 pt, pno. CG CGA1326.

Keyboard / Instrumental

● Miller, Aaron David. "Puer nobis" from *Introductions and Alternate Accompaniments for Piano*, vol. 3. Pno. AFP 9780800623593.
p ● Nelson, Ronald A. "Vårvindar friska" from *Easy Hymn Settings*, vol. 3. Org. AFP 9781451462562.
p ● Roberts, Al. "Vårvindar friska" from *We Belong to God*. Pno. AFP 9781451451801.
● Wold, Wayne L. "Veni Creator Spiritus" from *Light on Your Feet*, vol. 3. Org. AFP 9780806698021.

⊕ = global song   ✿ = praise song
● = relates to hymn of the day   p = available in Prelude Music Planner

Handbell

- Delancy, Lauran. "Come, Holy Ghost." 3 or 5 oct hb, opt 3 or 5 oct hc, L2. CPH 97-7416.

  Lamb, Linda. "Holy Spirit, Breath of God." 3-5 oct hb, opt 2 oct hc, L2. LOR 20/1470L.

- Moore, Boude. "Carillon on 'Puer nobis.'" 3 oct hb qrt, Cantabile Press. CP6156.

Wednesday, May 18

Erik, King of Sweden, martyr, died 1160

Erik, long considered the patron saint of Sweden, ruled from 1150 to 1160. He is honored for efforts to bring peace to the nearby pagan kingdoms and for his crusades to spread the Christian faith in Nordic lands. He established a protected Christian mission in Finland that was led by Henry of Uppsala. As king, Erik was noted for his desire to establish fair laws and courts and for his concern for the poor and sick. Erik was killed by a Danish army that approached him at worship on the day after the Ascension. He is reported to have said, "Let us at least finish the sacrifice. The rest of the feast I shall keep elsewhere." As he left worship he was killed.

Saturday, May 21

Helena, mother of Constantine, died around 330

Wife of the co-regent of the West, Helena (or Helen) was mother of Constantine, who later became Roman emperor. After he was converted to Christianity, he influenced her also to become Christian. From that point she lived an exemplary life of faith, particularly through acts of generosity toward the poor. She is also remembered for traveling through Palestine and building churches on the sites she believed to be where Jesus was born, where he was buried, and from which he ascended.

TIME AFTER PENTECOST
SUMMER

SUMMER

AUTUMN

NOVEMBER

PREPARING FOR SUMMER

After the festival of the Holy Trinity (May 22), congregations following the Revised Common Lectionary will spend the summer months working their way through scenes from the Gospel of Luke depicting Jesus' ministry in Galilee and movement toward Jerusalem. Careful readers will notice that the lectionary does not simply march the assembly through the third gospel sequentially. Rather, it pays special attention to stories unique to Luke's gospel, highlighting themes that are particularly Lukan: God's healing and reconciling power made available to all people, particularly the poor and the outcast.

A summer of healing

As the summer progresses, stories of healing, forgiveness, and new life take on progressive layers of depth and meaning. In the early weeks of summer, worshipers will listen as Jesus heals a centurion's slave, raises a widow's son, forgives a scandalous woman, and liberates a man possessed by demons. In each, personal experiences of healing and restoration are placed in a larger social and political context. These scenes, so intimate in their depiction of need and mercy, draw the assembly in and encourage them to bring their need for healing to Jesus.

As June gives way to July, worshipers will imagine themselves among the seventy whom Jesus sends out to announce peace, to share table fellowship, to cure the sick, and to proclaim the reign of God drawn near (Luke 10:8-9). The injunction to "love the Lord your God with all your heart, and with all your soul, and with all your strength, and with all your mind; and your neighbor as yourself" (Luke 10:27) is expanded upon with the parable of the good Samaritan (July 10) and the scene of Jesus' arrival in the home of Mary and Martha (July 17). Having been healed by Jesus, worshipers will hear the call to share the love we have received with neighbors both familiar and unfamiliar.

As summer draws to a close, Jesus draws closer to Jerusalem and we come to understand that his acts of healing have disrupted the status quo with consequences for all who choose to follow him. Having seen Jesus' willingness to confront the legalism and prejudice that keep people needlessly sick and suffering, disciples are confronted with difficult words and choices about what they will value more, their personal comfort or their public call.

Given this summer's persistent theme of healing, personal and societal, preachers and worship planners might choose to incorporate healing rites and topical hymnody into the assembly's worship. If the order for healing (*ELW*, p. 276) is unfamiliar to your congregation, consider including it at least once, or perhaps once a month, this summer. If this rite is already familiar to your worshiping community, consider including it weekly from May 29 through June 19 with locally prepared intercessions that connect Jesus' powerful acts of healing from each Sunday's readings with needs and concerns specific to your context. Or schedule a service of prayer around the cross on a Sunday or weekday evening. See the seasonal rites section for one possible order (pp. 208–210).

In addition to service music (ELW 218–221) and hymns (ELW 610–617) recommended for use within the order of healing, consider the following selections from *Singing Our Prayer: A Companion to Holden Prayer Around the Cross* (Augsburg Fortress, 2010): "Bring your best to our worst" (4), "Christ, our peace" (5), "For the healing of the nations" (12a), and "Heal us, Lord" (14). Congregations already familiar with music for worship from Taizé or Iona will be able to learn these simple pieces quickly and sing them continuously during the laying on of hands with prayer and anointing, or during communion.

A celebration of women

Time and again throughout the Gospel of Luke, the author expands upon material found in the other gospels or includes stories unique to this account that feature women as subjects of Jesus' ministry and equals among Jesus' followers. The summer kicks off with Jesus' healing of the centurion's servant (Luke 7:1-10; also in Matt. 8:5-13 and John 4:46-54) but continues the following week with a story unique to Luke concerning the healing of the widow's son at Nain (Luke 7:11-17). In Luke's hands, the story of the woman with the ointment is expanded beyond the other gospels and concludes with a specific naming of those women who joined Jesus' movement and funded it out of their own resources (Luke 7:36—8:3). Alone among the gospels is Luke's narration of Jesus in the home of Mary and Martha, where Mary takes her place at his feet in the posture of a disciple and is commended for having chosen the better part (Luke 10:38-42). As Jesus draws near to Jerusalem and his conflict with the temple authorities deepens, he heals a woman on the sabbath who has been bent over and frees her to stand straight (Luke 13:10-17).

While these stories fit within a larger Lukan motif of Jesus' preferential option for the poor and marginalized, the specificity of these stories should not be ignored. Jesus saw the ways that women's lives were jeopardized and diminished by patriarchy, and he responded to their plight, their pain, and their passion for his ministry by inviting them into community in ways that defied societal expectations. While Luke's examples may fall short of the stories of powerful and prophetic women's leadership we witness throughout the church today, we must acknowledge how radical they were in context and consider how they challenge us to reevaluate our own assumptions about who is and is not included in the church's community of leaders in our own time.

In many congregations, older members can still remember a time when only boys were allowed to be acolytes; only men were allowed to be not only pastors, but church council members and ushers. This summer's readings provide every congregation with an opportunity to revisit the spoken and unspoken traditions around congregational leadership and challenge us to pattern our ways of life together as signs of the reign of God, in which all people are invited to bring all of their gifts for the building up of the church and its ministries. Those who plan worship and schedule worship leaders should be especially attentive this summer to ensure that women's leadership at every level is visible to the congregation. Preachers who ensure that women's experiences, stories, and lives are central to their preaching will be showing great fidelity to these texts. (See 07_Summer.BiblicalWomen.pdf* for a selected bibliography of resources related to biblical women.)

Table fellowship

The first Sunday after the festival of the Holy Trinity narrates Jesus' healing of the centurion's servant. As Jesus nears the centurion's house, the man sends friends to say, "Lord, do not trouble yourself, for I am not worthy to have you come under my roof" (Luke 7:6). As the summer draws to a close, we will hear Jesus offer this advice about who we should invite into our homes: "When you give a banquet, invite the poor, the crippled, the lame, and the blind. And you will be blessed, because they cannot repay you, for you will be repaid at the resurrection of the righteous" (Luke 14:13-14).

Every Sunday as we gather for worship, there are people in the assembly who feel unworthy to receive Jesus into their lives. Every Sunday as we gather for worship, we invite all people to receive the means of grace at the font and at the table. In 2013 the ELCA, through an action at its Churchwide Assembly, committed itself to a conversation about the relationship between baptism and holy communion, and a review of its varied practices of eucharistic hospitality. Congregations of the ELCA have been asked to participate in this conversation in a number of ways, and materials for study and review are available online at www.elca.org/worship.

Be especially attentive this summer to the hymns selected for the offering and communion. While there is often a strong desire to select hymns that are familiar so that people can continue to sing as they move to and from the table, worship planners must also pay attention to the sung theology that shapes our understanding of the sacraments. This is the meal of unity (ELW 496, 498). It is also a foretaste of the feast to come, a glimpse of God's in-breaking reign of love and justice (ELW 462, 479). It is the sign of God's mercy and forgiveness (ELW 471, 483). Many hymns deftly weave these and still more images together. In this time of renewed discernment about our practices of table fellowship, the songs we sing as we take our places at the table will help us hear more clearly our Lord's call to extend the invitation to all people.

Environment

During these summer months, the image of the tree of life might serve to tie together several scriptural themes present in the lectionary texts. One of these themes is the creation itself. Many of the readings include images of trees, plants, fruits, water, and other elements of God's creation. Be especially attentive to opportunities to affirm connections between the created beauty that surrounds us and the God who entrusts us with its care. The tree of life image invites reflection on God's vision of wholeness for humankind in relationship with creation. For example, in your region, do these months produce an abundance of garden flowers? If so, consider suspending formal floral arrangements and inviting parishioners to share flowers from their gardens. Recruit a team to create casual floral arrangements that celebrate nature's diversity. Alternatively, could garden enthusiasts be invited to place early seasonal produce in baskets positioned around the worship space? Include in the prayers of intercession thanks for God's abundant provision. After worship, distribute the flowers or food among worshipers, homebound members, and/or residents in the neighborhood.

Another theme present in the lectionary texts is healing. The centurion and his slave, the widow and her son, the scandalous woman, the man possessed by demons—all are transformed by Jesus' compassionate intervention. Invite reflection on the manifold expressions of human frailty and the manifold ways in which God effects healing and restores wholeness. Reference Revelation 22:2, where the tree of life is described as being "for the healing of the nations."

The theme of table fellowship described earlier in this introduction prompts us to ask, Whom do we welcome? Whom do we exclude? In Ezekiel 31 the tree of life is described as "beautiful in its greatness, in the length of its branches; for its roots went down to abundant water" (v. 7). And of this tree we are told, "All the birds of the air made their nests in its boughs; under its branches all the animals of the field gave birth to their young; and in its shade all great nations lived" (v. 6). How does this image challenge us to adopt ever-wider circles of inclusion? Amplify this theme by using breads from a variety of cultures at communion over these months. Or create a seasonal processional cross inspired by the one described in the seasonal introduction to Autumn (p. 269; see 07_Summer.BreadCross.pdf)*.

Finally, as noted earlier, Luke's gospel includes stories of women whose lives intersected with Jesus in significant ways. How do these stories heighten appreciation for the broad span of the tree of life's canopy? Identify ways to celebrate these women's lives and the myriad ways that Jesus used their stories to broaden our understanding of who finds a place of welcome and belonging in him. See 07_Summer.BiblicalWomen.pdf* for a list of resources to empower your creativity.

So how might your congregation express visually the tree of life in a way that is as unique as the faith community where it will reside? Wood? Fabric? Paper? Metal? Glass? Let the gifts that God has placed in your midst inform the medium of expression. Some examples to jump-start your creative vision are available at 07_Summer.TreeOfLife.pdf*. Consider designing your visual to undergo changes as the Time after Pentecost progresses—from leaves in lighter greens to darker greens to autumn shades. Consider how to make your congregation's tree of life unique: leaves made from handprints or imprinted with handwritten scripture texts or words of thanks for gifts that empower service in your ministry context.

Seasonal Checklist

- If the summer worship schedule changes, notify local newspapers, update your website (especially so summer visitors can consider worshiping with you), and change listings on exterior signs and church voice mail.
- If your space is not air-conditioned, consider ways to help worshipers stay cool during warm weather.
- If outdoor services are held, make sure details for the service are covered thoroughly. Do an actual walk-through or rehearsal of the whole service to confirm what needs to be brought to the outdoor site.
- Omit the Kyrie (except on Holy Trinity).
- Use the Nicene Creed for Holy Trinity; use the Apostle's Creed for remaining summer Sundays.
- If the congregation is sending youth and/or adults on mission trips or to youth gatherings, use Blessing and Sending for Mission (*Evangelical Lutheran Worship Occasional Services for the Assembly*, pp. 159–160) on the Sunday prior to departure.
- Use Farewell and Godspeed (*Evangelical Lutheran Worship Occasional Services for the Assembly*, pp. 108–110) when people leave the congregation to move to a new community or to bid farewell to graduates leaving for college, other study, or other opportunities.

WORSHIP TEXTS FOR SUMMER

Confession and Forgiveness

All may make the sign of the cross, the sign marked at baptism,
as the presiding minister begins.
Blessed be the holy Trinity, + one God,
abounding in steadfast love toward us,
healing the sick and raising the dead,
showering us with every good gift.
Amen.

Let us confess our sin
in the presence of God and of one another.

Silence is kept for reflection.

Just and gracious God,
we come to you for healing and life.
Our sins hurt others and diminish us;
we confess them to you.
Our lives bear the scars of sin;
we bring these also to you.
Show us your mercy, O God.
Bind up our wounds,
forgive us our sins,
and free us to love,
for the sake of Jesus Christ, our Savior.
Amen.

The apostle Paul assures us:
"When we were dead in our trespasses,
God made us alive together with Christ,
nailing the record of our sins to the cross."
Jesus says to you, + "Your sins are forgiven."
Be at peace, and tell everyone
how much God has done for you.
Amen.

Offering Prayer

God of mercy and grace,
the eyes of all wait upon you,
and you open your hand in blessing.
Fill us with good things at your table,
that we may come to the help of all in need,
through Jesus Christ, our redeemer and Lord.
Amen.

Invitation to Communion

Christ invites you to a place of honor at this banquet.
Welcome to the feast.

Prayer after Communion

O God, as a mother comforts her child,
so you comfort your people,
carrying us in your arms
and satisfying us with this food and drink,
the body and blood of Christ.
Send us now as your disciples,
announcing peace and proclaiming
that the reign of God has come near;
through Jesus Christ, our Savior and Lord.
Amen.

Sending of Communion

O God of tender compassion,
as you healed the sick and welcomed the stranger,
bless those who leave this assembly
to share the gifts of this table
with our sisters and brothers
who are *sick/homebound/imprisoned.*
May they be sustained by the love and prayers
of this community,
and by the Bread of life that satisfies all hunger,
Jesus Christ our Lord.
Amen.

Blessing

The Lord bless you and keep you.
The Lord's face shine upon you with grace and mercy.
The Lord look upon you with favor
and + give you peace.
Amen.

Dismissal

Go in peace. Proclaim the good news.
Thanks be to God.

Seasonal Rites for Summer

Prayer Around the Cross: Beside Still Waters

A liturgy of healing prayer with the laying on of hands and anointing, based on Psalm 23. This and other Prayer Around the Cross liturgies should not be reproduced and placed in the hands of the assembly. Their intent is best realized when the services are conducted in semidarkness.

Preparation

*Written for two leaders (**L1** and **L2**) and a light bearer.*

A place for kneeling around a cross is prepared in the midst of the assembly. Small shells or bowls of oil are provided for anointing.

Write this or another simple prayer on 5" x 7" cards and place one near each bowl of oil:
Jesus Christ,
our savior and shepherd,
fill you with love,
mend you with mercy,
and grant you peace.

If this kind of liturgy is new to those gathered, a music leader may explain the nature of the singing (singing in the dark with no paper resource, chants sung repeatedly, etc.). The musician(s) teach any music that cannot easily be learned during the liturgy itself.

Gathering

People enter in silence and in near darkness. When all are gathered and silence has deepened and taken root, a simple repetitive chant is sung by the assembly. During this chant, a large lighted candle may be carried in and placed in a stand.

Suggestions for an opening chant:
To you all hearts are open   SP 43
O God, we call   SP 30
Nada te turbe / Nothing can trouble   SP 29

L1: We gather in the name of the triune God,
our healer, our hope, our only home.

L2: We come to hear the promises of God,
to pray for healing and for one another,
to give and to receive the anointing of oil

and the laying on of hands,
and to be sent into the world
as wounded healers and bearers of Christ's love.

L1: The room will be quite dark, inviting silence and stillness
as we immerse ourselves in scripture, song, and prayer.
The music during our prayer is simple and quickly learned.
Our singing is a way of breathing prayer to God.

L2: After the final blessing, you may remain here in prayer.
When you leave, do so quietly.

Brief silence.

L1: The peace of Christ be with you.
And also with you.

L1: Let us pray. *(pause)*
Lord Jesus Christ,
by your goodness and mercy
you guide your flock
to still waters and green pastures
where we are restored to life,
life abundant in you,
now and all the days of our lives.
Amen.

Silence.

Word

The musicians introduce a simple song or refrain drawn from Psalm 23, such as Still waters (SP 38) or the refrain of Shepherd me, O God (ELW 780). Then the assembly sings it once or twice. The psalm may be spoken or chanted by a cantor. If the psalm is chanted, choose a psalm tone that can follow and lead into the song or refrain.

Refrain

L1: The Lord is my shepherd,
    I shall not be in want.
The Lord makes me lie down in green pastures
    and leads me beside still waters.

L2: You restore my soul, O Lord,
 and guide me along right pathways
 for your name's sake.

Though I walk through the valley
of the shadow of death,
 I shall fear no evil;
for you are with me;
 your rod and your staff,
 they comfort me. (Psalm 32:1-4)

Refrain

L1: You prepare a table before me
 in the presence of my enemies;
you anoint my head with oil;
 and my cup is running over.

L2: Surely goodness and mercy
 shall follow me
 all the days of my life,
and I will dwell
 in the house of the Lord forever. (Psalm 23:5-6)

Refrain

Silence

L1: Let us pray. *(pause)*

Lord Jesus Christ, our good shepherd,
you give us new birth in the waters of baptism,
you anoint us with oil,
and you nourish us at your table with heavenly food.
In your goodness and mercy,
dispel the shadows of evil and death,
and lead us along safe paths,
that we may rest securely in you
and dwell in the house of the Lord,
now and forever, for your name's sake.*
Amen.

A time of silence is kept as the word dwells richly in the assembly.

Invitation to Laying On of Hands and Anointing

L2: A reading from James. *(pause)*
Are any among you suffering? They should pray.
Are any cheerful? They should sing songs of praise.
Are any among you sick?
They should call for the elders of the church
and have them pray over them,
anointing them with oil in the name of the Lord.
The prayer of faith will save the sick,
and the Lord will raise them up,
and anyone who has committed sins will be forgiven.
Therefore confess your sins to one another,
and pray for one another, so that you may be healed.
(James 5:13-16a)

L1: Those who desire the prayer of faith
and the laying on of hands
are invited to kneel at one of the cushions provided.
All who are drawn to be part of this ministry
are asked to watch
so that no one comes forward and is left kneeling alone—
rise and stand beside those who kneel.

L2: Place your hands upon the person's head.
Pray these or similar words:
"Jesus Christ, our savior and shepherd,
fill you with love, mend you with mercy,
and grant you peace."

L1: Use the oil provided to trace the sign of the cross on the person's forehead, a reminder of the baptismal grace that forgives, frees, and heals us, saying, "You are God's child, now and always."

During the following invitation, the light bearer lights one candle in each container of sand.

L1: The Lord is our shepherd, we need nothing more.
Come, you who are filled with anxiety, regret, or fear.
Christ leads you beside still waters.

L2: Come, you who long for reconciliation
between peoples and nations.
God has set a table in the presence of our enemies,
where we can feast with them on Christ's mercy.

L1: Come, you who walk in death's dark valley
and you who accompany others along the sorrow road.
God's comfort is yours.

L2: When the singing begins, you may come to the cross
to kneel or sit as beside still waters.
You who remain seated, sing the simple songs,
as our bodies, our breath, our hearts, our hands,
and our voices are joined in prayer.

Prayer at the Cross

*Songs and ostinato chants are sung while people come forward
to pray, and others to pray over them.*

Suggested music:
Still waters   SP 38—*if not sung earlier*
Shepherd me, O God   ELW 780—*if not sung earlier. The
assembly may sing this refrain as an ostinato chant, or a can-
tor may sing verses interspersed.*
Take, oh, take me as I am   SP 40
Bring your best to our worst   SP 4
Nade te turbe / Nothing can trouble   SP 29—*if not sung
earlier*
Precious Lord, take my hand   ELW 773

*When the prayers around the cross have come to a natural close
and the music has ended, silence is kept. Then the leader gathers
the prayers, commending them to God.*

Closing Prayer

L1: Gathering our many prayers into one, let us pray.
(pause)
We give thanks, O God,
that you have come to heal us,
and have called us to bring your healing to one another.
Fill us with your Spirit,
that we may be faithful to your call
and grateful for your power.
Send us into the world as healers in your name
through Jesus Christ, the great shepherd of the sheep.
Amen.

Sending

L1: The God of peace,
who brought again from the dead our Lord Jesus,
keep you in goodness and mercy, now and forever.
Amen.

L2: You may remain in silence for prayer.
When you leave, do so quietly.
Christ goes with you.

*The room stays quiet and dark until all have finished praying.
Music may continue awhile after the dismissal or may end, leaving
people to pray in silence.*

*Evangelical Lutheran Worship Leaders Edition © 2006, admin. Augsburg
Fortress, prayer 468, Psalm 23.

From Susan Briehl and Tom Witt, *Holden Prayer Around the Cross:
Handbook to the Liturgy,* third ed. (Augsburg Fortress, 2009), pp. 97–102.
Singing Our Prayer: A Companion to Holden Prayer Around the Cross
(Augsburg Fortress, 2009) is available in full score and assembly editions,
and as an audio CD. www.augsburgfortress.org

This and other Prayer Around the Cross liturgies should not be
reproduced and placed in the hands of the assembly. Their intent is best
realized when the services are conducted in semidarkness.

Resources for Memorial Day
Prayers

The armed forces of the nation

Almighty and everlasting God, whose providence guides your people in diligent service, bless the officers and enlisted women and men of the Army, Navy, Marines, Air Force, and Coast Guard as they perform the duties of their calling. Give them not only true love of country but also love of you and an understanding of your love for all people; so that, relying upon your guidance, they may courageously defend our nation from every foe, promote justice, honor, and unity among our people, and be a means of fostering mutual respect and understanding among all peoples of the world; through Jesus Christ, your Son and our Lord. Amen.

From *Prayer in Time of War for Church and Home*, prepared by the Common Service Book Committee of the United Lutheran Church in America, © 1942 United Lutheran Publication House. Additional prayers for individual branches of the military are available in *Evangelical Lutheran Worship Prayer Book for the Armed Services* (Augsburg Fortress, 2013), pp. 63–64.

Those who have given their lives

Eternal God, we give thanks for all those who have shown the greatest love by laying down their lives for others. We especially thank you for those in our military through-out history who have sacrificed their lives for their fellow citizens and for us who came after. As we remember their service, keep us mindful of all those for whom this day is a burden, and send your spirit of comfort to them. Be present with all the women and men who are serving in the military today. [Though they are at war] let them live for the peace known only from you. Help us to be worthy of their legacy, and keep us mindful of their service, that in all things we may live our lives in praise and thanksgiving to you; through Jesus Christ, our Savior and Lord. Amen.

From *Evangelical Lutheran Worship Prayer Book for the Armed Services* (Augsburg Fortress, 2013), p. 65.

Resources for Labor/Labour Day
Prayers

Almighty God, your Son Jesus Christ dignified our labor by sharing our toil. Guide us with your justice in the work-place, so that we may never value things above people, or surrender honor to love of gain or lust for power. Prosper all efforts to put an end to work that brings no joy, and teach us how to govern the ways of business to the harm of none and for the sake of the common good; through Jesus Christ our Lord. Amen. (*Evangelical Lutheran Worship*, p. 78)

Lord of life, you have given us six days on which to work, and modeled resting in your word on the sabbath. We give thanks for fair labor practices that offer time for rest and leisure as balance to our daily work. We pray for good and productive work in our daily professions and pursuits for the welfare of our neighbors. We pray for just and safe working conditions for all, for living wages, for honor and dignity in our employment. We pray that you work against all forces that steal human dignity or rob communities of the economic support they need from their labors to live sufficiently and well. For all those who defend the dignity of work, and all those who help us discover how to connect our faith to work, we give you thanks; through Jesus Christ our Lord. Amen.

God of justice, we remember before you those who suffer want and anxiety from lack of work. Guide the people of this land so to use our wealth and resources that all people may find suitable and fulfilling employment and receive just payment for their labor; through your Son, Jesus Christ our Lord. Amen. (*Evangelical Lutheran Worship*, p. 79)

O God, the heavens declare your glory and tell of your work in creation. From you come the gifts of our bodies and minds, our skills and abilities, and the opportunities to use these gifts in sustaining our lives and in helping our neighbors. We pray for those whose livelihood is insecure; for those who are bearing heavy burdens and stressful times at work; for those whose work is tedious or dangerous; for those who have experienced failures at work; for those who have lost a job; and for all who face any difficulty in their lives of labor. Surround them with your never-failing love; free them from restlessness and anxiety; keep them in every perplexity and distress; and renew them in facing the opportunities and challenges of daily life and work; through Jesus Christ, our Savior and Lord. Amen. (*Evangelical Lutheran Worship Occasional Services for the Assembly*, p. 407)

A Hand Blessing

The leader begins:
Look at your hands. Notice their power and gentleness. Let us bless these hands together. I invite you to say each phrase after me.

Blessed be the works of your hands, O Holy One. *echo*
Blessed be these hands that have touched life. *echo*
Blessed be these hands that have nurtured creativity. *echo*
Blessed be these hands that have held pain. *echo*
Blessed be these hands that have embraced with passion.
    echo
Blessed be these hands that have tended gardens. *echo*
Blessed be these hands that have closed in anger. *echo*
Blessed be these hands that have planted new seeds. *echo*
Blessed be these hands that have harvested ripe fields. *echo*
Blessed be these hands that have cleaned, washed, mopped,
    scrubbed. *echo*
Blessed be these hands that have become knotty with age.
    echo
Blessed be these hands that are wrinkled and scarred from
    doing justice. *echo*
Blessed be these hands that have reached out and been
    received. *echo*
Blessed be these hands that hold the promise of the future.
    echo
(Add others)
Blessed be the works of your hands, O Holy One. *echo*

Diann L. Neu, "A Hand Blessing," in *WATERwheel* Vol. 2, no. 1 (Winter 1989). Used by permission.

ELCA Social Statement on Economic Life (1999)

"Sufficient, Sustainable Livelihood for All" is the Evangelical Lutheran Church in America's social statement on economic life. The statement expresses ELCA teaching that economic activity is a means through which God's will is served for the thriving and well-being of humankind and the care of the earth. It recognizes that even though sin distorts human activity, we are called to practice economic activity justly and with special concern for those who live in poverty.

In this work, the church is guided by the biblically grounded imperative of "sufficient, sustainable livelihood for all." This means giving attention to the scope of God's concern ("for all"), the means by which life is sustained ("livelihood"), what is needed ("sufficiency"), and a long-term perspective ("sustainability"). The statement recognizes that these criteria may be in tension with one another, but it still provides a framework for discernment. Toward that purpose, it discusses commerce, law, vocation, public policy, work, human dignity, agriculture, business, and efforts to empower those who live in poverty.

Read or download the full social statement on "Economic Life: Sufficient, Sustainable Livelihood for All" in English or Spanish at www.elca.org/Faith/Faith-and-Society/Social-Statements/Economic-Life. The statement was adopted in 1999 by the ELCA Churchwide Assembly.

Interfaith Worker Justice Resources

Visit the Interfaith Worker Justice (IWJ) website (www.iwj.org) for many resources, suggestions, and a toolkit, including:
- Suggested biblical passages
- Sample sermons
- Prayers and litanies
- Information about hosting a Labor in the Pulpit speaker
- Encouraging conversation around practical solutions for today's workplace problems
- Suggestions for examining worker issues through your faith lens
- Bulletin inserts
- Ways to promote your Labor/Labour Day service
- Sample bulletin/newsletter/website announcement
- Information about finding an IWJ group near you

May 22, 2016
The Holy Trinity
First Sunday after Pentecost

"O Lord our Lord, how majestic is your name in all the earth!" Today we celebrate the name of God: holy blessed Trinity. There is no other day quite like this one in the church's year. There is no other god like ours. Praise Father, Son, and Holy Spirit!

Prayer of the Day

Almighty Creator and ever-living God: we worship your glory, eternal Three-in-One, and we praise your power, majestic One-in-Three. Keep us steadfast in this faith, defend us in all adversity, and bring us at last into your presence, where you live in endless joy and love, Father, Son, and Holy Spirit, one God, now and forever.

or

God of heaven and earth, before the foundation of the universe and the beginning of time you are the triune God: Author of creation, eternal Word of salvation, life-giving Spirit of wisdom. Guide us to all truth by your Spirit, that we may proclaim all that Christ has revealed and rejoice in the glory he shares with us. Glory and praise to you, Father, Son, and Holy Spirit, now and forever.

Gospel Acclamation

Alleluia. Holy, holy, holy is the [|] LORD of hosts;* God's glory fills [|] the whole earth. *Alleluia.* (Isa. 6:3)

Readings and Psalm
Proverbs 8:1-4, 22-31

In the Bible, wisdom has many faces. It is portrayed in terms sometimes human and sometimes divine. Often, it is personified as feminine. In this passage, Woman Wisdom is depicted not only as the first creation of God but also as God's helper, rejoicing in God's creation, especially in human beings.

Psalm 8

Your glory is chanted above the heavens. (Ps. 8:2)

Romans 5:1-5

Paul describes the life of faith with reference to God, Jesus, and the Holy Spirit. Even now, we have peace with God through Jesus, and our hope for the future is grounded in the love of God that we experience through Christ's Holy Spirit.

John 16:12-15

Jesus' ongoing presence with the disciples will be borne by the coming Spirit, who will guide them and communicate to them Jesus' will and glory.

Preface   Holy Trinity

Color   White

Prayers of Intercession

The prayers are prepared locally for each occasion. The following examples may be adapted or used as appropriate.

Rejoicing in the triune God, let us pray for the church, those in need, and all of God's creation.

A brief silence.

O Lord our sovereign, your name is majestic in all the earth. Enliven your church by your Spirit to live into the name bestowed on us in baptism. Lord, in your mercy,

hear our prayer.

Holy Wisdom, we praise and thank you for the mountains and hills, the earth and fields, the skies above, the fountains of the deep, and your delight in the human race. Lord, in your mercy,

hear our prayer.

Peace-bringing God, the nations of the world are ever and always dependent on the peace that only you give. Guide the leaders of nations to make choices that lead to peace. Lord, in your mercy,

hear our prayer.

Spirit of truth, heal us, reconcile us, break the bonds of the oppressed, give sanctuary to refugees, end the exile of those who are marginalized, and pour your love into all hearts. Especially we pray for . . . . Lord, in your mercy,

hear our prayer.

Father of Jesus, keep us mindful of how we use the names of others. Keep us from bearing false witness, and help us honor your name above all others. Lord, in your mercy,

hear our prayer.

Here other intercessions may be offered.

O God, you have called the saints your own. Gather us, with them, into your kingdom, in the promise of life forever with you. Lord, in your mercy,

hear our prayer.
We lift our prayers to you, O God, trusting your promise to hear us; through Jesus Christ our Lord.
Amen.

Images in the Readings

The Christian writings of the first century give only the beginnings of what became the developed doctrine of the Trinity of **Father, Son, and Spirit**. For Paul, how can the crucifixion bring God's glory? We have access to God through our Lord Jesus Christ on the cross and through the Spirit "poured" into our hearts at baptism. For John, how can we be assured of God's truth? Through the Son, the Father will send to the faithful the Spirit of truth.

The poem in Proverbs relies on the ancient Near Eastern literary image of **Woman Wisdom**. Some ancient religions, such as that in Egypt, assigned to a goddess the wisdom of the universe. Like the figure of Justice that we are familiar with, she knows truth and weighs it in her balance. Wisdom, in Hebrew *hokmah*, is a feminine noun and thus was easy to personify as a mighty woman. Scholars disagree on whether this imagery was merely a literary convention for early Judaism or instead pointed to popular belief in a goddess as Yahweh's consort. For Christians speaking Greek, the poem in John 1 exemplifies the replacement of Wisdom with the Word, *logos* being a masculine noun. Christ is our Woman Wisdom, who participated in God's creation of the world: see, for example, stanza 2 in "O come, O come, Emmanuel" (ELW 257).

Ideas for the Day

◆ St. Augustine maintained that it is valuable to "seek for some image of the Trinity in that which is decaying," and Christian preachers and teachers have been looking for good object lessons ever since. Flour, salt, and water combine to make dough. Apples are composed of seeds, skin, and flesh. Water can be found in liquid, solid, and vaporous forms. Augustine himself famously used the act of sight as a model for the Trinity: the object perceived, the image in the perceiver's mind, and the attention required to see comprise a "trinity" of perception. When encountered at impressionable ages, these imaginative models can leave deep impressions. The preacher may helpfully evoke memories of these Sunday school lessons on the Trinity, taking Augustine's dictum as permission to try (and often fail) to illustrate complicated theology with simple, understandable models drawn from the material world. The limitations of these earthly models may lead us into heresy, but attempting to do without them may leave us groping in the dark with neither vision nor imagination. Is theology primarily about "getting it right" or about inviting believers into an

imaginative and creative space that brings us closer in relation to the one who created all things? The perils of illustrating the Trinity provide an interesting test case for what we think theology is for and how we navigate the challenges theology presents, whether as preachers or as those in the pews.

◆ Lutheran teaching advises that Holy Baptism be administered "in the name of the triune God, Father, Son, and Holy Spirit," but warns that "washing with water in this name is much more than the use of a 'formula.'" Pastors and congregations are warned against misunderstanding trinitarian orthodoxy as a "magic formula or as a misrepresentation of the one God in three persons," and as cultural and theological conversations about the appropriateness of "Father" and "Son" language for God continue, it may be helpful to remind congregations that trinitarian language is neither magical, hierarchical, nor controlling, but rather serves as an invitation to deeper relationship and encounter with a God who is relational and egalitarian by God's very nature (*The Use of the Means of Grace*, 1997).

Connections with the Liturgy

The opening confession and forgiveness in *Evangelical Lutheran Worship* (p. 94) begins in the name of the Trinity. The standard greeting with which to begin the Sunday liturgy (p. 98) proclaims the Trinity. Our worship concludes with a trinitarian blessing. Christian worship begins and ends not with the usual social greetings of "Good morning" and "Bye, now." Rather, we are privileged to stand within and under uniquely Christian phrases: we give to one another and we receive the grace, love, and communion of the triune God.

Let the Children Come

View and discuss the painting *Trinity* by Andrei Rublev, based on the reading where Abraham and Sarah welcome three heavenly visitors for dinner (Gen. 18:2). God the Father, Son, and Holy Spirit join us at the table in loving, equal, and joyful relationship with one another. And then through the bread of life and the cup of salvation, they become one with the children of God. This love of God in Jesus Christ is poured into our hearts by the Holy Spirit in our baptism. Invite children to go to the baptismal font and mark a cross on their foreheads.

Assembly Song
Gathering

Come, all you people   ELW 819, TFF 138, WOV 717
Come, thou almighty King   ELW 408, LBW 522
All glory be to God on high   ELW 410, LBW 166

Psalmody and Acclamations

Burkhardt, Michael. "Psalm 8" from *Psalms for the Church Year*. 3 pt equal voices a cap or with org and/or hb. MSM 80-708.

Cherwien, David and Susan. "Two Psalm Settings (Psalm 8)." U/2 pt kybd, assembly, opt tr, 3 hb or hc. CG CGA1077.

Valentine, Timothy, SJ. "How Majestic Your Name." SAB, cant, assembly, gtr, kybd, opt inst. GIA G-4833.

(GA) ELW 175 with proper verse for Holy Trinity (tone in *ELW Accompaniment Edition: Service Music and Hymns*)

Hymn of the Day

Come, join the dance of Trinity   ELW 412   *KINGSFOLD*

Holy, holy, holy, Lord God Almighty!   ELW 413, LBW 165   *NICAEA*

Voices raised to you   ELW 845   *SONG OF PRAISE*

Offering

Now the silence   ELW 460, LBW 205

Holy, holy, holy   ELW 473, W&P 62

Communion

We eat the bread of teaching   ELW 518

Father, most holy   ELW 415, LBW 169

Gracious Spirit, heed our pleading   ELW 401, LS 66, TFF 103, WOV 687

Sending

Come to us, creative Spirit   ELW 687, WOV 758

Holy God, we praise your name   ELW 414, LBW 535

Additional Assembly Songs

Holy, holy   TFF 289, W&P 60

¡Santo, santo, santo!   LLC 371

Santo Espíritu, excelsa paloma   LLC 366

🌐 Anon. "Holy, Holy, Holy/Santo, santo, santo." U. *ELW*, p. 181.

🌐 Custodio, Bernardino. "Our Souls Are Full of Praises" from *Sound the Bamboo*. SATB. GIA G-6830.

✧ Byrd, Marc/Steve Hindalong. "God of Wonders" from CCLI.

✧ Getty, Keith, and Stuart Townend. "The Perfect Wisdom of Our God" from CCLI.

✧ Hart, Sarah/Jayme Thompson. "God with Us" from CCLI.

✧ Modlin, Rick. "Holy, Holy, Holy Cry" from *Spirit and Song*, vol. 4. OCP.

✧ Muglia, Chris. "Our God Is Here" from *Spirit and Song,* vol. 2. OCP.

✧ Sibelius, Jean/Kari Jobe/Jason Ingram. "Be Still My Soul (In You I Rest)" from CCLI.

Music for the Day
Choral

p Distler, Hugo. "Creator Spirit, Heav'nly Dove" from *Chantry Choirbook*. SAB. AFP 9780800657772.

p Highben, Zebulon. "Mothering God, You Gave Me Birth." SAB, gtr, fl. AFP 9781451424249.

p ● Martin, Joseph. "Our Song Shall Rise to Thee." SATB, pno. HOP C5811.

p Scott, K. Lee. "Christ Be with Me" from *New Songs of Gladness: Vocal Solos for Worship*. S/T, kybd. AFP 9781451486001.

Children's Choir

Burkhardt, Michael. "Praise and Honor" from *Praise and Honor: Six Anthems for Unison or Two-Part Voices and Orff Ensemble*. 2 pt, metallophone, xyl. MSM 55-4000.

Martin, Joseph M. "I Will Clap My Hands." U/2 pt, pno, opt perc/hb. LOR 10/3768L.

Petersen, Lynn. "We All Believe in One True God." 2 pt, vln/C inst, kybd. GIA G-4926.

Keyboard / Instrumental

p ● Cherwien, David M. "Kingsfold" from *Organ Plus*, vol. 2. Org, fl, ob. AFP 9780800678548.

● Farlee, Robert Buckley. "Nicaea" from *Augsburg Organ Library: Easter*. Org. AFP 9780800659363.

● Post, Piet. "Nicaea" from *Augsburg Organ Library: Summer*. Org. AFP 9780800676872.

p ● Shaw, Timothy. "Nicaea" from *My Redeemer Lives*. Pno. AFP 9781451451795.

Handbell

● Hopson, Hal H. "Variations on 'Kingsfold.'" 3 or 5 oct, L2+. AFP 1110703.

Krug, Jason W. "Abba Father." 3-5 oct hb, opt 3-4 oct hc, L2+. LOR 20/1707L.

● Moklebust, Cathy. "Toccata on 'Holy, Holy, Holy.'" 3 or 5 oct, L4+. CG CGB433.

Tuesday, May 24

Nicolaus Copernicus, died 1543; Leonhard Euler, died 1783; scientists

Remembering scientists such as Copernicus and Euler offers an opportunity to ponder the mysteries of the universe and the grandeur of God's creation. Copernicus is an example of a renaissance person. He formally studied astronomy, mathematics, Greek, Plato, law, medicine, and canon law. He also had interests in theology, poetry, and the natural and social sciences. Copernicus is chiefly remembered for his work as an astronomer and his idea that the sun, not the earth, is the center of the solar system.

Euler (oy-ler) is regarded as one of the founders of the science of pure mathematics and made important contributions to mechanics, hydrodynamics, astronomy, optics, and acoustics.

🌐 = global song   ✧ = praise song
● = relates to hymn of the day   p = available in Prelude Music Planner

Friday, May 27

John Calvin, renewer of the church, died 1564

John Calvin began his studies in theology at the University of Paris when he was fourteen. In his mid-twenties he experienced a conversion that led him to embrace the views of the Reformation. His theological ideas are systematically laid out in his *Institutes of the Christian Religion*. He is also well known for his commentaries on scripture. He was a preacher in Geneva, was banished once, and then later returned to reform the city under a theocratic constitution.

May 29, 2016
Time after Pentecost — Lectionary 9

God hears every prayer—the prayer of the outsider as well as the prayer of the insider. The attentive nature of our God is evident as God comes to us again and again in the word and in the supper. "Ascribe to the Lord the honor due the holy name; bring offerings and enter the courts of the Lord." Do it today.

Prayer of the Day

Merciful Lord, we do not presume to come before you trusting in our own righteousness, but in your great and abundant mercies. Revive our faith, we pray; heal our bodies, and mend our communities, that we may evermore dwell in your Son, Jesus Christ, our Savior and Lord.

Gospel Acclamation

Alleluia. God so loved the world that he gave his ' only Son,* so that everyone who believes in him should not perish, but have e- ' ternal life. *Alleluia.* (John 3:16)

Readings and Psalm
1 Kings 8:22-23, 41-43

King Solomon prays at the dedication of the temple in Jerusalem, built under his direction. Solomon prays that the temple will be a sign of God's presence and power, not only to the Israelites, but to all peoples.

Psalm 96:1-9

Declare the glory of the Lord among the nations. (Ps. 96:3)

Galatians 1:1-12

Paul, who started this church in Galatia, is angry and troubled that the congregation is confused by other teachers. As he begins this letter, Paul is direct with them about his desire for Christ's pure gospel to be the center of their lives.

Luke 7:1-10

A Roman centurion stands to lose a highly valued slave. Jewish leaders in Capernaum consider the centurion worthy, but the Gentile declares himself unworthy. In the midst of this tangle of attitudes, the centurion shows his understanding of authority and his testimony that Jesus has it, even authority over illness and death.

Semicontinuous reading and psalm
1 Kings 18:20-21 [22-29] 30-39

The Israelites have been enticed by King Ahab and his non-Israelite queen, Jezebel, to worship the Canaanite god Baal. So Elijah challenges the prophets of Baal to a contest. The contest proves that the Lord is indeed the true God, and the people turn back to the Lord.

Psalm 96

Ascribe to the Lord honor and power. (Ps. 96:7)

Preface Sundays

Color Green

Prayers of Intercession

The prayers are prepared locally for each occasion. The following examples may be adapted or used as appropriate.

Let us pray for the church, those in need, and all of God's creation.

A brief silence.

God of Israel, there is no one like you in heaven above or on earth beneath. Keep covenant with your church, and build us up as your people. Lord, in your mercy,

hear our prayer.

Creator God, we ascribe to you glory and strength. We praise you for the glory of your creation, and ask that you strengthen us to keep it and tend it as a gift and trust. Lord, in your mercy,

hear our prayer.

Ruler of the nations, you have brought together people from many lands. Give us grace to receive foreigners with hospitality, to be good guests in foreign lands, and to accompany one other in faith. Lord, in your mercy,

hear our prayer.

Healing God, we pray for all those who need to be made whole. We pray especially for . . . . Give us faith to trust that you are the presence that gives life. Lord, in your mercy,

hear our prayer.

Gracious God, we remember today those who laid down their lives for others. Give us the strength to live together as a faith community in humility and gentleness of spirit, maintaining the bond of peace. Lord, in your mercy,

hear our prayer.

Here other intercessions may be offered.

O God, you have called the saints your own. Gather us (*with the hymnwriter Jiří Tranovský*) into your kingdom, in the promise of life forever with you. Lord, in your mercy,

hear our prayer.

We lift our prayers to you, O God, trusting your promise to hear us; through Jesus Christ our Lord.

Amen.

Images in the Readings

The Roman Empire was as successful as it was because of the might and discipline of its armies. Thus for the gospels to describe a **Roman centurion** as coming to Jesus for help would have been an impressive image for early Christians. They could hope that the world's mightiest military power would eventually give way to faith in Christ, whose authority came not from the emperor, who was perhaps harsh, even vindictive, even insane, but rather from a loving God.

The Israelite **temple**, built by slave labor during Solomon's reign, was similar to other ancient Near Eastern temples, which were understood as the earthly residence of the deity who supported the dynasty. The devout came as close to the statue of the god or goddess as their status allowed. In Israel, the prohibition of statues meant that the ark of the covenant, a box holding precious items from Israelite history, stood for the presence of God. Thus God's history of faithfulness replaced a graven image. Some Christians have likened their churches to the temple. But as the rite of Dedication of a Church Building (*Occasional Services for the Assembly*, p. 146) says, remarking on the differences, "We are the temple of your presence, and this building is the house of your church."

Recent scholarship has shown that the term **gospel** had a pre-Christian use: to indicate some announcement of good news or benefaction issuing from the emperor or some proclamation about imperial power. Thus, although for us the word *gospel* has only pleasant connotations, and in our ears we hear some enthusiastic hymn singing, for Paul and other early Christians to call their message about Jesus "gospel" had a strong critical and countercultural edge. How do we capture this edge in our time, especially in a society that likes to describe itself as blessed by God?

Ideas for the Day

♦   All three lectionary texts address the question of how God will deal with perceived outsiders, whether a foreigner among Israel, a Gentile among Jews, or a centurion among oppressed peasants. Responding to outsiders is a perennial challenge for Christian communities, and yet the direction of all three biblical texts points to a God who sees no outsiders but only human beings in need of healing. So-called "outsider artists"—those who operate outside the regulated bounds of galleries, museums, and churches—sometimes hold up a mirror to a society that can so easily be divided into insiders and outsiders, and expose painful and sometimes beautiful reality. *Finding Vivian Maier* (Ravine Pictures, 2014) tells the story of one such outsider artist, a brilliant street photographer who kept her work hidden and died unknown before being discovered by a young filmmaker. A "foreigner" in every way, Maier's photographs reveal a common humanity: the need for healing found in the eyes of the stockbroker and the street person alike.

♦   In the Roman writer Vegetius's *De Re Militari*, the centurion is described as a strong, silent type: he is "vigilant, temperate, active and readier to execute the orders he receives than to talk" (Book II.14. Vegetius's work is available online at www.digitalattic.org). This is an image that might evoke the memory of actors like John Wayne and Gary Cooper. Not anxious to sit down to coffee with Jesus, Luke's centurion is wholly focused on the needs of his beloved servant. He sees in Jesus one who will understand him, even though the centurion is a man of action rather than words. In the lectionary passages to follow, Jesus will interact with other individuals who do not seem to fit the profile of an ideal disciple: a hysterical widow, a weeping woman, a demoniac. The preacher with a penchant for the theatrical may think of ways to dramatize these characters, or perhaps reference Hollywood actors like Wayne and Cooper to "sketch" them in the congregant's imagination: each one with a unique perspective on who Jesus is and what he represents.

Connections with the Liturgy

Solomon is described as spreading out his hands to heaven. Called the *orans*, the posture of raising one's hands in prayer is normal in some churches and is increasing at least among presiding ministers in others. With arms outstretched is how Jesus would have prayed. In the ancient world, the posture probably suggested that God resided up in the sky. For us, the gesture signifies the opening of the self in praise to God and in awareness of the community.

Some preachers begin their sermons by quoting Paul's greeting in Galatians 1:3.

Let the Children Come

Invite children to learn Psalm 96:1-2. "Sing to the LORD" is repeated three times in these verses. Most children could learn this short phrase by heart and it could be said or sung as a group. Simple motions could be added to make it even more joyful and inclusive of younger children.

Assembly Song
Gathering

O day of rest and gladness ELW 521, LBW 251

Christ is made the sure foundation ELW 645, WOV 747, LBW 367

Come, let us join in cheerful songs ELW 847, LBW 254

Psalmody and Acclamations

Ellingboe, Bradley. "Psalm 96:1-9" from PWC.

Harbor, Rawn. "Let the Heavens Rejoice (Psalm 96)." TFF 10.

Rennick, Charles. "Psalm 96: O Sing a New Song." SATB, cant, assembly, org, opt tpt. GIA G-4803.

Shute, Linda Cable. "Psalm 96:1-9," Refrain 1, from PSCY.

(GA) ELW 175 with proper verse for Lectionary 9 (tone in *ELW Accompaniment Edition: Service Music and Hymns*).

Hymn of the Day

Oh, praise the gracious power ELW 651, WOV 750 *CHRISTPRAISE RAY*

Strengthen for service, Lord ELW 497 *BUCKHURST RUN* LBW 218 *WIR DIENEN, HERR*

All Are Welcome ELW 641 *TWO OAKS*

Offering

Let the vineyards be fruitful ELW 183

O Christ, the healer, we have come ELW 610, sts. 1, 4; LBW 360, sts. 1, 4

Communion

We are all one in Christ ELW 643, LLC 470, LS 130, TFF 221

The church's one foundation ELW 654, LBW 369

Lord, keep us steadfast in your word ELW 517, LBW 230

Sending

I love to tell the story ELW 661, LBW 390, LS 154, TFF 228

In Christ there is no east or west ELW 650, TFF 214, LBW 359

Additional Assembly Songs

Come to Jesus TFF 156

Necesitado me encuentro, Señor LLC 529

I was glad W&P 68

⊕ Pangosban, Ben. "Sing a Song to God" from *Glory to God*. U. WJK 9780664238971.

⊕ Wanji tune/arr. Austin Lovelace. "Praise God, the Father" from *Set Free: A Collection of African Hymns*. SATB. AFP 9780806600451

✿ Beeching, Vicky. "Breath of God" from CCLI.

✿ Doerksen, Brian. "Hope of the Nations" from CCLI.

✿ Evans, Darrel. "Let the River Flow" from CCLI.

✿ Getty, Keith/Stuart Townend. "Every Promise" from CCLI.

✿ Maher, Matt. "Your Grace Is Enough" from CCLI.

✿ Tomlin, Chris/Christy Nockels/Nathan Nockels. "Where the Spirit of the Lord Is" from CCLI.

Music for the Day
Choral

Bedford, Michael. "Psalm 96." SATB, org, tpt in C. ECS 6207.

Burkhardt, Michael. "God of Grace and God of Glory." SATB, org, opt 2 tpt, timp, assembly. MSM 60-8015.

Schelat, David. "Praise the Lord, God's Glories Show." SAB, conga drm. OXF 9780193865518.

p Wood, Dale. "Jubilate Deo" from *Augsburg Easy Choirbook*, vol. 1. 2 pt mxd, org. AFP 9780800676025.

Children's Choir

Hopson, Hal H. "God's Glory Echoes through the Skies." U, org. HIN HMC 410.

Jothen, Michael. "O Sing Ye." U, kybd. BP BP1128.

Paulus, Stephen. "Hear My Words." 2 pt, kybd. HIN HMC 201.

Keyboard / Instrumental

p ● Childs, Edwin T. "Buckhurst Run" from *Communion Hymns for Organ*, vol. 2. Org. AFP 9781451424157.

● Lenz, Charles L. "Two Oaks" from *All Are Welcome*. Org. AFP 9781451424164.

p ● Miller, Aaron David. "Christpraise Ray" from *Introductions and Alternate Accompaniments for Piano*, vol. 7. Pno. AFP 9780800623654.

p ● Organ, Anne Krentz. "Buckhurst Run" from *Reflections on Hymn Tunes for Holy Communion*, vol. 2. Pno. AFP 9780800679095.

Handbell

Angerman, David. "Crown Him with Many Crowns." 2-3 oct, L1. ALF 12388.

● McAninch, Diane. "Prelude on 'All Are Welcome.'" 3-5 oct hb, opt 3 oct hc, opt fl, L3. GIA G-7083.

Sherman, Arnold. "Oh, Rest in the Lord." 3-5 oct, L2+. CG CGB469.

⊕ = global song   ✿ = praise song
● = relates to hymn of the day   p = available in Prelude Music Planner

Sunday, May 29

Jiří Tranovský, hymnwriter, died 1637

Jiří Tranovský (YEAR-zhee truh-NOF-skee) is considered the "Luther of the Slavs" and the father of Slovak hymnody. Trained at the University of Wittenberg in the early seventeenth century, Tranovský was ordained in 1616 and spent his life preaching and teaching in Prague, Silesia, and finally Slovakia. He produced a translation of the Augsburg Confession and published his hymn collection *Cithara Sanctorum* (Lyre of the Saints), the foundation of Slovak Lutheran hymnody.

Tuesday, May 31

Visit of Mary to Elizabeth

Sometime after the Annunciation, Mary visited her cousin Elizabeth. This occasion is sometimes referred to simply as "the Visitation." Elizabeth greeted Mary with the words "Blessed are you among women," and Mary responded with her famous song, the Magnificat. Luke's gospel tells that even John the Baptist rejoiced and leapt in his mother's womb when Elizabeth heard Mary's greeting. On this festival two women are seen: one, seemingly too old to have a child, bears the last prophet of the old covenant, and the other, quite young, bears the incarnate Word and the new covenant.

Wednesday, June 1

Justin, martyr at Rome, died around 165

Justin was born of pagan parents. At Ephesus he was moved by stories of early Christian martyrs and came under the influence of an elderly Christian man he met there. Justin described his conversion by saying, "Straightway a flame was kindled in my soul and a love of the prophets and those who are friends of Christ possessed me." Justin was a teacher of philosophy and engaged in debates about the truth of Christian faith. He was arrested and jailed for practicing an unauthorized religion. He refused to renounce his faith, and he and six of his students, one a woman, were beheaded.

Justin's description of early Christian worship around the year 150 is one of the foundations of the church's pattern of worship, East and West.

Friday, June 3

The Martyrs of Uganda, died 1886

Christianity had been introduced to Uganda after 1877, but was made available primarily to those in the court of King Mutesa. His successor, King Mwanga, was angered by these Christian members of the court whose first allegiance was not to him but to Christ. On June 3, 1886, thirty-two young men were burned to death for refusing to renounce Christianity. Other martyrs followed. But many were impressed by the confident manner in which these Christians went to their deaths, and the persecution led to a much stronger Christian presence in the country.

John XXIII, Bishop of Rome, died 1963

In his ministry as a bishop of Venice, John (then Archbishop Roncalli) was loved by his people. He visited parishes and established new ones. He had warm affection for the working class—he himself was the child of Italian peasants—and he worked at developing social-action ministries. At age seventy-seven he was elected bishop of Rome. Despite the expectation that he would be a transitional pope, he had great energy and spirit. He convened the Second Vatican Council to open the windows of the church and "let in the fresh air of the modern world." The council brought about great changes in Roman Catholic worship, changes that have influenced Lutherans and many other Protestant churches as well.

June 5, 2016
Time after Pentecost — Lectionary 10

The Time after Pentecost is a teaching time, a growing time, in the life of the church. Today's texts celebrate God's ability and intention to provide us with a new lease on life. To that end we gather today with the whole people of God to be instructed by the word and nourished in the blessed sacrament.

Prayer of the Day

Compassionate God, you have assured the human family of eternal life through Jesus Christ. Deliver us from the death of sin, and raise us to new life in your Son, Jesus Christ, our Savior and Lord.

Gospel Acclamation

Alleluia. A great prophet has ris- ¹ en among us!* God has looked favora- ¹ bly on us! *Alleluia.* (Luke 7:16)

Readings and Psalm

1 Kings 17:17-24

Having offered hospitality to Elijah, a widow in Zarephath loses her son to an illness. Through prayer, Elijah restores the boy to life, and the joyful mother acknowledges that Elijah is indeed a man of God.

Psalm 30

My God, I cried out to you, and you restored me to health. (Ps. 30:2)

Galatians 1:11-24

The apostle and church-planter Paul tells the story of his ministry given to him by Jesus Christ. In the midst of grave tension in his church in Galatia, he assures his congregation that his work is centered in the pure gospel of Jesus Christ, unlike the other teachers among them.

Luke 7:11-17

Jesus' ministry bears witness to God's coming reign, where the lowly are shown mercy and the dead are raised. Here, Jesus ministers to a widow by raising her only son to life.

Semicontinuous reading and psalm

1 Kings 17:8-16 [17-24]

During a severe drought in Israel, God tells Elijah to find lodging with a widow in Zarephath, in the region of Sidon, west of Israel. The widow, despite experiencing severe hardship, offers hospitality to Elijah and is rewarded with a miraculous abundance of food.

Psalm 146

The LORD lifts up those who are bowed down. (Ps. 146:8)

Preface   Sundays

Color   Green

Prayers of Intercession

The prayers are prepared locally for each occasion. The following examples may be adapted or used as appropriate.

Let us pray for the church, those in need, and all of God's creation.

A brief silence.

God, we praise you for revealing your gospel to prophets, preachers, and leaders in your church. Inspire their continuing faithful proclamation. Lord, in your mercy,
hear our prayer.

God of the living and the dead, work in your creation, and work through us, in such ways that lead to life for your creation and for all people. Lord, in your mercy,
hear our prayer.

God of the city, we pray for cities, urban areas, suburbs, small towns, and all communities. Look favorably on all lands; bring peace where there is conflict and cooperation where there is disagreement. Lord, in your mercy,
hear our prayer.

Holy One, you see the needs of those who suffer. When we are sick, tend to us and to our neighbors, and give us gratitude when we are well. We pray especially for . . . . Lord, in your mercy,
hear our prayer.

Giver of joy, make your presence known in this assembly. Give us such a clear and bold share of your Spirit that your life and vitality shine through us into our neighborhood. Lord, in your mercy,
hear our prayer.

Here other intercessions may be offered.

O God, you have called the saints your own. Gather us (*with Boniface, bishop and missionary,*) into your kingdom, in the promise of life forever with you. Lord, in your mercy,

hear our prayer.
We lift our prayers to you, O God, trusting your promise to hear us; through Jesus Christ our Lord.
Amen.

Images in the Readings

The growing practice of holding memorial services rather than funerals means that seldom are we gathered around a **corpse**. Our society hides real dead bodies and in films makes of dead bodies a safe entertainment. Many Christians never visit the graves of their beloved dead. Yet lying in the place of death is the future for us all. How in our culture can we hold genuine death before ourselves so that we can affirm the power of God over death?

In both the first reading and the gospel a **widow** represents everyone who is in greatest need.

Moses and **Elijah** were the two most revered prophets in the Israelite tradition. In the story of the transfiguration of Jesus, they figure as representatives of the Jewish connection with God. Elijah lived during the reign of King Ahab (869–850 BCE), who was remembered as having allowed the worship of Canaanite deities in Israel. Some first-century Jews believed that Elijah would return to announce the coming of God at the end of time: thus the inquiry of whether John the Baptist was Elijah and the comment by the bystanders at the crucifixion that Jesus had prayed for Elijah. Even today at the Jewish seder meal, a place is set at the table for Elijah, who is expected to arrive at Passover; the outside door is left ajar for his arrival, and a cup of wine gets surprisingly drained: well, did Elijah come, but we missed him?

Ideas for the Day

◆   One of the lesser-known decisions made at the Council of Nicaea is that no Christian should kneel. Since Christ is risen from the dead, the thinking goes, those who worship him also should remain in a posture of resurrection. Most of us break this instruction, sitting and kneeling for prayer. Today we hear of a child and mother who experience the Risen One's ability to bring new life from death. What would it mean if we gave up kneeling for one Sunday? If you pray or share the eucharist while kneeling, change your practice for one week and stand instead. Consider what it means to express faith in bodily motions.

◆   "Do not weep." "Young man, I say to you, rise!" A small urban church is planted in a changing neighborhood. Leaders in schools, coffee shops, and nonprofits use social media to inform the wider community how the neighborhood is improving with the hashtag #neighborhoodrising. Bread, rivers, people, and communities can all rise up. To what do you imagine the risen Christ speaking this promise now? Where is there weeping heard in your community? Direct intercessory prayers toward those who weep, and extend a hand of blessing toward a hurting place or upon a grief-stricken family as you pray.

◆   Funeral bulletins often list the dates of birth and baptism for the deceased. When it comes to listing the date of death, a recent trend is to announce it as the date when a person was "born into eternal life." While it is true that the dead are held in God, in eternal life, the trend seems to come from our uneasiness with words like *died*, *dead*, and *death*. Encourage the faithful to speak honestly about death, calling it by name, so that we may also speak boldly about resurrection. This may be a good day for discussing with the community what your funeral practices are and where they come from. How is a Christian funeral unique? How does it especially reflect trust in the resurrection of Christ? Melinda Quivik's *A Christian Funeral: Witness to the Resurrection* (Minneapolis: Augsburg Fortress, 2005) makes a great book study.

Connections with the Liturgy

Since at least the second century, Christian communities have thanked God in their Sunday prayers for those who died in the faith, especially those who provided an example of faithfulness in the face of persecution. Although medieval prayers sought the aid of the pious dead, current Protestant practice is informed by today's second reading: "They glorified God because of me." The outline for the weekly intercessions in *Evangelical Lutheran Worship* (pp. 105–106) concludes with a prayer of thanksgiving for the faithful departed. On both January 25 and June 29, the calendar of commemorations (pp. 15–16) provides special occasions to "glorify God because of" the apostle Paul.

Let the Children Come

Jesus raises the widow's son from the dead. What does it mean to come to life again? The psalmist writes about God removing our sackcloth—which was an uncomfortable garment made of goat's hair that people wore while in mourning or when repenting of sins—and then clothing us with joy (Ps. 30:11). In baptism our "sackcloth" is taken off and we are clothed with the risen Christ. Perhaps the children could have an opportunity to touch rough, scratchy fabric (burlap?) and then compare that feeling to how they feel when they wear their favorite play clothes.

Assembly Song
Gathering

Oh, worship the King   ELW 842, LBW 548

Arise, my soul, arise   ELW 827, LBW 516

When morning gilds the skies   ELW 853, LBW 546

Psalmody and Acclamations

Daigle, Gary. "I Will Praise You, Lord" from PCY, vol. 4.

Haugen, Marty. "Psalm 30," Refrain 2, from PSCY.

+ Chepponis, James. "Psalm 146." 2 cant, assembly, opt SATB, kybd, gtr, C inst, hb. GIA G-4227.

(GA) ELW 175 with proper verse for Lectionary 10 (tone in *ELW Accompaniment Edition: Service Music and Hymns*).

Hymn of the Day

Healer of our every ill   ELW 612, WOV 738   *HEALER OF OUR EVERY ILL*

Jesus lives, my sure defense   ELW 621, LBW 340   *JESUS, MEINE ZUVERSICHT*

O God beyond all praising   ELW 880, WOV 797   *THAXTED*

Offering

Have you thanked the Lord?   ELW 829, TFF 270

Oh, that I had a thousand voices   ELW 833, sts. 1-2; LBW 560, sts. 1-2

Communion

By gracious powers   ELW 626, WOV 736

Now we join in celebration   ELW 462, LBW 203

We come to you for healing, Lord   ELW 617

Sending

In thee is gladness   ELW 867, LBW 552

I'm so glad Jesus lifted me   ELW 860, LS 121, TFF 191, WOV 673

Additional Assembly Songs

To go to heaven   TFF 181

No tengas niedo de morir   LLC 536

Let us enter in   DH 32

⊕ Democratic Republic of Congo. "Mungu ni mwema/Know That God Is Good" from *My Heart Sings Out*. SATB. Church Publishing 9780898694741.

⊕ Spanish traditional. "When We Are Living/Pues si vivimos." U. ELW 639.

✩ Brumley, Albert. "I'll Fly Away" from CCLI.

✩ Hall, Mark. "If We Are the Body" from CCLI.

✩ Morgan, Reuben/Ben Fielding. "Mighty to Save" from CCLI.

✩ Tomlin, Chris/Ed Cash/Jesse Reeves. "Let God Arise" from CCLI.

✩ Smith, Martin. "Did You Feel the Mountains Tremble" from CCLI.

✩ Story, Laura. "Blessings" from CCLI.

Music for the Day
Choral

p   Brahms, Johannes. "Let Grief Not Overwhelm You" from *Chantry Choirbook*. SATB, org. AFP 9780800657772.

Farrar, Sue/arr. John Ness Beck. "Song of Joy." 2 pt, kybd. BP BP1214.

p   Haugen, Marty. "Now in This Banquet." 2 pt mxd, pno, gtr, 2 ww in C, assembly. GIA G-2918.

p ● Hopson, Hal. "O God, beyond All Praising." SATB, org, opt br qrt, timp, hb, assembly. AFP 9781451462418.

Children's Choir

Hildebrand, Kevin. "For You, O Lord, Have Delivered My Soul from Death." U, org. CPH 983866WEB.

p   Krunk, Kris. "Dance on the Water." U, pno. CG CGA1328.

p   Miller, Aaron David. "Psalm 30" from *Augsburg Easy Choirbook*, vol. 2. U, pno. AFP 9781451462104.

Keyboard / Instrumental

● Ashdown, Franklin D. "Healer of Our Every Ill" from *Augsburg Organ Library: Healing and Funeral*. Org. AFP 9781451462616.

● Sensmeier, Randall. "Healer of Our Every Ill" from *Ten Piano Essays*. Pno. GIA G-4856.

p ● Shaw, Timothy. "Thaxted" from *My Redeemer Lives*. Pno. AFP 9781451451795.

● Walther, Johann Gottfried. "Jesu, meine Zuversicht." Org. Various editions.

Handbell

p ● Larson, Lloyd. "O God beyond All Praising." 3-5 oct, L2. HOP 2632.

● McAninch, Diane. "Healer of Our Every Ill." 2-3 oct, L2. GIA G-7286.

p   Page, Anna Laura. "His Eye Is on the Sparrow." 3-5 oct, L3. CG CGB827.

Sunday, June 5

Boniface, Bishop of Mainz, missionary to Germany, martyr, died 754

Boniface (his name means "good deeds") was born Wynfrith in Devonshire, England. He was a Benedictine monk who at the age of thirty was called to missionary work among the Vandal tribes in Germany. His first missionary attempt was unsuccessful, but he returned two years later and was able to plant the gospel in an area filled with superstitious and violent practices. He led large numbers of Benedictine monks and nuns in establishing churches, schools, and seminaries. Boniface was also a reformer. He persuaded two rulers to call synods to put an end to the practice of selling church offices to the highest bidder. Boniface was preparing a group for confirmation on the eve of Pentecost when he and they were killed by a band of pagans.

Tuesday, June 7

Seattle, chief of the Duwamish Confederacy, died 1866

Noah Seattle was chief of the Suquamish tribe and later became chief of the Duwamish Confederacy, a tribal alliance. When the tribes were faced with an increasing number of white settlers, Seattle chose to live and work peacefully with them rather than engage in wars. After Seattle became a Roman Catholic, he began the practice of morning and evening prayer in the tribe, a practice that continued after his death. On the centennial of his birth, the city of Seattle—named for him against his wishes—erected a monument over his grave.

Thursday, June 9

Columba, died 597; Aidan, died 651; Bede, died 735; renewers of the church

These three monks from the British Isles were pillars among those who kept alive the light of learning and devotion during the Middle Ages. Columba founded three monasteries, including one on the island of Iona, off the coast of Scotland. That monastery was left in ruins after the Reformation but today is home to an ecumenical religious community. Aidan, who helped bring Christianity to the Northumbria area of England, was known for his pastoral style and ability to stir people to charity and good works. Bede was a Bible translator and scripture scholar. He wrote a history of the English church and was the first historian to date events *anno Domini* (A.D.), "year of our Lord." Bede is also known for his hymns, including "A Hymn of Glory Let Us Sing!" (ELW 393).

Saturday, June 11

Barnabas, Apostle

The Eastern church commemorates Barnabas as one of the Seventy commissioned by Jesus. Though he was not among the Twelve mentioned in the gospels, the book of Acts gives him the title of apostle. His name means "son of encouragement." When Paul came to Jerusalem after his conversion, Barnabas took him in over the fears of the other apostles, who doubted Paul's discipleship. Later, Paul and Barnabas traveled together on missions. At the Council of Jerusalem, Barnabas defended the claims of Gentile Christians in relation to the Mosaic law.

June 12, 2016
Time after Pentecost — Lectionary 11

The enormity of our sin is surpassed only by the mercy of God. We come, repentant, to the table of the Lord. In the body and blood of Jesus, in the announcement of our absolution, all our sins are forgiven. "Happy are they . . . whose sin is put away." Happy are we.

Prayer of the Day

O God, throughout the ages you judge your people with mercy, and you inspire us to speak your truth. By your Spirit, anoint us for lives of faith and service, and bring all people into your forgiveness, through Jesus Christ, our Savior and Lord.

Gospel Acclamation

Alleluia. In this is love, that God loved us and ǀ sent the Son* to be the atoning sacrifice ǀ for our sins. *Alleluia.* (1 John 4:10)

Readings and Psalm
2 Samuel 11:26—12:10, 13-15

King David seduced his neighbor Bathsheba and was responsible for the death of her husband, Uriah. God sends the prophet Nathan to confront the king. Nathan tells the king a parable and opens David's eyes to see his own guilt.

Psalm 32

Then you forgave me the guilt of my sin. (Ps. 32:5)

Galatians 2:15-21

Paul preaches on the power of God's grace to make us faithful. We are made right with God through Jesus Christ alone, through no work of our own. As a result, Christ's life has become our whole identity.

Luke 7:36—8:3

Through a dramatic encounter of rich and poor, righteous and sinner, Jesus teaches the relationship between receiving mercy and responding with a lavish outpouring of love. Jesus also provokes his host by claiming authority to forgive sins.

Semicontinuous reading and psalm
1 Kings 21:1-10 [11-14] 15-21a

Ahab and Jezebel ruled Israel in the days of Elijah. Misusing their royal power, they have Naboth the Jezreelite killed in order to seize the land that is his family inheritance. God sends the prophet Elijah to confront them with their sin.

Psalm 5:1-8

Lead me, Lord, in your righteousness; make your way straight before me. (Ps. 5:8)

Preface   Sundays

Color   Green

Prayers of Intercession

The prayers are prepared locally for each occasion. The following examples may be adapted or used as appropriate.

Let us pray for the church, those in need, and all of God's creation.

A brief silence.

Faithful God, inspire fidelity in your church. Guard it from temptation, and make it place of safety, welcome, and joy for all. Lord, in your mercy,

hear our prayer.

God of all that is, we encounter you not only in the grandeur of your creation, but in its smallest and quietest parts. Awaken us to your presence all around us. Lord, in your mercy,

hear our prayer.

God of power and might, call the nations of the world to recognize first your authority and justice. Guard all nations from unjust rulers, and bring forth your kingdom of righteousness and peace. Lord, in your mercy,

hear our prayer.

God of the lowly, help us recognize hospitality and generosity from unexpected sources, the humanity and goodness of those in prison, the faith and persistence of those who weep. Let our weakness be our strength. We pray especially for . . . . Lord, in your mercy,

hear our prayer.

God of new life, as you bring newcomers, visitors, and seekers into this assembly, give us hearts open to the new perspectives and gifts they bring. Lord, in your mercy,

hear our prayer.

Here other intercessions may be offered.

O God, you have called the saints your own. Gather us, with them, into your kingdom, in the promise of life forever with you. Lord, in your mercy,
hear our prayer.
We lift our prayers to you, O God, trusting your promise to hear us; through Jesus Christ our Lord.
Amen.

Images in the Readings

Probably because of his narrative skill, perhaps also because of the sexual overtones of his account, Luke's telling has become the most well known of the stories of **the anointing woman**. The title Christ means "the anointed one," and early baptisms included an anointing with scented oil, and so the several stories of Jesus being anointed by women were cited by the church fathers as pictures of baptism.

It was Pope Gregory in the seventh century who taught that this sinner woman was **Mary Magdalene**, although Luke 8:2 gives no hint that she was the character in the prior narrative. Yet the identification of Mary Magdalene as a prostitute had a long and successive run in Christian imagination. Recently the opposite use of sex—that Mary Magdalene was Jesus' wife—has gained popularity. Sex, sex, sex. Alas: can we stop this?

Luke lists "**some women**" who traveled with "the twelve" as part of Jesus' entourage as he traveled through Judea and Galilee. Scholars do not agree as to the historicity of such a traveling troupe.

According to Nathan's parable, in committing **adultery** with Uriah's wife, David is guilty of theft, which is emphasized over the murder of Uriah. That a man owns his wives just as he owns his sheep is seen also in the ninth and tenth commandments. The story does not apologize for a sexual ethic that we find foreign, even offensive. The Bible does not promulgate only one sexual ethic. Rather, the ethics of sex and marriage changed substantially over the centuries in which a nomadic people became urban dwellers. Christians do not agree as to how sexual ethics ought or ought not change in our time.

Ideas for the Day

◆   Jesus asks Simon, "Do you *see* this woman?" How well do we see our neighbors, or ourselves? Can we see like Jesus sees? Invite worshipers to sit in a spot different from their usual place. How does the view change? If your baptismal font is clear glass, invite children to gaze through the glass and water. Though the view itself may be blurred, this is how Jesus always sees us: through the waters of life. We are all children of God.

◆   The woman's gesture of love toward Jesus is lavish. Rarely are we this extravagant in our practice of faith in church. Maybe this is a good Sunday to pour abundant water into the font as people gather, or use rich, tasty bread and good wine at the eucharist. Maybe it is a good Sunday to use the order for healing and anoint the people with oil (*ELW*, pp. 276–278). Grocery store olive oil is perfect, perhaps lightly scented with bergamot (a citrusy, fresh scent). Just as you would come together to receive bread and wine, let the ushers guide people to worship assistants ready with oil and a towel. Each person can speak a request for prayer or receive a general blessing. As you make the sign of the cross on their foreheads or open palms, say, "May you be blessed, and may you be a blessing."

◆   Ephrem of Syria writes in the fourth century about the physical elements of worship that convey God's grace to us. Along with wine and bread, there is the beautiful oil. Notice how the oil, not the wine, is the element of joy in the final poetic line:

> Wheat, the olive and grapes, created for our use—
> the three of them serve You symbolically in three ways.
> With three medicines You healed our disease.
> Humankind had become weak and sorrowful and was failing.
> You strengthened her with Your blessed bread,
> and You consoled her with Your sober wine,
> and You made her joyful with Your holy chrism.
> ("Hymn 37," *Ephrem the Syrian: Hymns*, trans. Kathleen E. McVey [Mahwah, NJ: Paulist Press, 1989], 425)

Connections with the Liturgy

"Your sins are forgiven," calls out the pastor in the absolution, quoting Luke who is quoting Jesus (*ELW*, p. 96). At each confession and forgiveness, we join with the anointing woman to beg for forgiveness.

Let the Children Come

The gospel reading is filled with an abundance of tactile, sensual actions: bathing feet with tears and then wiping them with hair, anointing feet with precious moisturizers, kissing. These are the gestures that parents offer their young children: they bathe, dry, moisten, and kiss. All these actions done with love are signs of a parent's care for the life of this child. So it is in the liturgy. God comes to us and reveals a father's or a mother's love through simple actions: bathing, anointing, kissing. What is the fear that prevents so many of our churches from engaging in this evangelization of all the senses?

Assembly Song
Gathering

Praise the Lord! O heavens   ELW 823, LBW 540
Many and great, O God   ELW 837, WOV 794
Praise ye the Lord   ELW 872

Psalmody and Acclamations

Cooney, Rory. "I Turn to You" from PCY, vol. 4.

Helgen, John. "Psalm 32" from *ChildrenSing Psalms*. U, assembly, kybd.

Isele, David Clark/Hal H. Hopson. "Psalm 32" from TP.

+ Post, Marie. "Hear, O Lord, My Urgent Prayer" (alternate tune: PATMOS) from LUYH.

(GA) ELW 175 with proper verse for Lectionary 11 (tone in *ELW Accompaniment Edition: Service Music and Hymns*).

Hymn of the Day

How clear is our vocation, Lord   ELW 580   REPTON

O Jesus, joy of loving hearts   ELW 658, LBW 356   WALTON

O Christ, our hope   ELW 604, LBW 300   LOBT GOTT, IHR CHRISTEN

Offering

Change my heart, O God   ELW 801, W&P 28

Create in me a clean heart   ELW 188

Communion

There's a wideness in God's mercy   ELW 587/588, LBW 290

Just a closer walk with thee   ELW 697, TFF 253

Abide, O dearest Jesus   ELW 539, LBW 263

Sending

Sing praise to God, the highest good   ELW 871, LBW 542

Salvation unto us has come   ELW 590, LBW 297

Additional Assembly Songs

By grace we have been saved   W&P 25, ASG 4

If I have wounded any soul today   TFF 170

En el hambre   LLC 448

⊕ Park, Chung Kwan. "To My Precious Lord" from *Glory to God*. U. WJK 9780664238971.

⊕ Punjabi melody. "I'll Teach and Instruct You the Way You Should Go" from *Sound the Bamboo*. U. GIA G-6830.

✿ Hall, Mark/Matthew West. "Jesus, Friend of Sinners" from CCLI.

✿ Houston, Joel/Jonas Myrin. "Broken Vessels (Amazing Grace)" from CCLI.

✿ MacIntosh/Jonathan/Sarah MacIntosh/Vicky Beeching. "Salvation Day" from CCLI.

✿ Redman, Matt. " I Will Offer Up My Life" from CCLI.

✿ Scott, Kathryn. "Hungry" from CCLI.

✿ Tomlin, Chris/Ed Cash/Stephen Conley Sharp. "Made to Worship" from CCLI.

Music for the Day
Choral

p Bouman, Paul. "O God of Love" from *To God Will I Sing: Vocal Solos for the Church Year*. Solo, kybd, C inst. AFP 9780800674335.

p Kidwell, Sally. "There's a Wideness in God's Mercy." SATB, pno. AFP 9781451451696.

p Larson, Lloyd. "I Then Shall Live" from *Women in Song IV*. SSA, pno. HOP 8581.

p Raney, Joel. "Faithfulness." SATB, pno. HOP C5834.

Children's Choir

Hopkins, Edward J./arr. Ken Berg. "Search Me, O God." U, pno. CG CGA1245.

p Miller, Aaron David. "I Know the Lord's Laid His Hand on Me." U, solo, pno. AFP 9781451421590.

Telemann, G. P./arr. Hal H. Hopson. "O Lord, You Know Me." U, kybd. HIN HMC 779.

Keyboard / Instrumental

p ● Lind, Richard. "Lobt Gott, ihr Christen" from *Introductions and Alternate Accompaniments for Piano*, vol. 6. Pno. AFP 9780800623647.

● Nelson, Ronald A. "Walton" from *Easy Hymn Settings for Organ*, vol. 3. Org. AFP 9781451462562.

p ● Organ, Anne Krentz. "Repton" from *In Heaven Above*. Pno. AFP 9781451401912.

● Powell, Robert J. "Repton" from *Augsburg Organ Library: Autumn*. Org. AFP 9780800675790.

Handbell

p Gramann, Fred. "Jubilation." 3-6 oct, L2+. CG CGB833.

p Rogers, Sharon Elery. "My Heart Ever Faithful." 2-3 oct, L1+. CG CGB522.

Waugh, Timothy. "Repton Reminiscence." 2-3 oct, L2. ALF 42905.

Tuesday, June 14

Basil the Great, Bishop of Caesarea, died 379; Gregory, Bishop of Nyssa, died around 385; Gregory of Nazianzus, Bishop of Constantinople, died around 389; Macrina, teacher, died around 379

The three men in this group are known as the Cappadocian fathers; all three explored the mystery of the Holy Trinity. Basil was influenced by his sister Macrina to live a monastic life, and he settled near the family estate in Caesarea. Basil's Longer Rule and Shorter Rule for monastic life are the basis for Eastern monasticism to this day, and express a preference for communal monastic life over that of hermits. Gregory of Nazianzus (nah-zee-AN-zus) was sent to preach on behalf of the Orthodox faith against the Arians in Constantinople, though the Orthodox did not have a church there at the time. He defended Orthodox trinitarian and Christological doctrine, and his preaching won over the city.

Gregory of Nyssa (NISS-uh) was the younger brother of Basil the Great. He is remembered as a writer on spiritual life and the contemplation of God in worship and sacraments.

Macrina (muh-CREE-nuh) was the older sister of Basil and Gregory of Nyssa. She received an excellent education centered on the Bible, and when her fiancé died she devoted herself to the pursuit of Christian perfection. She was a leader of a community, based at the family estate, dedicated to asceticism, meditation, and prayer. Macrina's teaching was influential within the early church.

June 19, 2016
Time after Pentecost — Lectionary 12

This Sunday's texts paint startling pictures of the horrific—the demonic—nature of sin. The church's repeated celebration of the holy communion counters that tragic reality in a continued showing forth of the death of Jesus "until he comes." It is a dramatic declaration of "how much God has done for you."

Prayer of the Day

O Lord God, we bring before you the cries of a sorrowing world. In your mercy set us free from the chains that bind us, and defend us from everything that is evil, through Jesus Christ, our Savior and Lord.

Gospel Acclamation

Alleluia. Return ᵻ to your home,* and declare how much God has ᵻ done for you. *Alleluia.* (Luke 8:29)

Readings and Psalm
Isaiah 65:1-9

The prophet announces God's impatience. The people's self-absorption is idolatry, and images from pagan worship fill this reading. Like a vintner who crushes the grape to release the wine, God will use Israel's exile to establish a new community of the faithful.

Psalm 22:19-28

In the midst of the assembly I will praise you. (Ps. 22:22)

Galatians 3:23-29

For Paul, baptism is a powerful bond that unites people not only with God but with other believers. Those who call themselves children of God experience a transformation that removes prejudices of race, social class, or gender in favor of true unity in Christ.

Luke 8:26-39

Jesus' mission includes foreigners, and his authority extends to the casting out of demons. Some who witness Jesus' work are seized with confusion and fear, but the man who was healed is commissioned to give testimony of God's mercy and power.

Semicontinuous reading and psalm
1 Kings 19:1-4 [5-7] 8-15a

Elijah has defeated the prophets of Baal through the power of the Lord. Now, fleeing from Queen Jezebel, Elijah comes to Mount Horeb (another name for Sinai). God appears to him there not in power but in "a sound of sheer silence" and reassures him that he is not alone.

Psalms 42 and 43

Send out your light and truth, that they may lead me. (Ps. 43:3)

Preface   Sundays

Color   Green

Prayers of Intercession

The prayers are prepared locally for each occasion. The following examples may be adapted or used as appropriate.
Let us pray for the church, those in need, and all of God's creation.
A brief silence.
Gracious God, we pray for the church. *A brief silence.* Keep it faithful to you, so that your people here stand in witness to proclaim how much you have done for us in Jesus Christ. Lord, in your mercy,
hear our prayer.
We pray for the well-being of creation. *A brief silence.* Tend and nurture plants and animals, lands, seas, and skies.

Restore the vitality of lands and waters suffering from human misuse or natural disaster (*here specific concerns may be named*). Lord, in your mercy,
hear our prayer.

We pray for the nations. *A brief silence.* Work in and through governments, humanitarian organizations, and local partnerships to cast out the forces of evil and establish your life and peace. Lord, in your mercy,
hear our prayer.

We pray for all who suffer in body, mind, or spirit. *A brief silence.* Be with those who know demons of any kind, and clothe them with Christ's freedom and healing. Lord, in your mercy,
hear our prayer.

We pray for this congregation. *A brief silence.* Establish and renew our faith, strengthen our ministries (*especially*), and bless those preparing for baptism. Bless fathers and all who provide fatherly care in their vocation to raise up our children in love. Lord, in your mercy,
hear our prayer.

Here other intercessions may be offered.

O God, you have called the saints your own. Gather us, with them, into your kingdom, in the promise of life forever with you. Lord, in your mercy,
hear our prayer.

We lift our prayers to you, O God, trusting your promise to hear us; through Jesus Christ our Lord.
Amen.

Images in the Readings

Clothing the naked is one image for baptism. Evidence suggests that in the church's early centuries candidates were indeed baptized naked and then clothed in white. Contemporary albs are such white garments worn by the baptized. Some assemblies clothe their newly baptized in white, and at least infants can be baptized naked and thus become symbols for us all. This story recalls Genesis 3, in which God presumably kills some animals to get their skins to make clothes for the naked man and woman. In the parable of the prodigal son, the forgiving father clothes his son in "the best" robe. In today's second reading, Paul speaks of baptism as being clothed with Christ. Moreover, clothing the naked is often cited in the New Testament as one task given to the Christian community.

Scholars have suggested various proposals regarding the original purpose behind the Old Testament's kosher laws, which rendered **pigs** unclean. Anthropologists write that all cultures define what is appropriate for their tribe by delineating also what is alien, harmful, unclean. Jewish readers of this story (Matt. 8:28-34; Mark 5:1-20; Luke 8:26-39) may have noted that Jesus is kinder to the demons than to the pigs.

These readings are filled with reference to **outsiders**: Canaanite religious practice, a naked madman, a cemetery, the Roman legions, a swineherd. However, Paul calls Christians to live as if the outsider—the Greek, the slave, the woman—is one with the insider—the Jew, the free, the man. It is not surprising that many slaveholders of the antebellum South did not allow their slaves to be baptized, for that would have rendered the slave as one with the slave owner.

Ideas for the Day

◆ "Clothed and in his right mind," like many colloquialisms, has its origin in scripture. This well-used phrase often omits the part that precedes it: "They found the man from whom the demons had gone sitting at the feet of Jesus" (Luke 8:35). Clothed in the garment of baptism, we are in our "right mind" when we sit at Jesus' feet. Having the right mind may look a great deal like having the mind of Christ who emptied himself in love and took the form of a servant. And like the healed Gerasene, we tell others about Jesus and what Jesus has done for us.

◆ This is another appropriate day to consider using the order for healing following the hymn of the day (*ELW*, pp. 276–278). We often come bound in shackles and chains. Through the laying on of hands, prayer, and anointing, we receive the healing touch of Christ with these powerful words: "Father . . . drive away all sickness of body and spirit; make whole that which is broken; deliver [us] from the power of evil; preserve [us] in true faith, to share in the power of Christ's resurrection and to serve you with all the saints now and evermore" (*ELW*, p. 277).

◆ Jesus unbinds us in order that we may be bound! Freedom is discovered in Christian community where there are no distinctions and we are bound together in love. The hymn "No Longer" by Carolyn Winfrey Gillette is based on the reading from Galatians and proclaims the good news (www.carolynshymns.com/no_longer.html). The composer notes that divisiveness diverts us from our true calling to serve and work as one and "the life we live together is an answered prayer."

Connections with the Liturgy

In the sending at the close of each service of holy communion (*ELW*, pp. 93, 114–115), we are sent to return to our home and declare how much God has done for us. "Go in peace. Share the good news."

Let the Children Come

We often mistakenly think that in order for the church to be united, we must all agree. Because there is no longer Jew or Greek, slave or free, male or female (Gal. 3:28), we think that we must agree in all things. In so thinking, we mistake differences for divisions. Christ has not done away with our differences. Christ has overcome the power of our differences to divide us. The church is united not by the fact that we are all the same, but because Christ Jesus has made us all children of God through faith (Gal. 3:26). Children are not too young to understand that disagreeing is not the same as being divided.

Assembly Song
Gathering

The people walk   ELW 706, LLC 520
Rise, shine, you people   ELW 665, LBW 393
Drawn to the Light   ELW 593

Psalmody and Acclamations

Mummert, Mark. "Psalm 22:19-28," Refrain 2, from PSCY.
Schalk, Carl. "Psalm 22:19-28" from PWC.
+ Joncas, Michael. "As the Deer." Cant, SATB, assembly, org, opt str, ww, hp. GIA G-4883.
(GA) ELW 175 with proper verse for Lectionary 12 (tone in *ELW Accompaniment Edition: Service Music and Hymns*).

Hymn of the Day

Praise the One who breaks the darkness   ELW 843   NETTLETON
God, my Lord, my strength   ELW 795, LBW 484   PÁN BỬH
We come to you for healing, Lord   ELW 617   MARTYRDOM

Offering

Just as I am, without one plea   ELW 592, LBW 296
When we are living   ELW 639, LLC 462

Communion

When pain of the world surrounds us   ELW 704
I heard the voice of Jesus say   ELW 332/611, LBW 497, TFF 62
Lord of our life   ELW 766, LBW 366

Sending

God of grace and God of glory   ELW 705, LBW 415
Lead me, guide me   ELW 768, TFF 70, W&P 84

Additional Assembly Songs

I heard an old, old, story   TFF 97
Do, Lord, remember me   TFF 178
¿Por qué te nombro con miedo?   LLC 449
⊕ Anon. "We Are All One in Christ/Somos uno en Cristo." U. ELW 643.
⊕✿ Bell, John L. "One Is the Body" from *One Is the Body: Songs of Unity and Diversity*. SATB. GIA G-5790.
✿ Fielding, Ben/Sam Knock. "The Lost Are Found" from CCLI.
✿ Getty, Keith/Kristyn Getty/Stuart Townend. "Come, People of the Risen King" from CCLI.

✿ Getty, Keith/Kristyn Getty/Stuart Townend. "Creation Sings the Father's Song" from CCLI.
✿ Ingram, Jason/Reuben Morgan. "Forever Reign" from CCLI.
✿ Tomlin, Chris. "We Fall Down" from CCLI.

Music for the Day
Choral

Highben, Zebulon. "O God of Light." SATB, org, tpt, opt assembly. AFP 9781451462425.
Kemmer, George. "There Is a Balm in Gilead." SSA, pno. ECS 1.1990.
Mendelssohn, Felix/ed. Robert Van Howten. "As the Deer Longs." SAB, kybd. MSM CH-1115.
Shaw, Timothy. "Come, Thou Fount of Every Blessing." SAB, kybd. MSM 50-5310.

Children's Choir

Kosche, Kenneth T. "Bless God's Holy Name." 2 pt, kybd, opt hb. CG CGA766.
Parker, Alice. "Lord, Thou Hast Searched Me." U, kybd. HIN HMC 456.
p Powell, Susan. "I Praise the God of Grace." U, pno. CG CGA1300.

Keyboard / Instrumental

● Carlson, J. Bert. "Nettleton" from *Let It Rip! at the Piano*, vol. 1. Pno. AFP 9780800659066.
● Near, Gerald. "Nettleton" from *Laudes Domini*, vol. 2. Org. MSM 10-349.
p ● Roschke, Ronald. "Pán Bửh" from *Yours Is the Glory*. Org. AFP 9781451420876.
● Scheer, Greg. "Nettleton" from *Piano Plus Through the Year*, vol. 2. Pno, inst. AFP 9780800663728.

Handbell

● Morris, Hart. "Come, Thou Fount of Every Blessing." 3-6 oct, L4-. AGEHR AG36019.
p Page, Anna Laura. "God Is Our Refuge and Strength." 3-6 oct hb, opt fl, opt tpt, L3, CG CGB846. Opt SATB with pno and U voices, CG CGA1381. Opt full score, CG CGB845.
● Thompson, Karen. "What Shall I Render?" 3 or 5 oct hb, opt 3 oct hc, L3. ALF 42908.

⊕ = global song   ✿ = praise song   + = semicontinuous psalm
● = relates to hymn of the day   p = available in Prelude Music Planner

Tuesday, June 21

Onesimos Nesib, translator, evangelist, died 1931

Onesimos Nesib (oh-NESS-ee-mus neh-SEEB) was born into the Oromo people of Ethiopia. He was captured by slave traders and taken from his homeland to Eritrea, where he was bought, freed, and educated by Swedish missionaries. He translated the Bible into Oromo and returned to his homeland to preach the gospel. His tombstone includes a verse from Jeremiah 22:29, "O land, land, land, hear the word of the Lord!"

Friday, June 24

John the Baptist

The birth and life of John the Baptist are celebrated exactly six months before Christmas Eve. For Christians in the Northern Hemisphere, these two dates are deeply symbolic. John said that he must decrease as Jesus increased. According to tradition, John was born as the days are longest and then steadily decrease, while Jesus was born as the days are shortest and then steadily increase. In many countries this day is celebrated with customs associated with the summer solstice.

Saturday, June 25

Presentation of the Augsburg Confession, 1530

On this day in 1530 the German and Latin editions of the Augsburg Confession were presented to Emperor Charles of the Holy Roman Empire. The Augsburg Confession was written by Philipp Melanchthon and endorsed by Martin Luther and consists of a brief summary of points in which the reformers saw their teaching as either agreeing with or differing from that of the Roman Catholic Church of the time. In 1580 when the *Book of Concord* was drawn up, the unaltered Augsburg Confession was included as the principal Lutheran confession.

Philipp Melanchthon, renewer of the church, died 1560

Though he died on April 19, Philipp Melanchthon (meh-LAHNK-ton) is commemorated today because of his connection with the Augsburg Confession. Colleague and co-reformer with Martin Luther, Melanchthon was a brilliant scholar, known as "the teacher of Germany." The University of Wittenberg hired him as its first professor of Greek, and there he became a friend of Luther. Melanchthon was a popular professor—even his classes at six in the morning had as many as six hundred students. As a reformer he was known for his conciliatory spirit and for finding areas of agreement with fellow Christians. He was never ordained.

June 26, 2016

Time after Pentecost — Lectionary 13

We have no good apart from God. That makes our Lord's call to follow him an invitation to freedom. This is freedom to revel in the Spirit's fruits: love, joy, peace, patience, and the like. This is the path of life.

Prayer of the Day

Sovereign God, ruler of all hearts, you call us to obey you, and you favor us with true freedom. Keep us faithful to the ways of your Son, that, leaving behind all that hinders us, we may steadfastly follow your paths, through Jesus Christ, our Savior and Lord.

Gospel Acclamation

Alleluia. Lord, to whom ¹ shall we go?* You have the words of e- ¹ ternal life. *Alleluia.* (John 6:68)

Readings and Psalm

1 Kings 19:15-16, 19-21

In the story preceding today's reading, the prophet Elijah flees for his life to the security of God's mountain. There the Lord reveals to Elijah that there are still other faithful people in Israel and commissions him to anoint new leaders, including his own successor, Elisha.

Psalm 16

I have set the LORD always before me. (Ps. 16:8)

Galatians 5:1, 13-25

For Paul, the freedom Christ gives is not permission to do whatever we want. It is the invitation to be what we could not be otherwise. The power and guidance of Christ's Holy Spirit produce a different kind of life, one marked by the fruit of this Holy Spirit.

Luke 9:51-62

Jesus is unwavering in his commitment to his mission in Jerusalem and will not be swayed by pettiness. In a series of striking cases in point, he calls his disciples to a similar single-mindedness.

Semicontinuous reading and psalm

2 Kings 2:1-2, 6-14

Elijah's ministry is finished as he is taken up into heaven, and a new chapter begins as Elisha inherits the mantle and the spirit of his teacher. Like the great prophet Moses before

them, both Elijah and Elisha part a body of water through the power of the Lord.

Psalm 77:1-2, 11-20

By your strength you have redeemed your people. (Ps. 77:15)

Preface Sundays

Color Green

Prayers of Intercession

The prayers are prepared locally for each occasion. The following examples may be adapted or used as appropriate.

Let us pray for the church, those in need, and all of God's creation.

A brief silence.

Anointing God, you commission us for our ministry in daily life. You also call us to pass our faith and ministry on to the next generation. Inspire us in our equipping of others. Lord, in your mercy,
hear our prayer.

God of creation, you have given us all we need. Inspire us to honor your creation as an inheritance and trust. Lord, in your mercy,
hear our prayer.

God of the nations, the distractions of the world draw our attention away from you. Refocus us in our commitment to your ways and the justice you desire for the world. Lord, in your mercy,
hear our prayer.

Through the fruits of your Spirit, make us healers in the world. Bring love, joy, peace, patience, kindness, generosity, faithfulness, gentleness, and self-control into the lives of all in need. We pray especially for . . . . Lord, in your mercy,
hear our prayer.

Steadfast God, guide this congregation by your Spirit. Make us neighbors to each other, ready to be and receive strangers, and show us how to love our neighbors as you intend. Lord, in your mercy,
hear our prayer.

Here other intercessions may be offered.

O God, you have called the saints your own. Gather us, with them, into your kingdom, in the promise of life forever with you. Lord, in your mercy,

hear our prayer.

We lift our prayers to you, O God, trusting your promise to hear us; through Jesus Christ our Lord.

Amen.

Images in the Readings

All three readings assume that the hearer knows that oxen are **yoked** together to **plow** fields. Elisha is called away from plowing his fields, and he burns up the yokes; Paul refers to our being yoked to a law that cannot save; and Jesus likens the life of proclaiming the kingdom to plowing a field. Our task is to bring vibrancy to these images, which are so distant from most of our worshipers.

In Genesis, God does send **fire** down from heaven to destroy wicked cities. Luke calls believers to refrain from such retribution and instead to move on to another village. The fire that Luke describes is the illumination on the forehead of each believer's head at Pentecost.

Many Christian artists depicted the tree of life filled with the **fruit of the Spirit**: on the branches each fruit was labeled "love," "joy," "peace," and so on. In 1845, Nathaniel Currier also drew *The Tree of Death*, on which hung fruit corresponding to Paul's list of vices.

Ideas for the Day

♦ Søren Kierkegaard once said that Jesus wants followers not admirers. How do we make that leap? Perhaps this is a good time to unpack the questions surrounding holy baptism, such as the baptismal renunciations (*ELW*, p. 229) and the Affirmation of Christian Vocation, "Will you endeavor to pattern your life on the Lord Jesus, in gratitude to God and in service to others, at morning and evening, at work and at play, all the days of your life?" (*ELW*, p. 84). What are we called to leave behind? What does it look like to pattern our lives after Jesus to serve others in all aspects of life? How is being yoked to Jesus a life of radical freedom?

♦ In the movie *Chocolat* (Miramax, 2000), the mayor of a small French town has tight control over just about everything, including forced fasting and abstinence during Lent. He even writes the sermons for the priest. A woman comes to town and opens a chocolate shop. People secretly visit during Lent. In the end, the mayor, in his attempt to disband her work, surrenders to his own need for control and discovers a new kind of freedom. When freed from the need to be right, we are free to live for others and follow Jesus in the radical adventure of putting people before protocol. For freedom Christ has set us free!

♦ "A Christian is a perfectly free lord of all, subject to none. A Christian is a perfectly dutiful servant of all, subject to all" (Martin Luther, *On the Freedom of a Christian* [1520]).

Connections with the Liturgy

Thanksgiving at the Table VII (*ELW*, p. 67) asks God to "nurture in us the fruits of the Spirit, that we may be a living tree, sharing your bounty with all the world." Also, the listing of sins we confess in the order for corporate confession and forgiveness (*ELW*, p. 240) is an elaboration of Paul's list in Galatians 5. Both options for the words of forgiveness (p. 241) invoke the Holy Spirit as the power to reject such a life of "flesh" for the new life of baptism.

Let the Children Come

"If we live by the Spirit, let us also be guided by the Spirit" (Gal. 5:25). A farmer can't plow a straight line if he or she is looking backward. We can't follow Jesus if we are distracted by things around us that get us off track. It is important to trust that God will provide for us and the Holy Spirit will lead us on the journey. Invite a few children to wear blindfolds and a few others (who can be trusted with this responsibility) to lead them around. The blindfolded ones must trust their guides to lead them in a way that will keep them safe as God does for us.

Assembly Song
Gathering

Holy Spirit, ever dwelling ELW 582, LBW 523
Come, follow me, the Savior spake ELW 799, LBW 455
Oh, that I had a thousand voices ELW 833, LBW 560

Psalmody and Acclamations

Hopson, Hal H. "Psalm 16" from TP.
Wise, Raymond. "Thirteenth Sunday in Ordinary Time / C" from LP:LG.
+ True, Lori. "I Cry Before You." SATB, cant, assembly, gtr, kybd, C inst, vc. GIA G-5189.
(GA) ELW 175 with proper verse for Lectionary 13 (tone in *ELW Accompaniment Edition: Service Music and Hymns*).

Hymn of the Day

The Son of God, our Christ ELW 584, LBW 434 *SURSUM CORDA*
Come down, O Love divine ELW 804, LBW 508 *DOWN AMPNEY*
O Master, let me walk with you ELW 818, LBW 492 *MARYTON*

Offering

Beloved, God's chosen ELW 648, OBS 48
Draw us in the Spirit's tether ELW 470, WOV 703

Communion

O Jesus, I have promised   ELW 810, LBW 503

Let us ever walk with Jesus   ELW 802, LBW 487

Oh, that the Lord would guide my ways   ELW 772, LBW 480

Sending

Rise, O church, like Christ arisen   ELW 548, OBS 76

Oh, happy day when we shall stand   ELW 441, LBW 351

Additional Assembly Songs

Freedom is coming   TFF 46

God has smiled on me   TFF 190

What have we to offer?   W&P 156, DH 20

- South African. "Freedom Is Coming" from *Glory to God*. SATB. WJK 9780664238971.
- Swaziland melody. "We Will Walk with God/Sizohamba naye" from *Glory to God*. SATB. WJK 9780664238971.
- Brown, Brenton/Glenn Robertson. "All Who Are Thirsty" from CCLI.
- Cash, Ed/Jack Mooring/Leeland Mooring. "Follow You" from CCLI.
- Houston, Joel/Matt Crocker. "Search My Heart" from CCLI.
- Ligertwood, Brooke. "Lord of Lords" from CCLI.
- Rohman, Chris/Jason Ingram/Matt Hammitt. "Lead Me" from CCLI.
- Tomlin, Chris/Jason Ingram/Reuben Morgan. "I Will Follow" from CCLI.

Music for the Day
Choral

p   Cain, Robin/Phil Kadidlo. "Peace, Perfect Peace" from *With All My Heart: Contemporary Vocal Solos*, vol. 1. Solo, kybd. AFP 9780800676841.

- Hopson, Hal. "O Master, Let Me Walk with You." SATB, kybd, opt vln, vla or vc. MSM 50-9212.

p   Miller, Aaron David. "Psalm 30: I Will Exalt You, O My Lord" from *Augsburg Easy Choirbook*, vol. 2. U, pno. AFP 9780800677510.

p   Toolan, Suzanne. "The Call." SATB, opt kybd. GIA G-5326.

Children's Choir

Archer, Malcolm. "Gracious Spirit, Holy Ghost." 2 pt, kybd. GIA G-6492.

Buxtehude, Dieterich/arr. Michael Burkhardt. "My Jesus Makes My Heart Rejoice." U, pno, 2 vln, cont. CG CGA1356.

Marshall, Jane. "Dear Lord, Lead Me Day by Day." U, kybd, opt fl. CG CGA637

Keyboard / Instrumental

- Raabe, Nancy M. "Sursum corda" from *Grace and Peace*, vol. 2. Pno. AFP 9780800679019.
- Sedio, Mark. "Down Ampney" from *Augsburg Organ Library: Easter*. Org. AFP 9780800659363.

p ● Sedio, Mark. "Maryton" from *Come and Praise*, vol. 1. Org. AFP 9780800678500.

p ● Wonacott, Glenn. "Down Ampney" from *Introductions and Alternate Accompaniments for Piano*, vol. 9. Pno. AFP 9780800623678.

Handbell

- McChesney, Kevin. "O Master, Let Me Walk with Thee." 3-5 oct, L1. JEF JHS9419.
- Stephenson, Valerie. "Christ of the Upward Way." 3-5 oct hb, opt 3 oct hc, L2+. LOR 20/1202L.
- Wissinger, Kathleen. "Sketches on 'Down Ampney.'" 3-6 oct, L3+. LOR 20/1428L.

Monday, June 27
Cyril, Bishop of Alexandria, died 444

Remembered as an outstanding theologian as well as a contentious personality, Cyril defended the orthodox teachings about the person of Christ against Nestorius, bishop of Constantinople. Nestorius taught that the divine and human natures of Christ were entirely distinct, and therefore Mary could not be referred to as the *theotokos*, or bearer of God. This conflict, which also had roots in a rivalry for preeminence between Alexandria and Constantinople, involved all of the major Christian leaders of the time, including the patriarchs of Rome, Antioch, and Jerusalem, and finally also the emperor. In the end it was decided that Cyril's interpretation, that Christ's person included both divine and human natures, was correct.

Tuesday, June 28
Irenaeus, Bishop of Lyons, died around 202

Irenaeus (ee-ren-AY-us) believed that the way to remain steadfast to the truth was to hold fast to the faith handed down from the apostles. He believed that only Matthew, Mark, Luke, and John were trustworthy gospels. Irenaeus was an opponent of gnosticism and its emphasis on dualism. As a result of his battles with the gnostics, he was one of the first to speak of the church as "catholic." By catholic he meant that local congregations did not exist by themselves but were linked to one another in the whole church. He also maintained that this church was not contained within any national boundaries. He argued that the church's message was for all people, in contrast to the gnostics and their emphasis on "secret knowledge."

⊕ = global song   ☼ = praise song   + = semicontinuous psalm

● = relates to hymn of the day   p = available in Prelude Music Planner

Wednesday, June 29

Peter and Paul, Apostles

These two are an odd couple of biblical witnesses to be brought together in one commemoration. It appears that Peter would have gladly served as the editor of Paul's letters: in a letter attributed to him, Peter says that some things in Paul's letters are hard to understand. Paul's criticism of Peter is more blunt. In Galatians he points out ways that Peter was wrong. One of the things that unites Peter and Paul is the tradition that says they were martyred together on this date in 67 or 68. What unites them more closely is their common confession of Jesus Christ. Together Peter and Paul lay a foundation and build the framework for our lives of faith through their proclamation of Jesus Christ.

Friday, July 1

Catherine Winkworth, died 1878; John Mason Neale, died 1866; hymn translators

Neale was an English priest associated with the movement for church renewal at Cambridge. Winkworth lived most of her life in Manchester, where she was involved in promoting women's rights. These two hymn writers translated many hymn texts into English. Catherine Winkworth devoted herself to the translation of German hymns, nineteen of which are included in *Evangelical Lutheran Worship*; the fourteen hymn translations of John Mason Neale in the collection represent his specialization in ancient Latin and Greek hymns.

July 3, 2016
Time after Pentecost — Lectionary 14

God is the source of our nourishment. Our Lord's invitation to "take and eat . . . take and drink" is a repeated one. In the holy eucharist, in the word read and proclaimed, in the assembly of the people of God, the dominion of God has come near. Rejoice! Your name is written in heaven.

Prayer of the Day

O God, the Father of our Lord Jesus, you are the city that shelters us, the mother who comforts us. With your Spirit accompany us on our life's journey, that we may spread your peace in all the world, through your Son, Jesus Christ, our Savior and Lord.

Gospel Acclamation

Alleluia. Let the peace of Christ rule | in your hearts,* and let the word of Christ dwell | in you richly. *Alleluia.* (Col. 3:15, 16)

Readings and Psalm
Isaiah 66:10-14

Those who returned from the exile found that the hopes for the glorious restoration of Judah were not completely fulfilled. For these disappointed people, the prophet envisions salvation in the image of a nursing woman. Mother Jerusalem and a mothering God remind the community how they are sustained and supported.

Psalm 66:1-9

All the earth bows down before you and sings out your name. (Ps. 66:4)

Galatians 6:[1-6] 7-16

In the close of his letter to the Galatians, Paul encourages them to live as people made right with God through faith in Jesus Christ. Here Paul offers practical advice about how believers exercise common concern for one other in "the family of faith."

Luke 10:1-11, 16-20

Jesus commissions harvesters and laborers to go where he would go and do what he would do. Risking hardship and danger in exchange for the experience of great joy, they offer peace and healing as signs that the reign of God is near.

Semicontinuous reading and psalm
2 Kings 5:1-14

Naaman, a Syrian general, suffers from leprosy. In this passage Elisha miraculously cures his illness, but only after

Naaman realizes, with the help of his servants, that his real problem lies in his pride.

Psalm 30

My God, I cried out to you, and you restored me to health. (Ps. 30:2)

Preface   Sundays

Color   Green

Prayers of Intercession

The prayers are prepared locally for each occasion. The following examples may be adapted or used as appropriate.

Let us pray for the church, those in need, and all of God's creation.

A brief silence.

Gentle grower, send your church as laborers into your harvest. Make us joyful in sharing the good news of Jesus and make the harvest plentiful. Lord, in your mercy,
hear our prayer.

Creating God, bring about measured and healthy growth in fields and gardens through rain, wind, and sun. Lord, in your mercy,
hear our prayer.

Holy wisdom, you teach that we reap what we sow. Inspire leaders in our nation and throughout the world to sow the seeds of civility, peace, and goodwill. Lord, in your mercy,
hear our prayer.

Healer of all, we bring before you those in need of your healing presence. Do not be far off, but work your healing in the lives of all in need. We pray especially for . . . . Lord, in your mercy,
hear our prayer.

Holy friend, you call us to bear one another's burdens. Strengthen us in our commitment to the good of this congregation, our neighborhood, and our wider community. Lord, in your mercy,
hear our prayer.

Here other intercessions may be offered.

O God, you have called the saints your own. Gather us (*with the apostle Thomas*) into your kingdom, in the promise of life forever with you. Lord, in your mercy,
hear our prayer.

We lift our prayers to you, O God, trusting your promise to hear us; through Jesus Christ our Lord.
Amen.

Images in the Readings

Among the many images in today's readings (the city, breasts, a river, grass, law, loads, reaping, harvest, family,

circumcision, the cross, new creation, seventy, journey, lambs, wolves, heaven) are these:

During intertestamental times, Judaism popularized an alternative explanation for the origin of evil, to which Jesus refers (Luke 10:18). The sin of the first humans described in Genesis 3 only repeated among humankind the prior sin of the angels: some angels had wished to be like God, supported **Satan** in a rebellion, and after the "war in heaven" were expelled from the presence of God, going from the highest level of the universe to the lowest. For Luke, every instance of overcoming evil recalls God's victory over Satan. The earliest developed theory of atonement proposed that Satan had thought that because Christ was crucified, evil had won out, but the resurrection established Christ's victory over the forces of Satan. This theory is now more central to *The Lion, the Witch and the Wardrobe* than to most contemporary theologians.

In several biblical passages, **snakes** personify evil and incarnate the devil, perhaps because Canaanite religion depicted the goddess as a snake, whose shedding of its skin symbolized ongoing fertility. Still today the aboriginal religion of Australia depicts the creator deity as the rainbow serpent.

God is like a **mother**. For some Christians, this metaphor is disturbing, since it can be taken to contradict the traditional language of God as father. For other Christians, discovery of this passage is a gift of good news, the "gospel" reading for the day.

Ideas for the Day

◆   Today more people are on the move than at any other time in the history of the world. Whether motivated by the pull of opportunities generated by an increasingly global society or pushed by the inequalities and conflicts often exacerbated by that same phenomenon of globalization, this increased mobility brings both unprecedented opportunities and overwhelming challenges to our communities. On their first assignment, Jesus' disciples are sent out two by two; Jesus reminds them by this first mission that they are to be a people on the move—known as people of "the Way," called to take up their cross and follow. How does our own experience of mobility—moving to pursue a new job opportunity, following retirement, or following the breakup of a relationship—shape the way we hear Jesus' instructions to the disciples he sends out? How might it shape the way we receive those who are on the move coming into our communities?

◆   The Bible is filled with stories of people on the move. Similarly, many of our congregations have stories of immigrants who founded them or of moves following growth in the church or a moment of loss or crisis. Exploring these stories of earlier transitions can help us navigate the transitions we are confronting today. Together with Isaiah, who addressed people returning from exile, we can speak God's promise of comfort: "As a mother comforts her child, so I will comfort you; you shall be comforted in Jerusalem" (Isa. 66:13).

◆ Independence Day provides an opportunity to live in the tension between Jesus' call to his disciples to venture out with only the basics and God's promise to comfort the returning exiles. Independence and freedom are very much about opportunity, venturing out, setting one's own course. But they are also about protecting the rights of others, bearing one another's burdens (Gal. 6:2), recognizing as Martin Luther King Jr. did that "we are tied together in the single garment of destiny, caught in an inescapable network of mutuality. And whatever affects one directly affects all indirectly. For some strange reason I can never be what I ought to be until you are what you ought to be. This is the way God's universe is made; this is the way it is structured" ("Letter from Birmingham Jail," April 16, 1963).

Connections with the Liturgy

The rite for Blessing and Sending for Mission (*Occasional Services for the Assembly*, pp. 159–160) might be used this Sunday since the prayers apply Luke's description of the sending of the apostles to each of us.

Thanksgiving at the Table X (*ELW*, p. 69) acknowledges that no words we use when praising God are deep enough. So this thanksgiving describes God using opposite adjectives: God is mighty but also merciful. God is both majestic and motherly.

Let the Children Come

Today's reading from Isaiah images Jerusalem as a nursing mother, a mother who dandles her child on her knees. And God comforts us as a mother comforts her child (Isa. 66:13). Our assemblies include nursing infants, toddlers who delight us, and children who need comfort. Parents and caregivers need the love and support of the community of faith as they nurture their children in faith and prayer. Children need the love and support of this community, too, as they learn to trust God and grow in the Christian faith and life. How can each of us be a mothering, fathering presence in the lives of our congregation's children?

Assembly Song
Gathering

Rejoice, ye pure in heart ELW 873/874, LBW 553
Shout to the Lord ELW 821, W&P 124
All who hunger, gather gladly ELW 461

Psalmody and Acclamations

"Shout to the Ends of the Earth" from *Psallite* C-86 (verses 1-9). Cheri, Richard/Jalonda Robertson/arr. Thomas W. Jefferson. "Fourteenth Sunday in Ordinary Time / C" from LP:LG.

+ Daigle, Gary. "I Will Praise You, Lord" from PCY, vol. 4.
(GA) ELW 175 with proper verse for Lectionary 14 (tone in *ELW Accompaniment Edition: Service Music and Hymns*).

Hymn of the Day

To be your presence ELW 546 ENGELBERG
Lord, you give the great commission ELW 579, WOV 756 ABBOT'S LEIGH
Arise, my soul, arise! ELW 827, LBW 516 NYT YLÖS, SIELUNI

Offering

Mothering God, you gave me birth ELW 735, WOV 769
We plow the fields and scatter ELW 680/681, LLC 492, LBW 362, LS 102

Communion

O living Bread from heaven ELW 542, LBW 197
Here is bread ELW 483, W&P 58
Here I Am, Lord ELW 574, LS 138, TFF 230, WOV 752

Sending

The Spirit sends us forth to serve ELW 551, WOV 723
We all are one in mission ELW 576, WOV 755

Additional Assembly Songs

¡Vengan, vengan, vengan! LLC 389
Fill my cup, let it overflow TFF 127
In spirit and truth DH 73

⊕ Loh, I-to. "Sound a Mystic Bamboo Song" from *Glory to God*. SATB. WJK 9780664238971.

⊕ Zulu traditional. "We Will Follow/Somlandela" from *Worship and Song*. SATB. ABI 9781426709951.

✿ Angrisano, Steve/Tom Tomaszek. "Go Make a Difference" from CCLI.

✿ Boyd, Aaron/Andrew McCann/Ian Jordan/Peter Comfort/Peter Kernoghan/Richard Bleakley. "God of This City" from CCLI.

✿ Hall, Charlie/Kendall Combes. "Breathe" from CCLI.

✿ Hall, Charlie. "Salvation" from CCLI.

✿ Tomaszek, Tom. "Grateful" from CCLI.

✿ Tomlin, Chris/Ed Cash/Jesse Reeves. "Rejoice" from CCLI.

Music for the Day
Choral

p Grundahl, Nancy. "When I Survey the Wondrous Cross" from *Augsburg Choirbook for Women*. SSA, pno. AFP 9780800620370.

⊕ = global song   ✿ = praise song   + = semicontinuous psalm
● = relates to hymn of the day   p = available in Prelude Music Planner

p   Larson, Lloyd. "How Deep the Father's Love for Us" from
       Contemporary Classics for Two Voices. Solo/duet, pno. HOP
       8570.
p   Larson, Lloyd. "There Is an Everlasting Kindness (The Compassion
       Hymn)." SATB, pno, opt C inst. HOP C5803.
     Vasile, Paul. "Let All the World in Every Corner Sing." U, pno. MSM
       50-6405.

Children's Choir

     Rosebrock, Stephen. "Evening and Morning." 2 pt, kybd, fl. CPH
       983988WEB.
p   Scroggins, Debra. "An Instument of Thy Peace." 2 pt, pno. CG
       CGA1330.
     Sleeth, Natalie. "God Is Calling Us." U/2 pt, kybd. LOR 10/3767L.

Keyboard / Instrumental

●   Cherwien, David M. "Abbot's Leigh" from *Let It Rip! at the Piano*,
       vol. 2. Pno. AFP 9780800675806.
p ● Culli, Benjamin. "Abbot's Leigh" from *Praise the One*, vol. 3. Org.
       AFP 9781451424195.
p ● Kerr, J. Wayne. "Nyt ylös, sieluni" from *Organ Celebrations*. Org.
       AFP 9781451451740.
p ● Organ, Anne Krentz. "Engelberg" from *In Heaven Above*. Pno. AFP
       9781451401912.

Handbell

●   Afdahl, Lee. "Abbot's Leigh." 3-5 oct, L2+. HOP 2103.
●   Sherman, Arnold. "When in Our Music God Is Glorified." 3-6 oct
       hb, opt 3-4 oct hc, L3-, HOP 2414. Opt full score with br qnt,
       HOP 2414B. Opt org, HOP 2414P. Opt org and hb score, HOP
       2414D. Opt SATB, HOP 2414V.
     Tucker, Margaret. "Sunshine and Shadow." 3-5 oct hb, opt 2 oct hc,
       L3. CG CGB365.

Monday, July 4
Thomas, Apostle (transferred)

Thomas is perhaps best remembered as "Doubting Thomas." But alongside this doubt, the Gospel of John shows Thomas as fiercely loyal: "Let us also go, that we may die with him" (John 11:16). And John's gospel shows Thomas moving from doubt to deep faith. Thomas makes one of the strongest confessions of faith in the New Testament, "My Lord and my God!" (John 20:28). From this confession of faith, ancient stories tell of Thomas's missionary work to India, where Christian communities were flourishing a thousand years before the arrival of sixteenth-century missionaries.

Wednesday, July 6
Jan Hus, martyr, died 1415

Jan Hus was a Bohemian priest who spoke against abuses in the church of his day in many of the same ways Luther would a century later. He spoke against the withholding of the cup at the eucharist and because of this stance was excommunicated, not for heresy but for insubordination toward his archbishop. He preached against the selling of indulgences and was particularly mortified by the indulgence trade of two rival claimants to the papacy who were raising money for war against each other. He was found guilty of heresy by the Council of Constance and burned at the stake. The followers of Jan Hus became known as the Czech Brethren and eventually continued as the Moravian Church.

July 10, 2016
Time after Pentecost — Lectionary 15

To love the Lord your God with all your heart, soul, strength, and mind is to reflect God's mercy in responding to one's neighbor. That mercy found its most profound expression in the "gospel that has come to you"—namely the life, death, and resurrection of Jesus Christ. That gospel mercy comes to us again today: at the font, at the altar, and from the pulpit. It is very near to you.

Prayer of the Day

O Lord God, your mercy delights us, and the world longs for your loving care. Hear the cries of everyone in need, and turn our hearts to love our neighbors with the love of your Son, Jesus Christ, our Savior and Lord.

Gospel Acclamation

Alleluia. You shall love the Lord your God with ˡ all your heart,* and your neighbor ˡ as yourself. *Alleluia.* (Luke 10:27)

Readings and Psalm
Deuteronomy 30:9-14

Moses calls the people who are about to enter the promised land to renew the covenant God made with their ancestors. Through this covenant God gives life and asks for obedience. God's commandment is neither burdensome nor too far off, but dwells in the people's own hearts.

Psalm 25:1-10

Show me your ways, O Lᴏʀᴅ, and teach me your paths. (Ps. 25:4)

Colossians 1:1-14

The letter to the Colossians was written to warn its readers of various false teachings. The first part of the letter is an expression of thanks for the faith, hope, and love that mark this community, including a prayer for strength and courage from Paul.

Luke 10:25-37

Jesus is challenged to explain what is involved in obeying the greatest commandment. Jesus tells a parable rich in surprises: those expected to show pity display hard hearts while the lowly give and receive unexpected and lavish mercy.

Semicontinuous reading and psalm
Amos 7:7-17

Amos, a shepherd from the southern village of Tekoa, is called by God to preach against Israel, the Northern Kingdom, in a time of economic prosperity. Today's reading illustrates how Amos's stinging criticism of Israel alienated him from those in authority, including King Jeroboam and the priest Amaziah.

Psalm 82

Arise, O God, and rule the earth. (Ps. 82:8)

Preface   Sundays

Color   Green

Prayers of Intercession

The prayers are prepared locally for each occasion. The following examples may be adapted or used as appropriate.

Let us pray for the church, those in need, and all of God's creation.

A brief silence.

Gracious God, your word is very near to us, building up your church and keeping it faithful to your word. Make our witness to your love strong and clear. Lord, in your mercy,
hear our prayer.

God of creation, even the seas, the rocks, and the trees are our neighbors. Increase the vitality and beauty of your whole creation, and move us to work for its health and well-being. Lord, in your mercy,
hear our prayer.

Loving God, guide and direct the nations of the world to be good neighbors one to another, and to reach across the human barriers that divide us. Lord, in your mercy,
hear our prayer.

Protecting God, sustain police officers, firefighters, EMTs, and others who attend to public safety. Uphold those who are sick, injured, or who will die this day, and those who care for them. We pray especially for . . . . Lord, in your mercy,
hear our prayer.

Listening God, encourage this assembly in its ministries of prayer and service (*especially*). Enlarge our capacity for

hospitality and our willingness to welcome those who are not like us. Lord, in your mercy,
hear our prayer.
Here other intercessions may be offered.
O God, you have called the saints your own. Gather us, with them, into your kingdom, in the promise of life forever with you. Lord, in your mercy,
hear our prayer.
We lift our prayers to you, O God, trusting your promise to hear us; through Jesus Christ our Lord.
Amen.

Images in the Readings

Contemporary English retains many phrases that echo the King James translation of the Bible; one of the most commonly used is "a **good Samaritan**." Perhaps the fact that the story is so well known has encouraged preachers to turn the parable into an allegory that has numerous meanings. In one Christocentric interpretation, the good Samaritan is Christ, whose crucifixion has placed him outside the law, and yet who personifies mercy. If the good Samaritan is an image of Christ, we are the innkeepers, who are to care for the needy until Christ returns. July 11 is the commemoration of Benedict of Nursia, the sixth-century monk renowned for the inspiration that undergirds Benedictine religious communities. Part of Benedictine spirituality is the dictum that all visitors are welcomed as if they are Christ. Thus, every stranger is the man beaten by robbers whom we receive into our midst.

Much of our culture maintains the traditional expectation that one's **neighbor** is similar to oneself, whether in ethnicity, religion, or economic status. With this understanding, a neighborhood is an area that houses similar people, and this similarity affords people psychological comfort and identity support. Yet Luke's parable beckons us to a life of countercultural border crossing.

Both Deuteronomy and Colossians use the imagery of **fruit**. Each piece of fruit contains the seed, or is itself the seed, of new growth.

The Colossians reading includes the archetypal imagery of **darkness** as symbolic of evil and death. Recall that the synoptic gospels say that darkness accompanied the crucifixion; in John, the discourse in chapter 12 calls believers to live in the light. In today's reading, we have already been transferred out of darkness. Early Christians called baptism "enlightenment." It is important, however, to remember that if literalized, a symbol can have dangers: darkness is also a gift from God, a time for rest and growth.

Ideas for the Day

◆ With a "by invitation only" $2,500 annual fee, and a requirement to charge at least a quarter of a million dollars a year, the American Express Centurion card—known as

the "black card"—is a bit of a stretch for the average Joe. Membership has its benefits. In a world where resources are finite, who qualifies for "benefits" is a matter of extensive discussion. Many political lines are drawn along the question of who qualifies for the society's benefits. Keeping this in mind is helpful when approaching today's parable of the good Samaritan, as it helps us understand the importance of the question at the core of the story: "Who is my neighbor?" (Luke 10:29).

◆ Jesus' surprising use of the Samaritan in responding to the question of who the neighbor is—and therefore who qualifies for society's benefits according to Leviticus 19:18—muddies the water. Samaritans were outsiders but not clearly outsiders. They shared ancestry with the people of Israel and also shared their religious belief in the God of Abraham. When it comes to determining membership, Jesus is unwilling to make it a simple litmus test—a question of insider or outsider, Jew or Samaritan, legal or illegal. The question is one about individuals rather than stereotypes.

◆ Reflecting on this text, Jewish scholar Berel Dov Lerner writes, "The verse 'Love your neighbor as yourself' is not a slogan or proverb; it is a law which requires Jews to be as concerned for the welfare of their fellow Jew as they are for their own" ("Samaritans, Jews and Philosophers," www.academia.edu/150589/Samaritans_Jews_and_Philosophers). Jesus is looking to extend that high level of expectation to those of questionable origin, those whose status places them in a category they can never overcome. In our increasingly global society—where someone I don't even know makes my clothes, grows my food, and assembles my computer—I, too, must wrestle with the question: who, indeed, is my neighbor?

Connections with the Liturgy

The first option in *Evangelical Lutheran Worship* for a prayer of confession at the opening of weekly worship echoes today's gospel reading: "We have not loved [God] with our whole heart; we have not loved our neighbors as ourselves" (p. 95).

Let the Children Come

Who are our neighbors? Ask children about neighbors in their daily lives. Have they encountered people who are hurting at school or in the neighborhoods where they live? How did teachers, parents, or other adults help? Then broaden the definition of neighbors by showing pictures of people who live in your church's neighborhood and beyond. Ask how we can show Jesus' love to these neighbors. Teach children this simple sung refrain: "Jesu, Jesu, fill us with your love, show us how to serve the neighbors we have from you" (ELW 708).

Assembly Song

Gathering

Gather Us In ELW 532, WOV 718

Christ, Be Our Light ELW 715

Praise the Almighty! ELW 877, LBW 539

Psalmody and Acclamations

Cool, Jayne Southwick. "Psalm 25" from *ChildrenSing Psalms*. U/2 pt, assembly, kybd, opt perc.

Mathis, William H. Refrain for "Psalm 25" from *After the Prelude: Year A*. U/cant, hb. CG CGB658 (digital version), CGB659 (printed version). Use with ELW psalm tone 6 or 7 (in C).

Parker, Val. "Psalm 25: To You, O Lord, I Lift My Soul." SATB, assembly, kybd, gtr. OCP 21060.

+ Hopson, Hal. "Psalm 82" from TPP.

(GA) ELW 169 with proper verse for Lectionary 15.

Hymn of the Day

Lord, whose love in humble service ELW 712, LBW 423 BEACH SPRING

Will you let me be your servant ELW 659 THE SERVANT SONG

O God of mercy, God of light ELW 714, LBW 425 JUST AS I AM

Offering

The Word of God is source and seed ELW 506, WOV 658

Ubi caritas et amor ELW 642/653, WOV 665

Communion

Jesu, Jesu, fill us with your love ELW 708, LS 146, TFF 83, WOV 765

When we are living ELW 639, LLC 462

Build us up, Lord ELW 670

Sending

We Are Called ELW 720, LS 37, W&P 147

Lord of all nations, grant me grace ELW 716, LBW 419

Additional Assembly Songs

Su nombre es "El Señor" LLC 517

Toma mi mano, hermano LLC 390

Help me, Jesus TFF 224

⊕ Argentine folk melody. "May the God of Hope Go with Us/Canto de esperanza" from *Glory to God*. SATB. WJK 9780664238971.

⊕ Indian traditional. "Almighty God" from *Love and Anger: Songs of Lively Faith and Social Justice*. U. GIA G-4947.

✪ Brewster, Lincoln. "Love the Lord" from CCLI.

✪ Hall, Mark. "Lifesong" from CCLI.

✪ Hall, Charlie/Nathan Nockels/Stuart Townend. "Sending" from CCLI.

✪ Kendrick, Graham. "God of the Poor" from CCLI.

✪ Park, Andy, et al. "Friend of the Poor" from CCLI.

Music for the Day

Choral

p Anon. "Not unto Us, Lord" from *Augsburg Motet Book*. SAB. AFP 9781451423709.

p Butler, Eugene. "Hymn of Abundance." SATB, kybd. HOP C5822.

p ● Fleming, Larry L. "Humble Service." SATB. AFP 9780800646226.

p Merrill, William. "Rise Up, O Men of God." TTBB. AFP 9780800645731.

Children's Choir

Bach. J. S./arr. Stephen Roddy. "Rejoice, Ye Children of God." U, kybd, opt fl. FB JG2246.

p Patterson, Mark. "Come into God's Presence (Echo Song)" from *The Joy of Part Singing*. U/2 pt, kybd, metallophone, xyl. CG CGBK67.

Shaw, Timothy. "Teach Me Your Way." U/2 pt, kybd, opt C inst. CG CGA1081.

Keyboard / Instrumental

p ● Albrecht, Mark. "The Servant Song" from *Introductions and Alternate Accompaniments for Piano*, vol. 7. Pno. AFP 9780800623654.

Bon, Anna. "Allegro in D" from *Women Composers' Album*. Org. MSM 10-774.

● Organ, Anne Krentz. "Beach Spring" from *Woven Together*, vol. 1. Pno, inst. AFP 9780800658168.

p ● Wold, Wayne L. "Beach Spring" from *Light on Your Feet*, vol. 3. Org. AFP 9780806698021.

Handbell

p Compton, Matthew. "Through the Walk of Life." 3-7 oct, L4+. CG CGB813.

p ● Helman, Michael. "Lord, Whose Love through Humble Service." 3-5 oct hb, opt 3 oct hc, L3. CG CGB586.

p Larson, Lloyd. "I Then Shall Live (Finlandia)." 3-5 oct hb, L2+, HOP 2631. Opt pno/org and SAB, HOP C5800. Opt pno/org and SATB, HOP C5342.

Monday, July 11

Benedict of Nursia, Abbot of Monte Cassino, died around 540

Benedict is known as the father of Western monasticism. He was educated in Rome but was appalled by the decline of life around him. He went to live as a hermit, and a community of monks came to gather around him. In the prologue of his rule for monasteries he wrote that his intent in drawing up his regulations was "to set down nothing harsh, nothing burdensome." It is that moderate spirit that characterizes his rule and the monastic communities that are formed by

Order Now
Year A 2017

sundays and seasons

Sundays and Seasons Year A 2017

978-1-4514-9597-3 ....$39.00
(2 or more $32.00 ea.)

Sundays and Seasons: Preaching Year A 2017

Features new commentary and ideas for proclamation, contributed by practicing preachers as well as scholars, together with succinct notes on each day and its readings.

978-1-4514-9601-7 ....$29.00

NEW! Planning Guide and Preaching Combo Pack

Purchase *Sundays and Seasons* and *Sundays and Seasons: Preaching* together, and save!

978-1-5064-0103-4 ....$55.00
($68.00 if purchased separately)

Worship Planning Calendar Year A 2017

The perfect complement to *Sundays and Seasons*. Spiral-bound, this is both an appointment calendar and a workbook for preparing worship. Contains daily lectionary reading citations.

978-1-4514-9598-0 ....$22.00

Planning Guide and Calendar Combo Pack

Sundays and Seasons and *Worship Planning Calendar* work together to save you time and provide all you need to prepare engaging worship.

978-1-5064-0106-5 ....$51.00
($61.00 if purchased separately)

Sundays and Seasons.com

A rich and reliable resource for worship planning, Sundays and Seasons online worship planner follows the three-year lectionary cycle and provides everything you need to support your worship ministry in one convenient location, always accessible online. Learn more at sundaysandseasons.com

Words for Worship Year A 2017

This CD-ROM contains texts and graphical files with content from *Evangelical Lutheran Worship*. Also includes week-to-week elements from *Lectionary for Worship, Year A; Sundays and Seasons 2017*; and *Psalter for Worship Year A*, Evangelical Lutheran Worship edition.

978-1-4514-9604-8 ....$199.00

⊞ AUGSBURG FORTRESS

Worship Planning Resources
2017 Year A Order Form

To order by mail, detach, fold, and seal your completed card. Please be sure to attach postage. You can also order by calling 1-800-328-4648, faxing 1-800-722-7766, or visiting our online store at augsburgfortress.org.

SHIP TO _____

Address _____

City _____

State_____ ZIP _____

Phone _____

Email _____

BILL TO _____

Address _____

City _____

State_____ ZIP _____

Phone _____

METHOD OF PAYMENT *(select one)*

AF Account #_____

Credit Card #_____

Exp. Date_____ *Card must be valid through Oct. 2016. Products ship Sept. 2016.*

Signature_____
Signature required on all credit card orders.

Sundays and Seasons 2017
QTY: _____ 978-1-4514-9597-3 ....$39.00*
QTY: _____ SUNSEASONS ....Standing Order

Sundays and Seasons: Preaching Year A 2017
QTY: _____ 978-1-4514-9601-7 ....$29.00*
QTY: _____ SUNSEPREAC ....Standing Order

Planning Guide and Preaching Combo Pack 2017
QTY: _____ 978-1-5064-0103-4 ....$55.00*
QTY: _____ SUNSEAPPC ....Standing Order

Worship Planning Calendar 2017
QTY: _____978-1-4514-9598-0 ....$22.00*
QTY: _____ WRSHPPLNCL ....Standing Order

Planning Guide and Calendar Combo Pack 2017
QTY: _____ 978-1-5064-0106-5 ....$51.00*
QTY: _____ SUNSEAWPC ....Standing Order

Words for Worship 2017
QTY: _____ 978-1-4514-9604-8 ....$199.00*

Calendar of Word and Season 2017
QTY: _____ 978-1-4514-9602-4 ....$10.95*
QTY: _____ CALWRDSESN ....Standing Order

Church Year Calendar 2017
QTY: _____ 978-1-4514-9599-7 ....$1.95*

Church Year Calendar 2017 PDF
ONLINE 978-1-4514-9600-0 ....$9.96

Bread for the Day 2017
QTY: _____ 978-1-4514-9603-1 ....$8.95*

Ritual Lectionary, Year A
QTY: _____ 978-0-8066-5613-7 ....$115.00*

Study Edition Lectionary, Year A
QTY: _____ 978-0-8066-5614-4 ....$27.50*

The RCL: 20th Anniversary Annotated Edition
QTY: _____ 978-1-4514-3603-7 ....$30.00*

Prices do not include shipping. Prices valid through April 1, 2016.

Detach this card, fold it in half here, and seal the edges.

AUGSBURG FORTRESS
Attn: Mailing Center
P.O. Box 1209
Minneapolis, MN 55440-1209

Place
Stamp
Here

sundays
and
seasons

Order Now
for Year A 2017

Great gifts and useful resources for living the church's year!

Bread for the Day 2017

Bible readings and prayers for the full year. Follows the daily lectionary. Quantity discounts available.

978-1-4514-9603-1

Quantity	1–9	10–99	100–299	300–499	500–999	1,000+
Price	$8.95	$7.16	$6.71	$6.27	$5.37	$4.48

Calendar of Word and Season Year A 2017

Full-color wall calendar with room for adding family and church activities. Features beautiful art each month and identifies church festivals, national holidays, the color of the day, and Revised Common Lectionary citations. 8³/₈" x 10⁷/₈". Spiral-bound and punched for hanging.

978-1-4514-9602-4

Quantity	1–11	12–49	50–99	100–499	500+
Price	$10.95	$4.50	$3.50	$3.00	$2.50

Church Year Calendar Year A 2017

Provides dates, lectionary readings, hymn of the day, and the liturgical color for each Sunday and festival. The ideal time-saver for all who live by the liturgical year. Two-sided. 11" x 8½".

978-1-4514-9599-7

Quantity	1–11	12–99	100+
Price	$1.95	$0.83	$0.75

Lectionary for Worship, Ritual Edition Year A
978-0-8066-5613-7 .... *$115.00*

Lectionary for Worship, Study Edition Year A
978-0-8066-5614-4 .... *$27.50*

The Revised Common Lectionary: 20th Anniversary Annotated Edition
978-1-4514-3603-7 .... *$30.00*

Shipping and Handling

Prices and Product Availability are subject to change without notice.

Sales Tax: Exempt customers must provide Augsburg Fortress with a copy of their state-issued exemption certificate prior to purchase. Customers without tax-exempt status must add applicable state/province and local sales tax for their area. Canadian customers will be charged GST.

Shipping Charges are additional on all orders. U.S. and Canadian orders (except U.S. cash orders) are assessed actual shipping charges based on standard group rates. Additional shipping charges are assessed for expedited service requests and international shipments.

Return Policy: With proof of purchase, non-dated, in print product in saleable condition may be returned for credit. Please call Sales and Service at 1-800-328-4648 (U.S.) or 1-800-265-6397 (Canada) for assistance if you receive items that are damaged, defective, or were shipped in error. Specific return restrictions apply to some product lines. Please contact us prior to returning a special order item or item shipped directly from the manufacturer. Send U.S. order returns by a secure, prepaid, traceable method to the Augsburg Fortress Distribution Center, PBD Worldwide, c/o AF Distribution, 905 Carlow Dr., Unit B, Bolingbrook, IL 60490. Canadian orders may be returned to Augsburg Fortress Canadian Distribution Center, 500 Trillium Drive, Box 9940, Kitchener, Ontario N2G 4Y4.

it. Benedict encourages a generous spirit of hospitality, saying that visitors to Benedictine communities are to be welcomed as Christ himself.

He also valued the work of liberal Protestant scholars and believed social action was a first step on the path toward a united Christianity. He organized the Universal Christian Council on Life and Work, one of the organizations that in 1948 came together to form the World Council of Churches.

Tuesday, July 12

Nathan Söderblom, Bishop of Uppsala, died 1931

In 1930, this Swedish theologian, ecumenist, and social activist received the Nobel Prize for peace. Söderblom (zay-der-blom) saw the value of the ancient worship of the church catholic and encouraged the liturgical movement.

July 17, 2016
Time after Pentecost — Lectionary 16

Perhaps the church, at its best, is "all ears." Almighty God urges the faithful, again and again, to "listen up!"—to heed the word from above. So it was with Abraham and Sarah, with Mary and Martha, and the early church at Colossae. So it is today as we join the assembly to hear the word of God, the words of life.

Prayer of the Day

Eternal God, you draw near to us in Christ, and you make yourself our guest. Amid the cares of our lives, make us attentive to your presence, that we may treasure your word above all else, through Jesus Christ, our Savior and Lord.

Gospel Acclamation

Alleluia. Blessed are those who hold the word fast in an honest | and good heart,* and bear fruit with pa- | tient endurance. *Alleluia.* (Luke 8:15)

Readings and Psalm
Genesis 18:1-10a

The Lord visits Abraham and Sarah to tell them that the long-awaited promise of the birth of a child will be fulfilled for them in their old age.

Psalm 15

LORD, who may abide upon your holy hill? (Ps. 15:1)

Colossians 1:15-28

Sometimes Paul preaches with great attention to theological concepts. Here, however, Paul offers a mystical teaching, that the great mystery of God is "Christ in you." Because Christ is present in the church, Christians share in his life, suffering, and glory.

Luke 10:38-42

Jesus uses his visit to two sisters as an occasion to remind disciples that an important aspect of obedience is single-minded devotion to Jesus and his word.

Semicontinuous reading and psalm
Amos 8:1-12

Amos announces God's judgment upon the people of Israel, who sin by oppressing the poor and engaging in deceitful business practices. Amos uses a Hebrew wordplay: a basket of summer fruit (*qayits*) symbolizes the end (*qets*) of Israel. That end will come through a famine of hearing the word of the Lord.

Psalm 52

I am like a green olive tree in the house of God. (Ps. 52:8)

Preface Sundays

Color Green

Prayers of Intercession

The prayers are prepared locally for each occasion. The following examples may be adapted or used as appropriate.
Rooted in Christ and rising to serve, let us pray for the church, the world, and all in need.

A brief silence.

You open the doors of your church, Lord, to all who feel distant or estranged. Give us courage to share your good news through conversation and love. Hear us, O God.
Your mercy is great.

Cultivate in all people a care for the world you have made. Make us mindful of our impact on creation for the good of our neighbor and future generations. Hear us, O God.
Your mercy is great.

Reconcile and bring peace to communities that suffer (*especially*). Raise up and strengthen leaders and organizations that promote dialogue, hospitality, and restoration. Hear us, O God.
Your mercy is great.

Open our eyes to see those suffering any affliction, even ourselves. Open our lips to boldly beg relief in body or spirit for all in need (*especially*). Hear us, O God.
Your mercy is great.

Bless and keep safe campers, counselors, and families who experience the gift of outdoor ministry at camps this summer. Continue transforming them in Christ once they are safely home. Hear us, O God.
Your mercy is great.

Here other intercessions may be offered.

Comfort your children with the trust that your word is stronger than death. We remember saints and loved ones who have died and rest in you (*especially the missionary Bartolomé de Las Casas*). Hear us, O God.
Your mercy is great.

We lift our prayers to you, O God, trusting your promise to hear us; through Jesus Christ our Lord.
Amen.

Images in the Readings

Martha images those who serve; **Mary** images those who listen. We are to be both. Their home is our table.

The extraordinary amount of food and the considerable efforts in preparation suggest that the **meal of Abraham** symbolizes far more than a literal reading might indicate. That meal goes on through history, and we share in it each Sunday.

The ancient imagery of **Wisdom** hovers behind the hymn in Colossians. In pagan imagery borrowed by the Jewish tradition, Sophia was the goddess-like partner of the creator God. The ancient religious idea meant to affirm that the very order of creation testified to God. Christians continued this understanding. For example, Augustine said that if our knowledge about the universe conflicted with our biblical interpretation, it was our biblical interpretation that was wrong, for not only was the Bible extremely difficult to interpret, but also God's gracious power was indeed manifest in the created universe.

Ideas for the Day

♦ Rather than viewing Martha and Mary simply as characters in the gospel story, some commentators view them as archetypes of two aspects of Christian discipleship. Martha models service, hospitality, and action, and Mary exemplifies study, listening, and reflection. While some individuals may be more inclined to one than the other, both are important in individuals and in a community. Ask two people to share their experiences of growing in faith through service and study. This reading could challenge members of your community to spiritual growth by exploring the aspect with which they are less experienced or comfortable.

♦ When we gather for worship, we are both Martha and Mary—serving and listening. Highlight that dual presence in worship by assigning two people to play these parts periodically throughout the service. For example, after the welcome, Martha might stand up to comment on the importance of hospitality to the gathering time. Mary might stand up to introduce the readings or sermon. Martha could point out hospitality in the sharing of peace, then by helping to set the table at communion, while Mary participates in the thanksgiving at the table. Together they could send people forth, both to serve and to look and listen for God in daily life.

♦ Many people can identify with Martha's being "distracted by her many tasks." One can find plenty of advice on how to achieve balance in a life of many tasks, and also plenty of despair about ever reaching such a balance. In the article "A Centered Life" (*The Lutheran*, December 2007), former ELCA presiding bishop Mark Hanson suggests that we hope for a centered life instead of a balanced one. Whereas balance functions like law and requires too much of our control, a life centered on Jesus holds much greater possibility of grace and peace.

Connections with the Liturgy

Christians have seen both of today's stories as narrative illustrations of Sunday worship. We gather, we welcome the stranger, we attend to God's word, we receive a blessing, and we share a meal that the community has prepared but that God inhabits.

Let the Children Come

Have you ever witnessed a young child so deeply engaged in an activity—drawing, playing with blocks, picking up leaves—that all other distractions seem to fall away? Children are capable of deep concentration when they encounter something truly compelling. Like Mary listening at the feet of Jesus, other activities are put on hold in order to fully engage with what compels. How does your congregation provide opportunities for children to discover what is compelling *to them* about the language, gestures, symbols, rituals, and practice of faith?

Assembly Song
Gathering

Open now thy gates of beauty ELW 533, LBW 250

God, whose almighty word ELW 673, LBW 400

Dearest Jesus, at your word ELW 520, LBW 248

Psalmody and Acclamations

Haas, David. "They Who Do Justice" from PCY, vol. 3.

Traditional/arr. Wendell Whalum. "Psalm 15" from PAS 15C.

+ Wold, Wayne L. "Psalm 52" from PSCY.

(GA) ELW 169 with proper verse for Lectionary 16.

Hymn of the Day

Word of God, come down on earth ELW 510, WOV 716 *LIEBSTER JESU, WIR SIND HIER*

Open your ears, O faithful people ELW 519, WOV 715 *YISRAEL V'ORAITA*

Beloved, God's chosen ELW 648 *ANDREW'S SONG*

Offering

Lord, let my heart be good soil ELW 512, LS 83, TFF 131, W&P 52, WOV 713

We Are an Offering ELW 692, W&P 146

Communion

When the poor ones ELW 725, LLC 508

As rain from the clouds ELW 508

O Jesus, joy of loving hearts ELW 658, LBW 356

Sending

Listen, God is calling ELW 513, LS 79, TFF 130, WOV 712

O God of light ELW 507, LBW 237

Additional Assembly Songs

Open our eyes, Lord TFF 98, LS 31, W&P 113

All to Jesus I surrender TFF 235

Open our lives to the Word DH 8

⊕ Bell, John L. "As the Eyes of a Servant" from *We Walk His Way.* SATB. GIA G-7403.

⊕ Neto, Rodolfo Gaede. "For the Troubles and the Sufferings/ Pelas dores deste mundo" from *Glory to God.* SATB. WJK 9780664238971.

✿ Baloche, Paul. "Offering" from CCLI.

✿ Baloche, Paul/Lincoln Brewster/Paul Ingram. "Shout for Joy" from CCLI.

✿ Hughes, Tim. "Jesus You Alone" from CCLI.

✿ Redman, Matt. "The Heart of Worship" from CCLI.

✿ Scott, Kathryn. "Devotion" from CCLI.

Music for the Day
Choral

p Cherwien, David. "Give Me Jesus" from *To God Will I Sing: Vocal Solos for the Church Year.* Solo, kybd. AFP 9780800674335.

p Goeller, Dan. "You Are the Lord of Me" from *GladSong Choirbook: Contemporary Music for the Church Year.* SAB, kybd, C inst, assembly. AFP 9780800676087.

● Hobby, Robert. "Beloved, God's Chosen." 2 pt mxd, pno, fl. MSM 50-8707.

Miller, Mark. "Love Has Broken Down the Wall." SATB, pno. CG CGA1384.

Children's Choir

Barta, Daniel. "Lead Me in Your Truth." 2 pt, pno. CG CGA880.

Patterson, Mark. "A Prayer for Humility." U, pno. CG CGA989.

Schalk, Carl. "Thy Word Is Like a Garden, Lord." U, org, fl. CG CGA1089.

Keyboard / Instrumental

p ● Nelson, Ronald A. "Liebster Jesu, wir sind hier" from *Easy Hymn Settings for Organ,* vol. 3. Org. AFP 9781451462562.

p ● Organ, Anne Krentz. "Andrew's Song" from *Introductions and Alternate Accompaniments for Piano,* vol. 7. Pno. AFP 9780800623654.

p ● Powell, Robert J. "Liebster Jesu, wir sind hier" from *Our Cheerful Songs.* Org. AFP 9781451486070.

● Wold, Wayne L. "Yisrael v'oraita" from *Water, Word, Meal.* Org. AFP 9780800677552.

Handbell

Krug, Jason W. "Elation." 3-5 oct hb, opt 2 oct hc, L3+. RR BL5065. Opt perc, RR BP5065.

Lamb, Linda. "A Simple Prayer (Soliloquy)." 2-3 oct, L1. CG CGB816.

Raney, Joel. "Sweet Hour of Prayer." 3-5 oct, L3. HOP 2666.

Sunday, July 17

Bartolomé de Las Casas, missionary to the Indies, died 1566

Bartolomé de Las Casas was a Spanish priest and a missionary in the Western Hemisphere. He first came to the West while serving in the military, and he was granted a large estate that included a number of indigenous slaves. When he was ordained in 1513, he granted freedom to his servants. This act characterized much of the rest of Las Casas's ministry. Throughout the Caribbean and Central America, he worked to stop the enslavement of native people, to halt the brutal treatment of women by military forces, and to promote laws that humanized the process of colonization.

⊕ = global song ✿ = praise song + = semicontinuous psalm
● = relates to hymn of the day p = available in Prelude Music Planner

Friday, July 22

Mary Magdalene, Apostle

The gospels report Mary Magdalene was one of the women of Galilee who followed Jesus. She was present at Jesus' crucifixion and his burial. When she went to the tomb on the first day of the week to anoint Jesus' body, she was the first person to whom the risen Lord appeared. She returned to the disciples with the news and has been called "the apostle to the apostles" for her proclamation of the resurrection. Because John's gospel describes Mary as weeping at the tomb, she is often portrayed in art with red eyes. Icons depict her standing by the tomb and holding a bright red egg, symbol of the resurrection.

Saturday, July 23

Birgitta of Sweden, renewer of the church, died 1373

Birgitta (beer-GEE-tuh) was married at age thirteen and had four daughters with her husband. She was a woman of some standing who, in her early thirties, served as the chief lady-in-waiting to the queen of Sweden. She was widowed at the age of thirty-eight, shortly after she and her husband had made a religious pilgrimage. Following the death of her husband the religious dreams and visions that had begun in her youth occurred more regularly. Her devotional commitments led her to give to the poor and needy all that she owned, and she began to live a more ascetic life. She founded an order of monks and nuns, the Order of the Holy Savior (Brigittines), whose superior was a woman. Today the Society of St. Birgitta is a laypersons' society that continues her work of prayer and charity.

July 24, 2016

Time after Pentecost — Lectionary 17

Persistence in prayer evoked the admiration of Jesus and wins the attention of the Lord when Abraham intercedes for Sodom. The life of the baptized—to be rooted and built up in Christ Jesus the Lord—is to be rooted in prayer. God hears and answers prayer and so strengthens God's own. "When I called, you answered me; you increased my strength within me."

Prayer of the Day

Almighty and ever-living God, you are always more ready to hear than we are to pray, and you gladly give more than we either desire or deserve. Pour upon us your abundant mercy. Forgive us those things that weigh on our conscience, and give us those good things that come only through your Son, Jesus Christ, our Savior and Lord.

Gospel Acclamation

Alleluia. Ask, and it will be given you; search, and ¹ you will find;* knock, and the door will be o- ¹ pened to you. *Alleluia.* (Luke 11:9)

Readings and Psalm

Genesis 18:20-32

In today's reading, Abraham undertakes the role of a mediator between God and sinful humanity. Appealing to God's justice, Abraham boldly asks for mercy for the city of Sodom, for the sake of the few righteous people who are in it, including Abraham's nephew, Lot.

Psalm 138

Your steadfast love endures forever; do not abandon the works of your hands. (Ps. 138:8)

Colossians 2:6-15 [16-19]

Paul warns his congregation in Colossae about "the empty lure" of philosophies and traditions that compromise faith. Through the gift of faith, the church is mystically connected with Christ in his death and resurrection, which is enacted in baptism.

Luke 11:1-13

In teaching his disciples this prayer, Jesus also reminds them to focus on God's coming reign, God's mercy, and the strengthening of the community. Jesus encourages his disciples to child-like trust and persistence in prayer.

Semicontinuous reading and psalm
Hosea 1:2-10

Hosea's marriage to a faithless wife symbolizes Israel's faithlessness toward God. Even the names of Hosea's children—Jezreel (where Israel's idolatrous kings were killed), Lo-ruhamah ("not pitied"), and Lo-ammi ("not my people")—announce the nation's coming doom, countered by the proclamation that Israel remains a child of the living God.

Psalm 85

Righteousness shall go before the LORD. (Ps. 85:13)

Preface   Sundays

Color   Green

Prayers of Intercession

The prayers are prepared locally for each occasion. The following examples may be adapted or used as appropriate.
Rooted in Christ and rising to serve, let us pray for the church, the world, and all in need.
A brief silence.
Faithful God, through diverse cultures and countries, your Spirit weaves us together as one church. Help us all, your disciples, to ask for the things we need, confident that you hear us. Hear us, O God.
Your mercy is great.
Call us to notice places and people you created but we often forget. For busy places, for those working in the noon heat, in the silence of the night, and in care of your creation. Hear us, O God.
Your mercy is great.
Bring peace where strife is found, where homes have become battlegrounds (*especially*). Empower leaders and organizations to find solutions through persistence and faith. Hear us, O God.
Your mercy is great.
Turn our hearts to the cries of those in great need. Comfort and heal those who feel defined by situation, grief, or sickness (*especially*). Hear us, O God.
Your mercy is great.
Seek after us wherever we are found in these summer months. Grant safety to those who travel, sabbath rest to those who vacation, and perseverance to those who have no leisure time. Hear us, O God.
Your mercy is great.
Here other intercessions may be offered.
Join our prayers with those ancestors and saints who taught us to pray (*especially*). We remember those who have died in faith, with the comfort that your steadfast love endures forever. Hear us, O God.

Your mercy is great.
We lift our prayers to you, O God, trusting your promise to hear us; through Jesus Christ our Lord.
Amen.

Images in the Readings

The excerpt from Luke begins and concludes with the image of God as **Father**. Rare for first-century Jews, yet the standard title for Jupiter (which name elides Jove, that is, Zeus, and *pater*, father), Father has become the primary designation of the Christian God, perhaps because of this prayer and its doublet in Matthew. Christians continue to debate whether this image is something like the given name of God, and thus required for acceptable prayer. Much prayer in the Eastern Orthodox tradition is directed to the Trinity.

Abraham's pleading that God's power function with justice is an inspiration to Christians to beg God for justice in the world.

Sodom, in recollection of which the English language since the thirteenth century has designated sexual intercourse between a male and another male or an animal, is mentioned in Genesis 13:12-13 as Lot's choice for his home and as a city of "great sinners." Historically commonplace is the claim that especially cities are sexually immoral. In the description of Sodom in Genesis 19, Lot, Abraham's nephew, offers his neighbors his virgin daughters for sex, indicating that the gang rape of his daughters was preferable to the abuse of his male guests. The New Testament continues the tradition of identifying Sodom with evil. Christians continue a rancorous debate concerning whether the homosexual sex of males, perhaps also of females, is a sin. Historically, since the legal question concerned the use of the penis, female homosexuality was far less an issue.

The image in Colossians 2:14 is striking: it is as if the list of human sins is superimposed on the body of Jesus and thus **nailed** to the cross. In the image, God does the nailing, an idea that was developed in the church's theories of atonement, according to which God willed the death of Christ as the only way to triumph over evil.

Ideas for the Day

◆   With the emphasis on persistence in Luke and Genesis, it is easy to wonder whether God really requires that in order to hear our prayers. Frederick Buechner offers this perspective: "Be importunate, Jesus says—not, one assumes, because you have to beat a path to God's door before God will open it, but because until you beat the path maybe there's no way of getting to your door" (*Wishful Thinking* [San Francisco: HarperSanFrancisco, 1993]). Imagine the literal path "beaten" on the floor of your worship space over time by people coming to receive communion. Highlight the persistence of your faith community by calling attention to their footsteps as they tread that path once again.

◆   Prayer both reflects and creates intimacy with God, but it can be easily misunderstood when God becomes merely a "divine butler" and "cosmic therapist." Those terms come from *Soul Searching: The Religious and Spiritual Lives of American Teenagers* by Christian Smith and Melissa Lundquist Denton (New York: Oxford University Press, 2005). The authors found that teenagers (and adults!) practice a faith they called "moralistic therapeutic deism," even in the midst of established faith traditions. You can read a summary of their findings online in Smith's contribution to the 2005 Princeton (Seminary) Lectures on Youth, Church, and Culture. Contrast the faith they describe with the faith to which Jesus calls us, in which persistent prayer does not expect God to serve our own happiness but rather reshapes us and our desires.

◆   In Matthew's gospel, Jesus himself initiates the discussion of the Lord's Prayer. Here in Luke, however, the prayer is a response to one of his disciples who says, "Lord, teach us to pray." A quick search of "how to pray" on eHow.com suggests that many contemporary people share that desire. How might Jesus respond in our day? You could prepare a take-home list of prayer resources for individuals and families, including some possibilities for structuring daily prayer. Or use a video from the re:form confirmation curriculum, "Why should I pray the Lord's Prayer?" (Download the single session from wearesparkhouse.org.)

Connections with the Liturgy

The Lord's Prayer, albeit Matthew's longer version, has become the primary prayer of Christians. However, a personal application of its petitions has largely replaced the prayer's original eschatological intent. "Save us from the time of trial," from the 1975 English translation of the Lord's Prayer, is far truer to the original meaning than is the alternate idea that God leads us into temptation.

In the *Evangelical Lutheran Worship* rite of Holy Baptism (p. 228), the parents and the sponsors of the baptismal candidates promise to "teach them the Lord's Prayer."

Let the Children Come

"Knock, knock." "Who's there?" "Your children!" Perhaps the assisting minister could end each petition of the intercessory prayers today with the call, "O God, your children are knocking." Prepare the children to knock twice on the back of the pew or chair in front of them or another hard surface. Then all the people respond, "Hear our prayer." Or have the children sing Ken Medema's "Lord, listen to your children praying" (ELW 752) following each petition.

Assembly Song

Gathering

Now to the Holy Spirit let us pray   ELW 743, LBW 317
God the sculptor of the mountains   ELW 736, TFF 222
Jesus, the very thought of you   ELW 754, LBW 316

Psalmody and Acclamations

Cooney, Rory. "Psalm 138: On the Day I Called." Cant, SAB, assembly, kybd, gtr, fl. OCP 10474.
Joncas, Michael. "In the Sight of the Angels (Psalm 138)." SATB, cant, assembly, hp or kybd, opt fl, ob, vc. GIA G-7139.
+ Post, Marie J. "Lord, You Have Lavished on Your Land" (MELITA) from LUYH.
(GA) ELW 169 with proper verse for Lectionary 17.

Hymn of the Day

What a friend we have in Jesus   ELW 742, LBW 439   CONVERSE
Your will be done   ELW 741, TFF 243   MAYENZIWE
Our Father, God in heaven above   ELW 746/747   VATER UNSER

Offering

Let the vineyards be fruitful   ELW 182
Lord, listen to your children praying   ELW 752, LS 94, TFF 247, W&P 92, WOV 775

Communion

Break now the bread of life   ELW 515, LBW 235
O God in heaven   ELW 748
Day by day   ELW 790, WOV 746

Sending

Lord, teach us how to pray aright   ELW 745, LBW 438
What God ordains is good indeed   ELW 776, LBW 446

Additional Assembly Songs

I must tell Jesus   TFF 183
Sweet hour of prayer   TFF 242
Seek ye first   TFF 149, LS 90, W&P 122, WOV 783
🌐 Punjabi melody. "Jesus, Savior, Lord, Now to You I Come/Saranam, saranam" from *Glory to God*. SATB. WJK 9780664238971.
🌐 Rosas, Carlos. "The Lord's Prayer/Padre nuestro" from *Worship and Song*. SA. Abingdon Press 9781426709951.
✿ Cash, Ed/Matt Maher. "As It Is in Heaven" from CCLI.
✿ Houston, Joel/Matt Crocker/Scott Ligertwood. "Break Free" from CCLI.
✿ Miller, Tony. "Shepherd of My Soul" from CCLI.
✿ Peacock, Charlie. "In the Light" from CCLI.
✿ Powell, Aaron/Elias Dummer/Eric Fusilier/Josh Vanderlaan. "Manifesto" from CCLI.
✿ Roscoe, Jeffrey. "Let My Prayer Come like Incense" from *Spirit and Song*, vol. 1. OCP.

🌐 = global song   ✿ = praise song   + = semicontinuous psalm
● = relates to hymn of the day   p = available in Prelude Music Planner

Music for the Day

Choral

p • Keesecker, Thomas. "Our Father, God in Heaven Above" from *The New Gloria Deo*, vol. 2. 2 pt mxd, org. AFP 9781451424133.

p • McCartha, Charles. "What a Friend We Have in Jesus." SAB, kybd. AFP 9781451479508.

Shaw, Timothy. "Psalm 117." 2 pt mxd, kybd. CPH 98-3928.

p   Trinkley, Bruce. "Don't Be Weary, Traveler" from *Augsburg Choirbook for Men*. TB, pno. AFP 9780800676834.

Children's Choir

Coleman, Gerald Patrick. "Christ Is with Me." 2 pt, opt SATB, C inst, pno. CPH 983051.

Giamanco, Anthony. "Love Comes Trick-a-lin' Down." U/2 pt, kybd. GIA G-6216.

p   Keesecker, Thomas. "A Calypso Lord's Prayer" from *ChildrenSing in Worship*, vol. 2. U/2 pt, pno, opt fl, opt perc. AFP 9781451461152.

Keyboard / Instrumental

•   Hobby, Robert A. "Converse" from *Augsburg Organ Library: Summer*. Org. AFP 9780800676872.

p • Jordan, Elizabeth/Keith Kolander. "Mayenziwe" from *Introductions and Alternate Accompaniments for Piano*, vol. 8. Pno. AFP 9780800623661.

p • Powell, Robert J. "Vater unser" from *Mixtures: Hymn Preludes for Organ*. Org. AFP 9781451479553.

•   Raabe, Nancy M. "Vater unser" from *Grace and Peace*, vol. 6. Pno. AFP 9781451479621.

Handbell

p   Geschke, Susan E. "El Shaddai." 3-5 oct, L2+. HOP 2667.

p   Joy, Michael. "Clarion Call." 3-5 oct, L2+. CG CGB864.

•   Moklebust, Cathy. "Dixieland Swing on 'What a Friend We Have in Jesus.'" 3 or 5 oct hb, L5, CG CGB615. Opt full score with cl, tba, drms, perc, CG CGB614.

Monday, July 25

James, Apostle

James is one of the sons of Zebedee and is counted as one of the twelve disciples. Together with his brother John they had the nickname "sons of thunder." One of the stories in the New Testament tells of their request for Jesus to grant them places of honor in the kingdom. They are also reported to have asked Jesus for permission to send down fire on a Samaritan village that had not welcomed them. James was the first of the Twelve to suffer martyrdom and is the only apostle whose martyrdom is recorded in scripture. He is sometimes called James the Elder to distinguish him

from James the Less, commemorated with Philip on May 1, and James of Jerusalem, commemorated on October 23.

Thursday, July 28

Johann Sebastian Bach, died 1750; Heinrich Schütz, died 1672; George Frederick Handel, died 1759; musicians

These three composers have done much to enrich the worship life of the church. Johann Sebastian Bach drew on the Lutheran tradition of hymnody and wrote about two hundred cantatas, including at least two for each Sunday and festival day in the Lutheran calendar of his day. He has been called "the fifth evangelist" for the ways he proclaimed the gospel through his music. George Frederick Handel was not primarily a church musician, but his great work *Messiah* is a musical proclamation of the scriptures. Heinrich Schütz wrote choral settings of biblical texts and paid special attention to ways his composition would underscore the meaning of the words.

Friday, July 29

Mary, Martha, and Lazarus of Bethany

Mary and Martha are remembered for the hospitality and refreshment they offered Jesus in their home. Following the characterization drawn by Luke, Martha represents the active life, Mary the contemplative. Mary is identified in the fourth gospel as the one who anointed Jesus before his passion and who was criticized for her act of devotion. Lazarus, Mary's and Martha's brother, was raised from the dead by Jesus as a sign of the eternal life offered to all believers. It was over Lazarus's tomb that Jesus wept for love of his friend.

Olaf, King of Norway, martyr, died 1030

Olaf is considered the patron saint of Norway. In his early career he engaged in war and piracy in the Baltic and in Normandy. In Rouen, though, he was baptized and became a Christian. He returned to Norway, succeeded his father as king, and from then on Christianity was the dominant religion of the realm. He revised the laws of the nation and enforced them with strict impartiality, eliminating the possibility of bribes. He thereby alienated much of the aristocracy. The harshness that he sometimes resorted to in order to establish Christianity and his own law led to a rebellion. After being driven from the country and into exile, he enlisted support from Sweden to try to regain his kingdom, but he died in battle.

July 31, 2016
Time after Pentecost — Lectionary 18

Today's texts offer instruction and encouragement for all who are occasionally overwhelmed by the "unhappy business" of life. Jesus urges us to take care and be on guard against all kinds of greed. We who have died with Christ in holy baptism have also been raised with him and are encouraged to elevate our thinking, seeking the "things that are above." To that end we seek the sustenance of the Lord's supper and the encouragement of God's word.

Prayer of the Day

Benevolent God, you are the source, the guide, and the goal of our lives. Teach us to love what is worth loving, to reject what is offensive to you, and to treasure what is precious in your sight, through Jesus Christ, our Savior and Lord.

Gospel Acclamation

Alleluia. Blessed are the ¹ poor in spirit,* for theirs is the king- ¹ dom of heaven. *Alleluia.* (Matt. 5:3)

Readings and Psalm
Ecclesiastes 1:2, 12-14; 2:18-23

The teacher of wisdom who wrote Ecclesiastes sees that working for mere accumulation of wealth turns life into an empty game, a "vanity of vanities." Nevertheless, he asserts in the next verse, it is good to find enjoyment in one's work because such enjoyment is a gift from God.

Psalm 49:1-12

My mouth shall speak of wisdom. (Ps. 49:3)

Colossians 3:1-11

Life in Christ includes a radical reorientation of our values. Just as the newly baptized shed their old clothes in order to put on new garments, so Christians are called to let go of greed and take hold of a life shaped by God's love in Christ.

Luke 12:13-21

In God's reign, the "rich will be sent away empty." Jesus uses a parable to warn against identifying the worth of one's life with the value of one's possessions rather than one's relationship with God.

Semicontinuous reading and psalm
Hosea 11:1-11

Hosea compares God's love for Israel to the love parents have for their children. Whether teaching toddlers to walk or dealing with a child's rebellion, good parents continue to love their children as they try to lead them to life. In the same way, God's love will not let Israel go.

Psalm 107:1-9, 43

We give thanks to you, LORD, for your wonderful works. (Ps. 107:8)

Preface   Sundays

Color   Green

Prayers of Intercession

The prayers are prepared locally for each occasion. The following examples may be adapted or used as appropriate.

Rooted in Christ and rising to serve, let us pray for the church, the world, and all in need.

A brief silence.

O God, enliven the body of Christ with energy and creativity. Work through partnerships across towns, denominations, and ministry contexts, that Christ be shared with all. Hear us, O God.

Your mercy is great.

Guard your creation against greed and over-consumption. Restore polluted air and waters, protect animal habitats, and send new growth where it is needed. Hear us, O God.

Your mercy is great.

Break down barriers between neighborhoods, peoples, and nations (*especially*). Sustain community leaders, legislators, volunteers, peacemakers, and all who seek the good of their communities. Hear us, O God.

Your mercy is great.

Soothe furrowed and fevered brows. Give energy and compassion to caregivers, those who sit at bedsides or wait by the phone. Comfort all in need of healing (*especially*). Hear us, O God.

Your mercy is great.

Inspire our congregation to live in the present moment, O God, and to trust in you. In committee meetings, classrooms, and all ministries, give us flexibility to follow where you lead. Hear us, O God.

Your mercy is great.

Here other intercessions may be offered.

We give thanks for those who have died recently and across the ages (*especially*), and we rejoice in the hope of the resurrection. Hear us, O God.

Your mercy is great.

We lift our prayers to you, O God, trusting your promise to hear us; through Jesus Christ our Lord.

Amen.

Images in the Readings

Bigger and bigger **barns** filled with more and more stuff: that's us.

Ecclesiastes, the book titled "**Teacher,**" can give our lives no worthy direction. We turn to Christ, who is all and in all, who not only teaches but is the Word of God.

The author of Colossians recalls the phrase from Genesis 1:27 in which humankind is created in the **image of God**. Over the centuries Jews and Christians have debated what is meant by this image of God. For example, Thomas Aquinas posited that this image was rationality. The author of Colossians suggests that since Christ is the image of the invisible God (1:15), baptism returns us to Christ and his relationship with God.

Ideas for the Day

◆ For many in American culture, "bigger barns" looks like garages stuffed full and storage rental units crammed with excess. Many of us have enough wealth to accumulate and store up. Jesus' parable urges letting go of the need to find security in wealth and possessions and instead exploring the opportunities to help others that arise from excess wealth. A sermon could inspire a congregation to sponsor a community-wide garage sale, encouraging members and those in the neighborhood to empty out their "barns" and donate items, and using the money raised to feed hungry souls nearby and around the world.

◆ In economics there is a concept called "opportunity cost." Every time we save or spend, we are giving up the opportunity to use those resources for something else. Four dollars spent on an espresso drink is four dollars not put into a college savings fund. We daily make financial choices without consciously looking at the opportunity costs. Jesus' parable raises the issue of the opportunities lost when we do this, opportunities Jesus calls being "rich toward God." What opportunities exist in the congregation and community that need to be considered so the assembly can respond to God's gracious provisions by being rich toward God?

◆ Issues of food distribution and waste are a growing concern in a world where many are malnourished and hungry. ELCA World Hunger has resources that could be highlighted in connection with the gospel reading. Their "Feed the World Coin Box" could be distributed as "little barns" to put coins in, and instead of putting the money saved into the "bigger barns" of our savings and checking accounts, it could be given to the work of the church to alleviate hunger and promote justice. See www.elca.org/hunger.

◆ In the parable, Jesus encourages his listeners to live as if life were short and respond to God's generous love today. Henri-Frédéric Amiel, nineteenth-century Swiss philosopher and poet, said, "Life is short, and we have never too much time for gladdening the hearts of those who are traveling the dark journey with us. Oh be swift to love, make haste to be kind!" (*Amiel's Journal,* entry for December 26, 1868).

Connections with the Liturgy

Both the Apostles' and the Nicene Creeds use the image also in Colossians of God sitting on a throne above the sky with the heir apparent, or the prime minister, seated at God's right hand.

Let the Children Come

In the gospel Jesus says that a person's life does not consist in the abundance of possessions. A life lived in Christ is about being rich toward God. This is wisdom we all need in the midst of a culture that encourages and celebrates the acquisition of stuff. While some children are shopping for new school clothes, others have little to wear. Is it appropriate in your congregation to organize a late-summer "school clothes" project? Invite children to look through their drawers and closets for good clothes they do not need. Let them help wash, iron, and prepare them to be shared with children who need them.

Assembly Song
Gathering

Earth and all stars   ELW 731, LBW 558, LS 119

Lord, your hands have formed   ELW 554, WOV 727

How Great Thou Art   ELW 856, LBW 532

Psalmody and Acclamations

Howard, Julie/arr. Vera Lyons. "Let Not the Wise Glory in Their Wisdom" from PAS 49C.

Leckebush, Martin/I-to-Loh. "Come, One and All" (KIÚ-JI-IT) from LUYH.

+ Wold, Wayne L. "Psalm 107:1-9, 43," Refrain 1, from PSCY.

(GA) ELW 169 with proper verse for Lectionary 18.

Hymn of the Day

Jesus, priceless treasure   ELW 775, LBW 457   *JESU, MEINE FREUDE*

LBW 458   *GUD SKAL ALTING MAGE*

God, whose giving knows no ending   ELW 678, LBW 408
   RUSTINGTON

We give thee but thine own   ELW 686, LBW 410   *HEATH*

Offering

God, whose farm is all creation   ELW 734

Son of God, eternal Savior   ELW 655, sts. 1-2; LBW 364, sts. 1-2

Communion

Touch the earth lightly   ELW 739

Father, we thank you   ELW 478, WOV 704

When pain of the world surrounds us   ELW 704

Sending

The Lord now sends us forth   ELW 538, LLC 415

All depends on our possessing   ELW 589, LBW 447

Additional Assembly Songs

God has done marvelous things   W&P 51

Some folk would rather have houses   TFF 236

Cuando las bases de este mundo tiemblan   LLC 526

꙳ Lim, Swee Hong. "May the Love of the Lord" from *Glory to God*. U. WJK 9780664238971.

꙳ Manzano, Miguel. "When the Poor Ones/Cuando el pobre." U. ELW 725.

✧ Brewster, Lincoln/Paul Baloche. "Today Is the Day" from CCLI.

✧ Hall, Charlie/Edward Mote/Kendall Combes/Trent Austin/William Batchelder Bradbury. "The Solid Rock" from CCLI.

✧ Houston, Joel/Jonathon Douglass. "One Way" from CCLI.

✧ Maher, Matt. "Jericho" from *Spirit and Song*, vol. 2. OCP.

✧ Webster, Miriam. "Made Me Glad" from CCLI.

Music for the Day
Choral

p   de Silva, Chris. "Come, Receive the Living Bread." SATB, kybd, gtr, 2 C inst, str qrt. GIA G-8276.

p   Keesecker, Thomas. "I Lift My Eyes Up to the Hills" from *The New Gloria Deo*, vol. 2. SA(T)B, pno. AFP 9781451424133.

p   Mendelssohn, Felix/ed. K. Lee Scott. "The Lord Is Ever Watchful" from *Sing Forth God's Praise*. Solo, kybd. AFP 9780800675387.

p   Sedio, Mark. "Take My Life, That I May Be/Toma, oh Dios, mi voluntad." SATB, pno, fl. AFP 9780800658298.

Children's Choir

Messick, Pat. "Treasures in Heaven." U/2 pt, pno. CG CGA1252.

Fauré, Gabriel/arr. Jean Ashworth Battle. "Cantique de Jean Racine." U, kybd. HIN HMC1730.

p   Patterson, Mark. "Living God's Love." U/2 pt, pno, opt hb/hc. CG CGA1367.

Keyboard / Instrumental

● Bach, Johann Sebastian. "Jesu, meine Freude" from *Orgelbüchlein*. Org. Various editions.

● Raabe, Nancy M. "Rustington" from *Introductions and Alternate Accompaniments for Piano*, vol. 7. Pno. AFP 9780800623654.

p ●Shaw, Timothy. "Rustington" from *All Praise for Music*. Org. AFP 9781451401127.

● Wonacott, Glenn. "Jesu, meine Freude" from *Piano Plus Through the Year*, vol. 2. Pno, inst. AFP 9780800663728.

Handbell

● Lamb, Linda. "Jesus, Priceless Treasure." 3-5 oct hb, opt 3 oct hc, opt fl, L3. CPH 97-7467.

p   Tucker, Margaret. "Carillon and Bell Jubilee." 3-5 oct hb, opt 2 oct hc, L3. CG CGB779.

Wagner, Douglas. "Forever." 3-5 oct hb, L3, LOR 20/1452L. Opt acc CD, LOR A385. Opt full score with 2 tpt, tenor sax, tbn, elec gtr, elec bass, drms, LOR 30/2415L.

August 7, 2016
Time after Pentecost — Lectionary 19

Jesus says, "It is your Father's good pleasure to give you the kingdom." It is God's promise from the beginning—to Abraham, to the early church, and to the "little flock" of which we are a part today in assembly. Faith, God's baptismal gift, trusts the promises of God. Have no fear.

Prayer of the Day

Almighty God, you sent your Holy Spirit to be the life and light of your church. Open our hearts to the riches of your grace, that we may be ready to receive you wherever you appear, through Jesus Christ, our Savior and Lord.

Gospel Acclamation

Alleluia. Keep awake [1] and be ready,* for you do not know on what day your [1] Lord is coming. *Alleluia.* (Matt. 24:42, 44)

Readings and Psalm
Genesis 15:1-6

God promises childless and aging Abram that a child of his own will be his heir and that his descendants will number as many as the stars. Abram trusts God's promise, and through this faith he is considered righteous.

Psalm 33:12-22

Let your lovingkindness be upon us, as we place our hope in you. (Ps. 33:22)

Hebrews 11:1-3, 8-16

Abraham and Sarah exemplify the vision of faith that people of God enact in every age. Their hope and trust in God's promise allowed them to face an unknown future and to receive the promise of God.

Luke 12:32-40

Jesus encourages disciples to invest their hearts and live fully into God's reign. Instead of facing life with fear, those who know God's generosity are always ready to receive from God and to give to others.

Semicontinuous reading and psalm
Isaiah 1:1, 10-20

Isaiah announces God's displeasure with the offerings and sacrifices of a people who are without compassion. He urges them instead to do justice and defend the oppressed. Indeed, if they repent, the Lord promises, they will be made as clean as new-fallen snow.

Psalm 50:1-8, 22-23

To those who go the right way I will show the salvation of God. (Ps. 50:23)

Preface   Sundays

Color   Green

Prayers of Intercession

The prayers are prepared locally for each occasion. The following examples may be adapted or used as appropriate.

Rooted in Christ and rising to serve, let us pray for the church, the world, and all in need.

A brief silence.

Faithful God, encourage your church in new ventures of faith: new congregations, ministries, conversations, and partnerships. Hear us, O God.

Your mercy is great.

Creating God, the abundance of your creation fills us with awe and delight. Call us daily to be vigilant and responsible stewards of all you have made. Hear us, O God.

Your mercy is great.

Merciful God, calm the fears that produce wars, prejudice, and injustice. Equip governments, leaders, and peacemakers to be models of cooperation and reconciliation among the nations. Hear us, O God.

Your mercy is great.

Restoring God, comfort all who long for relief from circumstances of grief or sickness (*especially*). Bless hospitals, mental health facilities, and all places of healing. Hear us, O God.

Your mercy is great.

Steadfast God, we pray for those in life transitions that bring anxiety. Heal those hurt by broken promises, and sustain them with your never-ending love. Hear us, O God.

Your mercy is great.

Here other intercessions may be offered.

Heavenly Father, we give you thanks for all the saints who now enjoy unfailing treasure in heaven, and we rejoice that we are united with them in your love. Hear us, O God.

Your mercy is great.
We lift our prayers to you, O God, trusting your promise to hear us; through Jesus Christ our Lord.
Amen.

Images in the Readings

The slaves are waiting faithfully for the master to arrive, and then to their utter surprise the **master serves** them at table. John 13 elaborates this image with the narrative of the footwashing. We, who think that there ought to be no slaves and that the master should be serving everyone at table, find this image nowhere near as shocking as it was to Luke's audience.

Finally, even our most carefully chosen language fails to express the full mercy of God. We see this in the odd final image: the Son of Man, who at the end of time will judge evil and bridge the chasm between God and humankind, is a **thief** who breaks into our house. When we imagined that a thief might come, we were prepared by having set our house alarm, but then the thief came when we least expected it and carried off our treasures. It is a surprising way to describe the coming of Christ into our lives. Are we like a locked house, hiding inside from everything we fear?

Abraham, who is honored by Jews, Christians, and Muslims, is a central image of the life of faith. The biography given in Hebrews acclaims his faith, his journey to a new homeland, his descendants Isaac and Jacob, and the miraculous birth of his son. And yet, so like us, he died before he received the full measure of God's gifts, which are imaged throughout the Bible as life in the city beyond all cities.

A **shield** is a defensive weapon: God is our shield.

Ideas for the Day

◆ Jesus makes a connection between *fear* and *use of wealth*. He implies that living without fear by trusting God's goodness frees us to sell our possessions and help those in need. Stewardship is often the work of helping people face their fears about wealth and possessions, and find reason in God to be free of their fear. Here is a chance to see stewardship as the freedom from fear and the opportunity to act on faith.

◆ The image of our heart being where our treasure is can be reversed: our treasure is where our heart is. An interactive sermon could include people writing on a sticky note what they value in life, what they treasure, and sticking the note to themselves over their hearts. Placing the hand over the heart is a meaningful gesture of dedication. How does the good news of Christ empower people to dedicate themselves to what they treasure in God? Have the assembly place their hands over their hearts to dedicate themselves to what they treasure from God.

◆ There are thematic connections between the parable of the master who serves and Jesus washing his disciples' feet at the last supper in John's gospel. The assembly at worship is much like those who are "alert" in Jesus' parable, whom the master serves at table: they are here, watching and waiting for what God will do. The good news for the assembly is that Christ comes to serve them in the eucharistic meal. Consider including a footwashing ritual, perhaps during the communion distribution, and have assembly members wash each other's feet, embodying the presence and rule of Christ in their service to one another.

◆ Like Jesus' disciples, Abraham fears that the promises God makes might not come true. In his poem "Count the Stars," Michael Coffey explores how God's invitation to Abraham to count the stars in the sky is a call to live by faith instead of fear, even for people of faith today. The poem can be found at mccoffey.blogspot.com/2013/08/count-stars.html.

Connections with the Liturgy

Abraham and Sarah's receiving the gift of a child is cited as an example of God's mercies in Thanksgiving at the Table X (*ELW*, p. 69).

Let the Children Come

Before children can understand what it means to have treasures, they must be treasured at home and in your church family. Every Sunday have ushers welcome families with young children and seat them where children will be able to see and hear what is going on in worship. Teach greeters to welcome young ones by meeting their eyes (squatting down to eye level if physically able) and expressing their pleasure at seeing them. If our greatest treasure is God's love for us, then children will discover that this gift is for them as they are wrapped in the loving arms of their church family.

Assembly Song
Gathering

We've come this far by faith   ELW 633, TFF 197
God, who stretched the spangled heavens   ELW 771, LBW 463
Great is thy faithfulness   ELW 733, TFF 283, WOV 771

Psalmody and Acclamations

"The Earth Is Full of the Goodness of God" from *Psallite* C-59 (verses 1-14).

Morgan, Michael. "Rejoice, You Righteous, in the Lord" (ELLACOMBE) from PAS 33B.

Roberts, Leon C. "Nineteenth Sunday in Ordinary Time / C" from LP:LG.

+ Organ, Anne Krentz. "Psalm 50:1-8, 22-23," Refrain 2, from PSCY. (GA) ELW 169 with proper verse for Lectionary 19.

Hymn of the Day

Blessed assurance   ELW 638, TFF 118, WOV 699   *ASSURANCE*
Have no fear, little flock   ELW 764, LBW 476   *LITTLE FLOCK*
Be thou my vision   ELW 793, WOV 776   *SLANE*

Offering

Children of the heavenly Father   ELW 781, LBW 474, LS 167
Many and great, O God   ELW 837, WOV 794

Communion

Holy Spirit, truth divine   ELW 398, LBW 257
When memory fades   ELW 792
On Eagle's Wings   ELW 787, LS 163, W&P 110, WOV 779

Sending

My life flows on in endless song   ELW 763, WOV 781
What a fellowship, what a joy divine   ELW 774, TFF 220, WOV 780

Additional Assembly Songs

Time is filled with swift transition   TFF 231
El Señor es mi luz   LLC 537
Necesitado me encuentro, Señor   LLC 529

🌐 Garcia, Juan Luis. "God's Word Is Upright/La palabra del Señor" from *Glory to God*. U. WJK 9780664238971.
🌐 Plainsong, Mode V. "In a Deep, Unbounded Darkness" from *Glory to God*. U. WJK 9780664238971.
✧ Baloche, Paul. "All the Earth Will Sing Your Praises" from CCLI.
✧ Brown, Brenton/Paul Baloche. "Almighty" from CCLI.
✧ Carpenter, Kelly. "Draw Me Close" from CCLI.
✧ Chapman, John Wilbur/Mark Hall/Michael Bleecker. "Glorious Day (Living He Loved Me)" from CCLI.
✧ Mark, Robin. "Days of Elijah" from CCLI.

Music for the Day
Choral

p   Bach, Johann Sebastian. "Take Heart, Contented Be, and Restful" from *To God Will I Sing: Vocal Solos for the Church Year*. Solo, kybd. AFP 9780800674335.
p ● Ferguson, John. "Be Thou My Vision." SATB, org. AFP 9780800657932.
p   Raabe, Nancy. "Creator of the Stars of Night." 2 pt mxd, kybd. AFP 9781451401622.
p   Telemann, Georg Philip/ed. Joan Conlon. "Come, Enjoy God's Festive Springtime." U, kybd, vln. AFP 9780800646486.

Children's Choir

p   Helgen, John. "Keep Your Lamps Trimmed and Burning." U, opt desc, pno. AFP 9781451483871.
Keylock, Melissa/Jill Friersdorf. "The Prayer Perfect." U/2 pt, pno. Colla Voce 24-96755.
p ● Pooler, Marie. "Be Thou My Vision" from *Augsburg Easy Choirbook*, vol. 1. U, kybd, opt desc. AFP 9781451462159.

Keyboard / Instrumental

● Carlson, J. Bert. "Assurance" from *Blessed Assurance: A Piano Collection*. Pno. AFP 9780800658045.
p ● Dahl, David P. "Slane" from *The Organ Sings*. Org. AFP 9781451462609.
p ● Organ, Anne Krentz. "Slane" from *Be Thou My Vision*. Pno. AFP 9780800678524.
● Powell, Robert J. "Assurance" from *Prayerful Preludes*, set 2. Org. MSM 10-646.

Handbell

● Eithun, Sandra. "Blessed Assurance." 2-3 oct, L1, CG CGB683. 3-5 oct, L1, CG CGB684.
● Glasgow, Michael J. "Prayer for Guidance." 3-6 oct hb, opt 3 oct hc, L3+. JEF JHS9431.
● McFadden, Jane. "Have No Fear, Little Flock." 3-5 oct hb, opt 3 oct hc, L2. CPH 97-6922.

Monday, August 8
Dominic, founder of the Order of Preachers (Dominicans), died 1221

Dominic was a Spanish priest who preached against the Albigensians, a heretical sect that held gnostic and dualistic beliefs. Dominic believed that a stumbling block to restoring heretics to the church was the wealth of clergy, so he formed an itinerant religious order, the Order of Preachers (Dominicans), who lived in poverty, studied philosophy and theology, and preached against heresy. The method of this order was to use kindness and gentle argument, rather than harsh judgment, to bring unorthodox Christians back to the fold. Dominic was opposed to burning Christians at the stake. Three times Dominic was offered the office of bishop, which he refused so that he could continue in his work of preaching.

Wednesday, August 10
Lawrence, deacon, martyr, died 258

Lawrence was one of seven deacons of the congregation at Rome and, like the deacons appointed in Acts, was responsible for financial matters in the church and for the care of the poor. Lawrence lived during a time of persecution under the emperor Valerian. The emperor demanded that Lawrence surrender the treasures of the church. Lawrence gathered lepers, orphans, the blind and lame. He brought them to the emperor and said, "Here is the treasure of the church." This act enraged the emperor, and Lawrence was sentenced to death. Lawrence's martyrdom was one of the first to be observed by the church.

🌐 = global song   ✧ = praise song   + = semicontinuous psalm
● = relates to hymn of the day   p = available in Prelude Music Planner

Thursday, August 11

Clare, Abbess of San Damiano, died 1253

At age eighteen, Clare of Assisi heard Francis preach a sermon in a church in town. From that time, she determined to follow in his example of Christian living. With Francis's help (and against the wishes of her father) she and a growing number of companions established a women's Franciscan community, called the Order of Poor Ladies, or Poor Clares. She became a confidante and advisor to Francis, and in standing up against the wishes of popes for the sake of maintaining complete poverty, she helped inspire other women to pursue spiritual goals.

Saturday, August 13

Florence Nightingale, died 1910; Clara Maass, died 1901; renewers of society

When Florence Nightingale decided she would be a nurse, her family was horrified. In the early 1800s nursing was done by people with no training and no other way to earn a living. Florence trained at Kaiserswerth, Germany, with a Lutheran order of deaconesses. She returned home and worked to reform hospitals in England. Nightingale led a group of thirty-eight nurses to serve in the Crimean War, where they worked in appalling conditions. She returned to London as a hero and resumed her work there for hospital reform.

Clara Maass was born in New Jersey and served as a nurse in the Spanish-American War, where she encountered the horrors of yellow fever. She later responded to a call for subjects in research on yellow fever. During the experiments, which included receiving bites from mosquitoes, she contracted the disease and died. The commemoration of these women invites the church to give thanks for all who practice the arts of healing.

August 14, 2016

Time after Pentecost — Lectionary 20

The word of God is a refining fire. Jesus is the great divide in human history. He invites our undivided attention and devotion. Today, in the assembly, we are surrounded by "so great a cloud of witnesses." In the word and in the holy communion we are invited yet again to look to Jesus, "the pioneer and perfecter of our faith."

Prayer of the Day

O God, judge eternal, you love justice and hate oppression, and you call us to share your zeal for truth. Give us courage to take our stand with all victims of bloodshed and greed, and, following your servants and prophets, to look to the pioneer and perfecter of our faith, your Son, Jesus Christ, our Savior and Lord.

Gospel Acclamation

Alleluia. My sheep | hear my voice.* I know them, and they | follow me. *Alleluia.* (John 10:27)

Readings and Psalm

Jeremiah 23:23-29

Because Jeremiah preaches the unpopular message of God's judgment, he suffers rejection. Today's reading distinguishes between the true prophet, like Jeremiah, who speaks God's word, and the false prophet who misleads the people through dreams. One is like wheat; the other like worthless straw.

Psalm 82

Arise, O God, and rule the earth. (Ps. 82:8)

Hebrews 11:29—12:2

The author of Hebrews presents us with rich stories of faith. In a long list of biblical heroes, we find examples of trust in God that enabled them to face the trials of life faithfully. In addition to this "cloud of witnesses," we have Jesus, the perfect model of faithful endurance.

Luke 12:49-56

Jesus delivers harsh words about the purifying and potentially divisive effects of obedience to God's call. The way of the cross often leads followers to encounter hostility and rejection, even from those they love.

Semicontinuous reading and psalm
Isaiah 5:1-7

The prophet sings about a beautiful vineyard, carefully planted and cultivated, that nevertheless yields wild grapes. The owner therefore determines to destroy the vineyard, which represents the sinful people of Israel and Judah.

Psalm 80:1-2, 8-19

Look down from heaven, O God; behold and tend this vine. (Ps. 80:14, 15)

Preface   Sundays

Color   Green

Prayers of Intercession

The prayers are prepared locally for each occasion. The following examples may be adapted or used as appropriate.
Rooted in Christ and rising to serve, let us pray for the church, the world, and all in need.
A brief silence.
God near to us, increase your people's passion to share how Christ transforms lives. Raise up prophets in your church, Lord, to interpret the word and the world today. Hear us, O God.
Your mercy is great.
Renewing God, we pray for scorched places that need rain, those recovering from disaster, and those needing balance. Hear us, O God.
Your mercy is great.
God of power, administer justice. Pour your spirit of compassion and mercy into those who hold the lives of others in their hands. We pray for all who are persecuted or imprisoned for their beliefs. Hear us, O God.
Your mercy is great.
Compassionate God, save us from being overwhelmed by addictions, medical conditions, competition, and fear. Comfort all in need in body, mind, or spirit (*especially*). Hear us, O God.
Your mercy is great.
Give wisdom to our community, Lord. Help us discern your will for our life and ministry together, even when it may divide or challenge us. Hear us, O God.
Your mercy is great.
Here other intercessions may be offered.

We thank you, O God, for the great cloud of witnesses that surrounds us. Gather us with (*Maximilian Kolbe and Kaj Munk, martyrs of the church, and*) all the saints around your throne on the last day. Hear us, O God.
Your mercy is great.
We lift our prayers to you, O God, trusting your promise to hear us; through Jesus Christ our Lord.
Amen.

Images in the Readings

Luke's picture of the **divided family** contradicts many dreams about happy families united in faith. The early Christian movement brought about much family divisiveness, and in a post-Christian world, such divisions will likely increase. When churches describe church members in terms of family, they need to beware of naïveté: each individual image of faith is inadequate unless it stands with its opposite.

Jeremiah ridicules **dreams** as being unfaithful to the genuine word of God. Over the millennia, the world's religions have valued dreams as messages from the deities. In Christianity, the dreams of individuals are scrutinized by the community, which tests whether the dream serves Christ. Of course Christians have not always agreed about the value of specific dreams.

A **hammer** uses force to straighten things out. God's word is a hammer.

Ideas for the Day

◆   In today's gospel, Luke seeks to encourage his readers, many of whom had been rejected by their families. Keeping faith when it causes separation from loved ones is particularly painful. This gospel could be a starting point for creating a support group focused on family estrangement, particularly as caused by religion. Allow your group to be a place of grieving but also encouragement. A good resource is Dr. Joshua Colman's book *When Parents Hurt: Compassionate Strategies When You and Your Grown Child Don't Get Along* (New York: William Morrow, 2007).
◆   Family division and persecution were serious, often deadly possibilities for the earliest followers of Christ. In 2014, the story of Meriam Ibrahim was a disturbing reminder that this still happens today. Ibrahim was sentenced to death in Sudan for alleged apostasy from Islam, and to public flogging because her marriage to a Christian was not legally recognized. She gave birth to her second child while shackled in prison. In the *Wall Street Journal*, Charlotte Allen compared Ibrahim's story to that of third-century martyrs Perpetua and Felicity, who were also young African mothers (www.wsj.com/articles/charlotte-allen-meriam-ibrahim-and-the-persecution-of-christians-1403822908).

◆ Anti-Christian persecution is on the rise worldwide. Pope Francis has compared the plight of Christians today to that of the early church—even stating it is worse today. As of 2013, about 100 million Christians faced persecution around the world, in 111 countries. They are persecuted in more places than any other religious group, according to the Pew Forum on Religion and Public Life. How might your congregation respond to this crisis?

◆ The "great cloud of witnesses" described in Hebrews is composed not of passive observers but of cheering fans. To illustrate the idea of the witnesses as our "cheerleaders" rather than just observers (or judges), you could create a skit, reference a recent sporting event, or even make up your own "cheers" to encourage your assembly.

Connections with the Liturgy

Jeremiah proclaims that God fills heaven and earth. We sing this in the "Holy, holy, holy" of the eucharist: "Heaven and earth are full of your glory."

Let the Children Come

The prophet Jeremiah is playing peekaboo with God; sometimes God feels very near and sometimes very far away. Children, indeed all people, have this feeling too. Today's gospel initially may seem harsh and even scary for children (and parents), but Jesus is speaking of closeness and intimacy. Through baptism we are brought so close to God, through Jesus the Christ, we are a part of God's family. This whole family promises in baptism to nurture closeness and intimacy with God, so that the fire kindled in the waters of baptism can be nurtured in the child.

Assembly Song
Gathering

Here, O Lord, your servants gather   ELW 530
O Holy Spirit, enter in   ELW 786, LBW 459
Soli Deo Gloria   ELW 878

Psalmody and Acclamations

Hopson, Hal. "Psalm 82" from TPP.
Paradowski, John. "Psalm 82" from PWC.
+ Wold, Wayne L. "Psalm 80:1-2, 8-19," Refrain 2, from PSCY. (GA) ELW 169 with proper verse for Lectionary 20.

Hymn of the Day

All my hope on God is founded   ELW 757, WOV 782   *MICHAEL*
If God my Lord be for me   ELW 788, LBW 454   *IST GOTT FÜR MICH*
Lift high the cross   ELW 660, LBW 377   *CRUCIFER*

Offering

We place upon your table, Lord   ELW 467, LBW 217
Let the vineyards be fruitful   ELW 182

Communion

My faith looks up to thee   ELW 759, LBW 479
We come to the hungry feast   ELW 479, DH 84, WOV 766
All who love and serve your city   ELW 724, LBW 436

Sending

God of tempest, God of whirlwind   ELW 400
Rise up, O saints of God!   ELW 669, LBW 383

Additional Assembly Songs

Señor, ten piedad de tu pueblo   LLC 530
Beauty for brokenness   W&P 17
Let justice roll like a river   W&P 85

⊕ Brazilian traditional. "Here You Are Among Us/Tú estas presente" from *One Is the Body: Songs of Unity and Diversity.* U. GIA G-5790.

⊕ Meru (Kenya) tune/arr. Carl Kronberg. "O God's Lamb Most Holy" from *Set Free: A Collection of African Hymns.* SATB. AFP 9780806600451.

✿ Byrd, Marc/Matt Maher. "On the Third Day" from CCLI.
✿ Beeching, Vicky. "Stronger Than the Storm" from CCLI.
✿ Doerksen, Brian. "Refiner's Fire" from CCLI.
✿ Hall, Mark. "And Now My Lifesong Sings" from CCLI.
✿ Mooring, Leeland/Marc Byrd. "Beautiful Lord" from CCLI.
✿ Zschech, Darlene. "I Know It" from CCLI.

Music for the Day
Choral

p Ferguson, John. "Let the Whole Creation Cry." SAB, org. AFP 9780806698182.
p Hopson, Hal. "God, in Your Grace." SATB, pno. AFP 9781451451597.
● Howells, Herbert/arr. John Rutter. "All My Hope on God Is Founded." U, desc, org. Collegium CCS-201.
Ziegenhals, Harriet. "Tapestry." U, pno. CG CGA533.

Children's Choir

p Parker, Alice. "Many in One" from *Augsburg Choirbook for Women.* U/2 pt, kybd. AFP 9781451461688.
Thiman, Eric. "Eternal Ruler of the Ceaseless Round." U, kybd. NOV NOV401012.
Tucker, Margaret. "Prayer for Today." U, kybd, opt fl. CG CGA358.

Keyboard / Instrumental

● Burkhardt, Michael. "Michael" from *As Though the Whole Creation Cried,* vol. 1. Org. MSM 10-555.
● Cherwien, David M. "Crucifer" from *Let It Rip! at the Piano,* vol. 1. Pno. AFP 9780800659066.
● Cherwien, David M. "Lift High the Cross." Org. MSM 10-726.
p ● Raabe, Nancy M. "Crucifer" from *Foot-Friendly Preludes.* Org. AFP 9781451479539.

⊕ = global song   ✿ = praise song   + = semicontinuous psalm
● = relates to hymn of the day   p = available in Prelude Music Planner

Handbell

p   Geschke, Susan. "Joshua Fit the Battle of Jericho." 2 oct, L2. HOP
        2621.

•   McAninch, Diane. "Lift High the Cross." 2-3 oct, L2-. HOP 2357.
        Thompson, Karen. "Earth Has No Sorrow That Heaven Cannot
            Heal." 3-5 oct hb, opt 3-5 oct hc, L2. AGEHR AG35331.

Sunday, August 14

Maximilian Kolbe, died 1941; Kaj Munk, died 1944; martyrs

Father Kolbe was a Franciscan priest, born Raymond Kolbe.
After spending some time working in Asia, he returned
in 1936 to his native Poland, where he supervised a fri-
ary that came to house thousands of Polish war refugees,
mostly Jews. The Nazis were watching, however, and he was
arrested. Confined in Auschwitz, Kolbe gave generously of
his meager resources and finally volunteered to be starved
to death in place of another man who was a husband
and father. After two weeks, he was executed by a lethal
injection.

Kaj (pronounced KYE) Munk, a Danish Lutheran pastor
and playwright, was an outspoken critic of the Nazis, who
occupied Denmark during the Second World War. His plays
frequently highlighted the eventual victory of the Christian
faith despite the church's weak and ineffective witness. The
Nazis feared Munk because his sermons and articles helped
to strengthen the Danish resistance movement. He was
executed by the Gestapo on January 5, 1944.

Monday, August 15

Mary, Mother of Our Lord

The church honors Mary with the Greek title *theotokos*,
meaning God-bearer. Origen first used this title in the early
church, and the councils of Ephesus and Chalcedon upheld
it. Luther upheld this same title in his writings. The honor
paid to Mary as *theotokos* and mother of our Lord goes
back to biblical times, when Mary herself sang, "From now
on all generations will call me blessed" (Luke 1:48). Mary's
life revealed the presence of God incarnate, and it revealed
God's presence among the humble and poor. Mary's song,
the Magnificat, speaks of reversals in the reign of God: the
mighty are cast down, the lowly are lifted up, the hungry are
fed, and the rich are sent away empty-handed.

Saturday, August 20

Bernard, Abbot of Clairvaux, died 1153

Bernard was a Cistercian monk who became an abbot
of great spiritual depth. He was a mystical writer deeply
devoted to the humanity of Christ who emphasized the
inner human experience of prayer and contemplation. He
was critical of one of the foremost theologians of the day,
Peter Abelard, because he believed Abelard's approach to
faith was too rational and did not provide sufficient room
for mystery. Bernard's devotional writings are still read
today. His sermon on the Song of Solomon treats that Old
Testament book as an allegory of Christ's love for humanity. Bernard wrote several hymns that are still sung today
in translation, including "Jesus, the Very Thought of You"
(ELW 754).

August 21, 2016
Time after Pentecost — Lectionary 21

Remember the sabbath day. Call the sabbath a delight. This is the Lord's day, and the Lord will do for us what the Lord does: feed us, forgive us, help and heal us. Rejoice at all the wonderful things God is doing.

Prayer of the Day

O God, mighty and immortal, you know that as fragile creatures surrounded by great dangers, we cannot by ourselves stand upright. Give us strength of mind and body, so that even when we suffer because of human sin, we may rise victorious through your Son, Jesus Christ, our Savior and Lord.

Gospel Acclamation

Alleluia. The crowd ˈ was rejoicing* at the wonderful things that Je- ˈ sus was doing. *Alleluia.* (Luke 13:17)

Readings and Psalm
Isaiah 58:9b-14

The Lord promises those who have returned from exile that where justice and mercy prevail, the ruins will be rebuilt and light will rise in the darkness. It is a day for new beginnings.

Psalm 103:1-8

The Lord crowns you with mercy and steadfast love. (Ps. 103:4)

Hebrews 12:18-29

Using images of Moses from the Old Testament, the writer presents a striking vision of the new covenant of God made possible in Christ. There is no longer fear; only awe in the new promise in Christ into which we are invited.

Luke 13:10-17

Jesus heals a woman on the sabbath, offering her a new beginning for her life. When challenged by a narrow reading of the sabbath command, Jesus responds by expanding "sabbath work" to include setting people free from bondage.

Semicontinuous reading and psalm
Jeremiah 1:4-10

The call of the prophet Jeremiah does not depend on either Jeremiah's abilities or his age. God will give him the words to speak. Even before Jeremiah was born, God appointed him a prophet to the nations, to minister in the difficult years before the Babylonian exile.

Psalm 71:1-6

From my mother's womb you have been my strength. (Ps. 71:6)

Preface   Sundays

Color   Green

Prayers of Intercession

The prayers are prepared locally for each occasion. The following examples may be adapted or used as appropriate.

Rooted in Christ and rising to serve, let us pray for the church, the world, and all in need.

A brief silence.

Lord of all languages, we pray with and for Christians in worship all over the world. Make your church joyful to reflect the diversity of your people and the unity of your love. Hear us, O God.

Your mercy is great.

Your Spirit speaks in creation. We thank you for watered gardens, for abundant yield, for clean water, for sunlight, for communities where people and nature live in peace together. Hear us, O God.

Your mercy is great.

Remove the yoke of destructive partisanship, the pointing of the finger at our enemies, and bless nations in need (*especially*). Empower all to speak the truth, encouraging honorable leadership. Hear us, O God.

Your mercy is great.

Bring strength, health, and wholeness in the parched places of our lives. Bless those in need this day (*especially*) and surround them with care and hope. Hear us, O God.

Your mercy is great.

We pray for those who must be absent from this assembly while they work. Give them and all people sabbath rest. Refresh our hearts in Christ. Hear us, O God.

Your mercy is great.

Here other intercessions may be offered.

Our stories are shaped in community. We thank you for people young and old, women and men, who have witnessed to your love, and we remember those who have recently died (*especially*). Hear us, O God.
Your mercy is great.
We lift our prayers to you, O God, trusting your promise to hear us; through Jesus Christ our Lord.
Amen.

Images in the Readings

The **bent woman** is a striking image of all humanity. How is each of us bent?

By the early second century, the majority of Christians were Gentiles rather than Jews. Therefore, replacing **sabbath** observance with a communal meal on Sunday, which was a workday in the Roman Empire, was a logical religious development. Some Christians in the sixteenth century worked to reinstitute sabbath as the way to keep Sunday, but for many Christians throughout history, Sunday could not be a day of rest. One way we "keep sabbath" is by doing justice to the poor.

The poem from Isaiah anticipates that those returning from exile will rebuild Jerusalem, restoring its **streets**. Also in the book of Revelation, the resurrection is described as life in a city. Very few hymns continue this biblical tradition of seeing the city—its walls, streets, clean water, stored food, cooperative community—as a positive way to depict the presence of God. We can praise God, not only for trees, but also for libraries; not only for stars, but also for streetlights.

Ideas for the Day

◆   The image of the woman bent over is striking. Being "quite unable to stand up straight" (Luke 13:11) meant she couldn't look people in the eye. She was probably ignored and forgotten. But Jesus notices her. He sets her free from the "spirit that had crippled her" (v. 11). Unfortunately, many women still live under a spirit of oppression today. Women who work outside the home are often passed over for promotions and paid less for equal work. Women who choose to stay home and raise children are easily ignored and forgotten. Violence toward women is unacceptably high and unconscionably excused. There are many ways that women need justice and an advocate. Spur your congregation to notice the spirits that cripple women and to work toward setting them free in whatever way they can.

◆   In today's gospel, Jesus once again gets himself into trouble for healing on the sabbath. But his spin on it is important: "Woman, you are set free from your ailment" (Luke 13:12). Keeping the sabbath was meant to remind God's people that God had rescued them from bondage in the land of Egypt (Deut. 5:15). So the sabbath was the perfect occasion to set a person free through healing. If the sabbath is primarily understood as a day for healing, how might you encourage your congregation to keep sabbath? Healing can certainly be found in rest but also in forgiveness, feeding, working for justice, or helping others. How can you set someone (or yourself) free this sabbath?

◆   In the reading from Hebrews, God's is the "voice whose words made the hearers beg that not another word be spoken to them" (12:19). The God whom the Hebrews met at Sinai was terrifying and awesome. This is God as illustrated by C. S. Lewis in *The Lion, the Witch and the Wardrobe*. When the Pevensie children first hear that Aslan is a lion, they say, "Then he isn't safe?" and Mr. Beaver replies, "'Course he isn't safe. But he's good." We sometimes sterilize God, making God our buddy or sweet baby Jesus. We do well to remember that our God is not safe—but God is good.

Connections with the Liturgy

Jesus speaks of the sabbath as a day to set captives free. In the confession and forgiveness, we admit that since we remain captive to sin, we need Christ to free us from this bondage.

The fire that is not God and the fire that is: see *Evangelical Lutheran Worship*'s depiction of the Vigil of Easter, the first eucharist of the resurrection (p. 266). Christians surround the fiery God in "the light of Christ, rising in glory," dispelling the darkness of our hearts and minds.

Let the Children Come

When Jesus restores a woman to health on the sabbath, he reminds us that a vibrant, abundant life springs from coming close to him on the day of rest. The concept of restorative, playful rest is counter to many children's lives of overscheduled calendars and lack of free time. Add in a dose of abundant screen time with boredom, and the sabbath can pass by without a notice. How does your congregation model a different rhythm than the wider culture? How does your Christian assembly model for children life-giving rest on the sabbath?

Assembly Song
Gathering

God is here! ELW 526, WOV 719
Oh, for a thousand tongues to sing ELW 886, LBW 559, LS 185
Praise, praise, praise the Lord! ELW 875, TFF 278, W&P 116

Psalmody and Acclamations

Cherwien, David. "Psalm 103:1-8," Refrain 2, from PSCY.
Hopson, Hal. "Psalm 103" from TPP.
+   Kallman, Daniel. "Psalm 71:1-6" from PWC.
   (GA) ELW 169 with proper verse for Lectionary 21.

Hymn of the Day

O day full of grace   ELW 627, LBW 161   *DEN SIGNEDE DAG*

O day of rest and gladness   ELW 521, LBW 251   *ELLACOMBE*

Come, we that love the Lord   ELW 625, TFF 135, WOV 742
    MARCHING TO ZION

Offering

Create in me a clean heart   ELW 186

Taste and see   ELW 493, TFF 126

Communion

There is a balm in Gilead   ELW 614, TFF 185, WOV 737

I know that my Redeemer lives!   ELW 619, LBW 352

Rock of Ages, cleft for me   ELW 623, LBW 327

Sending

O God, our help in ages past   ELW 632, LBW 320

How firm a foundation   ELW 796, LBW 507, LS 80

Additional Assembly Songs

Come and taste   W&P 30

Jesus, we want to meet   TFF 145

Con gran gozo y placer   LLC 406

⊕ African American spiritual. "Jesus Is a Rock in a Weary Land." ELW 333.

⊕ Traditional, Nyanga, Zambia. "Chimwemwe mwa Yesu/Rejoice in Jesus." from *Agape: Songs of Hope and Reconciliation*. SATB. Lutheran World Federation. Out of print. Available on Amazon.com.

☼ Brown, Chris/Jane Williams/London Gatch/Mack Brock/Steven Furtick/Wade Joye. "In Your Presence" from CCLI.

☼ Fox, Kip. "Already Clean" from Kipfox.com and CCLI.

☼ Springer, Chris/Eric Nuzum. "Healing Waters" from CCLI.

☼ Tomlin, Chris/Christy Nockels/Daniel Carson/Matt Redman/Nathan Nockels. "Healing Is in Your Hands" from CCLI.

☼ Tomlin, Chris/Daniel Carson/Ed Cash/Jesse Reeves/Kristian Stanfill/Matt Redman. "The Name of Jesus" from CCLI.

Music for the Day
Choral

p   Ippolitov-Ivanov, Mikhail/arr. Arthur Becker. "Bless the Lord, O My Soul." SATB, opt kybd. GIA G-6125.

p   Larson, Lloyd. "You Are Mine" from *Contemporary Classics for Two Voices*. Solo/duet, pno. HOP 8570.

p   Miller, Aaron David. "Oh, Happy Day When We Shall Stand" from *Choral Stanzas for Hymns*, vol. 1. U, kybd. AFP 9780806698410.

p ● Shaw, Timothy. "We're Marching to Zion." SATB, snare drm, tri. AFP 9780800664275.

Children's Choir

p   Burrows, Mark. "Bwana Asifiwe (Lobe den Herren)." U/2 pt, pno, opt perc. CG CGA1311.

Handel, G. F./arr. Hal H. Hopson. "I Will at All Times Praise the Lord" from *G. F. Handel: A Collection of Anthems for Children, Youth and Adults*. U, kybd. CG CGC10.

Henderson, Ruth Watson. "Bless the Lord, O My Soul." U, kybd. HIN HMC1171.

Keyboard / Instrumental

p ● Bottomley, Greg. "Ellacombe" from *Piano Sunday Morning*, vol. 2. Pno. AFP 9781451462654.

p ● Raabe, Nancy M. "Ellacombe" from *Grace and Peace*, vol. 2. Pno. AFP 9780800679019.

p ● Sedio, Mark. "Den signede dag" from *Come and Praise*, vol. 1. Org. AFP 9780800678500.

● Wold, Wayne L. "Den signede dag" from *Augsburg Organ Library: Easter*. Org. AFP 9780800659363.

Handbell

p ● Honoré, Jeffrey. "Marching to Zion." 3 or 5 oct, L4. AFP 9781451421231.

● Larson, Katherine. "O Day Full of Grace." 3-5 oct hb, opt 2 oct hc, L4. CPH 97-6774.

● Sherman, Arnold. "Canticle of Praise." 3-5 oct, L4-. AGEHR AG35288.

Wednesday, August 24
Bartholomew, Apostle

Bartholomew is mentioned as one of Jesus' disciples in Matthew, Mark, and Luke. The list in John does not include him but rather Nathanael. These two are therefore often assumed to be the same person. Except for his name on these lists of the Twelve, little is known. Some traditions say Bartholomew preached in India or Armenia following the resurrection. In art, Bartholomew is pictured holding a flaying knife to indicate the manner in which he was killed.

August 28, 2016
Time after Pentecost — Lectionary 22

Invited and inviting—that is the nature of the church. By God's grace in holy baptism we have a place at the banquet table of the Lord. When, by the power of that same Spirit, humility and mutual love continue among us, the church can be more inviting still.

Prayer of the Day

O God, you resist those who are proud and give grace to those who are humble. Give us the humility of your Son, that we may embody the generosity of Jesus Christ, our Savior and Lord.

Gospel Acclamation

Alleluia. Take my yoke upon you, and ¹ learn from me;* for I am gentle and hum- ¹ ble in heart. *Alleluia.* (Matt. 11:29)

Readings and Psalm

Proverbs 25:6-7

The book of Proverbs is part of a collection of writings known as wisdom literature. Wisdom literature gave directions to Israel's leaders and people for the conduct of daily life. Today's reading is about humility.

or Sirach 10:12-18

The book of Sirach, like the book of Proverbs, is part of a collection of writings known as wisdom literature. In the reading for today, the writer of the book warns against the sin of pride, proclaiming that God will utterly overthrow the proud.

Psalm 112

The righteous are merciful and full of compassion. (Ps. 112:4)

Hebrews 13:1-8, 15-16

The conclusion of the letter to the Hebrews contains suggestions for the conduct of a holy life, all of which are shaped by God's love toward us in Jesus Christ.

Luke 14:1, 7-14

Jesus observes guests jockeying for position at the table. He uses the opportunity to teach his hearers to choose humility rather than self-exaltation. Jesus also makes an appeal for hosts to mimic God's gracious hospitality to the poor and the broken.

Semicontinuous reading and psalm

Jeremiah 2:4-13

God, who has been faithful in leading Israel through the wilderness into a good land, calls upon the heavens to witness the incredible foolishness of a people who, under the flawed leadership of priests, rulers, and prophets, willingly abandon God's life-giving water for leaky cisterns.

Psalm 81:1, 10-16

I feed you with the finest wheat and satisfy you with honey from the rock. (Ps. 81:16)

Preface   Sundays

Color   Green

Prayers of Intercession

The prayers are prepared locally for each occasion. The following examples may be adapted or used as appropriate.

Rooted in Christ and rising to serve, let us pray for the church, the world, and all in need.

A brief silence.

O God, guide leaders who speak your word to your people. Use your church's powerful witness and genuine invitation to welcome all to your banquet table. Hear us, O God.

Your mercy is great.

We thank you for tables of abundant food. Bless crops, farms, and industries, that as co-creators with you, we may provide responsibly from the earth for the sake of all. Hear us, O God.

Your mercy is great.

Break the bonds of captivity and injustice. Work in leaders and nations to bring peace and to advocate for the least of these. Especially we pray for . . . . Hear us, O God.

Your mercy is great.

Heal and comfort those we hold in our hearts and those who have asked for our prayers (*especially*). Bring hope to prisoners, refugees, and outsiders. Hear us, O God.

Your mercy is great.

Strengthen marriages, families, and friendships with mutual love and respect. Bless our congregation to be a place of support and care for healthy relationships. Hear us, O God.

Your mercy is great.

Here other intercessions may be offered.

Rejoicing in the promise of the heavenly banquet, we give thanks for all those who have died in faith (*especially Augustine, Bishop of Hippo, and Moses the Black, martyr*). Join us, with them, at the resurrection of the righteous. Hear us, O God.

Your mercy is great.

We lift our prayers to you, O God, trusting your promise to hear us; through Jesus Christ our Lord.

Amen.

Images in the Readings

The Bible often uses the image of a **wedding** to symbolize the covenant relationship between God and the people. Granting the culture in which this image arose, God is being compared to a groom who chooses, loves, and cares for the bride who, in turn, honors, obeys, and serves him. The image of the wedding feast includes the whole community in celebrating the commitment of the couple.

The reading from Proverbs seems to address the **lowly** who ought not get above their station. The reading from Luke seems to address the **wealthy** who host banquets. So we are all included.

The phrase "**entertaining angels unawares**" derives from the traditional English translation of today's Hebrews passage and has entered secular speech to suggest unsuspected religious outcomes. Moreover, our serving communion to the stranger is like welcoming angels.

The author of Hebrews uses the noun *sacrifice* as a metaphor. For Christians, literal sacrifices, that is, the killing of animals as gifts to the deities, are replaced by praising God and giving to the poor.

Ideas for the Day

◆ Check out Inspiration Kitchens (www.inspirationkitchens.org) in Chicago for a vision of what this feast described in today's gospel could look like today. Especially check out "Student Stories." These restaurants not only invite the poor, incarcerated, lame, and lowly to "Come up here" and eat, but also to cook, organize, manage, and host the meal!

◆ Do not preach that Jesus calls us to universally take the lowest seat, make ourselves less, and think little of ourselves. Not only is this message detrimental to many of those seated in our assemblies, but it is also not what Jesus is calling us to. Especially people of color, women, young people, and LGBTQ people have more than likely internalized that they do not belong at the top. Do not reinforce this message. Instead, reinforce that Jesus is granting tremendous agency in this passage. Jesus is entrusting us with the role of hosting a banquet with a generosity that says that in God we are so capable, so provided for, so wealthy that we do not need to rely on the system of reciprocity that our culture is dependent on.

◆ Trace the footsteps of vulnerability through this text. To show up and assume your position is to be invulnerable. To show up and take the lowest seat is to assume a vulnerable position. A host has a certain level of control when inviting friends to a party. To invite strangers, the poor, the outcast, and the lame leaves the host in a vulnerable position, encountering many unknowns. Notice Jesus' vulnerability in attending this meal at the Pharisee's home. Notice the way God goes about hosting a meal. It seems that God is a vulnerable host, encountering a great many unknowns.

◆ Notice the directions in this encounter. Who's going up? Who's coming down? Which direction has life in it for you? Moving up or being relinquished from the top? Jürgen Moltmann writes, "God became man that dehumanized men might become true men" (*The Crucified God* [Minneapolis: Fortress Press, 1993], 231). Moving down might free you to be less of a god and more of a human. Maybe there's freedom in being invited to take the lowest seat.

Connections with the Liturgy

Several of the prayers before and after communion in *Evangelical Lutheran Worship* make explicit the Christian conviction that "offerings," that is, "sacrifices," are now given not to the deities, but to all in need, "those who hunger in any way" (pp. 107, 64, 65, 114).

Let the Children Come

Unspoken lessons of hospitality and welcome are abundant in our church buildings. Children are especially attuned to unspoken messages. A place at the table or a clean, vibrant space conveys what words cannot fully convey: "This community values you and knows your worth!" However, the inverse is true too. Children can sense when they are a second thought or not truly welcomed by the community. The classrooms in a dark basement or cluttered corners are telling the children just how low they are in the community hierarchy. What does your church environment convey to children about their value?

Assembly Song
Gathering

Gather Us In   ELW 532, WOV 718

What is this place   ELW 524

Jesus, we are gathered   ELW 529, TFF 140

Psalmody and Acclamations

"How Blest Are Those Who Fear the Lord" (MELCOMBE) from PAS 112A.

Hopson, Hal. "Psalm 112" from TPP. U/cant, kybd, opt fl.

+ Schalk, Carl. "Psalm 81:1, 10-16" from PWC.

(GA) ELW 169 with proper verse for Lectionary 22.

Hymn of the Day

We Are Called   ELW 720, W&P 147   *WE ARE CALLED*

The trumpets sound, the angels sing   ELW 531, W&P 139
THE FEAST IS READY

Jesu, Jesu, fill us with your love   ELW 708, TFF 83, WOV 765
CHEREPONI

Offering

Let us go now to the banquet   ELW 523, LLC 410

Yours, Lord, is the glory   ELW 849, LLC 605

Communion

Lord of glory, you have bought us   ELW 707, LBW 424

Light dawns on a weary world   ELW 726

Where charity and love prevail   ELW 359, LBW 126

Sending

Voices raised to you   ELW 845

Lead on, O King eternal!   ELW 805, LBW 495

Additional Assembly Songs

Where charity and love prevail   TFF 84

Have thine own way, Lord   TFF 152

Lord, I want to be a Christian   TFF 234

⊕ Bunun melody. "Lord, We Thank You for This Food" from *Glory to God*. U. WJK 9780664238971.

⊕ Punjabi melody. "Blest Be God, Praised Forever" from *Glory to God*. U. WJK 9780664238971.

✿ Baloche, Paul. "I Will Boast" from CCLI.

✿ Brown, Brenton. "Humble King" from CCLI.

✿ Morgan, Reuben. "Emmanuel" from CCLI.

✿ Smith, Martin/Matt Redman. "Take It to the Streets" from CCLI.

✿ Thomas, Dylan/Joel Davies/Marty Sampson. "Came to My Rescue" from CCLI.

Music for the Day
Choral

p   Bender, Jan. "Whosoever Does Not Receive the Kingdom" from *To God Will I Sing: Vocal Solos for the Church Year*. Solo, kybd, opt trbl inst. AFP 9780800674335.

p   Hayes, Mark. "Welcome Table." SATB, pno. AFP 9780800676032.

p   Keesecker, Thomas. "Around You, O Lord Jesus." SAB, pno, opt hb. AFP 9780800664336.

p   Pasch, William. "When Invited to the Feast." 2 pt mxd, pno, opt SATB, assembly. AFP 9781451424096.

Children's Choir

Farrar, Sue. "Give Thanks." U/2 pt, kybd, opt hb. BP BP1317.

How, Martin. "Thy Kingdom Come, O God." U, org. GIA G-RA461.

p   Patterson, Mark. "I Want Jesus to Walk with Me." U, pno, opt desc. AFP 9781451421606.

Keyboard / Instrumental

● Cool, Jayne Southwick. "Chereponi" from *Piano Plus Through the Year*, vol. 2. Pno, inst. AFP 9780800663728.

p ● Kerr, J. Wayne. "Chereponi" from *Amen, We Praise Your Name: World Hymns for Organ*. Org. AFP 9781451486018.

● Miller, Aaron David. "The Feast Is Ready" from *Augsburg Organ Library: Autumn*. Org. AFP 9780800675790.

p ● Wonacott, Glenn. "We Are Called" from *Introductions and Alternate Accompaniments for Piano*, vol. 8. Pno. AFP 9780800623661.

Handbell

● Helman, Michael. "Jesu, Jesu, Fill Us with Your Love." 3-5 oct hb, opt 3 oct hc, L3. AFP 1111025.

● Prins, Matthew. "We Are Called." 2-3 oct, L2. GIA G-8543. 3-5 oct, L2. GIA G-8544.

p   Tucker, Sondra. "Morning Hymn (Father, We Praise Thee)." 3-5 oct, L1. CG CGB787.

Sunday, August 28

Augustine, Bishop of Hippo, died 430

Augustine was one of the greatest theologians of the Western church. Born in North Africa, he was a philosophy student in Carthage, where he later became a teacher of rhetoric. Much of his young life was a debauched one. As an adult he came under the influence of Ambrose, the bishop of Milan, and through him came to see Christianity as a religion appropriate for a philosopher. Augustine was baptized by Ambrose at the Easter Vigil in 387. He was ordained four years later and made bishop of Hippo in 396. Augustine was a defender of the Christian faith and argued, against the Donatists, that the holiness of the church did not depend on the holiness of its members, particularly the clergy, but that holiness comes from Christ, the head of the church. Augustine's autobiography, *Confessions*, tells of his slow movement toward faith and includes the line "Late have I loved thee."

Moses the Black, monk, martyr, died around 400

A man of great strength and rough character, Moses the Black was converted to Christian faith toward the close of the fourth century. Prior to his conversion he had been a thief and a leader of a gang of robbers. The story of his conversion is unknown, but eventually he became a desert

⊕ = global song   ✿ = praise song   + = semicontinuous psalm
● = relates to hymn of the day   p = available in Prelude Music Planner

monk at Skete. The change in his heart and life had a profound impact on his native Ethiopia. He was murdered when Berber bandits attacked his monastery.

Friday, September 2

Nikolai Frederik Severin Grundtvig, bishop, renewer of the church, died 1872

Grundtvig was one of two principal Danish theologians of the nineteenth century; the other was Søren Kierkegaard. Grundtvig's ministry as a parish pastor had a difficult start. He was officially censured after his first sermon, though he did receive approval a year later to be ordained. He served with his father for two years but was unable to receive a call for seven years after that. In 1826 he was forced to resign after he attacked the notion that Christianity was merely a philosophical idea rather than God's revelation made known to us in Christ and through word and sacrament. This belief would be a hallmark of Grundtvig's writing. He spent his last thirty-three years as a chaplain at a home for elderly women. From his university days he was convinced that poetry spoke to the human spirit better than prose. He wrote more than a thousand hymns, including "God's Word Is Our Great Heritage" (ELW 509).

TIME AFTER PENTECOST
AUTUMN

SUMMER

AUTUMN

NOVEMBER

PREPARING FOR AUTUMN

As autumn begins, congregations return from the more relaxed pace of summer to the demands of fall—the beginning of a new school year, the annual stewardship campaign, and soon enough, preparations for the holidays. As family calendars fill up and household budgets get stretched, the church hears Jesus' call to a costly discipleship that demands hard choices be made with our time and our money.

It's unfortunate that this season begins with the Labor/Labour Day weekend (Lectionary 23), over which attendance may be near its lowest, and concludes on Reformation Sunday (Lectionary 31) when many congregations will choose to use the texts for Reformation instead of those for Lectionary 31. The gospel reading for the first Sunday in September concludes, "So therefore, none of you can become my disciple if you do not give up all your possessions" (Luke 14:33). The gospel reading for the last Sunday in October reaches its climax when Zacchaeus the tax collector pledges *half* his possessions and fourfold repayment of those he has defrauded and Jesus declares, "Today salvation has come to this house. . . . For the Son of Man came to seek out and to save the lost" (Luke 19:8-9). In the weeks between these two bookends, congregations will follow as the Gospel of Luke explores the dangers of wealth and the temptation toward self-righteousness.

Back to school

Just as the summer months were marked by scene after scene of miraculous healing, these autumn months are filled with parables that are either exclusive to or greatly expanded by the Gospel of Luke. As Jesus heads toward Jerusalem, he is teaching the crowds, the Pharisees, and the disciples about the demands of discipleship and the dangers of wealth. Preachers, teachers, and worship leaders might help the assembly take note of this shift by incorporating the art of storytelling throughout Sunday morning worship and Christian education.

These parables are filled with memorable characters. The shepherd looks for the sheep and the woman her lost coin. The dishonest steward cuts deals. The rich man pleads with Father Abraham to send Lazarus to his brothers. The widow harangues the unjust judge. The Pharisee congratulates himself for not being like the tax collector. These scenes are ripe for chancel dramas. Invite the writers, actors, and other dramatists in the congregation to consider how they would present these stories. Rather than reducing these parables to a single meaning, assist the assembly in finding their own analogues for the people and relationships described by these tales.

Sunday school curricula that follow the lectionary, such as Spark or Whirl (wearesparkhouse.org), will very naturally introduce children to the parables of Jesus in age-appropriate ways that help them learn these stories by heart, internalizing them as foundational elements of our shared Christian narrative. Other pedagogies, such as Godly Play or Catechesis of the Good Shepherd, focus on giving children a primary experience of storytelling and meaning making that is as creative, generative, and open-ended as the parables themselves.

For adults, who have often been through years of schooling and been instilled with a desire to have "the answer" or to "get to the point," a Sunday morning adult forum or midweek book study on the parables might create the space needed to slow down and approach these stories with the type of playfulness and imagination that yields new meanings. Professor Amy-Jill Levine's book *Short Stories by Jesus: The Enigmatic Parables of a Controversial Rabbi* (HarperCollins, 2014) has nine chapters, which, while not corresponding exactly to the lectionary texts for this season, do line up neatly with the number of Sundays.

The dangers of wealth

From Jesus' early words this fall, calling disciples to give up all their possessions (Lectionary 23), to the parable of the rich man and Lazarus (Lectionary 26), the Gospel of Luke is unambiguous in its critique of wealth and the dangers it poses to those who want to follow Jesus. "No slave can serve two masters," Jesus says. "You cannot serve God and wealth" (Luke 16:13; Lectionary 25).

At first glance, the autumn texts may seem like a stewardship committee chair's dream come true. Look closely, however, and you'll find difficult words for those who become self-satisfied with their tithing and their public prayer (Lectionary 30). What then are we to say, or to sing, about these things?

Luke's gospel gives us some clues. Just as Jesus assures us that "there is joy in the presence of the angels of God over one sinner who repents" (Luke 15:10; Lectionary 24), so we also catch a glimpse of that repentance as Zacchaeus, a rich man and a tax collector, makes a spectacle of himself in his efforts to see the Lord (Lectionary 31). Rather than emphasizing our duty to give, which Jesus addresses rather dismissively as a motivation (Lectionary 27), worship planners and stewardship speakers can look for opportunities for the assembly to return to the Lord their God, offering glory and praise to the one who seeks out and saves those who are lost—which is all of us (Lectionary 28).

The offering is a wonderful place for the sung theology of the congregation to reflect Luke's emphasis on the joy that follows when those who were lost, especially those lost in their wealth, are found. Of course we will want to sing "Amazing grace, how sweet the sound" (ELW 779) and "Softly and tenderly Jesus is calling" (ELW 608). Beyond those familiar hymns, look for ones that express the simple joy of offering thanks, such as "To God our thanks we give" (ELW 682) or "Take my life, that I may be" (ELW 583). Consider also "God, whose giving knows no ending" (ELW 678) and "We give thee but thine own" (ELW 686).

Reformation Sunday

The final Sunday of October is still the day when many Lutheran congregations celebrate Reformation Day (October 31) by transferring the festival and its appointed texts to the Sunday gathering. While this festival is intended to celebrate the ongoing work of the Holy Spirit in reforming the church in every land and age, it has sometimes taken on a self-congratulatory spirit as Lutherans celebrate "the Reformation" and neglect to honor the Holy Spirit's reforming activity here and now. When we allow that spirit to enter our worship, we end up, ironically, sounding like the Pharisee who offers thanks to God that he is not like the tax collector (Lectionary 30).

If your congregation will be using the Reformation Sunday texts, endeavor to read them in relationship to the preceding weeks' texts. When the Jews who had believed in Jesus say to him, "We are descendants of Abraham and have never been slaves to anyone," he replies, "I know that you are descendants of Abraham; yet you look for an opportunity to kill me, because there is no place in you for my word" (John 8:33, 37). Having traveled with Jesus through the Gospel of Luke this fall, we will find in this exchange a reminder of the parable of the rich man and Lazarus (Lectionary 26) who come to recognize that their status as children of Abraham is not conditioned by the same criteria that defined them in life. Help the congregation make this connection more explicitly by pairing the traditional "A mighty fortress is our God" (ELW 503–505) with "The God of Abraham praise" (ELW 831).

Likewise, if your congregation will be using the Lectionary 31 texts, there are ample opportunities to connect the story of Zacchaeus the tax collector and the entire arc of Luke's gospel throughout the fall with Lutheran Reformation themes. Though Jesus began this season insisting that all who would follow him must give up all their possessions (Lectionary 23), on this day we hear the story of a rich tax collector who pledges only half his wealth—but with a spirit of sincere repentance—and is assured of his salvation (Luke 19:9-10). As with the Samaritan leper who returns to give praise to God (Lectionary 28), it is the grace we receive through faith the size of a mustard seed (Lectionary 27) that justifies us, not works of our own (Lectionary 30).

Whichever texts you choose to read this day, rather than treating Reformation Sunday as a festival that stands apart from the word of grace heard throughout these autumn months, let it be a joyous culmination of a season of offering thanks and praise to the God who seeks out and saves all who are lost, not because of who we are but because of who God is.

Environment

"Do not be weary in doing what is right" (2 Thessalonians 3:13; Lectionary 33) is an exhortation that summarizes this long season of God's people, the church, in the world. Look for ways to lift up the weekly rhythm of discipleship that gathers us together around word and sacrament and then sends us out to bear God's love and grace to our families, neighborhoods, schools, workplaces, communities, nation, and world.

If you developed a tree of life visual for the summer, its use will continue to be relevant during this time of reflection on and empowerment for a life of faith, ministry, and service:

- The people of God are "like trees planted by streams of water" (Ps. 1:3; Lectionary 23).
- Sinners find a place of welcome under the expansive canopy of God's grace (Lectionary 24).
- The tree of life bears witness to the cross by which Christ claimed us for God (Lectionary 25).
- True riches are found in sharing the abundance of God's provision with others (Lectionary 26).
- Even faith the size of a mustard seed is able to command trees to move (Lectionary 27).
- We find healing and hope in the waters (Lectionary 28).
- We are indebted to those who helped plant the seed of faith in our hearts and nurtured our growth in discipleship (Lectionary 29).

- All creation stands in need of God's forgiveness, and all creation is included in the embrace of God's love and mercy (Lectionary 30).
- Because growth comes by way of change, God's church needs always to be engaged in transformation and reformation (Reformation Sunday).

If Labor/Labour Day is observed in your ministry context, use that as an opportunity to emphasize God's calling of the baptized to ministries of daily life. Consider concluding worship with a sending rite that includes an anointing of worshipers' hands with the sign of the cross, accompanied by a simple phrase such as "Hearts to love; hands to serve," or "God's work; our hands." See also the suggestions for a Labor/Labour Day observance in the seasonal rites section (pp. 211–212). Or consider using the Affirmation of Christian Vocation in *Evangelical Lutheran Worship* as a way to recognize the various kinds of daily work in which the assembly is engaged.

If you created a bread processional cross for the summer (see page 205), use it to anchor the discipleship calling to become what we are privileged to receive: the body and blood of Christ, broken and poured out for the sake of the world. Link its use with an ingathering of wine to be used for communion during the coming year and/or a workshop to explore a variety of communion bread recipes.

This Time after Pentecost offers opportunities for seasonal rites and activities:

- Ask God's blessing on children and youth who are beginning a new school year, as well as college students who are leaving home to pursue academic studies.
- Schedule a blessing of animals—not only pets, but also wild animals, farm animals, and endangered species—to remind us of our calling to be responsible stewards of God's creation. One possible form is provided in the seasonal rites section (p. 273). Invite participation by the neighborhood and/or community in this blessing. The 08_Autumn.Animals.pdf* offers an image to assist those efforts.
- Celebrate the church's ecumenical diversity and the ongoing reformation of God's church by hosting a hymn festival. Invite neighboring congregations and organize a joint choir made up of their singers. Conclude the celebration with a time of fellowship with refreshments contributed by each of the congregations.

Seasonal Checklist

- If the worship schedule changes, notify local newspapers, update your website, and change listings on exterior signs and church voice mail.
- Consider using harvest decorations during autumn, from the first Sunday in September through the end of the church year.
- If a blessing of teachers and students will be held, see possible forms in the seasonal rites section.
- If Bibles will be distributed to young readers, consider having their parents or baptismal sponsors involved in physically handing over the Bibles, as a way to honor promises made at baptism. Words to accompany this action are provided in the seasonal rites section.
- For ideas for celebrating Canada's Day of Thanksgiving (October 10), see pages 331–333.
- Use the Kyrie, or reintroduce confession and forgiveness if this has been omitted during the summer months.
- Use the canticle of praise ("Glory to God") or a hymn equivalent, perhaps in alternation with Sundays when the Kyrie is used.
- Use the Nicene Creed for Reformation Sunday; use the Apostles' Creed for other Sundays in these months.
- If Affirmation of Baptism will be held on Reformation Sunday, begin making preparations.
- Begin planning for Advent 2016.

WORSHIP TEXTS FOR AUTUMN

Confession and Forgiveness

All may make the sign of the cross, the sign marked at baptism,
as the presiding minister begins.

Blessed be the holy Trinity, ✝ one God:
the only Sovereign, who dwells in light;
Christ Jesus, who came to save sinners;
the Holy Spirit, who lives within us.
Amen.

Let us confess our sin in the presence of God
and of one another.

Silence is kept for reflection.

God of overflowing grace,
we come to you with repentant hearts.
Forgive us for shallow thankfulness.
Forgive us for passing by the ones in need.
Forgive us for setting our hopes on fleeting treasures.
Forgive us our neglect and thoughtlessness.
Bring us home from the wilderness of sin,
and strengthen us to serve you
in all that we do and say;
through Jesus Christ, our Savior and Lord.
Amen.

There is joy in heaven over every sinner who repents.
By the grace of God in ✝ Christ Jesus,
who gave himself up for us all,
your sins are forgiven and you are made free.
Rejoice with the angels and with one another!
We are home in God's mercy, now and forever.
Amen.

Offering Prayer

Merciful God, as grains of wheat scattered upon the hills
were gathered together to become one bread,
so let your church be gathered together
from the ends of the earth into your kingdom,
for yours is the glory through Jesus Christ, now and forever.
Amen.

Invitation to Communion

Take hold of the life that really is life.
Come, take your place at the table.

Prayer after Communion

We come again to you, O God,
giving you thanks that in this feast of mercy
you have embraced us and healed us,
making us one in the body of Christ.
Go with us on our way.
Equip us for every good work,
that we may continue to give you thanks
by embracing others with mercy and healing;
through Jesus Christ, our Savior and Lord.
Amen.

Sending of Communion

Gracious God, you took the form of a servant,
offering yourself as food, comfort, and strength
to a sick and hurting world.
Anoint with a servant heart
those who take your word and sacrament
to our sisters and brothers
in their homes/in prisons/in hospitals.
Grant grace, mercy, healing, and hope
to those who feast on your body and blood
and receive your words of new life.
May we all recognize that we have a place and a home
in the body of our Lord Jesus Christ.
Amen.

Blessing

God Almighty send you light and truth
to keep you all the days of your life.
The hand of God protect you;
the holy angels accompany you;
and the blessing of almighty God,
the Father, the + Son, and the Holy Spirit,
be with you now and forever.
Amen.

Dismissal

Go in peace. Remember the poor.
Thanks be to God.

SEASONAL RITES FOR AUTUMN

Blessings for Teachers and Students

For the marvels of your creation,
we praise you, O God.
For the opportunity to explore and study,
we praise you, O God.
For those who guide us, teachers and mentors,
we praise you, O God.
Teach us your ways and guide us in your path,
for you are the creator of all that is, seen and unseen.
Amen.

or

Let us pray for all who are beginning a new school year,
that both students and teachers
will be blessed in their academic endeavors.

Almighty God, you give wisdom and knowledge.
Grant teachers the gift of joy and insight,
and students the gift of diligence and openness,
that all may grow in what is good and honest and true.
Support all who teach and all who learn,
that together we may know and follow your ways;
through Jesus Christ our Lord.
Amen.

Presentation of the Bible

*A representative of the congregation may present a Bible to each
person. These or similar words may be spoken:*
Receive this Bible.
Hear God's word with us.
Learn and tell its stories.
Discover its mysteries.
Honor its commandments.
Rejoice in its good news.
May God's life-giving word
inspire you and make you wise.

Blessing of Backpacks

*This blessing is suitable for a Sunday before school begins and
may be publicized for several Sundays beforehand. The ritual
may be modified to include adults, who could be encouraged in
advance to bring their smartphones, laptops, work boots, or other
tools of their trade. This blessing, however, focuses on children
starting the school year.*

*Have the children come forward at the appointed time, wearing
their backpacks. Mark 10:13-16, Romans 12:4-8, or another
appropriate scripture passage may be read once the children
have gathered.*

Dear God,
as we get ready to start another year in school,
we ask your blessing on these backpacks,
and especially on these children who will wear them.
As they do the very important work of being students,
bless them with
 eagerness to learn, that their world may grow large;
 respect for teachers and students,
 that they may form healthy relationships;
 love for nature,
 that they may become caretakers of your creation;
 happiness when learning is easy
 and stick-to-it-iveness when it is hard;
 faith in Jesus as their best teacher and closest friend.
We ask that you would protect these, your own children.
Watch over them and keep them safe
as they travel to and from school.
As they learn, help them also to discover
the different gifts that you have given each one of them
to be used in your work in the world.
As they hear the many voices that will fill their days,
help them to listen most carefully for your voice,
the one that tells them you will love them always,
no matter what.
We ask this in Jesus' name.
Amen.

Blessing of Animals

This service may be used entirely on its own, perhaps for an observance on or near the commemoration of Francis of Assisi, renewer of the church, died 1226 (October 4). Various elements of this order may also be incorporated into another worship service, though this material is not intended to replace the customary Sunday worship of the congregation. For practical reasons, this service may be conducted outdoors or in a facility other than a congregation's primary worship space.

Greeting and Prayer

The grace of our Lord Jesus Christ, the love of God, and the communion of the Holy Spirit be with you all.
And also with you.

Let us pray.
Sovereign of the universe, your first covenant of mercy was with every living creature. When your beloved Son came among us, the waters of the river welcomed him, the heavens opened to greet his arrival, the animals of the wilderness drew near as his companions. With all the world's people, may we who are washed into new life through baptism seek the way of your new creation, the way of justice and care, mercy and peace; through Jesus Christ, our Savior and Lord.
Amen.

or

Source and sustainer of life, we cherish the myriad works of your hands. Water, earth, and sky are yours, as are all their inhabitants, wild and tame. We thank you for creatures that nourish and serve us, befriend, enrich, entertain, and protect us. May we, who are made in your image, care for them well. And may your groaning yet wondrous creation rally and thrive, revealing to all who come after us your wise, redemptive, transfiguring love; through Jesus Christ, our Savior and Lord.
Amen.

Readings

Genesis 1:1, 20-28
Genesis 6:17-22
Psalm 8
Psalm 84:1-4
Psalm 148

The reading of scripture is followed by silence for reflection. Other forms of reflection may also follow, such as brief commentary, teaching, or personal witness; nonbiblical readings; interpretation through music or other art forms; or guided conversation among those present.

Song

God of the sparrow   ELW 740
Oh, that I had a thousand voices   ELW 833
All creatures, worship God most high!   ELW 835
All things bright and beautiful   WOV 767
This is my Father's world   ELW 824

Blessing of Animals

The leader may ask all who have brought pets or animals to the celebration to come forward for the following prayer.
The Lord be with you.
And also with you.
Let us pray.
Gracious God, in your love you created us in your image and made us stewards of the animals that live in the skies, the earth, and the sea. Bless us in our care for our pets and animals (*names of pets may be added here*). Help us recognize your power and wisdom in the variety of creatures that live in our world, and hear our prayer for all that suffer overwork, hunger, and ill treatment. Protect your creatures, and guard them from all evil, now and forever.
Amen.

Lord's Prayer

Blessing

Almighty God bless us,
and direct our days and our deeds in peace.
Amen.

September 4, 2016
Time after Pentecost — Lectionary 23

Called to contemplate the cost of discipleship today, we might be helped by translating Paul's request to Philemon into our prayer of the day: Refresh my heart in Christ. Strengthened by the company and forgiveness of Christ in the blessed sacrament and recalling God's grace in remembrance of baptism, we can be strengthened in this hour to "choose life"—to choose life in God as our own.

Prayer of the Day

Direct us, O Lord God, in all our doings with your continual help, that in all our works, begun, continued, and ended in you, we may glorify your holy name; and finally, by your mercy, bring us to everlasting life, through Jesus Christ, our Savior and Lord.

Gospel Acclamation

Alleluia. Let your face shine up- ¹ on your servant,* and teach ¹ me your statutes. *Alleluia.* (Ps. 119:135)

Readings and Psalm
Deuteronomy 30:15-20

Moses speaks to the Israelites, who are about to enter the land promised to their ancestors, Abraham, Isaac, and Jacob. In this passage, he lays out the stark choice before them: choose life by loving and obeying the Lord; or choose death by following other gods.

Psalm 1

They are like trees planted by streams of water. (Ps. 1:3)

Philemon 1-21

While Paul was in prison, he was aided by a runaway slave named Onesimus. The slave's master, Philemon, was a Christian friend of Paul. Paul told Onesimus to return to his master and encouraged Philemon to receive Onesimus back as a Christian brother.

Luke 14:25-33

Jesus speaks frankly about the fearsome costs of discipleship. Those who follow him should know from the outset that completing the course of discipleship will finally mean renouncing all other allegiances.

Semicontinuous reading and psalm
Jeremiah 18:1-11

God teaches Jeremiah a lesson at a potter's shop. Just as a potter is able to destroy an unacceptable vessel, starting over to refashion it into one of value, so God molds and fashions the nations, including Israel.

Psalm 139:1-6, 13-18

You have searched me out and known me. (Ps. 139:1)

Preface   Sundays

Color   Green

Prayers of Intercession

The prayers are prepared locally for each occasion. The following examples may be adapted or used as appropriate.

Rejoicing in the Spirit's work among us, let us pray for the church, the world, and all those in need.

A brief silence.

Let us pray for all congregations gathered around the word and sacraments, that they be strengthened in their discipleship through these means of grace. Lord, in your mercy,
hear our prayer.

Let us pray for the creation, that it thrives and flourishes. Make us good stewards of the land with all its vegetation, mammals, birds, and creatures of all kinds. Lord, in your mercy,
hear our prayer.

Let us pray for all who lead and direct us: for elected officials, school boards, pastors, bishops, trustees, councils, ministry teams, business owners, judges, and community organizers. Especially we pray for . . . . Lord, in your mercy,
hear our prayer.

Let us pray for refugees, immigrants, prisoners, and all who seek new life. Show life and prosperity to those who struggle with injury or illness (*especially*). Lord, in your mercy,
hear our prayer.

Let us pray for our congregation and community, that they be safe places for all, especially the young and mature. Revive and refresh our hearts as we receive the forgiveness of Christ. Lord, in your mercy,
hear our prayer.

Here other intercessions may be offered.

Let us remember with thanksgiving the dearly departed who rest from their labors (*especially*). Instruct us by their witness and bring us, with them, into the promised land. Lord, in your mercy,

hear our prayer.

Into your hands, O God, we commend all for whom we pray, trusting in your mercy; through your Son, our Lord and Savior, Jesus Christ.

Amen.

Images in the Readings

To **carry the cross** is an image that can be used as license to allow others to suffer, a kind of sacred "suck it up." However, the image does remind us that to follow Christ into the kingdom is to live by the countercultural values of the gospel.

For centuries, languages have spoken as if one's **heart** is the center of the self. Despite our knowledge about the brain, we still talk about loving someone "from the bottom of our heart." The beat inside the body, the pump of the blood: the heart can turn away from God, as if the self does not need the God who created and sustains it.

Although most of the world no longer maintains **slavery**, societies still have persons at the bottom of the pile who do the dirty work for little pay and who are unable to rise into a better economic situation. Early Christians popularized the language of family, for many believers had come to baptism individually, having left their natural family for the family of the church. The hope is that baptism impels us to treat all persons, even the hired help, as sisters and brothers.

Ideas for the Day

◆   This is the only time Philemon comes up in the Revised Common Lectionary. Dr. David Rhoads, professor emeritus of the Lutheran School of Theology, practices the art of biblical storytelling. Check out www.youtube.com/watch?v=48YWFNWvzK0 to watch him perform the book of Philemon. Consider telling the story this week rather than reading it.

◆   This gospel holds within itself some incongruities. Jesus compares a prospective disciple to a prospective tower builder and a king considering battle. The tower builder sits down and considers his resources. He's ready when he has everything he needs. The king would map his route, size up his enemy, and take inventory of his weapons. He's ready when he has everything he needs. Both the tower builder and the king are taking note of what they have. But here Jesus is calling the prospective disciple to give up everything: relationships, possessions, and even life itself. Disciples are ready when they have nothing. Our preparedness looks different. We are prepared for this venture when we have nothing and can show up empty-handed.

◆   Think of the people we've encountered in Luke's gospel so far who fit this bill for discipleship. Who are the people who can truly say that they are empty-handed? The leper in chapter 5 would have been isolated from kin and without possessions due to his disease. The dead son of the widow of Nain in chapter 7 was also completely cut off from kin and had nothing in death, yet his resurrection was a major catalyst for spreading the news about Jesus. The woman with the alabaster jar in chapter 7, the Gerasene demoniac and the hemorrhaging woman in chapter 8, the bent-over woman in chapter 13, and the man with dropsy at the beginning of chapter 14 all have impressive resumes according to Jesus' description of discipleship in today's gospel.

◆   Check out the story of Lawrence, deacon and martyr (commemorated on August 10), at www.catholic.org/saints/saint.php?saint_id=366. He brings before the Roman official the "treasures of the church," which turn out to be the sick and the outcast. These people just might be candidates for discipleship!

Connections with the Liturgy

We can think of the Affirmation of Baptism (*ELW*, pp. 234–237) as church members saying yes to Moses' call by once again rejecting sin, confessing the faith, and promising to continue in the covenant of their baptism. Such affirmation is a demonstration of our choosing the life of Christ.

Let the Children Come

As children begin to return to school, they will probably encounter a list of classroom rules posted on a bulletin board. We condition our children to follow the rules so that there is some sense of social order and safety. Jesus seems to discard one of the ten commandments (honor your parents) in the gospel text. This will catch the attention of children and parents alike! Discipleship is not about following rules for social order, but about living and loving in the body of Christ. Jesus is inviting his followers to look at old rules with a new way of thinking for the love of the whole world.

Assembly Song
Gathering

Praise and thanks and adoration ELW 783, LBW 470
Praise to the Lord, the Almighty ELW 858/859, LBW 543
Lift high the cross ELW 660, LBW 377, LS 88

Psalmody and Acclamations

Arnatt, Ronald. "Psalm 1." U or cant, assembly, kybd. ECS 5463.
Burkhardt, Michael. "Psalm 1" from *Psalms for the Church Year*. U, org. MSM 80-708.
Psalter, 1912, alt. "The One Is Blest" (WINCHESTER OLD) from LUYH.

+ Haugen, Marty. "Psalm 139:1-6, 13-18" from PSCY. (GA) ELW 170 with proper verse for Lectionary 23.

Hymn of the Day

Take up your cross, the Savior said ELW 667 *BOURBON* LBW 398 *NUN LASST UNS*

Change my heart, O God ELW 801, W&P 28 *CHANGE MY HEART*

Let us ever walk with Jesus ELW 802, LBW 487 *LASSET UNS MIT JESU ZIEHEN*

Offering

Come, my way, my truth, my life ELW 816, LBW 513

Take my life, that I may be ELW 583/685, LBW 406

Communion

I want to walk as a child of the light ELW 815, LS 36, WOV 649

Come, follow me, the Savior spake ELW 799, LBW 455

Around you, O Lord Jesus ELW 468, LBW 496

Sending

We have seen the Lord ELW 869

Will you come and follow me ELW 798, W&P 137

Additional Assembly Songs

A Dios gloria, alabanza LLC 577

I can hear my Savior calling TFF 146

Must Jesus bear the cross alone TFF 237

Japanese traditional. "Praise to God" from *My Heart Sings Out*. U. Church Publishing 9780898694741.

Loh, I-to. "Search Me, O God" from *Glory to God*. U. WJK 9780664238971.

Cloninger, Claire/Don Moen. "I Offer My Life" from CCLI.

Corum, Casey. "Offering of Love" from CCLI.

Gaither, Gloria/William Gaither. "Jesus Is Lord of All" from CCLI.

Ingram, Jason/Matt Hammitt. "You Are My Treasure" from CCLI.

Kendrick, Graham/Paul Baloche. "What Can I Do" from CCLI.

Tomlin, Chris/Isaac Watts/J.D. Walt/Jesse Reeves/Lowell Mason. "The Wonderful Cross" from CCLI.

Music for the Day
Choral

Killman, Daniel. "You Shall Be as the Tree." SATB, desc, kybd. MSM 50-7041.

p Raabe, Nancy. "The Fullness of God." 2 pt mxd, pno, low inst. AFP 9781451462494.

p Raabe, Nancy. "Tune My Heart to You" from *With All My Heart: Contemporary Vocal Solos*, vol. 2. Solo, kybd. AFP 9780800676858.

Rutter, John. "God Be in My Head." SATB. OXF 9780193854154.

Children's Choir

p Haydn, Joseph/arr. Patrick Liebergen. "Come Follow Me Forever." 2 pt, kybd. GIA G-5387.

p Horman, John D. "Psalm 1" from *ChildrenSing Psalms*. U, kybd. AFP 9781451460865.

How, Martin. "Bless, O Lord, Us Thy Servants." U/2 pt/3 pt mxd/equal voices, org. GIA G-4182.

Keyboard / Instrumental

p ● Albrecht, Mark. "Change My Heart" from *Introductions and Alternate Accompaniments for Piano*, vol. 9. Pno. AFP 9780800623678.

p ● Manz, Paul. "Lasset uns mit Jesu ziehen" from *Augsburg Organ Library: Marriage*. Org. AFP 9781451486025.

p ● Powell, Robert J. "Lasset uns mit Jesu ziehen" from *Mixtures: Hymn Preludes for Organ*. Org. AFP 9781451479553.

p ● Stevens, Wendy Lynn. "Bourbon" from *How Sweet the Sound*. Pno. AFP 9780806696966.

Handbell

● Behnke, John. "Let Us Ever Walk with Jesus." 3 oct, L2. CPH 97-7106.

● Cota, Patricia Sanders. "Change My Heart, O God." 3-5 oct hb, opt 2 oct hc, L3. HOP 2136.

p Eithun, Sandra. "Steal Away." 3-6 oct hb, opt 3-5 oct hc, L2+. CG CGB775.

Friday, September 9

Peter Claver, priest, missionary to Colombia, died 1654

Peter Claver was born into Spanish nobility and was persuaded to become a Jesuit missionary. He served in Cartagena (in what is now Colombia) by teaching and caring for the slaves. The slaves arrived in ships, where they had been confined in dehumanizing conditions. Claver met and supplied them with medicine, food, clothing, and brandy. He learned their dialects and taught them Christianity. He called himself "the slave of the slaves forever." Claver also ministered to the locals of Cartagena who were in prison and facing death.

September 11, 2016
Time after Pentecost — Lectionary 24

The grumbling of the Pharisees and the scribes in today's gospel is actually our holy hope: This Jesus welcomes sinners and eats with them. That our God wills to seek and to save the lost is not only a holy hope, it is our only hope. As Paul's first letter to Timothy reminds us, "The saying is sure and worthy of full acceptance, that Christ Jesus came into the world to save sinners." Thanks be to God.

Prayer of the Day

O God, overflowing with mercy and compassion, you lead back to yourself all those who go astray. Preserve your people in your loving care, that we may reject whatever is contrary to you and may follow all things that sustain our life in your Son, Jesus Christ, our Savior and Lord.

Gospel Acclamation

Alleluia. There is joy in the presence of the an- ¹ gels of God* over one sinner ¹ who repents. *Alleluia.* (Luke 15:10)

Readings and Psalm
Exodus 32:7-14

While Moses is on Mount Sinai, the people grow restless and make a golden calf to worship. Today's reading shows Moses as the mediator between an angry God and a sinful people. Moses reminds God that the Israelites are God's own people and boldly asks mercy for them.

Psalm 51:1-10

Have mercy on me, O God, according to your steadfast love. (Ps. 51:1)

I Timothy 1:12-17

The letters to Timothy are called the Pastoral Epistles because they contain advice especially intended for leaders in the church. Here the mercy shown to Paul, who once persecuted the church, is cited as evidence that even the most unworthy may become witnesses to the grace of God.

Luke 15:1-10

Jesus tells two stories that suggest a curious connection between the lost being found and sinners repenting. God takes the initiative to find sinners, each of whom is so precious to God that his or her recovery brings joy in heaven.

Semicontinuous reading and psalm
Jeremiah 4:11-12, 22-28

The sinfulness of the people will surely bring their destruction. God's searing wind of judgment, in the form of a massive foreign army, will reduce the land to its primeval state of waste and void, as it was at the beginning of Genesis.

Psalm 14

The LORD looks down from heaven upon us all. (Ps. 14:2)

Preface   Sundays

Color   Green

Prayers of Intercession

The prayers are prepared locally for each occasion. The following examples may be adapted or used as appropriate.

Rejoicing in the Spirit's work among us, let us pray for the church, the world, and all those in need.

A brief silence.

Gracious God, we thank you for your word that strengthens the weak and the faint in heart. We thank you for your word that encourages the believer and saves sinners. Hear us, O God.

Your mercy is great.

We pray for those places in our world ravaged by fires or floods (*especially*). Restore the land, and bless the efforts of those who work to save and protect it. Hear us, O God.

Your mercy is great.

We pray for the leaders of nations and all those in positions of authority. Guide them as they make decisions for the good of all. Lead them in the ways that make for peace. Hear us, O God.

Your mercy is great.

We pray for those who suffer as the result of war, violence, terrorism, or natural disaster. And we pray for those who willingly serve others in dangerous situations: first responders, firefighters, emergency medical personnel, members of the military, law enforcement (*and others we name now*). Hear us, O God.

Your mercy is great.

We pray for our congregation. Prepare us to welcome newcomers. Make this a place of hope for the least of these in our community. Be with those who are sick, injured, or in any need (*especially*). Hear us, O God.

Your mercy is great.

Here other intercessions may be offered.

Let us remember with thanksgiving the blessed dead who rest from their labors (*especially*). Gladden us by their lives of faith, and at the last day unite us in the joy of heaven. Hear us, O God.

Your mercy is great.

Into your hands, O God, we commend all for whom we pray, trusting in your mercy; through your Son, our Lord and Savior, Jesus Christ.

Amen.

Images in the Readings

That we are sheep is a familiar image for Christians. That we are lost coins and Christ the **woman sweeping** is a far less common metaphor, and it provides us a biblical occasion to image God as a female. People who are lost still have value. Our culture of individual freedom makes it uncomfortable for many in the church to sweep assiduously, searching for those who are lost, hoping to bring them back into the worshiping community.

Luke's pattern of presenting stories of **both men and women** is an inspiration to preachers.

The **calf** of Exodus 32 probably recalls the statue of the bull in which many ancient religious traditions imaged the divine, as if the god resembled the bull's male potency. In much of our culture, the "gold" part of the calf is what is worshiped.

To be described as **stiff-necked** is to imagine ourselves unwilling to turn our heads to see something different, to look in a new direction. In the exodus story, even God can turn around and so see us in a new way.

Ideas for the Day

◆ Boxing and mixed martial arts events often begin with an announcer's dramatic words: "Let's get ready to rumble!" The crowd now knows that the fight is about to begin, and they turn their full attention to the ring where the fighters will meet. The passage we read today from Luke 15 turns our attention toward another kind of conflict, and we seem to hear a voice cry out: "Let's get ready to grumble!" Grumbling voices continue to impact our ministries, and their complaints can sometimes keep us from turning our attention toward people and issues that are easily ignored and avoided. What kind of grumbling is heard in your congregation or community as you do ministry that is challenging and perhaps unpopular?

◆ September 11, 2001, is a day the world will never forget. Remembering this day of suffering and anguish also brings to mind stories of profound courage and compassion. Luke's parables show a man and a woman who search diligently for something they have lost. Today is a time to remember not only what has been lost, but also what has been found, recovered, and celebrated as people all around us continue to work together to heal and restore important things that are too easily broken or lost. Who should you remember today because they refused to give up on a person or an idea that others said was lost and not worth the effort to reclaim?

◆ Imagine how the lost sheep felt at each stage of the story. Abandoned and forgotten. Remembered, rescued, and restored. And then, of course, there's that ride on the shoulders of the shepherd. A popular story about God's faithful presence in our lives describes a scene on the beach where two sets of footprints appear side by side. This represents God's accompaniment and companionship during life's journeys. When we find ourselves fearful and anxious because suddenly only one set of footprints can be seen, we may ask, "Where is God?" The story of the lost sheep reminds us to imagine and celebrate the joy of hearing God say to us, "These are the times that I was carrying you."

Connections with the Liturgy

Each Sunday's worship can replicate today's parables from Luke: we begin by acknowledging that we are lost, and we conclude with the entire community rejoicing over God's forgiveness.

The psalm includes the line "Create in me a clean heart, O God," which some assemblies sing at the offering (ELW 185–188).

Let the Children Come

The feeling of being lost is scary: losing a parent's hand in a crowd, being in the wrong aisle in the market, or being overwhelmed in a new class at school. The wider culture often values the smartest, most beautiful, or perhaps just the most sensational, leaving children with a sense they must live up to a strange set of expectations. Jesus' parable of the lost sheep comforts us all, revealing that everyone is God's own beloved. How does your community convey to children their unique value and worth in your assembly? In your greater community? In the whole world?

Assembly Song
Gathering

Immortal, invisible, God only wise   ELW 834, LBW 526

All people that on earth do dwell   ELW 883, LBW 245

Spread, oh, spread, almighty Word   ELW 663, LBW 379

Psalmody and Acclamations

Browning, Carol. "Lord Jesus Christ." SATB, cant, assembly, kybd, gtr. GIA G-5905.

Marshall, Jane. "Create in Me, O God." U, desc or C inst, assembly, kybd.

Mayernik, Luke. "A Broken Heart." SATB, cant, assembly, kybd, gtr, fl. GIA G-7196.

+ Shute, Linda Cable. "Psalm 14," Refrain 2, from PSCY. (GA) ELW 170 with proper verse for Lectionary 24.

Hymn of the Day

Savior, like a shepherd lead us ELW 789, TFF 254 BRADBURY
LBW 481 HER TIL VIES

Amazing grace, how sweet the sound ELW 779, LBW 448 NEW BRITAIN

Lord, speak to us that we may speak ELW 676, LBW 403 CANONBURY

Offering

O Christ, your heart, compassionate ELW 722, sts. 1, 3

Lord, who the night you were betrayed ELW 463, st. 1, LBW 206, st. 1

Communion

Softly and tenderly Jesus is calling ELW 608, TFF 155, WOV 734

Chief of sinners though I be ELW 609, LBW 306

You satisfy the hungry heart ELW 484, WOV 711

Sending

Come, thou Fount of every blessing ELW 807, LBW 499, TFF 108

O Zion, haste ELW 668, LBW 397

Additional Assembly Songs

All the way my Savior leads me TFF 259

Oh, let the Son of God enfold you TFF 105, W&P 130

One in a hundred LS 156

Anon. "Jesus Knows the Inmost Heart" from Glory to God. U. WJK 9780664238971.

Anon. Sri Lanka. "This Is the Story" from Sound the Bamboo. U. GIA G-6830.

Hall, Mark. "Praise You with the Dance" from CCLI.

Park, Andy, et al. "King of the Broken" from CCLI.

Park, Andy. "The River Is Here" from CCLI.

Redman, Matt. "Dancing Generation" from CCLI.

Smith, Martin. "Singer's Song" from CCLI.

Wyeth, John/Robert Robinson/Thomas Miller. "Come, Thou Fount, Come, Thou King" from CCLI.

Music for the Day
Choral

p Haugen, Marty. "O God, Why Are You Silent?" SATB, kybd, gtr. GIA G-6099.

p Neswick, Bruce. "Hearken to My Voice, O Lord, When I Call" from The Augsburg Choirbook: Sacred Choral Music of the Twentieth Century. 2 pt, org. AFP 9780800656782.

Shaw, Timothy. "Amazing Grace." SSA. CPH 98-4009.

p Wonacott, Glenn. "Sing Praise to God." SAB, kybd. AFP 9781451401738.

Children's Choir

p Edwards, Rusty/arr. Wayne Wold. "Rejoice! I Found the Lost." U/2 pt, kybd. AFP 9781451484090.

p Horman, John D. "The Lost Coin" from Sing the Stories of God's People. U, kybd. AFP 9780800679453.

p ● Roberts, William Bradley. "Savior, Like a Shepherd Lead Us." U, kybd, C inst. AFP 9781451462227.

Keyboard / Instrumental

● Biery, Marilyn. "New Britain" from Hymn-Tune Miniatures for the Church Year. Pno. MSM 15-829.

● Hobby, Robert A. "New Britain" from For All the Saints, vol. 1. Org. AFP 9780800675370.

● Kallman, Daniel. "Bradbury" from Three Hymns for Two Violins and Piano. Pno, 2 vln. MSM 20-971.

p ● Sedio, Mark. "Canonbury" from Come and Praise, vol. 2. Org. AFP 9780806696928.

Handbell

● Lamb, Linda. "Amazing Grace (My Chains Are Gone)." 3-5 oct hb, opt 3 oct hc, L3. LOR 20/1599L.

● Ringham, William. "Lord, Speak to Me That I May Speak." 3-5 oct, L3. LOR 20/1208L.

● Tucker, Sondra. "Savior, like a Shepherd Lead Us." 3-5 oct hb, opt 3 oct hc, L3. LOR 20/1425L.

Tuesday, September 13

John Chrysostom, Bishop of Constantinople, died 407

John was a priest in Antioch and an outstanding preacher. His eloquence earned him the nickname "Chrysostom" ("golden mouth"), but it also got him into trouble. As bishop of Constantinople he preached against corruption among the royal court. The empress, who had been his supporter, sent him into exile. His preaching style emphasized the literal meaning of scripture and its practical application. This interpretation stood in contrast to the common style at the time, which emphasized the allegorical meaning of the text.

= global song   = praise song   + = semicontinuous psalm
● = relates to hymn of the day   p = available in Prelude Music Planner

279

Wednesday, September 14

Holy Cross Day

Helena, the mother of Constantine, made a pilgrimage to Israel to look for Christian holy sites. She found what she believed were the sites of the crucifixion and burial of Jesus, sites that modern archaeologists believe may be correct. Here Constantine built two churches. The celebration of Holy Cross Day originated with the dedication of the Church of the Resurrection in 335. Today the festival provides the church an opportunity to lift up the victory of the cross with a spirit of celebration that might be less suitable on Good Friday.

Friday, September 16

Cyprian, Bishop of Carthage, martyr, died around 258

Cyprian worked for the unity of the church and cared for his flock in North Africa during a time of great persecution. During Cyprian's time as bishop many people had denied the faith under duress. In contrast to some who held the belief that the church should not receive these people back, Cyprian believed they should be welcomed into full communion after a period of penance. He insisted on the need for compassion in order to preserve the unity of the church. His essay *On the Unity of the Catholic Church* stressed the role of bishops in guaranteeing the visible, concrete unity of the church. Cyprian was also concerned for the physical well-being of the people under his care. He organized a program of medical care for the sick during a severe epidemic in Carthage.

Saturday, September 17

Hildegard, Abbess of Bingen, died 1179

Hildegard lived virtually her entire life in convents, yet was widely influential within the church. After an uneventful time as a nun, she was chosen as abbess of her community. She reformed her community as well as other convents. Around the same time, she began having visions and compiled them, as instructed, in a book she called *Scivias*. Hildegard's importance went beyond mysticism. She advised and reproved kings and popes, wrote poems and hymns, and produced treatises in medicine, theology, and natural history. She was also a musician and an artist.

September 18, 2016
Time after Pentecost — Lectionary 25

As we are invited today to consider what it means to be managers (rather than owners) of all that we have, it is crucial to recall that we are bought with a price. "Christ Jesus, himself human, . . . gave himself a ransom for all." Apart from the generosity of God we have nothing—we are nothing. By God's gracious favor we have everything we need.

Prayer of the Day

God among us, we gather in the name of your Son to learn love for one another. Keep our feet from evil paths. Turn our minds to your wisdom and our hearts to the grace revealed in your Son, Jesus Christ, our Savior and Lord.

Gospel Acclamation

Alleluia. Live your life in a manner worthy of the gos- ¹ pel of Christ;* strive side by side for the faith ¹ of the gospel. *Alleluia.* (Phil. 1:27)

Readings and Psalm
Amos 8:4-7

Amos was called by God to prophesy in the Northern King-dom of Israel. Peace and prosperity in Israel led to corrupt business practices and oppression of the poor. The prophet declares that God will not tolerate such a situation.

Psalm 113

The Lᴏʀᴅ lifts up the poor from the ashes. (Ps. 113:7)

1 Timothy 2:1-7

The Pastoral Epistles offer insight into how early Christians understood many practical matters, such as church admin-istration and worship. The church's focused prayer for oth-ers is an expression of the single-minded passion God has toward us in Jesus.

Luke 16:1-13

Jesus tells the curious story of a dishonest man who cheats his employer and then is commended by him for having acted so shrewdly. Jesus wonders why his own followers are less creative and diligent in their stewardship given that they are managers of a far more valuable household.

Semicontinuous reading and psalm
Jeremiah 8:18—9:1

Jeremiah's primary task as God's prophet was to announce the terrible destruction that awaited the people of Judah and Jerusalem because of their sin. In this passage, a grief-stricken Jeremiah anguishes over the sadness of that message and weeps for his people.

Psalm 79:1-9

Deliver us and forgive us our sins, for your name's sake. (Ps. 79:9)

Preface   Sundays

Color   Green

Prayers of Intercession

The prayers are prepared locally for each occasion. The following examples may be adapted or used as appropriate.

Rejoicing in the Spirit's work among us, let us pray for the church, the world, and all those in need.

A brief silence.

Giver of the feast, bless your church and all who hunger and thirst. Nourish us richly with your word and meal, and send us as signs of your living presence in the world. Lord, in your mercy,

hear our prayer.

Ruler of the earth, bring forth an abundant harvest from fields, orchards, and gardens. Renew fields that will soon lie fallow. Feed and protect all wild creatures. Lord, in your mercy,

hear our prayer.

God of the nations, we pray for places in the world affected by conflict, war, and turmoil (*especially*). We pray that your perfect peace and order be restored. Lord, in your mercy,

hear our prayer.

God of our weary years, we remember before you those among us who are sick or who are recovering from illness or surgery (*especially*). Lord, in your mercy,

hear our prayer.

God our beginning and ending, we thank you for hope even in the midst of despair. Visit this assembly with your light and truth. Lord, in your mercy,

hear our prayer.

Here other intercessions may be offered.

God of our silent tears, we remember the faithful departed who make up the great cloud of witnesses (*especially Dag Hammarskjöld, renewer of society, whom we commemorate today*). Gather us all in praise around your throne. Lord, in your mercy,
hear our prayer.
Into your hands, O God, we commend all for whom we pray, trusting in your mercy; through your Son, our Lord and Savior, Jesus Christ.
Amen.

Images in the Readings

Luke's warning about **wealth** and his attention to the poor are hard to hear in a capitalist country. Some Christians have replaced it with a point of view found in the Old Testament, that God gives wealth as a reward for religious faithfulness. So it is that Christians do not agree about how to have and use money.

Orthodox Jews are to maintain the practice of never handling money on the **sabbath**. The idea is that if human effort reaches for more money, then resting in God means the cessation of caring about worldly goods. In early Christianity, those assembling for the communal meal—which was not held on the sabbath—were to contribute money for the needs of the poor as one way to offer thanks to God.

First Timothy calls Christ our **ransom**. The ransom theory of atonement understands that humans are captive to sin, captured by the devil, and Christ offers himself to the devil in order to ransom, that is, to buy back, believers to God. This ancient battle practice of ransom is seen in C. S. Lewis's novel *The Lion, the Witch and the Wardrobe*, when Aslan offers the White Witch his own life in exchange for Edmund's. Much current political practice refuses to negotiate with kidnappers, thus making ransom a somewhat archaic idea.

Ideas for the Day

♦ Road trips require preparation. The car or van needs to be ready for the long drive and packed with supplies for the journey—and the driver should be well rested. None of this will keep some passengers from growing impatient and asking along the way: "Are we there yet?" As the prophet Amos describes greedy merchants who can't wait for the sabbath to end so they can resume their deceitful practices, we realize that our own impatience is never completely harmless. What happens in our lives today that makes us impatient with one another, impatient with the process of change, and even impatient with God? How can our faith prepare us for the difficult journeys of life that will require both patience and perseverance?

♦ Reality shows present unscripted stories about the lives of celebrities as well as ordinary people who face challenges as they try to solve their problems. Jesus seems very comfortable with stories about real people as he describes how a dishonest man who is about to lose his job makes deals that will benefit him when he is unemployed. This parable is about what people may choose to do when they are pushed to the margins of society. What stories can you share about people in your congregation or parish who are not successful in finding adequate employment, housing, and health care? How do you acknowledge the reality of their struggles to make ends meet as you tell the story of Jesus and his love?

♦ Many people are surprised to learn that money is typically quite dirty and full of germs, and it is wise to wash your hands after handling currency. Criminals today use a process called *money laundering* to hide their illegal funds, but their money remains a sign of greed and corruption. Perhaps Jesus anticipates this paradox as he compares true riches with dishonest wealth. Good stewards want the money that passes through our hands to become a sign of grace and generosity as we make financial decisions that reflect our values and our faith. How we handle money can reveal God's cleansing power working in our hearts.

Connections with the Liturgy

The imagery of believers as children of light is important in the rite of baptism. The Welcome (*ELW*, p. 231) with the presentation of the baptismal candle calls the baptized to live in the light of God. The early Christian church called baptism enlightenment.

Each week in the prayers of intercession, we heed the call to pray for rulers (1 Tim. 2:1).

Let the Children Come

This is the time of year that families may begin to feel like they are serving two masters, the family calendar and God's abundant life. The family calendar is often packed with soccer practice, homework, dance classes, chores, and slumber parties—all promising abundant life but often only delivering busyness. Sometimes the church community becomes exasperated with the participation of children and their families. How is the church countercultural in promising God's abundant life? How does your community's programming for children and families offer a much-needed renewal to Christ's peace? How does your community draw families into a real sense of shalom?

Assembly Song
Gathering

God, who stretched the spangled heavens   ELW 771, LBW 463
He comes to us as one unknown   ELW 737, WOV 768
Let justice flow like streams   ELW 717, TFF 48, WOV 763

Psalmody and Acclamations

"You Have Shown You Love Us" from *Psallite* C-200.

Morgan, Michael. "Bless the Lord, O Saints and Servants" (AUSTRIAN HYMN) from PAS 113B.

+   Frey, Marvin V. "Psalm 79:1-9" (refrain: *KUM BA YAH*, in D minor) from PAS 79A.

(GA) ELW 170 with proper verse for Lectionary 25.

Hymn of the Day

There's a wideness in God's mercy ELW 587 *ST. HELENA*
  ELW 588, LBW 290 *LORD, REVIVE US*

Let streams of living justice ELW 710 *THAXTED*

By gracious powers ELW 626 *TELOS* WOV 736 *BERLIN*

Offering

We Are an Offering ELW 692, W&P 146

Create in me a clean heart ELW 187

Communion

Borning Cry ELW 732, W&P 69, WOV 770

Be thou my vision ELW 793, WOV 776

Lord of all nations, grant me grace ELW 716, LBW 419

Sending

Holy God, holy and glorious ELW 637

O Christ, our hope ELW 604, LBW 300

Additional Assembly Songs

Guide my feet TFF 153

Make me a channel of your peace W&P 95, LLC 527

Put on love DH 78

⊕ Mexican traditional. "Dios está aquí/God Is Here Today" from *My Heart Sings Out*. U. Church Publishing 9780898694741.

⊕ Bell, John L. "Goodness Is Stronger Than Evil." SATB. ELW 721.

✿ Getty, Kristyn. "What Grace Is Mine" from CCLI.

✿ McCloghry, Jill. "We the Redeemed" from CCLI.

✿ Mooring, Jack/Leeland Mooring. "Thief in the Night" from CCLI.

✿ Redman, Matt. "God of Our Yesterdays" from CCLI.

✿ Ruis, Daniel. "You're Worthy of My Praise" from CCLI.

Music for the Day
Choral

p   Cherwien, David. "O Healing River" from *To God Will I Sing: Vocal Solos for the Church Year*. Solo, kybd. AFP 9780800674335.

p ● Ellingboe, Bradley. "There's a Wideness in God's Mercy." SATB, pno. AFP 9780800676544.

p ● Roberts, William Bradley. "By Gracious Powers." U or SATB, pno. AFP 9780800678210.

p   Tierney, Patrick. "Purify My Heart (Refiner's Fire)." SATB, pno. HOP C5850.

Children's Choir

Dexheimer-Pharris, William/arr. Mark Sedio. "Take My Life, That I May Be" from *Augsburg Easy Choirbook*, vol. 2. U/2 pt, pno, fl, perc, opt gtr. AFP 9780800677510.

p   Patterson, Mark. "Sing for Joy, Sing Together." U/2 pt, pno, opt fl, fc. CG CGA161.

Savoy, Thomas F. "God Be in My Head." 2 pt, org, opt SATB. GIA G-4786.

Keyboard / Instrumental

●   Cherwien, David. "Thaxted" from *Organ Plus One*. Org, tpt. AFP 9780800656188.

●   Farlee, Robert Buckley. "Thaxted" from *Augsburg Organ Library: Autumn*. Org. AFP 9780800675790.

p ● Organ, Anne Krentz. "Telos" from *Introductions and Alternate Accompaniments for Piano*, vol. 6. Pno. AFP 9780800623647.

●   Raabe, Nancy M. "St. Helena" from *Grace and Peace*, vol. 6. Pno. AFP 9781451479621.

Handbell

Glasgow, Michael J. "Healing Spirit." 3-7 oct hb, opt fl, opt perc, L3-. CG CGB754.

●   Helman, Michael. "Prelude on 'Thaxted.'" 3-6 oct hb, opt 3-5 oct hc, L3. AGEHR AG36045.

●   Tucker, Sondra. "There's a Wideness in God's Mercy." 3-5 oct, L3. AFP 0800674901.

Sunday, September 18
Dag Hammarskjöld, renewer of society, died 1961

Dag Hammarskjöld (HAH-mar-sheld) was a Swedish diplomat and humanitarian who served as secretary general of the United Nations. He was killed in a plane crash on this day in 1961, in what is now Zambia, while he was on his way to negotiate a cease-fire between the United Nations and the Katanga forces. For years Hammarskjöld had kept a private journal, and it was not until that journal was published as *Markings* that the depth of his Christian faith was known. The book revealed that his life was a combination of diplomatic service and personal spirituality, and of contemplation on the meaning of Christ in his life and action in the world.

Wednesday, September 21

Matthew, Apostle and Evangelist

Matthew ("Levi" in the gospels of Mark and Luke) was a tax collector for the Roman government in Capernaum. Tax collectors were distrusted because they were dishonest and worked as agents for a foreign ruler, the occupying Romans. In the gospels, tax collectors are mentioned as sinful and despised outcasts, but it was these outcasts to whom Jesus showed his love. Matthew's name means "gift of the Lord." Since the second century, tradition has attributed the first gospel to him.

September 25, 2016

Time after Pentecost — Lectionary 26

Consideration of and care for those in need (especially those "at our gate," visible to us, of whom we are aware) is an essential component of good stewardship. It is in the sharing of wealth that we avoid the snare of wealth. It is the one whom death could not hold—who comes to us risen from the dead—who can free us from the death grip of greed.

Prayer of the Day

O God, rich in mercy, you look with compassion on this troubled world. Feed us with your grace, and grant us the treasure that comes only from you, through Jesus Christ, our Savior and Lord.

Gospel Acclamation

Alleluia. You know the generous act of our Lord Jesus Christ, that though he was rich, yet for your sakes he ˡ became poor,* so that by his poverty you might ˡ become rich. *Alleluia.* (2 Cor. 8:9)

Readings and Psalm

Amos 6:1a, 4-7

The prophet Amos announces that Israel's great wealth is a cause not for rejoicing but rather for sorrow, because God's people have forgotten how to share their wealth with the poor. The wealthy will be the first to go into exile when judgment comes.

Psalm 146

The Lord gives justice to those who are oppressed. (Ps. 146:7)

1 Timothy 6:6-19

Timothy is reminded of the confession he made at his baptism and of its implications for daily life. His priorities will be different from those of people who merely want to be rich.

Luke 16:19-31

Jesus tells a parable in which the poor one is "lifted up" and the rich one is "sent away empty." Jesus makes it clear that this ethic of merciful reversal is not new but is as old as Moses and the prophets.

Semicontinuous reading and psalm

Jeremiah 32:1-3a, 6-15

In the year before Jerusalem fell to the Babylonians, when the siege had already begun, Jeremiah, imprisoned in the king's palace, purchased a piece of land. The purchase of the land is a sign of hope that God will restore the people to life in the land after the exile.

Psalm 91:1-6, 14-16

You are my refuge and my stronghold, my God in whom I put my trust. (Ps. 91:2)

Preface Sundays

Color Green

Prayers of Intercession

The prayers are prepared locally for each occasion. The following examples may be adapted or used as appropriate.

Rejoicing in the Spirit's work among us, let us pray for the church, the world, and all those in need.

A brief silence.

God, we thank you for the church, its mission, and its ministry. Help us to be examples of the faith and to pursue righteousness in all we say and do. Lord, in your mercy,
hear our prayer.

We pray for the well-being of all creation. Make us wise stewards of your rich and beautiful world. Lord, in your mercy,
hear our prayer.

Ruler of the nations, we pray for peace in places of conflict and war (*especially*). We pray for exiles, refugees, and those far from home. Lord, in your mercy,
hear our prayer.

We pray for all those who are lonely or homebound, those who are trapped in any kind of prison of body, mind, or spirit, and for those who are sick or injured. Especially we pray for . . . . Lord, in your mercy,
hear our prayer.

God who sits high but looks low, we pray for our brothers and sisters who struggle to make ends meet. Provide for all of our physical and spiritual needs. Lord, in your mercy,
hear our prayer.

Here other intercessions may be offered.

We remember and give thanks for all your saints in light and for those who have recently died (*especially*). Thank you for the good foundation of their lives and witness. Lord, in your mercy,
hear our prayer.

Into your hands, O God, we commend all for whom we pray, trusting in your mercy; through your Son, our Lord and Savior, Jesus Christ.
Amen.

Images in the Readings

Lazarus is lying at the **gate**. The rich man lives in a gated community, safe from thieves, careful to keep the poor distant from his sight. Most gates keep the insiders in and the outsiders out. Yet John's gospel says that Christ is the gate: he is the opening to all the needy and the homeless.

In that the parable depicts the dead man crying out for water because he is in **flames**, it is clear that this is not a literal description of the afterlife. When also we are thirsty, Christ is the water of life. God does have mercy on us and offers water to cool our tongue.

First Timothy contrasts our love of money with the Christian **treasure**, which is the hope for life that comes from and radiates God.

The author of 1 Timothy believes in the resurrection of believers to eternal life rather than the **immortality** of the soul: God alone is immortal. Christians have suggested several different ways to imagine the end of human life and the endlessness of God, sometimes with the simplistic imagery of today's parable.

Ideas for the Day

◆ The beautiful song from Central America, "Enviado soy de Dios," is translated in English: "The Lord now sends us forth" (ELW 538; LLC 415). The refrain states with extraordinary clarity: "The angels are not sent into our world of pain to do what we were meant to do in Jesus' name; that falls to you and me." This is a powerful reminder that the evangelical mission of God's church is not assigned to any of the celestial beings. It is exclusively the work of God's people, mortal sinners who are saved by grace and shaped by the struggles of this world. Jesus' parable teaches us that those who proclaim the message of the holy gospel must be called, equipped, and sent from the ranks of the living!

◆ Jesus' parable introduces us to a rich man who eats a feast every day but refuses to share anything with Lazarus. He is very selfish; evil has captured his heart. After both men die, Lazarus is comforted while the rich man is denied even a drop of water. This dichotomy still exists for people who live at opposite ends of the economic spectrum. How can our church serve as a bridge that crosses the great chasm separating the haves and the have-nots? Are there stories we can share that show how more equitable relations between rich and poor communities are possible?

◆ My five brothers are on the wrong path, the rich man says as he begs Abraham to send someone to warn them "so that they will not also come into this place of torment." Lutherans don't have the reputation of being a church of "warners" who preach fire and brimstone and eternal damnation. Yet our faith is grounded in both law and gospel, and as we invite others to take hold of the life that really is life (1 Tim. 6:19), we do warn about sin and judgment. We warn about urgent environmental and ecological concerns and other social justice issues, especially the scandal of poverty in an age of unprecedented wealth and prosperity. We actually speak a lot of warnings about a lot of things. What warnings are central to the work God has entrusted to you as you do ministry in Jesus' name?

Connections with the Liturgy

In the second century, Justin wrote that on Sunday the worshiping community collected money and goods for the needy, and each Sunday worshiping assemblies respond to the call in 1 Timothy to be generous and ready to share with others. See the offering (*ELW*, p. 106). Those churches that institute contributions by direct bank withdrawal do well to continue at each Sunday liturgy a symbolic weekly generosity to the poor.

Let the Children Come

If you spend time with the average three-year-old, you may notice the word *mine* come up in the conversation. Sharing is not a built-in skill, nor is it even possible to teach very young children. Listening to the story-within-a-story of Lazarus and the rich man, one may wonder if sharing is possible to learn in our lifetime! This little allegory helps guide the church to wonder who is hungry at our gates. Good stewardship comes from turning the word *mine* into a sharing way of life. It is not a one-time lesson to be taught, but an ongoing modeling of sharing God's abundance.

Assembly Song
Gathering

Creating God, your fingers trace   ELW 684, WOV 757

Where cross the crowded ways of life   ELW 719, LBW 429, LLC 513

Golden breaks the dawn   ELW 852

Psalmody and Acclamations

Chepponis, James. "Psalm 146." 2 cant, assembly, opt SATB, kybd, gtr, C inst, hb. GIA G-4227.

Gelineau, Joseph. "Psalm 146" from ACYG.

+ Farlee, Robert Buckley. "Psalm 91:1-6, 14-16" from PWC. (GA) ELW 170 with proper verse for Lectionary 26.

Hymn of the Day

We raise our hands to you, O Lord   ELW 690   *VI REKKER VÅRE HENDER FREM*

Son of God, eternal Savior   ELW 655, LBW 364   *IN BABILONE*

Lord, thee I love with all my heart   ELW 750, LBW 325   *HERZLICH LIEB*

Offering

All who hunger, gather gladly   ELW 461

Lord of glory, you have bought us   ELW 707, sts. 1-2; LBW 424, sts. 1-2

Communion

Let us go now to the banquet   ELW 523, LLC 410

O bread of life from heaven   ELW 480, LBW 197

Lord, whose love in humble service   ELW 712, LBW 423

Sending

O God of every nation   ELW 713, LBW 416

God of grace and God of glory   ELW 705, LBW 415

Additional Assembly Songs

I'd rather have Jesus   TFF 233

En medio de la vida   LLC 512

Feliz el hombre   LLC 540

⊕ Manzano, Miguel. "When the Poor Ones/Cuando el pobre." U. ELW 725.

⊕ Soahuku traditional. "Haleluya Puji Tuhan/Alleluia, Praise the Lord" from *Agape: Songs of Hope and Reconciliation*. 2 pt. Lutheran World Federation. Out of print. Available on Amazon.com.

✿ Brown, Brenton. "Amazing God" from CCLI.

✿ Cantelon, Ben/Tim Hughes. "Happy Day" from CCLI.

✿ Green, Melody. "There Is a Redeemer" from CCLI.

✿ Morgan, Reuben/Robert Fergusson. "We Will See Him" from CCLI.

✿ Smith, Martin/Stuart Garrard. "Everything" from CCLI.

✿ Zschech, Darlene. "It Is You" from CCLI.

Music for the Day
Choral

p Berger, Jean. "A Rose Touched by the Sun's Warm Rays." SATB. AFP 9780800645557.

p Carter, John. "They Who Wait for the Lord." SATB, pno, cl or C inst. AFP 9780806698427.

p Lund, Emily. "Nearer, Still Nearer." SATB, pno. CG CGA1293.

p Wold, Wayne L. "For the Least." 2 pt mxd, kybd. AFP 9781451462326.

Children's Choir

Burkhardt, Michael. "The Lord Now Sends Us Forth/Enviado soy de Dios." 2 pt trbl/SATB, pno, perc, opt assembly. MSM 50-5412.

p Simon, Julia. "Where Is Your Treasure?" 2 pt, pno. AFP 781451461350.

Wagner, Douglas E. "Song of Gentleness." U, kybd/hb. BP BP1192.

Keyboard / Instrumental

● Krebs, Johann Ludwig. "Herzlich lieb." Org. Various editions.

● Miller, Aaron David. "Vi rekker våre hender frem" from *Introductions and Alternate Accompaniments for Piano*, vol. 7. Pno. AFP 9780800623654.

● Sedio, Mark. "In Babilone" from *Let It Rip! at the Piano*, vol. 2. Pno. AFP 9780800675800.

● Walther, Johann Gottfried. "Herzlich lieb." Org. Various editions.

Handbell

● Griffin, Jackie. "Festive Celebration." 5 oct hb, L3, FTT 201885HB. Br qnt, FTT 201885B. Org, FTT 201885O. Timp, FTT 201885P. Full score, FTT 201885M. Complete set (8 hb pt, 1 of each other pt), FTT 201885.

p Krug, Jason W. "Jerusalem." 3-5 oct, L3+. HOP 2664.

Ryan, Michael. "On Eagle's Wings." 2-3 oct, L2. LOR 20/1518L.

⊕ = global song   ✿ = praise song   + = semicontinuous psalm
● = relates to hymn of the day   p = available in Prelude Music Planner

Thursday, September 29

Michael and All Angels

On this festival day the church ponders the richness and variety of God's created order and the limits of human knowledge of it. The scriptures speak of angels (the word means "messengers") who worship God in heaven, and in both testaments angels speak for God on earth. They are remembered most vividly as they appear to the shepherds and announce the birth of the Savior. Michael is an angel whose name appears in Daniel as the heavenly being who leads the faithful dead to God's throne on the day of resurrection. In Revelation, Michael fights in a cosmic battle against Satan.

Friday, September 30

Jerome, translator, teacher, died 420

Jerome is remembered as a biblical scholar and translator. Rather than choosing classical Latin as the basis of his work, he translated the scriptures into the Latin that was spoken and written by the majority of the persons in his day. His translation is known as the Vulgate, from the Latin word for *common*. While Jerome is remembered as a saint, he could be anything but saintly. He was well known for his short temper and his arrogance, although he was also quick to admit to his personal faults. Thanks to the work of Jerome, many people received the word in their own language and lived lives of faith and service to those in need.

October 2, 2016
Time after Pentecost — Lectionary 27

A little faith goes a long way is our Lord's point in the gospel. A mustard seed's-worth has miraculous potential. The patience, tenacity, and endurance required for the life of faith are the blessings received in water and the word (holy baptism), bread and wine (holy communion), the word read and proclaimed in this assembly. Anticipate them. Receive them with thanksgiving.

Prayer of the Day

Benevolent, merciful God: When we are empty, fill us. When we are weak in faith, strengthen us. When we are cold in love, warm us, that with fervor we may love our neighbors and serve them for the sake of your Son, Jesus Christ, our Savior and Lord.

Gospel Acclamation

Alleluia. The word of the Lord en- ǀ dures forever.* That word is the good news that was an- ǀ nounced to you. *Alleluia.* (1 Pet. 1:25)

Readings and Psalm
Habakkuk 1:1-4; 2:1-4

Injustice and violence in the time leading up to the Babylonian exile move this prophet to lament: How can a good and all-powerful God see evil in the world and seemingly remain indifferent? God answers by proclaiming that the wicked will perish, but the righteous will live by faith.

Psalm 37:1-9

Commit your way to the Lord; put your trust in the Lord. (Ps. 37:5)

2 Timothy 1:1-14

This message written from Paul to Timothy is a personal message of encouragement. In the face of hardship and persecution, Timothy is reminded that his faith is a gift of God. He is encouraged to exercise that faith with the help of the Holy Spirit.

Luke 17:5-10

On the way to Jerusalem, Jesus instructs his followers about the power of faith and the duties of discipleship. He calls his disciples to adopt the attitude of servants whose actions are responses to their identity rather than works seeking reward.

Semicontinuous reading and psalm
Lamentations 1:1-6

Jeremiah's announcement of destruction has become a reality. Now Judah is in exile in Babylon. The book of Lamentations contains five poems mourning the exile. In this passage, Jerusalem is portrayed as a widow with no one to comfort her.

Lamentations 3:19-26

Great is your faithfulness, O Lord. (Lam. 3:23)

or **Psalm 137**

Remember the day of Jerusalem, O Lᴏʀᴅ. (Ps. 137:7)

Preface Sundays

Color Green

Prayers of Intercession

The prayers are prepared locally for each occasion. The following examples may be adapted or used as appropriate.

Rejoicing in the Spirit's work among us, let us pray for the church, the world, and all those in need.

A brief silence.

Increase the faith of your church, O God. Raise up faithful parents and grandparents, prophets and teachers who know, love, and spread your gospel. Hear us, O God.

Your mercy is great.

Tend and nurture the lands and seas, O God. Raise up faithful stewards of all you have entrusted to human care. Hear us, O God.

Your mercy is great.

Save the nations, O God. Raise up faithful leaders who strive for peace and justice in the midst of violence and destruction. Especially we pray for . . . . Hear us, O God.

Your mercy is great.

Guard those in need, O God. Raise up faithful advocates and caretakers for those who are oppressed, poor, lonely, imprisoned, bereaved, or sick. Especially we pray for . . . . Hear us, O God.

Your mercy is great.

Give vision to this congregation, O God. Raise up faithful teachers, staff, volunteers, worship leaders, and council members who serve with purpose, joy, boldness, and love. Hear us, O God.

Your mercy is great.

Here other intercessions may be offered.

You abolished death, O God. Thank you for all those you called according to your purpose and who now rest in your light (*especially*). Hear us, O God.

Your mercy is great.

Into your hands, O God, we commend all for whom we pray, trusting in your mercy; through your Son, our Lord and Savior, Jesus Christ.

Amen.

Images in the Readings

The **mustard seed** shows up again in the synoptic parable of the kingdom. Mustard was used in the ancient Mediterranean as a condiment and thus was a valued plant. It is not a particularly small seed.

The New Revised Standard Version of the Bible reintroduces the language of "**slaves**" in some places that many other translations use the more palatable "servant." The Bible was written in a slave culture and does not condemn it. This biblical imagery became central to the thought of Martin Luther who, since he doubted that people had much genuine control over themselves, instead spoke of us as enslaved either to God or to evil. "We are captive to sin," says one of the confessions of sin in *Evangelical Lutheran Worship* (p. 95).

Lois and Eunice are remembered as having raised Timothy in the faith, just as multitudes of mothers and grandmothers have raised their children as Christians. We can pray in today's intercessions for all these mothers and grandmothers. Historically, many theologians have described the church itself as Mother Church, like Lois rearing the next generation.

Thanks to marathons, we know well Habakkuk's image of **runners** being able to read a sign as they rush past. So, as we run through life—indeed, in our culture most of us spend much of life running—may we see the sign of the word of God, held up by the church, and may we read there an encouragement to our faith in the race that really matters.

Ideas for the Day

◆ Anyone with a smartphone or computer can access incredible amounts of information, but the human spirit longs for much more than this. We hunger and thirst for an encounter with the living God. Habakkuk was called to write a vision that people on the move could easily access, a vision so plainly written and visible that a runner could read it. How does your faith community discern and share the vision God has given you? How does technology assist you? Who do you imagine is watching and waiting or even running to see and hear what the Lord is saying to you?

◆ Today we are given a wonderful story of how God's power can impact an entire family. Can you imagine some of the things that Eunice and Lois shared with Timothy through the years? Their love of Christ seems so beautifully contagious—a fire that never stopped burning and a faith that never stopped growing. Not everyone is raised in a home like this, but Jesus promises to bring us together in relationships that will encourage our faith to grow stronger and deeper. How have you seen God connect people with new friends and companions who become like sisters and brothers and even mothers and fathers who help nurture the gift of faith?

◆ Some trees have roots so deep that even hurricanes and tornadoes cannot uproot them. The same can be said for long-standing institutions that seem completely resistant to the forces of change. Refusing to merely quantify what faith is, Jesus boldly claims that even the smallest sort of faith can uproot the sturdiest of trees. His words remind us that we are not always willing to trust God's transforming power to make all things new. "Increase our faith," we continue to pray, so that we will serve together in ministries that call us to do what we ought to have done. How has God placed risky and difficult work in your hands that became a significant test of your faith?

Connections with the Liturgy

The Timothy reading speaks of the "laying on of hands." Christians continue the ancient practice of the laying on of hands, first described in the Bible when the dying Isaac blesses his sons (Gen. 48:14). *Evangelical Lutheran Worship* suggests the laying on of hands in baptism (p. 231), the affirmation of baptism (p. 236), confession and forgiveness (pp. 241, 244), and marriage (p. 289), as well as in several of the occasional services, such as ordination. The gesture evolved from the natural human sign of affection and usually symbolizes a prayer for God to bless the recipient, such as when parents bless their children each morning when they leave for school. Historically especially in ordination, it came also to denote a transfer of power.

Let the Children Come

Jesus promises amazing things can come from the tiniest of beginnings through faith. Little children are so often seen as the "future of the church." How many times have you heard (or thought), "If only we had more children and families, then our church would grow"? Doesn't that place a lot of responsibility on ones so small? Children and their families are not a special or set-apart division of the church, but equal and unique members, each with particular gifts and limitations. We can trust in our Lord to abundantly pour out blessings on the whole church through the life-giving waters of baptism.

Assembly Song
Gathering

Open now thy gates of beauty   ELW 533, LBW 250

Joyful, joyful we adore thee   ELW 836, LBW 551

Lord Jesus Christ, be present now   ELW 527, LBW 253

Psalmody and Acclamations

Perry, Michael. "Commit Your Way to God the Lord" (ROCKINGHAM) from PAS 37A.

Raabe, Nancy. "Psalm 37:1-9," Refrain 2, from PSCY.

+ Nicholson, Paul. "Lamentations 3:19-26" from PSCY.

+ Bash, Ewald. "By the Babylonian Rivers" (KAS DZIED JA) from PAS 137A.

(GA) ELW 170 with proper verse for Lectionary 27.

Hymn of the Day

We've come this far by faith   ELW 633, TFF 197   THIS FAR BY FAITH

How firm a foundation   ELW 796, LBW 507   FOUNDATION

Take, oh, take me as I am   ELW 814   TAKE ME AS I AM

Offering

We place upon your table, Lord   ELW 467, LBW 217

Lord, let my heart be good soil   ELW 512, LS 83, TFF 131, W&P 52, WOV 713

Communion

Healer of our every ill   ELW 612, WOV 738

Come, ye disconsolate   ELW 607, TFF 186

O Jesus, I have promised   ELW 810, LBW 503

Sending

On our way rejoicing   ELW 537, LBW 260

O God, my faithful God   ELW 806, LBW 504

Additional Assembly Songs

Yield not to temptation   TFF 195

Bring forth the kingdom   W&P 22, LS 35

That Christ be known   W&P 133

🌐 Caribbean Pentecostal chorus. "If You Only Had Faith/Si tuvieras fe" from *Glory to God*. U. WJK 9780664238971.

🌐 Lucio, Evy. "Soul, Adorn Yourself with Gladness/Vengo a ti, Jesús amado." U. ELW 489.

✿ Baloche, Paul. "Open the Eyes of My Heart" from CCLI.

✿ Brewster, Lincoln. "Let the Praises Ring" from CCLI.

✿ Kerr, Ed/Paul Baloche. "I Confess My Trust" from CCLI.

✿ Tomlin, Chris/Louie Giglio/Matt Maher. "I Lift My Hands" from CCLI.

✿ Zschech, Darlene. "The Potter's Hand" from CCLI.

Music for the Day
Choral

Bedford, Michael. "Now to Praise the Name of Jesus." SATB, kybd. PRE 392-41243.

● Koch, Paul. "How Firm a Foundation." 2 pt mxd, org. MSM 50-0008.

p Organ, Anne Krentz. "Come and Find the Quiet Center." SAB, kybd, fl, opt assembly. AFP 9780800675097.

p Raabe, Nancy. "God's Plan." 2 pt mxd, pno, cl. AFP 9781451479348.

Children's Choir

Hopson, Hal. "We Are the Children of Light." U, pno, opt desc, opt tamb, opt hb. HOP C5080.

Marcello, Benedetto/arr. Dale Grotenhuis. "Teach Me Now, O Lord." 2 pt, kybd. GIA 50-9418.

p Wilkinson, Sandy. "Be Strong!" U/2 pt, pno. CG CGA1325.

🌐 = global song   ✿ = praise song   + = semicontinuous psalm
● = relates to hymn of the day   p = available in Prelude Music Planner

Keyboard / Instrumental

p ● Ashdown, Franklin D. "Foundation" from *Postludes on Hymns of Faith and Assurance*. Org. AFP 9781451479560.

p ● Carter, John. "This Far by Faith" from *Introductions and Alternate Accompaniments for Piano*, vol. 6. Pno. AFP 9780800623647.

● Hobby, Robert A. "Foundation" from *Three Hymns of Praise*, set 8. Org. MSM 10-543.

● Stover, Harold. "Foundation" from *Organ Plus Anthology*, vol. 1. Org, inst. AFP 9781451424256.

Handbell

p Cota, Patricia. "Barcarole (Peace in the Storm)." 3-5 oct, L2+. HOP 2643.

● Eithun, Sandra. "How Firm a Foundation." 2-3 oct, L1+. CG CGB305. 3-5 oct, L1+. CG CGB743.

Krug, Jason W. "Faith, Hope, and Love." 3-6 oct hb, opt 2 oct hc, L2. LOR 20/1570L.

Tuesday, October 4

Francis of Assisi, renewer of the church, died 1226

Francis was the son of a wealthy cloth merchant. In a public confrontation with his father, he renounced his wealth and future inheritance and devoted himself to serving the poor. Francis described this act as being "wedded to Lady Poverty." Under his leadership the Order of Friars Minor (Franciscans) was formed, and they took literally Jesus' words to his disciples that they should take nothing on their journey and receive no payment for their work. Their task in preaching was to "use words if necessary." Francis had a spirit of gladness and gratitude for all of God's creation. This commemoration has been a traditional time to bless pets and animals, creatures Francis called his brothers and sisters. A prayer and a hymn attributed to St. Francis are included in *Evangelical Lutheran Worship* (p. 87, #835).

Theodor Fliedner, renewer of society, died 1864

Fliedner's (FLEED-ner) work was instrumental in the revival of the ministry of deaconesses among Lutherans. While a pastor in Kaiserswerth, Germany, he also ministered to prisoners in Düsseldorf. Through his ministry to prisoners, he came in contact with Moravian deaconesses, and it was through this Moravian influence that he was convinced that the ministry of deaconesses had a place among Lutherans. His work and writing encouraged women to care for those who were sick, poor, or imprisoned. Fliedner's deaconess motherhouse in Kaiserswerth inspired Lutherans all over the world to commission deaconesses to serve in parishes, schools, prisons, and hospitals.

Thursday, October 6

William Tyndale, translator, martyr, died 1536

William Tyndale was ordained in 1521, and his life's desire was to translate the scriptures into English. When his plan met opposition from King Henry VIII, Tyndale fled to Germany, where he traveled from city to city, living in poverty and constant danger. He was able to produce a New Testament in 1525. Nine years later he revised it and began work on the Old Testament, which he was unable to complete. He was captured, tried for heresy, and burned at the stake. Miles Coverdale completed Tyndale's work, and the Tyndale-Coverdale version was published as the "Matthew Bible" in 1537. For nearly four centuries the style of this translation has influenced English versions of the Bible such as the King James (Authorized Version) and the New Revised Standard Version.

Friday, October 7

Henry Melchior Muhlenberg, pastor in North America, died 1787

Muhlenberg (MYOO-len-berg) was prominent in setting the course for Lutheranism in North America. He helped Lutheran churches make the transition from the state churches of Europe to a new identity on American soil. Among other things, he established the first Lutheran synod in America and developed an American Lutheran liturgy. His liturgical principles became the basis for the Common Service of 1888, used in many North American service books for a majority of the past century. That Muhlenberg and his work are remembered today was anticipated at his death. The inscription on his grave reads, in Latin, "Who and what he was, future ages will know without a stone."

October 9, 2016
Time after Pentecost — Lectionary 28

It's a miracle! Multiple miracles! The waters of holy baptism have healed us. The body and blood of Jesus in holy communion have made us clean. We have died with Christ and been raised with him. For all this we have returned to offer thanks. From this place we are sent on our way rejoicing to share the good news.

Prayer of the Day

Almighty and most merciful God, your bountiful goodness fills all creation. Keep us safe from all that may hurt us, that, whole and well in body and spirit, we may with grateful hearts accomplish all that you would have us do, through Jesus Christ, our Savior and Lord.

Gospel Acclamation

Alleluia. Give thanks in all | circumstances;* for this is the will of God in Christ Je- | sus for you. *Alleluia.* (1 Thess. 5:18)

Readings and Psalm
2 Kings 5:1-3, 7-15c

Naaman, a Syrian general, suffers from leprosy. In this passage Elisha miraculously cures his illness, but only after Naaman realizes, with the help of his servants, that he also needs healing for his pride. This foreign general then acknowledges the sovereignty of the God of Israel.

Psalm 111

I will give thanks to the LORD with my whole heart. (Ps. 111:1)

2 Timothy 2:8-15

Though Paul is chained as a prisoner, he reminds Timothy that the word of God is never shackled or confined. He encourages his young friend to proclaim that word of freedom in an honest and upright life as well as in his teaching and preaching.

Luke 17:11-19

Jesus' mission includes making the unclean clean again. Unexpectedly, a cleansed Samaritan leper becomes a model for those who would praise and worship God and give thanks for God's mercy.

Semicontinuous reading and psalm
Jeremiah 29:1, 4-7

Ten years before the destruction of Jerusalem, many leaders of Judah were taken to Babylon. Jeremiah sends a letter to those exiles encouraging them, as they live in that strange place, to raise families and even to pray for the welfare of Babylon. God will restore them in due time.

Psalm 66:1-12

God has kept us among the living. (Ps. 66:9)

Preface   Sundays

Color   Green

Prayers of Intercession

The prayers are prepared locally for each occasion. The following examples may be adapted or used as appropriate.
Set free by the truth of God's gracious love, we pray for the church, the world, and all of God's good creation.
A brief silence.
O God, we pray for the church on earth. Make us one in spirit wherever we meet and however we worship. Hear us, O God.
Your mercy is great.
We pray for the health of the life-giving waters of creation (*here local water sources may be named*). Guard them from misuse and pollution. Hear us, O God.
Your mercy is great.
We pray for leaders in our town, our region, our country, and across the globe (*especially*). Equip them to work for justice for all people. Hear us, O God.
Your mercy is great.
We pray for those who are sick or in pain, for those who feel unclean in body or spirit, and for all in need of healing (*especially*). Hear us, O God.
Your mercy is great.
We pray for this assembly. Send your Spirit to inspire in us words and deeds of healing in our neighborhood and wider community. Hear us, O God.

Your mercy is great.

Here other intercessions may be offered.

We give thanks for the faithful departed (*especially*), and we wait for the day when we join them in thanks and praise around your heavenly throne. Hear us, O God.

Your mercy is great.

Into your hands, faithful God, we place ourselves and our prayers, spoken and unspoken, trusting in your mercy; through Jesus Christ, our Savior.

Amen.

Images in the Readings

Although there is no evidence that first-century lepers lived in isolated enclaves such as depicted in the film *Ben-Hur*, the practice of quarantining those with **leprosy** reflects not only the mistaken medical judgment that the disease is highly contagious, but also the psychological desire to keep undesirables away. Each society has its lepers. As usual in the gospels, if there are folks who have been placed on the other side of a line, there is where we will find Christ.

Samaritans were ethnically and religiously distinct from the Judeans. It is characteristic of the human phenomenon of religion that it embraces the insiders in the protection of their beliefs and distances itself from those who are other. Thus often religion gives its adherents a secure identity in contrast with the outsider who is somehow dangerous. The religion of Jesus Christ as described by Luke hopes to be different in this regard: Christ embraces the outsider.

Some of the church fathers likened Naaman immersing himself seven times in the **Jordan** to Christians washing in baptismal waters. This water runs through centuries of stories of God's faithful people, washing away what destroys God's intent, bringing people from the old life to the new.

The passage from 2 Timothy speaks of the word of God as not being **chained**. Some Protestants were taught that the medieval church chained copies of the scriptures to shelves in monastic libraries to prevent access to them. Actually, handwritten manuscripts of the Bible were so valuable that such chains protected them from theft so that the few persons educated enough to read the Latin could do so. Yet the image can remain a metaphor for the church: when are we "chaining" the word of God? Keep in mind that the same passage remonstrates church leaders to "rightly explain the word of truth."

Ideas for the Day

◆ The word *eucharist* derives from the Greek word *charis*, "thanksgiving." As the leper was cleansed by Jesus, so in the Lord's supper we receive forgiveness, hope, and a future. From these gifts, there is much for which to give thanks. Put pens and sticky notes at the ends of pews or chair rows. As worshipers return from communion, invite them to note something from their experience of receiving communion for which they give thanks. Provide a place where these thanksgivings can be posted and easily seen. Call it your "Charis Center," and invite people to add thanksgivings through the end of the church year.

◆ In baptism we are promised forgiveness, life, and salvation; the same gifts given to those healed in today's gospel. Toward the close of worship, ask worshipers to reflect on how they might show thanks for the gift of baptism in daily life this week. Maybe they have a gift to share, need to forgive someone, or know someone who needs an invitation. Encourage everyone to share one or two of their thoughts with a fellow worshiper, family member, or friend after worship or on the way home.

◆ *Charis* can also mean "gift." Survey the congregation, asking how their individual gifts might be offered up in thanksgiving in or outside of church. Such gifts might include leadership, care, time, carpentry, or music. Use this survey in planning for worship, mission, and ministry.

◆ Ask children to draw a picture of what they think the man who returned to Jesus looked like as he gave thanks. Or they could draw a picture of themselves giving thanks. With permission, use one or more of these drawings for the cover of your congregation's Thanksgiving bulletin or as projected art.

Connections with the Liturgy

Each Sunday we can join with the lepers to sing "Have mercy on us" (*ELW*, p. 98).

"Let us give thanks to the Lord our God," is said each Sunday as we keep eucharist. During the twentieth century, many Protestants recovered the ancient practice of giving thanks to God in a substantial prayer before joining together at the table of the Lord. To those who refuse to pray such a prayer, one might ask: In this prayer, we thank God for creation, the history of salvation, the mercy of Christ, the food on this table, and the presence of the Holy Spirit: how bad can that be? "It is right to give our thanks and praise."

Let the Children Come

Have you ever taken a walk outside with a young child? Have you noticed how they seem to stop at every little thing? The bustling anthill, the tree root making a crack in the sidewalk, the exoskeleton left behind by the cicada—all miracles. Sometimes it is hard for us to see and recognize God's miracles all around us. Sometimes it takes the unexpected observer to notice and wonder at God's abundant grace to help us notice too. How can we foster communities that allow the outsiders or the unexpected ones to be our teachers?

Assembly Song
Gathering
Remember and rejoice   ELW 454

Praise and thanksgiving be to God   ELW 458, LBW 191

We know that Christ is raised   ELW 449, LBW 189

Psalmody and Acclamations
Cherwien, David. "I Will Give Thanks to the Lord." U, org, opt hb. CPH 98-2930.

Dudley-Smith, Timothy. "Rejoice in God, My Heart" (LEONI/YIGDAL) from PAS 111D.

Pavlechko, Thomas. "Psalm 111" from SMP.

+ Farlee, Robert Buckley. "Psalm 66:1-12," Refrain 2, from PSCY. (GA) ELW 170 with proper verse for Lectionary 28.

Hymn of the Day
Oh, that I had a thousand voices   ELW 833, LBW 560   O DASS ICH TAUSEN ZUNGEN HÄTTE

Baptized in water   ELW 456, WOV 693   BUNESSAN

O Christ, the healer, we have come   ELW 610, LBW 360   DISTRESS

Offering
The peace of the Lord   ELW 646, LLC 471

Have you thanked the Lord?   ELW 829, TFF 270

Communion
O Christ the same   ELW 760, WOV 778

Waterlife   ELW 457, W&P 145

I am the Bread of life   ELW 485, WOV 702

Sending
We are baptized in Christ Jesus   ELW 451, WOV 698

Now thank we all our God   ELW 839/840, LBW 533/534

Additional Assembly Songs
Thank you, Lord   TFF 293

I am thanking Jesus   TFF 286, LS 101

Al Dios creador damos gracias   LLC 502

⏣ Brazilian. "Give Thanks to the Lord Our God/Rendei graças ao Senhor" from My Heart Sings Out. U. Church Publishing 9780898694741.

⏣ Matsikenyiri, Patrick. "Jesus, We Are Gathered/Jesu, tawa pano." SATB. ELW 529.

✧ Collins, Chris/Edwin Othello Excell/John Newton/Todd Agnew. "Grace like Rain" from CCLI.

✧ Eichelberger, Brian/Zach Bolen. "Made Alive" from CCLI.

✧ Groves, Eric Daniel/Jonathan Stockstill. "Healing Is Here" from CCLI.

✧ Guglielmucci, Mike. "Healer" from CCLI.

✧ Johnson, Brian/Jeremy Riddle/Joel Taylor. "For the Sake of the World" from CCLI.

✧ West, Matthew. "Blessed Assurance" from Praisecharts.

Music for the Day
Choral
p ● Ferguson, John. "Oh, That I Had a Thousand Voices." SATB, org, br qrt, opt assembly. AFP 9781451402513.

p Dengler, Lee. "Put on Love." SAB, pno. AFP 9781451420784.

p Helgen, John. "Baptized and Set Free." SATB, pno. AFP 9781451420661.

p Rosewall, Michael. "Now Thank We All Our God." 2 pt mxd, kybd. AFP 9780800623852.

Children's Choir
p Benson, Robert A. "What Shall We Give to God?" from ChildrenSing in Worship, vol. 3. U, kybd, opt desc, opt C inst. AFP 9781451476620.

Folkemer, Stephen. "Banned and Banished." SA/SAB, org. GIA G-4907.

Schram, Ruth Elaine. "Giving Thanks." U/2 pt, pno. SHW 884088636098.

Keyboard / Instrumental
● Floeter, Valerie A. "Distress" from Piano Plus Through the Year, vol. 2. Pno, inst. AFP 9780800663728.

● Near, Gerald. "Bunessan" from Laudes Domini, vol. 2. Org. MSM 10-349.

p ● Nelson, Ronald A. "O dass ich tausend Zungen hätte" from Easy Hymn Settings, vol. 3. Org. AFP 9781451462562.

● Raabe, Nancy M. "O dass ich tausend Zungen hätte" from Grace and Peace, vol. 1. Pno. AFP 9780800677602.

Handbell
Lamb, Linda. "How Majestic Is Your Name." 3-5 oct, L3. Ring Praise! RP7518.

● Moklebust, Cathy. "Morningdance." 3-5 oct, L3. CG CGB218.

Morris, Hart. "Faithful Promises." 3-5 oct, L4-. BP HB267.

Monday, October 10, 2016
Day of Thanksgiving (Canada)
See Day of Thanksgiving (U.S.A.), pp. 331–333.

Saturday, October 15
Teresa of Ávila, teacher, renewer of the church, died 1582
Teresa of Ávila (AH-vee-la) is also known as Teresa de Jesús. She chose the life of a Carmelite nun after reading the letters of Jerome. Frequently sick during her early years as a nun, she found that when she was sick her prayer life flowered, but when she was well it withered. Steadily her life of faith and prayer deepened, and she grew to have a lively

⏣ = global song   ✧ = praise song   + = semicontinuous psalm
● = relates to hymn of the day   p = available in Prelude Music Planner

sense of God's presence with her. She worked to reform her monastic community in Ávila, which she believed had strayed from its original purpose. Her reforms asked nuns to maintain life in the monastic enclosure without leaving it and to identify with those who are poor by not wearing shoes. Teresa's writings on devotional life have enjoyed a wide readership.

October 16, 2016
Time after Pentecost — Lectionary 29

Pray always. Do not lose heart. This is the encouragement of the Christ of the gospel today. Persistence in our every encounter with the divine will be blessed. Wrestle with the word. Remember your baptism again and again. Come regularly to Christ's table. Persistence in our every encounter with the divine will be blessed.

Prayer of the Day

O Lord God, tireless guardian of your people, you are always ready to hear our cries. Teach us to rely day and night on your care. Inspire us to seek your enduring justice for all this suffering world, through Jesus Christ, our Savior and Lord.

Gospel Acclamation

Alleluia. The word of God is liv- | ing and active,* able to judge the thoughts and intentions | of the heart. *Alleluia.* (Heb. 4:12)

Readings and Psalm
Genesis 32:22-31

Returning to the home he had fled many years before after stealing his brother's birthright and his father's blessing, Jacob wrestles all night long with a divine adversary who ultimately blesses him and changes his name to "Israel," a name that means "he wrestles with God."

Psalm 121

My help comes from the Lord, the maker of heaven and earth. (Ps. 121:2)

2 Timothy 3:14—4:5

Paul continues his instruction of Timothy, his younger colleague in ministry, by emphasizing the importance of faithful teaching despite opposition.

Luke 18:1-8

Jesus tells a parable of a hateful judge who is worn down by a widow's pleas. Jesus is calling God's people to cry out for justice and deliverance. For if an unethical judge will ultimately grant the plea of a persistent widow, how much more will God respond to those who call.

Semicontinuous reading and psalm
Jeremiah 31:27-34

After uttering many oracles of judgment, Jeremiah announces a day of hope when God will make a new covenant with Israel and Judah, a covenant written upon their hearts and sealed with God's forgiveness.

Psalm 119:97-104

Your words are sweet to my taste, sweeter than honey to my mouth. (Ps. 119:103)

Preface   Sundays

Color   Green

Prayers of Intercession

The prayers are prepared locally for each occasion. The following examples may be adapted or used as appropriate.
Set free by the truth of God's gracious love, we pray for the church, the world, and all of God's good creation.
A brief silence.
Protector of all, you guard your people from evil. Help your church to provide sanctuary for all who are in need. Hear us, O God.

Your mercy is great.
Creator of all, you made the sun, the moon, and the stars. Bless efforts to restore clean air, that your pure light may shine in the world. Hear us, O God.
Your mercy is great.
Keeper of all life, you provide justice for the nations. Call upon leaders and judges, lawyers and advocates to proclaim your justice where injustice rules. Hear us, O God.
Your mercy is great.
Nurturing healer, you reach out to those who have lost heart. Ease their suffering, relieve their pain, comfort the dying, and calm the troubled (*especially*). Hear us, O God.
Your mercy is great.
God of unfailing love, you are our first and best teacher. Guide all who teach in schools, homes, churches, seminaries, and in public life. Let your love shine forth in their teaching. Hear us, O God.
Your mercy is great.
Here other intercessions may be offered.
Holy One, you bless all those who cry out to you. We give thanks for the persistent witness of your blessed saints who now rest in your just and righteous presence. Hear us, O God.
Your mercy is great.
Into your hands, faithful God, we place ourselves and our prayers, spoken and unspoken, trusting in your mercy; through Jesus Christ, our Savior.
Amen.

Images in the Readings

If medieval Christianity focused obsessively on Christ as an exacting **judge** of all, many contemporary Christians so stress God's loving forgiveness that they forgo attention to God as judge. We are far distant from the countless European churches in which the entire front of the sanctuary was painted with a scene of the final judgment, with luminous good guys ascending to heaven on Christ's right and wretched, ugly creatures falling into the mouth of hell on his left. Yet in the creed we affirm that Christ will judge the living and dead. We pray in the confession for forgiveness and in our Sunday intercessions for an increase of justice in the world.

If Judaism dwells on the idea of **wrestling with God**, of harassing God with prayer, many contemporary Christians have inherited a religious quietism that is strong on patience and weak on persistence in prayer. God has promised to give food to the hungry, peace to the faithful: let us keep up our petitions, bothering God until God acts.

The image of **itching ears** is most appropriate for our time, when individuals seek perpetual novelty and continuous entertainment that "suits their own desires."

Ideas for the Day

◆   Many people are uncomfortable with prayer simply because they have never been taught to pray. They might think it's a matter of technique, which they don't believe they have, or a matter of having a special connection to God, which they don't believe they possess. Dedicate an educational event or a retreat to teaching worshipers to pray as the widow in today's text. Note that she was persistent, direct, and honest. No prayer "technique" is more important than this. And as Jesus points out in the parable, if the judge listened to the widow, who had no real connection to him apart from her "bothering," God will surely heed the prayers of the faithful.

◆   Teach children the prayer, "Come, Lord Jesus, be our guest; let these (your) gifts to us be blessed." Some children may use this as a prayer before meals at home. Ask those who know the prayer to help teach it to children who don't. After all have learned the prayer, invite them to lead the assembly in the prayer during worship. This little grace does not have to serve only as a table prayer at home; it might also be appropriate as an offering prayer before communion.

◆   Teach the prayer, "Be present at our table, Lord; be here and everywhere adored; these mercies bless and grant that we may strengthened for thy service be." Invite the congregation to sing the prayer as a response to the Lord's supper, as well as at a congregational meal (tune: OLD HUNDREDTH; ELW 883). Note similarities between the Lord's supper and a fellowship meal in your church newsletter, in the worship folder, or in projected content.

◆   Intersperse prayer during the sermon. The preacher might pause to pray or assign several people to do so. As an alternative, design an entire sermon as an exercise in prayer. Use this as an occasion both to teach persistent prayer and to engage in it.

Connections with the Liturgy

Each Sunday, when perhaps at worship we have wrestled with God, we are sent away with God's blessing. Each Sunday we are instructed in the inspired scripture, and we receive the proclaimed message. Each Sunday we join with the widow to plead for justice in the world. It is as if the weekly assembly is enacting this Sunday's readings.

Let the Children Come

The parable of the woman persistently beseeching the unjust judge is the model Jesus offers for prayer life. It conveys a whole gamut of feelings: humor, exasperation, determination, persistence, and trust. So often we teach children prayers handed down to us from others, but how can we model for children a more conversational prayer life with God? The nurturing of a vibrant, relational faith is enriched with ancient words, but also involves lifting up real human needs. How does your community leave space for children's voices to pray? How do adults model for children trust in God through their spoken prayers?

Assembly Song
Gathering
Lead me, guide me   ELW 768, TFF 70, W&P 84
In my life, Lord, be glorified   ELW 744, TFF 248, W&P 89
Holy, holy, holy, holy   ELW 762, LLC 273, TFF 203, W&P 61

Psalmody and Acclamations
Bedford, Michael. "Psalm 121" from *ChildrenSing Psalms*. U, kybd, 4 hb.
O'Brien, Frances Patrick. "Our Help Is from the Lord." SAB, cant, assembly, kybd, opt gtr, fl, vc. GIA G-5449.
+   Hopson, Hal. "Psalm 119 (97-104)" from TPP.
(GA) ELW 170 with proper verse for Lectionary 29.

Hymn of the Day
Day by day   ELW 790, WOV 746   *BLOTT EN DAG*
Give Me Jesus   ELW 770, TFF 165, WOV 777   *GIVE ME JESUS*
Lord, teach us how to pray aright   ELW 745, LBW 438   *SONG 67*

Offering
Your will be done   ELW 741, TFF 243
Lord, listen to your children praying   ELW 752, LS 94, TFF 247, W&P 92, WOV 775

Communion
Lord, take my hand and lead me   ELW 767, LBW 333
My faith looks up to thee   ELW 759, LBW 479
If you but trust in God to guide you   ELW 769, LBW 453

Sending
Evening and morning   ELW 761, LBW 465
What a fellowship, what a joy divine   ELW 774, TFF 220, WOV 780

Additional Assembly Songs
I shall not be moved   TFF 147
Los que confían en Jehová   LLC 534
Let my prayer be a fragrant offering   W&P 86
Lee, Song. "To the Hills I Lift My Eyes" from *Glory to God*. U. WJK 9780664238971.
Sedio, Mark. "Alleluia Verse in African Style" from *Global Choral Sounds*. SATB, perc. CPH 98-3610.
Hall, Mark/Matthew West. "Courageous" from CCLI.
Houston, Joel. "From the Inside Out" from CCLI.
Hughes, Tim. "God of Justice" from CCLI.
Kirkland, Eddie. "Here and Now" from CCLI.
Myrin, Jonas/Matt Redman. "How Great Is Your Faithfulness" from CCLI.

Riddle, Jeremy/Josh Farro/Phil Wickham. "This Is Amazing Grace" from CCLI.

Music for the Day
Choral
p ● Hayes, Mark. "Day by Day." SATB div, pno. AFP 9780800658342.
p   Hopson, Hal. "We See the Mountains Lifted High before Us." 2 pt mxd, pno. CG CGA1291.
Kodály, Zoltán. "Psalm 121." SATB div. B&H M-060035562.
p ● Lau, Robert. "Give Me Jesus." SATB, opt solo, kybd. AFP 9780800678128.

Children's Choir
p   Neswick, Bruce. "Hearken to My Voice, O Lord, When I Call" from *The Augsburg Choirbook: Sacred Choral Music of the Twentieth Century*. SA/TB, org. AFP 9781451467017.
Perkey, Christine. "Evening Prayer (Jesus, Tender Shepherd, Hear Me)." 2 pt, kybd. HIN HMC 1708.
p   Wold, Wayne. "Build New Bridges" from *ChildrenSing in Worship*, vol. 3. U/2 pt, kybd. AFP 9781451476545.

Keyboard / Instrumental
●   Billingham, Richard. "Give Me Jesus" from *Augsburg Organ Library: Summer*. Org. AFP 9780800676872.
p ● Carlson, J. Bert. "Blott en dag" from *Drawn to the Light*. Org. AFP 9781451462586.
●   Cherwien, David. "Give Me Jesus" from *Eight for Eighty-Eight*, vol. 2. Pno. AFP 9780800657321.
●   Porter, Rachel Trelstad. "Blott en dag" from *Day by Day*. Pno. AFP 9780800656326.

Handbell
●   Behnke, John. "Give Me Jesus." 4-6 oct hb, opt 3-5 oct hc, L4. AGEHR AG46025.
p ● McFadden, Jane. "Two More Swedish Melodies for Handbells ('Blott en dag' and 'Bred dina vida vingar')." 3-4 oct hb, opt 2-4 oct hc, L2. AFP 9781451421040.
Moklebust, Cathy. "I Will Lift Mine Eyes unto the Hills (Psalm 121)." 3-5 oct hb, L2, CG CGB529. Opt full score with org, CG CGB528.

Monday, October 17
Ignatius, Bishop of Antioch, martyr, died around 115
Ignatius was the second bishop of Antioch, in Syria. It was there that the name "Christian" was first used to describe the followers of Jesus. Ignatius is known to us through his letters. In them he encouraged Christians to live in unity sustained with love while standing firm on sound doctrine. Ignatius believed Christian martyrdom was a privilege.

When his own martyrdom approached, he wrote in one of his letters, "I prefer death in Christ Jesus to power over the farthest limits of the earth. . . . Do not stand in the way of my birth to real life." Ignatius and all martyrs are a reminder that even today Christians face death because of their faith in Jesus.

Tuesday, October 18

Luke, Evangelist

St. Luke is identified by tradition as the author of both Luke and Acts. Luke is careful to place the events of Jesus' life in both their social and religious contexts. Some of the most loved parables, including the good Samaritan and the prodigal son, are found only in this gospel. Luke's gospel has also given the church some of its most beautiful songs: the Benedictus sung at morning prayer, the Magnificat sung at evening prayer, and the Nunc dimittis sung at the close of the day. These songs are powerful witnesses to the message of Jesus Christ.

October 23, 2016

Time after Pentecost — Lectionary 30

Genuine repentance and pretentious piety stand in stark contrast in the gospel and all around us. All creation stands in need of God's forgiveness. Keep the faith. God's people—"all who have longed for his appearing"—shall be accounted righteous for Jesus' sake. Our God is merciful to sinners. For all this the assembly glorifies God forever.

Prayer of the Day

Holy God, our righteous judge, daily your mercy surprises us with everlasting forgiveness. Strengthen our hope in you, and grant that all the peoples of the earth may find their glory in you, through Jesus Christ, our Savior and Lord.

Gospel Acclamation

Alleluia. All who exalt themselves | will be humbled,* but all who humble themselves will | be exalted. *Alleluia.*
(Luke 18:14)

Readings and Psalm
Jeremiah 14:7-10, 19-22

In a time of drought, the people pray for mercy, repenting of their sins and the sins of their ancestors. They appeal to God to remember the covenant, to show forth God's power, and to heal their land by sending life-giving rain.

or Sirach 35:12-17

The author of this wisdom book urges his audience to give generously to God. He also asserts that God is a just judge who does not show partiality but listens to the prayers of the oppressed and the poor.

Psalm 84:1-7

Happy are the people whose strength is in you. (Ps. 84:5)

2 Timothy 4:6-8, 16-18

The conclusion of this letter to a young minister offers a final perspective on life from one who is now facing death. Though others have let him down, Paul is sure of his faith in the Lord, who has stood by him and lent him strength.

Luke 18:9-14

The coming reign of God will involve unexpected reversals of fortune with judgment rooted in mercy. Jesus tells a parable in which the one who humbles himself is exalted and the one who exalts his own righteousness is humbled.

Semicontinuous reading and psalm
Joel 2:23-32

The prophet interprets the event of a plague of locusts as a sign of God's judgment. Today's reading points beyond the judgment to a day when prosperity will return, when God's spirit will be poured out on the people, and when everyone who calls on the Lord's name will be saved.

Psalm 65

Your paths overflow with plenty. (Ps. 65:11)

Preface Sundays

Color Green

Prayers of Intercession

The prayers are prepared locally for each occasion. The following examples may be adapted or used as appropriate.

Set free by the truth of God's gracious love, we pray for the church, the world, and all of God's good creation.

A brief silence.

Only you are righteous, O God. Lead your church to true repentance so that we reflect your light and truth to the world. Hear us, O God.

Your mercy is great.

Only you can bring rain, O God. Be with those who lack clean water or must walk miles to quench their thirst. Hear us, O God.

Your mercy is great.

Only you can judge the nations, O God. Raise up leaders with humble hearts so that your peace spreads across the earth. Hear us, O God.

Your mercy is great.

Only you can bring healing, O God. Be with all whose hearts ache, who hold out empty hands, who long for forgiveness. Comfort the grieving and heal the sick (*especially*). Hear us, O God.

Your mercy is great.

Only you know the depths of our hearts, O God. Call this congregation to loving action in your name and open our eyes to what you are doing among us. Hear us, O God.

Your mercy is great.

Here other intercessions may be offered.

Those who live in your house are happy, O God. Keep us by your grace until we join (*James of Jerusalem, martyr, and all*) the saints around your throne. Hear us, O God.

Your mercy is great.

Into your hands, faithful God, we place ourselves and our prayers, spoken and unspoken, trusting in your mercy; through Jesus Christ, our Savior.

Amen.

Images in the Readings

A danger among Christians is a kind of **humility** contest, a competition to the bottom. Former Israeli prime minister Golda Meir famously said, "Don't be humble: you are not that great."

Pharisees were a lay sect of devout Jews who observed a rigorous legalism and separated themselves out from others to maintain their religious purity. They honored both the written and the oral Torah. Paul was a Pharisee. Although certainly many Pharisees were devout believers, they received bad press in the New Testament because their piety was exclusionary, even of the need for Christ. Pharisees gained dominance in Judaism after Rome's destruction of the temple in 70 CE. In Martin Luther's exposition of this parable, he shows that the Pharisee has kept all the commandments, but that, says Luther, is not what saves.

The Roman Empire hired representatives of conquered peoples to work as **tax collectors**, who negotiated their own pay by overcharging their own community. Although the deceit involved in their trade has always been condemned, over the centuries Christians have debated to what extent believers can cooperate with evil governments. The New Testament usually stresses the obedience of Christians to their government, although for example the book of Revelation might be seen as seditious.

Jeremiah's plea speaks of God's **heart** (v. 19). Ancient peoples thought of the heart, not as a bodily organ that pumps blood through the body, but as the center of the affections. Thus the image is not as anthropomorphic as one might first think.

Besides the Pharisee and the tax collector, the readings include many other images: drought, stranger, traveler, warrior, wanderers, healing, God's throne, libation, good fight, race, crown, judge, lion's mouth, attack, kingdom of heaven. These readings make clear that the Bible is made up of metaphors.

Ideas for the Day

◆ "Yet you, O Lord, are in the midst of us, and we are called by your name; do not forsake us!" (Jer. 14:9b). Jeremiah gives a full-throated lament but at the same time affirms that God is "in the midst." God is right in the middle of the disaster Israel is experiencing, not watching from a distance. This doesn't make the lament any less real or heartfelt, and Jeremiah's words could easily be applied to our world today: "Why have you struck us down so that there is no healing for us? We look for peace, but find no good; for a time of healing, but there is terror instead" (v. 19b). How would you write this passage in a way that relates to a situation in your life, congregation, community, or world? How often do you use the phrase "in the midst," and what does it mean to you?

◆ The passage from 2 Timothy 4 is often used at funerals, particularly verse 7: "I have fought the good fight, I have finished the race, I have kept the faith." This verse is meaningful and comforting to many people; others will be reminded of the negative impact that can come from using a "fight" metaphor for illness, particularly cancer. Read more about "The Problem with 'Fighting' Cancer" on the science and medicine site blogs.plos.org (http://blogs.plos.org/?s=fighting+cancer).

◆ The song "Recovering Pharisee" by Buddy Greene includes the line "I'm a sinner and a saint simultaneously," a reference to *simul justus et peccator* and Martin Luther's teaching on sin and justification. To identify with either the Pharisee or the tax collector misses the point; we're not either/or, we're both/and.

◆ "I thank God that I'm not like . . ." Even if we don't come out and say it that way in our prayers, most of us have experienced feeling good at the expense of others and judging others to be less than ourselves. The internet is often a venue where people, emboldened by the distance of virtual interaction, engage in various forms of self-righteous judgment. On BuzzFeed, a site that often features lists making fun of people, a staff member posted an article titled "Everyone on the Internet Is an Actual Person" (July 30, 2014). The article encourages posters and commenters to remember the humanity of people with unfortunate tattoos, awkward family photos, and fledgling guitar skills.

Connections with the Liturgy

In the rite of confession and forgiveness (*ELW*, pp. 94–96), the Kyrie (pp. 98–99), the "Glory to God" (p. 100), the "Lamb of God" (p. 112), and one option for blessing (p. 114), we stand with the tax collector to ask for God's mercy. He stood "far off," yet in our baptism we stand front and center, seeing the face of God in Jesus Christ.

Let the Children Come

Children, especially older elementary-aged children, are very concerned about justice. Is the slice of cake equal? Who was standing in line first? "My hand was raised first, and the teacher still didn't call on me!" Jesus' parable of the Pharisee and tax collector provides a helpful focus for our work for justice: self-reflection. Maslow's hierarchy of needs ranks self-actualization at the top of human needs. Even though it is a skill for the mature, children can see and learn authentic confession and forgiveness by generous practice of it by the adults in their lives. The words "I'm sorry" and "I forgive you" are precious gifts.

Assembly Song
Gathering

How small our span of life   ELW 636

In a lowly manger born   ELW 718, LBW 417

Praise to you, O God of mercy   ELW 208, W&P 119, WOV 790

Psalmody and Acclamations

Duba, Arlo D. "How Lovely, Lord, How Lovely" (MERLE'S TUNE) from PAS 94C.

Haugen, Marty. "How Lovely Is Your Dwelling Place" (PROSPECT). SATB, cant, gtr, kybd, C inst. Assembly part available on OneLicense.net. GIA G-5242.

+ Dudley-Smith, Timothy. "Every Heart Its Tribute Pays" (ST. GEORGE'S WINDSOR) from PAS 65E.

(GA) ELW 170 with proper verse for Lectionary 30.

Hymn of the Day

Our Father, we have wandered   ELW 606, WOV 733   HERZLICH TUT MICH VERLANGEN

You Are Mine   ELW 581, W&P 158   YOU ARE MINE

Love divine, all loves excelling   ELW 631, LBW 315   HYFRYDOL

Offering

Seed that in earth is dying   ELW 330, sts. 1, 3

For the fruit of all creation   ELW 679, WOV 760, LBW 563

Communion

O Lord, we praise you   ELW 499, LBW 215

Out of the depths I cry to you   ELW 600, LBW 295

O God of love, O King of peace   ELW 749, LBW 414

Sending

Guide me ever, great Redeemer   ELW 618, LBW 343

You are the way   ELW 758, LBW 464

Additional Assembly Songs

God forgave my sin in Jesus' name   TFF 187

Un nuevo amanecer   LLC 469

All to Jesus I surrender   TFF 235

⊕ Amis tribe, Taiwan. "O Give Thanks to the Lord" from *My Heart Sings Out*. U. Church Publishing 9780898694741.

⊕ Park, Sung-ho. "Everyone Who Longs for the Boundless Love of God" from *Glory to God*. U. WJK 9780664238971.

✿ Hudson, Bob. "Humble Thyself in the Sight of the Lord" from CCLI.

✿ Kendrick, Graham. "O Lord, the Clouds Are Gathering" from CCLI.

✿ Redman, Matt. "Facedown" from CCLI.

✿ Redman, Matt. "You Must Increase" from CCLI.

✿ Tomlin, Chris/Louie Giglio/Henri Abraham César Malan. "Take My Life" from CCLI.

Music for the Day
Choral

● Davis, Sidney. "Love Divine, All Loves Excelling." 2 pt, kybd. MSM 50-9408.

p Hampton, Keith. "He's Got the Whole World." SATB, solo. AFP 9780800659608.

p Miller, Aaron David. "Lord Jesus, Think On Me" from *The New Gloria Deo: Music for Small Choirs*. SAB, pno. AFP 9780806698403.

Vaughan Williams, Ralph. "O How Amiable." SATB, org. OXF 9780193851245.

⊕ = global song   ✿ = praise song   + = semicontinuous psalm
● = relates to hymn of the day   p = available in Prelude Music Planner

Children's Choir

Grier, Gene/Lowell Everson. "Come and Go with Me/Standing in the Need of Prayer." 2 pt, kybd. GIA G-5871.

Kosche, Kenneth. "How Lovely Is Your Dwelling Place." 2 pt, kybd. MSM 50-6302.

Powell, Robert J. "Bless to Me, O God." U, pno/org. PAR 9931.

Keyboard / Instrumental

• Blair, Dallas. "Hyfrydol" from *Hymn Introductions and Descants for Trumpet and Organ*, set 3. Org, tpt. MSM 20-141.

• Brahms, Johannnes. "Herzlich tut mich verlangen." Org. Various editions.

p • Raabe, Nancy M. "Herzlich tut mich verlangen" from *Grace and Peace*, vol. 2. Pno. AFP 9780800679019.

p • Sedio, Mark. "Hyfrydol" from *Augsburg Organ Library: Marriage*. Org. AFP 9781451486025.

Handbell

Lamb, Linda. "Love Divine, All Loves Excelling (Meditation on 'Beecher')." 3-5 oct hb, opt 3 oct hc, L2. CG CGB749.

McChesney, Kevin. "How Lovely Is Thy Dwelling Place." 3-5 oct, L3. CG CGB253.

• Tucker, Sondra. "You Are Mine." 3-5 oct hb, opt 2 oct hc, L3. GIA G-7063.

Sunday, October 23

James of Jerusalem, martyr, died around 62

James became an early leader of the church in Jerusalem. He is described in the New Testament as the brother of Jesus, and secular historian Josephus calls James the brother of Jesus, "the so-called Christ." Little is known about James, but Josephus reported that the Pharisees respected James for his piety and observance of the law. His enemies had him put to death.

Wednesday, October 26

Philipp Nicolai, died 1608; Johann Heermann, died 1647; Paul Gerhardt, died 1676; hymnwriters

These three outstanding hymnwriters all worked in Germany during times of war and plague. When Philipp Nicolai was a pastor in Westphalia, the plague killed thirteen hundred of his parishioners. One hundred seventy people died in one week. His hymns "Wake, Awake, for Night Is Flying" (ELW 436) and "O Morning Star, How Fair and Bright!" (ELW 308) were included in a series of meditations he wrote to comfort his parishioners during the plague. The style of Johann Heermann's hymns moved away from the more objective style of Reformation hymnody toward expressing the emotions of faith. Among his hymns is the plaintive text "Ah, Holy Jesus" (ELW 349). Paul Gerhardt lost a preaching position at St. Nicholas Church in Berlin because he refused to sign a document stating he would not make theological arguments in his sermons. The author of beloved hymns such as "O Sacred Head, Now Wounded" (ELW 351), some have called Gerhardt the greatest of Lutheran hymn writers.

Friday, October 28

Simon and Jude, Apostles

Little is known about Simon and Jude. In New Testament lists of the apostles, Simon the "zealot" or Cananaean is mentioned, but he is never mentioned apart from these lists. Jude, sometimes called Thaddeus, is also mentioned in lists of the Twelve. At the last supper Jude asked Jesus why he had chosen to reveal himself to the disciples but not to the world. A traditional story about Simon and Jude says that they traveled together on a missionary journey to Persia and were both martyred there.

October 30, 2016
Reformation Sunday

On this day we celebrate the heart of our faith: the gospel of Christ—the good news—that makes us free! We pray that the Holy Spirit would continue to unite the church today in its proclamation and witness to the world. In the waters of baptism we are made one body; we pray for the day that all Christians will also be one at the Lord's table.

Prayer of the Day

Almighty God, gracious Lord, we thank you that your Holy Spirit renews the church in every age. Pour out your Holy Spirit on your faithful people. Keep them steadfast in your word, protect and comfort them in times of trial, defend them against all enemies of the gospel, and bestow on the church your saving peace, through Jesus Christ, our Savior and Lord, who lives and reigns with you and the Holy Spirit, one God, now and forever.

or

Gracious Father, we pray for your holy catholic church. Fill it with all truth and peace. Where it is corrupt, purify it; where it is in error, direct it; where in anything it is amiss, reform it; where it is right, strengthen it; where it is in need, provide for it; where it is divided, reunite it; for the sake of your Son, Jesus Christ, our Savior, who lives and reigns with you and the Holy Spirit, one God, now and forever.

Gospel Acclamation

Alleluia. If you continue in my word, you are truly ' my disciples,* and you will know the truth, and the truth will ' make you free. *Alleluia.* (John 8:31-32)

Readings and Psalm
Jeremiah 31:31-34

The renewed covenant will not be breakable, but like the old covenant it will expect the people to live upright lives. To know the Lord means that one will defend the cause of the poor and needy (Jer. 22:16). The renewed covenant is possible only because the Lord will forgive iniquity and not remember sin. Our hope lies in a God who forgets.

Psalm 46

The LORD of hosts is with us; the God of Jacob is our stronghold. (Ps. 46:7)

Romans 3:19-28

Paul's words stand at the heart of the preaching of Martin Luther and the other Reformation leaders. No human beings make themselves right with God through works of the law. We are brought into a right relationship with God through the divine activity centered in Christ's death. This act is a gift of grace that liberates us from sin and empowers our faith in Jesus Christ.

John 8:31-36

Jesus speaks of truth and freedom as spiritual realities known through his word. He reveals the truth that sets people free from sin.

Preface   Sundays

Color   Red

Prayers of Intercession

The prayers are prepared locally for each occasion. The following examples may be adapted or used as appropriate.

Set free by the truth of God's gracious love, we pray for the church, the world, and all of God's good creation.

A brief silence.

Righteous God, write your law on our hearts. Unite your church. Let your word spread throughout the earth. Hear us, O God.

Your mercy is great.

Earth-maker, show your power and goodness in the mountains, the depths of the sea, the rivers, and all of your creation. Teach us how to care for our earthly home. Hear us, O God.

Your mercy is great.

Source of hope, you make wars to cease in all the world. Visit places devastated by war and conflict (*especially*). Break the bow, shatter the spear, and bring your perfect peace. Hear us, O God.

Your mercy is great.

God our refuge and strength, you are a very present help in trouble. Comfort those who are sick or in pain, the lonely and grieving, those without a home or meaningful work. Especially we pray for . . . . Hear us, O God.

Your mercy is great.

Faithful God, call this assembly to remember the everlasting covenant you have made with us. Shape us to live in the freedom Christ gives us and to welcome others into this way of life. Hear us, O God.
Your mercy is great.

Here other intercessions may be offered.

God our stronghold, the saints from every age gather around your throne. Help us to wait with patience and joy until that day when we too see you face to face. Hear us, O God.
Your mercy is great.

Into your hands, faithful God, we place ourselves and our prayers, spoken and unspoken, trusting in your mercy; through Jesus Christ, our Savior.
Amen.

Images in the Readings

The gospel's image of **freedom** presents a challenge to contemporary North Americans and perhaps to other Western societies as well, since popularly "freedom" is understood as the right of the individual to live out personal choices. John's gospel suggests instead that the freedom granted in Christ is the freedom of the son who remains in the father's house and does the will of that father. Sixteenth-century Christians used this proclamation of freedom to leave behind church regulations of the medieval church, but even Martin Luther wrote detailed interpretations of the ten commandments, understood as "law" for Christian use. We are free to be obedient children.

A **covenant** was a legal agreement in which the master promised protection because the participants met certain obligations. Ancient Israelites adopted this cultural category for their understanding of the relationship that God had offered the chosen people. Christians continued to use this language in articulating the renewed relationship with God that was affected through Christ. Particularly Methodists have kept this language alive in referring to the Baptismal Covenant and in their annual Covenant Renewal ceremonies. Lutherans understand the covenant as God's continuing mercy given in word and sacrament.

Ideas for the Day

◆ Polaris is an organization dedicated to eradicating modern slavery (polarisproject.org). Their tagline is "Freedom happens now," and they take their name from the North Star that guided slaves to freedom in the United States. One goal of the organization is to shed light on the truth that slavery is not something that happened in the past to other people; it is something happening right now, and it impacts all people.

◆ "I will put my law within them, and I will write it on their hearts; and I will be their God, and they shall be my people" (Jer. 31:33b). What words are written on your heart? Share something you've memorized with the congregation, take time during worship to give people a chance to practice and memorize verses from Romans 8, or host an "On Our Hearts" festival where people of all ages share poems, passages, prayers, and other words they've memorized and keep close to their hearts as a way to remember the love and grace of God.

◆ In his Lutheran Confessions class, Dr. Timothy Wengert told the story of a woman who walked into a Lutheran church during worship on Sunday morning feeling unloved and unlovable. She'd never been to a Lutheran church before; she was desperate. During the words of the confession, she felt terrible, and the weight of her sin was oppressive. Then the pastor said, "I therefore declare to you *the entire forgiveness of all your sins*." And the woman said, out loud, "That's all it takes?" She was overwhelmed, and her life was changed forever by hearing the good news that God gives the *entire* forgiveness of *all* our sins, completely apart from anything we do.

◆ *Alive Inside* (2014, Projector Media) is a documentary about the profound impact music can make on patients with dementia. Patients who can't remember the names of their children are able to remember lyrics of songs; patients who are uncommunicative suddenly brighten and sing along when a favorite song is played for them. Music, like the law and love of God, is written on our hearts.

Connections with the Liturgy

In the opening confession and forgiveness of Holy Communion (*ELW*, p. 95), we confess that "we are captive to sin." This language recalls Jesus' words in today's gospel that we are slaves to sin.

The *Evangelical Lutheran Worship* baptismal rite (p. 231) announces that the newly baptized are now daughters and sons of God. We now have a place in God's house forever. The baptismal sponsors promise to help the newly baptized live "in the covenant of baptism," recalling the imagery from Jeremiah. The new covenant is sealed by Christ's blood, poured out for us in the weekly meal of grace (pp. 108, 109).

Let the Children Come

If you've ever had a child who is afraid of a monster under the bed or noise in the closet, you may know how hard it is to convince them not to be afraid. How we long to liberate them from the fear keeping them afraid and you awake. The truth is liberating. See? There is nothing under the bed. See? Nothing in the closet. In today's gospel, Jesus proclaims to his disciples, "The truth will make you free." When the nations are in an uproar and kingdoms totter, we can be still and know that God is God.

Assembly Song
Gathering

A mighty fortress is our God   ELW 503–505, LBW 228/229, LS 81, TFF 133

Christ is made the sure foundation   ELW 645, WOV 747, LBW 367

Salvation unto us has come   ELW 590, LBW 297

Psalmody and Acclamations

Cherwien, David. "Psalm 46: God Is Our Refuge." U, assembly, org. MSM 80-800.

Folkening, John. "Psalm 46" from *Six Psalm Settings with Antiphons*. SATB, U or cant, assembly, opt kybd. MSM 80-700.

Gelineau, Joseph. "Psalm 46" from ACYG.

Harbor, Rawn. "The Lord of Hosts Is with Us (Psalm 46)." TFF 6.

(GA) Chepponis, James. "Festival Alleluia." Assembly, cant, org, opt SATB, br qrt/qnt, timp, suspended cymbal, fl, hb. MSM 80-847A.

Hymn of the Day

Lord, keep us steadfast in your word   ELW 517, LBW 230   *ERHALT UNS, HERR*

The church's one foundation   ELW 654, LBW 369   *AURELIA*

The church of Christ, in every age   ELW 729, LBW 433   *WAREHAM*

Offering

That priceless grace   ELW 591, TFF 68

We are all one in Christ   ELW 643, LLC 470, LS 130, TFF 221

Communion

Dear Christians, one and all, rejoice   ELW 594, LBW 299

For by grace you have been saved   ELW 598

O Word of God incarnate   ELW 514, LBW 231

Sending

Built on a rock   ELW 652, LBW 365

Father, we thank you   ELW 478, WOV 704

Additional Assembly Songs

For by grace   W&P 38

Praised be the rock   TFF 290

Dios es nuestro amparo   LLC 553

Kim, Seung Nam. "God Is Our Help, Refuge, and Strength" from *Glory to God*. U. WJK 9780664238971.

Latin American traditional. "Dios es nuestro amparo/God Will Be Our Refuge" from *Psalms for All Seasons: A Complete Psalter for Worship*. SATB. Brazos Press 9781592554447.

Doerksen, Brian/Steve Mitchinson. "Fortress 144" from CCLI.

Fragar, Russell. "Holy Spirit Rain Down" from CCLI.

Houston, Joel/Matt Crocker. "Scandal of Grace" from CCLI.

Cowart, Benji/Jacob Sooter/Tyler Miller. "I'm Going Free (Jailbreak)" from CCLI.

Moffitt, David/Sue C. Smith/Travis Cottrell. "The Lamb Has Overcome" from CCLI.

Music for the Day
Choral

p • Bach, Johann Sebastian. "Lord, Keep Us Steadfast in Your Word" from *Bach for All Seasons Choirbook*. SATB, opt kybd. AFP 9780800658540.

p   Betinis, Abbie. "Blessed Be the Lord, My Rock" from *Augsburg Motet Book*. SAB. AFP 9781451423709.

p • Ferguson, John. "The Church's One Foundation." SATB div, org, br qrt, opt assembly. AFP 9780800658311.

p   Organ, Anne Krentz. "The Gift of Grace." SATB, org. AFP 9781451462500.

Children's Choir

p   Helgen, John. "That Priceless Grace" from *Augsburg Easy Choirbook*, vol. 1. U, pno, opt desc. AFP 9781451462241.

Kosche, Kenneth T. "Bless God's Holy Name." 2 pt, kybd, opt hb. CG CGA766.

p   Patterson, Mark. "Psalm 46" from *ChildrenSing Psalms*. U or 2 pt, kybd. AFP 9781451460964.

Willan, Healy. "Te Deum laudamus/We Praise Thee, O God." U, kybd. CPH 981059PODWEB.

Keyboard / Instrumental

• Buxtehude, Dietrich. "Erhalt uns, Herr." Org. Various editions.

p • Miller, Aaron David. "Wareham" from *Chorale Preludes for Piano in Traditional Styles*. Pno. AFP 9780800679033.

• Organ, Anne Krentz. "Aurelia" from *Piano Reflections for the Church Year*. Pno. AFP 9780800674748.

p • Raabe, Nancy M. "Aurelia" from *Foot-Friendly Preludes*. Org. AFP 9781451479539.

Handbell

• Afdahl, Lee. "The Church of Christ in Every Age." 3-5 oct hb, opt 3-5 oct hc, L2. AGEHR AG35306.

• Eithun, Sandra. "Lord, Keep Us Steadfast in Thy Word." 3-5 oct, L2+, CPH 97-7116.

• Garee, Betty. "The Church's One Foundation." 5 oct, L1, SHW HP5263.

= global song   = praise song   + = semicontinuous psalm
● = relates to hymn of the day   p = available in Prelude Music Planner

303

October 30, 2016
Time after Pentecost — Lectionary 31

"God loves us all, both big and small," a child's verse declares. The sins of the world are covered. We are able to stand tall before God our righteous judge because in the person of Jesus "salvation has come to this house"—to our house today. In Christ Jesus God seeks us out to save us.

Prayer of the Day

Merciful God, gracious and benevolent, through your Son you invite all the world to a meal of mercy. Grant that we may eagerly follow his call, and bring us with all your saints into your life of justice and joy, through Jesus Christ, our Savior and Lord.

Gospel Acclamation

Alleluia. Today salvation has come | to this house,* for the Son of Man came to seek out and to | save the lost. *Alleluia.* (Luke 19:9, 10)

Readings and Psalm
Isaiah 1:10-18

Isaiah announces God's displeasure with the offerings and sacrifices of a people who are without compassion. He urges them instead to do justice and defend the oppressed. Indeed, if they repent, the Lord promises, they will be made as clean as new-fallen snow.

Psalm 32:1-7

All the faithful will make their prayers to you in time of trouble. (Ps. 32:6)

2 Thessalonians 1:1-4, 11-12

This letter of Paul begins with a typical salutation, blessing, and words of praise for what God is accomplishing among the recipients. By remaining faithful and growing spiritually during hardship, the Thessalonian Christians have become witnesses to the glory of God.

Luke 19:1-10

Jesus encounters Zacchaeus, a rich man who is also a lost sinner. Moved by Jesus' acceptance of him, Zacchaeus becomes a model of discipleship. In immediate response to being restored to God's people, Zacchaeus ministers to the poor and seeks reconciliation with those whom he has wronged.

Semicontinuous reading and psalm
Habakkuk 1:1-4; 2:1-4

Injustice and violence in the time leading up to the Babylonian exile move this prophet to lament: How can a good and all-powerful God see evil in the world and seemingly remain indifferent? God answers by proclaiming that the wicked will perish, but the righteous will live by faith.

Psalm 119:137-144

Grant me understanding, that I may live. (Ps. 119:144)

Preface   Sundays

Color   Green

Prayers of Intercession

The prayers are prepared locally for each occasion. The following examples may be adapted or used as appropriate.

Set free by the truth of God's gracious love, we pray for the church, the world, and all of God's good creation.

A brief silence.

Continue to reform your church, O God. Unite it in mission. Teach it to grow in service. Send it to those who do not yet know your love. Hear us, O God.

Your mercy is great.

Call us to repent of our destructive actions toward your beautiful creation. Help us to leave our children and grandchildren a world in which to live and thrive. Hear us, O God.

Your mercy is great.

Call the nations to account, O God. Show leaders and governments the way to peace. Awaken in us a desire for the well-being of all people, both our friends and our enemies. Hear us, O God.

Your mercy is great.

Show your mercy to all those who call on you in times of trouble. Provide for the poor, heal the sick, and comfort the grieving. Especially we pray for . . . . Hear us, O God.

Your mercy is great.

Teach us to welcome the stranger as Christ himself. Prepare us to receive newcomers and visitors in this assembly with true hospitality and gracious care. Hear us, O God.
Your mercy is great.

Here other intercessions may be offered.

We give thanks for all the faithful witnesses and renewers of the church who have gone before us (*especially*) and who now enjoy eternal life with you. Hear us, O God.
Your mercy is great.

Into your hands, faithful God, we place ourselves and our prayers, spoken and unspoken, trusting in your mercy; through Jesus Christ, our Savior.
Amen.

Images in the Readings

Zacchaeus means "innocent." Perhaps the name is meant to be ironic, perhaps an expression of his repentance. We too have defrauded our neighbors, and we too are called by God to a life of justice; we can be seen by God as innocent, thanks to the death and resurrection of Christ.

Solemn assemblies is a summary term for all the religious practices both of ancient Israel and of contemporary Christians. Biblical passages like this one inspired especially those believers called Pietists to refuse to participate in the rituals of public worship. Yet most Christians have read such passages as calls to concomitant lives of justice. Our "hands are full of blood": let us hope that the blood of our acts of violence is washed clean so that we can take into our hands the chalice of the blood of Christ.

Snow and wool are white. Contemporary Christians need to use with care the images that depict goodness as white and evil as black or red, especially as long as the society refers to skin tones with these words.

Ideas for the Day

◆ Isaiah is relentless in demanding more than simple window dressing in the practice of faith. He demands a change of heart that issues in changed behavior. That's exactly what happens with Zacchaeus. His encounter with Jesus issues in such a change that he is willing to make amends that significantly affect his pocketbook. We open ourselves to be changed every Sunday in the encounter with Christ in the spoken and proclaimed word. We often forget that in our complacency. See Annie Dillard's essay "An Expedition to the Pole": "Does anyone have the foggiest idea what sort of power we so blithely invoke? . . . It is madness to wear ladies' straw hats and velvet hats to church; we should all be wearing crash helmets" (in *Teaching a Stone to Talk* [New York: HarperPerennial, 1982], 58).

◆ Zacchaeus might be a difficult figure for our hearers to connect with. Either he's a cartoonish figure, or we point to him as one of "those" greedy people. Cyril of Alexandria wrote that he was "a man entirely abandoned to greed, whose only goal was the increase of his gains" (*Ancient Christian Commentary on Scripture, New Testament*, vol. 3, ed. Art Just Jr. [Downers Grove, IL: InterVarsity, 2003], 289–290). But it's not just the wealthy who are concerned about increasing their gains. The stock market has become a middle-class institution also. Print and broadcast media are replete with commercials for help with "wealth management." We suddenly discover that most of us have more in common with Zacchaeus than we thought. Yet we also share with Zacchaeus that we are counted worthy of Christ's mercy. Christ comes into our house today and is himself the host at the meal of mercy and salvation.

◆ At the end of Charles Dickens's *A Christmas Carol*, after Ebenezer Scrooge has been confronted with the harmful consequences of his greed and miserliness, he awakens and revels in the joy of his newfound generosity. An encounter with Jesus brings us face-to-face with the radicalness of grace and the power of the good news. Zacchaeus shows us what an encounter with Jesus can mean: the gift of being restored to community and the joy of generosity.

Connections with the Liturgy

Echoes of Isaiah 1:16-17 and Luke 19:8 are heard in the charge to the baptized and to their sponsors. All who are called into the assembly of faith promise to "care for others and the world God made, and work for justice and peace," to "strive for justice and peace in all the earth" (*ELW*, pp. 228, 236).

Let the Children Come

The story of Zacchaeus is a favorite among children. Maybe it is because of the children's song. Or maybe it is because Zacchaeus is "short in stature" and must climb a tree to see Jesus. Or maybe it is something more substantial. Perhaps children like the character of Zacchaeus because he is complex. He doesn't do what is expected of him, but he does far more than is expected of him. Jesus treats him with respect. The character of Zacchaeus shows children that Jesus values and treats all people with respect, including them. How does your community model value and respect for all people, including children?

Assembly Song
Gathering

God loved the world   ELW 323, LBW 292

Praise, my soul, the God of heaven   ELW 864/865, LBW 549

Lord, I lift your name on high   ELW 857, W&P 90

Psalmody and Acclamations

Cooney, Rory. "I Turn to You" from PCY, vol. 4.

Helgen, John. "Psalm 32" from *ChildrenSing Psalms*. U, assembly, kybd.

+ Hopson, Hal. "Psalm 119 (137-144)" from TPP.

(GA) ELW 170 with proper verse for Lectionary 31.

Hymn of the Day

Salvation unto us has come   ELW 590, LBW 297   *ES IST DAS HEIL*

Jesus loves me!   ELW 595, TFF 249   *JESUS LOVES ME*

Love consecrates the humblest act   ELW 360, LBW 122
TWENTY-FOURTH

Offering

All creatures, worship God most high!   ELW 835, sts. 1-2;
LBW 527, sts. 1-2

Let the vineyards be fruitful   ELW 181

Communion

Here is bread   ELW 483, W&P 58

We come to the hungry feast   ELW 479, DH 84, WOV 766

You have come down to the lakeshore   ELW 817, LLC 560, TFF 154,
WOV 784

Sending

Sent forth by God's blessing   ELW 547, LBW 221

Jesus calls us; o'er the tumult   ELW 696, LBW 494

Additional Assembly Songs

Be not dismayed whate'er betide   TFF 200

Entre el vaivén de la ciudad   LLC 513

Glory and praise to our God   W&P 43

⊕ Ghanian folk tune. "Jesu, Jesu, Fill Us with Your Love." U. ELW 708.

⊕ South African. "God Welcomes All" from *Glory to God*. U. WJK
9780664238971.

☼ Fielding, Ben. "Kingdom Come" from CCLI.

☼ Fields, Todd. "Salvation's Chorus" from CCLI.

☼ Heaslip, Eoghan/Neil Bennetts. "The King Has Come" from CCLI.

☼ Nockels, Christy/Nathan Nockels. "My Heart Your Home" from
CCLI.

☼ Smith, Martin. "I've Found Jesus" from CCLI.

☼ Wickham, Phil. "God of Our Salvation" from CCLI.

Music for the Day

Choral

p ● Distler, Hugo. "Salvation unto Us Has Come" from *Chantry
Choirbook*. SATB. AFP 9780800657772.

p ● Hassell, Michael. "Jesus Loves Me." SATB, pno, sax. AFP
9780800656515.

p LaBarr, Cameron. "Amen Siakudumisa." 3 pt, perc. CG CGA1355.

p Young, Philip. "Jesus Calls Us." SATB, org. AFP 9781451479386.

Children's Choir

Lavore, Roman. "Go Climb a Sycamore Tree." U, pno. HIN
HMC294.

Mendelssohn, Felix/arr. Ronald A. Nelson. U/2 pt, pno. "How
Lovely Is Your Dwelling." CG CGA1017.

Potter, Kenney. "Where Shall I Go from Your Spirit?" 2 pt, kybd. CG
CGA916.

Keyboard / Instrumental

● Bach, Johann Sebastian. "Es ist das Heil" from *Orgelbüchlein*. Org.
Various editions.

● Cool, Jayne Southwick. "Jesus Loves Me" from *Piano Plus Through
the Year*, vol. 2. Pno, inst. AFP 9780800663728.

p ● Organ, Anne Krentz. "Twenty-Fourth" from *Lamb of God*. Pno.
AFP 9781451424232.

● Proulx, Richard. "Es ist das Heil" from *Augsburg Organ Library:
Epiphany*. Org. AFP 9780800659349.

Handbell

● Glasgow, Michael. "Jesus Loves Me." 2-6 oct hb or hc, opt dbl
ensemble, L2+. RR BL5055. Opt full score, RR FS5055. Opt
pno, RR BP5055.

p Page, Anna Laura. "Stand by Me." 3-5 oct hb, opt 3 oct hc, L3. CG
CGB780.

Waldrop, Tammy. "Variations on 'Zacchaeus Was a Wee Little
Man.'" 2-3 oct, L2+. Ring Out! Press RO3226.

Monday, October 31

Reformation Day

By the end of the seventeenth century, many Lutheran
churches celebrated a festival commemorating Martin
Luther's posting of the Ninety-Five Theses, a summary of
the abuses in the church of his time. At the heart of the
reform movement was the gospel, the good news that it is by
grace through faith that we are justified and set free.

Tuesday, November 1

All Saints Day

The custom of commemorating all of the saints of the
church on a single day goes back at least to the third century. All Saints celebrates the baptized people of God, living
and dead, who make up the body of Christ. We remember
all who have died in the faith and now serve God around
the heavenly throne.

Thursday, November 3

Martín de Porres, renewer of society, died 1639

Martín was the son of a Spanish knight and Ana Velázquez, a freed black slave from Panama. Martín apprenticed himself to a barber-surgeon in Lima, Peru, and was known for his work as a healer. Martín was a lay brother in the Order of Preachers (Dominicans) and engaged in many charitable works. He was a gardener as well as a counselor to those who sought him out. He was noted for his care of all the poor, regardless of race. His own religious community described him as the "father of charity." His work included the founding of an orphanage, a hospital, and a clinic for dogs and cats. He is recognized as an advocate for Christian charity and interracial justice.

TIME AFTER PENTECOST
NOVEMBER

PREPARING FOR NOVEMBER

The month of November is full of holidays, both religious and secular. All Saints Sunday (November 6) is followed by Veterans Day (November 11), and Christ the King (November 20) is followed by Thanksgiving in the United States (November 24). Because the secular holidays emphasize honoring the memory of those who have given their lives in service and giving thanks for the abundance of the earth, it's easy to understand why our religious holidays have adopted a similarly retrospective quality. The texts for November, however, are not primarily concerned with the past, but instead focus on the future reign of God in which the world will be ruled with righteousness. In this they have more in common with another date on the secular calendar: Election Day (November 8).

As the United States responds to the results of what is sure to be another hotly contested presidential election, the Christian calendar offers the worshiping assembly a triptych of texts and images for the three Sundays in November before the new church year begins that invites us to step back and view the events that govern this world through the long lens of a salvation history in which God is the ultimate actor.

All Saints

On the Sunday before Election Day, congregations observing All Saints will hear the prophet Daniel given an interpretation of his dream of the "four great beasts" that emerge from the sea (Dan. 7:3). One of the attendants in the heavenly court tells him, "The holy ones of the Most High shall receive the kingdom and possess the kingdom forever" (Dan. 7:18). Worship planners might consider adding omitted verses 13-14 as well:

> As I watched in the night visions, I saw one like a human being coming with the clouds of heaven. And he came to the Ancient One and was presented before him. To him was given dominion and glory and kingship, that all peoples, nations, and languages should serve him. His dominion is an everlasting dominion that shall not pass away, and his kingship is one that shall never be destroyed.

This addition strengthens the resonance with the reading from Ephesians, which connects Daniel's image of the "one like a human being" to our Lord Jesus Christ, whom God seated "at his right hand in the heavenly places, far above all rule and authority and power and dominion, and above every name that is named, not only in this age but also in the age to come" (Eph. 1:20-21). Taken together, these two passages affirm a continuity between the Hebrew scriptures and the Christian testimony that God is moving in history and assure the faithful that their hope lies not in the empires of this world, but in the reign of God.

It is in Luke's gospel that we finally hear the "stump speech" for God's candidate, Jesus, in this presentation of contrasting worldviews. Here we learn that the reign of God will enfold the poor, the hungry, the disconsolate, and the persecuted. Luke's beatitudes go one step further, pronouncing a word of judgment on those who have reaped the benefits of the present age at the expense of those who have suffered in it. Once again, this connects the prophetic vision of Jesus with the prophet Daniel's vision of the world well cared for in God's dominion.

If all of this sounds a little too much like Christ the King come early, just wait. On that day the texts will speak more directly to the character of divine leadership modeled by Jesus. On this day, the emphasis in the texts is on the contrasting nature of the empires of this world and the compassionate reign of God that has become our inheritance as those "marked with the seal of the promised Holy Spirit" (Eph. 1:13). For this reason, congregations might choose to celebrate All Saints Sunday as a baptismal festival, welcoming new members into the body of Christ even as we give thanks for the witness of those who have joined the church triumphant.

On this first of three Sundays in November that look forward to the in-breaking reign of God, let the assembly's song shape their imagination as they claim their citizenship in God's new world order. Daniel's vision of the "one like a human being" and Paul's assurance that Jesus sits at God's right hand are clearly heard in "Lo! He comes with clouds descending" (ELW 435). The dual words of consolation and condemnation in Luke's beatitudes find expression in the African American spiritual "I've got a robe" (TFF 210). Congregations open to including folk and popular music in worship might find Carrie Newcomer's "Room at the Table" from the album *A Permeable Life* (Available Light Records, 2014) an appropriate choice for offering or communion song.

Lectionary 33

On the Sunday after Election Day, the assembly will be reminded that theirs is not the first generation to live in deeply divided and polarized times. This may be a consolation to those who have grown weary of political ads and rhetoric designed to depress voter turnout by demoralizing the electorate. In this context, Jesus' words in Luke's gospel may sound painfully familiar: "Nation will rise against nation, and kingdom against kingdom" (Luke 21:10). To people who have just come through such a national struggle, scripture offers these words from Malachi: "But for you who revere my name the sun of righteousness shall rise, with healing in its wings" (Mal. 4:2).

The turmoil of the nations brings persecution for those who are faithful to God's vision for a world restored, and opportunities for testimony as well (Luke 21:13). The themes introduced on All Saints Sunday are further developed this week as we come to understand more fully what it means to live as members of God's beloved community in a world divided by fear and violence. "Brothers and sisters," advises the second letter to the Christians at Thessalonica, "do not be weary in doing what is right" (2 Thess. 3:13).

In his book *Healing the Heart of Democracy: The Courage to Create a Politics Worthy of the Human Spirit* (San Francisco: Jossey-Bass, 2011), Parker Palmer writes about the need for all citizens to reclaim the work of democracy as something that we are each doing, unceasingly, in countless ways every day of our lives. "The common good is rarely served," he says, "if citizens are not speaking and acting in these local venues, gathering the collective power necessary to support the best and resist the worst of our leaders as they decide on matters that affect all of us" (p. 23). Congregations can be centers for strengthening this kind of public speech, especially as they reclaim and embrace the practice of offering testimony in worship. A number of books have been published in recent years exploring the theology and practice of Christian testimony, including Thomas Long's *Testimony: Talking Ourselves into Being Christian* (San Francisco: Jossey-Bass, 2004) and Lillian Daniel's *Tell It like It Is: Reclaiming the Practice of Testimony* (Lanham, MD: Rowman & Littlefield, 2006).

Christ the King

If All Saints Sunday served to remind us that we belong to a divine commonwealth by virtue of our baptism, and Lectionary 33 encouraged us to be relentless in our witness to the values of that new community, then Christ the King seeks to assure us that the reign of God is ultimately in Jesus' merciful hands.

The prophet Jeremiah picks up the theme first introduced on All Saints Sunday, contrasting the insufficient leadership of this world with the compassionate leadership of God's chosen one. "I will raise up shepherds over them who will shepherd them," says the Lord to the prophet, "and they shall not fear any longer" (Jer. 23:4). While the letter to the Colossians affirms that in Christ Jesus "all things in heaven and on earth were created, things visible and invisible, whether thrones or dominions or rulers or powers" (Col. 1:16), Luke's gospel shows us Jesus ruling from the humility of the cross. In a scene that summarizes Jesus' ministry to the forgotten and the outcasts, Jesus offers forgiveness to a criminal in the very hour of his own death. We, who are also sinners, rejoice in knowing that Jesus' words to the criminal are God's words to us as well: "Today you will be with me in Paradise" (Luke 23:43).

Planning worship on this day means holding the tension between the ways we continue to mock the lordship of Jesus and the ways that God is eternally confirming Jesus as Lord of all. Craft prayers and prepare music that allow honest confession and transcendent affirmation to exist side by side. Be sure to balance the surety of hymns like "Jesus shall reign" (ELW 434) and the joy of "Soon and very soon" (ELW 439) with the humility of music like "Jesus, remember me" (ELW 616) and the theology of the cross found in "Lift high the cross" (ELW 660).

Environment

How does your faith community relate to the biblical concepts of harvest and first fruits? Growing crops of grain, fruits, or vegetables? Raising livestock? Constructing buildings or highways? Programming computers? Stitching quilts? Matriculating in school? Realizing milestones in programs or ministries? Welcoming new members? Gathering offerings for special projects? Consider how these (and other) experiences might be celebrated with joy and thanksgiving through inclusion in the prayers, provision of visual displays, and/or projection of digital ministry-in-daily-life images while the offering is gathered.

Be intentional about making All Saints a celebration not only of those within your faith community who have completed their baptismal journeys within the past year, but also of the saints of every time and place with whom we are in holy communion.

• During the weeks leading up to All Saints, provide greeting cards for parishioners to send to those within and beyond the congregation who have lost loved ones during the previous year (see 09_November.AllSaints Card.pdf)*.

- If your congregation has a funeral pall, consider displaying it in worship and using it as an opportunity to talk about how the pall symbolizes the robe of Christ's righteousness, conferred in baptism, that envelops the baptized throughout the journey from life to death to new life.
- Bring in the parish registry and talk about the names recorded in it (births, baptisms, confirmations, marriages, deaths). Make a connection between the registry and the names indelibly etched in God's book of life (Job 19:23; Lectionary 32).
- If feasible, prepare paper rubbings of the grave markers of those who have died and display them in the worship space.
- During the prayers of intercession, speak the name of each person being remembered, followed by a moment of silence, the tolling of a handbell, and the lighting of a taper from the paschal candle for placement in a large sand-filled basin (or basins).
- As worshipers come to communion, provide opportunities for them to light additional tapers in remembrance of loved ones. Consider singing a simple, repetitive refrain that could be sung from memory, such as "Jesus, remember me" (ELW 616) or "O Lord, hear my prayer" ("The Lord is my song") (ELW 751). Remind worshipers that the saints who have gone before us are in our midst and present with us at the table.

This month includes a thanksgiving observance in the United States. Consider how the congregation might participate in a project that would extend the theme of thankfulness throughout the month. One possibility would be to embrace a slightly longer than usual time for the offering. Worshipers could use ten or so prepared strips of paper to record things for which they are thankful to God, each week focusing on a differing theme.

- November 6: the names of people who have or continue to bless their lives, enrich their faith, and/or encourage them in their journey of life and faith.

- November 13: phrases from scripture, hymnody, or liturgy that have been a source of blessing, guidance, or hope.
- November 20: expressions of thankfulness for what it means to have been claimed as God's children and to experience life under God's reign of justice, peace, mercy, and compassion.

Assemble the strips of paper into chains of thanksgiving. Use the chains as garlands to surround the worship space (see www.greenweddingshoes.com/backyard-colorful-paper-chain-wedding-leslie-nolan for inspiration) or use them to create a more structured installation (see www.pinterest.com/pin/266064290459451668 for one example).

Seasonal Checklist

- Consider using harvest decorations during November, from All Saints Sunday through the end of the church year.
- Publicize any special food collections and arrange for delivery to the appropriate agency after the collection.
- Provide a book of remembrance for All Saints Sunday and the month of November in which names of loved ones may be written and remembered aloud in prayer. If candles are lit, order these in advance and prepare to display them appropriately.
- Incorporate names of those who have died into a baptismal remembrance or into the prayers of intercession on All Saints Sunday. Or prepare a sung litany. See *Music Sourcebook for All Saints through Transfiguration* (Augsburg Fortress, 2013) for guidance.
- Omit the Kyrie.
- Use the canticle of praise ("This is the feast").
- Use the Nicene Creed for the festivals of All Saints and Christ the King; use the Apostles' Creed for other Sundays in November.
- Continue planning for Advent 2016.
- Begin publicizing the schedule of Advent and Christmas worship services.

WORSHIP TEXTS FOR NOVEMBER

Confession and Forgiveness

All may make the sign of the cross, the sign marked at baptism,
as the presiding minister begins.
In the name of God the Father of glory;
in the name of God the + Son, our Redeemer;
in the name of God the holy and life-giving Spirit.
Amen.

The Sun of righteousness shall rise
with shining beams of healing.
Let us gather under the wings of God's mercy.

Silence is kept for reflection.

Gracious God,
we acknowledge that we are sinners
and we confess our sins—
those known to us that burden our hearts,
and those unknown to us but seen by you.
We know that before you nothing remains hidden,
and in you everything is revealed.
Free us from the slavery of sin;
liberate us from the bondage of guilt;
and work in us that which is pleasing in your sight;
for the sake of Jesus Christ our Lord. Amen.

With a heart full of mercy and compassion,
God saves us and + forgives us all our sins.
Christ, the dawn from on high, shines upon us
and by the light of the Holy Spirit
guides our feet into the way of peace.
Amen.

Offering Prayer

Merciful God, as grains of wheat scattered upon the hills
were gathered together to become one bread,
so let your church be gathered together
from the ends of the earth into your kingdom,
for yours is the glory through Jesus Christ, now and forever.
Amen.

Invitation to Communion

Share in the inheritance of all the saints.
Come to the table prepared for you.

Prayer after Communion

We give you thanks, shepherding God,
that you have gathered your scattered flock again this day,
feeding us richly with the food of Paradise.
Accompany us as we serve you all the days of our lives,
and gather us with the saints in the day of our death;
through Jesus Christ, our Redeemer and Lord.
Amen.

Sending of Communion

Gracious God, you took the form of a servant,
offering yourself as food, comfort, and strength
to a sick and hurting world.
Anoint with a servant heart
those who take your word and sacrament
to our sisters and brothers
in their homes/in prisons/in hospitals.
Grant grace, mercy, healing, and hope
to those who feast on your body and blood
and receive your words of new life.
May we all recognize that we have a place and a home
in the body of our Lord Jesus Christ.
Amen.

Blessing

God who loves us,
who gives us eternal consolation and good hope,
comfort your hearts
and strengthen them in every good work and word;
and the blessing of almighty God,
Father, ✛ Son, and Holy Spirit,
be among you and remain with you forever.
Amen.

Dismissal

Go in peace. Christ is with you.
Thanks be to God.

SEASONAL RITES FOR NOVEMBER

Thanksgiving for Saints of the Congregation

A litany may be sung on All Saints Day or at other times when remembering and giving thanks for the lives of the saints, especially those from a particular congregation. This litany needs to be prepared well in advance by inviting congregational members to submit names and attributes of people they wish to include.

Music for this litany may be found in Music Sourcebook for All Saints through Transfiguration (Augsburg Fortress, 2013) #S507.

The cantor establishes a drone either hummed by all or carried by the organ, a shruti box, or other sustaining instrument. If the drone is carried by an instrument, the assembly may sing only the responses and not the drone.

Leader (*improvised chant, monotone, or spoken*):
O God of the pilgrim's way, we give thanks for those in generations past who have been examples for us of God's love at work in the world. As we pray, we know that we are surrounded by this great, rejoicing cloud of witnesses. Yet even as we name these holy ancestors, we thank God for others whose names we never knew or have forgotten, who showed us the meaning of life in Christ.

Cantor (*improvises the remembrances*):
For blessed *name*, compassionate teacher of children.
For blessed *name*, thoughtful companion.
For blessed *name*, artisan of simple beauty.

Assembly: We give thanks.

At the end of the litany, the leader intones the closing collect:
Leader (*improvised chant, monotone, or spoken*):
Holy God, we honor these, our ancestors in faith
and members of our family.
We, too, seek to do your will: guide us.
We, too, desire to be your servants: strengthen us.
We, too, long to know you clearly: teach us.
And in time, bring us to our eternal home of peace and joy.

Assembly: Amen.

Preparation

The following list may be helpful in constructing appropriate attributes, or other brief, poetic phrases may be created. The worship folder only needs to have the people's response printed and the list of names of those being remembered.

Teacher
Compassionate teacher of children
Teacher of your holy word
Learned bearer of knowledge

Doctor, nurse, psychologist, counselor, caregiver
Benevolent caregiver
Healer of mind and spirit
Skilled and helpful healer
Compassionate healer

Altar/Flower Guild member, sacristan
Preparer of holy vessels
Gifted arranger of God's natural beauty

Choir member, instrumentalist, organist
Singer of God's praise
Singer of beautiful song
Master/Mistress of music

Council, governing board, committee member
Steward of our earthly gifts
Trustee of God's beauty and our sacred space
Leader and wise counsel

Artists, writers, composers
Artisan of simple beauty
Gifted writer and poet
Creator in color and joy
Designer of symmetry and balance
Skilled composer of beautiful music

Other
Hospitable example
Thoughtful companion
Generous and gracious provider
Courageous homemaker
Caretaker of God's creation
Protector of family
Advocate of the world's needy
Home of quiet endurance
Tireless servant to the poor

Text by Marilyn Haskel from Music Sourcebook for All Saints through Trans-figuration. *© 2013 Augsburg Fortress.*

Resources for Veterans Day
Prayer

Almighty and ever-living God, we give you thanks for the men and women who have served and defended our country and the values of freedom and justice we hold so dear. Help us be mindful of the sacrifices they made and the hardship endured by their families and friends, so that we never take for granted the privileges they have secured for us. Hear us, we pray, through Jesus Christ, our Savior and Lord. Amen.

From Evangelical Lutheran Worship Prayer Book for the Armed Services *(Augsburg Fortress, 2013), 66. See also "Those who have given their lives" in the seasonal rites for summer, page 211.*

Care for Returning Veterans

We sometimes need to be reminded to welcome and care for those who are placed on the edges of society, particularly people who have experienced war and combat. We are called to love, serve, and welcome the strangers at our doors, not only by official mandate of our church, but by Jesus Christ when he says, "I was a stranger and you welcomed me."

"Care for Returning Veterans" is a daylong workshop developed by the Evangelical Lutheran Church in America for use in congregations, synods, and other ministry settings. The workshop includes a multimedia presentation that deals with "the veteran's experience"— psychological impacts, moral impacts, spiritual impacts, family impacts, and referrals and resources. The components of the workshop are available as a free DVD that includes a PowerPoint multimedia presentation with videos, script, and print materials.

The "Care for Returning Veterans" workshops have been developed in response to these needs and the call to love and serve our neighbor. It is not a complete response—it might well be called "Welcoming Returning Veterans 101," but it is a first step to assist pastors, caregivers, congregations, and others who want to put out the welcome mat for our returning veterans and their families. Call the ELCA at 800-638-3522 to request a copy. See more at www.elca.org/Our-Work/Leadership/Federal-Chaplaincy-Ministries/Care-for-Returning-Veterans.

November 6, 2016

All Saints Sunday

In holy baptism God makes saints out of sinners. In holy communion God forgives the sins of all the saints. In the assembly today we give thanks for all the saints "who from their labors rest," who have fought the good fight, who have gained the crown. In the same breath we petition our God for the strength to hear and to heed the admonitions of the Lord Jesus in today's gospel. Recalling that we have been sealed by the Spirit and sustained by the Savior's body and blood, we keep on keeping on as God gives us breath, to the praise of God's glory.

Prayer of the Day

Almighty God, you have knit your people together in one communion in the mystical body of your Son, Jesus Christ our Lord. Grant us grace to follow your blessed saints in lives of faith and commitment, and to know the inexpressible joys you have prepared for those who love you, through Jesus Christ, our Savior and Lord, who lives and reigns with you and the Holy Spirit, one God, now and forever.

Gospel Acclamation

Alleluia. They are before the ¹ throne of God,* and the one who is seated on the throne will ¹ shelter them. *Alleluia.* (Rev. 7:15)

Readings and Psalm

Daniel 7:1-3, 15-18

The book of Daniel was written in the second century B.C.E., when the Syrian king Antiochus Epiphanes was severely persecuting the Jews. Daniel's vision of the four beasts serves to proclaim the message that human kings will come and go, but the kingdom will ultimately belong to God and to God's people.

Psalm 149

Sing the LORD's praise in the assembly of the faithful. (Ps. 149:1)

Ephesians 1:11-23

After giving thanks for the faith of the Ephesians, Paul prays that they might understand the wisdom, hope, and power of God that is embodied in Jesus Christ.

Luke 6:20-31

In echoes of the prophet Isaiah and Mary's song of praise, Jesus reveals surprising things about who enjoys blessing and who endures woe. He invites his disciples to shower radical love, blessing, forgiveness, generosity, and trust, even to enemies and outsiders.

Preface   All Saints

Color   White

Prayers of Intercession

The prayers are prepared locally for each occasion. The following examples may be adapted or used as appropriate.

With the people of God gathered here and throughout the world, we offer our prayers for the church, those in need, and all of creation.

A brief silence.

For the church and its leaders, that we continue to proclaim the gospel of salvation to every corner of the earth, so that all embody the hope of eternal life, let us pray.

Have mercy, O God.

For the well-being of creation, for the seas and their creatures, for those preparing for changing weather, and for those who serve as good stewards of God's gifts, let us pray.

Have mercy, O God.

For peace among nations, for governments and electorates, for all who rule and have authority at any level, that they rule with justice, keeping in mind those who have no power, let us pray.

Have mercy, O God.

For the troubled and terrified, the poor and hungry, the abuser and abused, those who weep, those suffering from malaria or any sickness (*especially*), that God lift up people to provide care and consolation, let us pray.

Have mercy, O God.

For those who lead and support music in this assembly, that our song may point us all to Christ; for the newly baptized (*especially those baptized today*), that the Holy Spirit guides them in love and service, following the example of our Lord, let us pray.

Have mercy, O God.

Here other intercessions may be offered.

In thanksgiving for all the saints, known and unknown, who have died in the faith, that they serve as witnesses to the inheritance granted to us by Jesus Christ, let us pray.

Have mercy, O God.
Almighty God, you have promised to hear those who call upon your name. We commend all our spoken and silent prayers to you, trusting in your abundant mercy; through your Son, Jesus Christ our Lord.
Amen.

Images in the Readings

To be a **saint** is to be made holy by baptism and by life in the body of Christ.

Matthew writes, "Blessed are **the poor** in spirit" (5:3), but Luke writes, "Blessed are you who are poor" (6:20). Who is "poor"? *Evangelical Lutheran Worship* gives as one option for the dismissal "Go in peace. Remember the poor," a phrase taken from Galatians 2:10. We are all in some way poor, and we ask for God's blessings. But spiritualizing the phrase ought not lead us to forget Paul's original meaning to the Galatians: there are people who are desperately poor, hungry, and dispossessed, and as Christians we are to serve them. We are the body of Christ, offering food to the poor.

"Turn **the other cheek**" is an English expression urging nonviolence in all things. Some Christian denominations that hold this ethical injunction literally—for example, refusing to serve in the armed forces or to sue in court—keep before the rest of us the seriousness of this as a sign of the life of the baptized.

Even though some worshipers might be upset by this, today's intercessions will include a petition for those who are deemed our **enemies**, for God's blessings on them and for the betterment of their lives.

What are for us all, and for each of us individually, the **four beasts**?

Ideas for the Day

◆   In the worship spaces of St. Gregory of Nyssa Episcopal Church in San Francisco and the Cathedral of Our Lady of the Angels in Los Angeles, stunning artwork reminds the gathered assembly of the parade of saints that accompanies our worship. At St. Gregory's, the saints are painted around the rotunda as they join the assembly dancing around the eucharistic table (www.allsaintscompany.org/icons/dancing-saints). At the Los Angeles Cathedral, the side walls of the sanctuary are lined with stunning tapestries of saints who join the assembly in their procession to the altar (www.olacathedral.org).

◆   Blessing can be a difficult and slippery notion. Partly, it's because culturally we bless everything from boats to bodies. Maybe that's how it should be. In the ordinariness of daily living, we pause to recognize the source of all our living, the source of all that we are and all that we have. To bless is to create space for gratitude and wonder. We are blessed by God in Christ, made saints; we, in turn, bless

God, as the saints of old did in Psalm 149. The saints whose names we remember, and those whose names we do not, lived in the world with all of its hurt and brokenness, and somehow gave expression to God's presence and action in their own lives.

◆   The Ephesians reading makes a strong connection between baptism and the All Saints Day remembrance of those who have gone before us. In baptism, we receive the promise of an everlasting inheritance, we begin living into it immediately, and we live into its fullness as we pass through the gate of death. Many congregations light a candle for the newly baptized within the baptismal rite; consider a reflection of that practice, lighting a separate candle as each of the names of those who have died in the parish are read. If the font is visible to the congregation, a floating candle in the font can be a powerful evocation of the fulfillment of the gift of baptism for those who have died.

Connections with the Liturgy

As the conclusion of the intercessions each Sunday (*ELW*, p. 106), we thank God for those who have died over the past week and for those listed in the commemorations (pp. 15–17). This practice keeps in our minds the whole company of saints that has preceded and surrounds us. Usual Lutheran practice thanks God for the lives of the faithful departed but does not pray for the dead, because they are already in the hands of God.

One of the optional prayers of the day in the funeral rite (p. 281) prays that all who mourn will be comforted. In today's gospel, Jesus promises that the weeping of the saints will finally give way to laughter.

Let the Children Come

As part of the intercessory prayer today, invite one of the youth to read the names of those who have died in the last year (practice any tricky pronunciations). Grief and loss are experienced by all ages. It can be very meaningful to allow time during worship for candles to be lighted in memory of loved ones who have died. If your church has a cemetery, invite those who wish to walk outside after worship and visit the graves of those who have died in the last year. Share stories and prayers as these faithful departed are lovingly remembered and entrusted to God's care still.

Assembly Song
Gathering

Ye watchers and ye holy ones   ELW 424, LBW 175

In heaven above   ELW 630, LBW 330

You servants of God   ELW 825, LBW 252

Psalmody and Acclamations

Pavlechko, Thomas. "Psalm 149" from SMP.

Pelz, Walter L. "Psalm 149" from PWC.

Schwandt, Daniel E. "Psalm 149" from PSCY.

(GA) Chepponis, James. "Festival Alleluia." Assembly, cant, org, opt SATB, br qrt/qnt, timp, suspended cymbal, fl, hb. MSM 80-847A.

Hymn of the Day

By all your saints   ELW 420, LBW 177   KING'S LYNN   ELW 421   KUORTANE

Shall we gather at the river   ELW 423, TFF 179, WOV 690   HANSON PLACE

Sing with all the saints in glory   ELW 426, WOV 691   MISSISSIPPI

Offering

For all your saints, O Lord   ELW 427, LBW 176

For all the saints   ELW 422, sts. 1, 3; LBW 174, sts. 1, 3

Communion

Behold the host arrayed in white   ELW 425, LBW 314

In our day of thanksgiving   ELW 429

Blest are they   ELW 728, LS 143, WOV 764

Sending

Give thanks for saints   ELW 428

Jerusalem, my happy home   ELW 628, LBW 331

Additional Assembly Songs

Oh, when the saints go marching in   TFF 180

Swing low, sweet chariot   TFF 171

Deep river   TFF 174

Bell, John L. "Blest Are the Poor in Spirit" from *My Heart Sings Out*. SATB. Church Publishing 9780898694741.

Cuban traditional. "Aleluya entre tu pueblo/Alleluia in the Heavens" from *Laudate Omnes Gentes/Praying Together*. U. Gütersloher Verlagshaus. Out of print; available on Amazon.com.

Cash, Ed/Sarah Reeves. "Let Us Rise" from CCLI.

Fee, Steve. "Send Me Out" from CCLI.

Fielding, Ben/Sam Knock. "The Lost Are Found" from CCLI.

Millard, Bart. "I Can Only Imagine" from CCLI.

Tomlin, Chris/Ed Cash/Jesse Reeves. "Let Your Mercy Rain" from CCLI.

Music for the Day
Choral

p Ellingboe, Bradley. "Behold a Host, Arrayed in White." SAB, pno. AFP 9780806698212.

p Haydn, Franz Joseph. "Through Every Age, Eternal God" from *Augsburg Motet Book*. SAB. AFP 9781451423709.

Jenkins, Steve. "Around the Throne." SATB, org, fl, opt tri. MSM 50-8102.

p ● Martinson, Joel. "By All Your Saints" from *Augsburg Easy Choirbook*, vol. 2. 2 pt mxd, org. AFP 9780800677510.

Children's Choir

Bedford, Michael. "Blessed Are They: The Beatitudes." U/2 pt, org, fl. CG CGA1025.

Fauré, Gabriel. "Pie Jesu." U, org, opt pno, opt hp. MSM 50-9906.

Vaughan Williams, Ralph. "He That Is Down Need Fear No Fall." U, pno. OXF 9780193419506.

Keyboard / Instrumental

● Biery, James. "Mississippi" from *Augsburg Organ Library: Healing and Funeral*. Org. AFP 9781451462616.

● Cherwien, David. "Hanson Place" from *Organ Plus One*. Org, inst. AFP 9780800656188.

p ● Lasky, David. "King's Lynn" from *In Praise of God*. Org. AFP 9781451420869.

p ● Raabe, Nancy M. "Hanson Place" from *Grace and Peace*, vol. 2. Pno. AFP 9780800679019.

Handbell

Glasgow, Michael. "Faith of the Saints." 3-7 oct hb, opt 2 oct hc, opt tpt, L2+. LOR 20/1614L.

● Helman, Michael. "Shall We Gather at the River." 3-5 oct hb, opt 3-5 oct hc, L3. LOR 20/1578L.

Ingram, Bill. "Saints Medley." 3-5 oct, L3. RW 8234.

November 6, 2016
Time after Pentecost — Lectionary 32

We worship on the first day of the week because our Savior was raised on that day. Every Sunday is a little Easter. This Sunday feels more like Easter than many as the appointed texts celebrate the reality of the resurrection. Live it up this Lord's day. Our God is the God of the living.

Prayer of the Day

O God, our eternal redeemer, by the presence of your Spirit you renew and direct our hearts. Keep always in our mind the end of all things and the day of judgment. Inspire us for a holy life here, and bring us to the joy of the resurrection, through Jesus Christ, our Savior and Lord.

Gospel Acclamation

Alleluia. Jesus Christ is the firstborn | of the dead;* to him be glory and dominion forev- | er and ever. *Alleluia.* (Rev. 1:5, 6)

Readings and Psalm

Job 19:23-27a

Job suffers the loss of children, wealth, and health. Accused by his companions of wrongdoing, he knows himself to be innocent. Here, in the midst of his suffering, Job clings to the radical hope that his vindicator, his redeemer, lives; and that one day he himself will see God.

Psalm 17:1-9

Keep me as the apple of your eye; hide me under the shadow of your wings. (Ps. 17:8)

2 Thessalonians 2:1-5, 13-17

Paul writes to encourage the church at Thessalonica in a time of confusion and opposition. Here, the confusion concerned the return of Christ. Paul writes to those who were allowing their concern over Jesus' imminent return to divert them from the central teachings of the gospel.

Luke 20:27-38

The Sadducees, who do not believe in the resurrection of the dead, try to trap Jesus. They formulate the convoluted case of a serial widow who marries a succession of seven brothers. Jesus responds by teaching about God, to whom all are alive and in whom all relationships are fulfilled.

Semicontinuous reading and psalm
Haggai 1:15b—2:9

Haggai called on the exiles who had returned from Babylon to rebuild the temple. The rebuilt temple, however, pales in comparison with the first temple, built by Solomon. Haggai's message of encouragement and promise of future splendor gives hope to the people and to their leaders, Zerubbabel and Joshua.

Psalm 145:1-5, 17-21

Great is the LORD and greatly to be praised! (Ps. 145:3)

or Psalm 98

In righteousness will the LORD judge the world. (Ps. 98:9)

Preface Sundays

Color Green

Prayers of Intercession

The prayers are prepared locally for each occasion. The following examples may be adapted or used as appropriate.

With the people of God gathered here and throughout the world, we offer our prayers for the church, those in need, and all of creation.

A brief silence.

For all leaders of the church and their ministries, for pastors, musicians, lay leaders, and theologians, that the blessings and promises of God be proclaimed to the ends of the earth, let us pray.

Have mercy, O God.

For the marvelous works of God, for animals who live on dry land and creatures who live in the sea, that all creation will grow and thrive, let us pray.

Have mercy, O God.

For leaders who govern at all levels to work for just causes, for those voting in elections, for local and national governments to care for their people, and for advocates who speak for the voiceless, let us pray.

Have mercy, O God.

For the sick and their caregivers, the poor and their advocates, and the grieving and those who provide consolation (*especially*), that all who call upon you, O God, find refuge, comfort, and protection, let us pray.

Have mercy, O God.

For those who travel, for those inquiring about the gift of baptism and new life in Christ, for those from our congregation unable to attend worship, and for our families and friends, let us pray.

Have mercy, O God.

Here other intercessions may be offered.

For the witness of the faithful departed, that with them we proclaim that our Redeemer lives and on the last day will raise us up, let us pray.

Have mercy, O God.

Almighty God, you have promised to hear those who call upon your name. We commend all our spoken and silent prayers to you, trusting in your abundant mercy; through your Son, Jesus Christ our Lord.

Amen.

Images in the Readings

For tens of thousands of years, humans have speculated about an **afterlife**. Ancient graves yield personal possessions that the mourners assumed would be useful in the afterlife. Greek philosophy taught the immortality of the soul—thus no need for eating utensils. Medieval theology imagined the afterlife as a heavenly court in which believers entered into the presence of God. Some nineteenth-century Christians described heaven as an everlasting family picnic in paradise. Luke's description of the life of the resurrection relies on imagination about angels, whom the Bible describes in various ways. For Christians, all speculation about the life of the resurrection rests in our faith that after death Jesus Christ was transformed into new life and that God will do the same for all the baptized. We can be grateful for the reading from 2 Thessalonians, which describes even God's gift of comfort in this life as "eternal."

Job wishes that his religious hope be engraved on a **rock**. For us, Christ is such a rock.

The "**lawless one,**" usually referred to as the antichrist of 1 John, has been a source of perpetual speculation by Christians, repeatedly throughout history identified as whoever was the current monster of evil. But when are we Christians living lawlessly, opposed to the things of Christ?

Ought Christians be theologically conservative, as were the **Sadducees**, and as the author of 2 Thessalonians urges in verse 15, or theologically liberal, as were the Pharisees, and as the author of 2 Thessalonians implies when describing faith in a triune God (v. 13)?

Ideas for the Day

◆ Contemporary Christian thought often separates the resurrection of the body from the soul, dismissing the former and focusing on the everlasting nature of the latter. More and more, funerals (with the body present) are being replaced with memorial services that take place after the body has been buried or the ashes interred. It is interesting to note how this coincides with cultural messages that increasingly make our bodies our enemies—not fit enough, not beautiful enough, not young enough. Do we resist the idea of the resurrection of the body because we hate the idea of waiting until some undetermined future for the resurrected life to begin, or because we hate the idea of spending eternity in bodies we have come to despise?

◆ In her book *Honoring the Body: Meditations on a Christian Practice* (San Francisco: Jossey-Bass, 2002), Stephanie Paulsell addresses the gifts and challenges of honoring our bodies, our neighbors' bodies, and our bodies' (physical) longing for God. Is it possible that God longs, not only for our love, but for the *physicality* of our love, enfleshed? Prayers or a litany today might include acknowledgment of the goodness of our physical being and the solid createdness of all nature, along with expressions of hope and longing for the new creation that is filled with physical wholeness and delight.

◆ While not the core of today's message, Jesus' words about marriage (or lack thereof) in the next life provide an opportunity to address the situations of those in this age who do *not* marry. Many congregations celebrate and publicly support the institution of marriage but fail to acknowledge the giftedness of the lives of those who remain single, either by choice or by circumstance. Although a common mark of the social structures of Jesus' day and ours, marriage is not necessary to one's full personhood. Congregations who regularly mark the celebrations of wedding anniversaries in their prayers might choose, instead, to pray for those who praise God and reflect God's goodness through covenants of friendship and service that are often overlooked, and unsupported, by society and the church.

Connections with the Liturgy

Every Sunday we are called by God to receive the proclamation of the good news (2 Thess. 2:14). The concluding verses of the second reading are parallel to the options for each Sunday's final blessing (*ELW*, pp. 114–115). This Sunday these verses might serve as the blessing.

Let the Children Come

Psalm 17 includes the poignant verse, "Keep me as the apple of your eye; hide me under the shadow of your wings" (Ps. 17:8, *ELW*) All children long to feel secure, protected, and loved. Strive to make your church home a place of warmth and hospitality for children. Exchange hugs and handshakes with them during the peace. Teach greeters to welcome each child with a smile. Learn the children's names—all of them! Display children's artwork throughout your church building. These are all ways children will sense that God' house is their home.

Assembly Song
Gathering

O day full of grace ELW 627, LBW 161, LS 71
Blessed be the name ELW 797
Sing with all the saints in glory ELW 426, WOV 691

Psalmody and Acclamations

Busarow, Donald. "Psalm 17:1-9" from PSCY.
Cherwien, David. "Psalm 17:1-9" from PWC.
+ Mummert, Mark. "Psalm 145:1-5, 17-21," Refrain 2, from PSCY.
+ Psalm 98; see Lectionary 33.
(GA) ELW 168 with proper verse for Lectionary 32.

Hymn of the Day

The day of resurrection! ELW 361 *ELLACOMBE* LBW 141
  HERZLICH TUT MICH ERFREUEN
I know that my Redeemer lives! ELW 619, LBW 352 *DUKE STREET*
Christ Jesus lay in death's strong bands ELW 370, LBW 134 *CHRIST LAG IN TODESBANDEN*

Offering

For the bread which you have broken ELW 494, LBW 200
Strengthen for service, Lord ELW 497, LBW 218

Communion

Neither death nor life ELW 622
How sweet the name of Jesus sounds ELW 620, LBW 345
Now We Remain ELW 500, W&P 106

Sending

Jesus lives, my sure defense ELW 621, LBW 340
At the Lamb's high feast we sing ELW 362, LBW 210

Additional Assembly Songs

Jesus, we want to meet TFF 145
Lord, this day we've come to worship TFF 137
Come! Come! Everybody worship LS 73
⦿ Chinese traditional. "May the Lord, Mighty God" from *My Heart Sings Out*. 2 pt. Church Publishing 9780898694741.
⦿ Kolling, Miria T. "God Extends an Invitation/Nuestro Padre nos invita." U. ELW 486.
✿ Beach, Walker. "Victorious" from CCLI.
✿ Egan, Jon. "I Am Free" from CCLI.
✿ Lee, Jonathan/Sarah Hart. "More Than Enough" from CCLI.

✿ Maher, Matt/Mia Fieldes. "Christ Is Risen" from CCLI.
✿ Tomlin, Chris/Daniel Carson/Jason Ingram/Jesse Reeves. "Awake My Soul" from CCLI.

Music for the Day
Choral

p ● Hopson, Hal. "I Know That My Redeemer Lives." SATB, assembly, org. GIA G-5862.
p Jennings, Kenneth. "Sing to the Lord a New Song." SATB, org, br qrt, timp. AFP 9780800621551.
p Pelz, Walter. "I Will Exalt You, O God." SATB, org, tpt. AFP 9781451451610.
p Sedio, Mark. "Once He Came in Blessing" from *Augsburg Easy Choirbook*, vol. 1. 2 pt mxd, org, fl. AFP 9780800676025.

Children's Choir

p Bach, J. S./arr. Patrick Liebergen. "Sing Together! Psallite!" U/2 pt, pno, opt 2 fl. CG CGA1354.
Kosche, Kenneth. "Keep Me as the Apple of Your Eye." U/2 pt, kybd. CG CGA800.
p LaBarr, Cameron F. "Amen Siakudumisa." 3 pt trbl, opt perc. CG CGA1355.

Keyboard / Instrumental

● Bach, Johann Sebastian. "Christ lag in Todesbanden" from *Orgelbüchlein*. Org. Various editions.
Corelli, Archangelo. "Largo and Allegro" from *Organ Plus!* vol. 1. Org, 2 inst. MSM 20-810.
● Miller, Aaron David. "Ellacombe" from *Eight Chorale Preludes for Manuals Only*, vol. 1. Org. AFP 9780800677560.
p ● Organ, Anne Krentz. "Duke Street" from *Piano Reflections on Hymns of the Faith*. Pno. AFP 9780806698069.

Handbell

● Evanovich, Joshua. "Prelude on 'Duke Street.'" 2-3 oct, L2. GIA G-8541.
● Ingram, Bill. "I Sing the Mighty Power of God." 3-7 oct, L3. GIA G-7326.
● Lohr, Alan. "Christ lag in Todesbanden." 5 oct hb, opt 2 oct hc, L4. SF 118349.

Monday, November 7

John Christian Frederick Heyer, died 1873; Bartholomaeus Ziegenbalg, died 1719; Ludwig Nommensen, died 1918; missionaries

Three missionaries are commemorated on this date. Heyer was the first missionary sent out by American Lutherans. Ordained in 1820, he established Sunday schools and taught at Gettysburg College and Seminary. Heyer became

⦿ = global song   ✿ = praise song   + = semicontinuous psalm
● = relates to hymn of the day   p = available in Prelude Music Planner

a missionary in the Andhra region of India. During a break in his mission work he received the MD degree from what would later be Johns Hopkins University.

Bartholomaeus Ziegenbalg (ZEEG-en-balg) was a missionary to the Tamils of Tranquebar on the southeast coast of India. The first convert to Christianity was baptized about ten months after Ziegenbalg began preaching. His missionary work was opposed by the local Hindus and also by Danish authorities in that area. Ziegenbalg was imprisoned for his work on a charge of converting the natives. Today, the Tamil Evangelical Lutheran Church carries on his work.

Ludwig Ingwer Nommensen was born in Schleswig-Holstein, Germany. In the early 1860s he went to Sumatra to serve as a Lutheran missionary. His work was among the Batak people, who had previously not seen Christian missionaries. Though he encountered some initial difficulties, the missions began to succeed following the conversion of several tribal chiefs. Nommensen translated the scriptures into Batak while honoring much of the native culture.

Friday, November 11

Martin, Bishop of Tours, died 397

Martin's pagan father enlisted him in the army at age fifteen. One winter day, a beggar approached Martin for aid, and he cut his cloak in half and gave a portion to the beggar. Later, Martin understood that he had seen the presence of Christ in that beggar, and this ended his uncertainty about Christianity. He soon asked for his release from his military duties, but he was imprisoned instead. After his release from prison he began preaching, particularly against the Arians. In 371 he was elected bishop of Tours. As bishop he developed a reputation for intervening on behalf of prisoners and heretics who had been sentenced to death.

Søren Aabye Kierkegaard, teacher, died 1855

Kierkegaard (KEER-keh-gore), a nineteenth-century Danish theologian whose writings reflect his Lutheran heritage, was the founder of modern existentialism. Though he was engaged to a woman he deeply loved, he ended the relationship because he believed he was called to search the hidden side of life. Many of his works were published under a variety of names, so that he could reply to arguments from his own previous works. Kierkegaard's work attacked the established church of his day—its complacency, its tendency to intellectualize faith, and its desire to be accepted by polite society.

November 13, 2016

Time after Pentecost — Lectionary 33

The end is near. There is no doubt about it. The warnings are dire. The tone of today's texts is ominous. But the baptized know how to live in the "meantimes." The baptized are strengthened for the living of these days in word and sacrament. The baptized rally around the invitation of the apostle: "Brothers and sisters, do not be weary in doing what is right."

Prayer of the Day

O God, the protector of all who trust in you, without you nothing is strong, nothing is holy. Embrace us with your mercy, that with you as our ruler and guide, we may live through what is temporary without losing what is eternal, through Jesus Christ, our Savior and Lord.

Gospel Acclamation

Alleluia. Stand up and ¹ raise your heads,* because your redemption is ¹ drawing near. *Alleluia.* (Luke 21:28)

Readings and Psalm

Malachi 4:1-2a

Malachi, whose name means "my messenger," warns that the day of the Lord is coming. On that day, the evil will be destroyed like stubble in a fire, but the "sun of righteousness" will shine on those who fear God.

Psalm 98

In righteousness will the LORD judge the world. (Ps. 98:9)

2 Thessalonians 3:6-13

Some members of the Thessalonian community, because of their belief in the nearness of Christ's return, had ceased to work, living off the generosity of other members of the community. Paul warns them bluntly that if they want to eat, they need to work.

Luke 21:5-19

As history moves toward God's fulfillment there will be frightening signs and events. Before the end, believers will draw strength from their relationship to God and shall be given the words they need to testify and to endure without fear.

Semicontinuous reading and psalm

Isaiah 65:17-25

Addressing the exiles who had returned to Jerusalem from Babylon, the prophet proclaims a vision of a future time of peace and prosperity. Though the returned exiles are experiencing hard times, God is about to do a new thing.

Isaiah 12:2-6

In your midst is the Holy One of Israel. (Isa. 12:6)

Preface Sundays

Color Green

Prayers of Intercession

The prayers are prepared locally for each occasion. The following examples may be adapted or used as appropriate.

With the people of God gathered here and throughout the world, we offer our prayers for the church, those in need, and all of creation.

A brief silence.

For the church, for missionaries and teachers, clergy and laity, and all ministers who proclaim the gospel in word and deed, that the Sun of righteousness enlighten the whole earth, let us pray.

Have mercy, O God.

For rivers and lakes, hills and mountains, fruit and vegetables, and animals great and small, that creation thrive and that we care for all God has given us, let us pray.

Have mercy, O God.

For all in authority at the local, state, provincial, national, and international levels, for those who advocate for equity, and for relief workers and their supporters, let us pray.

Have mercy, O God.

For those who hunger or thirst, for those who doubt or are terrified, for those who suffer in body, mind, or spirit, and for caregivers, that all experience the healing and comfort given through Christ, let us pray.

Have mercy, O God.

For those gathered in this place to hear the gospel and receive the good gifts of God through Christ Jesus, that guided by the Holy Spirit, we serve our neighbor who is in need, let us pray.

Have mercy, O God.

Here other intercessions may be offered.

In thanksgiving for men and women of every time and place who have died in Christ, and that we follow their examples of faithful living, let us pray.

Have mercy, O God.

Almighty God, you have promised to hear those who call upon your name. We commend all our spoken and silent prayers to you, trusting in your abundant mercy; through your Son, Jesus Christ our Lord.

Amen.

Images in the Readings

Apocalyptic imagery arises periodically when a people are so downtrodden that they cannot foresee any relief from their suffering unless a cataclysm destroys everything and the earth begins anew. Thus, for example, the Jews living under the oppression of the Roman Empire popularized this literary genre. Natural disasters, political injustices, religious persecution, and family disruptions could, however, be seen positively, since they were signs that God would soon intervene to end evil once and for all. Thus "law" and "gospel" meet. Such apocalyptic tendencies are thriving also in our time.

The **temple** in Jerusalem had once again been rebuilt and refurbished. Yet it was again and finally to be destroyed, and currently its ruined wall is all that remains. For Christians, Christ is our temple, and the members of the church are its building stones. May God keep us from being thrown down!

The passage from Malachi refers to "neither **root nor branch**" left after God's fire destroys evil. What stands behind this passage is the ancient Near Eastern image of the nation-state as a tree of life, its height and strength likened to the power of the government.

In an ancient example of the cultural adaptation of religious symbolism, the Hebrew prophet appropriates an image of Shamash, the enemy's **sun god**, when speaking of the coming promise of the God of Israel.

Ideas for the Day

◆   In his book *Testimony: Talking Ourselves into Being Christian*, Thomas G. Long addresses the tension many Christians feel about sharing their faith: "Many people who hunger for the experience of God are nevertheless put off by people who go around talking about God all the time, and thoughtful Christians don't want to generate this response" ([San Francisco: Jossey-Bass, 2004], 23). Yet testimony is an important part of the Christian life. This would be an excellent day to include testimony from someone who is prepared to talk about their faith, to encourage worshipers unfamiliar with the practice.

◆   Many apocalyptic books and movies focus on warnings of destruction. Nonbelievers may experience this kind of testimony more as bullying than anything else. As we face dire warnings about dramatic climate change, rapidly changing global economies, and escalating warfare and famine, how does the church testify to the goodness of God's provision in the midst of fear without diminishing the seriousness of what we might be facing?

◆   Many postapocalyptic books and movies of popular culture illustrate the aftermath of devastating destruction by depicting people scavenging for water and food, building shelters out of whatever comes to hand, and keeping warm at fires built out of found wood. It's interesting to note that a significant percentage of the world's population already lives this kind of life. For these people, such a life isn't "the end of the world," but simply the way their life has always been. What exactly are the things we fear losing at the return of Christ? What are the systems and structures of privilege we cannot imagine living without but which might well fall in the presence of God?

◆   In the sacrament of the table, we are surrounded by a great cloud of witnesses, united with all before us who have died in Christ. Many of the saints lived lives relatively free from fear; others lived and died in the midst of prejudice, persecution, and violence. Yet they all live in Christ. Remembering their presence with us can give us courage and strength for *all* of the "end days."

Connections with the Liturgy

Both the Nicene Creed and the Apostles' Creed speak of the coming of Christ to judge the living and the dead. It is this judgment of which Luke speaks and in anticipation of which the rivers of Psalm 98 are clapping their hands.

Let the Children Come

We all have fears and worries. Help young and old alike let go of some of those fears and worries—give everyone a piece of paper or a note card and ask them to draw or write down some of those fears and worries. Have the children collect the fears and worries and place them in a suitable container near the altar or baptismal font. Then lead the assembly in a prayer asking God to help us let go and place all things in God's hands. The hymn "Have no fear, little flock" (ELW 764) or "Shepherd me, O God" (ELW 780) could be played and/or sung during the drawing, writing, and collecting.

Assembly Song
Gathering

My hope is built on nothing less   ELW 596/597, LBW 293/294, TFF 192

On Jordan's stormy banks I stand   ELW 437, TFF 49

All my hope on God is founded   ELW 757, WOV 782

Psalmody and Acclamations

Behnke, John. "Psalm 98: Sing to the Lord a New Song." SATB, cant, assembly, kybd, 2 tpt, hb. CPH 983666WEB.

Hesla, Bret. "Shout unto God (Psalm 98)" from *Justice, Like a Base of Stone*. AFP 9780800623562.

Marshall, Jane. "Psalm 98." U, kybd, assembly. CG CGA427.

+ Isaiah 12:2-6; see Vigil of Easter.

(GA) ELW 168 with proper verse for Lectionary 33.

Hymn of the Day

Lord of our life   ELW 766, LBW 366   *ISTE CONFESSOR*

Rise, O Sun of righteousness   ELW 657   *SONNE DER GERECHTIGKEIT*

When peace like a river   ELW 785, TFF 194, LBW 346   *VILLE DU HAVRE*

Offering

Goodness is stronger than evil   ELW 721

We give thee but thine own   ELW 686, LBW 410

Communion

If God my Lord be for me   ELW 788, LBW 454

Come with us, O blessed Jesus   ELW 501, LBW 219

O day of peace   ELW 711, WOV 762

Sending

God, my Lord, my strength   ELW 795, LBW 484

Let all things now living   ELW 881, LBW 557

Additional Assembly Songs

Like a ship that's tossed and driven   TFF 251

Jesús es todo para mí   LLC 532

Oh, I woke up this morning   TFF 166

⊕ Bell, John L. "Kyrie eleison" from *My Heart Sings Out*. SATB. Church Publishing 9780898694741.

⊕ Dexter, Noel. "The Right Hand of God." from *Global Songs 2*. SATB. AFP 9780800656744. ELW 889.

✿ Carr, David/Mac Powell/Mark D. Lee/Tai Anderson. "Children of God" from CCLI.

✿ Cowart, Benji/Michael Weaver. "Redeemed" from CCLI.

✿ Kirkland, Eddie/Steve Fee. "Everything Falls" from CCLI.

✿ Sampson, Marty. "God Is Great" from CCLI.

✿ Redman, Beth/Matt Redman. "You Never Let Go" from CCLI.

Music for the Day
Choral

p ● Burroughs, Bob. "Deep River." SATB, pno. GIA G-7008.

● Clausen, René. "It Is Well with My Soul." SSAATTBB, org. MSM 50-5211.

p ● Nelson, Eric. "It Is Well with My Soul" from *Augsburg Choirbook for Men*. TTBB, pno. AFP 9780800676834.

p ● Perkins, Scott. "The Beautiful Land." SAB, pno. AFP 9781451485752.

Children's Choir

p Bach, J. S./arr. Hal H. Hopson. "Lift High Every Voice" from *Three Unison Anthems from Master Composers*. U, pno. CG CGA1299.

Potter, Kenney. "The Earth Is the Lord's." 2 pt trbl, pno. HIN HMC 2091.

Sleeth, Natalie. "Good and Simple Gifts." U/2 pt, kybd. LOR 10/3843L.

Keyboard / Instrumental

p ● Bottomley, Greg. "Ville du Havre" from *Piano Sunday Morning*, vol. 2. Pno. AFP 9781451462654.

Douglas-Pennant, Adela. "Postlude: Introduction and Fugue" from *Women Composers' Album*. Org. MSM 10-774.

● Organ, Anne Krentz. "Partita on 'Sonne der Gerechtigkeit'" from *Reflections on Hymn Tunes for Holy Communion*, vol. 1. Pno. AFP 9780800654979.

● Tallis, Thomas. "Iste confessor." Org. Various editions.

Handbell

● Afdahl, Lee. "At the Lamb's High Feast." 3-5 oct hb, opt 2 oct hc, L2+. CPH 97-7309.

p McKlveen, Paul A. "Take My Life and Let It Be." 3-5 oct hb, opt 3 oct hc, L3. CG CGB539.

● Tucker, Margaret. "It Is Well with My Soul (When Peace like a River)." 3-6 oct hb, opt 3 oct hc, L3. CG CGB511.

Thursday, November 17

Elizabeth of Hungary, renewer of society, died 1231

This Hungarian princess lived her entire life in east-central Germany, and is often called Elizabeth of Thuringia. Married to a duke, she gave large sums of money, including her dowry, for relief of the poor and sick. She founded hospitals, cared for orphans, and used the royal food supplies to feed the hungry. Though she had the support of her husband, her generosity and charity did not earn her friends within the royal court. At the death of her husband, she was driven out. She joined a Franciscan order and continued her charitable work, though she suffered abuse at the hands of her confessor and spiritual guide. Her lifetime of charity is particularly remarkable when one remembers that she died at the age of twenty-four. She founded two hospitals, and many more are named for her.

⊕ = global song   ✿ = praise song   + = semicontinuous psalm
● = relates to hymn of the day   p = available in Prelude Music Planner

November 20, 2016

Christ the King
Last Sunday after Pentecost — Lectionary 34

Jeremiah's promise of the execution of "justice and righteousness in the land" finds ironic fulfillment in the execution of Jesus of Nazareth, the King of the Jews. It appears so utterly contradictory that the king should be crucified with the criminal. This victory appears for all the world as ignominious defeat. Yet through the gate of death our Lord opens the door to paradise.

Prayer of the Day

O God, our true life, to serve you is freedom, and to know you is unending joy. We worship you, we glorify you, we give thanks to you for your great glory. Abide with us, reign in us, and make this world into a fit habitation for your divine majesty, through Jesus Christ, our Savior and Lord, who lives and reigns with you and the Holy Spirit, one God, now and forever.

Gospel Acclamation

Alleluia. Blessed is the one who comes in the name ˈ of the Lord.* Blessed is the coming kingdom of our an- ˈ cestor David. *Alleluia.* (Mark 11:9)

Readings and Psalm

Jeremiah 23:1-6

Today's reading builds on the common ancient Near Eastern metaphor of the king as shepherd. Judah's unjust rulers have caused their people, their "flock," to be scattered. Nevertheless, the Lord will raise up a new and righteous shepherd who will rule a restored Judah.

Psalm 46

I will be exalted among the nations. (Ps. 46:10)

Colossians 1:11-20

An early Christian hymn praises the mystery of the political, personal, and mystical Christ, the one who was present at creation and is eternally reigning with God.

Luke 23:33-43

Amid scoffing and slander from those who sarcastically call him Messiah and king, Jesus reveals that to be Messiah and king is to give one's life for others. Here he uses his power to welcome a despised sinner to paradise but puts his own death into God's hands.

Semicontinuous reading and psalm

Jeremiah 23:1-6

Today's reading builds on the common ancient Near Eastern metaphor of the king as shepherd. Judah's unjust rulers

have caused their people, their "flock," to be scattered. Nevertheless, the Lord will raise up a new and righteous shepherd who will rule a restored Judah.

Luke 1:68-79

You have raised up for us a mighty Savior. (Luke 1:69)

Preface   Ascension *or* Sundays

Color   White *or* Green

Prayers of Intercession

The prayers are prepared locally for each occasion. The following examples may be adapted or used as appropriate.

With the people of God gathered here and throughout the world, we offer our prayers for the church, those in need, and all of creation.

A brief silence.

For Christ's church on earth and for those who proclaim the good news of your reign, that all divisions cease, let us pray.
Have mercy, O God.

For your creation in all its beauty, for water and land, plants and animals, and for those who advocate for the just use of the earth, that all creatures enjoy life abundant, let us pray.
Have mercy, O God.

For government leaders, for those who provide justice and safety, and for those in war-torn places (*especially*), that all be guided by the peace of the Lord, let us pray.
Have mercy, O God.

For the alienated, for the sick and suffering, for those living with HIV/AIDS, and for those in need of reconciliation (*especially*), that God provide them with skilled medical practitioners and counselors, let us pray.
Have mercy, O God.

For those traveling this week, for those gathered with family and friends, for protection from inclement weather, and for the body of Christ gathered here, let us pray.
Have mercy, O God.

Here other intercessions may be offered.

In thanksgiving for all the saints who lived their lives giving thanks to God and are now at rest, that their witness strengthen our confidence in the resurrection to eternal life, let us pray.

Have mercy, O God.

Almighty God, you have promised to hear those who call upon your name. We commend all our spoken and silent prayers to you, trusting in your abundant mercy; through your Son, Jesus Christ our Lord.

Amen.

Images in the Readings

On this Sunday, many churches praise Christ as **king**. Currently on the world scene some nations have rejected monarchies, some maintain figurehead monarchs, and some, while not using the term *king*, maintain heads of state with absolute, even ruthless, power over the people. The Bible promises that God's power and majesty differ radically from the reign of human monarchs. Thus we need to use the image of king as correcting the image of king. Several hymns do a splendid job of playing the image against itself. Some churches prefer the phrase "the reign of Christ" as stressing Christ's activity rather than his status: unfortunately, English has the problem of the homonym *rain*. A welcome alternative is "the sovereign Christ."

Jeremiah writes about the people as the **flock**. Much art in the church has engrained in our imagination the lone lost lamb, but here it is the entire flock, the full fold, that is shepherded by God.

The writer of Colossians contrasts **light** with darkness. We think of baptism as God's gift of light into the darkness of our human nature.

Perhaps John Calvin was right that God ought never be drawn in art, since such depictions can only serve to make God smaller than do the scriptures. Colossians offers to Christians the most important **image of God**: Christ, in whom is all the fullness of God. Christ is head of the body, and so we can glimpse at least part of God by looking at one another.

Ideas for the Day

◆ This is the last Sunday of the liturgical year, a New Year's Eve of the church year. The secular new year prompts resolutions for the coming year. Rather than inviting people to make their resolutions for faithfulness (which will never last, because resolutions never do), consider the resolutions or promises Jesus makes to us. In the cross, what does Jesus resolve to do? This could be introduced by a list of common resolutions, such as getting in shape, a reminder of the high failure rate, and an invitation to turn to Jesus and his saving acts.

◆ Stories of human kings (and queens) always seem to revolve around palace politics and the various schemes people craft as they seek to gain or maintain their power.

In Christ the king, we see something completely different. Here is a king who does not care about gaining or maintaining power. In fact, Jesus is willing to give up all power for the sake of the whole world. Strength through weakness is hard for the world to understand, but in Jesus it is powerful beyond measure.

◆ The movie *42* (Warner Bros., 2013) tells the story of Jackie Robinson breaking the color barrier in major league baseball. Early in the film, Branch Rickey, the owner of the Brooklyn Dodgers, is interviewing Jackie Robinson and trying to decide if he wants to sign him. At one point in the interview, Jackie asks Branch, "You want a player who doesn't have the guts to fight back?" Branch responds, "No, I want a player with the guts not to fight back." This is a modern image of the suffering servant. This is the true strength of Jesus.

Connections with the Liturgy

Every time we sing the "Glory to God" (*ELW*, pp. 99–100), we call God the heavenly king, and we praise Christ as seated at the right hand of the Father. In the Lord's Prayer, we give to God the kingdom, the power, and the glory forever.

Let the Children Come

Christ is our king yet is like no other king the world has ever known. Show kids a picture of a stereotypical king with a golden crown, robes, and scepter, and then a picture of Jesus wearing a crown of thorns. How is Jesus different from a "normal" king? How is he similar? Talk about what it means that Christ is our king and invite the children to offer suggestions for what it means that he is the ruler of our lives. Sing "Jesus, remember me" (ELW 616), a direct quote from today's gospel, as a communion song. Even prereaders can learn this simple refrain by heart.

Assembly Song
Gathering

Jesus shall reign   ELW 434, LBW 530

Christ is the king!   ELW 662, LBW 386

All hail the power of Jesus' name!   ELW 634, LBW 328/329, TFF 267

Psalmody and Acclamations

Cherwien, David. "Psalm 46" from PWC.

Erickson, Rick. "Psalm 46," Refrain 2, from PSCY.

Gelineau, Joseph. "Psalm 46" from ACYG.

+ Luke 1:68-79; see Second Sunday of Advent.

(GA) ELW 168 with proper verse for Christ the King.

Hymn of the Day

Beautiful Savior   ELW 838, LBW 518   *SCHÖNSTER HERR JESU*

Rejoice, for Christ is king!   ELW 430   *LAUS REGIS*

+ = semicontinuous psalm

Blessing, Honor, and Glory ELW 433, W&P 21 *BLESSING, HONOR, AND GLORY*

Offering

Savior, like a shepherd lead us ELW 789, TFF 254, LBW 481

Let the vineyards be fruitful ELW 184

Communion

At the name of Jesus ELW 416, LBW 179

O Christ, what can it mean for us ELW 431

The head that once was crowned ELW 432, LBW 173

Sending

Soon and very soon ELW 439, LS 2, TFF 38, W&P 128, WOV 744

Crown him with many crowns ELW 855, LBW 170

Additional Assembly Songs

O Christ the King, anointed TFF 294

The King of glory LS 8, W&P 136

Before the Ancient One, Christ stands CBM 58

⊕ Cárdenas, Casiodoro. "I Will Exalt My God, My King/Te exaltaré, mi Dios, mi Rey" from *Glory to God*. U. WJK 9780664238971.

⊕ Lee, Sunkyung. "Dream On, Dream On" from *Glory to God*. U. WJK 9780664238971.

✿ Crowder, David. "O Praise Him" from CCLI.

✿ Fox, Kip. "Thieves on a Cross" from Kipfox.com and CCLI.

✿ Kendrick, Graham/Paul Baloche. "Creation's King" from CCLI.

✿ McGranahan, James/Jeremy Johnson/Paul Marino. "Hallelujah for the Cross" from CCLI.

✿ Tomlin, Chris/Ed Cash. "All Bow Down" from CCLI.

✿ Tomlin, Chris/Daniel Carson/Ed Cash/Jason Reeves. "Jesus Messiah" from CCLI.

Music for the Day
Choral

p Carlson, J. Bert. "Lift High the Cross." SATB, org. AFP 9781451479393.

p Ferguson, John. "The Head That Once Was Crowned with Thorns." SATB, org, br qrt. GIA G-3750.

Owens, Sam Batt. "Lo! He Comes with Clouds Descending." SAB, kybd. MSM 50-0203.

p Schrader, Jack. "Soon and Very Soon." 2 pt mxd, pno. HOP C5825.

Children's Choir

Bowen, Kathy C. "As I Wander." U/2 pt, kybd. LOR 10/3001K.

Kosche, Kenneth T. "Let the Whole Creation Cry." U/2 pt, kybd. LOR 10/2493K.

p Patterson, Mark. "Let All the World in Every Corner Sing" from *ChildrenSing: Seven Anthems for Elementary Age Singers*. U, kybd, tamb. AFP 9781451461060.

Keyboard / Instrumental

• Burkhardt, Michael. "Schönster Herr Jesu" from *Three Hymn Improvisations for Organ*. Org. MSM 10-654.

p •David, Anne Marie. "Schönster Herr Jesu" from *Snow on Snow*. Pno. AFP 9781451486100.

p •Maynard, Lynette. "Blessing, Honor, and Glory" from *Introductions and Alternate Accompaniments for Piano*, vol. 3. Pno. AFP 9780800623616.

p •Weber, Jacob B. "Laus Regis" from *Christ Is King*. Org, AFP 9781451486032.

Handbell

• Eithun, Sandra. "Beautiful Savior." 3-5 oct hb, opt 3-5 oct hc, L2. GIA G-7939.

p Glasgow, Michael J. "No Dark Valley." 3-7 oct hb, opt 3-6 oct hc, L3+/4-, HOP 2665. Opt gtr, opt bass, opt vln, opt banjo or mandolin, HOP 2665P. Opt acc CD, HOP A514.

p Ingram, Bill. "Holy God, We Praise Your Name." 2-3 oct, L1. CG CGB847.

Wednesday, November 23

Clement, Bishop of Rome, died around 100

Clement was the third bishop of Rome and served at the end of the first century. He is best remembered for a letter he wrote to the Corinthian congregation, still having difficulty with divisions in spite of Paul's canonical letters. Clement's writing echoes Paul's. "Love . . . has no limits to its endurance, bears everything patiently. Love is neither servile nor arrogant. It does not provoke schisms or form cliques, but always acts in harmony with others." Clement's letter is also a witness to early understandings of church government and the way each office in the church works for the good of the whole.

Miguel Agustín Pro, martyr, died 1927

Miguel Agustín Pro grew up among oppression in Mexico, where revolutionaries accused the church of siding with the rich. He was a Jesuit priest who served during a time of intense anticlericalism, and therefore he carried out much of his ministry in private settings. He worked on behalf of the poor and homeless. Miguel and his two brothers were arrested, falsely accused of throwing a bomb at the car of a government official, and executed by a firing squad. Just before the guns fired, he yelled, "¡Viva Cristo Rey!" which means "Long live Christ the king!"

November 24, 2016
Day of Thanksgiving (U.S.A.)

Every gathering for worship has elements of thanksgiving. When we are nourished with God's bounty in holy communion, when we partake of Jesus' word that gives life to the world, and even when two or three of us simply join our hearts in prayer to make our requests known to God, we do so "with thanksgiving." Let us give thanks to the Lord, who is good and whose mercy endures forever.

Prayer of the Day

Almighty God our Father, your generous goodness comes to us new every day. By the work of your Spirit lead us to acknowledge your goodness, give thanks for your benefits, and serve you in willing obedience, through Jesus Christ, our Savior and Lord.

Gospel Acclamation

Alleluia. God is able to provide you with every blessing ˈ in abundance,* so that by always having enough of everything, you may share abundantly in ev- ˈ 'ry good work. *Alleluia.* (2 Cor. 9:8)

Readings and Psalm
Deuteronomy 26:1-11

The annual harvest festival called the Feast of Weeks provides the setting for today's reading. This festival celebrates the first fruits of the produce of the land, offered back to God in thanks. As they bring their offerings, worshipers remember and proclaim God's gracious acts on behalf of Israel.

Psalm 100

Enter God's gates with thanksgiving. (Ps. 100:4)

Philippians 4:4-9

Paul urges the Christians at Philippi to rejoice, to be thankful, and to dwell on everything worthy of praise.

John 6:25-35

The day after he multiplies bread to feed five thousand people, Jesus is pursued by the crowds clamoring for more bread. Recalling the image of manna in the wilderness, Jesus promises to provide the true bread from heaven that will never fail. Jesus himself is that bread of life.

Preface   Weekdays

Color   of the season

Prayers of Intercession

The prayers are prepared locally for each occasion. The following examples may be adapted or used as appropriate.

With the people of God gathered here and throughout the world, we offer our prayers for the church, those in need, and all of creation.

A brief silence.

For the church, bishops, pastors, and lay leaders, for those who proclaim the gospel through preaching, music, and action, and for all people gathered in prayer, that they know the Lord is near, let us pray.

Have mercy, O God.

For fields and all the food that they yield, for those who plant and harvest, and for those who care for land, sea, and air, that creation continue to reveal God's goodness, let us pray.

Have mercy, O God.

For leaders in government at every level, for police and firefighters, and for judges and attorneys, that all in authority justly use power and promote peace, let us pray.

Have mercy, O God.

For the afflicted, oppressed, hungry, and homeless, that God raise up advocates for them; for the sick, suffering, and grieving (*especially*), that God send them compassionate caregivers, let us pray.

Have mercy, O God.

For those traveling, for those anxious with holiday activities, for those absent from worship, and for our families and friends, that all the events of our lives be grounded in the love of Christ, let us pray.

Have mercy, O God.

Here other intercessions may be offered.

In thanksgiving for the faithful departed (*especially North American Lutheran pastors Justus Falckner, Jehu Jones, and William Passavant*), that their witness to the spread of God's word may inspire us in our doings, let us pray.

Have mercy, O God.

Almighty God, you have promised to hear those who call upon your name. We commend all our spoken and silent

prayers to you, trusting in your abundant mercy; through your Son, Jesus Christ our Lord.
Amen.

Images in the Readings

The reading from John speaks about **heaven**. In biblical speech, the term *heaven*, or *the heavens*, usually refers to the sky or to that vastness that is beyond the earth, and so it came to refer to the realm of God, who is above and beyond everything. Only much later in history did the word *heaven* come to suggest an everlasting family reunion. John's gospel uses the imagery of a three-tiered universe in saying that Christ comes down from heaven. We might say that Christ is present on earth as God among us. In the sacrament, we eat him. On earth, we consume heaven.

The **first fruits** described in Deuteronomy are a poignant addition to our celebration of Thanksgiving Day. Some Christians use this holiday as a time to contribute food gifts to the needy. The United States is one nation in which there is a growing gap between the haves and the have-nots.

Ideas for the Day

♦ God's people gather for worship, giving thanks for all of God's blessings, knowing full well a great many people throughout the world remain hungry and lack basic necessities. Even as this reality is lifted up, there is an opportunity to offer people a way to respond to those challenges. Could this be a day when the entire offering is designated for the ELCA World Hunger Appeal or to Canadian Lutheran World Relief? If your congregation gathers in an ecumenical setting, you might designate a local feeding ministry.

♦ Thanksgiving is one of those holidays that seems to transcend religion. Everyone celebrates. As Christians gather to worship, it is an opportunity to remind them of the difference between the generic thoughts and expressions of thanksgiving and the Christian's response. As followers of Jesus, we know who to thank. We know daily bread comes as a gift from our good and gracious God. Anyone can be grateful, but we know who deserves our gratitude and praise.

♦ The autumn days recall harvest celebrations. Lift this up by decorating your chancel area with baskets of vegetables like pumpkins, potatoes, apples, carrots, onions, and more. Cornstalks can stand tall and bales of straw can help stage the display. Following the holiday, the fresh food can be shared with the congregation or donated to a food pantry.

Connections with the Liturgy

As the art by He Qi in *Evangelical Lutheran Worship* (p. 89) suggests, each time we gather for worship we are giving

thanks to God for the food before us and for the food who is Christ. The fish on the plate reminds us of the early Christian creed, "Jesus Christ, God's Son, Savior," a phrase whose acronym in Greek forms the word *ichthus*, meaning "fish."

Let the Children Come

In worship, we give thanks to God before we share the meal of communion. We even call it the "great thanksgiving" (*ELW*, pp. 107–112). We give thanks—again—*after* we have shared communion (*ELW*, p. 114). In addition to a prayer at the beginning of a meal, some families also offer a "return of thanks" at the end of the meal. The words of Psalm 136:1 work well as a thanksgiving at the conclusion of a meal: "O give thanks to the Lord, for he is good, for his steadfast love endures forever." Invite families to try it at the Thanksgiving meal and then keep on doing it!

Assembly Song
Gathering

God extends an invitation   ELW 486, LLC 397

As saints of old   ELW 695, LBW 404

We praise you, O God   ELW 870, LBW 241

Psalmody and Acclamations

Hopson, Hal. "Psalm 100" from TPP.

Lim, Swee Hong/arr. John Bell. "All People Living on the Earth." SATB, pno, gtr, assembly, C inst. GIA G-8011.

Roberts, William Bradley. "Psalm 100" from PSCY.

Trapp, Lynn. "Psalm 100." SATB, assembly, org, 2 C inst. MSM 80-704.

(GA) ELW 168 with proper verse for Thanksgiving.

Hymn of the Day

Sing to the Lord of harvest   ELW 694, LBW 412   *WIE LIEBLICH IST DER MAIEN*

Praise and thanksgiving   ELW 689, LBW 409   *BUNESSAN*

Come, ye thankful people, come   ELW 693, LBW 407   *ST. GEORGE'S, WINDSOR*

Offering

We Are an Offering   ELW 692, W&P 146

Accept, O Lord, the gifts we bring   ELW 691, WOV 759

Communion

By your hand you feed your people   ELW 469

I am the Bread of life   ELW 485, WOV 702

Soul, adorn yourself with gladness   ELW 488/489, LBW 224, LLC 388

Sending

We plow the fields and scatter   ELW 680/681, LLC 492, LBW 362, LS 102

As rain from the clouds   ELW 508

Additional Assembly Songs

Aquí del pan partido tomaré   LLC 384

Te damos gracias   LLC 394

How to reach the masses   TFF 227

Loh, I-to. "The Rice of Life" from *Glory to God*. U. WJK 9780664238971.

Taiwanese melody. "Let Us Come to Worship God" from *Glory to God*. U. WJK 9780664238971.

Angrisano, Steve/Sarah Hart. "We Remember, We Believe"

Angrisano, Steve/Tom Tomaszek. "Come to the Lord" from CCLI.

Curry, Craig. "Hungry, I Come" from CCLI.

Kendrick, Graham. "Banquet" from CCLI.

Zschech, Darlene/Michael W. Smith/Andy Makken. "I Am Yours" from CCLI.

Music for the Day
Choral

p Lasky, David. "I Sing the Mighty Power of God." SATB, org. AFP 9780806697161.

Mozart, Wolfgang Amadeus/arr. Hal Hopson. "Come, Be Joyful." 2 pt mxd, kybd. MSM 50-7302.

p Parker, Alice. "For the Fruit of All Creation." 2 pt or SATB, kybd, opt assembly. GIA G-6264.

Rutter, John. "All Things Bright and Beautiful." 2 pt, kybd. HIN HMC-663.

Children's Choir

Greene, Maurice/arr. Michael Burkhardt. "To God the Mighty God." 2 pt trbl, kybd, opt trbl inst, opt cont. MSM 50-6103.

Halls, David. "It Is Good to Give Thanks to the Lord." U, org. PAR PPMO 0609.

Ziegenhals, Harriet. "A Time to Celebrate." U/2 pt/SATB, kybd, trumpet. GIA G-4715.

Keyboard / Instrumental

• Maynard, Lynette. "Wie lieblich ist der Maien" from *Introductions and Alternate Accompaniments for Piano*, vol. 7. Pno. AFP 9780800623654.

• Miller, Aaron David. "Bunessan" from *Eight Chorale Preludes for Manuals Only*, vol. 1. Org. AFP 9780800677560.

p • Organ, Anne Krentz. "St. George's, Windsor" from *Reflections on Hymn Tunes for the Fall Festivals*. Pno. AFP 9780800663834.

• Powell, Robert J. "Bunessan" from *Organ Tunes from the British Isles*. Org. AFP 9780800678746.

Handbell

• Eithun, Sandra. "Sing to the Lord of Harvest." 2-3 oct, L2. CPH 97-7418.

• Larson, Lloyd. "Raise the Songs of Harvest." 3-5 oct, L3-. BP HB279.

p • Shackley, Larry/Arnold Sherman. "Morning Has Broken." 3-5 oct, L3+. HOP 2634.

Thursday, November 24

Justus Falckner, died 1723; Jehu Jones, died 1852; William Passavant, died 1894; pastors in North America

A native of Saxony, Falckner was the son of a Lutheran pastor and, seeing the stresses his father endured, did not plan on becoming a pastor himself, though he studied theology in Halle. Instead, he joined with his brother in the real estate business in Pennsylvania. Through this business he became acquainted with a Swedish pastor in America, and finally he decided to become ordained. He served congregations in New York and New Jersey. Not only was he the first Lutheran ordained in North America, but he published a catechism that was the first Lutheran book published on the continent.

Jones was a native of Charleston, South Carolina. Ordained by the New York Ministerium in 1832, he became the Lutheran Church's first African American pastor. Upon returning to South Carolina he was arrested under a law prohibiting free blacks from reentering the state, so he was unable to join the group of Charlestonians he had been commissioned to accompany to Liberia. For nearly twenty years Jones carried out missionary work in Philadelphia in the face of many difficulties. There he led in the formation of the first African American Lutheran congregation, St. Paul's, and the construction of its church building.

William Passavant created and nurtured a new level of organized social ministry in western Pennsylvania. It was the seed of the system of social services that is now known as Lutheran Services in America. Passavant and his legacy sought to serve the poorest of the poor, providing shelter, medical, and living assistance.

Friday, November 25

Isaac Watts, hymnwriter, died 1748

Isaac Watts was born in England to a family of nonconformists, people who thought the Church of England had not carried its reforms far enough. As a youth, Watts complained to his father about the quality of hymnody in the metrical psalter of his day. That was the start of his hymn-writing career. He wrote about six hundred hymns, many in a two-year period beginning when he was twenty years old. Some of Watts's hymns are based on psalms, a nonconformist tradition. When criticized for writing hymns not taken from scripture, he responded that if we can pray prayers that are not from scripture but written by us, then surely we can sing hymns that we have made up ourselves. Ten of Watts's hymn texts are in *Evangelical Lutheran Worship*, including "O God, Our Help in Ages Past" (ELW 632).

Resources

Lectionaries

Lectionary for Worship Year C. Augsburg Fortress, 2006. The Revised Common Lectionary. Each reading is "sense-lined" for clearer proclamation of the scriptural texts. New Revised Standard Version. Available in study (includes reader helps) and ritual editions. Also available on sundaysandseasons. com.

§ *Revised Common Lectionary Daily Readings.* Consultation on Common Texts. Fortress Press, 2005.

Readings for the Assembly (C). Gordon Lathrop and Gail Ramshaw, eds. Augsburg Fortress, 1997. The Revised Common Lectionary. Emended NRSV with inclusive language. Available on sundaysandseasons.com

§ *The Revised Common Lectionary: Twentieth Anniversary Annotated Edition.* Consultation on Common Texts. Fortress Press, 2012. The most definitive source for the RCL and the most authoritative explanation of how it came to be developed. Includes marginal notes that identify sources and rationale for lectionary choices. With a foreword by Gordon Lathrop and a new historical introduction.

Worship Books

Evangelical Lutheran Worship. Augsburg Fortress, 2006. Available in pew, leaders ritual, leaders desk, gift, pocket, and enlarged print editions.

Evangelical Lutheran Worship Accompaniment Edition: Liturgies. Augsburg Fortress, 2006. Complete keyboard accompaniments for all ten holy communion settings and additional music within liturgies. Simplified edition also available.

Evangelical Lutheran Worship Accompaniment Edition: Service Music and Hymns (2 vols; Compact Edition, 1 vol.). Augsburg Fortress, 2006. Full accompaniments to all hymns and songs in the pew edition, #151–893. Simplified Keyboard and Guitar editions for service music and hymns also available.

§ *Evangelical Lutheran Worship Occasional Services for the Assembly.* Augsburg Fortress, 2009. Rites and prayers for use on particular occasions in the worshiping assemblies of congregations and synods, such as ministry rites, dedications, and blessings.

§ *Evangelical Lutheran Worship Pastoral Care:* Occasional Services, Readings, and Prayers. Augsburg Fortress, 2008. An essential tool for caregivers conducting the church's ministry of care outside the worshiping assembly.

Evangelical Lutheran Worship Prayer Book for the Armed Services: For Chaplains and Other Military Personnel. Augsburg Fortress, 2013. Pocket-sized edition includes resources for individual daily devotion, prayers for various circumstances selected and composed especially for use by service members, several assembly service orders featuring ecumenical texts, and the texts of 26 psalms and 65 hymns and national songs. Intended for use by active and reserve service members and their families and friends, pastors and congregations who minister to them, chaplains, and veterans.

Libro de Liturgia y Cántico. Augsburg Fortress, 1998. A complete Spanish-language worship resource. Leader edition (2001) includes additional psalms and indexes.

New Hymns of Praise. Taosheng Publishing House, Hong Kong, 2011. Joint venture of the ELCA and the Evangelical Lutheran Church in Hong Kong. The majority of the 143 hymns and songs can be sung in either Mandarin or Cantonese and all include an English text. Keyboard accompaniments for all the hymns are also provided.

Ritos Ocasionales. Augsburg Fortress, 2000. Spanish language version of rites and prayers for various occasions and circumstances.

* *Santa Comunión / Holy Communion.* Augsburg Fortress, 2014. Bilingual Spanish/English edition of Setting Seven from *Evangelical Lutheran Worship,* including texts and liturgical songs in both languages. Assembly and leaders editions.

This Far by Faith: An African American Resource for Worship. Augsburg Fortress, 1999. A supplement of worship orders, psalms, service music, and hymns representing African American traditions and developed by African American Lutherans.

Worship Planning Tools, Indexes, Calendars

∞ www.preludemusicplanner.com. A subscription-based online music planning tool. Create comprehensive plans. Browse, preview, and download music from multi-publisher library. Search music based on lectionary days, keywords, skill level and more. Store your usage history. Upload and organize your own library.

∞ www.sundaysandseasons.com. A subscription-based online worship planning tool. Browse, select, and download content for worship planning and worship folder preparation.

∞ Evangelical Lutheran Worship Liturgies CD-ROM. Augsburg Fortress, 2006. Liturgical material from pew edition in editable text files; assembly singing lines provided as graphics.

Indexes to Evangelical Lutheran Worship. Augsburg Fortress, 2007. Indexes the hymns and songs in Evangelical Lutheran Worship. Includes extensive lectionary, scripture, and topical indexes.

Choral Literature for Sundays and Seasons. Bradley Ellingboe, ed. Augsburg Fortress, 2004. A comprehensive listing of time-tested choral works, indexed to the readings for each Sunday and principal festival of the three-year lectionary. Includes information on voicing, instrumentation, composers, and publishers.

* *Calendar of Word and Season 2016: Liturgical Wall Calendar.* Augsburg Fortress, 2015. Features artwork by Christina Saj, Kathrin Burleson, and Corinne Vonaesch. A reference tool for home, sacristy, office.

* *Church Year Calendar 2016.* Augsburg Fortress, 2015. A one-sheet calendar of lectionary citations and liturgical colors for each Sunday and festival of the liturgical year. Appropriate for bulk purchase and distribution. Also available in downloadable format.

* denotes new or newer print resource
∞ denotes electronic or Web resource
334 § denotes print resource also available as an ebook

* ∞ *Words for Worship: 2016, Year C.* Augsburg Fortress, 2015. CD-ROM includes lectionary readings, worship texts, seasonal rites, and more for use in worship folders and other self-published materials.
* *Worship Planning Calendar 2016.* Augsburg Fortress, 2015. A two-page per week calendar helpful for worship planners, with space to record appointments and notes for each day. Specially designed to complement Sundays and Seasons. Features the CCT daily lectionary.

Westermeyer, Paul. *Hymnal Companion to Evangelical Lutheran Worship.* Augsburg Fortress, 2010. Background and insightful commentary on all 650 hymns, both text and music, together with biographical information on hymn writers and composers. Expanded indexes.

Worship Support

Boesenecker, Andrew, and James Graeser. *A Field Guide to Contemporary Worship: How to Begin and Lead Band-Based Worship.* Augsburg Fortress, 2011. A guide for anyone thinking about starting a contemporary worship service and an essential reference work for those wondering about the nuts and bolts of instrumentation, arranging, working with microphones and speakers, and much more.

§ Brugh, Lorraine, and Gordon Lathrop. *The Sunday Assembly.* Augsburg Fortress, 2008. A resource to guide leaders in their understanding and interpretation of the *Evangelical Lutheran Worship* resources. Focuses on holy communion.

§ Bushkofsky, Dennis, and Craig Satterlee. *The Christian Life: Baptism and Life Passages.* Augsburg Fortress, 2008. Contains detailed information on holy baptism and its related rites, as well as marriage, healing, and funeral.

∞ *Fed and Forgiven: Communion Preparation and Formation.* Augsburg Fortress, 2009. A comprehensive set of resources for leading children, youth, and adults into the sacrament of holy communion. Leader Guide with CD-ROM for all ages. Learner Resources for PreK-K, Grades 1-3, Grades 4-6, and adults. Supplementary DVD.

∞ *Go Make Disciples: An Invitation to Baptismal Living.* Augsburg Fortress, 2012. An ecumenical handbook offering a basic "how to" and a collection of updated resources for preparing adults for baptism or affirmation of baptism, and for Christian discipleship. Appropriate for a wide range of Protestant denominations, especially Lutheran, Episcopal, Anglican, United Methodist, Presbyterian, and Reformed. Supplementary CD-ROM available separately.

* § Hoyer, Christopher G. *Getting the Word Out: A Handbook for Readers.* Practical helps and spiritual wisdom for those who serve as lectors in the assembly. Augsburg Fortress, 2013.

Huffman, Walter C. *Prayer of the Faithful: Understanding and Creatively Leading Corporate Intercessory Prayer,* rev. ed. Augsburg Fortress, 1992. A helpful treatment of communal prayer, the Lord's Prayer, and the prayers of the people.

* *In These or Similar Words: Crafting Language for Worship.* Practical guidance for worship leaders and congregations wishing to craft new language for worship locally. Augsburg Fortress, 2015.

∞ *Leading Worship Matters: A Sourcebook for Preparing Worship Leaders* with accompanying DVD and CD-ROM. Augsburg Fortress, 2013. Practical, succinct, easy-to-use tools and resources to plan, execute, and evaluate worship leadership training. Covers assisting ministers, readers/lectors, altar guild/sacristans, intercessors, acolytes, ushers, greeters, communion ministers, and more.

§ Ramshaw, Gail, and Mons Teig. *Keeping Time: The Church's Years.* Augsburg Fortress, 2009. Contains detailed information on Sundays, seasons, festivals, and commemorations, as well as daily prayer.

§ Scharen, Christian. *Serving the Assembly's Worship: A Handbook for Assisting Ministers.* Practical helps and spiritual wisdom for those who serve as assisting ministers in the assembly. Augsburg Fortress 2013.

∞ *Washed and Welcome: A Baptism Sourcebook.* Augsburg Fortress, 2010. Resources to support a congregation's total baptismal ministry and the participation of God's people in the lifelong gift of baptism. Includes CD-ROM.

Choral Collections

* *Assembly Required.* Augsburg Fortress, 2010, 2014. Volume 1 includes four liturgical songs for choir and assembly. Volume 2 includes four songs for the Easter Vigil. Volume 3 includes liturgical music for holy communion.

Augsburg Choirbook, The. Augsburg Fortress, 1998. Kenneth Jennings, ed. Sixty-seven anthems primarily from twentieth-century North American composers.

Augsburg Choirbook for Advent, Christmas, and Epiphany. Augsburg Fortress, 2007. Thirty-three anthems, mostly easy-to-medium difficulty, for the Christmas cycle.

Augsburg Choirbook for Men. Augsburg Fortress, 2004. Fourteen anthems for two- to four-part male chorus.

Augsburg Choirbook for Women. Augsburg Fortress, 2006. Diverse selections for choirs of all ages and abilities from high school through adult.

Augsburg Easy Choirbook, vol. 1. Augsburg Fortress, 2003. Fourteen unison and two-part mixed anthems for the church year.

Augsburg Easy Choirbook, vol. 2. Augsburg Fortress, 2005. Sixteen anthems for the church year; accessible, quality music for the smaller, less-experienced choir.

Augsburg Motet Book. Augsburg Fortress, 2013. Zebulon M. Highben, ed. Over thirty classic anthems and new motets, edited with optional accompaniments.

Bach for All Seasons. Augsburg Fortress, 1999. Richard Erickson and Mark Bighley, eds. Offers movements from cantatas and oratorios presented with carefully reconstructed keyboard parts and fresh English texts. Instrumental parts available.

Chantry Choirbook. Augsburg Fortress, 2000. Choral masterworks of European composers spanning five centuries, many with new English translations, and indexed for use in the liturgical assembly throughout the year.

Choral Stanzas for Hymns. 2 vols. Augsburg Fortress, 2010–2011. More than 150 reproducible arrangements of selected hymn stanzas for choirs to sing in alternation with assemblies.

* denotes new or newer print resource
∞ denotes electronic or Web resource
§ denotes print resource also available as an ebook

GladSong Choirbook. Augsburg Fortress, 2005. Eleven titles for fall, Advent, and Christmas use, plus Reformation, Thanksgiving, All Saints, Christ the King, Epiphany, and communion.

Hear Our Prayer. Augsburg Fortress, 2007. A collection of sung prayer responses to be used between the petitions of the prayers of intercession or as a call or closing to prayer.

* *St. Olaf Choirbook for Men.* Augsburg Fortress, 2015. Christopher Aspaas, ed. Fourteen new and classic anthems scored for male voices.

The New Gloria Deo: Music for Small Choirs. Augsburg Fortress, 2010 (vol. 1), 2012 (vol. 2). Twelve anthems written with small ensembles in mind by Aaron David Miller and Thomas Keesecker.

Vocal Descants for the Church Year. Based on hymns in Evangelical Lutheran Worship. Augsburg Fortress, 2008. 250 descants, mostly reproducible, for adding color and brilliance to hymn singing.

Wade in the Water: Easy Choral Music for All Ages. Augsburg Fortress, 2007. A collection of two- and three-part choral music for the less-experienced singer.

Hymn and Song Collections

As Sunshine to a Garden: Hymns and Songs. Rusty Edwards. Augsburg Fortress, 1999. Forty-six collected hymns from the author of "We all are one in mission."

Come, Beloved of the Maker: Hymns of Susan Palo Cherwien. Augsburg Fortress, 2010. Thirty-four hymn texts by Cherwien, following up on her previous collection, *O Blessed Spring* (Augsburg Fortress, 1997). Each text is presented with a harmonized tune.

Earth and All Stars: Hymns and Songs for Young and Old. Herbert F. Brokering. Augsburg Fortress, 2003. A collection of hymn texts by the popular writer.

Justice like a Base of Stone. Bret Hesla. Augsburg Fortress, 2006. A collection of peace and justice songs in a variety of styles, easily taught to the congregation. Audio CD also available.

Pave the Way: Global Songs 3. Bread for the Journey. Augsburg Fortress, 2004. Eighteen songs from around the world, with performance notes. Also available: *Global Songs Local Voices* (1995) and *Global Songs 2* (1997).

∞ *Singing Our Prayer: A Companion to Holden Prayer Around the Cross. Shorter Songs for Contemplative Worship.* Augsburg Fortress, 2010. A collection of short, simple songs for worship. Available in full score and assembly editions, and audio CD.

Worship & Praise. Augsburg Fortress, 1999. A collection of songs in various contemporary and popular styles, with helps for using them in Lutheran worship.

Instrumental Collections

* *Augsburg Organ Library.* Augsburg Fortress, 2000–2014. A multi-volume collection of carefully selected organ music classics of the 20th and 21st centuries from a variety of publishers, organized according the seasons of the church year and primary liturgical contexts. Healing and Funeral (2013) is particularly useful for funerals, memorial services, services of healing, as

well as Sundays when the lectionary explores themes of healing, death, and dying. Marriage (2014) offers 40 musical settings for marriage, 17 of those based on hymn tunes.

* *Evangelical Lutheran Worship Festival and Ensemble Settings of Holy Communion.* Augsburg Fortress, 2008–2015. Additional instrumentation and choral elaboration for Evangelical Lutheran Worship Settings One, Two, Six, Seven, Eight, and Nine.

Hymn Accompaniments for Handbells: Advent and Christmas. Augsburg Fortress, 2010. Fourteen settings by Lee J. Afdahl to introduce and accompany hymns.

Hymns for Ensembles: Instrumental Accompaniments for Ecumenical Hymns. 2 vols. Augsburg Fortress, 2010–2011. More than 100 orchestrations of hymns old and new. Full score with keyboard part; parts for various instruments on CD-ROM, included.

In Heaven Above: Piano Music for Funerals and Memorials. Augsburg Fortress, 2011. More than fifty arrangements by various composers of favorite hymns of comfort, hope, and celebration of the saints.

Introductions and Alternate Accompaniments. Augsburg Fortress, 2007–2009. Two 10-volume series, one for organ and one for piano, covering every *Evangelical Lutheran Worship* hymn and song. Various composers.

Let It Rip! at the Piano (2 vols.) and *Pull Out the Stops* (2 vols.). Augsburg Fortress, 2000–2005. Collections for piano and organ respectively, each containing introductions and varied musical accompaniments by various composers for more than 100 widely used hymns and songs.

Organ Plus Anthology, vol. 1. Augsburg Fortress, 2012. Hymn arrangements by various composers for organ and one or two instruments.

Piano Plus: Hymns for Piano and Treble Instrument, Advent/Christmas. Augsburg Fortress, 2006. *Through the Year, 2009.* Arrangements by various composers that range in difficulty from simple cradle songs to jazz, and span numerous world cultures and several centuries.

Psalm Collections

See p. 351.

Preparing Music for Worship

∞ www.preludemusicplanner.com. A subscription-based online music planning tool. Create comprehensive plans. Browse, preview, and download music from multi-publisher library. Search music based on lectionary days, keywords, skill level and more. Store your usage history. Upload and organize your own library.

Boesenecker, Andrew, and James Graeser. *A Field Guide to Contemporary Worship: How to Begin and Lead Band-Based Worship.* Augsburg Fortress, 2011. A guide for anyone thinking about starting a contemporary worship service and an essential reference work for those wondering about the nuts and bolts of instrumentation, arranging, working with microphones and speakers, and much more.

* denotes new or newer print resource
∞ denotes electronic or Web resource
336 § denotes print resource also available as an ebook

Cherwien, David. *Let the People Sing! A Keyboardist's Creative and Practical Guide to Engaging God's People in Meaningful Song.* Concordia, 1997. Emphasis on the organ.

Bradley Ellingboe, ed. *Choral Literature for Sundays and Seasons.* Augsburg Fortress, 2004. A comprehensive listing of time-tested choral works, indexed to the readings for each Sunday and principal festival of the three-year lectionary. Includes information on voicing, instrumentation, composers, and publishers.

∞ *Evangelical Lutheran Worship* Liturgies Audio CD, vols. 1, 2, 3. Augsburg Fortress, 2006, 2010. Complete recordings of Holy Communion Settings One–Ten and Daily Prayer.

∞ *Evangelical Lutheran Worship Hymns* Audio CD, vols. 1 and 2. Augsburg Fortress, 2006, 2007. Recordings of four dozen hymns and songs from Evangelical Lutheran Worship, both new and familiar. Performed by choirs from St. Olaf and Lenoir Rhyne colleges.

Farlee, Robert Buckley, ed. *Leading the Church's Song.* Augsburg Fortress, 1998. Various contributors, with musical examples and audio CD, giving guidance on the interpretation and leadership of various genres of congregational song.

∞ *Favorite Hymns Accompanied.* John Ferguson, organist. Augsburg Fortress, 2005. A 2-CD set of 52 widely known hymns played without singing.

Highben, Zebulon M., and Kristina M. Langlois, eds. *With a Voice of Singing: Essays on Children, Choirs, and Music in the Church.* Minneapolis: Kirk House Publishers, 2007.

Musicians Guide to Evangelical Lutheran Worship. Augsburg Fortress, 2007. An introduction to the music, including specific suggestions for each liturgical music item, service music item, and hymn.

Soli Deo Gloria: Choir Devotions for Year A (Craig Mueller), *Year B* (Jennifer Baker-Trinity), and *Year C* (Wayne L. Wold). Augsburg Fortress, 2009–2011.

Weidler, Scott, and Dori Collins. *Sound Decisions.* Evangelical Lutheran Church in America, 1997. Theological principles for the evaluation of contemporary worship music.

§ Westermeyer, Paul. *The Church Musician,* rev. ed. Augsburg Fortress, 1997. Foundational introduction to the role and task of the church musician as the leader of the people's song.

§ ———. *Te Deum: The Church and Music.* Fortress Press, 1998. A historical and theological introduction to the music of the church.

§ Wold, Wayne L. *Preaching to the Choir: The Care and Nurture of the Church Choir.* Augsburg Fortress, 2003. Practical helps for the choir director.

Preparing Environment and Art

Chinn, Nancy. *Spaces for Spirit: Adorning the Church.* Chicago: Liturgy Training Publications, 1998. Imaginative thinking about ways to treat visual elements in the worship space.

§ Christopherson, D. Foy. *A Place of Encounter: Renewing Worship Spaces.* Augsburg Fortress, 2004. An exploration of principles for planning and renewing worship spaces.

Crowley, Eileen D. *A Moving Word: Media Art in Worship.* Augsburg Fortress, 2006. An exploration of how visual elements in worship can enhance the assembly's understanding of the gospel.

∞ *Evangelical Lutheran Worship* Graphics CD-ROM. Augsburg Fortress, 2011. Contains more than 100 graphic images that appear in the *Evangelical Lutheran Worship* family of resources, including the pew edition, Pastoral Care, Occasional Services for the Assembly, and more. Color images are provided as both TIFF and JPG files; black-and-white versions of the images are provided as TIFF files.

Giles, Richard. *Re-Pitching the Tent: Reordering the Church Building for Worship and Mission.* Collegeville, MN: The Liturgical Press, 1999.

Huffman, Walter C., S. Anita Stauffer, and Ralph R. Van Loon. *Where We Worship.* Minneapolis: Augsburg Publishing House, 1987. Study book and leader guide.

Mazar, Peter. *To Crown the Year: Decorating the Church through the Seasons.* Chicago: Liturgy Training Publications, 1995.

* § Stauffer, S. Anita. *Altar Guild and Sacristy Handbook.* Fourth revised edition. Augsburg Fortress, 2014. Revised and expanded edition of this classic on preparing the table and the worship environment.

Seasons and Liturgical Year

Of the Land and Seasons. Assembly and leader/accompaniment editions. Augsburg Fortress, 2013. A worship service connected to the change of the seasons in farming, orchards, or natural settings. Intended for quarterly use. This is a revised edition of the resource first published in 1990. The pattern and language have been reshaped to coordinate with the liturgies of Evangelical Lutheran Worship.

Worship Guidebook for Lent and the Three Days. Augsburg Fortress, 2009. A collection of insights, images, and practical tips to help deepen your congregation's worship life during the days from Ash Wednesday to Easter. A companion to *Music Sourcebook for Lent and the Three Days.*

Music Sourcebook for Lent and the Three Days. Augsburg Fortress, 2010. This collection includes 100 assembly songs, many of them reproducible, greatly expanding the repertoire for the assembly and its leaders during the days from Ash Wednesday to Easter.

Music Sourcebook for All Saints through Transfiguration. Augsburg Fortress, 2013. This collection offers a rich selection of assembly songs, mostly newly composed and many of them reproducible, for use during the days of November, Advent, Christmas, Epiphany, and the Time after Epiphany.

§ Ramshaw, Gail. *The Three-Day Feast: Maundy Thursday, Good Friday, Easter.* Augsburg Fortress, 2004. A little history and a lot of suggestions about how these services can enrich the assembly's worship life.

Children

* *ChildrenSing at Christmas.* Augsburg Fortress, 2015. Anne McNair and William McNair. Nine songs for young singers, useful independently or combined into a service of lessons and carols.

* *ChildrenSing Around the World.* Augsburg Fortress, 2014. A collection of global songs that span the church year by various composers. Reproducible singer pages.

* denotes new or newer print resource
∞ denotes electronic or Web resource
§ denotes print resource also available as an ebook

ChildrenSing in Worship. Augsburg Fortress, 2011–2013. Three volumes of anthems by various composers. Reproducible choral parts.

ChildrenSing Psalms. Marilyn Comer, ed. Augsburg Fortress, 2009. Collection of psalms for all seasons keyed to the lectionary.

Patterson, Mark. *ChildrenSing, ChildrenSing with Instruments,* and *Young ChildrenSing.* Augsburg Fortress, 2004–2006. Short anthems for young singers.

∞ *Fed and Forgiven: Communion Preparation and Formation.* (See Worship Support)

Kids Celebrate Worship Series. Augsburg Fortress, 2006–2007. A series of seasonal and topical 8-page booklets that introduce children and their families to worship and Evangelical Lutheran Worship. Pre-reader and young reader versions. Includes ideas and helps for parents, pastors, educators, and children's choir directors.

Our Worship Book (2006). A kid-friendly introduction to Evangelical Lutheran Worship.

Sunday Worship (2006). Focuses on the gathering, word, meal, sending pattern of Holy Communion.

Advent & Christmas (2006). Introduction to the Advent-Christmas season with activities.

Lent & Easter (2006). Introduction to the seasons of Lent and Easter with activities.

Three Amazing Days (2006). Introduction to Maundy Thursday, Good Friday, and the Easter Vigil.

Holy Communion (2007). Introduction to the sacrament of holy communion.

Baptism (2007). Introduction to the sacrament of holy baptism and baptismal living.

Our Prayers (2007). Focuses on how and when the assembly prays in worship, and prayer in the home.

The Bible (2007). Introduction to the ways in which scripture is used in worship.

LifeSongs (children's songbook, leader book, and audio CDs). Augsburg Fortress, 1999. A well-rounded selection of age-appropriate songs, hymns, and liturgical music that builds a foundation for a lifetime of singing the faith.

Living the Promises of Baptism: 101 Ideas for Parents. Augsburg Fortress, 2010. Concrete ideas for celebrating with children (infant to upper elementary) the gifts of baptism in daily living.

Ramshaw, Gail. *Every Day and Sunday, Too.* Augsburg Fortress, 1996. An illustrated book for parents and children. Daily life is related to the central actions of the liturgy.

———. *Sunday Morning.* Chicago: Liturgy Training Publications, 1993. A book for children and adults on the primary words of Sunday worship.

∞ *Washed and Welcome: A Baptism Sourcebook.* (See Worship Support)

Ylvisaker, Anne. Illustrated by Claudia McGehee. *Welcome, Child of God.* Augsburg Fortress, 2011. A board book about baptism for infants and toddlers.

Daily Prayer Resources

Briehl, Susan, and Tom Witt. *Holden Prayer Around the Cross: Handbook to the Liturgy.* Augsburg Fortress, 2009. Practical suggestions for planning and leading flexible orders for contemplative prayer. Includes fourteen liturgies in the Prayer Around the Cross format.

∞ *Singing Our Prayer: A Companion to Holden Prayer Around the Cross. Shorter Songs for Contemplative Worship.* (See Hymn and Song Collections)

§ Bread for the Day 2016: Daily Bible Readings and Prayers. Augsburg Fortress, 2015. Daily scripture texts for individual or group prayer based on the daily lectionary in Evangelical Lutheran Worship.

Cherwien, David. *Stay with Us, Lord: Liturgies for Evening.* Augsburg Fortress, 2001. Settings for Evening Prayer and Holy Communion, full music and congregational editions.

Haugen, Marty. *Holden Evening Prayer.* Chicago: GIA, 1990.

Haugen, Marty, and Susan Briehl. *Unfailing Light.* Chicago: GIA, 2004.

Makeever, Ray. *Joyous Light Evening Prayer.* Augsburg Fortress, 2000.

Miller, Aaron David. *Behold Our Light: Music for Evening Worship.* Augsburg Fortress, 2013. Settings of the musical selections needed for evening prayer or an evening communion service, scored for cantor, assembly, piano, and optional C instrument. Includes a service of light, setting of Psalm 139, Magnificat, intercessory prayers, and blessing, as well as a gospel acclamation, Sanctus, and Nunc dimittis.

§ *Revised Common Lectionary Daily Readings.* Consultation on Common Texts. Fortress Press, 2005.

Worship Studies, series

Worship Matters Series. Augsburg Fortress, 2004–2011. The series explores a range of worship-related topics.

§ Christopherson, D. Foy. *A Place of Encounter: Renewing Worship Spaces* (2004).

Crowley, Eileen D. *A Moving Word: Media Art in Worship* (2006).

§ Dahill, Lisa. *Truly Present: Practicing Prayer in the Liturgy* (2005).

§ Lathrop, Gordon. *Central Things: Worship in Word and Sacrament* (2005).

§ Quivik, Melinda. *A Christian Funeral: Witness to the Resurrection* (2005).

§ Ramshaw, Gail. *A Three-Year Banquet: The Lectionary for the Assembly* (2004).

§ ———. *The Three-Day Feast: Maundy Thursday, Good Friday, Easter* (2004).

§ Rimbo, Robert A. *Why Worship Matters* (2004).

§ Stewart, Benjamin. *A Watered Garden: Christian Worship and Earth's Ecology* (2011).

§ Torvend, Samuel. *Daily Bread, Holy Meal: Opening the Gifts of Holy Communion* (2004).

§ ———. *Flowing Water, Uncommon Birth: Christian Baptism in a Post-Christian Culture* (2011).

§ Wengert, Timothy, ed. *Centripetal Worship: The Evangelical Heart of Lutheran Worship* (2007).

Ylvisaker, John. *What Song Shall We Sing?* (2005).

* denotes new or newer print resource
∞ denotes electronic or Web resource
338 § denotes print resource also available as an ebook

Worship Studies, individual titles

Worship Matters: An Introduction to Worship. Multiple authors. Augsburg Fortress, 2012. A 5-session adult course that illuminates the whys and hows of Christian worship so that worshipers might experience a deeper appreciation of their community's worship. Leader guide and participant book.

∞ *Go Make Disciples: An Invitation to Baptismal Living.* Multiple authors. Augsburg Fortress, 2012. An ecumenical handbook offering a basic "how to" and a collection of updated resources for preparing adults for baptism or affirmation of baptism, and for Christian discipleship. Appropriate for a wide range of Protestant denominations, especially Lutheran, Episcopal, Anglican, United Methodist, Presbyterian, and Reformed. Supplementary CD-ROM available separately.

§ *The Christian Life: Baptism and Life Passages.* Augsburg Fortress, 2008.

§ *Keeping Time: The Church's Years.* Augsburg Fortress, 2009.

§ *The Sunday Assembly.* Augsburg Fortress, 2008.

§ *Inside Out: Worship in an Age of Mission.* Thomas Schattauer, gen. ed. Fortress Press, 1999. Lutheran seminary teachers address the mission of the church as it pertains to various aspects of worship.

§ Lathrop, Gordon. *The Four Gospels on Sunday: The New Testament and the Reform of Christian Worship.* Fortress Press, 2011. Lathrop demonstrates that the Gospels can remain a true catalyst for liturgical theology and liturgical renewal, as well as an inspiring link to the faith and convictions of the earliest followers of the Christian way.

§ ———. *Holy Ground: A Liturgical Cosmology.* Fortress Press, 2003.

§ ———. *Holy People: A Liturgical Ecclesiology.* Fortress Press, 1999.

§ ———. *Holy Things: A Liturgical Theology.* Fortress Press, 1998.

Principles for Worship. Renewing Worship, vol. 2. Augsburg Fortress, 2002. Principles for language, music, preaching, and worship space in relationship to the Christian assembly. Also available in Spanish.

Ramshaw, Gail. *Christian Worship.* Fortress Press, 2009. An engaging textbook on 100,000 Sundays of Christians at worship.

Senn, Frank. *Christian Liturgy: Catholic and Evangelical.* Fortress Press, 1997. A comprehensive historical introduction to the liturgy of the Western church with particular emphasis on Lutheran traditions.

§ ———. *Introduction to Christian Liturgy.* Fortress Press, 2012. This general introduction explores the meaning, history, and practice of worship in Eastern and Western, Catholic and Protestant traditions: the theology of worship, the historical development of the eucharist and the prayer offices, the lectionary and customs of the church year, other sacramental rites, and the use of music and the arts.

§ ———. *The People's Work: A Social History of the Liturgy.* Fortress Press, 2006. The first book to document the full history of ordinary Christians' liturgical expression.

Use of the Means of Grace: A Statement on the Practice of Word and Sacrament, The. Evangelical Lutheran Church in America, 1997. Also available in Spanish and Mandarin versions.

Web Sites

∞ www.preludemusicplanner.com. A subscription-based online music planning tool. Create comprehensive plans. Browse, preview, and download music from multi-publisher library. Search music based on lectionary days, keywords, skill level and more. Store your usage history. Upload and organize your own library.

∞ www.sundaysandseasons.com. A subscription-based online worship planning tool. Browse, select, and download content for worship planning and worship folder preparation. Complements *Sundays and Seasons.*

∞ www.alcm.org. Association of Lutheran Church Musicians. Links to conferences and resources available through this pan-Lutheran musicians' organization. Also a bulletin board and placement service.

∞ www.elca.org/worship. Evangelical Lutheran Church in America. Monthly WorshipNews e-newsletter.

∞ www.theworkofthepeople.com. Visual media for worship based on the Revised Common Lectionary, including videos, loops, and stills.

∞ www.worship.ca. Lift Up Your Hearts: The worship and spirituality site of the Evangelical Lutheran Church in Canada. Contains a variety of resources and news about events related to Lutheran worship.

Preaching Resources

§ Brueggemann, Walter. *The Practice of Prophetic Imagination: Preaching an Emancipating Word.* Fortress Press, 2012.

Craddock, Fred, et al. *Preaching through the Christian Year.* Three volumes for Cycles A, B, C. Valley Forge, PA: Trinity Press International, 1992, 1993. Various authors comment on the Sunday readings, psalms, and various festival readings.

§ Elements of Preaching series. O. Wesley Allen, series editor. Fortress Press, 2008–. Guides to the art and craft of preaching. Authors include Ronald Allen, Teresa Fry Brown, Mary Foskett, Jennifer Lord, Marvin McMickle, James Nieman, Melinda Quivik.

*§ Fortress Biblical Preaching Commentaries series. Fortress Press, 2013–. With their focus on the biblical books themselves and working with the realities of the lectionary, these volumes are useful in tandem with more extensive commentaries as well as with seasonal lectionary materials.

§ Hedahl, Susan K. *Proclamation and Celebration: Preaching on Christmas, Easter, and Other Festivals.* Fortress Press, 2012.

§ Lose, David J. *Preaching at the Crossroads: How the World—and Our Preaching—Is Changing.* Fortress Press, 2013.

§ Ramshaw, Gail. *Treasures Old and New: Images in the Lectionary.* Fortress Press, 2002. A creative unfolding of forty images drawn from the lectionary readings.

§ Rhodes, David, H. Paul Santmire, and Norman C. Habel, eds. *The Season of Creation: A Preaching Commentary.* Fortress Press, 2011. Scholars who have pioneered the connections between biblical scholarship, ecological theology, liturgy, and homiletics provide here a comprehensive resource for preaching and leading worship in this new season.

* denotes new or newer print resource
∞ denotes electronic or Web resource
§ denotes print resource also available as an ebook

∞ Sloyan, Gerard. *Preaching from the Lectionary: An Exegetical Commentary with CD-ROM*. Fortress Press, 2003. Exegetical analysis of each text from the RCL.

§ Stiller, Brian. *Preaching Parables to Postmoderns*. Fortress Press, 2005. An introduction to postmodern sensibilities and how it informs preaching the parables.

*∞ *Sundays and Seasons: Preaching*. Augsburg Fortress, 2014–. Multiple contributors. Encourages and provides helps for lectionary preaching, taking into account all the readings for the day, in addition to the rest of the worship service and the day itself in the church year. Features new commentary and ideas for proclamation, contributed by practicing preachers as well as scholars, together with succinct notes on each day and its readings.

∞ www.homileticsonline.com. An online sermon preparation resource including illustrations and visuals.

∞ www.newproclamation.com. An online sermon preparation resource that combines in-depth exegesis with homiletic advice from practicing preachers.

∞ www.workingpreacher.org. A resource for preachers from the Center for Biblical Preaching at Luther Seminary.

Periodicals

Call to Worship: Liturgy, Music, Preaching, and the Arts. Offers insight and inspiration for pastors, church musicians, artists, and other worship leaders. Quarterly. Published by the Office of Theology and Worship of the Presbyterian Church (USA).

Catechumenate: A Journal of Christian Initiation. Chicago: Liturgy Training Publications. Published six times a year with articles on congregational preparation of older children and adults for the celebration of baptism and eucharist.

CrossAccent. Journal of the Association of Lutheran Church Musicians. Publication for church musicians and worship leaders in North America. www.alcm.org.

Faith & Form. Journal of the Interfaith Forum on Religion, Art and Architecture. www.faithandform.com.

Liturgy. Quarterly journal of The Liturgical Conference. Each issue explores a worship-related issue from an ecumenical perspective. customerservice@taylorandfrancis.com.

Worship. Collegeville, MN: The Order of St. Benedict, published through The Liturgical Press six times a year. One of the primary journals of liturgical renewal among the churches.

Key to Hymn and Song Collections

* Indicates resources whose hymns or psalm refrains are, at least in part, included in the online worship planning tool Sundays and Seasons.com.

ASG*   As Sunshine to a Garden. Augsburg Fortress.

BOL*   Bread of Life. Augsburg Fortress

CBM   Come, Beloved of the Maker. Augsburg Fortress.

DH*   Dancing at the Harvest. Augsburg Fortress.

ELW*   Evangelical Lutheran Worship. Augsburg Fortress.

GS2*   Global Songs 2: Bread for the Journey. Augsburg Fortress.

GS3   Global Songs 3: Pave the Way. Augsburg Fortress.

LBW*   Lutheran Book of Worship. Augsburg Fortress.

LLC   Libro de Liturgia y Cántico. Augsburg Fortress.

LS*   LifeSongs. Augsburg Fortress.

MSB1*   Music Sourcebook for Lent and the Three Days. Augsburg Fortress.

MSB2*   Music Sourcebook for All Saints through Transfiguration. Augsburg Fortress.

OBS*   O Blessed Spring: Hymns of Susan Palo Cherwien. Augsburg Fortress.

SP*   Singing Our Prayer: A Companion to Holden Prayer Around the Cross. Augsburg Fortress.

TFF*   This Far by Faith. Augsburg Fortress.

W&P*   Worship & Praise. Augsburg Fortress.

WOV*   With One Voice. Augsburg Fortress.

Key to Psalm Collections

There are several new psalm collections included in this year's musical recommendations. The refrains included in the resources below may be reprinted with a OneLicense.net copyright license. Exceptions to this are *Psalms for All Seasons* and *Lift Up Your Hearts*, both of which contain psalm settings from a variety of publishers, some, but not all, of which are covered under the OneLicense.net license. In other cases (e.g., *Psalter for Worship* and *Psalm Settings for the Church Year*), permission to reproduce refrains is included with volume purchases. Psalm collections below that follow the Roman Lectionary are marked with [RL] at the end of the comments. Although the psalms appointed for the Roman Lectionary and the Revised Common Lectionary [RCL] are not identical, there is sufficient overlap to make these volumes very useful for those who follow the RCL.

ACYG   *Arise, Come to Your God: Forty-Seven Gelineau Settings of the Revised Grail Psalms.* GIA. This collection of psalm settings is an excerpted and edited volume of the Gelineau psalm settings included in the Psalter section of *Worship, Fourth Edition* (2011). Many of the original Gelineau collections are now out of print, so this new collection is a most welcome addition.

ChildrenSing Psalms. Marilyn Comer, ed. Augsburg Fortress. This collection of 15 of the more well-known psalms is a must-have for anyone working with children's choirs. Reproducible singer pages and assembly refrains.

COJ:S   *Cry Out with Joy: Christmas, Triduum, Solemnities & Other Celebrations.* GIA. Like *The Lyric Psalter*, when completed this four-volume set will also include volumes for years A, B, and C. Unlike *The Lyric Psalter*, verses are chanted rather than through-composed. Composers include David Haas, Kathleen Harmon, Stephen Pishner, Paul Tate, and Lori True. [RL]

DH   Ray Makeever. *Dancing at the Harvest.* Augsburg Fortress. This collection of songs includes lyrical settings of selected psalms with refrains and through-composed verses.

LP:LG   *Lectionary Psalms: Lead Me, Guide Me.* GIA. Refrains and psalm verse accompaniments composed in gospel style. These settings work well with *Evangelical Lutheran Worship* Holy Communion Setting Six or another gospel setting of the liturgy. [RL]

LP:W4   *Lectionary Psalms: Joseph Gelineau, SJ and Michel Guimont* (as found in *Worship, Fourth Edition*). GIA. Psalms in this volume are presented with a single refrain that may be used with a Gelineau tone or a tone by Michel Guimont. [RL]

LUYH   *Lift Up Your Hearts: Psalms, Hymns, and Spiritual Songs.* Faith Alive Resources. Includes all 150 psalms in a variety of settings for assembly singing.

PAS   *Psalms for All Seasons: A Complete Psalter for Worship.* Calvin Institute of Christian Worship, Faith Alive Christian Resources, and Brazos Press. In addition to each of the 150 psalms and

several canticles presented in multiple sung settings, this volume contains a comprehensive introduction to psalmody, several services of prayer, and extensive appendixes and indexes.

PCY   *Psalms for the Church Year.* Multi-volume. GIA. Each volume includes well-known psalm settings by various composers. This year, selections are recommended from volumes 1–4.

PRCL   Michel Guimont. *Psalms for the Revised Common Lectionary.* GIA. Responsorial psalms. May be accompanied by organ, piano, or guitar.

PS1   *Psalm Songs 1: Advent–Christmas–Epiphany.* Augsburg Fortress. This 3-volume set provides interesting settings of more common psalms. All settings include guitar chords and many have parts for other solo instruments.

PS2   *Psalm Songs 2: Lent–Holy Week–Easter.*

PS3   *Psalm Songs 3: Ordinary Time.*

Psallite   *Psallite: Sacred Song for Liturgy and Life.* Liturgical Press. This set of resources includes an accompaniment edition for each lectionary year and one volume for cantor/choir. In addition to lectionary psalms, provides biblically based songs that can be used at other times in the liturgy. [RL]

PSCY   *Psalm Settings for the Church Year.* 2 vols. Mark Mummert, ed. Augsburg Fortress. A collection of psalm settings in a wide variety of styles and structures. Includes all psalms used in the RCL.

PWC   *Psalter for Worship: Year C.* Augsburg Fortress. The third of three volumes of psalm refrains by various composers with Evangelical Lutheran Worship psalm tones. Coordinates with Celebrate and Today's Readings inserts. Includes a CD-ROM with reproducible psalm texts, refrains, and tones.

SMP   Thomas Pavlechko, arr. *St. Martin's Psalter.* Augsburg Fortress. Refrains and psalm tones based on familiar hymns in Anglican chant style. Uses the *Evangelical Lutheran Worship* psalm version. Published on CD-ROM, it includes reproducible parts for choir.

TLP:C   Tony Alonzo/Marty Haugen. *The Lyric Psalter: Year C.* GIA. This set contains four editions, one for each of the three years of the lectionary and one for solemnities, feasts, and special occasions. Each has a companion volume of descants for C-instrument. Psalm verses are through-composed and can be sung by a cantor. [RL]

TLP:S   Tony Alonzo/Marty Haugen. *The Lyric Psalter: Solemnities, Feasts, and Other Occasions.* GIA. [RL]

TPP   *The People's Psalter.* MorningStar. Responsorial psalm settings that make use of folk tunes from around the world. Includes settings for every psalm in the three-year lectionary.

Key to Music for Worship

acc	accompaniment	eng hrn	English horn	narr	narrator	tamb	tambourine
bar	baritone	fc	finger cymbals	ob	oboe	tba	tuba
bng	bongos	fl	flute	oct	octave	tbn	trombone
br	brass	glock	glockenspiel	opt	optional	tpt	trumpet
bsn	bassoon	gtr	guitar	orch	orchestra	timp	timpani
cant	cantor	hb	handbells	org	organ	trbl	treble
ch	chimes	hc	handchimes	perc	percussion	tri	triangle
cl	clarinet	hp	harp	picc	piccolo	U	unison
cont	continuo	hpd	harpsichord	pno	piano	UE	upper elementary
cym	cymbal	hrn	horn	pt	part	vc	violoncello
DB	double or string	inst	instrument	qnt	quintet	vcs	voices
	bass	kybd	keyboard	qrt	quartet	vla	viola
dbl	double	LE	lower elementary	rec	recorder	vln	violin
desc	descant	M	medium	sax	saxophone	wch	windchimes
div	divisi	MH	medium high	sop	soprano	ww	woodwind
drm	drum	ML	medium low	str	strings	xyl	xylophone
		mxd	mixed	synth	synthesizer		

Key to Music Publishers

ABI	Abingdon		(MorningStar)	MAR	Maranatha	SEL	Selah
AFP	Augsburg Fortress	FB	Fred Bock Music	MFS	Mark Foster (Shawnee)	SF	SoundForth
AG	Agape (Hope)	FLG	Flagstaff Publications	MMP	Masters Music		Publications
AGEHR	American Guild of Eng-	FTT	From the Top Music		Publication	SHW	Shawnee
	lish Handbell Ringers	GIA	GIA Publications	MSM	MorningStar Music	SMP	Sacred Music Press
ALF	Alfred	HAL	Hal Leonard	NOV	Novello (Shawnee)		(Lorenz)
AUR	Aureole	HIN	Hinshaw Music Co.	OCP	Oregon Catholic Press	WAL	Walton
BAR	Bärenreiter	HOP	Hope	OXF	Oxford University Press	WAR	Warner/Belwin
BP	Beckenhorst Press	HWG	H.W. Gray (Warner)	PAR	Paraclete	WJK	Westminster/John Knox
CG	Choristers Guild	INT	Integrity (Capitol CMG)	PET	C.F. Peters	WLP	World Library
CPH	Concordia	JEF	Jeffers	PRE	Presser		Publications
DUR	Durand (Presser)	KJO	Kjos	RR	Red River Music	WRD	Word Music
EAR	EarthSongs	LOR	Lorenz	RW	Ringing Word	WT	WorshipTogether.com
ECS	E. C. Schirmer	LP	The Ligurgical Press		Publications		

A Note on Music Listings

Please note that some choral and instrumental music in the day listings may be out of print. We are unable to research whether musical pieces from other publishers are still available. Why do we still list music if it is out of print? Primarily because many music planners may have that piece in their files, and can consider it for use. If a planner wishes to use a piece that has gone out of print, that may still be possible. For Augsburg Fortress resources, call 800/421-0239 or e-mail copyright@augsburgfortress.org to inquire about onetime reprint rights or to see whether a piece may be available on preludemusicplanner.org, or by print on demand.

343